Edward
Burne-Jones

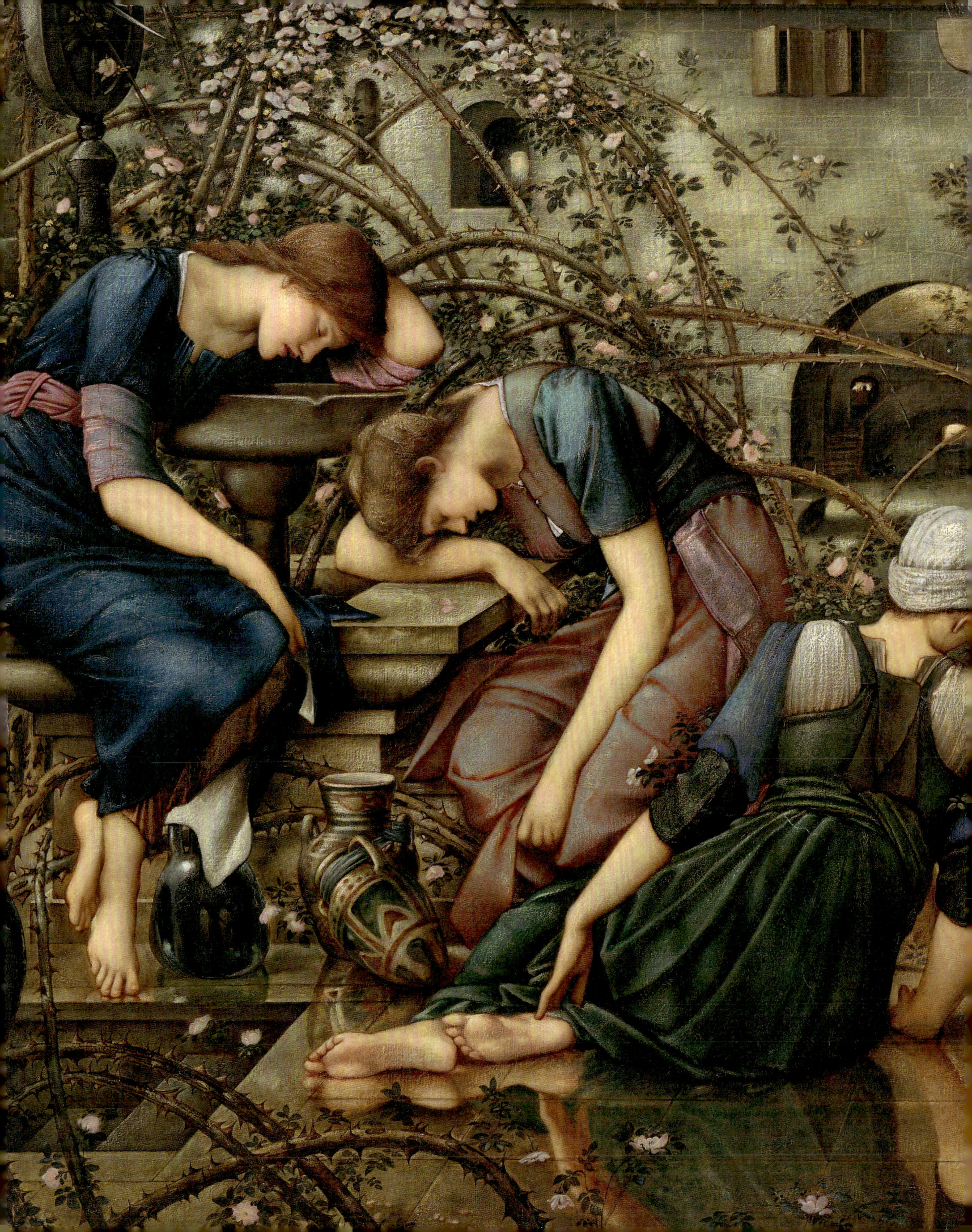

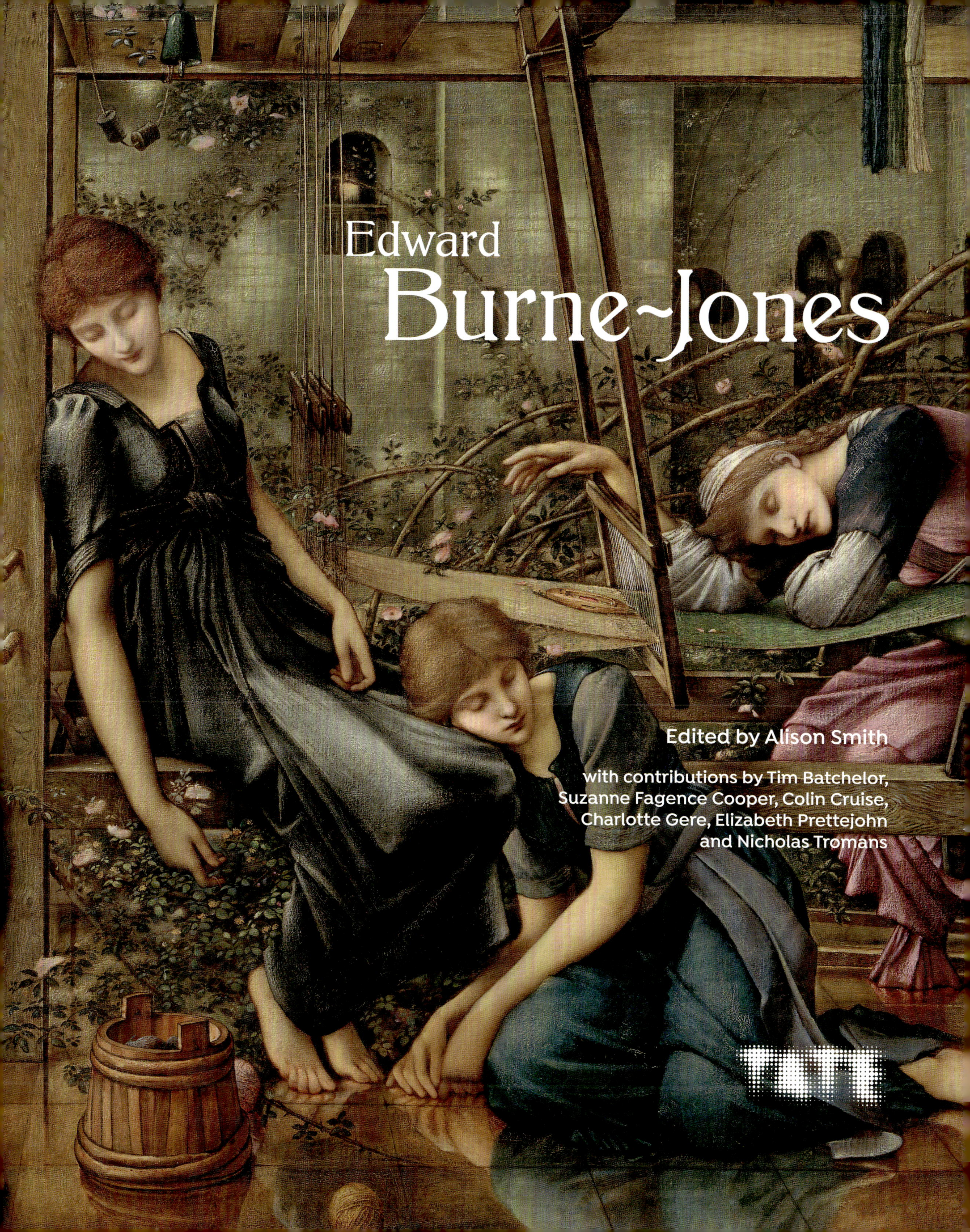

Edward Burne-Jones

Edited by Alison Smith

with contributions by Tim Batchelor, Suzanne Fagence Cooper, Colin Cruise, Charlotte Gere, Elizabeth Prettejohn and Nicholas Tromans

First published 2018 by order of the Tate Trustees
by Tate Publishing, a division of Tate Enterprises Ltd,
Millbank, London SW1P 4RG
www.tate.org.uk/publishing

on the occasion of the exhibition
Edward Burne-Jones

Tate Britain, London
24 October 2018 – 24 February 2019

Supported by Tate Patrons and Tate Members

A catalogue record for this book is available from the British Library

ISBN 978 1 84976 574 9 (hardback)
ISBN 978 1 84976 599 2 (paperback)

Distributed in the United States and Canada by ABRAMS, New York

Project Editor: Alice Chasey
Production: Roanne Marner
Picture Researcher: Deborah Metherell
Designed by Maggi Smith, Sixism Ltd
Colour reproduction by DL Imaging Ltd, London
Printed in Italy by Conti Tipocolor, Florence

All works by Edward Burne-Jones unless otherwise stated.

Paperback cover: *Laus Veneris* 1873–8, detail of no.94
Frontispiece: *The Garden Court* 1885–90, detail of no.125

Measurements of artworks are given in centimetres, height before width, before depth.

MIX
Paper from responsible sources
FSC www.fsc.org FSC® C016114

Contents

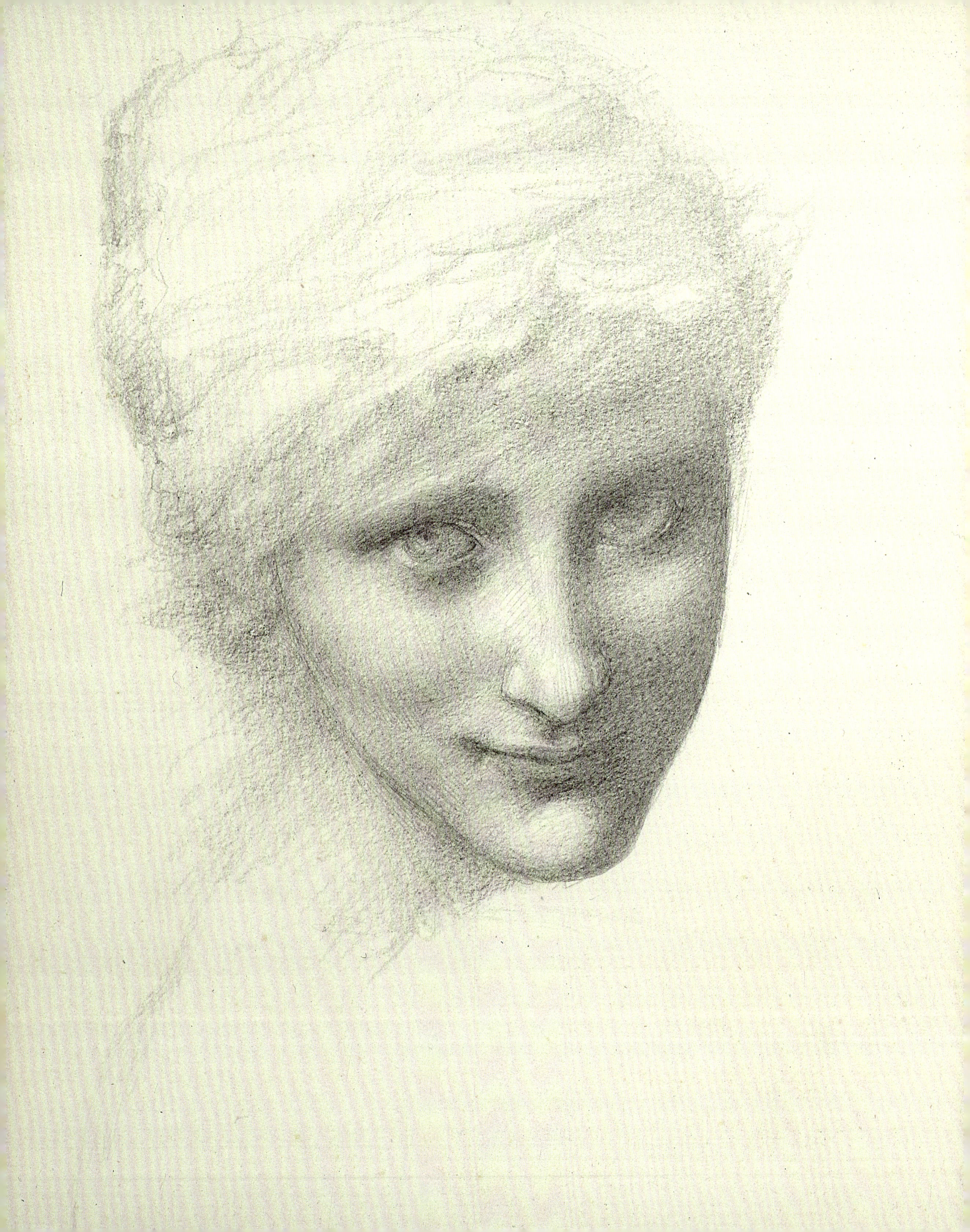

Director's Foreword

ALEX FARQUHARSON, DIRECTOR, TATE BRITAIN

As the home of British art, Tate has an outstanding collection of the works of Edward Burne-Jones. This includes two of his most famous paintings: *King Cophetua and the Beggar Maid* 1844 and *The Golden Stairs* 1880, which have been on almost permanent display since they entered the collection in 1900 and 1924 respectively, numbering among the most popular works in Tate's British collection.

It might be surprising to hear that Tate has only devoted one major exhibition to the artist which was the large retrospective held in 1933 to commemorate the centenary of Burne-Jones's birth. Since then he has featured in exhibitions devoted to the Pre-Raphaelite and Symbolist movements, most recently the 2012 show *Pre-Raphaelites: Victorian Avant-Garde*, but he rarely appears on his own terms. Indeed it was left to Birmingham, the artist's home town, to organise the 1998 centenary exhibition; and the last exhibition in London was the 1975 Hayward exhibition.

More than a generation has passed since the 1975 London show so it is high time we looked at Burne-Jones afresh. By focusing on many of his greatest productions this exhibition asks us to appreciate him as the great artist he became in his day: a visionary in the tradition of William Blake, one of the great draughtsmen in British art, and a pioneer of the Arts and Crafts movement in breaking down the barriers between media in seeking to beautify the world. A few of Burne-Jones's artistic peers achieved greater fame and commercial success in Britain, but none equalled the influence his mature work had on European art in the last two decades of the nineteenth century.

At the time of the Hayward exhibition the works of Burne-Jones found echoes in 1970s counter culture and fashion. He is no less relevant today for the ways his works disrupt traditional gender roles and make the imaginary possible – influencing the current vogue for fantasy in literature and cinema.

This exhibition was proposed and developed by Alison Smith, former Lead Curator, Nineteenth-Century British Art at Tate Britain. Since leaving the organisation in 2017 to join the National Portrait Gallery as its Chief Curator she has continued working on the project in close collaboration with Assistant Curator Tim Batchelor who took over as project manager supported by Kiko Noda as registrar.

We are grateful to the curators and external contributors Colin Cruise, Suzanne Fagence Cooper, Charlotte Gere, Elizabeth Prettejohn and Nicholas Tromans for their insightful writing in this publication.

Following its exhibition in London the exhibition will tour in a reduced version to the Prins Eugens Waldemarsudde in Stockholm, Sweden, and KODE Art Museums and Composer Homes, Bergen, Norway, in the first ever presentation of Burne-Jones's work in Scandinavia. For this I would like to thank Knut Ljøgodt, Director, Nordic Institute of Art, for championing the tour, and our partners in Sweden and Norway headed by Karin Sidén, Director of Prins Eugens Waldemarsudde and Petter Snare, Director of KODE.

On behalf of Tate I would like to extend our gratitude to all the lenders, private and institutional, who have supported the exhibition with generous loans from their collections. Many of the works have not been seen in public for many years allowing a whole new generation of visitors a unique opportunity to view the creations of this extraordinary artist.

We are particularly grateful to the Trustees of the Faringdon Collection for the loan of the 'Briar Rose' series. When the four main paintings were installed in the saloon at Buscot Park, Burne-Jones painted additional decorative panels to create a contiguous scheme. The whole scheme, comprising of fourteen paintings, is shown here for the first time since they were installed there in the 1890s.

The exhibition was made possible by the provision of insurance through the Government Indemnity Scheme. On behalf of Tate Britain I would like to thank HM Government for providing Government Indemnity, and the Department for Digital, Culture, Media and Sport and Arts Council England for arranging this indemnity.

Head study for mermaid in *The Depths of the Sea* 1886 (detail, no.90)

Acknowledgements

ALISON SMITH

Many people have contributed to the making of this exhibition and publication. Further to the acknowledgments made by Alex Farquharson in his Foreword, we would like to thank all those at Tate Britain whose enthusiasm and commitment have enabled the exhibition to be transformed from a dream into reality. Particular thanks are due to Kirsten Cowie in the press office, Pandora Ryan, Senior Marketing Manager, Jenny Batchelor, Head of Interpretation, and Alice Chasey, Roanne Marner, Deborah Metherell and Emilia Will in Tate Publishing for overseeing the production of the catalogue. Thanks also to Colin Grant for editing the catalogue and to Maggi Smith for the beautiful design. New research into Burne-Jones's materials and techniques has been specially carried out for the exhibition in the conversation department for which we are indebted to Rachel Scott, Joyce Townsend, Alastair Johnson and Rebecca Hellen.

Among those who have offered advice and support during the development of this project we would like to thank: Jasmine Allen, Raymond Asquith, Rowan Bain, Martin Beisly, Terry Bloxham, Stephanie Boydell, Etienne Bréton, Peter Brown, Julius Bryant, Thomas Scott Buckle, Stephen Calloway, Juliet Ceresole, Christofer Conrad, Caroline Corbeau-Parsons, Andrea D' Agosto, Caroline Dakers, Ana Debenedetti, Josceline Dimbleby, Harriet Drummond, Lisa Edwards, Mark Evans, Grant Ford, Ted Gott, Valérie Haerden, Colin Harrison, James and Lucinda Henderson, Lynn Hulse, Carol Jacobi, Andrew Lloyd Webber, Rupert Maas, Fiona MacCarthy, Fiona Mann, Anna Mason, Dan Matthews, Patrick McMahon, Sarah Miller, Julie Milne, Jane Munro, Peter and Renate Nahum, Victoria Osborne, Caroline Palmer, Victoria Partridge, Sandra Penketh, Alex Patterson, Anne Pritchard, the Rev. Austin K. Rios, Paul Reeves, Andrew Renton, Gabriele Rossi Rognoni, Mariela Saldias, Mark Samuels Lasner, Ben Sparkes, Serena Thirkell, Sian Tipler, Simon Toll, Piers Townshend, Nicholas Tromans, Roger Vlitos, William Waters.

Anyone writing on Burne-Jones is in the fortunate position of being able to draw upon the scholarship of the late John Christian. His painstaking research on the artist remains an invaluable source of information, not least his collaboration with Stephen Wildman in providing detailed catalogue entries for the 1998 Burne-Jones exhibition held in Birmingham, New York and Paris. Being in a position to draw upon this rich body of material, we have felt free in this publication to take a different approach in exploring some of the themes that underpin Burne-Jones's art and legacy, knowing that anyone interested in the details of the works themselves can access the 1998 catalogue freely online.

Pomona c.1885 (detail, no.149)

(overleaf)
Phyllis and Demophoön 1870 (detail, no.25)

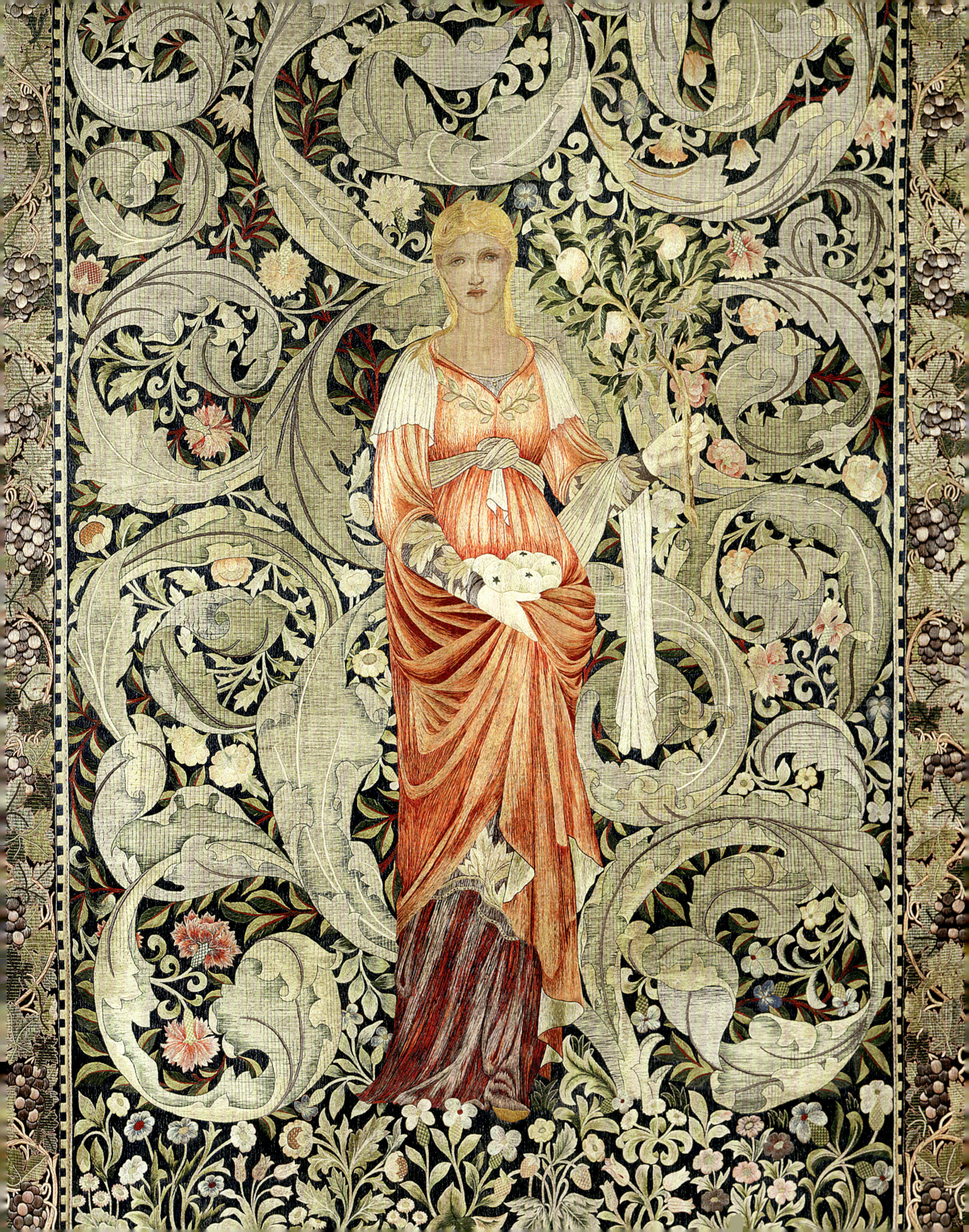

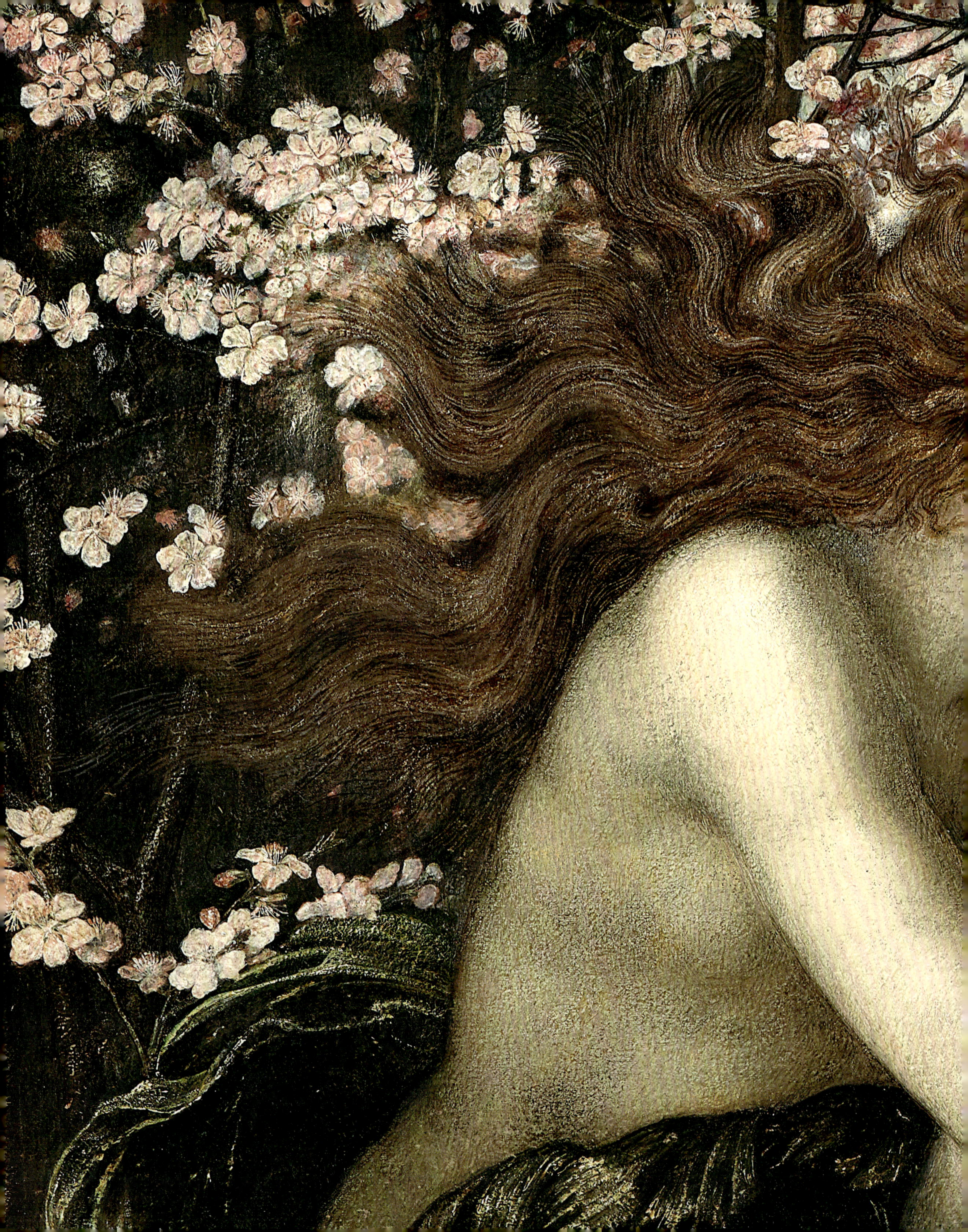

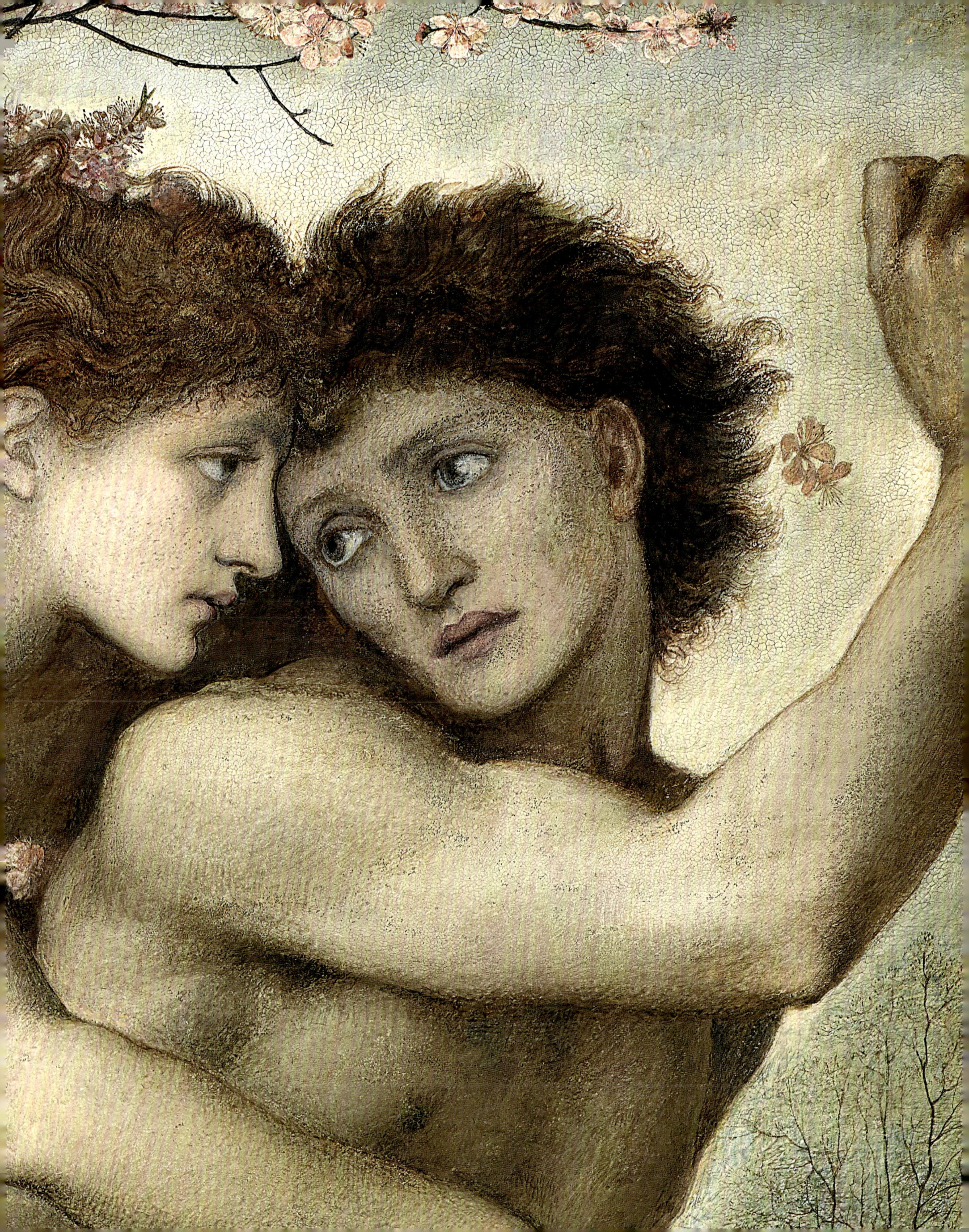

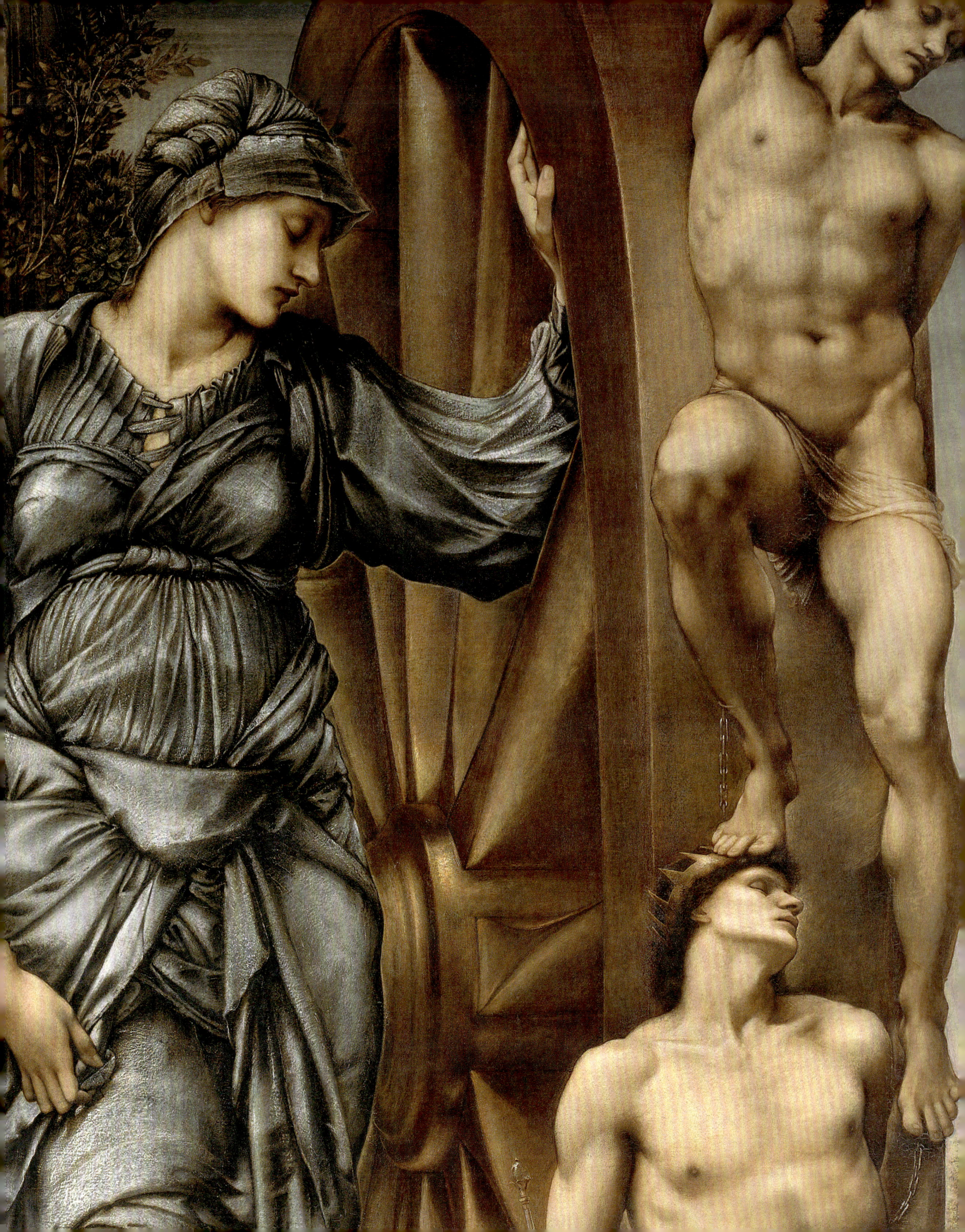

Burne-Jones: Intellectual, Designer, People's Man

ELIZABETH PRETTEJOHN

Edward Burne-Jones (in conversation, 29 May 1897):
'I've learned to know Beauty when I see it, and that's the best thing.'
Thomas Rooke (his studio assistant): 'And to shew it to us.'[1]

Art historians and curators are now acknowledging the greatness and importance of Edward Burne-Jones (the museum director Sir John Pope-Hennessy, for example, thought him one of the three greatest British artists of all time).[2] Yet they have failed to observe that his career and practice were in significant respects unlike those of any other artist of his generation. The difference is not one of degree; it is a difference in kind. Critics and historians have tried to assimilate his work to that of more familiar artistic practices, to see him, for example, as a 'second-generation Pre-Raphaelite', a proto-symbolist, or a traditionalist who set himself against the development of modernism, yet he cannot be made to fit any of those art-historical pigeonholes. Biographers have fared somewhat better in producing a convincing account of Burne-Jones's distinctiveness, but at the cost of making him a mere eccentric, endearing or slightly sinister according to one's tastes. Nor will that do: Burne-Jones lived for his work, and we cannot understand the man unless we find some way to come to terms with that work, different as it is from anything our art-history textbooks can explain.

The first thing to note is its very extent, whether that is calculated in number of objects or in square metres. It has been estimated that Burne-Jones made over 270 drawings for stained glass between 1872 and 1878 – a prolific period, but not unusually so, and at the same time he was designing his largest cycles of mural paintings, with all their myriads of preparatory drawings.[3] So daunting is the quantity that there is as yet no complete catalogue of Burne-Jones; we simply do not know how many works he made in total – far too many to be easily summarised in one exhibition or exhibition catalogue. That leads to a closely related second point: almost without exception, the artistic ideas that generated this vast body of production originated in the realm of applied or decorative art – in William Morris's phrase, 'the lesser arts'.[4] Those artistic ideas came, eventually, to inform some of the greatest works of modern fine art: *The Beguiling of Merlin*, *The Golden Stairs*, *King Cophetua and the Beggar Maid*, *The Wheel of Fortune* (nos. 93, 95, 98, 97), exhibited to tremendous acclaim at the international exhibitions of the later nineteenth century and much more influential on the history of western modernism than the textbooks have yet acknowledged. These, however, were a minority in Burne-Jones's artistic production, and in any case they derived from a primary impulse in the applied arts. Burne-Jones was not a fine artist. Art-historical interpretations fail when they attempt to treat him as though he were.

The Wheel of Fortune 1883 (detail, no.97)

The tendency to assimilate Burne-Jones's story to more orthodox narratives about nineteenth-century artists is strange, since his difference from other artists is not difficult to explain. Burne-Jones was educated at Oxford, one of England's great medieval universities, and not at art school. He had almost no artistic training of any of the standard kinds: he never attended an academy or a school of industrial design; he did not train in the studio or atelier of an established artist (except, briefly, that of Dante Gabriel Rossetti, of which more below); although he sporadically took part in drawing or life classes, he was never regularly enrolled as an art student. It is worth pausing for a moment to reflect on the point: all students of the Pre-Raphaelite movement know it to be a fact, and yet no one remarks on its singularity. Is there any other important artist of the nineteenth century who received a university education and never attended an art school? Is there, indeed, any other artist of the entire western tradition (from the Renaissance through to the present day) who was educated entirely as an intellectual and not as a practitioner?

The answer is no, and there are (at least) two kinds of entailment. First, Burne-Jones's education and outlook were entirely independent of the art-school system that (in modern art) is usually called 'academic'; more completely than any French artist of the avant-garde, he was a non-academic artist.[5] He was also thoroughly opposed to art academies and academic modes of training throughout his life. That art-political stance is more familiar among modern artists; indeed it is almost obligatory for any artist who wished to assert vanguard or avant-garde status after the early nineteenth century, but Burne-Jones is alone in being able to claim genuinely that he never had an 'academic' art education. The closest parallels are such naïve artists as Alfred Wallis or the 'Douanier' Rousseau, but Burne-Jones was not naïve: on the contrary, he was highly educated and highly sophisticated. True, he became a master of simple or childlike expression in both words and images, but that mastery was achieved through a lifetime of careful thought and research.

In the first place, then, Burne-Jones's unorthodox formation as an artist places him at an extreme of avant-gardism; in his intellectual habits, he is more like a conceptual artist of today or the non-professional Chinese scholar-painters of the Ming and earlier dynasties, known as literati, than he is like a studio-trained practitioner of the mainstream western tradition. On the other hand, his artistic development was also deeply embedded in a history and tradition with which he was fascinated from the start and in which he became impressively learned: the Renaissance tradition in which the artist aspires to the status of intellectual rather than artisan, enshrined in art theory from Leon Battista Alberti's *Della pittura* (1435–6) to Joshua Reynolds's *Discourses* to the students of the Royal Academy (1769–90). In Burne-Jones's own generation this Renaissance ideal was given fuller historical context in Jacob Burckhardt's *Civilization of the Renaissance in Italy* (1860) and adapted to modern philosophy in Walter Pater's *Studies in the History of the Renaissance* (1873). Equally important was first-hand knowledge and intensive study of Renaissance works of art through the burgeoning collections of the National Gallery and other museums and libraries, and through travel. Burne-Jones's four trips to Italy shaped his practice in ways that would have been inconceivable in any earlier generation.

Typically, artists have their career decision made for them – someone notices their talent, usually in early youth, and encourages them to develop it.[6] Burne-Jones, however, decided to be an artist before he knew whether he had any special talent for it – indeed, his first experiments, the illustrations to Archibald Maclaren's book of 1857, *The Fairy Family* (no.4), might have failed to inspire confidence that there was any likelihood of success. Often his aims and outlook have been contrasted to those of his lifelong best friend and collaborator, William Morris, but they took the decision to become artists together in 1855, and the two went about it in exactly the same way. Having resolved to be an artist, Burne-Jones (like Morris) made himself good at it; he was driven not so much by talent as by mind and will. Eventually

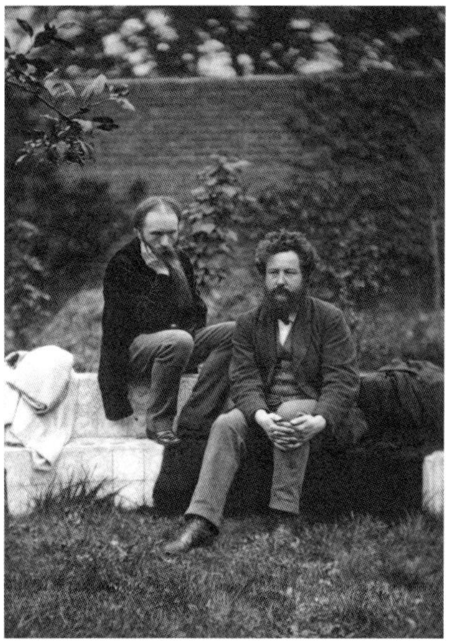

Fig.1
FREDERICK HOLLYER
Edward Burne-Jones and William Morris, 1874
National Portrait Gallery, London

he developed very considerable skill and even more impressive expertise, but this was not talent and not precisely genius, at least as that concept was theorised in the eighteenth- and nineteenth-century tradition of philosophical aesthetics, as something innate and irrational. Burne-Jones's expertise was deliberate and willed, not an aptitude that came unbidden. If, in the end, he did not take his Oxford degree, it was nonetheless the habit of application and the procedure of systematic research, developed at school and university, that made it possible for him to become one of the foremost artists in the world by the end of his life. His was the approach of an intellectual, not an artisan.

In the terms of philosophical aesthetics, what Burne-Jones possessed was not talent, aptitude or genius: it was judgement.[7] Much has been made of his childhood surroundings in squalid Birmingham, deprived of beauty. Somehow he taught himself to recognise the beautiful when he saw it, or (in philosophical terms) to make the judgement of taste: in a thirteenth-century manuscript at Oxford, a ruined abbey by the Thames, the Arena Chapel, or his own studio. Nineteenth-century and modern artists have made art for all manner of reasons – to tell important truths or promote worthwhile values. Burne-Jones approached art-making rather as a philosopher in the new discipline of aesthetics: to find out what is beautiful.

Intellectual

Unlike Morris, and many other committed social reformers of his generation, Burne-Jones had experienced genuine poverty, as well as unhappiness, in his childhood; even as a young adult, before he began to earn, he knew what it was to go hungry. His father, Edward Richard Jones, had a small picture- and mirror-framing business near the Society of Arts and New Street Station in Birmingham, so he should probably be described as lower-middle class, but he was not financially successful and seems not to have been particularly good at his job. Heartbroken after the death of his wife within days of childbirth, he was unable to provide either material or emotional comforts for the child. The transition from the poor and motherless child, born Edward Jones in 1833, to Sir Edward Burne-Jones, Bart, internationally famous and wealthy late-Victorian artist, was possible partly because his father was prepared to endure hardship for his son's sake.[8] Above all, it was enabled by an enlightened institution: King Edward's School, Birmingham, where the young Burne-Jones, evincing intellectual promise, was encouraged to transfer, aged fifteen, from the commercial to the classical department, in which he could learn Greek as well as Latin, like a gentleman, and prepare for university. He duly entered Exeter College, Oxford, in 1853 and there began his lifelong friendship with Morris, who had been at an elite public school (Marlborough) but was impressed by the superior classical knowledge of his new friend, trained at King Edward's.

Both young men needed the best available education because they were aiming for careers in the Church. That meant a serious commitment to public service, which transmuted in Morris's case to Marxian Socialism and in both men's cases to a determination to make beauty and art available to all people. It also meant serious theological learning, for which the ancient languages – traditional signs of elite education – were a means to an end. Before going up to Oxford, Burne-Jones had already persuaded his father to move from the evangelical St Mary's Church to the higher Anglican St Paul's, and he was inspired by the writings of John Henry Newman, leader of the Oxford (or 'Tractarian') Movement; he even flirted with the idea of converting, like his hero, to Roman Catholicism. That would have made impossible his marriage to Georgiana MacDonald, daughter of a Methodist minister, and it did not happen; later in life Burne-Jones made disparaging remarks about the Church of England and seems to have lost confidence in institutionalised religion of any kind. Perhaps he attended the parish church in Rottingdean, in which his daughter Margaret was married and where his ashes were eventually interred. In London, though, from the mid-1860s onwards, Sunday mornings were sacrosanct, instead, to planning the week's art-making with Morris.[9] For both men the change of career, from Church to art, was a matter of conviction and not motivated by worldly considerations.

It does not follow, however, that Burne-Jones lost interest in Christianity or Christian art. It is impossible to gauge the precise nature of Burne-Jones's own faith. His later letters and studio conversations are littered with references to Christian belief and aspects of theology, hedged about by a good deal of wit or irony and tempered by scepticism. The following, reported by his studio assistant Thomas Rooke, is typical:

> *I love Christmas Carol Christianity, I couldn't do without Medieval Christianity. The central idea of it and all it has gathered to itself made the Europe that I exist in. The enthusiasm and devotion, the learning and the art, the humanity and Romance, the self denial and splendid achievement that the human race can never be deprived of, except by a cataclysm that would all but destroy man himself, all belong to it.*[10]

It would be a mistake to take such statements, made in casual conversation (and recorded ad hoc), as logically reasoned positions. On the other hand, it was Burne-Jones's theological education that developed his intellect. A series of letters from his teenage years shows him fascinated by the doctrinal minutiae that differentiated the various Christian sects past and present, from Antinomians and Arians to Calvinists and Arminians.[11] From such debates, and particularly those in the writings of Newman and the other Oxford Movement theologians that caught the imagination of his generation, he learned exact thinking. That may, paradoxically, have destroyed his belief in any particular doctrine, but it gave him an analytical habit that is crucial to understanding his art.

What difference did it make, that Burne-Jones was educated at university, rather than art school? An obvious fact, although still one that needs underlining, is that he seldom chose subject matter of the sort that was familiar at the Royal Academy; he has been called a 'literary' painter but the literature he read was different from that of the many Victorian painters who chose subjects from Shakespeare, the English novel or familiar operas, plays and poems. Instead he drew inspiration from medieval and classical legends, epics, myths and romances: texts that were objects of scholarly study in the nineteenth century, and particularly in the sense that they existed in multiple versions, open to diverse interpretations. A few times, early in his career, Burne-Jones 'illustrated' characters from a particular text: Browning's *Childe Harold*, Rossetti's *The Blessed Damozel*, Meinhold's *Clara* and *Sidonia von Bork* (nos.17, 18), Chaucer's *Legend of Good Women* and *Assembly of Fowls*. Chaucer was a favourite writer from these early experiments through to the great collaborative project of the 1890s, the Kelmscott Press edition of *The Works of Geoffrey Chaucer* (no.152). Yet the fascination with Chaucer has much to do with the retelling of stories or legends that go further back – the 'good women' are those of ancient mythology, Alcestis, Dido, Cleopatra. As important as Chaucer's *Canterbury Tales* are the new tales of William Morris's vast narrative poem, *The Earthly Paradise*, published in three instalments from 1868 to 1870: new, or new-old, for Morris (like Chaucer) provides new tellings of traditional stories from classical and medieval literature. Morris's verses were originally to have hundreds of illustrations by Burne-Jones in a combined word-and-image project that proved impossibly ambitious. Yet the idea of retelling old tales in multiple forms – in words and images, pictures and objects, stained glass or painted furniture, designs on ceilings or caskets or gems, mosaics or parchments – remains the guiding thread. In the heyday of the Victorian 'subject picture', artists sought subjects that were as 'original' as possible – ideally, subjects that had never been treated before. Burne-Jones had no interest in originality of this sort. Indeed one suspects that a subject attracted him precisely to the extent that it connected his work to other works of art or literature that had gone before.

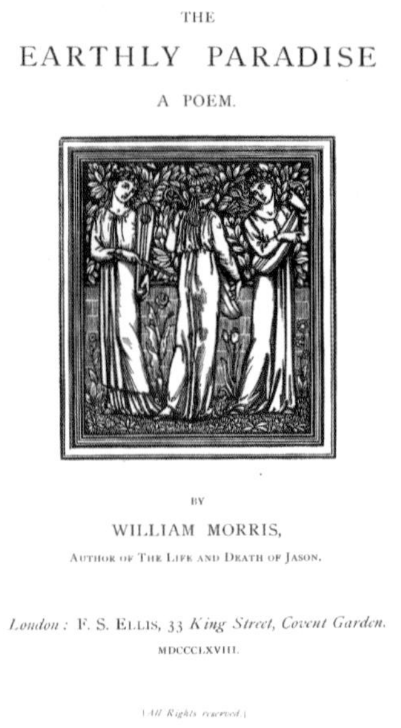
THE

EARTHLY PARADISE

A POEM.

BY

WILLIAM MORRIS,

AUTHOR OF THE LIFE AND DEATH OF JASON.

London: F. S. ELLIS, 33 *King Street, Covent Garden.*

MDCCCLXVIII.

(*All Rights reserved.*)

1
WILLIAM MORRIS
The Earthly Paradise 1868
Book, 18.8 × 13.5 × 4 (book closed)
Collection of Stephen Calloway

Fig.2
Study of feet for *The Golden Stairs* c.1878 (detail, no.30)

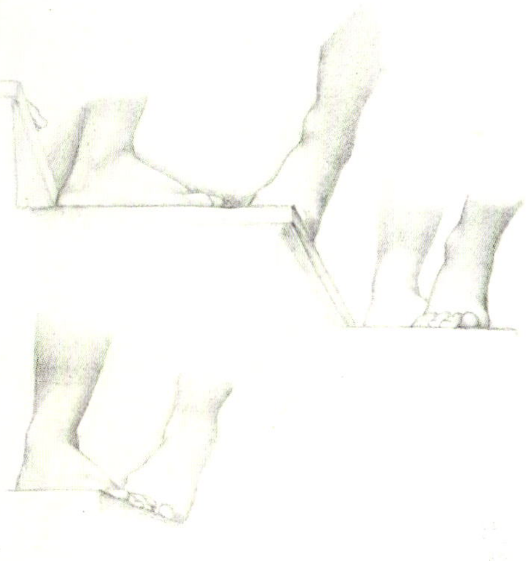

Often Burne-Jones preferred subjects that had already been interpreted more than once. Examples in the current exhibition include *The Beguiling of Merlin* (no.93), which features characters popularised by Tennyson's *Idylls of the King* (1859) but in Burne-Jones's version closer to those of Malory's *Morte d'Arthur* (1485); and *Phyllis and Demophoön* (no.25), based on a story from Chaucer's *Legend of Good Women* (late fourteenth century) also found in the *Heroides* by the Latin poet Ovid (43 BC–AD 17). This layering of sources, in which it is important to remember and compare all of the earlier versions of an event or legend, might be called a creative or artistic version of advanced textual scholarship or exegesis, in which every source is precisely identified and documented. Burne-Jones's school and university experience of Greek and Latin texts, with their commentaries, and of biblical criticism instilled in him the habit of thinking this way, and in his own lifetime the disciplines of comparative mythology and comparative religion, with their close links to anthropology and psychology, were being developed. It is not unlikely, in fact, that Burne-Jones's way of suggesting visual connections was itself an influence on the pioneers of those new disciplines, such as the comparative mythographer James Frazer, author of *The Golden Bough* (1890), the cultural anthropologist Edward Burnett Tylor and the Cambridge Ritualists, Jane Ellen Harrison and Gilbert Murray. Burne-Jones's approach to pictorial storytelling seems to epitomise what we now call 'intertextuality', or (in the words of Roland Barthes) 'a multi-dimensional space in which a variety of writings, none of them original, blend and clash ... a tissue of quotations drawn from the innumerable centres of culture'.[12]

Designer

The preceding discussion makes Burne-Jones seem principally an artist of ideas, or – as we might phrase it in the twenty-first century – a conceptual artist first and foremost. And indeed critics, from his own day to ours, have often found fault with the visual and material aspects of his art. Some have accused him of poor drawing; others of lacking the deep and visceral engagement with paint as substance that distinguishes the best work of his contemporaries in the standard modernist canon, such as the French impressionists and post-impressionists.[13] These critiques articulate persistent discomforts that have been felt even by the artist's greatest admirers, and yet there is something systematically wrong-headed about them. By measuring Burne-Jones's work against standardised expectations for a painter of his generation, they fail to acknowledge the exceptional coherence of a style that is instantly recognisable – what for want of a more precise analysis has been called the 'Burne-Jonesiness' of Burne-Jones.[14]

Rather than describing Burne-Jones as a painter, it might be truer to say that he was a designer, in the full sense of the word: *disegno*, in the Italian of Vasari's *Lives of the Artists*, is the virtue of his art, its motive or generative power. Anecdotal accounts may present him as languid and dreamy, in stark contrast to the explosive energy of Morris, so memorably portrayed in Burne-Jones's own caricatures. Perhaps, though, friends found such caricatures funny precisely because they called attention to a paradox in Burne-Jones's artistic personality: the way in which melancholic diffidence somehow coexisted with incessant activity, endless fiddling with pencil or pen, a seeming inability ever to leave off designing something. As the younger artist Graham Robertson put it, 'to draw was his natural mode of expression – line flowed from him almost without volition'.[15]

This compulsion for *disegno* accounts not only for the innumerable quantity of extant drawings, but also for the ungovernable variety of things in them: jewels, birds, helmets, plants, shields, wing feathers, hands, disconnected faces, unidentifiable details from old pictures or manuscripts, and above all draperies – crinkled, folded, crumpled, rippled, ruffled, or crystallised. It also helps to account for the seemingly superfluous paraphernalia that could irritate critics throughout the artist's career: the strange wooden platform on which the Virgin Mary kneels (no.21), the elaborate joinery of Noah's Ark (no.9), the tiny nudes (with their reflections in the glassy water) who grace the background of *The Mill* (fig.3), the intricate sandals of the angels in *The Morning of the Resurrection* (no.99).

One traditional meaning for *disegno* is the antithesis of *colorito*, colouring, and some critics have cited Burne-Jones's practice of letting Morris (or his assistants) add the colours to his black-and-white designs for stained glass to argue that his method was essentially that of a draughtsman – one who designs lines to be 'coloured in'. That, however, fails to account for the wide variety of colour worlds in Burne-Jones's work, which must surely be integral to the conception, not afterthoughts – from the jewel-like colours of the early watercolours to the steely greys of the Perseus series and the touches of gold that shimmer on the dark paper of some of Burne-Jones's later drawings. Perhaps the critics are right that Burne-Jones did not think entirely as an oil painter, like his colleagues trained in academies or the Parisian teaching ateliers: his colours recall much wider ranges of materials, metals, stones, jewels, mirrors, inks, mosaics, textiles. 'I like a picture so much better under glass; it's like a kind of aetherial varnish', he told Rooke in 1897; for Burne-Jones pictures are simply another kind of crafted object.[16]

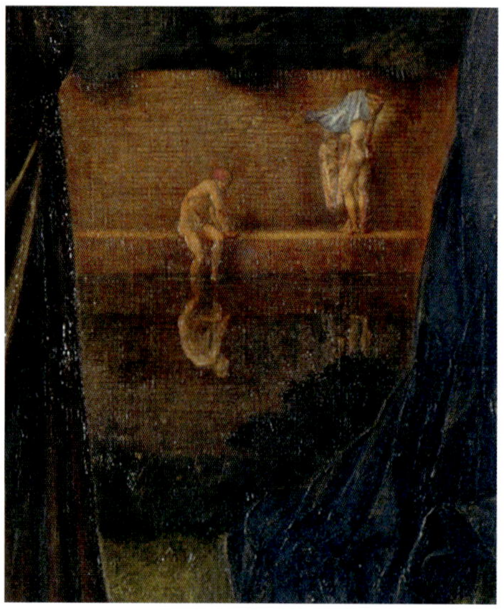

Fig.3
The Mill 1870–1882 (detail, no.92)

Rather than the academy or atelier, the home or birthplace for Burne-Jones's works is something more like the *bottega*, or workshop, of a Renaissance artist. He learned his trade by apprenticing himself, first in 1856 to Dante Gabriel Rossetti, and for the rest of his life he revered Rossetti's judgement: 'I wonder what Rossetti would have said to this', he remarked in 1897; 'I have never done anything without saying that to myself ... Always wondered whether he'd approve it and be pleased with it or whether he'd say it was rubbish.'[17] But he knew that Rossetti was only a little ahead of him in technical accomplishment, and from his first visit to Italy in 1859 he made himself the apprentice of the great masters of the Renaissance itself. He had, of course, to learn by studying their extant works rather than the methods and techniques for making them, which may account for the unconventionality with which he used materials himself – as Robertson put it, 'whether working in oil, in water colour, in pastel or in pure line, he appeared wilfully to ignore the possibilities of his medium and to put it to uses for which it was never intended'.[18] However, by imitating the Italian old masters he became capable by the end of the 1860s of dazzling technical accomplishment. A drawing such as the study of 1873 for the never completed subject from Spenser, *The Masque of Cupid* (no.47), demonstrates a proficiency worthy of an old master – Luca Signorelli, perhaps, whose frescoes at Orvieto, teeming with nudes, Burne-Jones had admired on his third Italian journey in 1871.[19] This is a far cry indeed from the often charming, but decidedly awkward, figure drawing of Burne-Jones's first efforts. Another example is the large watercolour, *Phyllis and Demophoön* of 1870 (no.25), with its clear echo of Botticelli's *Primavera*: Burne-Jones was one of the first artists seriously to study that forgotten masterpiece. *Phyllis and Demophoön* caused the end of Burne-Jones's first attempt at engaging with the nineteenth-century exhibition system, at the Old Water Colour Society in the 1860s; he was obliged to withdraw the work after a member of the public complained about its nudity, and subsequently resigned from the society.

By this date Burne-Jones's own studio at the Grange, Fulham (fig.4), was beginning to resemble a Renaissance *bottega*, with assistants to help cope with an increasingly unwieldy workload. Although he returned to the London exhibition scene with the opening of the Grosvenor Gallery in 1877, and subsequently widened his fame by showing in Paris and in the major international exhibitions of the later nineteenth century, the production of easel paintings for exhibition was never more than a fraction of the studio's output, which also spilled into a garden building; from 1880 the Burne-Joneses also had a second house, with smaller studio space, in Rottingdean on the Sussex coast. A photograph of the garden studio at the Grange shows the walls lined with massive works, including the ten full-scale cartoons for the Perseus series (fig.5, see pp.185–95).

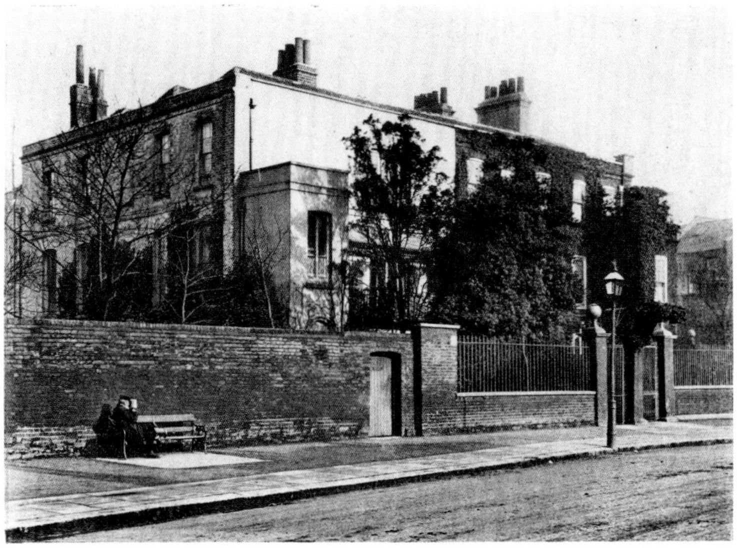

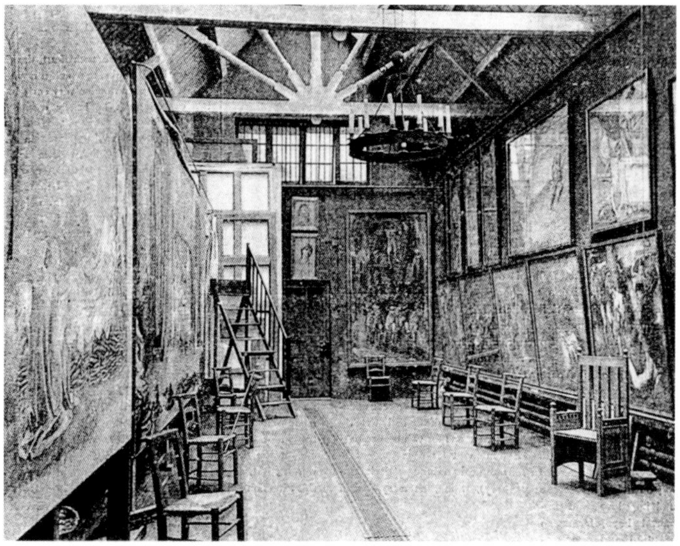

Fig.4
The Grange, North End Lane, Fulham
(Illustrated in *Burne-Jones* 1904, vol. 2)

Fig.5
FREDERICK HOLLYER
Interior of the Garden Studio at the Grange, Fulham, showing the Perseus series cartoons on the right-side wall

Despite his diffidence Burne-Jones was a confident studio chief, and the output of the studio, in conjunction with the Morris firm, was on a scale that would have been inconceivable for a lone artist-genius of the kind celebrated in modernist art criticism. Like many Renaissance *botteghe*, however, Burne-Jones's studio was unable to keep pace with its commitments. Additional studio space had to be rented to accommodate the largest painting of all, *The Sleep of King Arthur in Avalon*, not quite finished at Burne-Jones's death and now in Puerto Rico (fig.6). Six-and-a-half metres wide and teeming with Burne-Jonesian artefacts in a setting of burnished metalwork, Mantegnesque rocks and the thousand flowers of a medieval tapestry, this marked the culmination of Burne-Jones's fascination with Arthurian legend, and some critics have seen the sleeping King Arthur as an analogue for Morris. If the painting remains unfinished, so does the legend in which Arthur is destined, some time in the future, to return, Christlike, and open a new era.

Art for the people[20]

'A good artist ought to work only for public purposes; no private person ought to own pictures.'[21] The thought sounds like Morris, but it is from a studio conversation of Burne-Jones – to whom the poet William Allingham referred in 1866 as 'a People's Man'.[22] A cliché, often repeated, has it that Morris failed to achieve his socialist aims because his firm's products were too expensive for ordinary people to buy. That view is only plausible, however, if the firm's massive production for churches is discounted. Stained-glass windows made by the Morris firm, to designs by Burne-Jones, are available in vast quantity for anyone to see, and they are all over the world: from Ottawa to Calcutta, Boston to Rome. In 1881 Burne-Jones received a commission to provide mosaics for the American Episcopal Church in Rome, his best opportunity to realise the ambition recorded by his wife Georgiana: 'I want big things to do and vast spaces, and for common people to see them and say Oh! – only Oh!'[23] In the event Burne-Jones never saw the mosaics, which were finally completed under the supervision of his studio assistant, Thomas Rooke, in 1907. The resplendent interior, however, survives to give a shock of beauty to any visitor who wanders into the little-visited church on the Via Nazionale, just a step from Rome's main railway station (fig.7).

In a sense, the commitment to social reform that first inspired the two Oxford undergraduates to seek careers as clergymen was best realised, after their conversion to art as a mission, by work for churches. Both Burne-Jones and Morris might, then, have taken heart from the public visibility of their ecclesiastical work. Yet there always

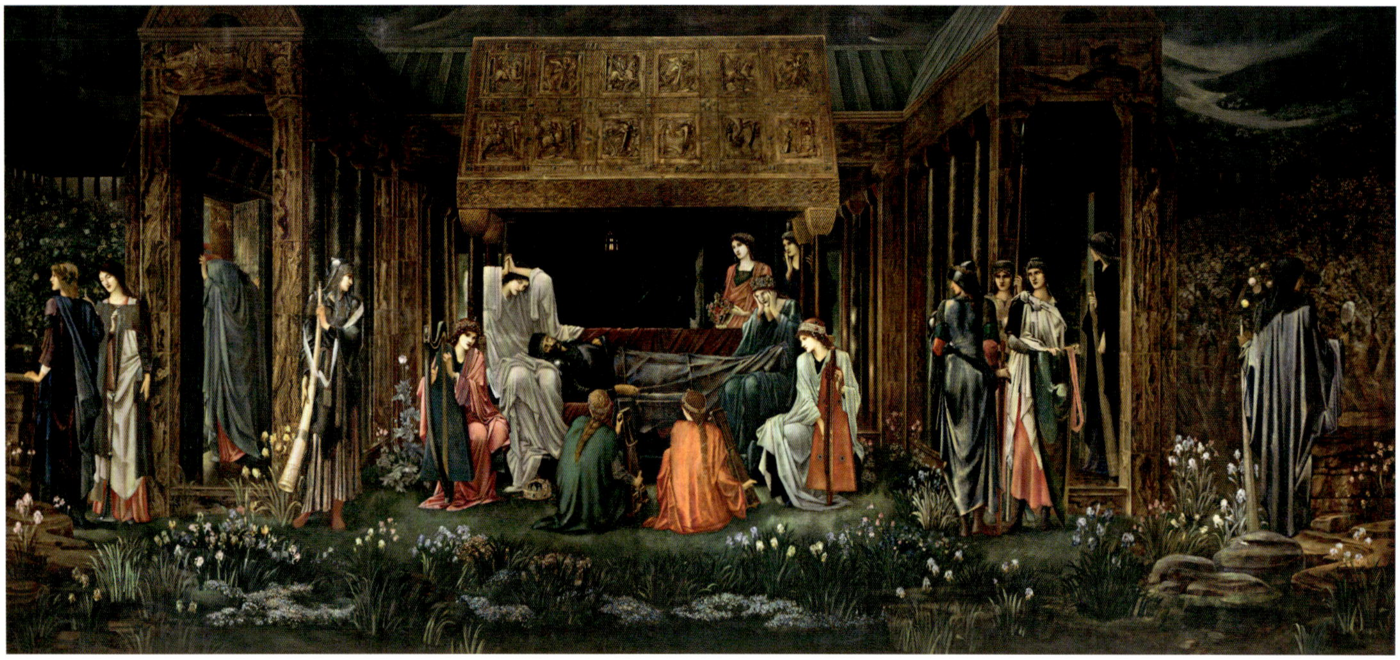

Fig.6
The Sleep of King Arthur in Avalon 1881–98
Oil on canvas
279.4 × 650.2
Museo de Arte de Ponce, Puerto Rico

remained the sense of an unfulfilled dream: 'if I could I would work only in public buildings and in choirs and places where they sing', as Burne-Jones put it in 1888.[24]

Perhaps it is in the nature of such dreams to remain unfulfilled, at least in the imperfect world of modern reality. No words come to mind more readily, in relation to Burne-Jones and his work, than those related to dreams or dreaming. They occur compulsively in texts on the artist, from Rossetti's famous estimate on first meeting – 'One of the nicest young fellows in – Dreamland'[25] – to a remark quoted so often that its original source has become occluded: 'I mean by a picture a beautiful, romantic dream of something that never was, never will be – in a light better than any light that ever shone – in a land no one can define or remember, only desire – and the forms divinely beautiful – and then I wake up, with the waking of Brynhild.'[26] Often these references are read to imply dreaming as an escape or withdrawal from reality, and yet that is a narrow interpretation. Dreaming may also point the way to a utopian or emancipatory future in politics,[27] or to the deepest secrets of the psyche: Sigmund Freud's *Interpretation of Dreams* was published in 1900, the year that Burne-Jones's *Dream of Launcelot at the Chapel of the San Graal* appeared in Paris at the last of the Universal Expositions to feature his work (no.100). Perhaps it was in relation to theories of dreaming that Wyndham Lewis, encountering Burne-Jones's work in 1948, called him a 'pioneer of surrealism'; the comment indicates a more extensive legacy for the artist than current art-historical orthodoxy acknowledges.[28]

If the dream is such a compelling figure for the pictorial world created by Burne-Jones, that is not because it is opposed to reality. It is because, while we are looking, it becomes our reality, as observed in a thoughtful account of 1907 by the critic T. Martin Wood:

> *Painter never lived more in a fairyland of his own making than Burne-Jones, yet a curious reality enters into the strangest of his conceptions ... The air of reality he carried into everything convinces us, we accept these things and they seem so true because whether it be the branches that support the shed, or the flowers and nodding grass that make a carpet for Our Lady, everything is drawn with a realism that would cheat us by its seeming appearance of 'every-day.' Never attempting subterfuge in vagueness, or escaping a difficulty in indefiniteness of form, everything in his art is as clear and*

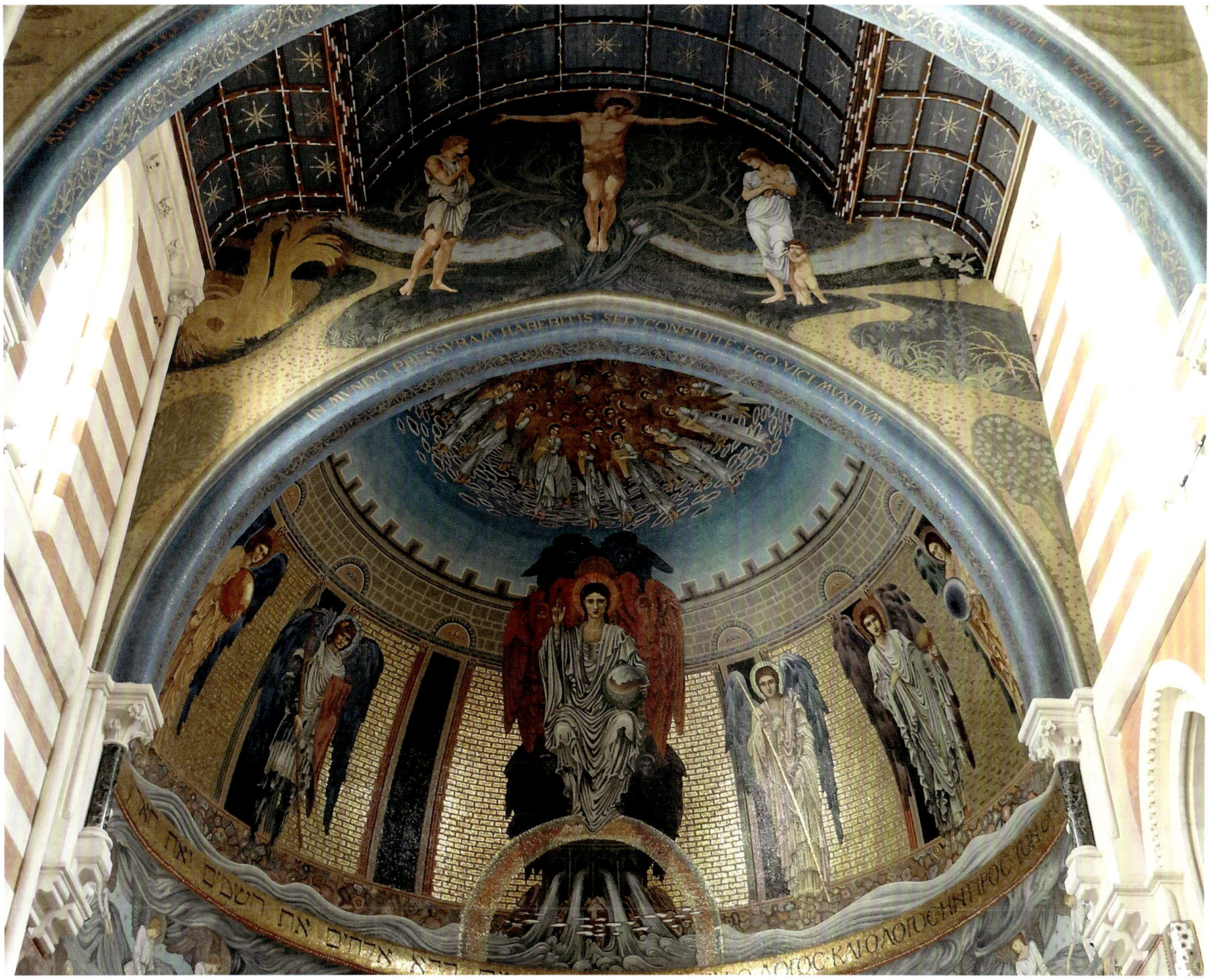

Fig.7
Mosaics in St Paul's Within-the-Walls, Rome, completed 1907

precise as he was clear in his own mind as to how he wished to view these things. From the realism he wedded with his fantasy springs his unusual power of making history an illusory thing, and so it is we feel that in whatever remote place and in however strange a way he has depicted them these things happened so in an older time.[29]

The wording recalls Ruskin's defence of the Pre-Raphaelite Brotherhood in 1851: 'they will draw either what they see, or what they suppose might have been the actual facts of the scene they desire to represent, irrespective of any conventional rules of picture-making'.[30] Burne-Jones never relinquished the Pre-Raphaelite aspiration to clarity of observation, and yet he used his art to make visible things that cannot, or cannot yet, be seen in everyday reality. In a story recounted by Georgiana Burne-Jones, a little girl watched the artist at work on the watercolour version of *The Star of Bethlehem* (the composition represented in this exhibition as a tapestry, no.148). When she asked him 'whether he believed in it, he answered: "It is too beautiful not to be true."'[31]

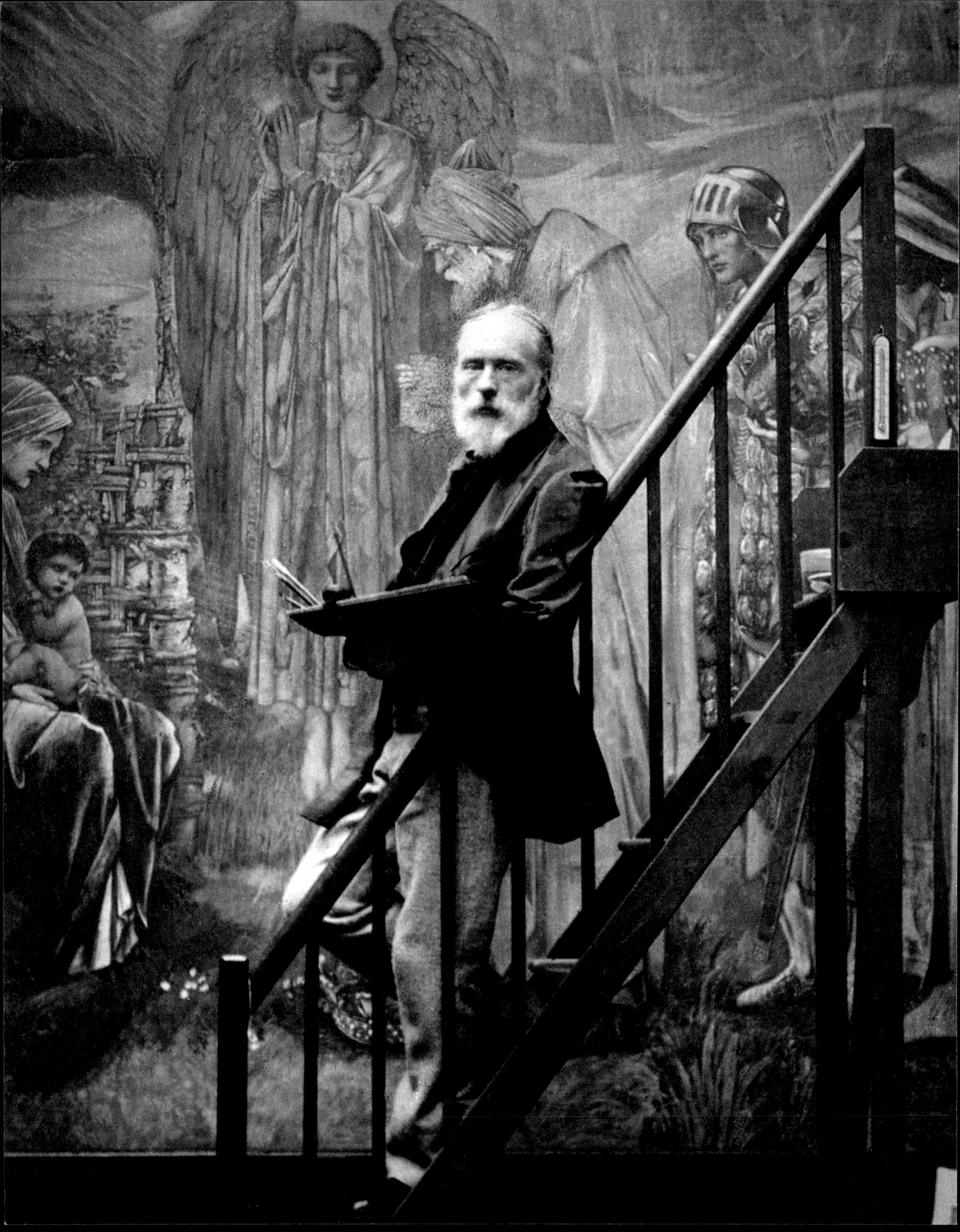

At Work: Burne-Jones's Studio, Materials and Techniques

ALISON SMITH

For an artist known as the quintessential Victorian visionary dreamer, it may seem something of a paradox that Burne-Jones's creations should have a hard crystalline quality. Far from being light and airy, his pictures are workman-like and solid, so that draperies have the weight and feel of stone, and flowers a precious metallic nature, with each part bound into the composition through wiry interlacing patterns of line. It follows that Burne-Jones is not what one would typically call a painter's painter, the kind of artist responsive to the intrinsic properties of a medium, be it the viscosity of oil that lends itself so well to mimesis or the fluid transparency of watercolour used for conveying atmosphere and distance. The very look of unfinished work was repellent to him. He disliked impressionist painting and the improvised brushwork made fashionable by painters such as John Singer Sargent, Arthur Melville and Philip Wilson Steer.[1] Rather he responded to the more resistant techniques and materials traditionally used for engraving, stained glass and mosaic, finding the limitations and discipline imposed by these practices more suited to what he wanted to achieve with his own craft, which was to embed his imagery in architecture so it could exist in creative tension with its surrounds and resonate within a setting.

Because he was happiest working in a fixed environment, Burne-Jones was uneasy with the notion of an itinerant picture. He would worry incessantly about how his paintings were displayed at public exhibition, as on the occasion when the young Conservative politician Arthur Balfour lent *The Wheel of Fortune* (no.97) to the Exposition des Beaux-Arts in Brussels, where it was badly hung on a wooden partition, much to the artist's dismay.[2] This kind of anecdote would indicate that Burne-Jones primarily thought of his art in architectural and decorative terms. Indeed, from the time he first embraced Tractarianism in Birmingham and went on to develop the arts and crafts ethos with William Morris, he approached his art as a form of craft rather than as a professionalised activity. Having received no specialised art training himself, he was not particularly interested in established traditions of painting, but rather upheld the idea that an artist's work should embrace different practices in seeking to transform the world. Together with Morris he strove to elevate the applied arts from their position of being 'lesser' to the fine or pictorial arts. This would explain Burne-Jones's ability to work across different media, expressing his ideas in watercolour, gouache and oil, as well as trying his hand at relief sculpture and designing for stained glass, tapestry, embroidery, mosaic, ceramic, book illustration and jewellery. Many of his paintings developed out of decorative schemes (see nos.123–7), while others involved applied techniques, such as the triptych he made for St Paul's in Brighton (no.12), which incorporates pastiglia (low-relief plaster decoration) and metal leaf. It would be true to say that all of his pictures look decorative, distinguished by clearly compartmentalised compositions, rhythmic dispositions of line and an all-over patterned surface. 'I love to work in that fettered way, and am better in a prison than

Fig.8
BARBARA LEIGHTON
Edward Burne-Jones on a stepladder in his garden studio at the Grange in front of *The Star of Bethlehem*, 27 July 1890.
Printed by Frederick Hollyer
Platinum print
33.3 × 25.7
National Portrait Gallery, London

in the open air always,' Burne-Jones once said, which would suggest that limitation was in some way liberating, in enabling him to create a structure around which he could best express the elusive themes of dream and enchantment that were so central to his vision.[3]

Looking at Burne-Jones's art from a contemporary perspective, when artists work freely across different media, it is easy to admire the interdisciplinary nature of his practice. However, this has not always been the case. Key to the western tradition since the Renaissance has been the distinction between the fine and applied arts, with the former associated with the mind and intellect, and the latter serving a more functional purpose necessitating skills of application and repetition. The division has not always worked in Burne-Jones's favour. Writing in the 1930s, the Irish poet R.N.D. Wilson described him as a mere decorator, contending that the artist's obsession with technique masked an inherent inability to confront reality or give meaning and focus to his designs. Apropos *King Cophetua and the Beggar Maid* (no.98), Wilson wrote dismissively: 'It is a purely decorative work, full of an exquisite handling of minute detail, but devoid of any single compelling purpose.'[4] Others went further in ascribing to Burne-Jones a 'feminine' sensibility, Ruskin being among the first to make the connection when he wrote to the painter George Frederic Watts: 'Jones, with all his power, paints still weakly as a woman – is essentially a woman – because he paints what he *likes* in defiance of what *is*.'[5] This kind of gendered criticism was used to single Burne-Jones out as a radical outsider in his own day and continues to divide opinion. Although recently hailed as a progressive artist on account of his ambiguous trans-sexual bodily types, the decorative nature of his work continues to invite the occasional misogynistic slur: he was, for example, recently described by one critic as 'mimsy'.[6]

The ideal of craftsmanship was of course key to Burne-Jones's mission of public service, which, as he expressed in private to his intimate friend Helen Mary (May) Gaskell, was 'to work and work & make a lovely world and to ask for no wages'.[7] Malcolm Bell, who was also close to Burne-Jones as the nephew of his brother-in-law Edward Poynter, maintained that Burne-Jones prized the decorative arts for being popular, democratic and available to all. And unlike the fine arts, which involved just the undivided attention of one maker, the decorative arts were more inclusive, in that execution could be entrusted to a number of skilled workers.[8] These would have included the weavers who created intricate tapestries out of Burne-Jones's and Morris's designs, the engravers who cut their blocks, and the women with whom both men collaborated over embroidery. Despite their diverging opinions on art and Socialism, Burne-Jones was at one with Morris in viewing art-making as a form of honest labour and a viable basis for a truly egalitarian society. Like Morris, he prided himself on being an artisan rather than a professional painter pandering to the appetites of the rich. He professed a dislike for comfortable furniture and for fashionable male attire, preferring the garb of labourers 'who work at laying gas pipes & have corduroys' and who 'look real & alive & natural'. He was known to be an indefatigable worker: in his studio by 9.00 am every day, hard at work until dinner apart from a short break for lunch, and then spending the rest of the evening drawing cartoons for stained glass.[9] As if to empathise with the ordinary worker, Burne-Jones littered his workbooks with the lamenting refrain of constant work, exploitation and poor remuneration.

The studio

The image Burne-Jones projected of a craftsman devoted to improving the world does not sit comfortably with either the introspective character of his work or the private and unconventional nature of his practice. Such a contradiction was embedded in the way he ran his workshop, for which, unlike the elegant show-studios adopted by many of his contemporaries, Burne-Jones favoured something more plain and functional. Recalling his first visit to the artist's residence, the Grange, in Fulham, the painter and aesthete W.G. Robertson described the studio as 'a huge barrack of a place, like a schoolroom or a gymnasium'.[10] The Burne-Joneses had moved to this large eighteenth-century house in 1867 when Burne-Jones had decided that he needed more space than the narrow room available to him at their residence in Kensington Square. The main studio (fig.9) was a large room on the first floor in the north wing, off which an adjacent drawing room acted as a gallery where visitors could view his finished pictures. Beyond this was a more intimate studio where he painted his portraits and to which only close friends were admitted; it was here that Burne-Jones painted the portraits of Amy Gaskell and Madeleine Deslandes (nos.121, 122). The large studio soon became so crowded that in 1876 he added a smaller room for storing stacks of canvases, cartoons and working materials; and from 1882 he had recourse to a long white rough-cast structure called the Garden Studio, (fig.10), designed to his specification by the architect and designer W.A.S. Benson, where he could work during the summer months.[11] In addition to the Grange, Burne-Jones had access to the large studio of fellow artist Roddam Spencer Stanhope on Campden Hill; and his final monumental composition, *The Sleep of King Arthur in Avalon* (fig.6), was painted at 9 St Paul's Studios (now 151 Talgarth Road), reputedly the largest workshop of this kind in the city.

The large studios available to Burne-Jones from 1867 are indicative of the dramatic surge in productivity that set in from around this time. After 1875, when the original partnership dissolved, Burne-Jones became Morris & Co.'s sole designer for stained glass, producing many cartoons for windows alongside his other works. The orders he made from his main supplier, the colourman Charles Roberson, rose markedly at this time, and to keep pace with the rate of production, he started to employ assistants on the lines of a Renaissance workshop. Their task was to transfer his designs to canvas and undertake some preliminary underpainting in dead colour. Most were hired on a temporary basis and included Charles Fairfax Murray, who assisted from 1866 to 1871, and Thomas Rooke, who joined in 1869 to

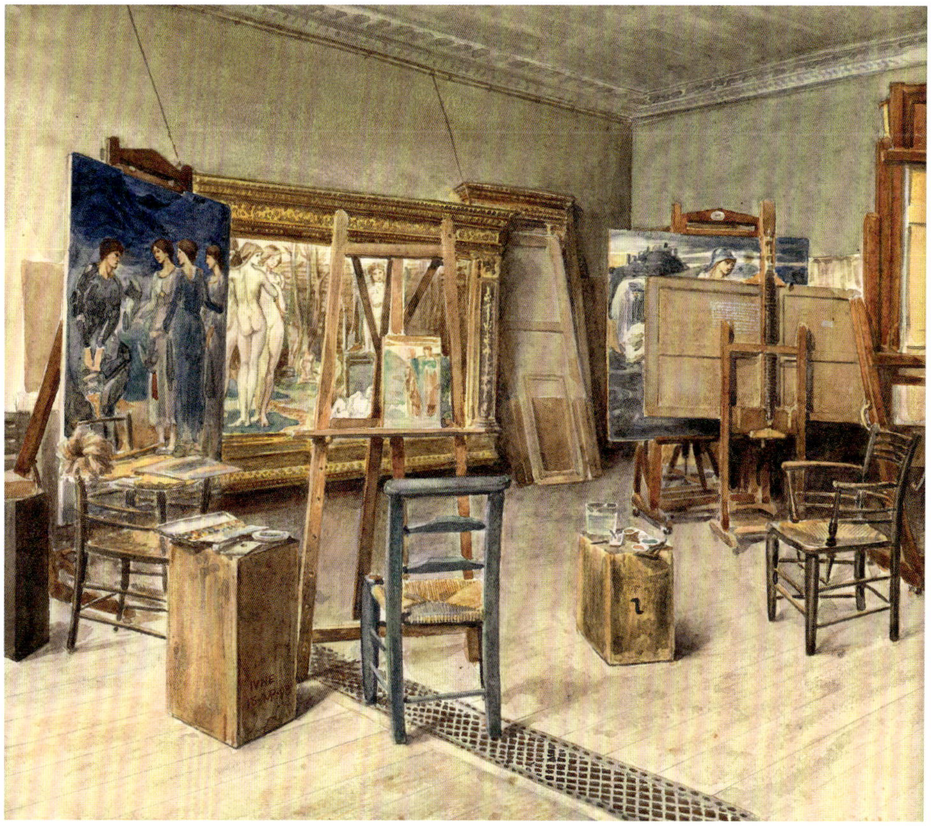

Fig.9
AMBROSE POYNTER
The Studio at the Grange 18 June 1898
Watercolour
26 × 30.5
Private collection

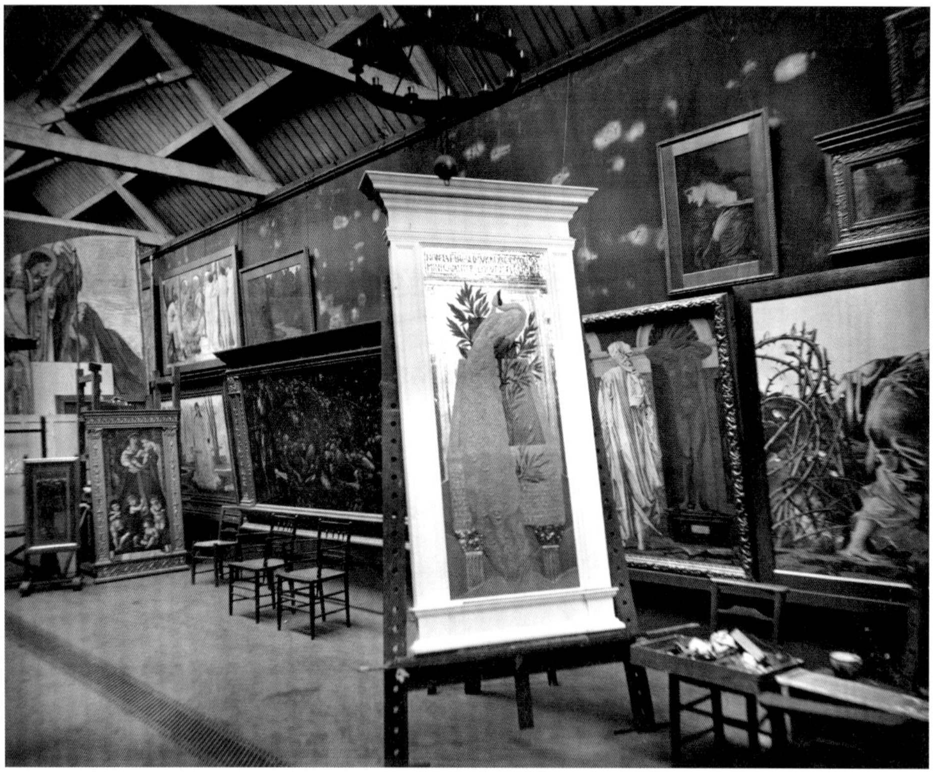

Fig.10
FREDERICK HOLLYER
The interior of Edward Burne-Jones's garden studio at the Grange, 1887
Historic England Archive

help with perspective and remained the artist's chief studio assistant until his death in 1898.[12] Distinguishing Burne-Jones's hand from that of his assistants is no easy matter, especially as their services were dispensed with once the underpainting was complete, although it can be discerned in unfinished paintings where the base layers are exposed, such as in nos.49 and 63. Rooke's diaries provide insight into how closely the two men worked together from 1894 in bringing a number of unfinished pictures to completion: the final touches for *Love and the Pilgrim* (no.101), for instance, occupied them on and off from 2 November 1895 to 3 April 1897, when Burne-Jones completed the crown of birds.[13]

The main evidence for the studio comes from Burne-Jones's own caricatures and comments, the descriptions of his contemporaries, plus a few paintings and photographs. The last present an empty space devoid of human presence with rows of pictures lining the walls or waiting completion on easels. Burne-Jones appears in only two of these images: the photograph by Barbara Leighton (later Sotheby) that shows him standing on the high steps he used to complete the upper portions of *The Star of Bethlehem*, and Philip Burne-Jones's portrait of his father painting away at his easel (figs.8, 11). Both present a master painter in command of his environment, a far cry from the image evoked in Burne-Jones's own caricatures of an exhausted dishevelled figure despairing over his own creations. In fact, contrary to the image of an organised workshop evoked by many of the photographs, most first-hand accounts of the studio present a picture of utter chaos. Rooke recalls that it was barely possible to cross from one side to the other so dense was the clutter, while the art critic Joseph Comyns Carr found the sheer mess of the place at odds with the ordered completeness of the designs emanating from the artist's hand.[14] It would seem that only Burne-Jones himself had a complete overview of how the studio functioned with its innumerable props, books and studies piled all over the place, and was constantly anxious lest anything be moved or cleaned (fig.12).

The mysterious aura surrounding the studio would help explain why so little is known about Burne-Jones's practice apart from what has been handed down

Fig.11
PHILIP BURNE-JONES
Sir Edward Burne-Jones 1898
Oil on canvas
76.2 × 52.2
National Portrait Gallery, London

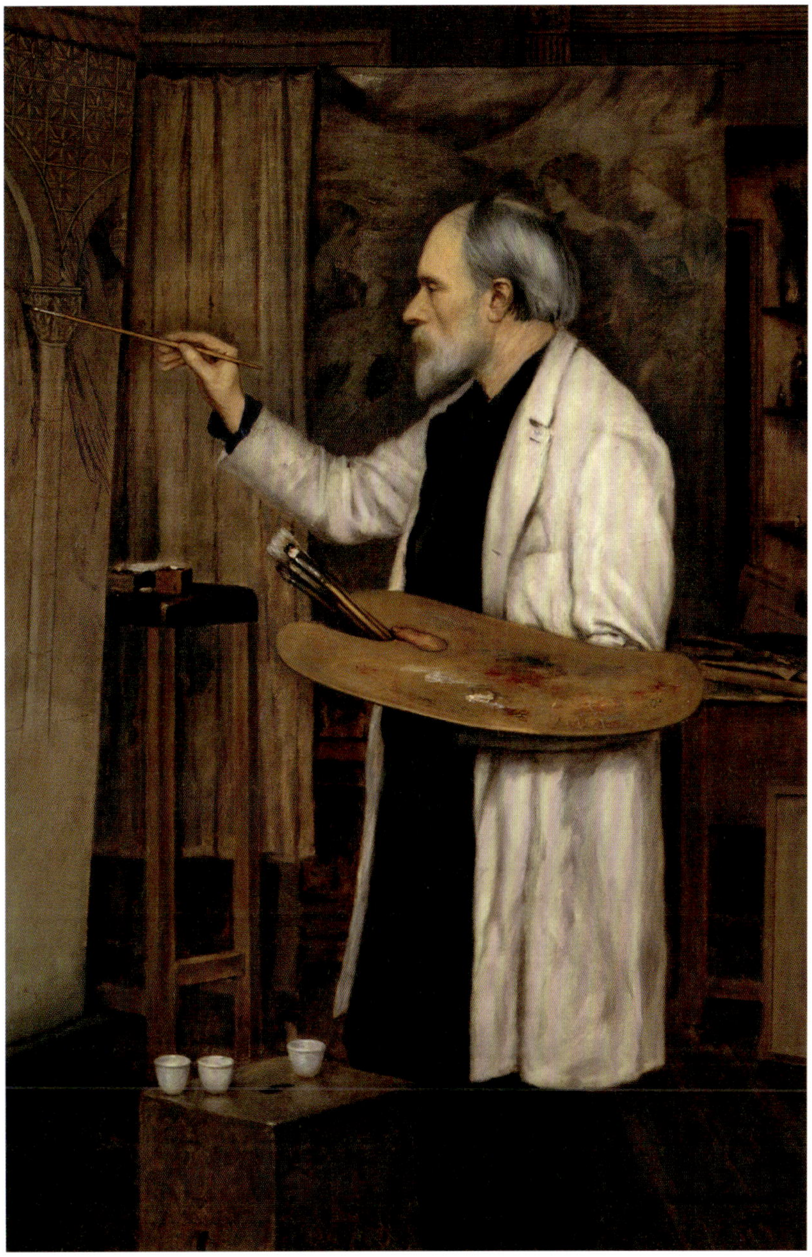

through the written testimonies of contemporaries. Rooke writes that he was wary of answering queries about his technique, and according to Burne-Jones's wife Georgiana, he had a rule that no one should be admitted to the studio in his absence.[15] It was in this sealed-off environment that he could reconcile the dual aspects of his practice – to complete a work to the highest possible standard so it might be released into the world, but yet to keep it hidden and close to himself. Although a consummate technician in aspiring to create something permanent and durable, Burne-Jones was also highly experimental in the way he employed his materials. To this day there has been very little technical analysis of his work, especially of the paintings in oil. While this can partly be ascribed to the durability of his materials and methods (Tate conservation has, for instance, never had a need to carry out any restoration treatment on *The Golden Stairs* or *King Cophetua*), it also relates to the private and idiomatic ways in which he employed his materials and which extend back to his early work in watercolour.

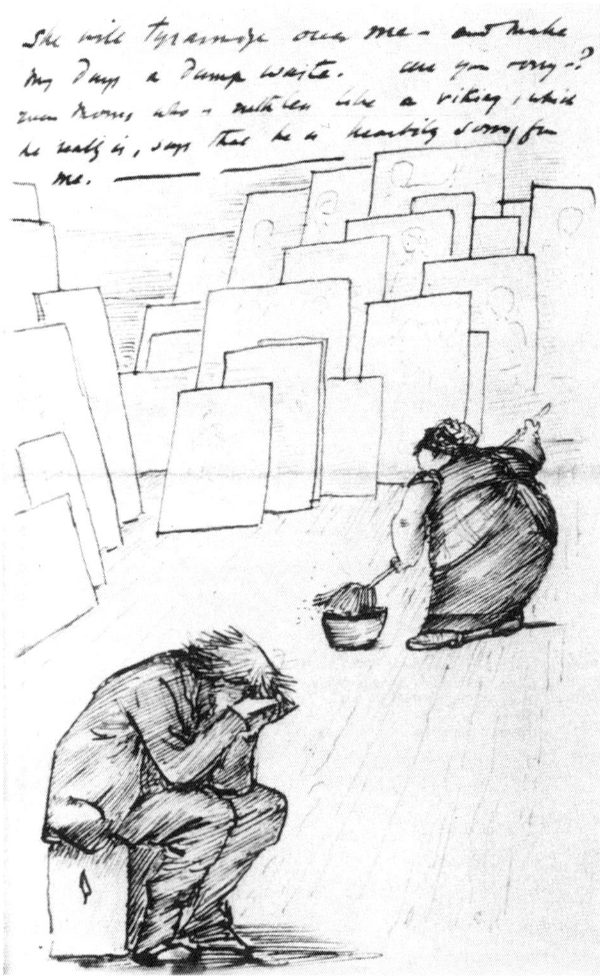

Fig.12
The Artist's despair at the cleaning of his 'Augean Studio', from the Album *Letters to Katie*, 1890s
Pen and ink
22.2 × 17.8
Private collection

Watercolour

Burne-Jones could be said to have started his career as a painter in watercolour, a medium traditionally accorded an indeterminate position between painting and drawing. Despite the efforts of the Society of Painters in Water-Colours (founded in 1804 and subsequently known as the Old Water Colour Society) and the New Society (established in 1834) to elevate its status, watercolour was still ranked beneath oil because of its association with the feminine, the amateur and the domestic. Being an 'amateur' himself (an artist who had received no formal training), Burne-Jones had been encouraged by his first mentor, Dante Gabriel Rossetti, to follow his own instincts. Discovering that oil made him physically sick, he took to working in pen and ink using hatching and stippling and employing a metal scraper to soften form and create texture – a process he subsequently transferred to his early work in watercolour, in defiance of the conventional association of the medium with transparency and fluidity of technique. For this he employed the latest pigments on the market, showing a particular predilection for madder carmine and vermillion, which he treated in a heavy way by adding bodycolour (an opaque water-based paint now called gouache) and ox gall (an acidic brown ink) for greater density.[16] Encouraged by Rossetti, who used a similar method, he applied paint thickly and then scraped into the hardened surface so that the work as a physical object could complement the sinister and magical subjects that caught his imagination.

The self-consciously wilful nature of Burne-Jones's method was only possible because of the strength of the supports he employed, which in many cases consisted of two pieces of heavy cartridge paper mounted on canvas and wrapped around a

Fig.13
Clerk Saunders 1861 (detail, no.19)

stretcher. *Clerk Saunders* (no.19) was painted on such a surface, on which the artist then applied zinc white to provide a clean and relatively non-absorbent coating for laying in colour. Paint was employed thinly for the faces and hands of the two figures but elsewhere built up in thick layers to evoke the 'sad and rainy' brown landscape of the morbid ballad that had inspired the painting. For further expressive effect he hatched fine parallel lines into the dry paint, adopting a 'scraperboard' technique to expose the underlying white as seen in the rose stalks on the right and the heavy leaden sky (fig.13).[17] In subjecting his materials to violent treatment for expressive, psychological ends, Burne-Jones would have felt emboldened by the radical ideas concerning the independence of artistic expression being formulated within the Rossetti circle at the time – a tendency further encouraged by his friendship with the poet Algernon Charles Swinburne and the painter Simeon Solomon.

Burne-Jones's early years can be summed up as a period of trial and error during which he discovered what pigments worked for him and what proved to be fugitive and troublesome. Some of the early watercolours, such as *Clerk Saunders* and *Merlin and Nimue* (no.20), now appear dark and muddy in contrast to early descriptions of their glowing colour. He soon discovered that Rossetti was not an ideal teacher in this respect, noting with hindsight that he lacked 'any stern morality about his work': 'He would have the very easiest method of painting and didn't care in the least whether it was lasting or not ... I used to say to him, "why do you paint with colours that you know are not permanent?" but he wouldn't listen to me.'[18] As he developed confidence in his own vision, Burne-Jones became more fastidious about the material side of his practice. He made a point of acquainting himself with the researches of the chemist and colourman George Field into the permanence of pigments and, apart from using traditional colours like red lead, chrome (yellow) and Antwerp blue, splashed out on the more costly, longer-lasting, newly introduced materials such as Field's vermillion so beloved by the Pre-Raphaelite Holman Hunt, another stickler for durability.[19]

As Burne-Jones developed as a watercolour painter in the 1860s, he became less dependent on Rossetti's influence. In 1864 he was elected Associate of the Old Water Colour Society, a by now rather conservative organisation with a strong emphasis on landscape. Although Burne-Jones was by no means unique in using complex mixed-media techniques, his method served to emphasise the flatness and texture of paint itself rather than evoke atmosphere and distance, thereby setting him apart from other painters. During this period his watercolours increased in size as he experimented with larger sheets and stronger supports to sustain the weight and tension of his pigments, and from 1865 he started to use moist paints in collapsible screw-cap tubes on a more regular basis.[20] These not only aided the thicker, drier application of colour but allowed him to work from dark to light, as well as paint on coloured papers and grounds. Employing hoghair brushes used for oil, he created dense layered surfaces, scumbling powdery highlights over dark colour (see nos.22 and 23) and resorting to smaller sables for finishing. As his palette began to soften, he continued to experiment with the latest pigments, including the new green-blue ceruleum, cobalt blue and violet – colours with a jewel-like quality that often counteracted the melancholy themes of his works, creating a tension between surface appearance and hidden, implied meaning.

The pastel-like chalky appearance of Burne-Jones's watercolours owed much to his application of zinc white, the opaque pigment (prepared from zinc oxide) he used in increasing quantities from 1862 onwards. Since it was first introduced in the 1830s, this 'white' for highlights proved to be contentious in watercolour circles with many purists regarding it as a lazy shortcut and a betrayal of the medium's characteristic transparency. Rather than using thin washes of watercolour and allowing the paper to provide the highlights, Burne-Jones went to the opposite extreme by coating his paper with a ground of zinc white and then covering it with thick layers of watercolour and gouache applied in the manner of oil paint. Fairfax Murray describes how he achieved magical results by mixing the colour on the surface with the white ground, which involved slightly moistening the colour and sometimes working it up as far as the paper, often spoiling the brush in the process by breaking and spreading the hairs. 'This trick is so dangerous to the uninitiated,' he warned, but with constant practice it invariably worked for Burne-Jones.[21] In his later years he added gold and aluminium (see no.145) to enhance the ornate effect, a technique about as far removed from traditional watercolour painting as possible.

The intermedial nature of Burne-Jones's art – his habit of transposing one medium into another so it is difficult to distinguish between them – marks him out as one of the most innovative painters of his time. W.G. Roberston recalled:

> *Whether working in oil, in water colour, in pastel or in pure line, he appeared wilfully to ignore the possibilities of his medium and to put it to uses for which it was never intended. In watercolour he would take no advantage of its transparency, but load on body colour and paint thickly in gouache; when he turned to oil he would shun the richness of impasto, drawing thin glazes of colour over careful drawings in raw umber heightened with white; if he used pastel, it was to imitate oil.*[22]

Even artists and connoisseurs were sometimes incapable of distinguishing one medium from another: John Ruskin, for instance, on a visit to the artist's studio with Cardinal Manning, mistook the oil painting *The Mirror of Venus* for watercolour, informing his companion that it was 'pure watercolour, my lord'.[23]

Burne-Jones's methods also singled him out as a rebel, and inevitably parallels were drawn between the way he corrupted his materials and the unwholesome character of his work with its inversion of conventional gender stereotypes and overall feeling of enervation. Such criticisms only exacerbated the artist's anxiety about releasing his pictures into the public domain. Added to this was his concern that his paintings should not be mistreated due to any confusion over the media

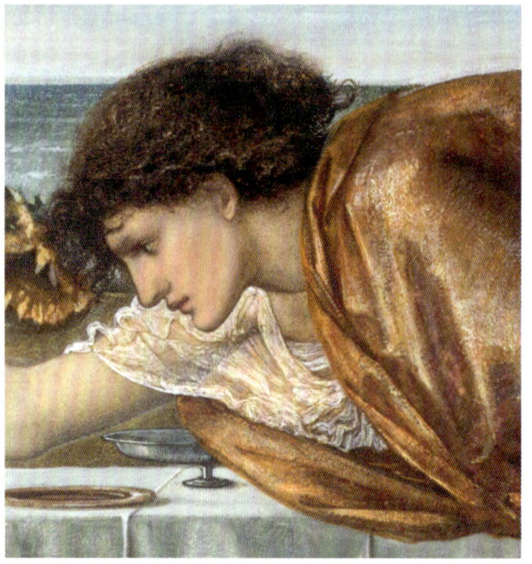

Fig.14
Wine of Circe 1863–9 (detail, no.23)

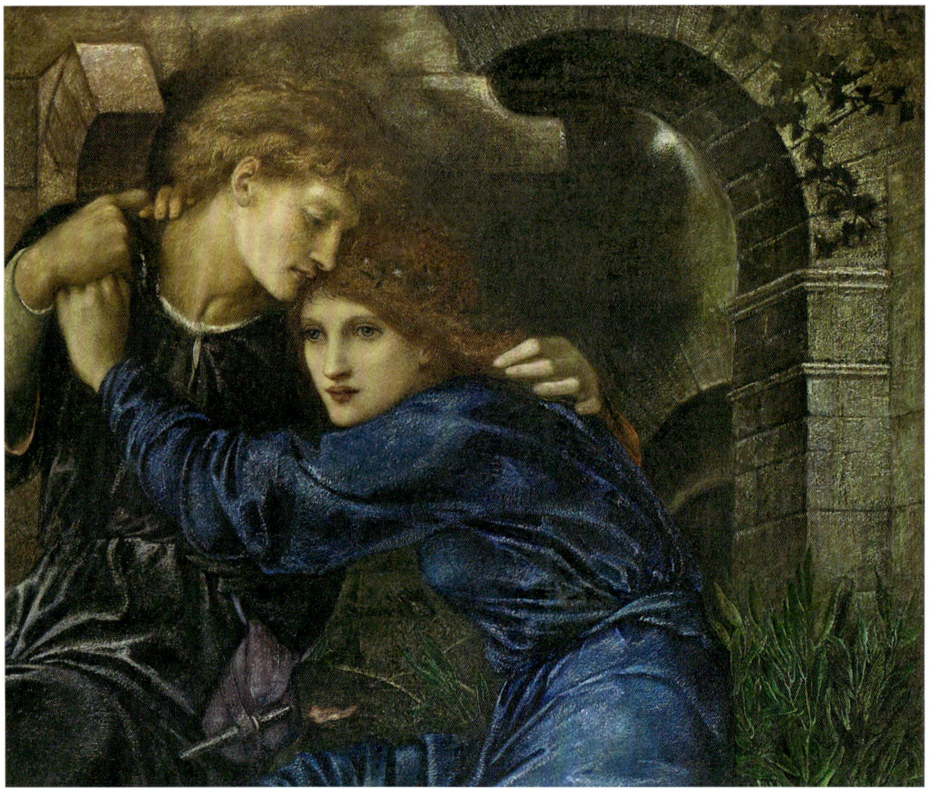

Fig.15
Love Among the Ruins 1870–3 (detail, no.91)

employed, to which end he would paste instructions on the reverse about how best to handle them. An inscription appended to *Love among the Ruins* (fig.15, no.91), the artist's largest watercolour to date, warned that it would 'be injured by the slightest moisture'.[24] Widely regarded in Burne-Jones's day as one of his greatest achievements – with its theme of decay and ruination underscoring the power of love symbolised by the sad embrace of the lovers – it marked a decisive shift in the critical reception of his work. Formerly hostile critics praised the painting for its haunting sentiment and extraordinary technique, the *Art Journal* declaring that a whole chapter could be dedicated to it, so completely did it 'illustrate the beginning, progress and end of much that is, and has been, done in recent watercolour art'.[25] After it entered the collection of the watercolour enthusiast Frederick Craven, the painting was lent on five separate occasions to public exhibitions, including the Exposition Universelle in Paris in 1878. Returning to Paris in 1893 for exhibition at the Sociétié Nationale des Beaux-Arts, it was taken to Goupil's Gallery to be photographed and in the process of preparation was accidentally damaged by the application of egg white across the surface to give an extra glaze; apparently no one had seen the label on the back, convinced by its size and the thick handling of paint that it was an oil. Although later restored (the albumen removed with ox gall), Burne-Jones suffered much grief in the interim, which reputedly inspired his arch-rival, James Whistler, to comment: 'Didn't I always say the man knew nothing about painting ... They take his oils for water-colours and his water-colours for oils.'[26]

Oil

Burne-Jones's shift towards painting in oil followed hard on his resignation from the Old Water Colour Society in 1870. In leaving a body that only accepted works in watercolour, he was now open to working in a wider range of materials than hitherto, and given that his works were often mistaken for oils, being matt and opaque, it was inevitable that he should branch out in the medium, especially as it encouraged working on a large scale. His orders of painting materials from Roberson's increased dramatically at this time, and alongside pigments included paper and canvases of all sizes – some with distinct dimensions such as the infill panels for the *Briar Rose* cycle at Buscot Park (no.127), listed as either ¾ inch or ⅞ inch thick.[27] As with his early watercolours, painting in oil did not come instinctively to Burne-Jones, or so he discovered to his dismay when working on *The Beguiling of Merlin* (no.93). Finding that the paint would not adhere to the surface, he blamed his supplier, Roberson, complaining to Frederick Leyland (who commissioned the painting) that 'there are spots innumerable in it where the paint will not bite the canvas, and where eventually it will, chip off and shew ruinous gaps'.[28] Fiona Mann has recently suggested that this may have been due to either the unprimed absorbent canvas used for the work or his experimentation with a medium called Bonomi's Preparation.[29] Apart from the medium employed, it would appear that the process adopted by Burne-Jones for his oils was very similar to what he used for watercolour: he would paint thinly in oil building up layers and then add scumbles to impart a dry crumbly texture. Fairfax Murray describes it as follows:

> *on the grey ground preparation he, when perfectly dry, scumbled strong colour and when that was dry repainted first the light in strong body with very dry powdery white, usually pure, and the half tones with white mixed with colour; this when dry was glazed again and this process was continued until the picture was completed – no medium of any kind being used throughout –a little turpentine being used sometimes to thin the colour and blotting paper to take the surplus oil out of some the colours occasionally.*[30]

Whether working in watercolour or oil, it mattered to Burne-Jones that his paintings should look dry and hard, to which end he was sparing in his use of binding medium. Although he ordered regular amounts of copal resin to make his paint more fluid, he never took to gelled mediums, such as Roberson's Medium, which the Pre-Raphaelites used to lend transparency and gloss to their works, confessing to the art critic Harry Quilter that he found the shine 'horrible'.[31] Rather he inclined to the lean or dry use of paint used by his friend George Frederic Watts, adopting a method by which he would blot or squeeze out the oil binder to allow for a thin matt texture, as used for the head of the king in *King Cophetua* (no.98). In order to speed up the drying process, Burne-Jones employed turpentine as a diluent and developed a method for slowing evaporation – a compound of equal amounts of copal, linseed oil and spike oil (of lavender) that he used sparingly, pouring out just a few drops each day.[32] In his posthumous account of his father's practice, Philip Burne-Jones recalls that Burne-Jones never painted into a tacky or half-dry surface, preferring to wait until each accumulated area had dried so as to preserve purity of colour.[33] It was a painstaking process and meant it was vital that he fix the design in the initial stages, lest he was compelled to start again. Such was the case with *The Rock of Doom* from the Perseus series (no.139). Here he found himself straying from his original concept by filling up the background with incidental detail, which necessitated three days of work taking it all out, so he could start again. According to Philip, Burne-Jones was scrupulous in 'scraping, turpenting and even chloroforming out original errors before painting over it'.[34]

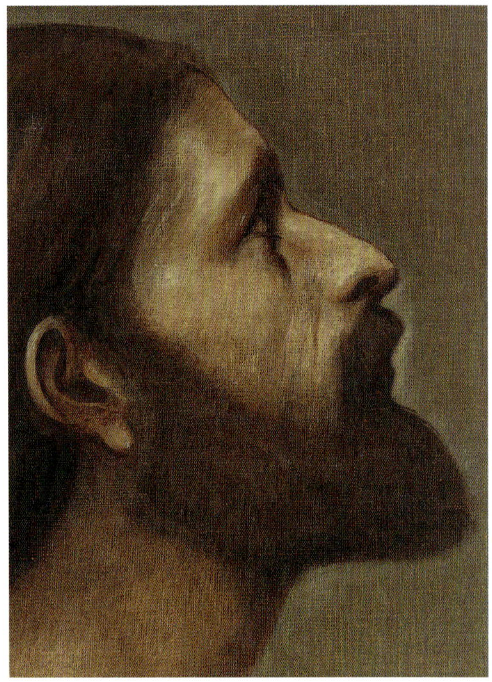

Fig.16
Portrait Head of King Cophetua c.1883–4 (detail, no.113)

The specific challenges of painting in oil required that Burne-Jones work on multiple projects at any given time so he could build up his compositions layer by layer. It encouraged productivity, but also repetition, as he moved between one project and another. The system he developed for layering in paint he referred to as the 'bones' of composition – the bodily metaphor suggesting that the structure had to be established first before he could add the upper layers of 'flesh', 'skin' and 'hair'.[35] Describing the process, Philip recalls how his father would start with a rough sketch, from which he would work towards a larger drawing on brown paper approximately the size of the finished work itself, and at the same time produce studies from models for each constituent part. For his largest works he often produced a full-scale study in pastel or watercolour as for *King Cophetua* and *Love and the Pilgrim* (no.101), which were both preceded by cartoons in pastel. Once the cartoon was complete, assistants would trace and transfer the design to canvas and then draw it in in monochrome, as already described, before Burne-Jones himself took over. If a painting was to be varnished, it had to wait several years for which he would often paste instructions on the reverse.[36]

Throughout his career, whether he was working on vellum, paper or canvas, or designing for stained glass, tapestry and mosaic, Burne-Jones aimed at creating something permanent and lasting. To this end he was scrupulous in his choice of pigment, apparently never employing a colour about whose durability chemists expressed any doubt, despite the restrictions this imposed on his palette.[37] Instead he would create dense tapestry-like effects by building up colour in complex mixes of varied thickness as in *King Cophetua*, where the overall gold-brown tonality is enlivened by touches of rose madder, vermillion, cobalt blue, ultramarine and emerald green.[38] In many works the canvas weave is prominent (as in no.98), especially in the areas where the paint is lean, and on occasion, he would paint on the reversed unprimed side to enhance the effect, as with the head study of Benson for *King Cophetua* (no.113 and see detail above, fig.16) .

All Burne-Jones's paintings represent a synthesis of different processes: painting, engraving, gilding, sculpting and weaving, all combined in a non-hierarchical way. It was an approach that had more to do with craft than with spontaneous execution, which would explain the extraordinary lengths he would go to in order to fabricate the imaginary world of his pictures, including designing many of the accessories that feature in them. Dresses were made to his specification by Aglaia Coronio (as for no.95), while Benson made countless objects including armour, crowns and musical

Fig.17
Designs for armour, jewellery and musical instruments, reproduced in Aymer Vallance, 'The Decorative Art of Edward Burne-Jones', *The Easter Art Annual*, 1900

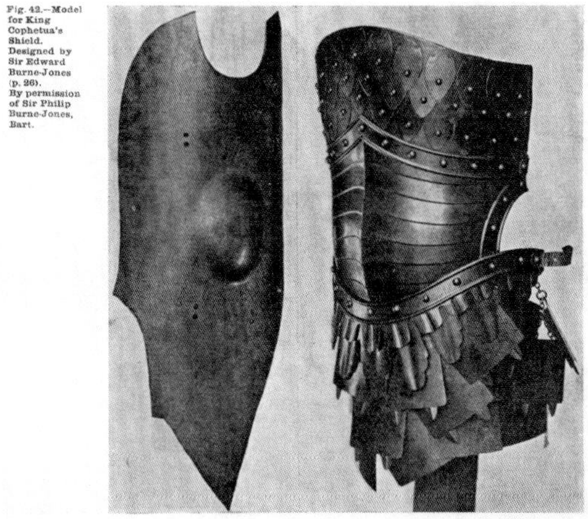

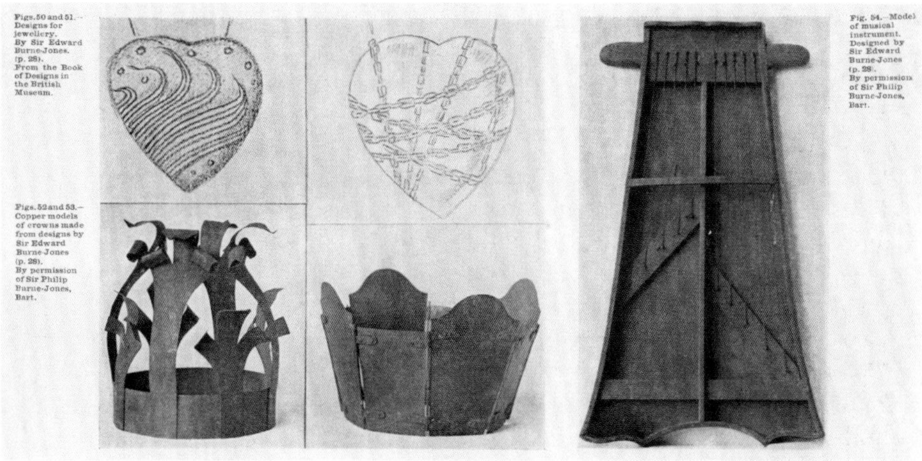

instruments (fig.17). Burne-Jones even designed a snake for the Perseus series, which he modelled in wax with the help of the ceramicist William de Morgan.[39] The purpose of these substitutes was not just to make the counterparts in the paintings appear real and solid, but to imbue each painting with an imaginary reality of its own, so it appeared, in the artist's words, as 'a reflection of a reflection of something purely imaginary', divorced from association with any historical time. 'I don't want to pretend that this isn't a picture', Burne-Jones is recorded as saying, meaning that he was not interested in offering a window onto the world or in communicating temporality, but that he aspired to create something that was both imaginary and real, something that was not of this world yet existed as a decorative object in its own right.[40]

Burne-Jones's ideal of a continuity of media reminds us of his desire to find large spaces in which he could locate his works where people could gaze on them in silent awe in the spirit of the Middle Ages. It was inevitable he should dislike bright light and the way pictures were presented at public exhibition ('the dazzle is simply barbarous,' he once complained), preferring the dim light of church interiors.[41] The slow, patient workmanlike nature of Burne-Jones's art placed him at odds with the idea of painting as a commodity, and certainly everything in his practice was made in defiance of the 'realist' mindset of his day. Rather he used the very substance of the materials he employed to craft an alternative world that was compelling to behold while remaining deeply personal. The uniqueness of his methods, in combining experimentation with craftsmanship, was central to this mission.

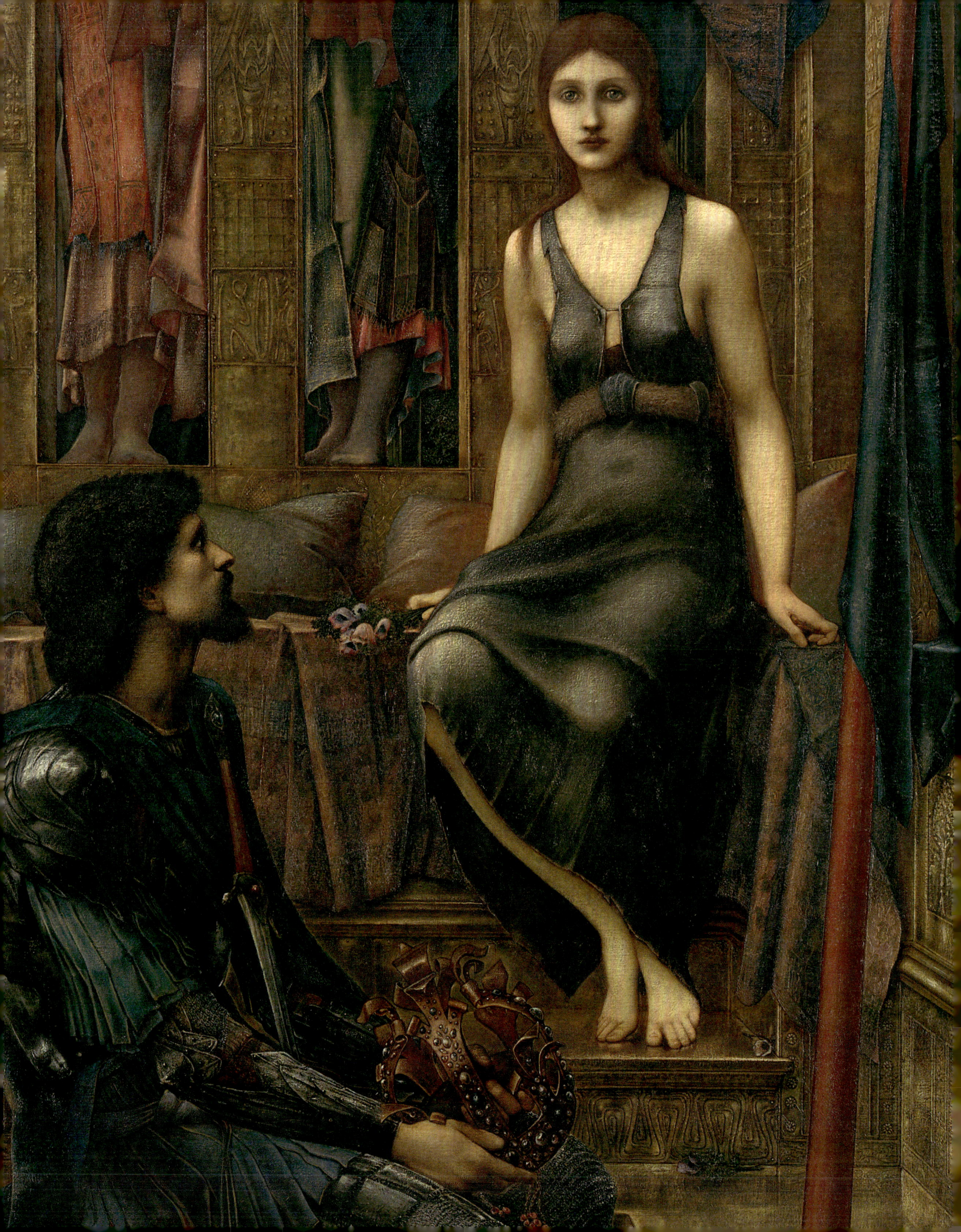

'Girlish Dreams': Burne-Jones in the Twentieth Century

NICHOLAS TROMANS

Georgiana Burne-Jones's biography of her husband, begun at his death in 1898 and published in two volumes in 1904, has consistently been admired for its elegance, clarity and – within the limits that frame any biographer – honesty. A century later, Burne-Jones's most recent biographer, Fiona MacCarthy, was still swift to praise. MacCarthy quotes Wilfrid Scawen Blunt, the poet, traveller and always opinionated man-of-action, as finding the *Memorials of Edward Burne-Jones* to be 'a thorough woman's book'. She concurs: 'It is the woman's sense of the importance of domestic background and emotional history that distinguishes her book from the event-centred biographies of men written by men that were de rigueur at the period.'[1] It was perhaps fitting that Burne-Jones should have been memorialised in this less masculine manner, given the gender-shifting reputation of his work itself, to which charges of effeminacy had attached for many years. In 1879 the human forms in his pictures were said to be such as 'every man who respects his manhood and every woman who values her honour must regard with disgust'. His way of inhabiting the styles of the old masters was 'entirely opposed to the originative masculine temper', thought one distinguished art critic. Ruskin, evidently taking a different definition of artistic manliness, had written to the artist G.F. Watts (both themselves the subject of some scorn on account of an alleged want of virility) that Burne-Jones, in generating his own imagined world and declining to confront hard reality, was in essence a woman.[2]

Burne-Jones's allies had to get used to dealing with this sort of thing. Joseph Comyns Carr, writing in the introduction to the catalogue of the 1898–9 memorial exhibition at the New Gallery, saw this perceived effeminacy as the central charge against his friend:

> *There are men so constituted that all delicate beauty seems to move them to resentment ... who go about the world constantly reassuring themselves of their own virility by denouncing what they conceive to be the effeminate weakness of others. To this class the art of Burne-Jones came in the nature of a personal offence. They raged against it; warning their generation not to yield to its insidious and enervating influence.*[3]

Rudyard Kipling, Georgiana's nephew, may perhaps have been one of those with doubts about some of Burne-Jones's unheroic imagery. But his love for the man was sure. Raw from the artist's funeral, he wrote: 'His work was the least part of him. It is him that one wants – the size and strength and the power and the jests and the God given sympathy of the man. He *knew*.'[4] In retrospect, Kipling might be taken to have spoken for the following generation's approach to Burne-Jones, which was so often based on a nostalgia for the artist himself – the Pre-Raphaelite from

King Cophetua and the Beggar Maid 1898 (detail, no.98)

unpromising Birmingham who had come from nowhere in particular to being almost embarrassingly well connected (not least through his wife and her remarkable sisters); who had gone to Oxford as Ned Jones and died as Sir Edward Coley Burne-Jones, Baronet; and who had made a work of art of himself more perfect than any dandy.

The public fascination with Burne-Jones's art had begun in the 1870s and reached a fever pitch by the 1890s, the years that nostalgics would often later represent as almost having belonged to him. During that decade, Burne-Jones became the sign of taking art seriously (or *too* seriously), especially among women, who were expected to own reproductions rather than the real thing. Thus Burne-Jones prints are said to have been the rage among women undergraduates at Oxford, while Proust imagined his character the Duchesse d'Alpes as using the same images as instruments of her civilising mission among her friends.[5] It was indeed during the 1890s that Burne-Jones became a celebrity in Europe, following the great impact made by *King Cophetua and the Beggar Maid* (no.98) at the Exposition Universelle of 1889. This is now a well-told story, and Burne-Jones's prestige among the French symbolists is understandably held up as key evidence of his art-historical significance. But their passion was soon spent, lasting we are told only into the mid-1890s.[6] Léonce Bénédite, Director of the Musée du Luxembourg, the French capital's premier museum of modern art, interpreted the affair as a confusion over politics. According to Bénédite, the inherently elitist symbolists could not understand, love him as they did, why Burne-Jones felt the need to reach out to the masses through his decorative schemes. To a French connoisseur, political art was beefy and brown – like Courbet – and nothing like the etiolated elegance of the Englishman.[7] The greatest of the Belgian symbolists, Fernand Khnopff, saw things similarly. To Khnopff, Burne-Jones's reputation had been built by the cultured few, whose lead the public had subsequently followed until 'the world had given him not merely the most universal celebrity, but even, alas! had granted him popularity'.[8] Picasso, on a visit to England decades later (to attend a meeting in Sheffield of the Soviet-directed World Peace Council in 1950), told the surrealist artist Roland Penrose that, when he arrived in Paris in 1900, he had originally intended to keep going on to London in pursuit of the works of Burne-Jones that he had already admired in reproduction in Barcelona.[9] That sounds rather too like a fable to be entirely literal and specifically recalls the story in Huysmans's 1884 novel *À rebours* of Jean des Esseintes, the literary archetype of the uncompromising European aesthete who endlessly contemplates a visit to aristocratic England but never quite makes it.

Burne-Jones lived to feel for himself the fading of his magic in the marketplace, as works came back from exhibition unsold.[10] The studio sale that usually followed an artist's death was held in his case with almost unseemly hurry, possibly because the family was aware that prices for the master's work were already failing. The artist's legacy to his profession however seemed assured: his model of other-worldly beauty remained an exemplar for some at least down to the 1940s.[11] That legacy was institutionalised through Morris & Co., who continued to supply 'Burne-Jones' windows well into the twentieth century, and at the art schools of Birmingham and other towns and cities where Burne-Jones, in his guise as Pre-Raphaelite decorator, appeared an apt foundation on which to build a symbolism compatible with civic responsibility. There was even a flurry of efforts to interpret him as the great modern Christian painter.[12] But this Edwardian afterglow of decent liberal dreaming soon risked being made to look uselessly tired by the arrival in London of post-impressionism. Burne-Jones's son Philip, himself an artist of real talent but, it seems, constrained by his own snobbery, unhelpfully drew the contrast as extremely as possible by joining in the ignorant denunciation of the new styles – cubism, fauvism and the like – as degenerate, echoing (apparently without any self-awareness) the very language used against his father's more unsettling visions.[13] The British intelligentsia of the inter-war years turned its back on Burne-Jones more in sadness than in contempt. An anonymous writer in the *Guardian* in 1920 put the case clearly

Fig.18
Film still from *The Beggar Maid*, 1921, directed by Herbert Blaché, USA
George Eastman Museum, Rochester, NY

and calmly. A nation had returned from the Great War furiously disillusioned; Burne-Jones may have offered a vision of melancholy that spoke to the progressives of a previous generation, but we now knew that 'Burne-Jones in his home was a red, jovial man' and somehow that said it all.[14]

Those who persisted with Burne-Jones into the twenties and thirties were often only able to do so in a self-consciously defeated mode. Some made a sort of aesthetic virtue of this, taking their cue from the master's own reflections on separation and loss. The artist and collector Graham Robertson, a self-styled figure of the 1890s, wrote touchingly about Burne-Jones in his memoirs and edited a little book of the artist's illustrated letters to Katie Lewis, the young daughter of one of his patrons.[15] Little girls indeed feature strongly in this phase of Burne-Jones's afterlife. His granddaughter Angela Thirkell became a successful popular novelist, but before this, in 1931, she published *Three Houses*, an irresistible slice of autobiography describing a childhood spent in the London and Sussex homes of the Burne-Jones clan. She recalls her grandfather listing out possible subjects for pictures he might draw for her, including such characters as the Fen Ganger and Mist Walker.[16] These sound rather like the denizens of Middle Earth, and it was in fact at just the time of the publication of *Three Houses* that another romantic storyteller came up with the first line of a story for his children: 'In a hole in the ground there lived a hobbit.'[17] The coincidence is worth noting, as the legacy of Burne-Jones for popular fantasy imagery and literature in the twentieth century would be interesting to explore.

Here then was the kind, jovial Burne-Jones in full effect. But what about his pictures? *King Cophetua* was acquired through public subscription for the new Tate Gallery in 1900 and remained the artist's physical memorial in the London gallery world. Its idea of the humble raised up suggested – albeit with the genders reversed – his own social promotion earned entirely on account of his beautiful mind. It drew the prolonged attention of visiting Bolshevik leader Lev Kamenev in 1920, and was even translated into a film the following year (fig.18).[18] As for exhibitions, there was none to speak of following the artist's death until the Tate was encouraged to celebrate the centenary of Burne-Jones's birth in 1933.[19] Those behind this project – Ernest Seymour Thomas, an Egyptologist at the Pitt Rivers Museum in Oxford, and William Rothenstein, Principal of the Royal College of Art – were entirely aware they were cutting at ninety degrees against the grain of the 1930s London art-scene.

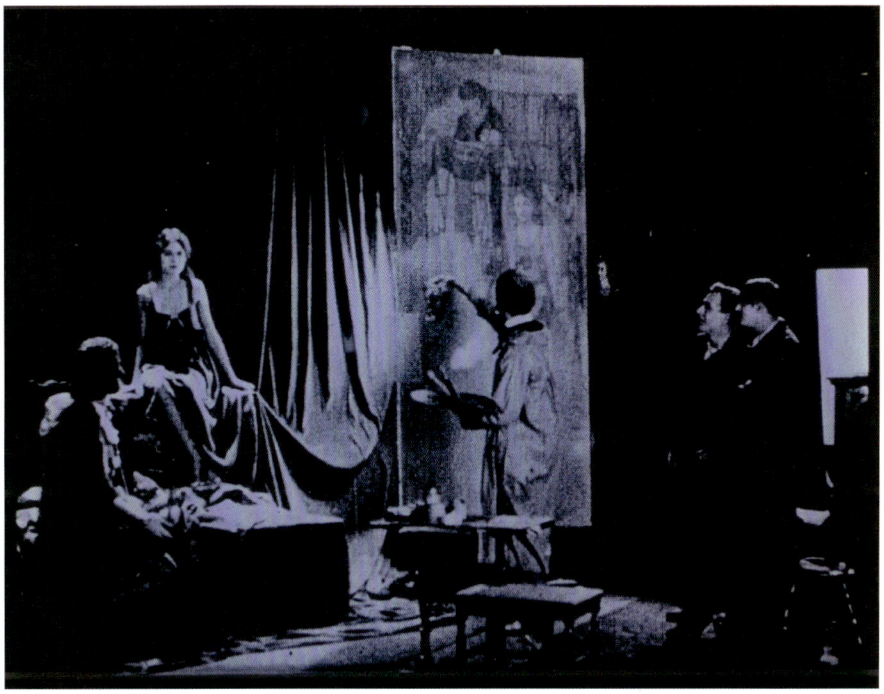

This pleasure in bloody-minded anti-fashion has often characterised Burne-Jones's most passionate supporters since. At the same time, the artist's extended family was now so distinguished that it was a toss-up whether to invite Kipling or the former Conservative Prime Minister Stanley Baldwin (another nephew) to open the show. In the event Baldwin did the honours, offering a movingly personal testament to the artist and the importance of his vision. Graham Robertson's words about that vision now being 'utterly scorned and rejected' and the opening party being populated by the 'forlorn' were part of the fighting-a-losing-battle talk of the old guard in defence of their hero. The exhibition was in fact apparently well attended, although mainly by older people: *The Times* leader writer felt the show's *raison d'être* was to allow those of a certain age to recapture their youth.[20] The critics as a rule tried to be constructive. In the same paper, a reviewer emphasised the deeply personal nature of Burne-Jones's art, writing that the imagery on show at the Tate was essentially 'an externalisation of that very mysterious thing, sexual preference'.[21] P.G. Konody, a writer with excellent modernist credentials, pointed out to his readers in the *Daily Mail* that the lines and rhythms of Burne-Jones were echoed in contemporary British painting by artists including Stanley Spencer, Tristram Hillier and Edward Burra.[22] An older artist, Robert Anning Bell, raised in the arts and crafts movement, reported a less positive response: '"Anything to do with Camelot makes me sick"' said 'one of our vivid young moderns at a casual mention of Burne-Jones.' Andrew Fincham, in the *Observer*, felt that Burne-Jones's atmosphere could simply not be recaptured in the twentieth century, and that even if younger people were drawn to his pictures, the path to his art was cut off: 'They may want to escape from life, but the road of escape does not lead to any land of faery.'[23]

Possibly it was the decision to honour Burne-Jones publicly in 1933 that caused a couple of authors surveying British art in that year to put their foot down. For a seriously committed modernist polemicist such as W.H. Wilenski, who published a book on *English Painting* in 1933, it seems understandable that Burne-Jones would simply be invisible to him as art. He could scarcely begin to make his case with such a reputation still in his way. Burne-Jones denied reality; modernism therefore had to come to confront it: he had dealt 'in the shadows not the substance of art' (as one reviewer of the Tate exhibition had put it).[24] C.H. Collins Baker was a different case: his objections to Burne-Jones in his broad survey of *British Painting* constitute a late discharge from the waning discourse of the degeneration of British manliness. The vocabulary used by the recently retired Surveyor of the King's Pictures would be comic were it not so aggressively homophobic and misogynistic. In a splenetic few sentences Burne-Jones is condemned as having produced only 'a thin memory of girlish dreams' suffering from 'anaemia'; he lacked 'virility' and created pictures that are 'sweet' and 'maidenly'; he was nothing more than 'a weakling aesthete' whose 'chaste' followers would have fared better 'in a manlier school'.[25] This is the kind of purple-faced parade-ground criticism denounced by Comyns Carr in 1898, and indeed has a genealogy, relevant to Burne-Jones, that goes back to the 1840s and outrage against the allegedly unmanly practices of the Tractarians.[26]

Such a strongly negative reaction at least presumes some human connection, some aesthetic and indeed political response. Certainly Collins Baker's emotional tirade helps make sense of the larger twentieth-century attitude towards Burne-Jones, rather more so than do the occasional positive attempts to place the artist within the history of art. We have noted Konody's comparison with surrealist-influenced painters of the 1930s. In a very brief piece of 1948 Wyndham Lewis, the vorticist pioneer, suggested it would be satisfying to hang Burne-Jones's Perseus series in a room with pictures by the surrealists Delvaux and Dalí, while in 1940, in an extended and thoughtful article, the painter and designer Robin Ironside reconnected Burne-Jones with the symbolists who had responded to him so enthusiastically.[27] Neither of these writers was anything like mainstream in their thinking, however, and the successful filing of an artist in their proper pigeon-hole does not constitute a revival. Burne-Jones was only thoroughly reimagined in Britain from the 1960s when masculinity became open for debate again following the waning of a decades-long phase of pervasive cultural militarism and the abandonment of empire.

If there was a specific moment, then it was 1969. In that year appeared (Lord) David Cecil's double biography of Burne-Jones and the Romantic landscape painter Samuel Palmer, *Visionary and Dreamer: Two Poetic Painters.* Reviewing it in the *Observer*, Philip Toynbee confessed he found Burne-Jones deeply disturbing – 'I am violently repelled by his dreams,' he wrote – and described his reaction of hurrying back to the concrete world of the senses as if to calm a panicked sense of its having been lost.[28] This inducement of death-anxiety was also picked up by Timothy Hilton in his brilliant introduction to *The Pre-Raphaelites* (1970), where he wrote of the paradoxically unsettling experience of entering Burne-Jones's world

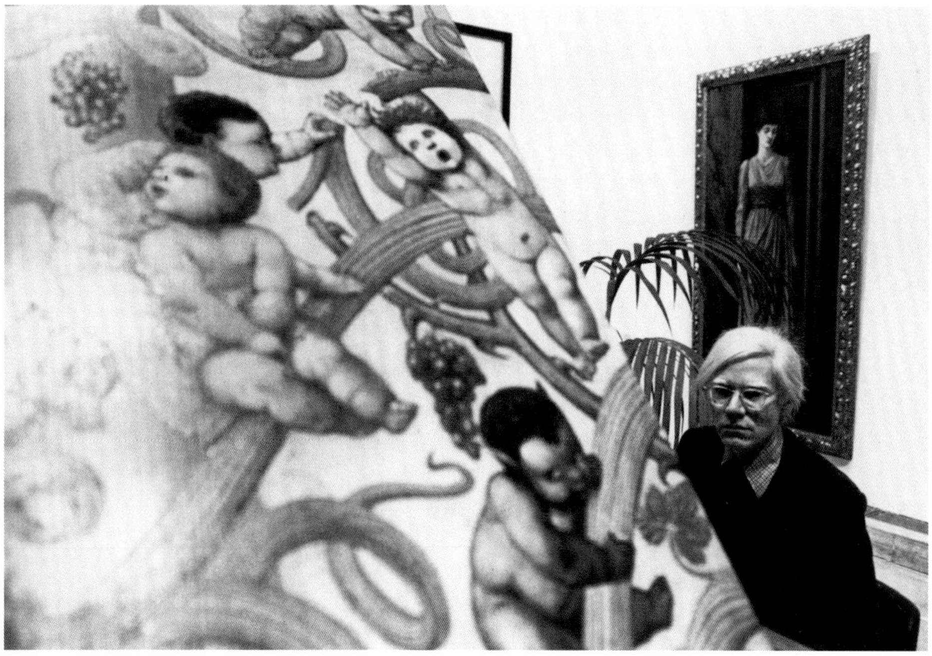

Fig.19
ROGER PERRY
Andy Warhol with *The Graham Piano* at the Edward Burne-Jones exhibition, Hayward Gallery, London, 5 November 1975–4 January 1976
Victoria and Albert Museum

where 'all disturbance has been hushed' – unsettling because 'it is not soothing to be becalmed'.[29] For Freud, thanatophobia was an irrational mental state brought on by (what else?) childhood trauma. Here was surely a theme ripe for investigation, but although Martin Harrison and Bill Waters, in their 1973 monograph on Burne-Jones, enticingly introduced their subject as an artist who 'reaches the vocabulary of the unconscious itself', this psychoanalytic reading of Burne-Jones was not taken forwards other than through the conventional biographic mode.[30]

Penelope Fitzgerald, like Angela Thirkell, was a successful novelist who opened her writing career with a book about Burne-Jones. Her lucid, empathetic and thoroughly researched biography was begun in 1969 and published in 1975.[31] As the author blurb on the dust-jacket of the book explained by way of introduction to a newcomer, Fitzgerald's credentials as a writer were underwritten by the renown of her relatives, not least her uncle Ronald Knox, that latter-day Newman who represented all that was most intellectually attractive in Catholic thought to the Oxford of the inter-war years. Her grandfather was Edmund Arbuthnott Knox, who had been rector of St Philip's in Birmingham when Burne-Jones's *Last Judgement* window was installed there in the 1890s. The novelist wrote tenderly of her memories of this sublime screen of colour 'through whose ruby-red glass the light streamed in at evensong'.[32]

By the early 1970s the art market was making much of Burne-Jones, and not just in Britain. In 1971 Kenneth A. Lohf, the distinguished Columbia University librarian, held an exhibition at the bibliophile Grolier Club in New York of his collection of Burne-Jones items assembled in recent years, and in 1972 the London dealers Hartnoll and Eyre mounted an exhibition exploring *Burne-Jones et l'influence des préraphaélites* in a commercial gallery on the rue St Denis in Paris.[33] Julian Hartnoll recalls that holding the exhibition in Europe made sense, as this was where the leading edge of the Burne-Jones market was to be found, among collectors who had come to the English artist via the revived taste for international movements such as symbolism and especially art nouveau. It was also in the early 1970s that Andrew Lloyd Webber began his collection of works by Burne-Jones, which now has no rival in private hands. His route was, it seems, rather different, the composer having inherited something of a Tractarian taste from his father, who had been organist and choirmaster at All Saints, Margaret Street, one of London's great High Church institutions.[34]

When a large retrospective of Burne-Jones's work was eventually shown in London in 1975, there was a widespread sense that it was about time, too (fig.19). The venue was the beautifully brutalist Hayward Gallery within the Southbank Centre arts complex: it had opened as recently as 1968 under the management of the Arts Council. It was the Chairman of the Council's Art Panel, John Pope-Hennessy, who apparently suggested the idea in 1972. Pope-Hennessy, then also Director of the V&A, felt Burne-Jones would be the natural successor to the Hayward's exhibition of *French Symbolist Painters* held in that year. He recalled in his memoirs that he had noticed the parallels between Burne-Jones's male figures and the marketing of men's fashions in contemporary London, and that this had convinced him that the younger generation were ready to rediscover Britain's lost symbolist. But as John Christian, the curator of the 1975 exhibition, later noted without bitterness, Pope-Hennessy had rather rewritten history in attributing to himself alone this *aperçu*: the Burne-Jones revival was already under way.[35] Nevertheless, Pope-Hennessy's referencing of male fashion is surely crucial to explaining what was happening. With homosexual acts between men only decriminalised – and arguably then only partially – in 1967, there was a sharp edge to such swinging fashion statements as David Bowie's appearance in a Michael-Fish-designed 'man-dress' on the cover of his 1971 album *The Man Who Sold the World*. On a promotional tour of the United States that year, Bowie would on occasion bring out the dress, and much later recalled: 'In New York I was very impressed by transvestites; they were kind of Pre-Raphaelite, there was something about the Edward Burne-Jones/Rossetti thing that I thought was a purist new energising of the British spirit.'[36] There is no space here to attempt an unpacking of that intriguing statement, but clearly here was a homage to a forgotten Victorian aestheticism, now again becoming – just – accessible. Bowie's revelatory New York experiences included introductions to the Factory scene and so to Lou Reed, to whose post-Velvet Underground refashioning Bowie would prove instrumental as producer of the *Transformer* album of 1972. In 1975 Reed was photographed in London, posing in black plastic and looking like nothing so much as Perseus in Burne-Jones's great series, then on show at the Hayward (fig.20). Andy Warhol, meanwhile, was captured at the exhibition itself (fig.19).

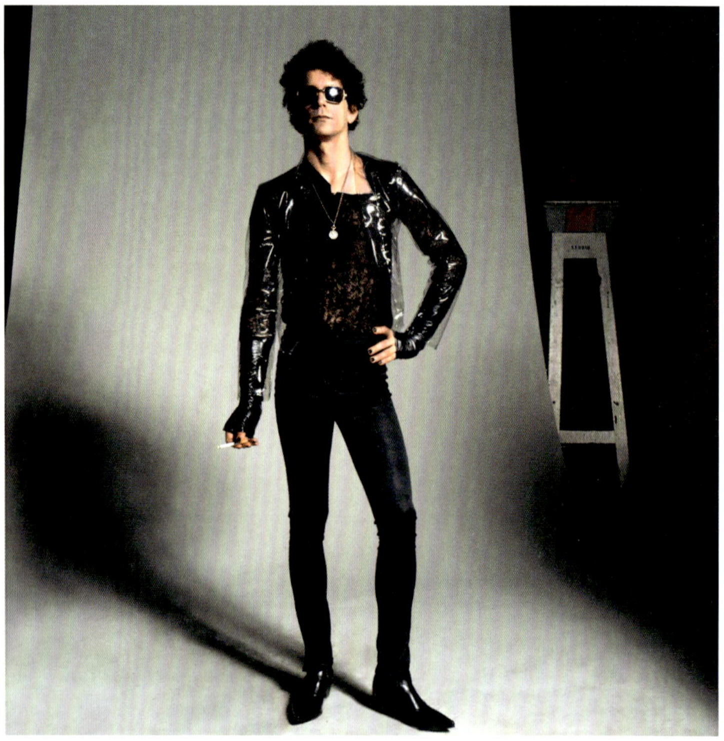

Fig.20
MICK ROCK
Lou in Plastic 1975
Courtesy Mick Rock

Seeking to sketch in any zeitgeist, such as that enveloping the new embrace of Burne-Jones, can perhaps too quickly become a pleasurable process of joining-the-dots. Did connoisseurs now respond to Burne-Jones with eyes attuned to the disturbingly cool post-pop imagery of artists like Richard Hamilton or Gerhard Richter, in which compelling found images were refracted between media (fig.21)? Where is Burne-Jones within *Monty Python and the Holy Grail* (fig.22)? Both were in the mix, alongside the perennial fascination with the Pre-Raphaelites' love lives. Colin MacInnes, another Burne-Jones-related novelist (he was the son of Angela Thirkell, making him the artist's great-grandson), reviewed the Hayward exhibition in 1976. He pointed to the representation of the Pre-Raphaelites on television as being based on the cliché of Victorian intellectuals expounding aesthetics of purity and grace while actually preoccupied with bed-hopping (he was certainly thinking of the previous year's BBC drama series *The Love School*).[37] In a disorienting moment of cultural simultaneity, MacInnes, famous as a chronicler of a new teenage identity in the 1950s, addressed – to a readership braced for the onslaught of Punk – his affectionate memories of Georgiana Burne-Jones. He felt regretful that she would have seen the 1970s revival as an exercise only in taste, rather than a fuller grasping of Burne-Jones's aspiration for an art that might 'regenerate the spirit'. But for those

Fig.21
GERHARD RICHTER
Annunciation after Titian 1973
Oil on canvas
125 × 200
Gerhard Richter Archive

Fig.22
Film still from the Castle Anthrax scene in *Monty Python and the Holy Grail*, 1975, directed by Terry Gilliam and Terry Jones

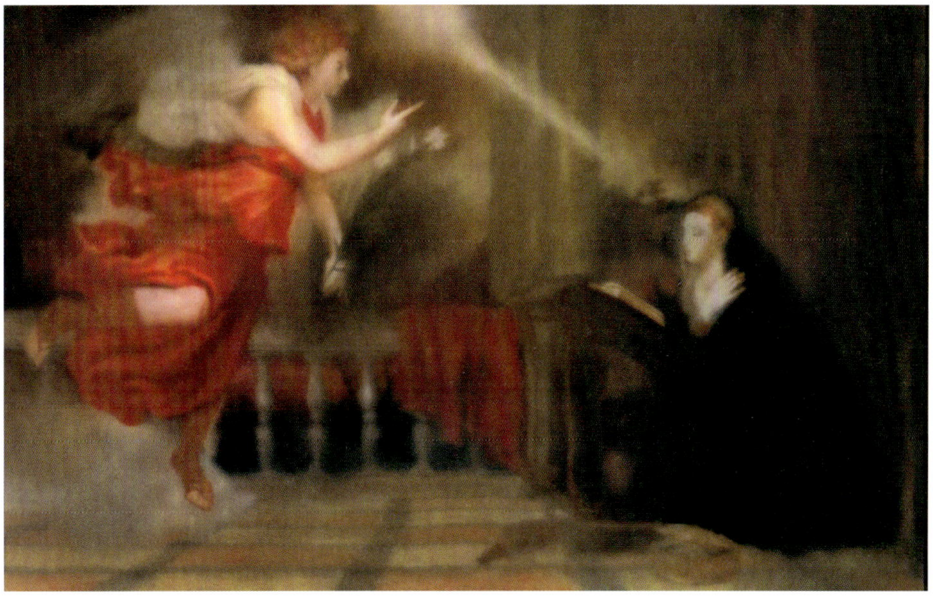

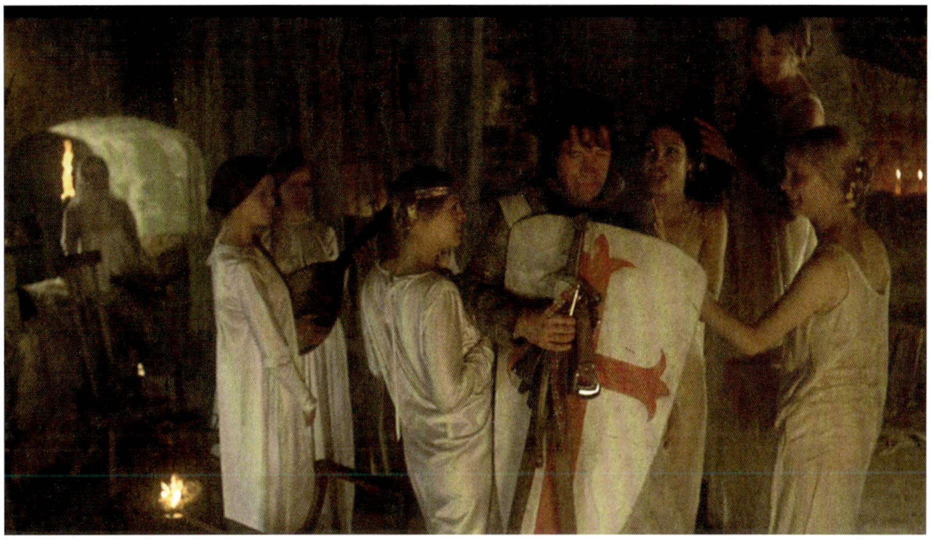

of us not personally related to Burne-Jones, it does not seem reasonable to expect us to enter blithely into his world 'that nothing can disturb' (the artist's own words) and to be able to find there 'peace for our souls', as Stanley Baldwin encouraged his audience to believe they might in 1933.[38] The accusation that the Pre-Raphaelites shared the supposed hypocrisy of their contemporaries – imagining perfect alternative worlds while scrabbling around clumsily in their fleshly actuality – now seems a vice scarcely restricted to the Victorian age. Searching biographical work by Jan Marsh, Fiona MacCarthy and others has offered more human resolutions, or more complete pictures, of that apparent contradiction. We can now, thanks to twentieth-century readings of Burne-Jones, recognise his art as emerging from within a turbulent and passionate mind: the separate world he created was in some sense a deeply private and necessary refuge for himself, rather than a merely dishonest evasion. If we cannot follow him there, or even if we are alarmed at the deathly stillness of his vision, we can still find imagery in which something urgent is at stake, and therefore feel the startling presence of another human being.

(overleaf)
The Wise and Foolish Virgins
c.1859 (detail, no.8)

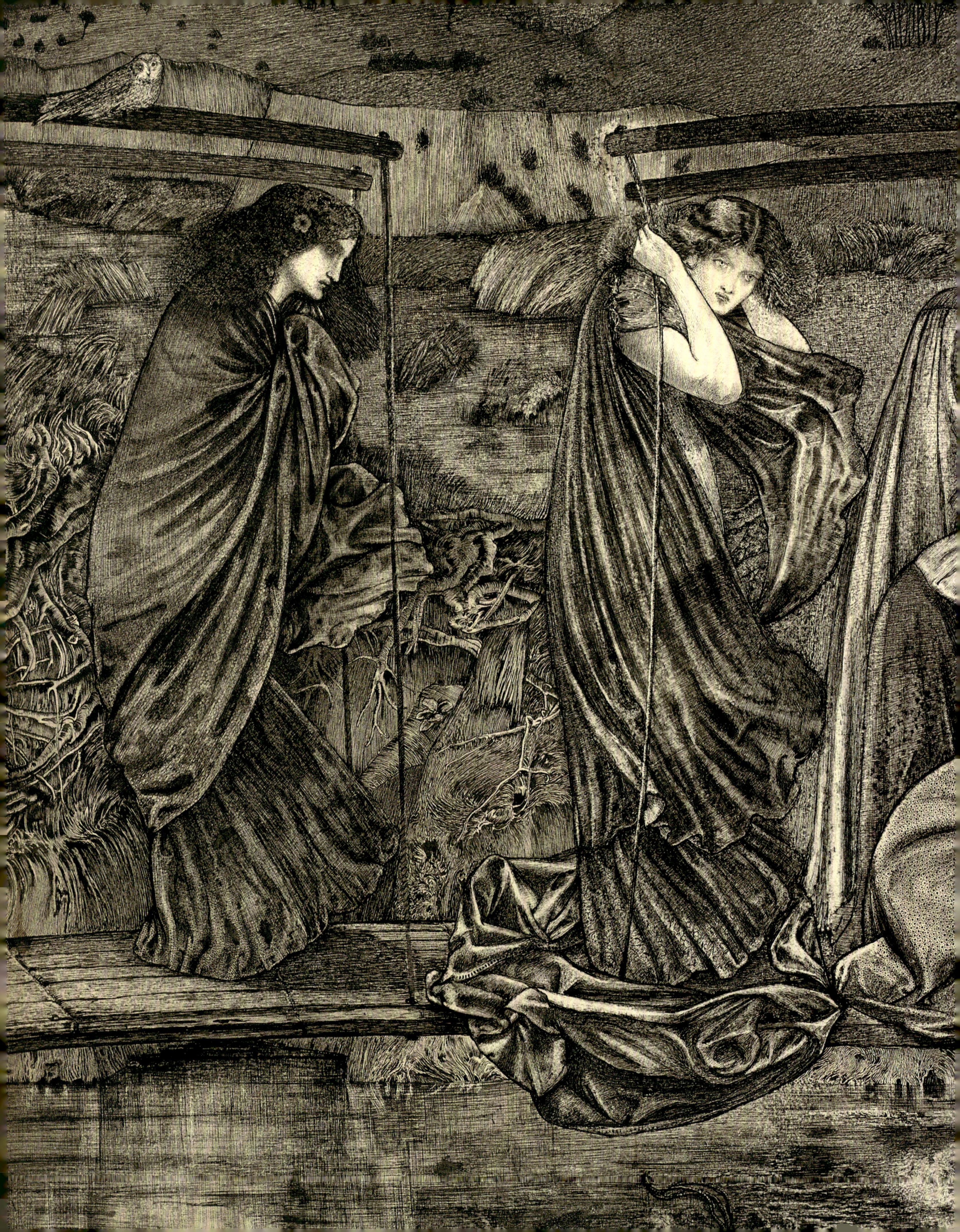

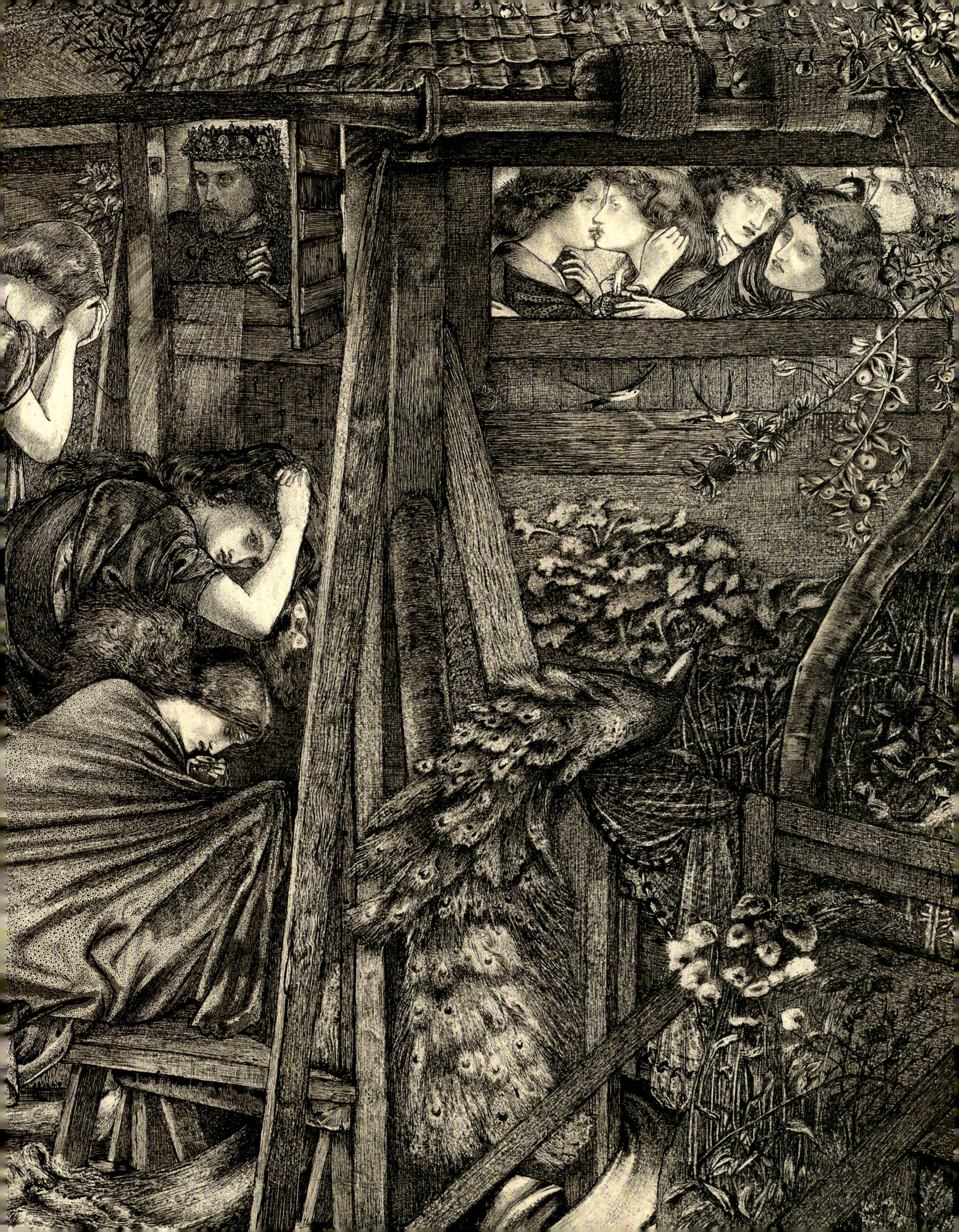

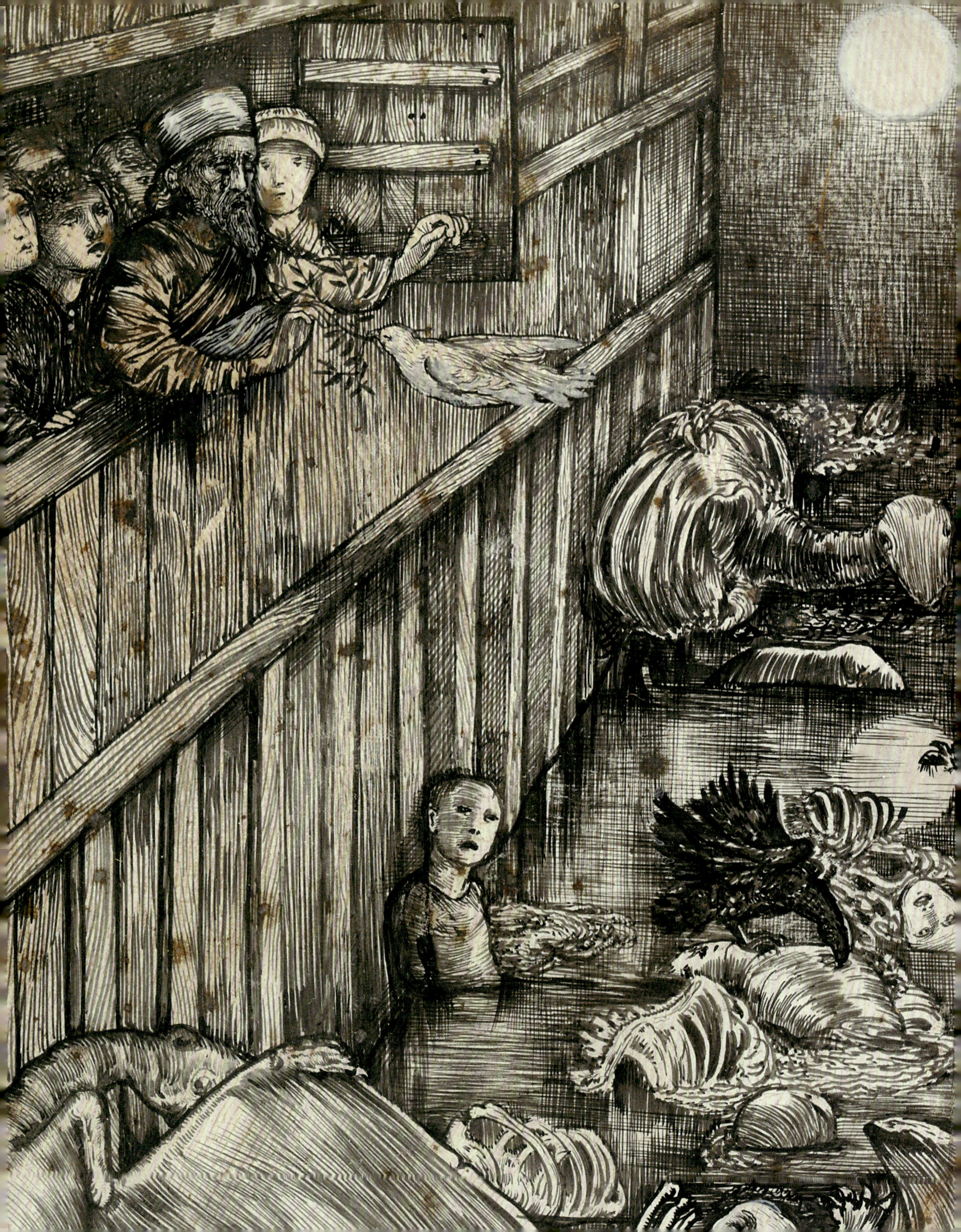

Apprentice to Master: 1856–70

ALISON SMITH

Birmingham in the early nineteenth century was widely synonymous with 'Brummagem'. This was the term used to describe the cheap, sometimes shoddy, mass-produced goods made in the city that came to represent the antithesis of Burne-Jones's rarefied vision of beauty. He was born there in 1833, the only surviving child of an unassuming frame-maker and his more gregarious wife, who died within a week of her son's birth. Christened plain Edward Jones ('Burne' was a later addition), he received a dour, evangelical upbringing. Birmingham, then a rapidly expanding industrial city, was not the kind of place to excite the imagination, reeking, as one contemporary described it, 'of oil and smoke and sweat and drunkenness'.[1] In 1844 he entered King Edward's School, destined for a career in commerce, but around 1848 decided on a future in the Church, a change in direction that was strongly influenced by the Tractarian or High Church movement, which provided an outlet for the young man's growing dissatisfaction with the mechanistic values of modern Britain. The appeal was partly aesthetic, for, in reaffirming the roots of Anglicanism in the Roman Catholic Church, the Tractarians sought to bring back the ritual and decorative richness associated with medieval religious practice that had been lost in Britain since the Reformation. But the calling was primarily spiritual, fuelling a genuine striving for holiness, as the artist later said of his then hero, the leading Tractarian, Catholic convert and founder of the Birmingham Oratory, John Henry Newman: 'In an age of sofas and cushions he taught me to be indifferent to comfort; and in an age of materialism he taught me to venture all on the unseen.'[2]

Driven by a strong sense of vocation, without the means yet of expressing it, Burne-Jones was at this stage of his life more interested in theology, literature and history than art. He did, however, demonstrate an early aptitude for drawing that led him to attend evening classes at the local Government School of Design. In 1853 he went up to Exeter College, Oxford, intent on being ordained. It was here he met his lifelong friend and collaborator, William Morris, who had arrived with a similar sense of mission. Set on establishing a brotherhood but disillusioned with the inward-looking intellectual culture at Oxford, both men underwent a crisis of purpose and embraced Christian Socialism, finding an outlet for their shared love of medievalism in the romances of Chaucer and Malory. The turning point came in 1854–5: having discovered the Pre-Raphaelites, who were likewise immersed in the writings of John Ruskin and other modern prophets, and having experienced the glory of Gothic architecture on a tour of the cathedrals of northern France, Morris and Burne-Jones converted to art as an alternative expression of service. In January 1856 Morris apprenticed himself to the architect G.E. Street, and in May Burne-Jones abandoned his degree to seek out the painter Dante Gabriel Rossetti in London with a view to becoming an artist. For a student of divinity to suddenly renounce the life

The Return of the Dove to the Ark 1863 (detail, no.9)

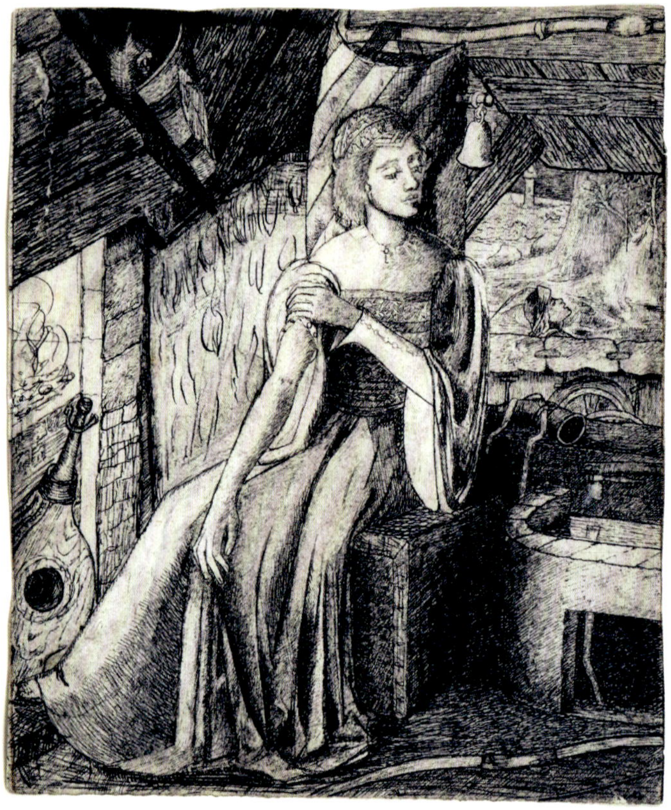

2
Cupid's Daughter by his Forge c.1857
Graphite, pen and ink on paper, 13.8 × 12.1
William Morris Gallery,
London Borough of Waltham Forest

3
Cupid's Forge 1861
Watercolour, bodycolour and gum arabic laid down on linen, 32.5 × 50
Private collection courtesy of Peter Nahum.
Renate Nahum. Agency

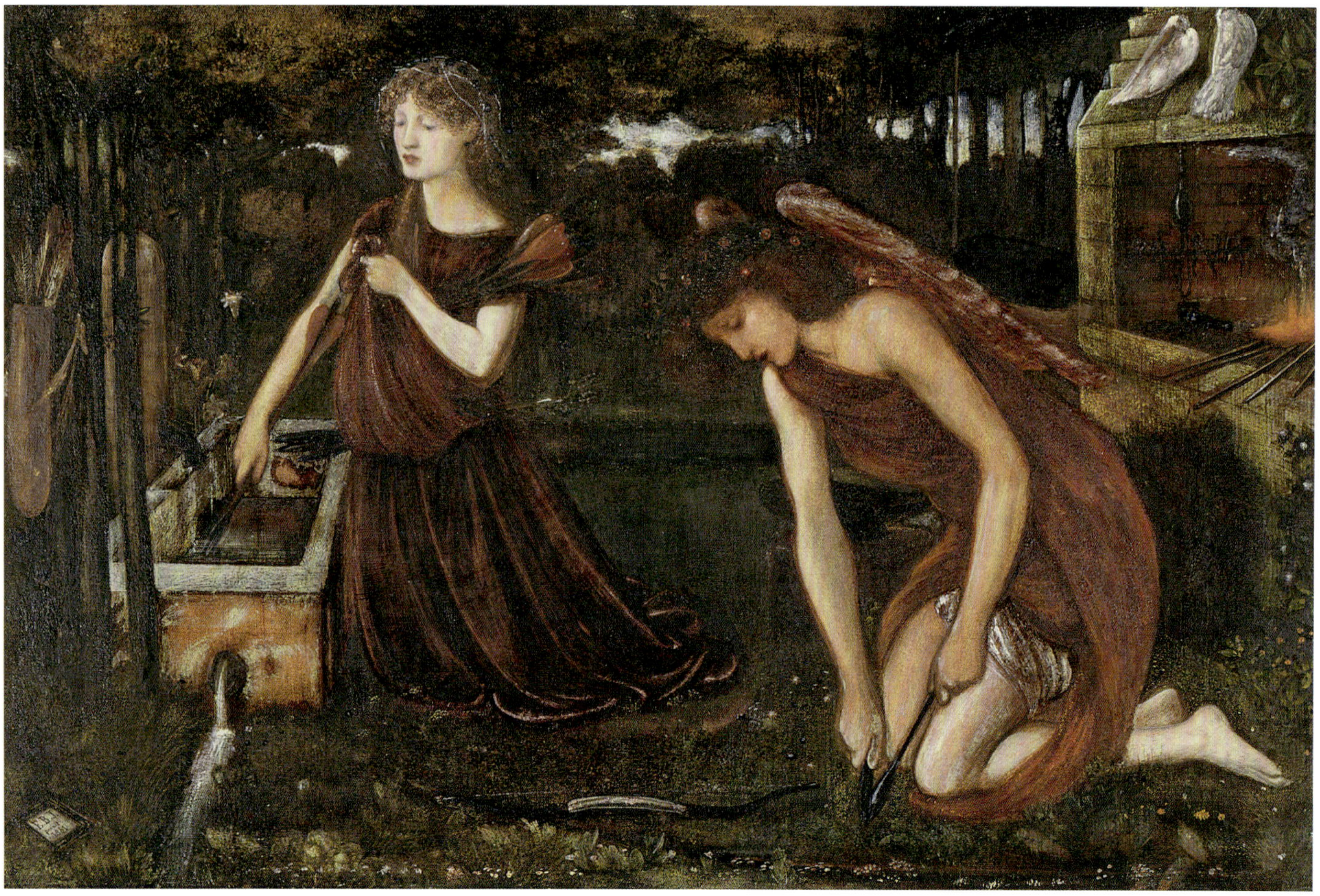

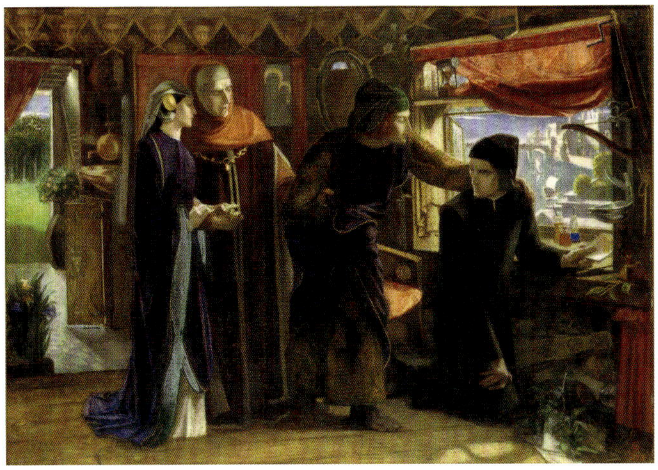

Fig.23
DANTE GABRIEL ROSSETTI
Dante Drawing an Angel on the Anniversary of Beatrice's Death 1853
Watercolour
22 × 32
Ashmolean Museum, University of Oxford

of a college man in order to become an artisan would have seemed to many of his contemporaries a drastic downgrading of social ambition, however well connected he may have been. Throwing caution to the wind and overlooking the practical question of how he was to actually learn his craft, he started on the new path, placing his faith in the spirit of creativity above all other considerations.

Just prior to meeting Rossetti, Burne-Jones had shown stirrings of his own distinct manner in the illustrations he produced for *The Fairy Family* (no.4), a compilation of the fairy lore of Europe commissioned by the Oxford pioneer of physical education, Archibald Maclaren. These drawings encapsulate the passions of the artist's youth – Gothic architecture and romantic literature – and although he was soon to dismiss them as mere juvenilia, they reveal, in their richness of imaginative detail and penchant for the quaint and grotesque, exactly what drew him to Rossetti and the Pre-Raphaelites in the first place.[3] As the only member of the original Pre-Raphaelite Brotherhood who steadfastly refused to concede to the demands of the art market, Rossetti was the perfect choice for the aspiring novice. Rossetti's contempt for conventional art education, together with his abiding belief in the imagination, fuelled Burne-Jones's confidence that he too would become an artist, despite coming to the profession relatively late in life. Apart from taking evening life classes at Leigh's, one of the few independent drawing schools in London, he saw no need for any formal training, believing wholeheartedly in his mentor. Indeed, what little education he received was during the mornings he spent in Rossetti's studio, learning more about what it meant to be a painter than the craft itself. As he later recalled: 'He [Rossetti] taught me to have no fear or shame of my own ideas; to design perpetually, to seek no popularity, to be altogether myself.'[4]

The influence of Rossetti's poetic evocations of the Middle Ages is apparent in one of the few drawings to survive from Burne-Jones's apprenticeship (no.2). Probably based on Chaucer's dream poem, the *Assembly of Fowls*, it shows Cupid's daughter by his forge preparing to temper his darts (possibly an early study for no.3).[5] Burne-Jones was soon to make rapid strides away from the stiff, rather hesitant penwork displayed in this scene, as he refined his technique by restricting himself to working almost exclusively in black and white, with many drawings executed on vellum (nos.5 and 7). Although indebted to Rossetti in terms of their dense texture and tilted perspective, these early drawings show an artist in growing command of his own vision. As a group, they depict an eclectic range of literary, biblical and historical subjects and are packed with detail that accumulates to form a rippling tapestry-like effect across the surface. A mood of quiet melancholy pervades each scene: the figures are self-contained and impassive, as if detached from the narrative action, which lends the images a poetic quality that lifts them beyond mere illustration. Described by Rossetti as 'marvels of finish and imaginative detail, unequalled by *anything* unless perhaps Albert Dürer's finest works', the drawings delight in a Ruskinian attention to natural observation, affirming the artist in his belief that drawing from a sunflower represented 'a whole school and education in itself'.[6] The largest and most ambitious, *Buondelmonte's Wedding* (no.7), illustrates the event that precipitated the Guelph and Ghibelline conflict in medieval Florence

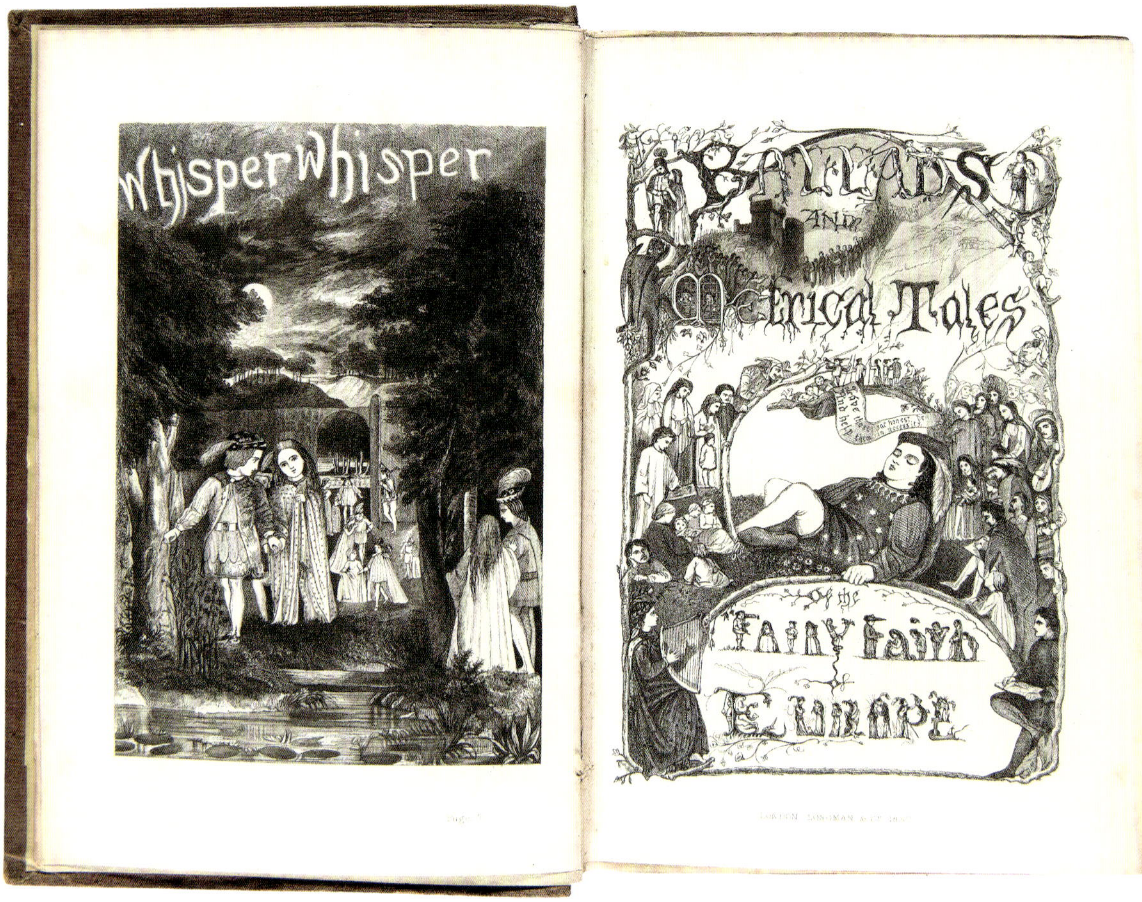

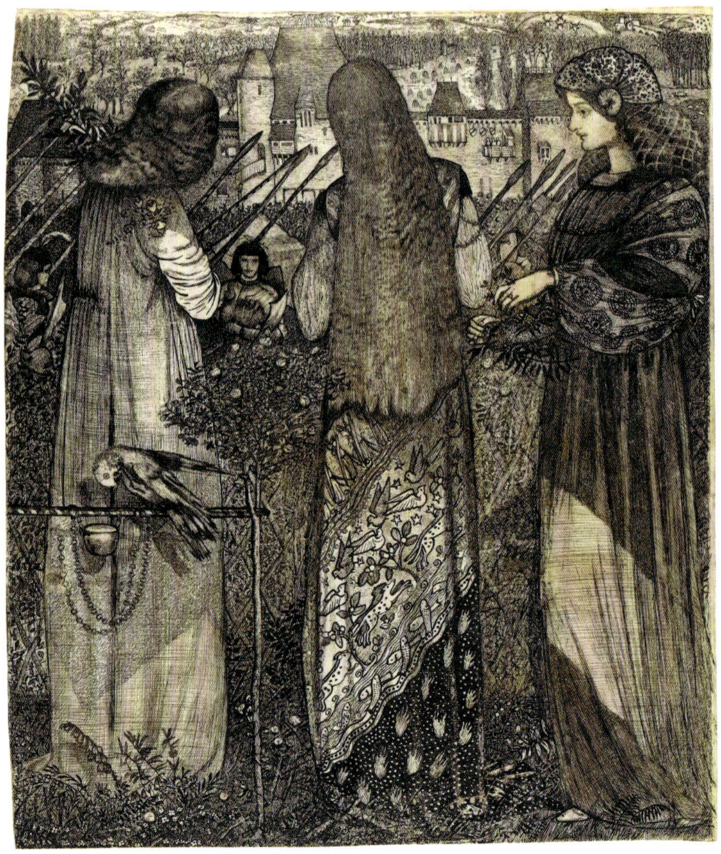

4
ARCHIBALD MACLAREN
The Fairy Family: A Series of Ballads and Metrical Tales Illustrating the Fairy Mythology of Europe 1857
Book illustrated by Burne-Jones
19 × 14 × 3 (book closed)
Collection of Stephen Calloway

5
Going to the Battle 1858
Pen and ink with grey wash on vellum
22.3 × 19.5
The Syndics of the Fitzwilliam Museum, University of Cambridge

6
Childe Roland 1861
Pen and ink and wash on paper,
43 × 24
The Trustees of the Cecil Higgins
Art Gallery (The Higgins Bedford)

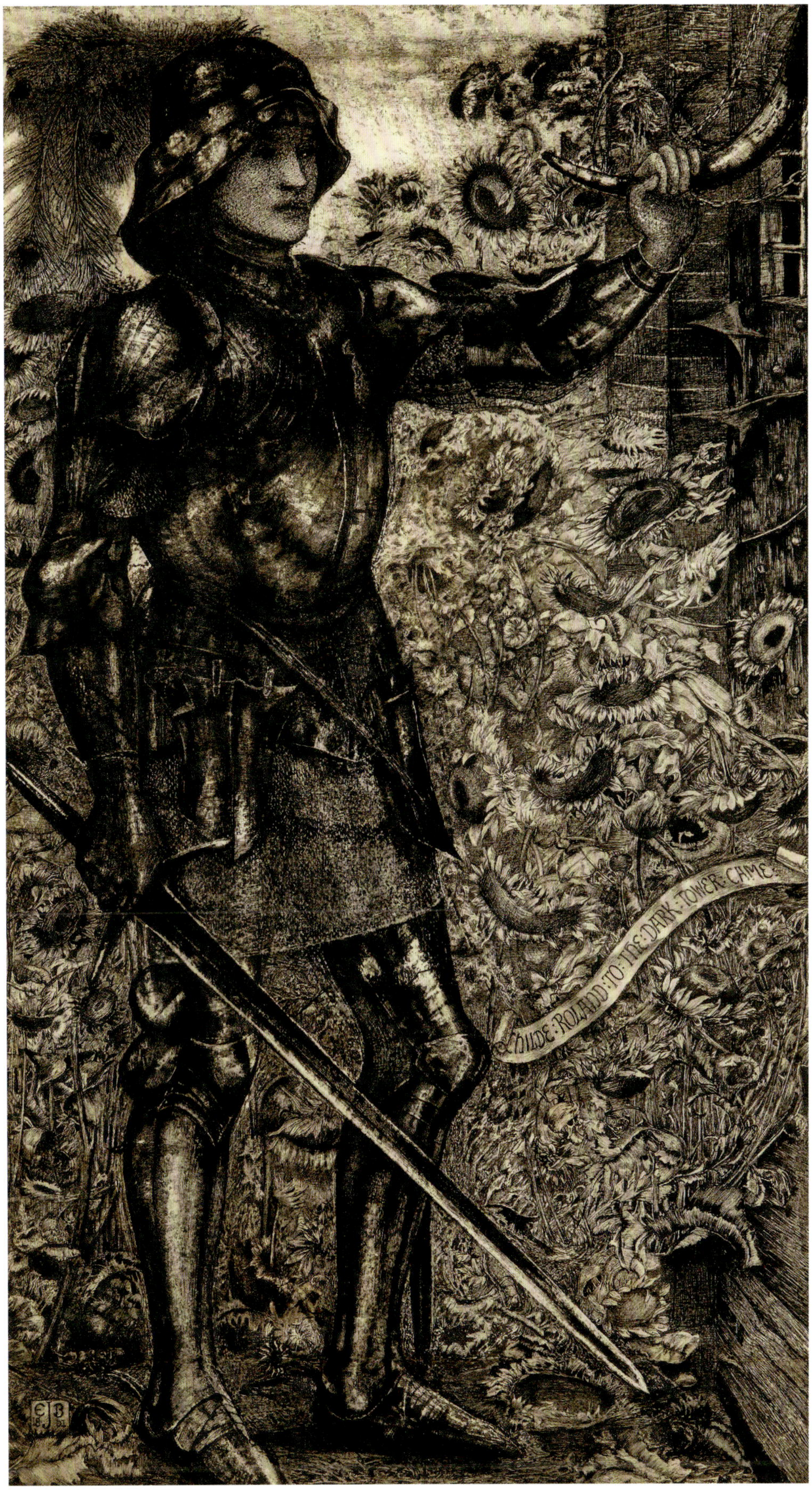

7
Buondelmonte's Wedding 1859
Pen and ink with some grey wash on vellum, 25.5 × 77
The Syndics of the Fitzwilliam Museum, University of Cambridge

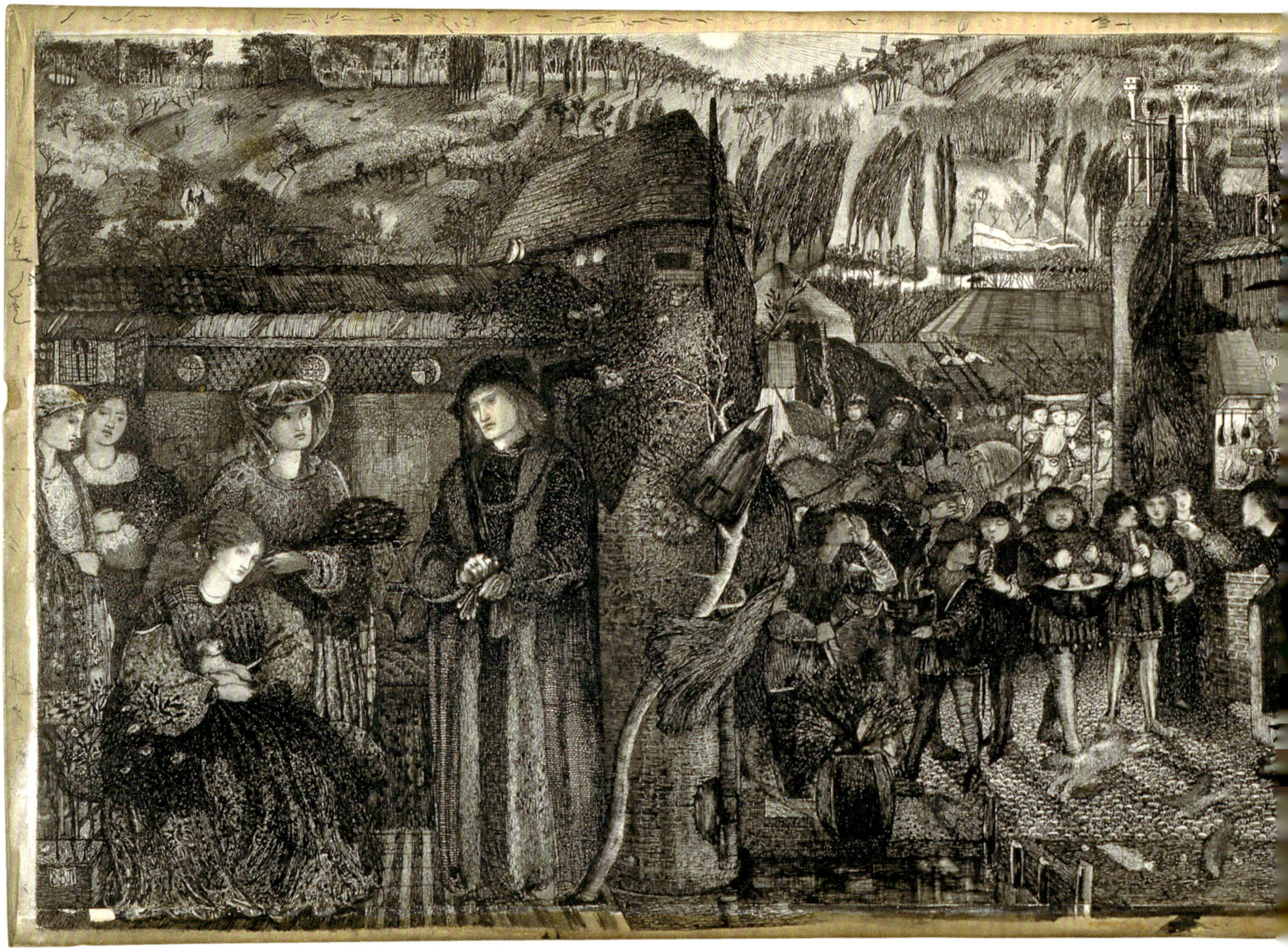

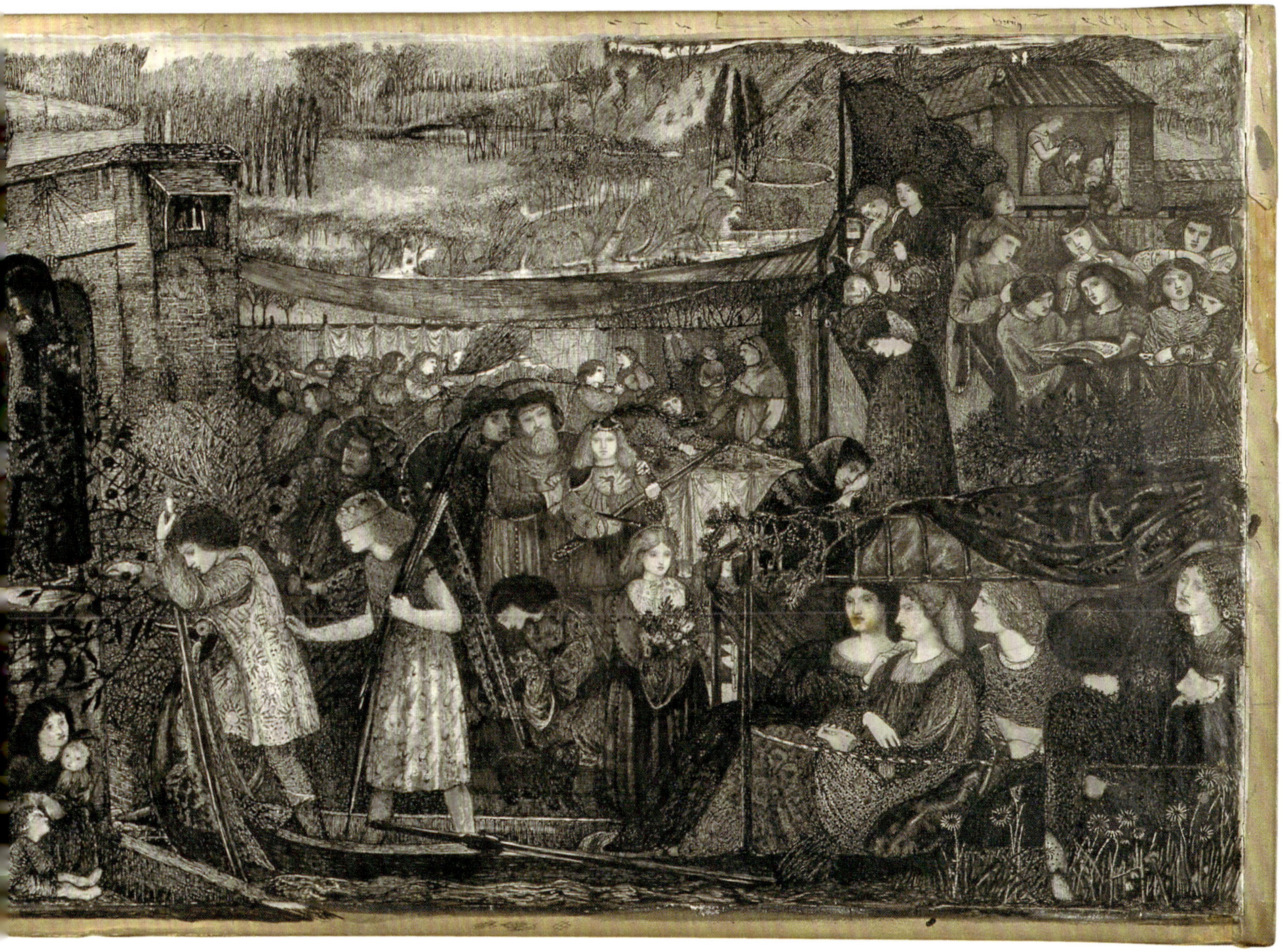

8
The Wise and Foolish Virgins c.1859
Pen and ink and grey wash, 45.5 × 60.5
Private collection

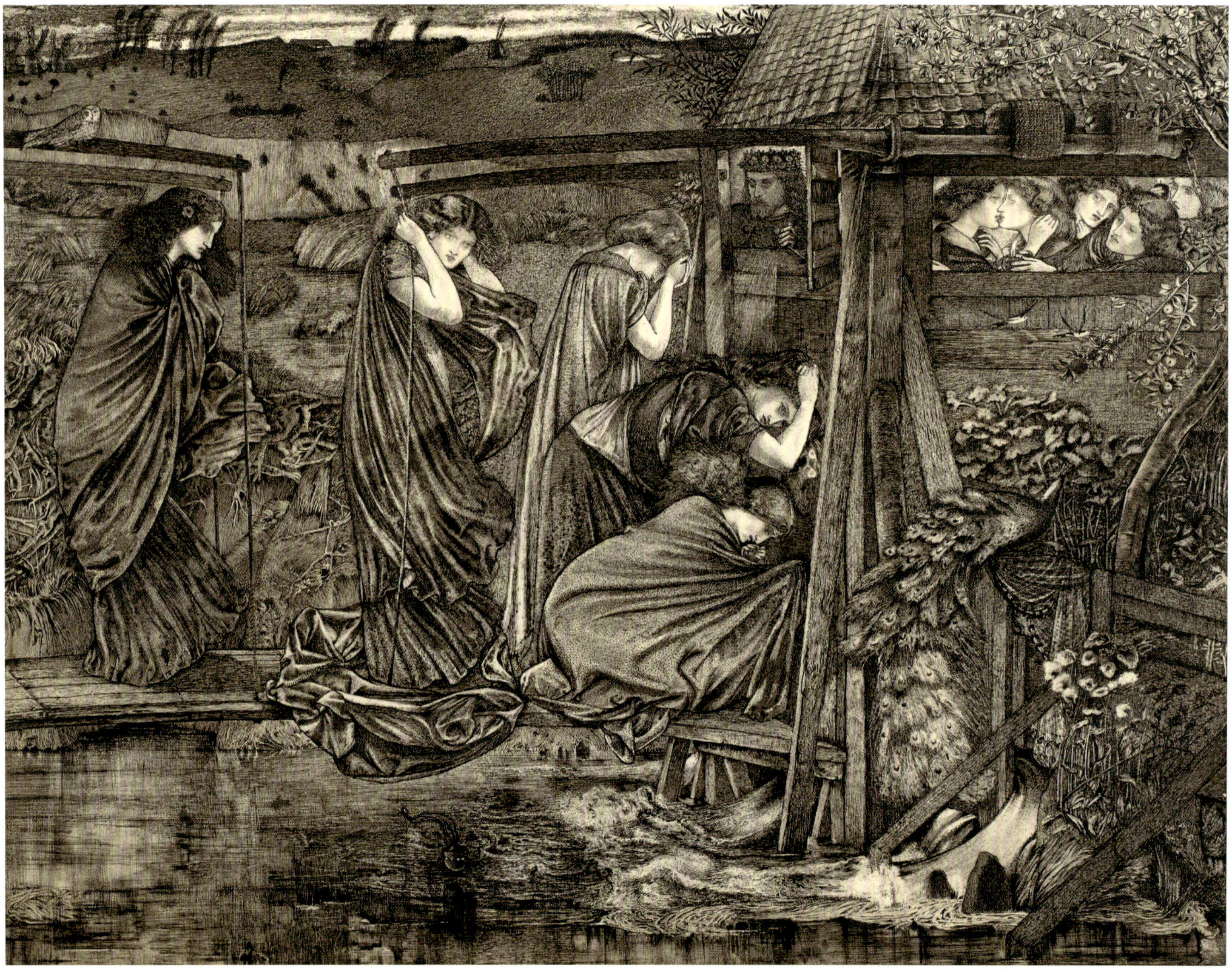

9
The Return of the Dove to the Ark 1863
Pen and ink on paper, 10.2 × 8.9
Victoria and Albert Museum

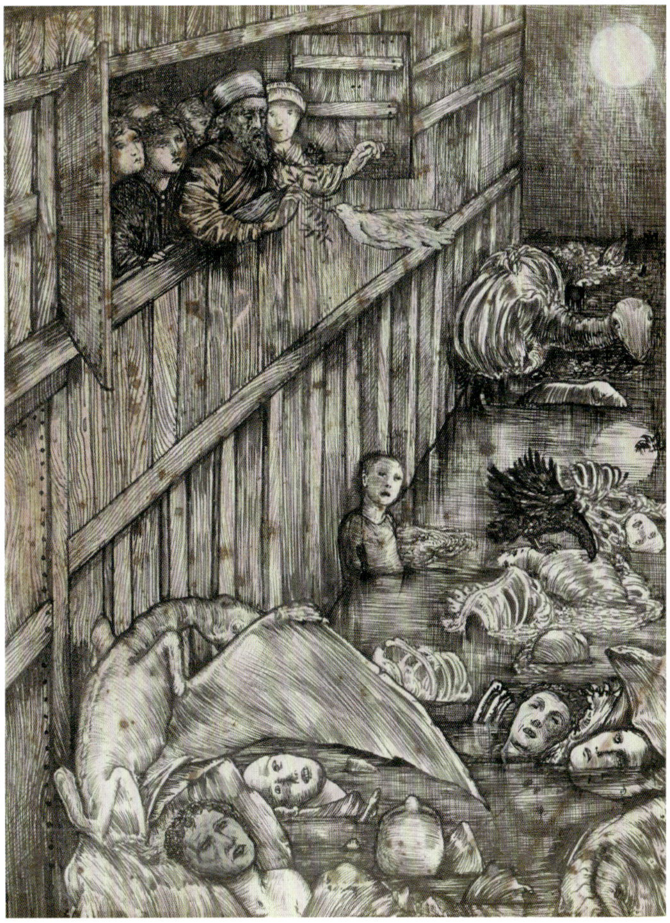

and, according to the artist, contains over a hundred figures.[7] It certainly overwhelms in its *horror vacui*; the piling-on of incident interrupts the narrative flow and threatens incoherence. Although such characteristics might be regarded as typical of the unprofessional artist (they are certainly not the work of a trained academician), the drawings are a marvel to behold and invite addictive looking. The self-conscious naivety of design and extreme compression of detail lend each image an authenticity that bridges the distance between the Middle Ages and the present day, inviting comparison with the intensity of Samuel Palmer's exuberant Shoreham landscapes. Nevertheless, Burne-Jones's obsession with detail was a characteristic he was soon to abandon, thereafter simplifying his designs and attempting a broader, more relaxed style of workmanship.

Burne-Jones's move into colour in the early 1860s was facilitated by his initial work in stained glass. At Rossetti's suggestion, James Powell and Sons of Whitefriars approached him in 1856 about making designs for their firm. As one of the leading manufactures of stained glass before the establishment of Morris & Co., Powell and Sons were at the forefront of championing the revival of medieval techniques of glass

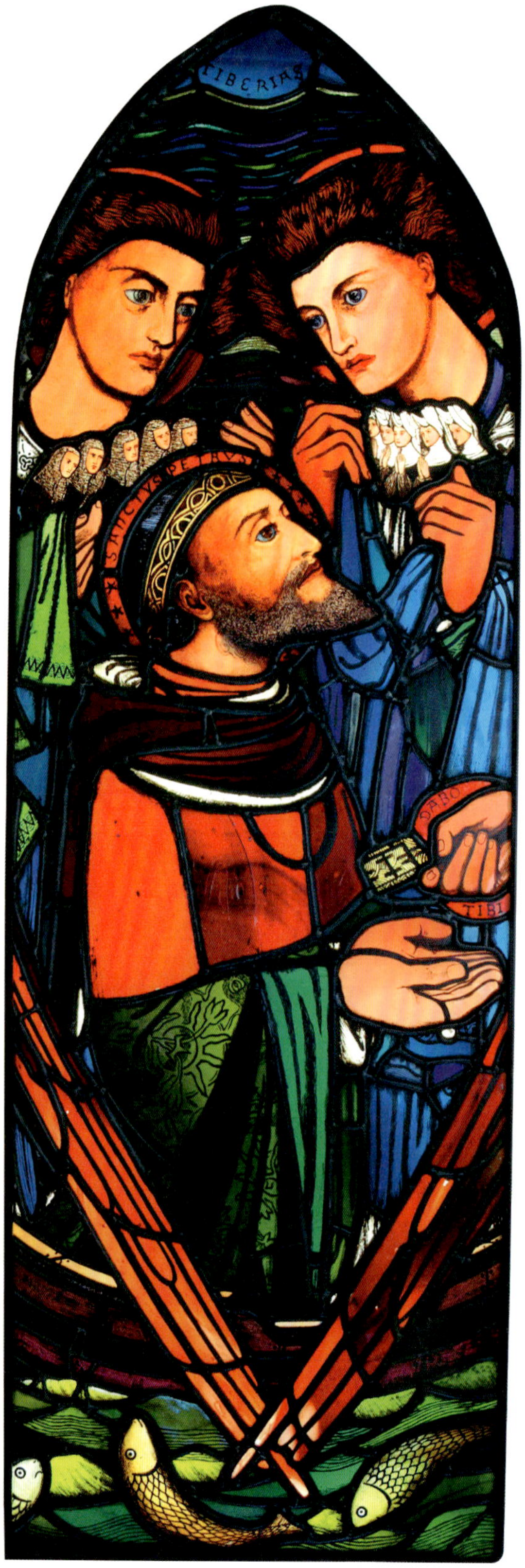
TIBERIAS

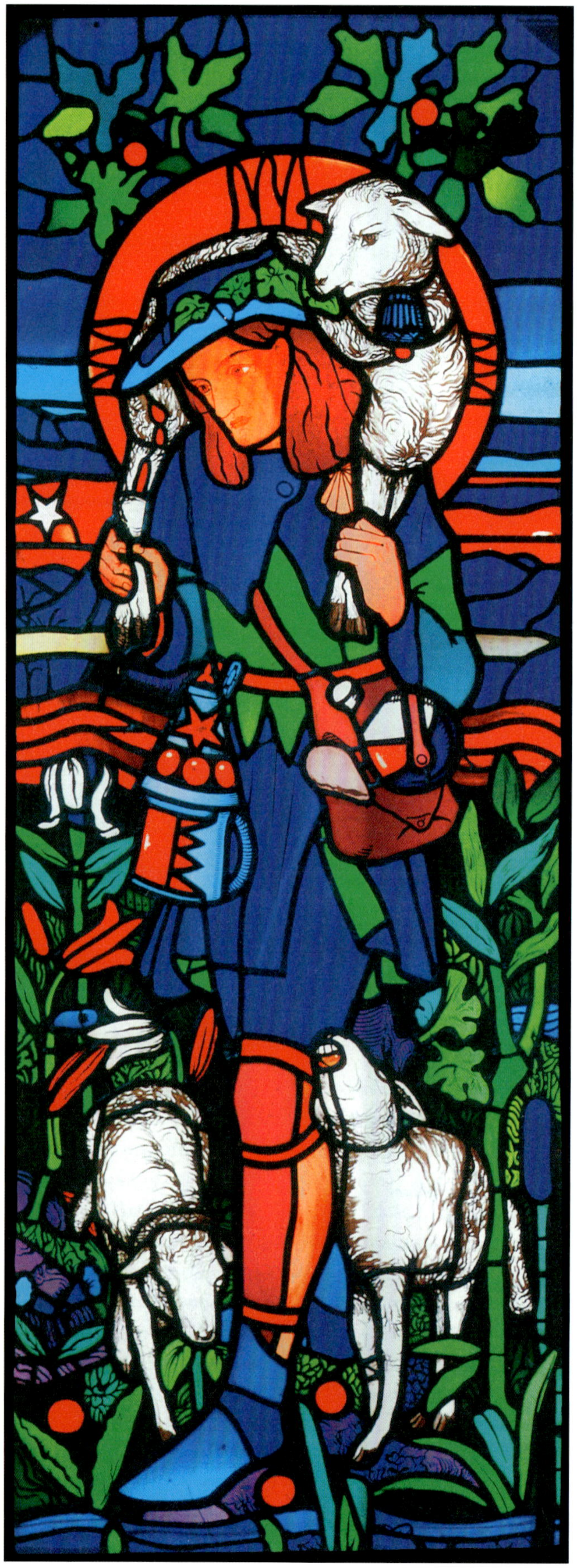

10
The Calling of St Peter c.1857
Stained and painted glass, 107.2 × 35.6
Victoria and Albert Museum

11
The Good Shepherd 1857–61
Stained-glass panel, 132 × 50.8
Birmingham Museums Trust

production, in reaction to the abandonment of mosaic leading and the adoption of a more pictorial approach that set in after the Renaissance. For this Powell's drew on the research of the glass connoisseur, Charles Winston, who maintained that to be true to the medium a window should depend on the medieval system of a dense network of lead lines framing small pieces of brilliant coloured glass for maximum visual impact.[8] Although executed in black and white, Burne-Jones's early drawings employ a similar method, with strong black lines and cross-hatching enhancing the overall, sparkling light effect. Designing for stained glass was therefore not such a leap for him as might be supposed but rather a matter of thinking on a larger scale and in colour, while maintaining preciousness of detail. Two single-light panels executed by Powell's from designs by Burne-Jones, *The Calling of St Peter* and *The Good Shepherd* (nos.10, 11), were revolutionary for the time in the way they combine Pre-Raphaelite naturalism with extreme stylisation. The colours are extraordinarily vivid and intense, with the mosaic-like pattern of deep rubies, blues and greens accentuating the scattered patches of white, and the lead lines are arranged so close in places to almost block the light.[9]

Burne-Jones became Powell's chief designer until he joined forces with Morris's firm in 1861, so instinctively did he take to the medium, understanding its limitations as its fundamental strength. Stained glass also enabled him to fulfil his original decision to become an artist-craftsman by reaching out to a broad audience through spiritually uplifting works. In keeping with the aims of the Ecclesiological Society, which approached art and architecture as a form of religious ministry and with which he had been involved since his Oxford days, Burne-Jones sought to revitalise modern Christianity through the production of beautiful and meaningful forms of church decoration. A major opportunity had presented itself in 1860 when he was asked to paint an altarpiece for the church of St Paul's in Brighton by one of the 'high priests' of the Tractarian movement, his friend the architect G.F. Bodley. Built at the instigation of the Tractarian, Father Arthur Douglas Wagner, St Paul's was one of the largest churches on the south coast with a reputation as a hotbed of Ritualism. Painted altarpieces were rare in the Church of England, due to a long-standing emphasis on the word above material culture and altarpieces in particular being associated with Roman Catholic idolatry, and this was no exception. It was to be placed behind the high altar in the chancel and took the form of a Renaissance-style triptych with the two outer panels depicting the Annunciation and the central compartment representing the Adoration of the Kings and Shepherds, following the format adopted by Rossetti for a similar triptych altarpiece *The Seed of David* for Llandaff Cathedral. The design itself is a curious blend of sixteenth-century Venetian and earlier Florentine painting, examples of which Burne-Jones had studied during his first visit to Italy in 1859, with the hieratic lateral panels contrasting with the naturalism of the central scene in which an attendant maid dries a cloth over a brazier and a shepherd plays a bagpipe.[10] This human element was reinforced by the artist's use of his friends as models: the Virgin Mary and first king were based on Jane and William Morris, and the shepherd with the pipe, on the poet Swinburne, with Burne-Jones himself shown bending into the scene behind him. As his largest and most ambitious commission to date, he was determined to get it right. Aware perhaps of a proclivity to overload his designs, Burne-Jones felt dissatisfied with the triptych once it was installed behind the altar, as it was difficult to read from the other end of

12
The Annunciation and the Adoration of the Magi 1861
Oil paint on three canvases, 108.6 × 73.7, 108.6 × 156.2, 108.6 × 73.7
Tate

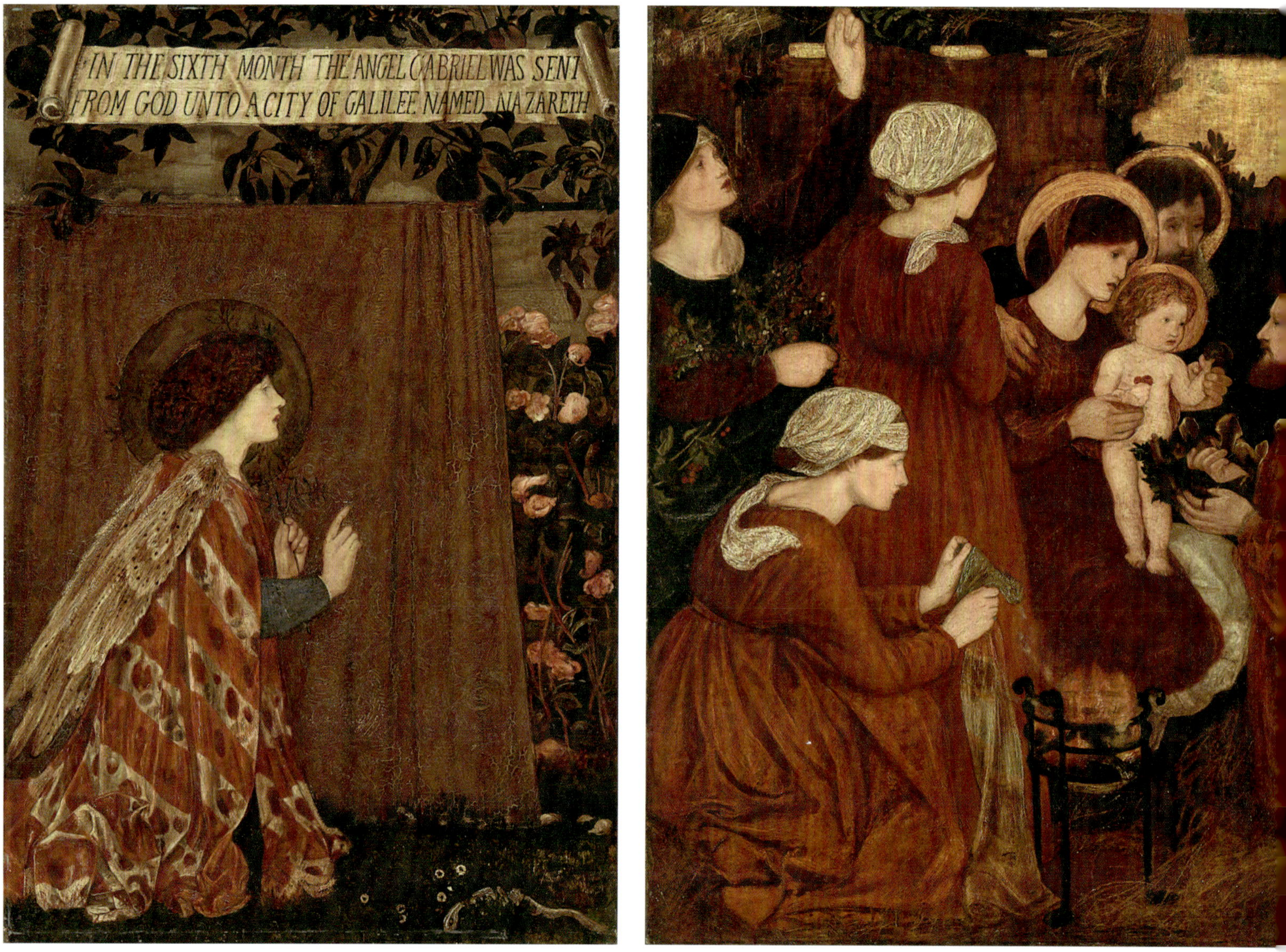

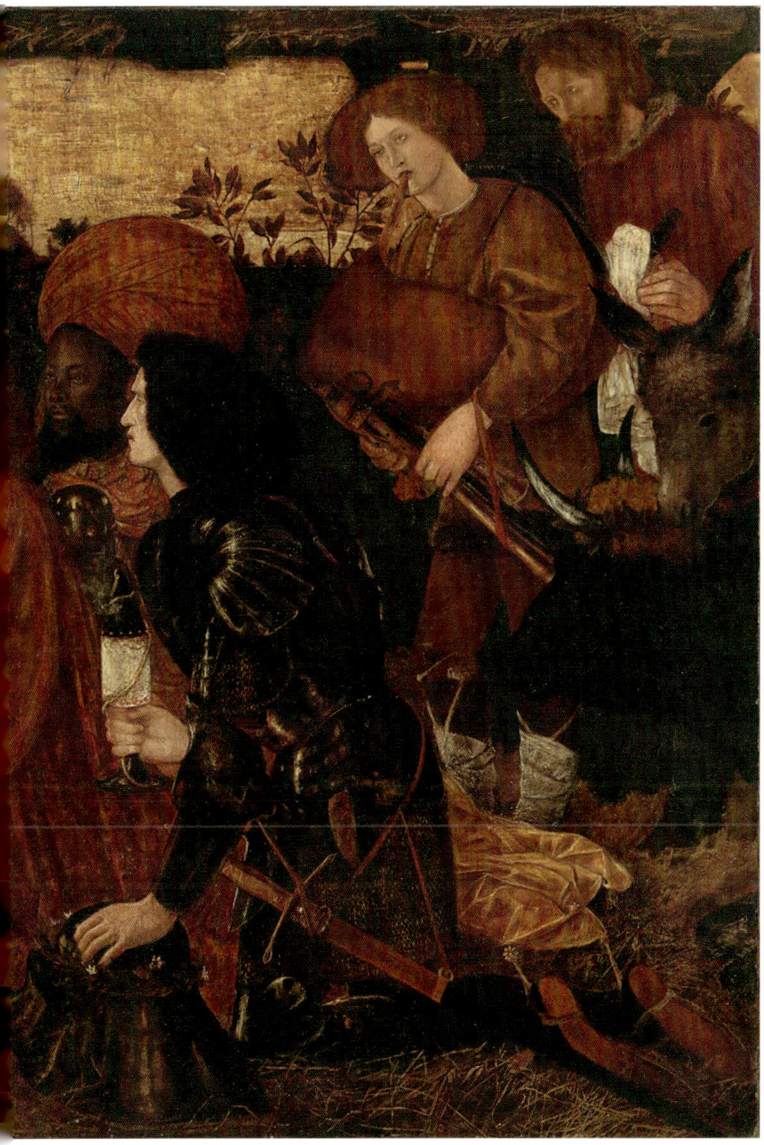

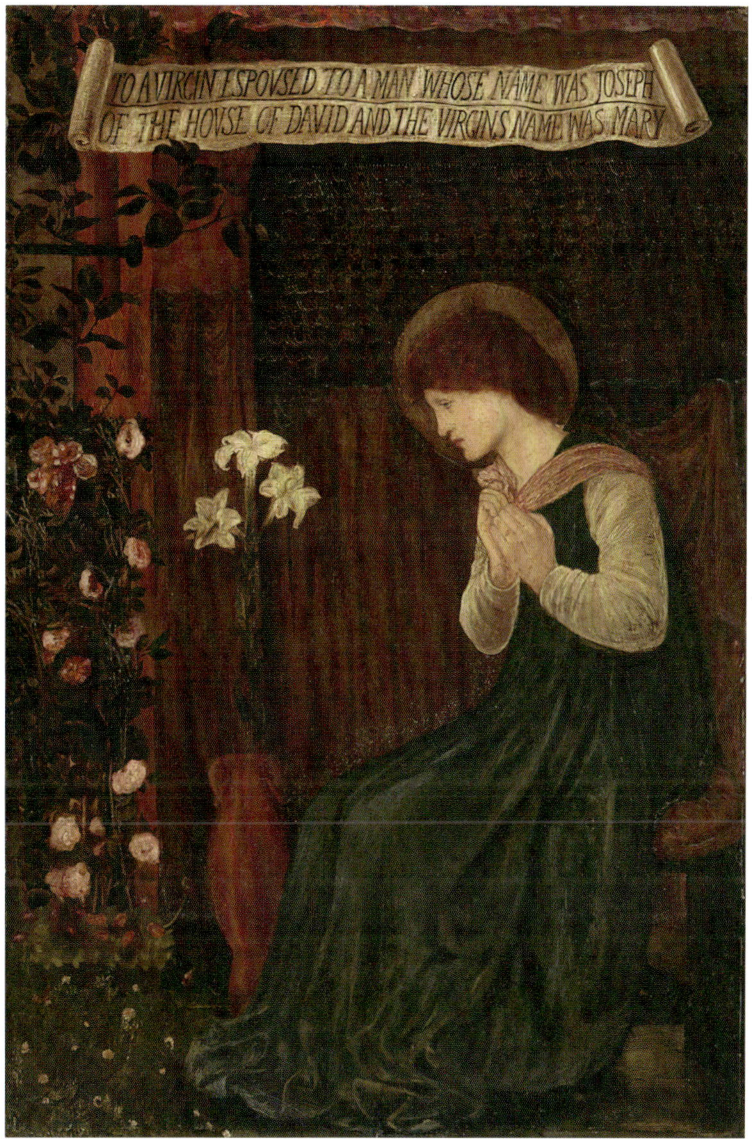
TO A VIRGIN ESPOVSED TO A MAN WHOSE NAME WAS JOSEPH
OF THE HOVSE OF DAVID AND THE VIRGINS NAME WAS MARY

13
The God of Love and Alceste from Chaucer's *Legend of Good Women* 1861–4
Stained and painted glass, 46.8 × 50.7
Victoria and Albert Museum

the long chancel and almost impossible to see from behind the rood screen in the nave (fig.24). Within a year he had repainted it, reducing the figures from eleven to six and focusing attention on the allegorical role of the kings as worshippers in the tradition of early Netherlandish altarpieces.[11]

Working for the Church was to provide Burne-Jones with inspiration for the rest of his life. It was also his main source of income, which became more of an imperative following his marriage in 1860 to Georgiana Macdonald, the daughter of a Methodist minister whom he had known since the early 1850s, and the children that ensued (Philip was born in 1861, Margaret in 1866). In 1861 he became one of the seven partners in the design collective Morris & Co., which, under Morris's lead, sought to improve the lives of all classes through the production of beautiful, useful objects for both ecclesiastical and domestic settings. This enterprise continued the friendship between Morris and Burne-Jones, allowing them to share their love of all things medieval and develop their literary interests over collaborative works. Morris became the firm's main pattern designer and Burne-Jones its principal figure designer, producing, according to an account book, 786 designs for stained glass between 1861 and 1898.[12] From this time onwards Burne-Jones's approach to glass became more subtle as seen in the more emphatic use of white glass and yellow stain in two panels inspired by Chaucer's *Legend of Good Women*, a long dream poem in which the poet is introduced by Amor (Love) to famous women from antiquity who suffered for their love (nos.13, 14). In their respective interpretations of Chaucer the two artists sought to capture in their own art something of what they described as the poet's half-pagan, half-Christianised treatment of antiquity, as seen in the classical reposeful figures that dominate the panels and are surrounded by touches of natural and fantastic detail, including a dragon-like serpent at Cleopatra's feet.

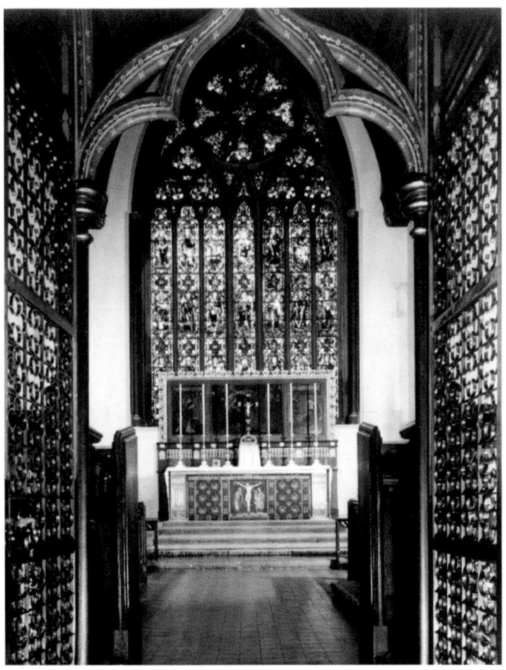

Fig.24
Second version of Edward Burne-Jones's triptych behind the altar at St Paul's Church, Brighton
St Paul's Church, Brighton

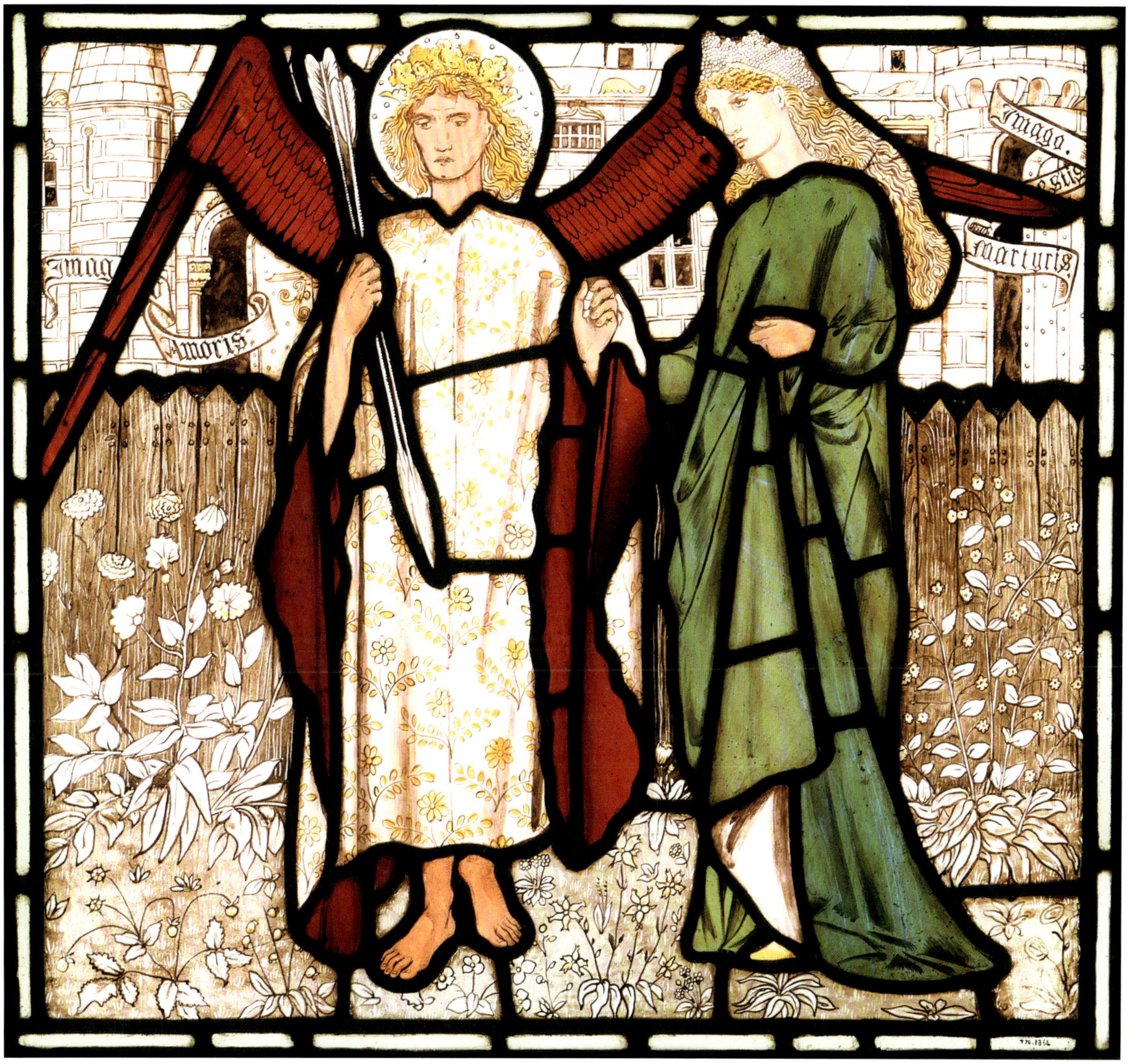
Amoris
Imago.
martyris

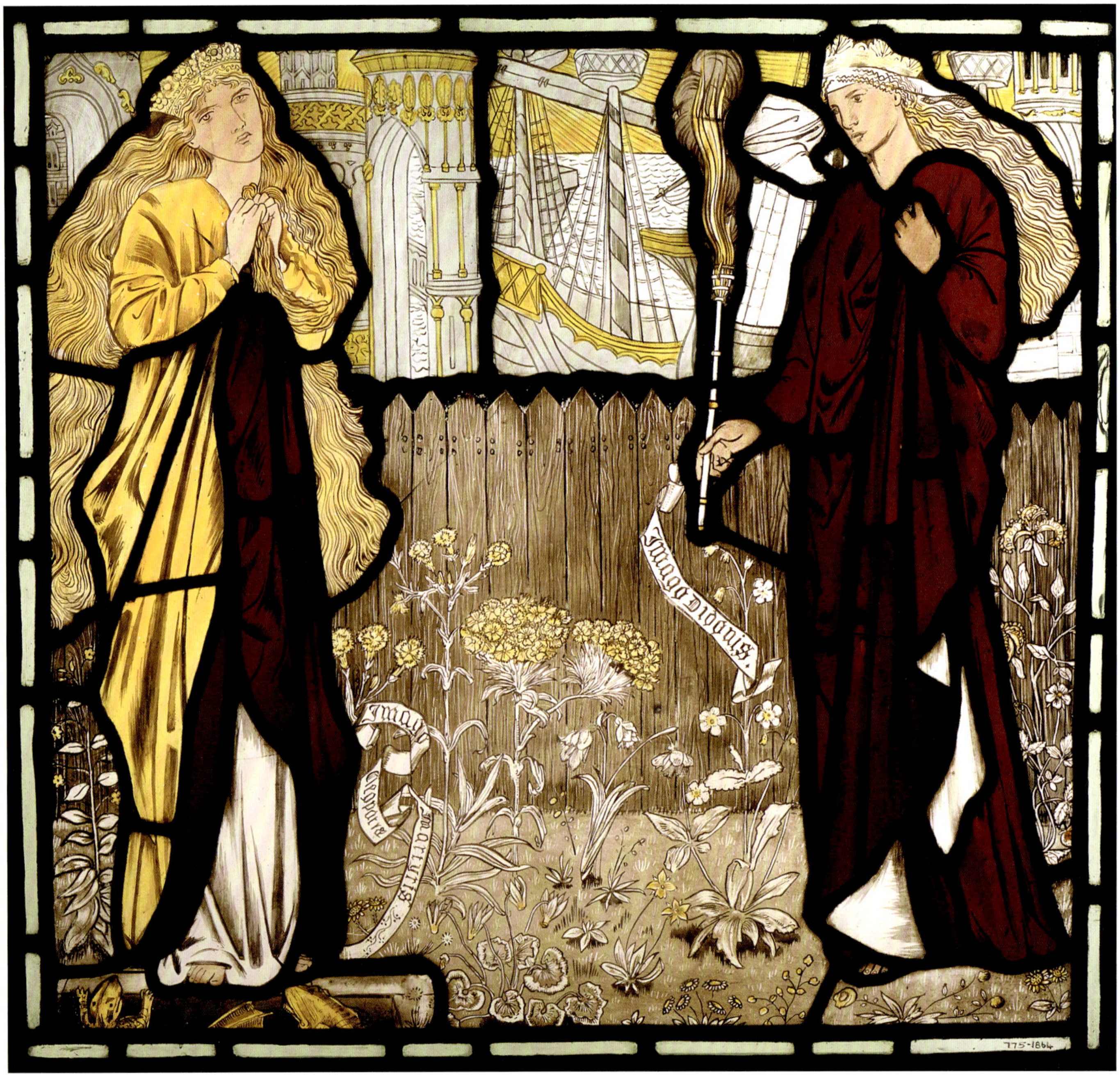
Imago Didonis.
Martyris
775-1864

14 (opposite)
Dido and Cleopatra from Chaucer's *Legend of Good Women* 1861–4
Stained-glass panel, 47 × 50.4
Victoria and Albert Museum

15
Geoffrey Chaucer 1863
Ceramic tile painted by William Morris after a design by Edward Burne-Jones, 15.3 × 15.3
Victoria and Albert Museum

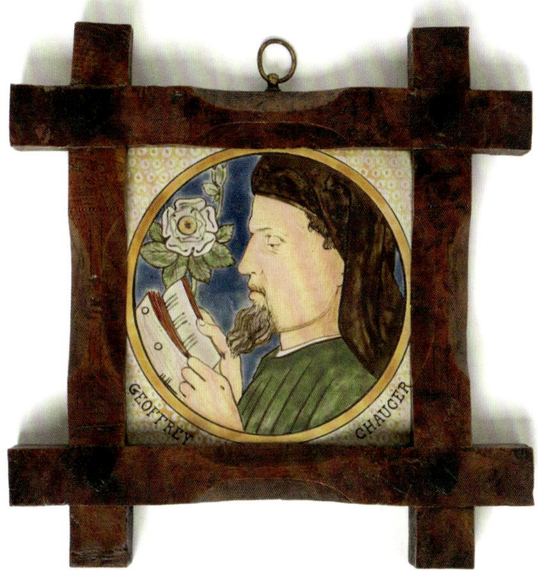

The dichotomies of pleasure and pain and of life and death that characterise so much of Burne-Jones's early non-ecclesiastical work also help explain why, just a few years earlier, he decided to adorn the lower (almost unseen) panel of a piano, given to him and Georgiana as a wedding gift, with a frieze showing Death knocking at the door of a garden, in which maidens recline languidly listening to music (no.16). Loosely based on a similar scene with seated figures in a fourteenth-century *Triumph of Death* in the Campo Santo, Pisa, this sombre picture would have complemented the melancholy airs Georgiana performed at the piano and, like the drolleries in the medieval manuscripts he so admired, suggests that death is ever present on the margins, mocking the transient pleasures of music, which for Burne-Jones epitomised the kind of otherworldly experience he sought to capture in his art.

This humble piece of decoration also marks a change in direction, away from the intricate black-and-white manner that had so enraptured Rossetti, to something more dreamy and introspective in mood and less pernickety in terms of design. Finding that his pen-and-ink drawings were not particularly 'saleable things', Burne-Jones branched out into painting in colour using watercolour combined with gouache, which became his chosen medium.[13] The first works Burne-Jones executed in watercolour were dark and opaque in appearance and comprise a kind of domestic grotesque, with sinister subjects (many based on unnatural relationships) disclosing a hidden threat of menace. In one scene the enchantress Nimue outwits the wizard Merlin by luring him into a grave (no.20); another shows a dead man reaching out to embrace his beloved (no.19); and in one small painting the witch Sidonia von Bork plots to destroy an entire royal family (no.18). Following Rossetti, Burne-Jones initially refrained from exhibiting his works in public, finding instead a sympathetic audience in the patrons who had supported the early Pre-Raphaelites. These included wealthy industrialists such as the Leeds stockbroker, Thomas Plint (owner of nos.7, 8), and the Newcastle lead manufacturer, James Leathart, who bought the two *von Bork* paintings and *Merlin and Nimue* (no.17,18,20).

16
Ladies and Death 1860
Painted wooden panel on an upright piano made by Frederick Priestley, painted gilt and gesso on wood, with a layer of shellac over gilded areas
33 × 125.7
Victoria and Albert Museum

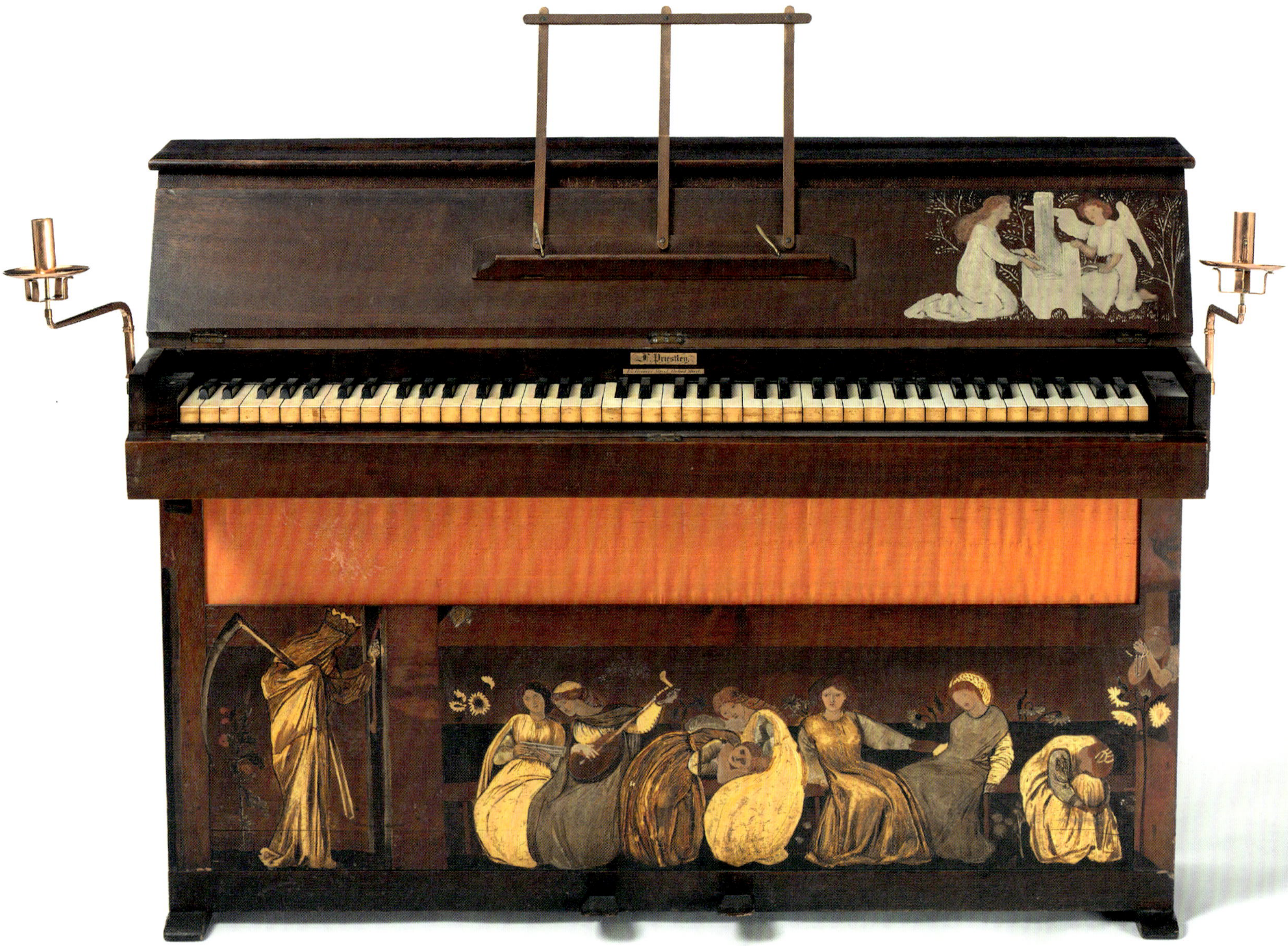

17
Clara von Bork 1560 1860
Watercolour and gouache on paper, 34.2 × 17.9
Tate

18
Sidonia von Bork 1560 1860
Watercolour and gouache on paper, 33.3 × 17.1
Tate

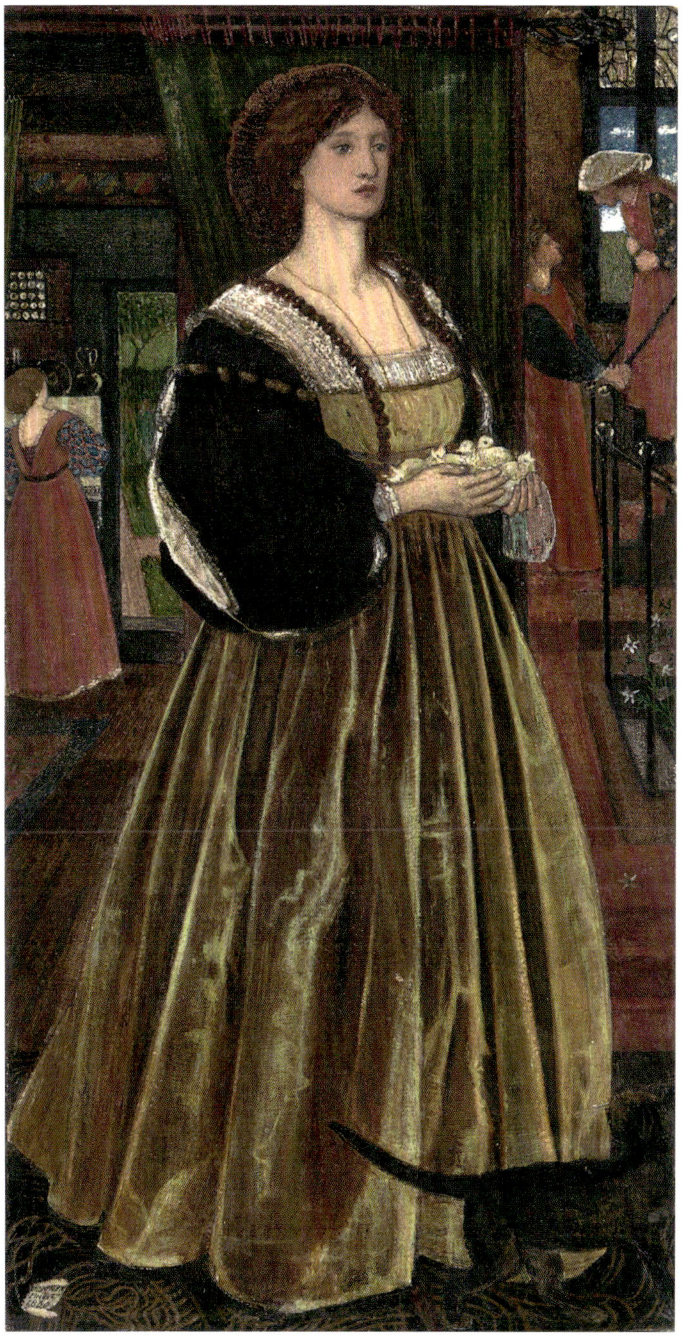

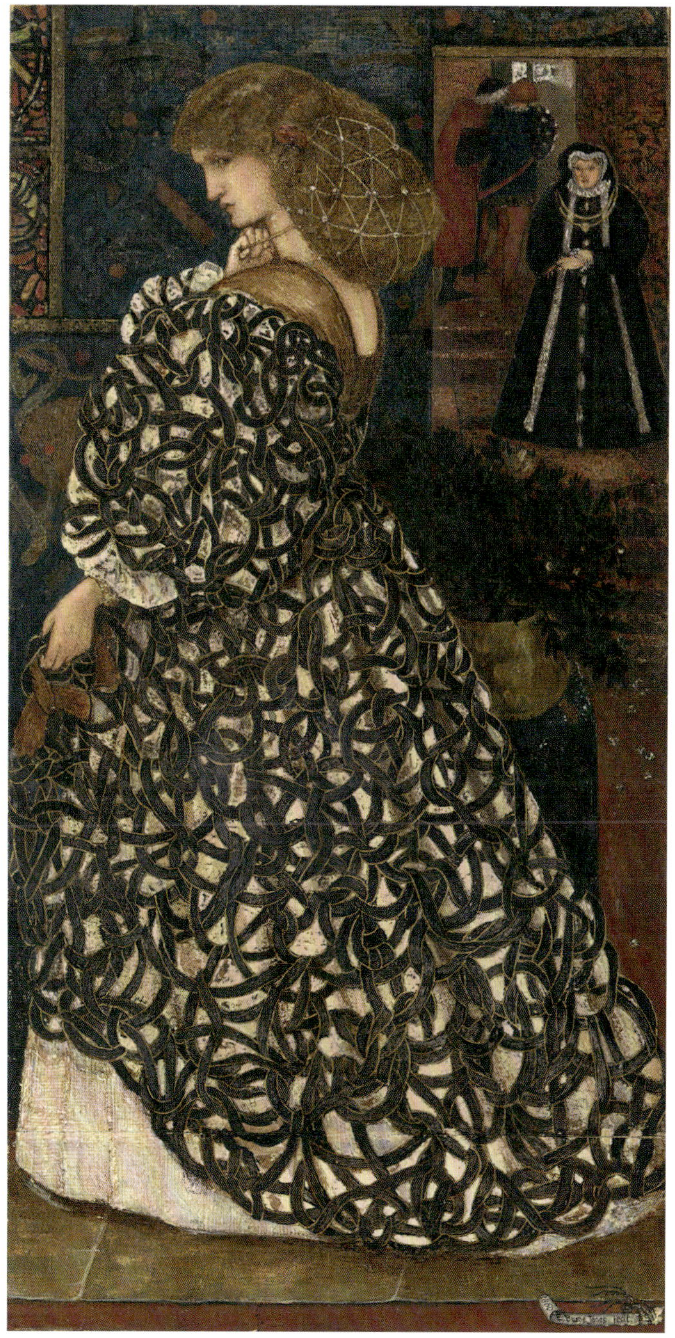

19
Clerk Saunders 1861
Watercolour on paper, 69.9 × 41.8
Tate

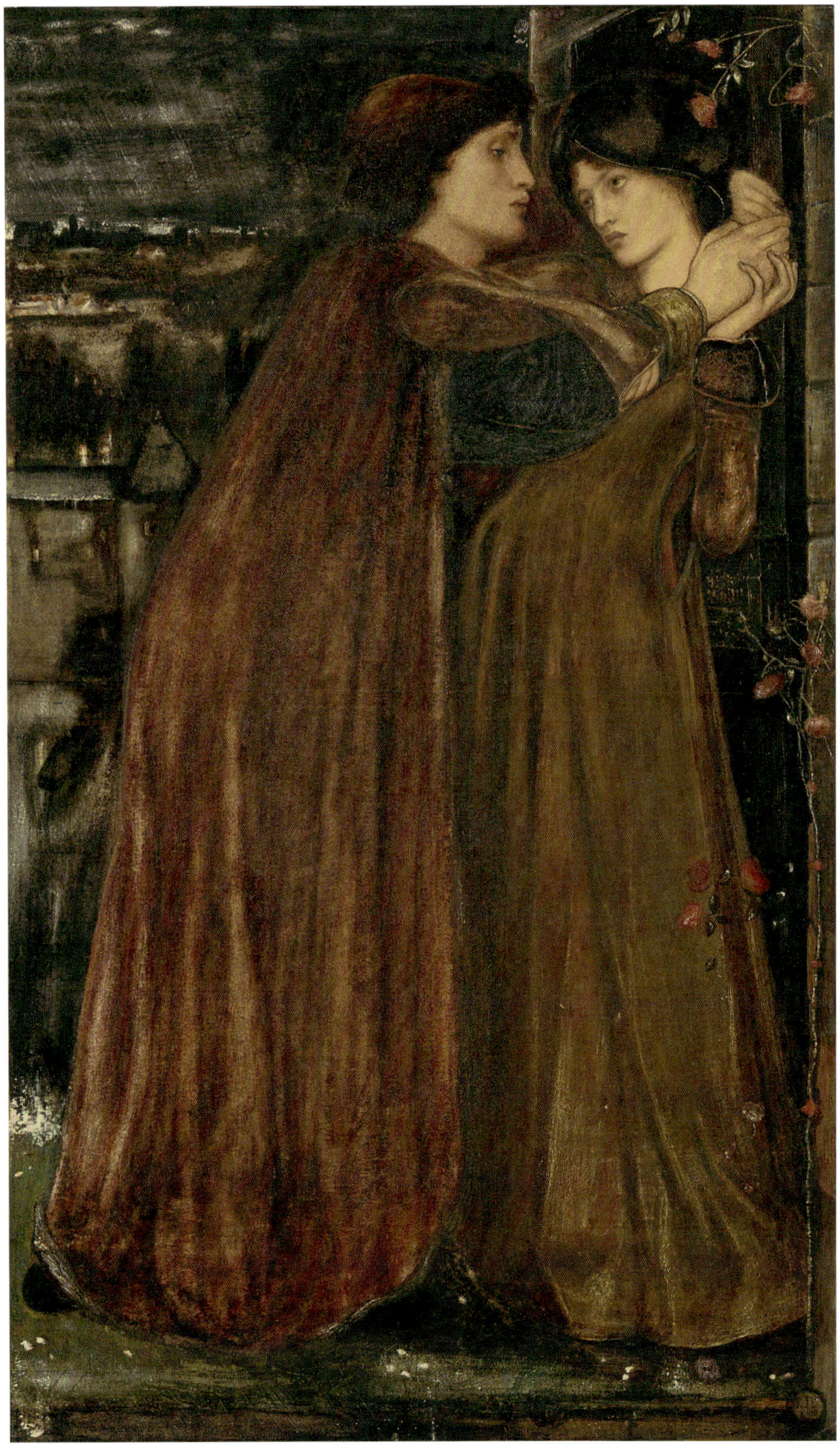

20
Merlin and Nimue 1861
Watercolour and bodycolour on paper, 64.2 × 52.1
Victoria and Albert Museum

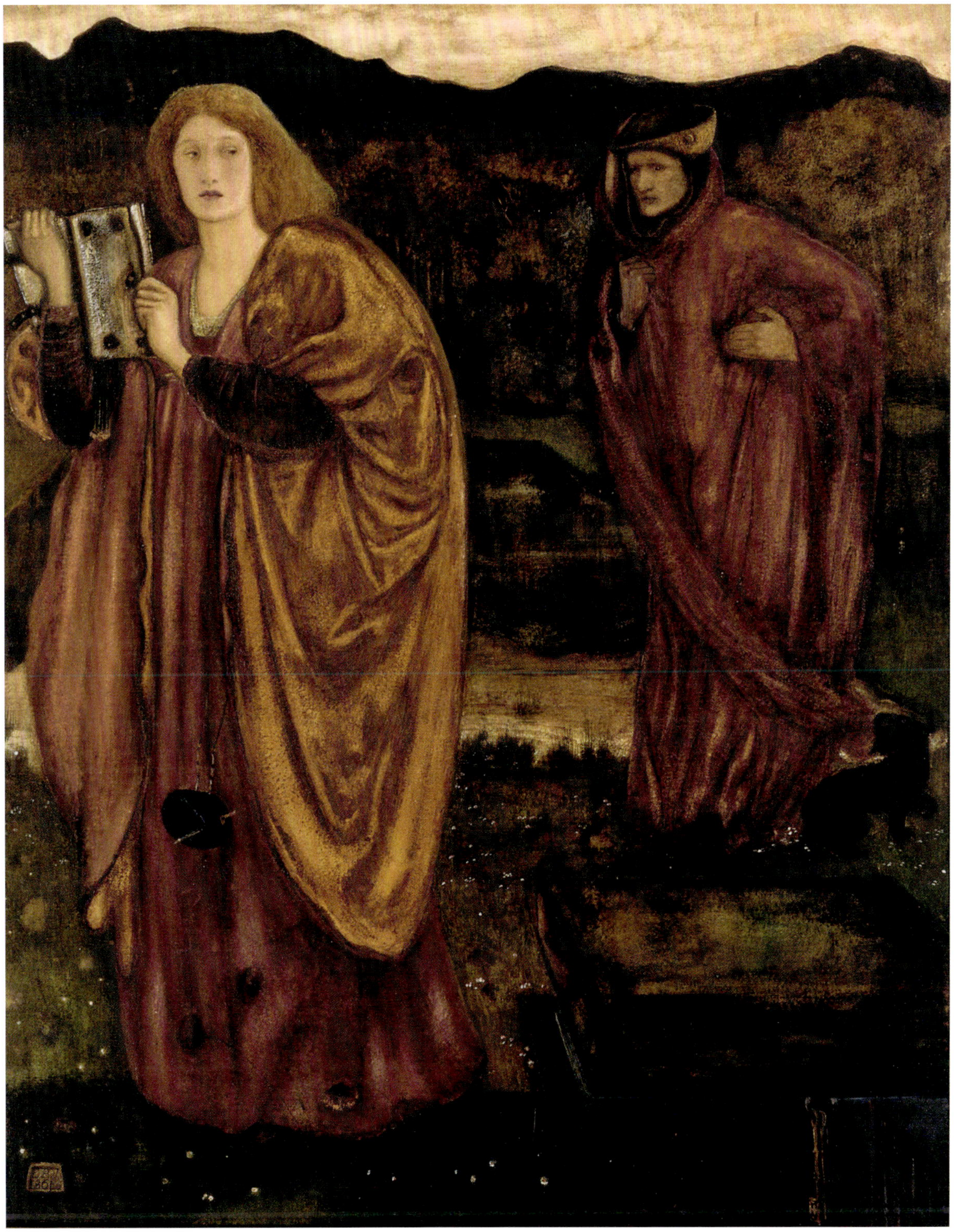

As his reputation grew within this select circle, Burne-Jones felt emboldened to put his head above the parapet and face a broader audience at public exhibition. In 1864 he was made an Associate of the Old Water Colour Society (OWCS, previously Society of Painters in Water-Colours), going on to exhibit some twenty-three works with the institution until his dramatic resignation in 1870. Burne-Jones's strange, melancholy subjects and idiomatic use of watercolour put him on course for a rocky ride with more conservative members of the society, who made a point of expressing their disapproval by skying his pictures and ignoring him. The press too was generally hostile, finding his works archaic and extreme. Despite this, the OWCS exhibitions were significant in introducing Burne-Jones to the men who were to become his most important patrons: the Liberal MP for Glasgow, William Graham, who bought *Le Chant d'Amour* (no.22), and the Liverpool shipping magnate, Frederick Leyland, the first owner of *The Wine of Circe* and *Phyllis and Demophoön* (nos.23, 25). 'Loved by the initiate few and laughed at by the profligate many', Burne-Jones's exhibits also attracted the attention of like-minded artists, notably Walter Crane, Edward Clifford and Henry Holiday, who looked up to him as the leader of a new 'poetic' school.[14]

The dramatic transformation in Burne-Jones's style was to find full expression in his exhibits of the late 1860s. These mark a further phase of development away from what Ruskin disparaged as a fancy for painting 'nasty black and brown things' to a lighter and more lyrical mode of expression. Ruskin himself was influential here in encouraging greater repose and tranquillity as the corollary to the morally uplifting subjects he hoped his protégé would now depict, and in 1862 funded a further visit to Italy so Burne-Jones could learn from the Venetian artists the writer deemed worthy of emulation.[15] Burne-Jones's Giorgionesque *Le Chant d'Amour* could be said to mark the culmination of this Venetian phase, with its rich colour and enigmatic musical subject in which a knight listens to a love song performed by a woman accompanied by the blindfolded figure of Love at the bellows. For Burne-Jones the shift towards a more graceful and balanced kind of composition was also a matter of wanting to draw better, as encouraged by his artist friend, George Frederic Watts, and to keep pace with his coevals who were producing equally experimental work but in a more classical vein. The latter included Frederic Leighton, Edward Poynter and James Whistler, all of whom were accomplished draughtsmen and proficient in drawing the nude, having received a thorough training on the Continent. As if to catch up on lost time, Burne-Jones made studies from classical Greek sculpture in the British Museum, gaining in the process a greater understanding of volume, anatomy and proportion. The increased emphasis on rhythm and interval in his work also developed in tandem with his collaborative work with Morris over illustrations for the latter's epic verse cycle, *The Earthly Paradise* (no.1). These designs introduced into Burne-Jones's practice the idea of a sequence of images in which each episode could exist as a discrete stand-alone composition that could be adapted in different media.

The full extent of Burne-Jones's development as an artist is apparent in two of the watercolours he exhibited at the OWCS in 1869, *The Lament* (no.24) and the Homeric *Wine of Circe*, the last of which sealed his reputation as a painter of rare imagination. Both works are indicative of his close study of classical Greek sculpture in the frieze-like disposition of forms and heavy drapery folds. The figures in *The Lament* relate to a group of seated deities on the Parthenon frieze, while *Circe* appears to have been suggested by a relief of a charioteer from the Mausoleum at Halicarnassus, also in the British Museum.[16] Other inventive adaptations of source material include the herm emerging from palm fronds and the censer entwined with serpents. The strong emphasis on architecture in both works not only allows for a crisper, more solid treatment of form but helps frame the attitudes of the figures, underscoring, on the one hand, the pensive interior emotion of *The Lament* with its chanting and meditating figures and, on the other, the steely determination of the sorceress fixing her potion as Odysseus's men approach in the distance. In keeping with the aesthetic tendency of the time, both works are composed in a particular colour key with the predominant orange-yellow in *Circe* dramatising the daily ritual performed by the enchantress in chime with the course of the sun (indicated by the wilting sunflowers on the left). By contrast, the alternate play of red and blue in *The Lament* complements the reflective mood evoked by the imagined sounds of the bell harp, reinforcing the dual emphasis on performance and receptivity, love and grief. The idea of correspondence between different art forms comes to the fore in these works, with painting linked to both poetry and music. Indeed, in an ekphrastic response to *Circe* Rossetti penned a sonnet responding to the colour of the painting and the idea of 'ruined passion' conveyed to him by the prowling panthers at the goddess's feet.

It has often been observed that the faces in Burne-Jones's work resemble one other, making it difficult to distinguish between the sexes (the figure on the right of *The Lament* has, for instance, been identified as both male and female). This tendency was to become more marked as he developed as a figure painter, resulting in a widespread perception that his art was abnormal in ways that might now be labelled 'queer', in departing from stereotypical models of masculine and feminine identity. This issue came to a head at the OWCS in 1870 when he exhibited *Phyllis and Demophoön* (no.25), which reinterpreted Ovid's legend to show Phyllis physically reappearing to reclaim the lover who had abandoned her and caused her to be transformed into an almond tree. More than any other work to date, this picture resonated on a personal level, with the face of Phyllis based on that of the Greek sculptress Maria Zambaco, with whom the artist was conducting a tempestuous extra-marital affair at the time. While the recoiling figure of Demophoön may reflect Burne-Jones's ambivalent feelings about the entanglement, as is often claimed, this was not the immediate cause of the controversy that ensued. Rather it was the wan depiction of Demophoön, torn between his guilt and desire, that made the work appear so repellent; the critic Tom Taylor in *The Times* noted with disapproval that there was 'no true characterisation of sex between the Demophoön and the Phyllis', while the *Illustrated London News* likened it to the decadent 'amatory poetry of the Swinburne school', with which the artist was associated.[17] Following a complaint to the society concerning the full-frontal nudity of the Demophoön, Burne-Jones was asked to alter the picture to make it more acceptable to public taste. He refused, withdrew it and, at the close of the exhibition, handed in his resignation, determined to pursue his own vision as the master of his own making.

21
The Annunciation (the Flower of God) 1862
Bodycolour on paper, 61 × 53.3
Private collection

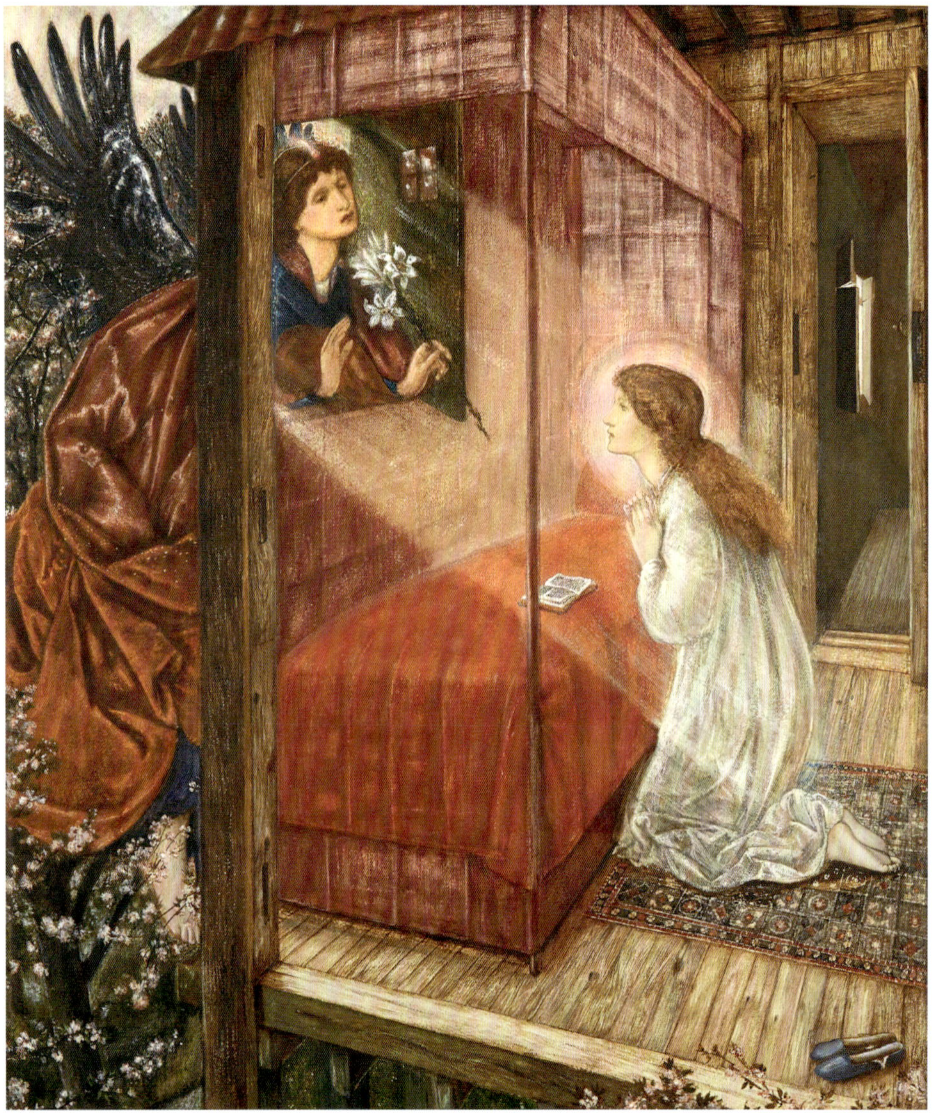

22
Le Chant d'Amour (The Love Song) 1865
Watercolour and bodycolour on paper, 54.9 × 77.7
Museum of Fine Arts, Boston

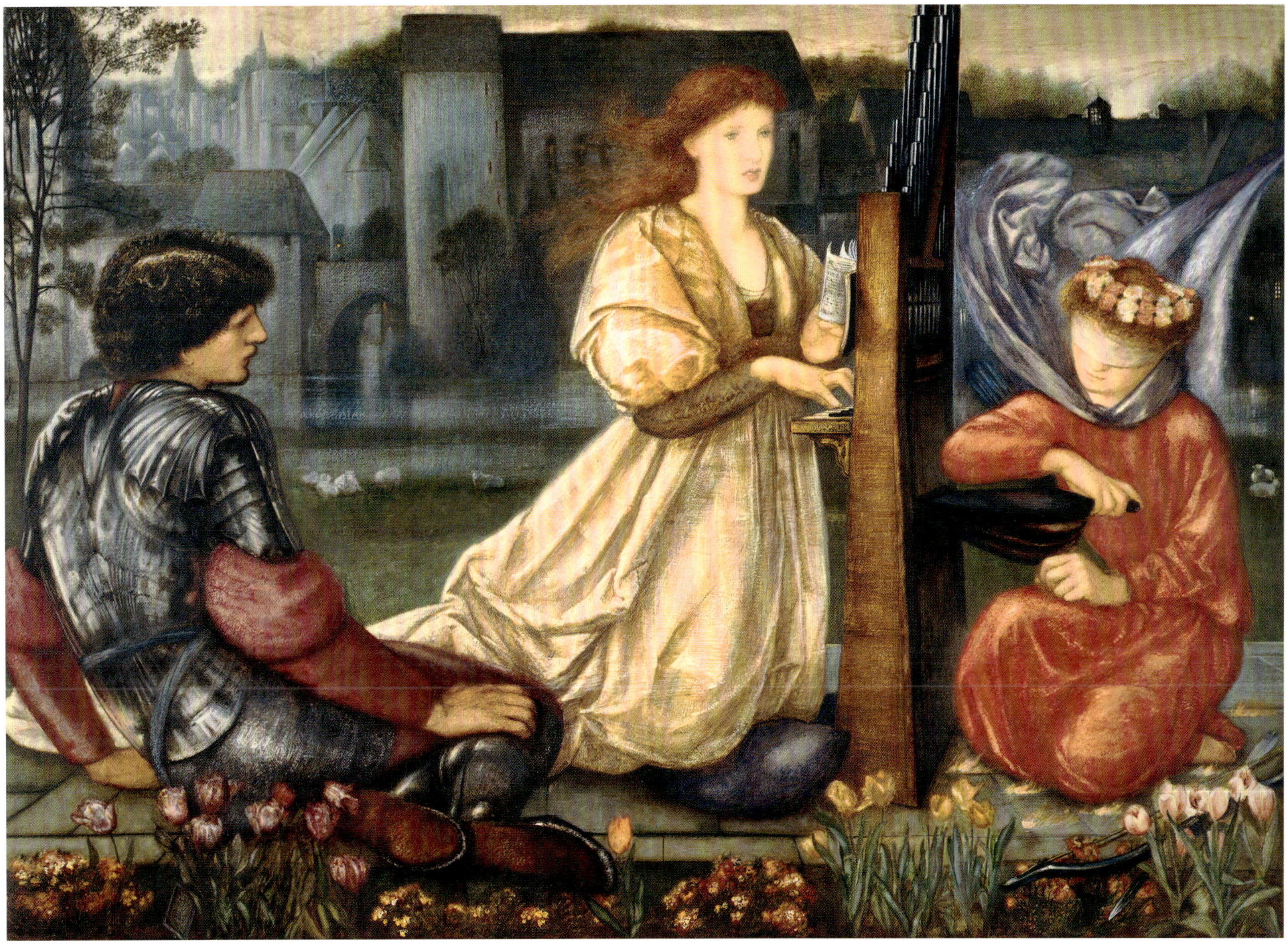

23
The Wine of Circe 1863–9
Watercolour and bodycolour on paper, 71.1 × 101.6
Private collection

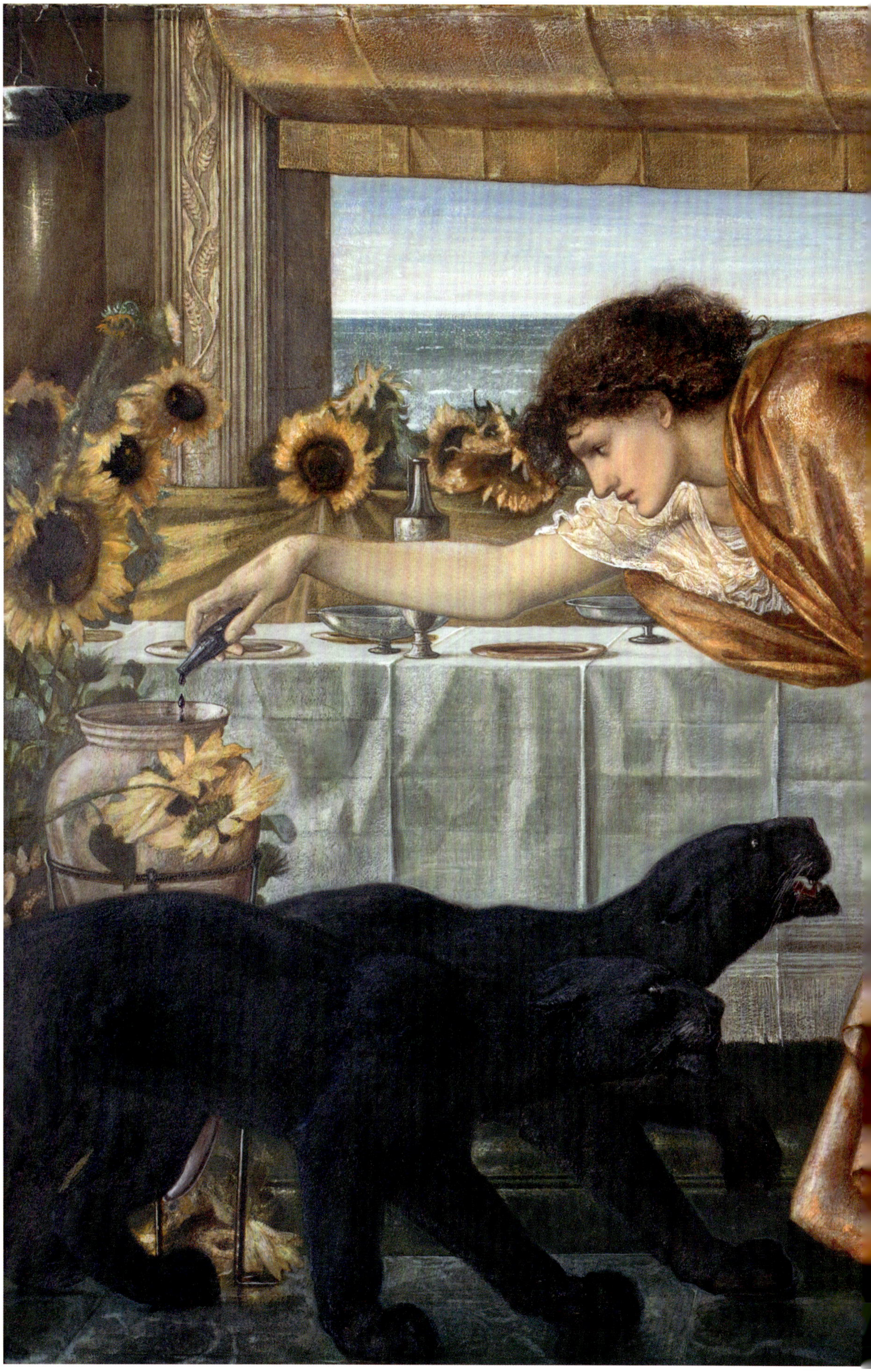

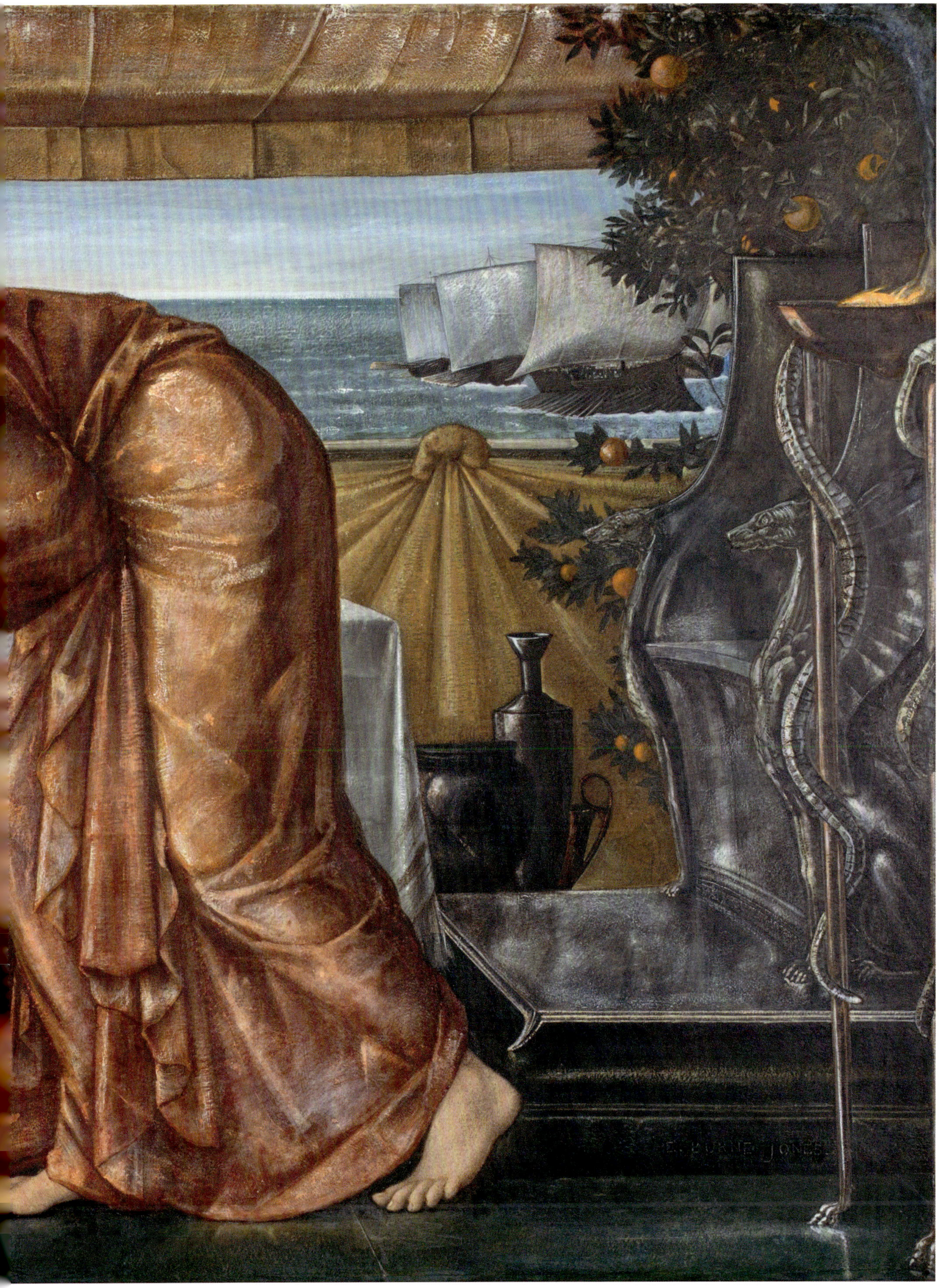
E. BURNE-JONES

24
The Lament 1865–6
Watercolour and bodycolour on paper mounted on canvas, 47.5 × 79.5
William Morris Gallery, London Borough of Waltham Forest

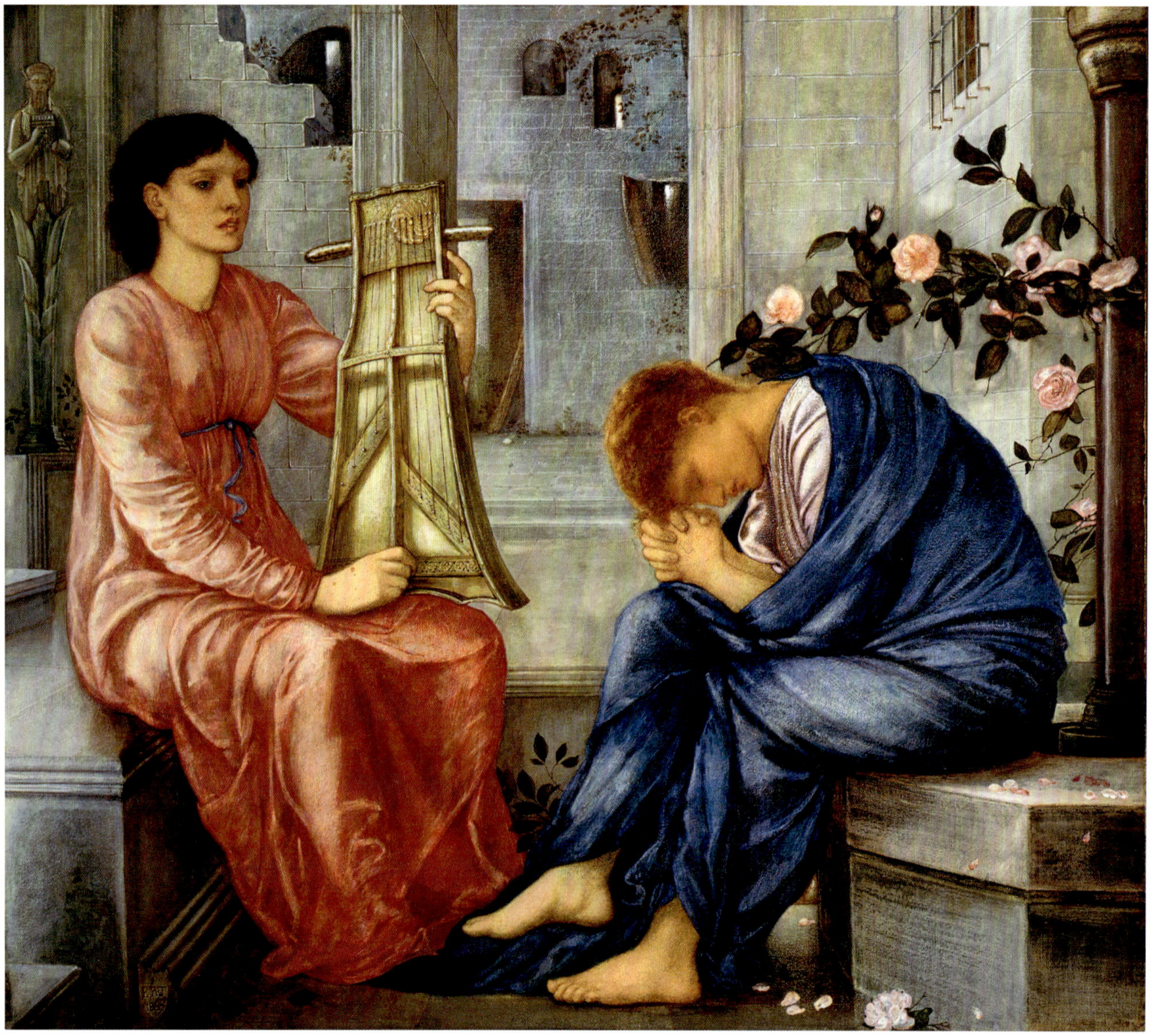

25
Phyllis and Demophoön 1870
Bodycolour and watercolour on paper, 91.5 × 45.8
Birmingham Museums Trust

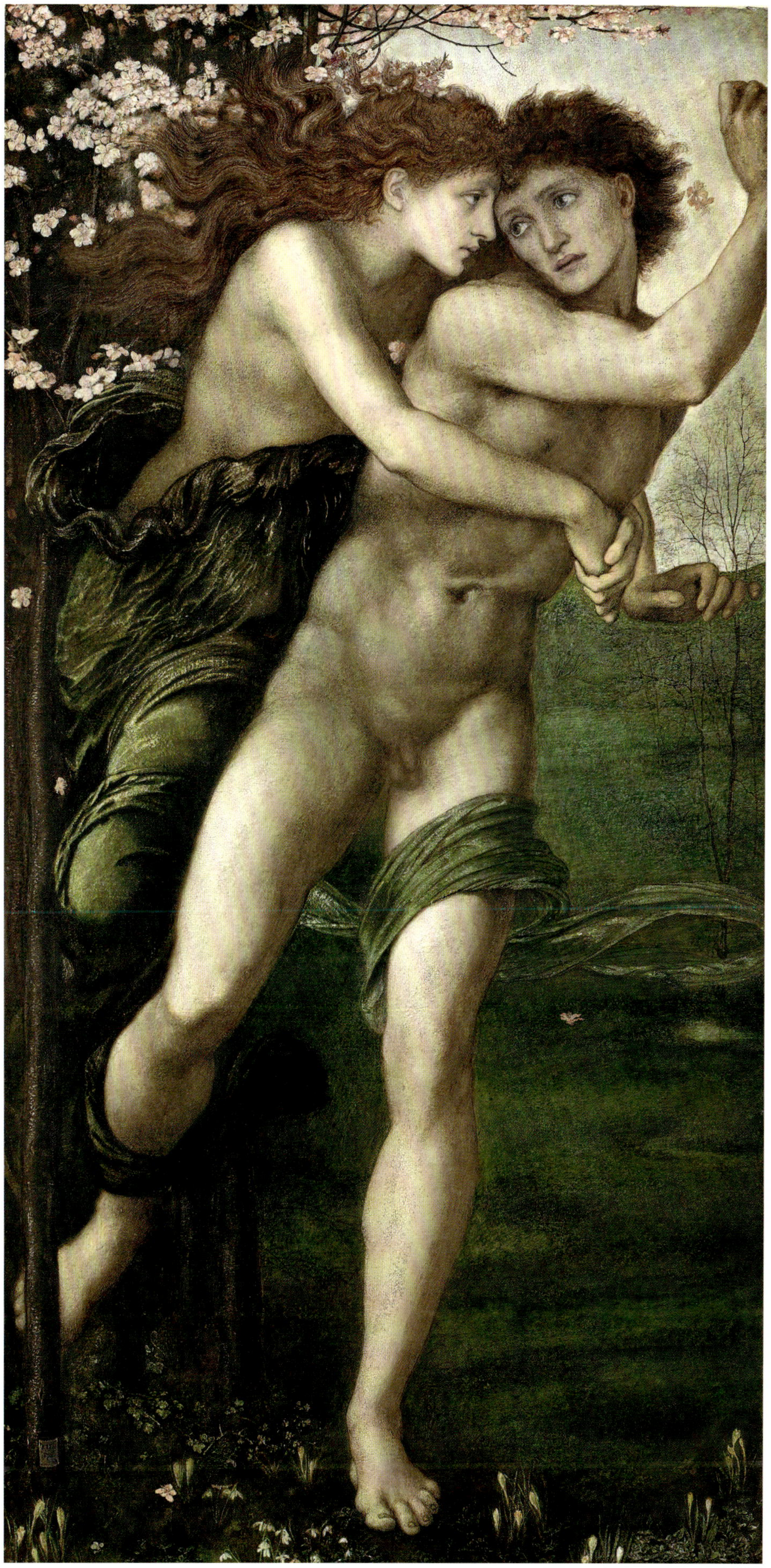

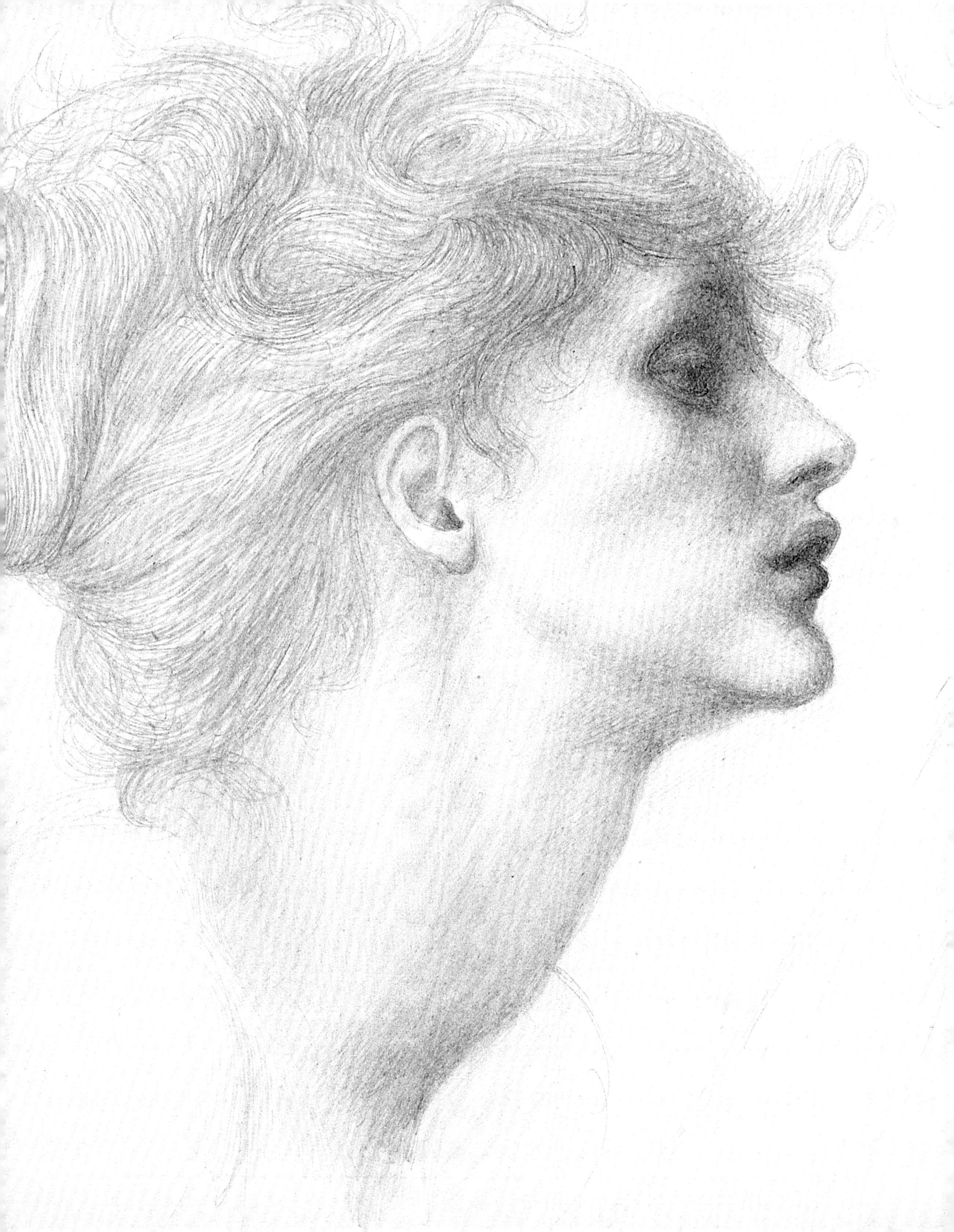

‘An impassioned imagination’: Burne-Jones as a Draughtsman

COLIN CRUISE

In his introductory essay to the catalogue for a memorial exhibition of Burne-Jones’s drawings held at the Burlington Fine Arts Club in 1899, the critic and poet Cosmo Monkhouse identified an ‘impassioned imagination’ as a characteristic of the artist.[1] Although it was not the first exhibition devoted to the artist’s drawings, it was the most comprehensive overview of his career presented solely through works on paper and related media. It ranged from early pen-and-ink on vellum works – such as *Going to the Battle* 1858[2] (no.5) – to studies for the various versions of the story of Perseus (c.1875–85; nos.71, 72, 73) and *The Romaunt de la Rose* (nos.59, 61, 63). There were sections on portraits, designs for books and decorative schemes, stained glass and embroidery, as well as ‘humorous sketches’. The volume of illustrated letters to Helen Mary Gaskell (no.87), making what must have been its first public appearance, was included in a case displaying ‘Painted Books and Sketches’.[3]

What was it about sketches and studies, incomplete works and marginalia that helped the public in a pursuit of Burne-Jones’s imagination? This question forces us to look closely at the drawings themselves, to recognise their special qualities, the artist’s skill and his powers of invention and visualisation. In these works, too, we can detect the influences on his choices of medium, technique and subject, some of them idiosyncratic, others traditional or revived from historical examples. However, at the end of the nineteenth century, exhibitions and publications had already fed a public fascination with drawing. Aestheticism had fuelled a taste for preparatory or fragmentary studies, chiefly for old master drawings but also for drawings by contemporary artists such as Burne-Jones, G.F. Watts and Frederic Leighton; all of them were compared favourably to the great artists of the Renaissance.

Drawing: the presence and personality of the artist

This new interest in the history of drawing took it out of the province of connoisseurs and collectors into a more varied constituency of artists, poets, historians and the gallery-visiting public. The taste was anticipated by British artists of previous generations such as Sir Joshua Reynolds and Sir Thomas Lawrence, whose impressive collections stimulated systematic museum collecting and curation in Britain. Drawing became emblematic of the art of the past, particularly of the great geniuses of the Renaissance. Several of the mid-nineteenth-century writers on the subject were well known to Burne-Jones. Algernon Charles Swinburne, one of his closest friends for a time, wrote his ‘Notes on Designs of the Old Masters at Florence’ in 1864 after a visit to the neglected collection of drawings at the Uffizi. He detected an ‘indefinable grace and grave mystery’ in Leonardo’s designs, a quality found also by Walter Pater writing not only on Leonardo but on Botticelli and Michelangelo, too.[4] Both critics perceived a dark mysteriousness in the paintings and drawings of these artists. Their highly personal encounters with the drawn mark drew special attention

Desiderium 1873 (detail, no. 68)

26
Study for *The Golden Stairs: Frances Graham at the foot of the stairs*
c.1876–80
Graphite on paper, 25.4 × 14
Courtesy of Mrs Dianne Roberts

27
Study for *The Golden Stairs*
c.1876–80
Graphite on paper, 25.2 × 13.8
Courtesy of Mrs Dianne Roberts

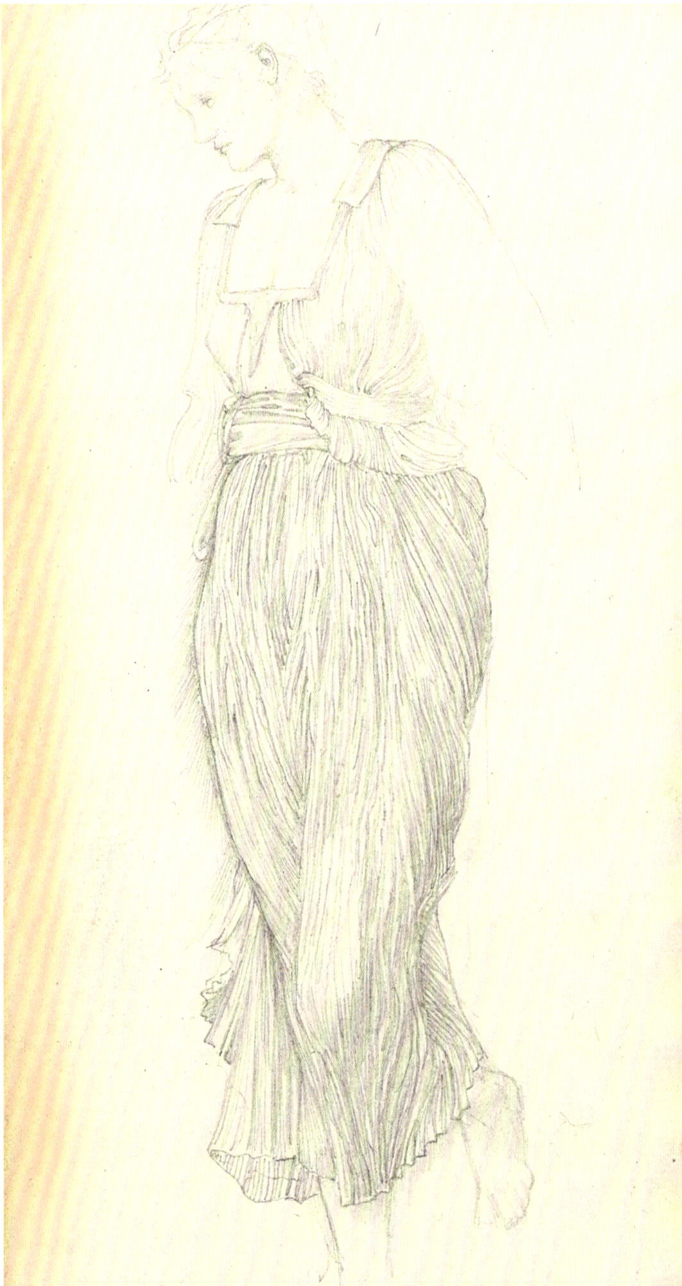

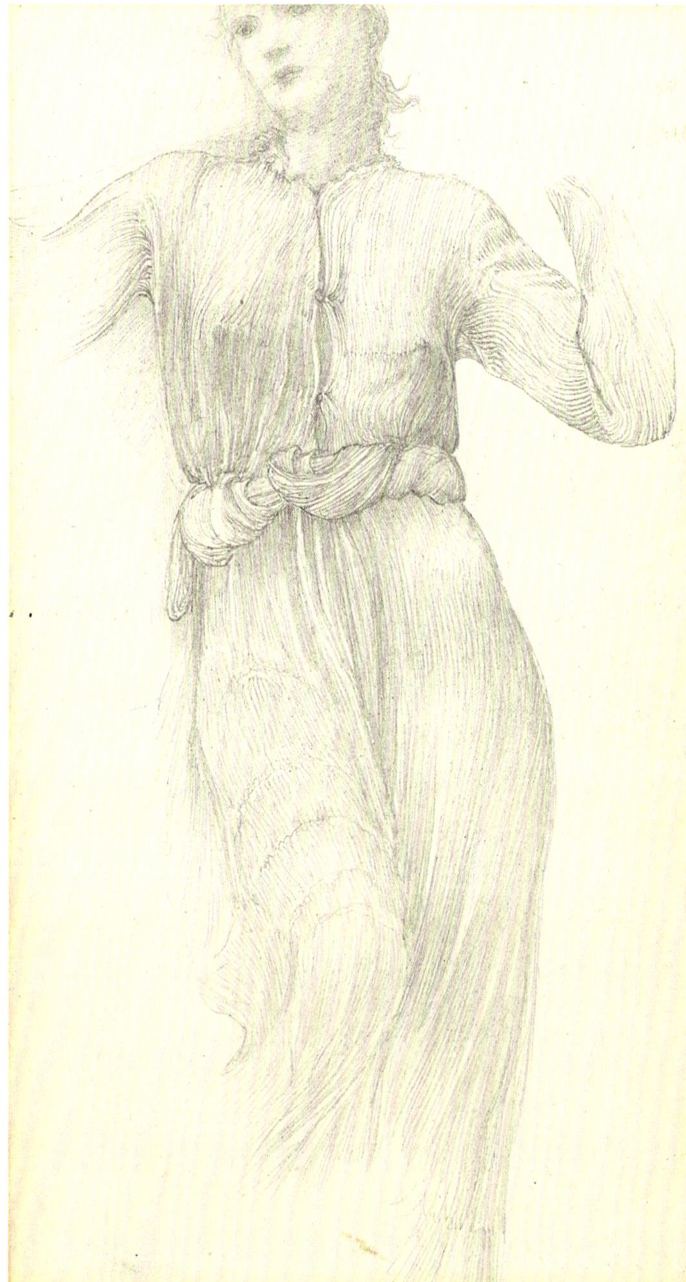

28
Study for *The Golden Stairs*
c.1876–80
Graphite on paper, 25.2 × 13.8
Courtesy of Mrs Dianne Roberts

29
Study for *The Golden Stairs*
c.1876–80
Graphite on paper, 25.2 × 13.8
Courtesy of Mrs Dianne Roberts

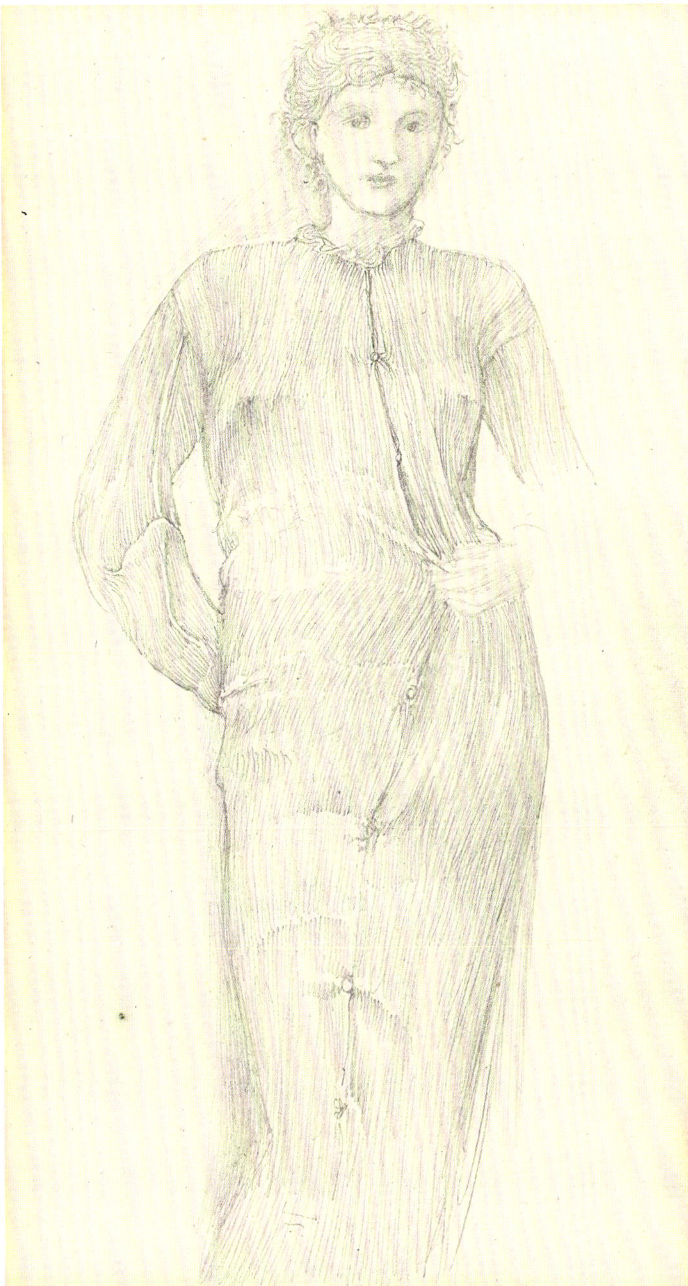

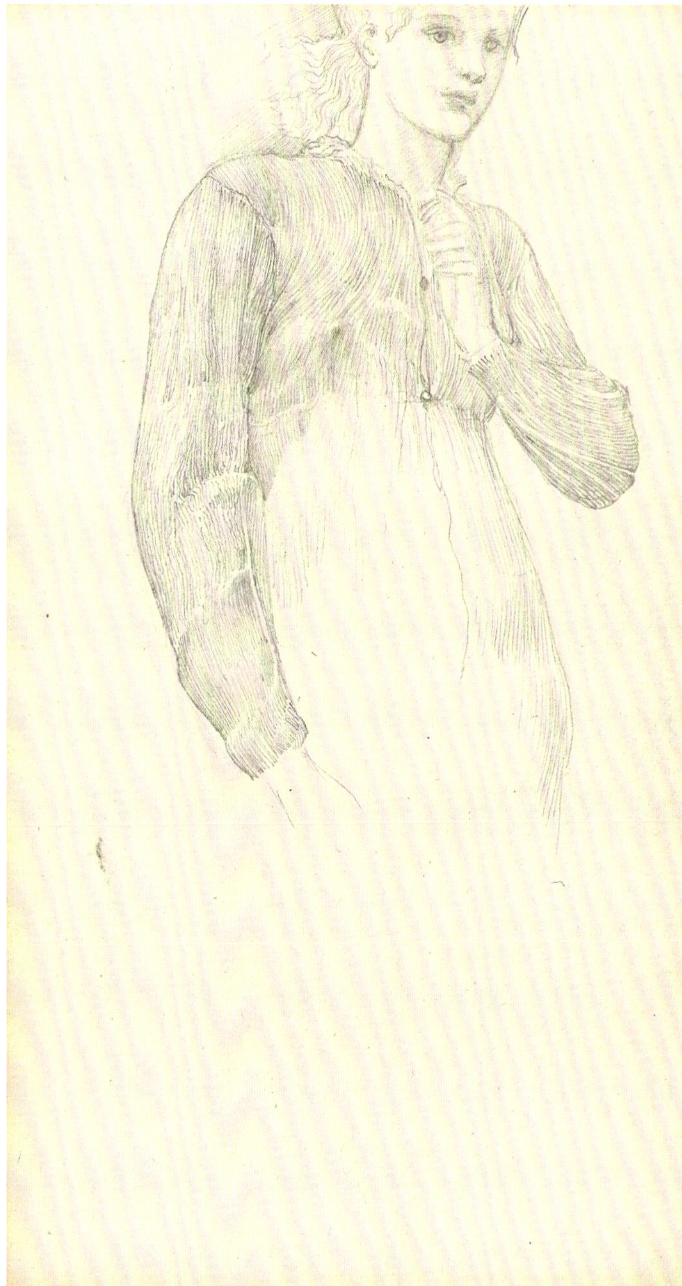

to the function of drawing as a primary tool of the artist, as revelatory and visionary rather than descriptive.

In 1893 John Addington Symonds ruminated on theories and practices of drawing in his biography of Michelangelo, one of the inspirations for Burne-Jones's later works: 'The simplicity of a sketch, the comparative rapidity with which it is produced, the concentration of meaning demanded by its rigid economy of means, render it more symbolical, more like the hieroglyph of its maker's mind, than any finished work can be.'[5] For Symonds a painting does not afford 'the involuntary revelation of the artist's soul' nor offer a glimpse of 'the mysteries of his genius and to its limitations' in the way that a drawing can.

Between 1877 and 1879 rival Winter Exhibitions at the Grosvenor Gallery and Burlington House bombarded the London art-viewing public with hundreds of works – chiefly drawings – by Michelangelo, Mantegna, Leonardo and Raphael, as well as the recently rediscovered Botticelli, and many other artists of lesser repute. These exhibitions not only permitted a new visibility for 'archaic drawings' and the techniques that produced them, such as metalpoint, but also drew attention to the provisional, the obscure, even – as in the case of silverpoint – the nearly invisible. Something similar happened with the work of contemporary artists. Having attained a huge if unexpected fame at the inaugural exhibition of the Grosvenor Gallery in 1877, Burne-Jones was one of the select artists whose drawings began to attract public attention. In the wake of the old master exhibitions and at the height of his fame, his work was displayed, as a matter of course, in selections of modern drawings.

Burne-Jones was included in the Fine Art Society's Winter Exhibition of 1889, which was devoted to works on paper. His drawings were displayed alongside Leighton, Albert Moore, Watts, Alma-Tadema and others. His contributions were described by the *Athenaeum* as 'charmingly graceful': a 'Floral study, lilies exquisitely drawn' (also shown at the 1899 exhibition and now in the Philadelphia Museum of Art) reminded the reviewer of 'Da Vinci in his best mood', and a sheet of drawings from the life was singled out for note: '[It] brings us to that pure type of the Renaissance which the artist has always affected. It is one of the numerous studies for the "Golden Stairs", that famous picture of maidens clad in white descending a staircase [no.95].'[6] This, too, might have struck the reviewer as Leonardesque (a term that crept into critical currency at the time). Burne-Jones made so many studies for these figures, many of them fragmented body parts – hand, wrists and feet – and all in a manner that clearly betrays the influence of the great Florentine draughtsman's sheets of elegant life studies (nos.30, 31). The drawing now known as *Desiderium* (no.68) was on show here, as it was to be in the 1899 exhibition, just beginning its fame as one of the artist's most beautiful depictions of the female head.

Influences and developments

By the time he made his decision to become an artist – he was twenty-two and studying Theology at Oxford – Burne-Jones had already developed an unmistakable graphic style. In deciding to pursue a career in art later than most artists he avoided the course of instruction at the Royal Academy Schools undergone by almost all professional artists working in Britain. While Burne-Jones had freedom to invent detailed and fantastic compositions, with their awkwardly drawn figures outlined in black ink, his contemporaries were performing laborious exercises

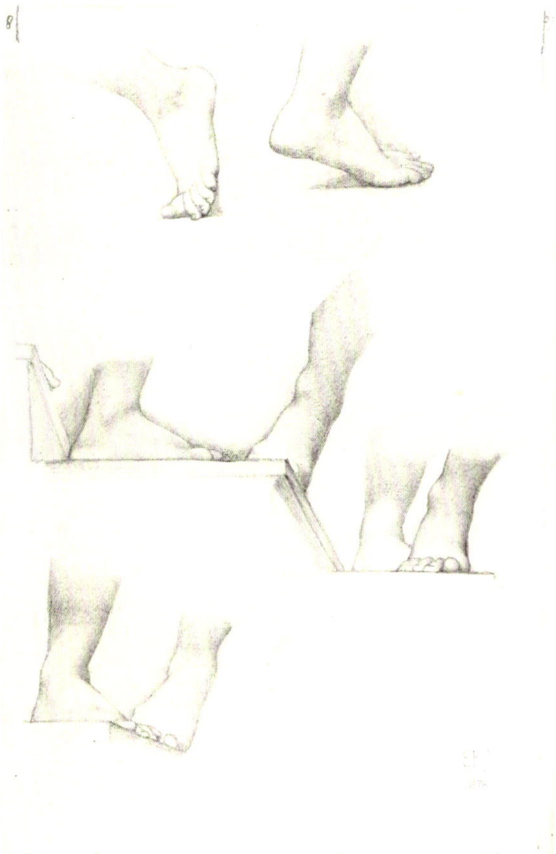

30
Study of feet for *The Golden Stairs* c.1878
Graphite on paper, 26.4 × 17.5
The Syndics of the Fitzwilliam Museum, University of Cambridge

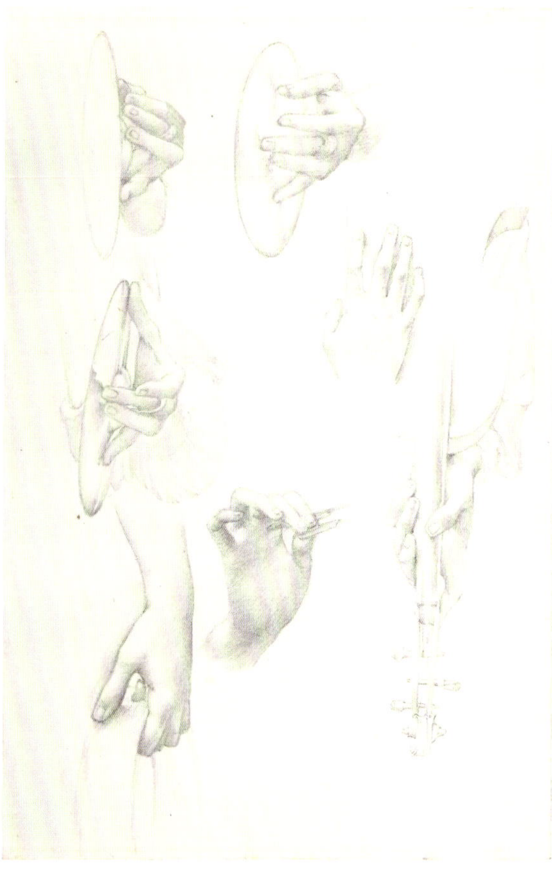

31
Study of hands with cymbals and holding a violin for *The Golden Stairs* c.1878
Graphite on paper, 26.3 × 17.5
The Syndics of the Fitzwilliam Museum, University of Cambridge

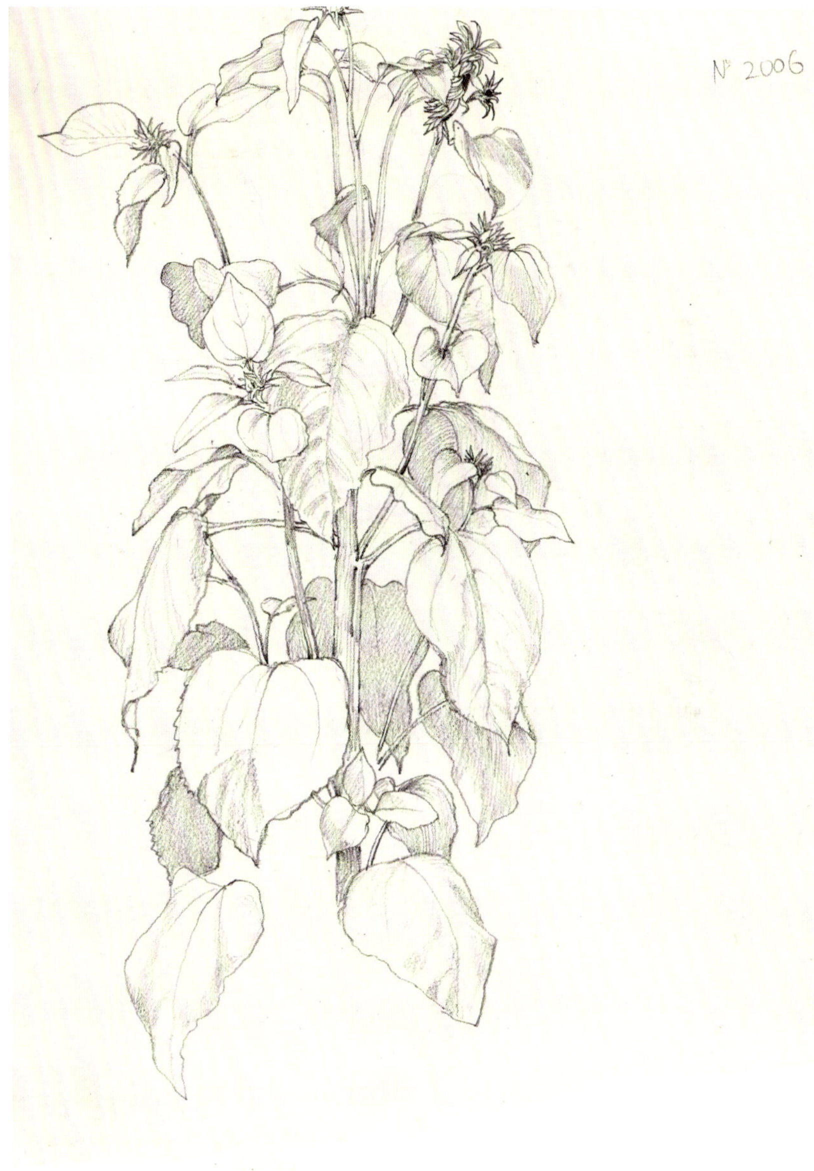

32
Plant study for *Love and the Pilgrim*
1877–97
Graphite on paper, 31.2 × 21.6
The Syndics of the Fitzwilliam Museum, University of Cambridge

at the Royal Academy Schools; their syllabus started with drawing from casts of antique sculpture and progressed slowly to the most advanced stage, the study of the nude figure. At this time Burne-Jones's ideas were presented in independent graphic works not intended as preparations for paintings; drawing was the first and final form of the expression of his ideas.[7] In his minutely finished and densely patterned drawings such as *Going to the Battle* (no.5), *Childe Roland* (no.6) and *Buondelmonte's Wedding* (no.7), the highly stylised forms suggest a knowledge of the medieval period but are far from being slavish copies of earlier works. Rather, they are imaginative reinterpretations of the art of the past in which the artist's lack of academic technique was not seen as an impediment. Indeed, the awkwardness of their compositional structures, the lack of perspective and failure to conform to conventional standards of beauty and proportion might be seen as virtues, increasing that quality of 'intensity' found in Rossetti's designs.

After he came under the influence of old master drawings, Burne-Jones made numerous studies before undertaking any work of significant scale. The extraordinary care taken in the graphite *Study of the Maid for 'King Cophetua and the Beggar Maid'* (no.34), for example, shows the importance he placed on drawing as a preparatory and investigative stage in the making of complex figure works. His expectations for draughtsmanship changed as different ambitions for his ideas and different audiences for them emerged. In a pivotal work such as *Ezekiel and the Boiling Pot*, we can see the ways in which life drawings (nos.35, 36) were incorporated into an image. Compositional studies (nos.37, 38) suggest the more autonomous workings of the artist's imagination, at that date usually unencumbered by expectations of 'correct drawing'. In the final version (1861; no.39), executed in ink and watercolour on vellum – its surface worked over and scratched – the figure of the prophet is transformed, his powerful, irascible personality dominates the left side of the picture in contrast to the daughters of Sodom who lounge in the background.[8]

While still undergraduates at Oxford, Burne-Jones and William Morris found themselves in a Pre-Raphaelite circle that included two of their heroes, Rossetti and Ruskin. Burne-Jones was caught between the 'two opposing forces' of Pre-Raphaelitism – 'Ruskinianism' and 'Rossettianism' – with their differing approaches to the art of the past – and the role of the modern artist. As Colin Harrison has observed: 'It is a measure of his greatness that his own personality gloriously conquered both forces.'[9] Early in 1856 he was invited to meet Rossetti at his rooms at Chatham Place by Blackfriars Bridge. Rossetti was working on *Fra Pace*, a watercolour depicting a monkish illuminator engrossed in drawing a mouse.[10] A shared, if by this time somewhat dated, enthusiasm for medievalist subjects was an obvious bond between the two men. Rossetti was in the process of transforming earlier Victorian modes of medievalism; for him it became a highly personal form for exploring feelings of various degrees of emotional intensity. His version of the past was a potent example for Burne-Jones, whose drawings – such as *Cupid's Forge* (no.3) – betray the influence of his new friend. There is a strong sense of a shared aesthetic in the early friendship of the two men. However, the influence was not all in one direction. Rossetti's *Mary Magdalene at the Door of Simon the Pharisee* (fig.25), for example, in which Burne-Jones's profile stands in for Christ's, strongly suggests the intricately detailed, highly patterned passages characteristic of such drawings as *The Wise and Foolish Virgins* (no.8).

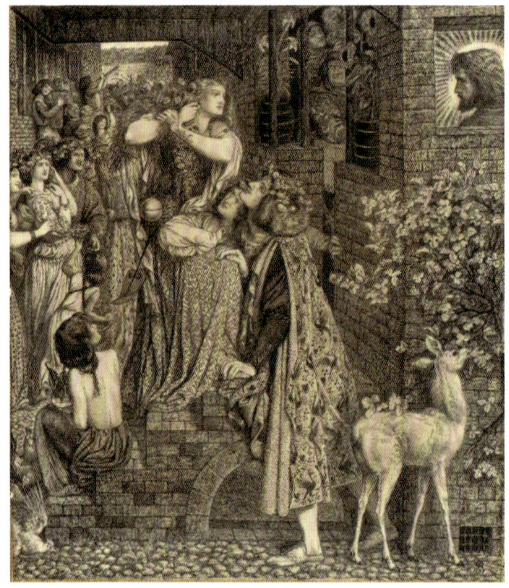

Fig.25
DANTE GABRIEL ROSSETTI
Mary Magdalene at the Door of Simon the Pharisee 1858
Pen and Indian ink on paper mounted on fine linen on a stretcher
50.8 × 45.7
The Fitzwilliam Museum, Cambridge

33
Study of Seated Figure for *The Garden Court* in the *Briar Rose* Series c.1873
Graphite on paper, 12.6 × 17.9
Tate

34
Study of the Maid for *King Cophetua and the Beggar Maid* 1883
Graphite on paper, 30.2 × 19.1
Tate

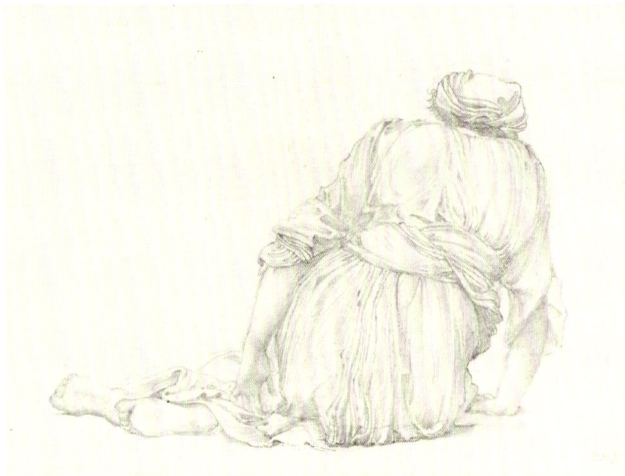

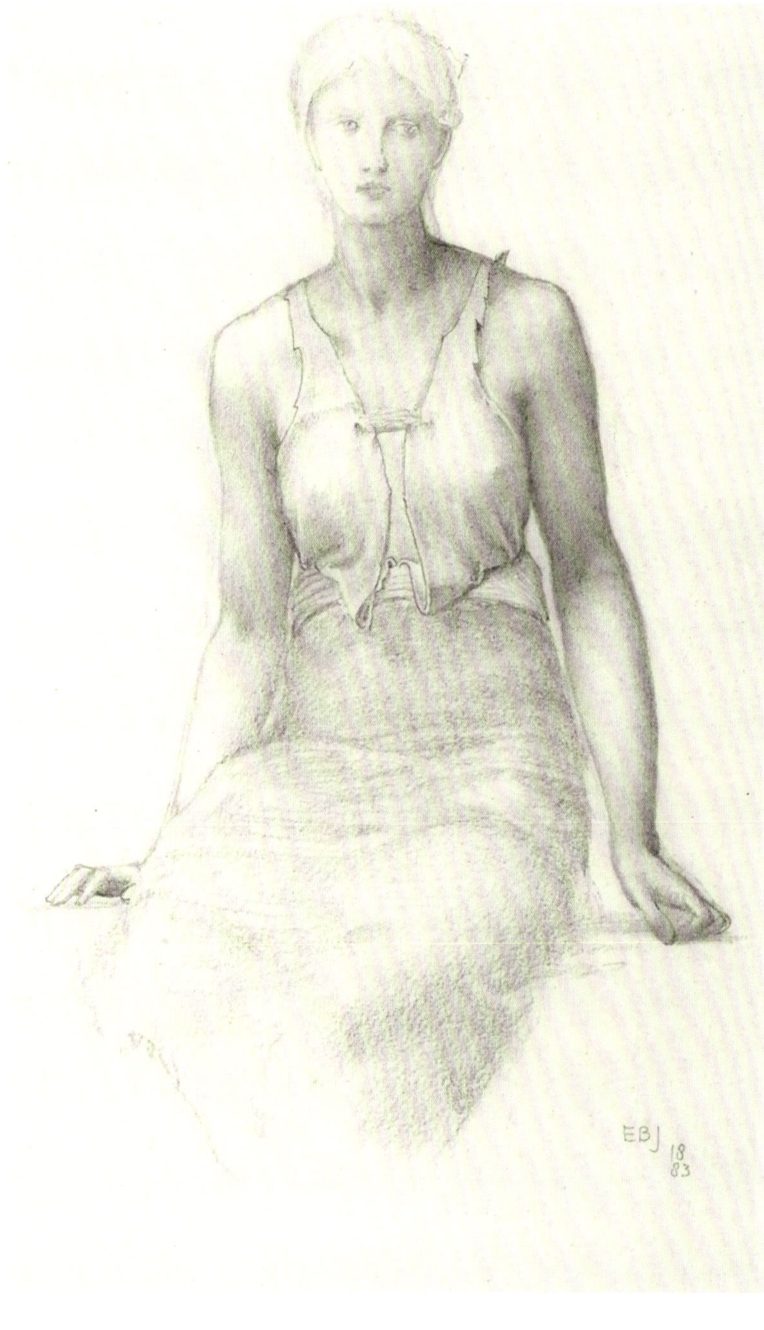

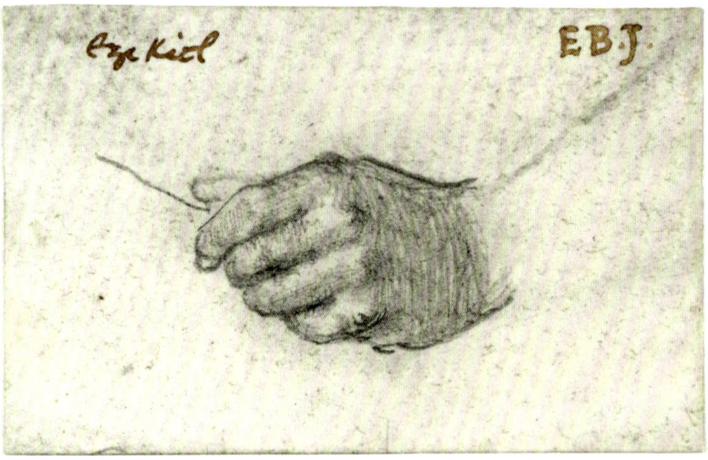

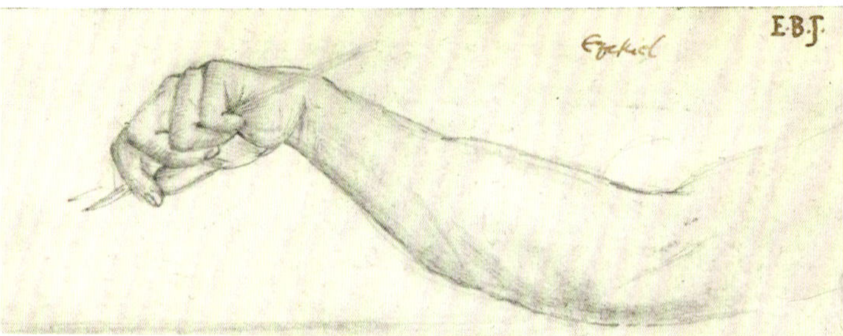

35
Study of Ezekiel's Hand for *Ezekiel and the Boiling Pot* c.1860
Graphite on paper, 4.4 × 11.7
Tate

36
Study of Ezekiel's Arm and Hand for *Ezekiel and the Boiling Pot* c.1860
Graphite on paper, 3.5 × 5.7
Tate

37
Composition Study for *Ezekiel and the Boiling Pot* c.1860
Graphite on paper, 17.8 × 13.3
Tate

38
Composition Study for *Ezekiel and the Boiling Pot* c.1860
Graphite on paper, 18.1 × 13.3
Tate

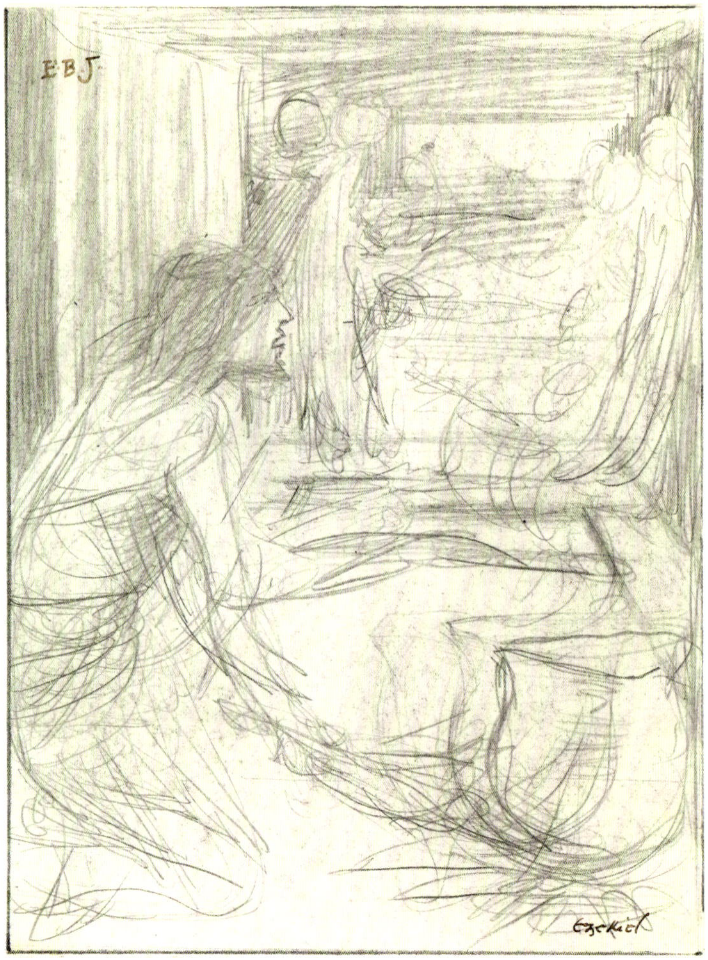

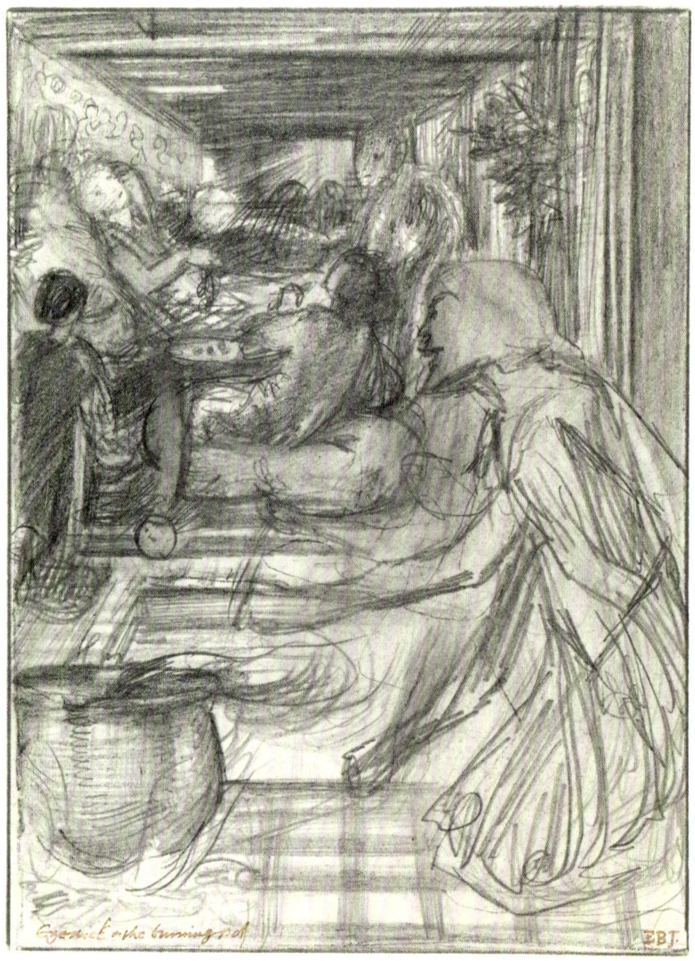

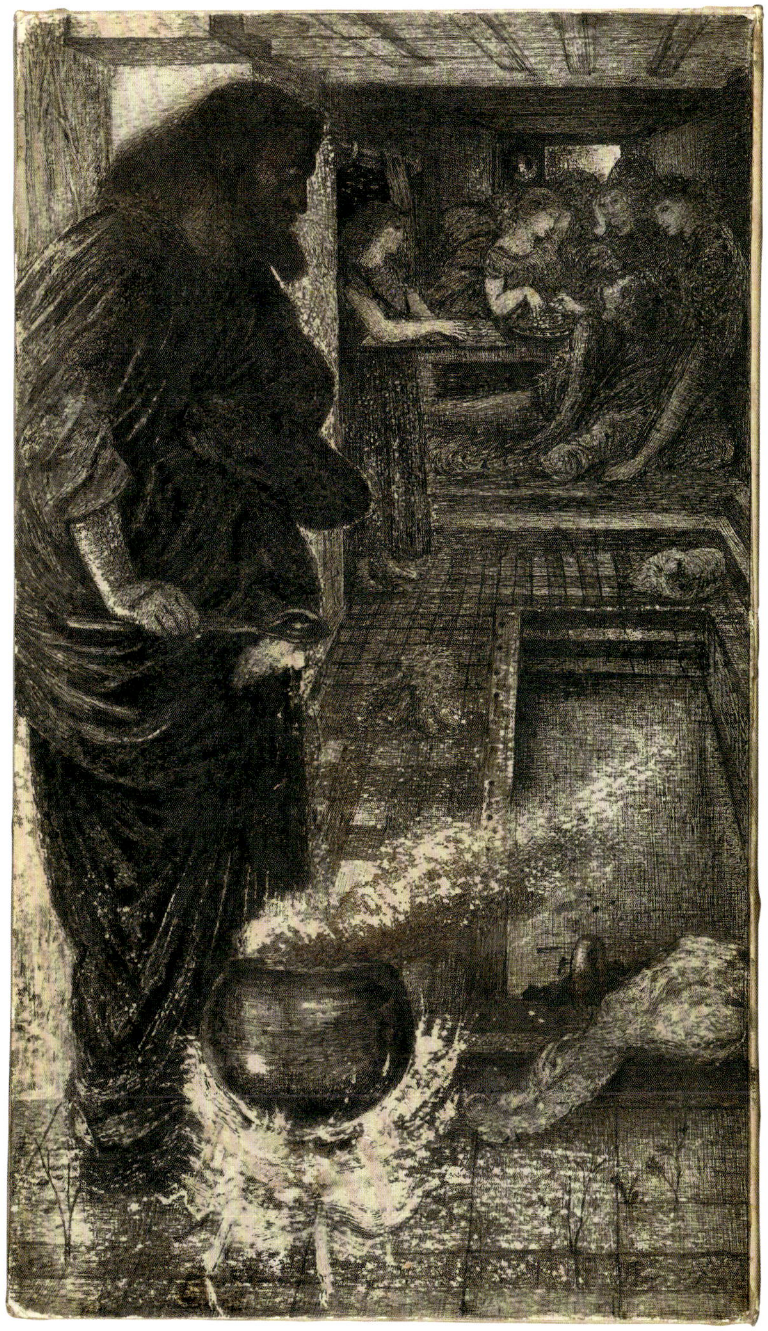

39
Ezekiel and the Boiling Pot 1861
Ink and watercolour on vellum mounted on canvas, 26 × 15.2
Tate

Both artists admired the works of Albrecht Dürer, particularly his prints. As early as 1859 Burne-Jones had confessed an ambition to emulate, if not to rival, Dürer. In a letter to Louisa Macdonald, his future sister-in-law, he proposed a project that would combine their joint skills and would 'make people say that Albert Dürer has come back again'.[11] Later, in 1865, Ruskin presented Burne-Jones with 'perfect impressions' of the engravings *The Knight and Death*, *St Hubert*, *The Fall of Man* and *Melencolia*, as well as several woodcuts.[12] Their influence can be seen in several works including *Gualdrada Donati Presenting her Daughter to Buondelmonte* (no.40) which contains a visual quotation from Dürer's *The Knight and Death* in the figure of Buondelmonte on horseback. The inclusion of a quotation from one of Dürer's allegories allows for the suggestion of a narrative of violent death encroaching into a story about the celebration of marriage.[13]

40
Gualdrada Donati Presenting her Daughter to Buondelmonte c.1860
Pen and ink with graphite on paper, 23.3 × 39.3
The Ashmolean Museum, University of Oxford

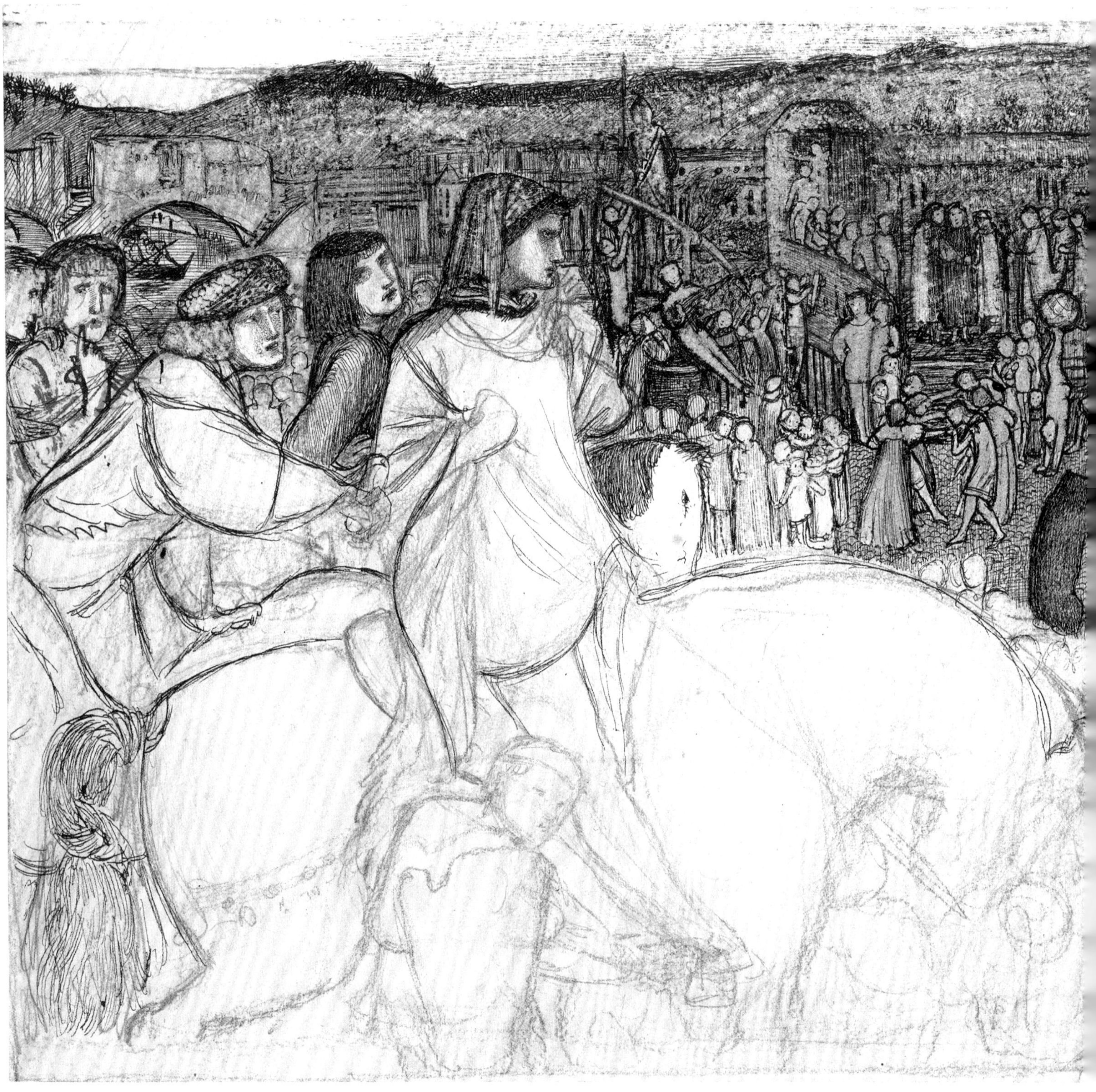

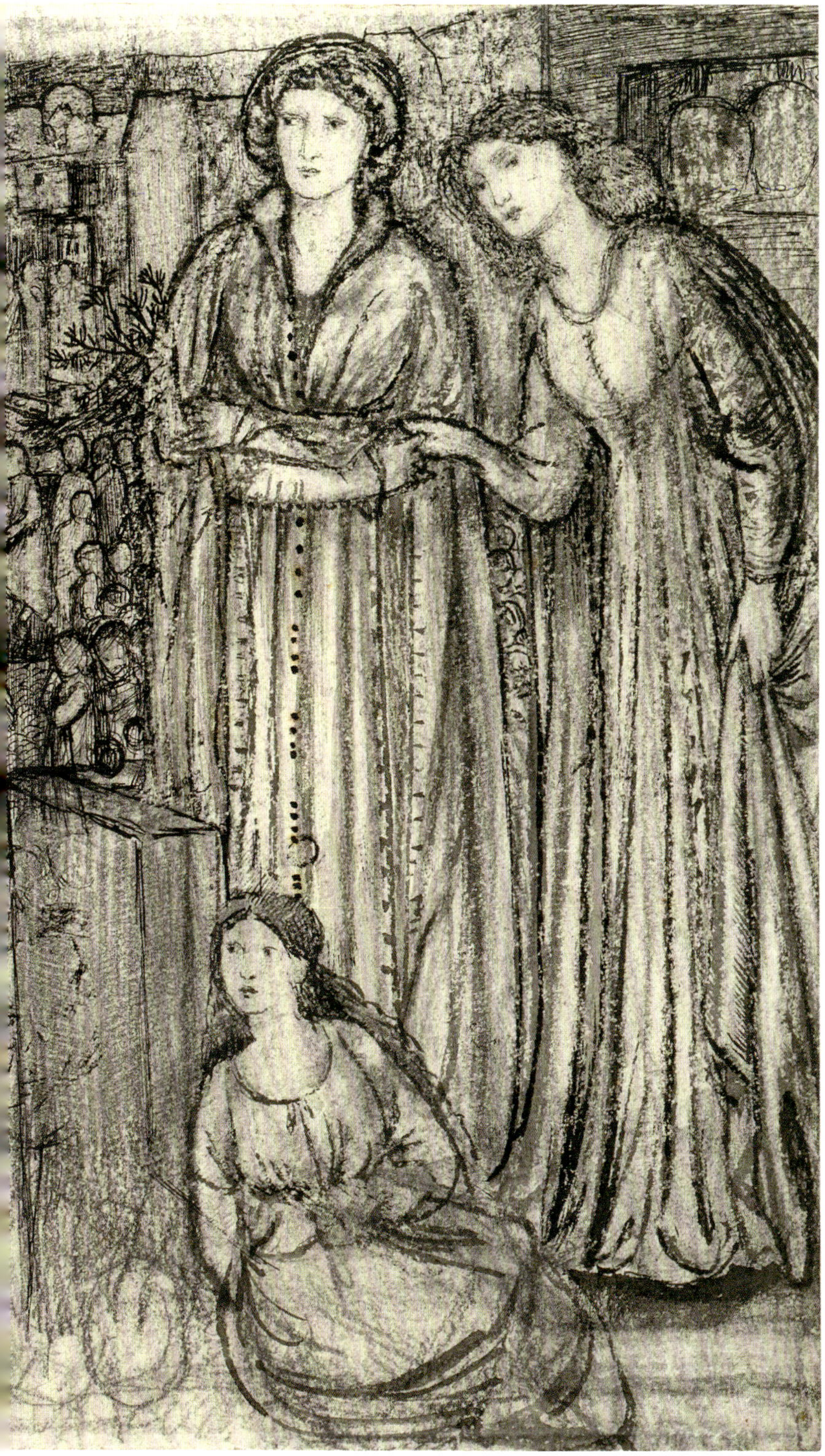

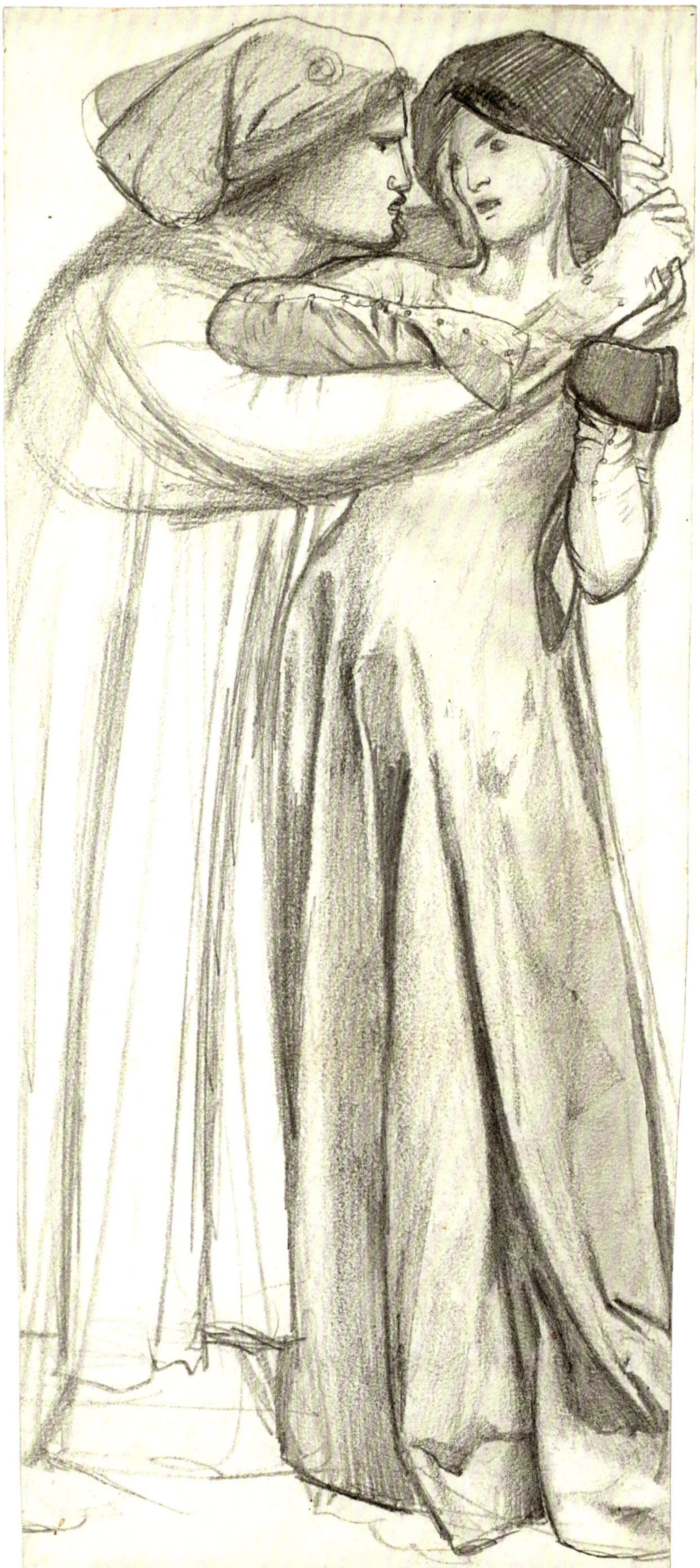

41
Composition Study for *Clerk Saunders* c.1861
Graphite on paper, 40.3 × 18.5
Tate

42
Sketch of Two Seated Figures for possibly *The Backgammon Players* c.1861
Graphite on paper, 21 × 22.5
Tate

43
Sketch of Two Seated Figures for *Le Chant d'Amour*
c.1862–5
Graphite on paper, 19 × 30
Tate

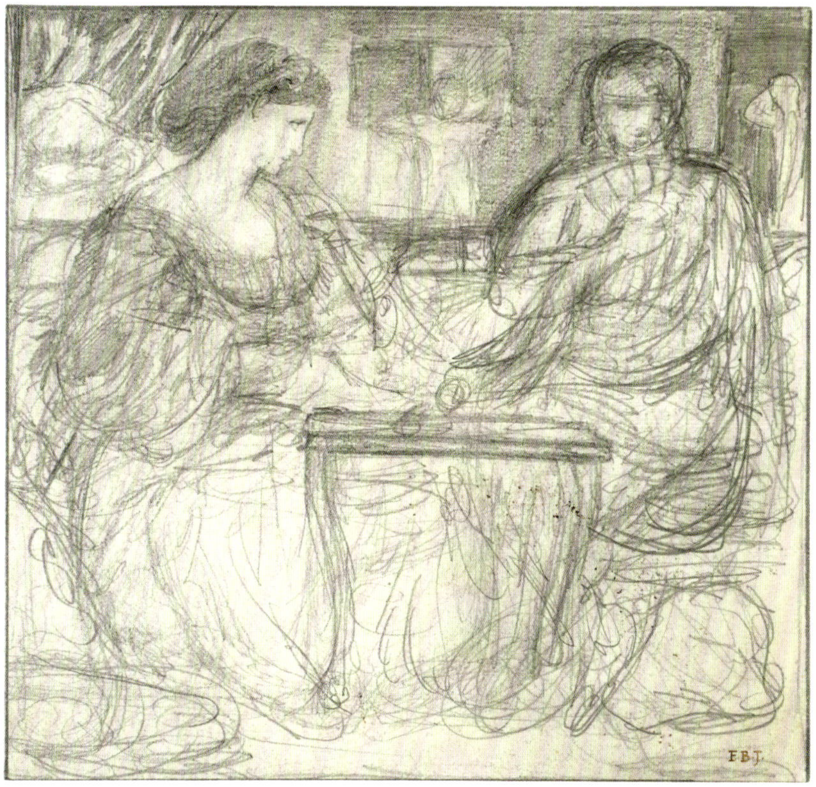

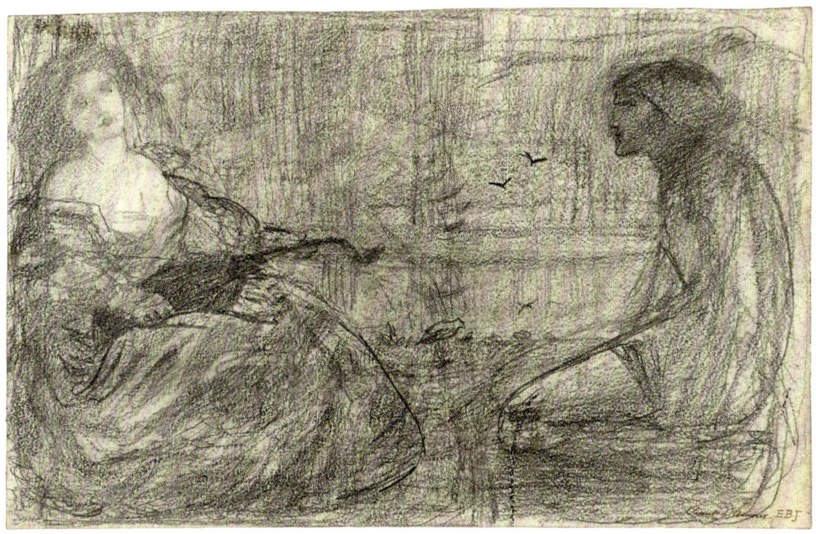

Gradually, a new type of work emerged, still imbued with Rossetti's influence but subtly changed. In *Clerk Saunders* (nos.19, 41), inspired by a ghostly ballad of the Scottish Borders – a source shared with Elizabeth Siddal – Burne-Jones confines the composition to two figures who occupy all the picture space. We can see the change in the searching stare that locks together the male and female figures – one insistent, the other wavering. Although this was one of the works that heralded the artist's move towards creating colour harmonies in watercolour – and from thence into mixed media painting – the drawing reveals the underlying horror initiated in the composition: the ghostly lover forcing himself on a living woman. Not all his compositions of the time are quite so fraught: the early sketches for *The Backgammon Players* c.1861 (no.42) and *Le Chant d'Amour* c.1862–5 (no.43) – both involving two figures who sit opposite one another – show that the characteristic stillness was in place before his refined colour sensibility worked its magic in the finished works.

Although they were first introduced in 1856, Burne-Jones's friendship with Ruskin developed more fully after the Rossetti period ended. He benefited from Ruskin's advice and patronage particularly in supporting the first two formative trips to Italy in 1859 and 1862. By the 1860s Ruskin had begun to regret his influence on some aspects of contemporary visual art, including Rossetti's 'intense' watercolours and the pursuit of medievalism; he sought a 'classical grace and tranquility' in Burne-Jones's work and began to advise him on a way towards this goal.[14] A new relationship to Renaissance traditions of *disegno* and close study was initially encouraged by Ruskin's patronage. However, it had an unexpected result in helping produce in his protégé's work a more highly charged aesthetic sensibility that was not encouraged by Ruskin.

Other friendships were important, too, and perhaps helped counterbalance Ruskin's somewhat insistent pedagogy. His patron, William Graham, with his interest in Mantegna, Carpaccio and Bellini, was a significant influence in forming Burne-Jones's tastes. So, too, was G.F. Watts with his various enthusiasms for Italy, Michelangelo and classical myth. Both men were important in liberating Burne-Jones from Rossetti's medievalism. In the case of Michelangelo it was not the nude figure in itself that became so important to Burne-Jones but the drawn marks that describe and express it. His sketchbook drawings of the nude and the many studies for the male figures depicted in *The Wheel of Fortune* (no.44) and for the *Briar Rose* sequence (no.33) are heavily dependent on Michelangelo. They show how study from the life could help articulate meaning through marks rather than through pose alone. These drawn marks describe a sense of inner motive and struggle within figures that, in the studies, seem to flicker with life. In addition, these drawings herald a change of painting style that accommodates his experiments with old master chiaroscuro. We can see the transition from graphic media to paint in *Souls on the Banks of the River Styx* (nos.45, 46, 48), *Venus Discordia* (no.49) and *Stella Vespertina* (no.50). A radical breakdown of the barriers between drawing and painting can be found in the artist's daring uses of bodycolour and metallic pigment in combination with pastel, chalk and other more traditional media in studies such as nos.77–79 and *A Woman Playing a Cithara* (no.51).

Burne-Jones's art changed during his copying practices, through which he learned, by emulation, new approaches to unfamiliar media and new compositional devices. In the several copies undertaken for Ruskin in his first trips to Italy we can see the artist being challenged by demands in draughtsmanship that his early work had not required of him. In a drawing commissioned by Ruskin, *Study of the Head of Bacchus* (no.57) after Tintoretto's *Venus Officiating at the Marriage of Bacchus and Ariadne* 1577–8, the use of soft pencil produces subtle gradations of light and shade that were unavailable to him in his earlier use of pen and ink. While the use of printed sources, such as Dürer's engravings, had been well explored by him in his earliest drawings, photographic images of paintings and drawings became increasingly important as aide-memoires, too. They functioned as a kind of model book, like those employed in Italian Renaissance workshops. Copying from these sources had a direct impact on his work. His extensive collection of photographs of works of art, bound together in many volumes, contained hundreds of images acquired from major international commercial photographic firms.[15]

44
Study for the King in *The Wheel of Fortune* 1879
Graphite on paper, 27.2 × 18
The British Museum, London

45
Two studies on one sheet for the left-hand figure and central crouching figure in *Souls on the Banks of the River Styx* c.1873
Graphite on paper, 24.1 × 16.5
Peter Nahum. Renate Nahum. Agency

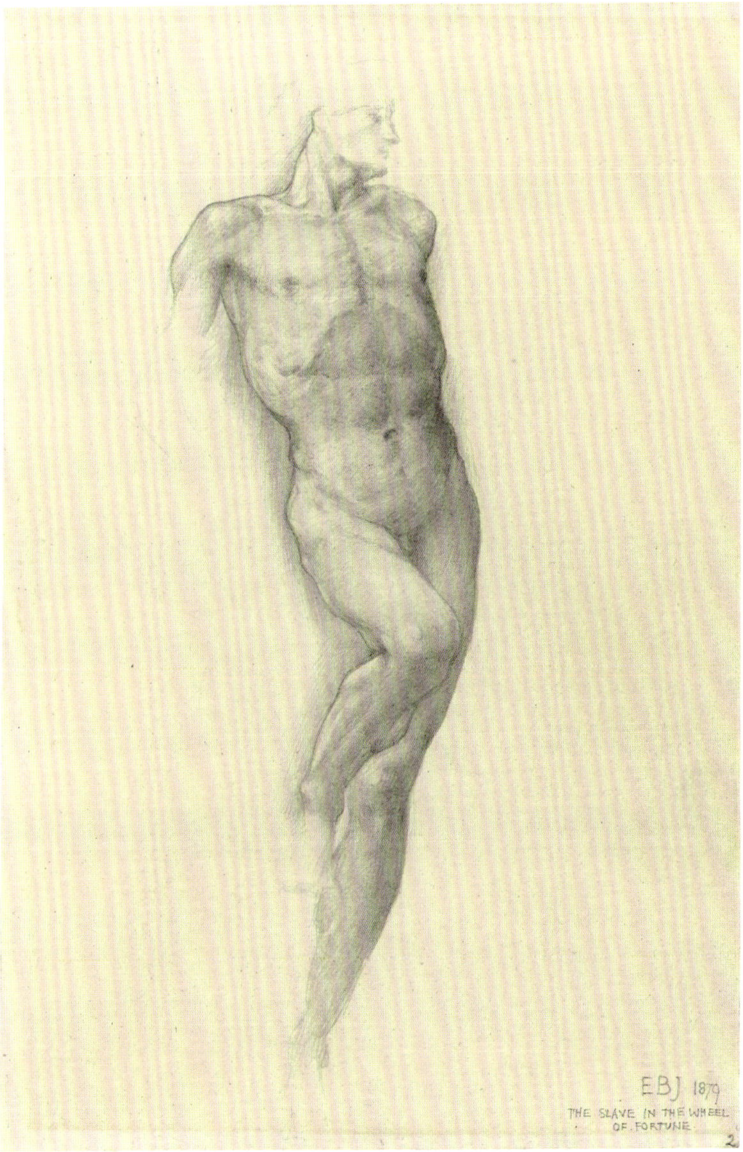

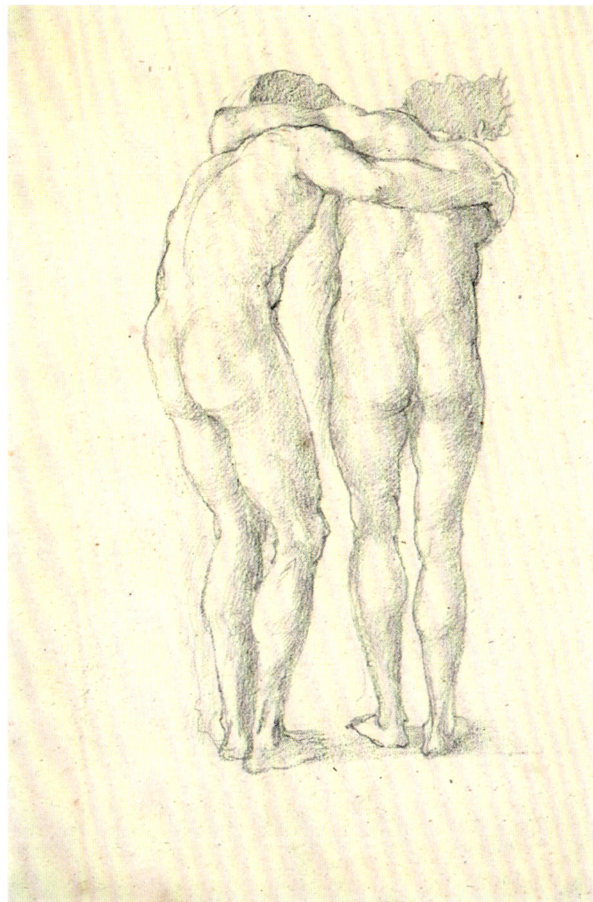

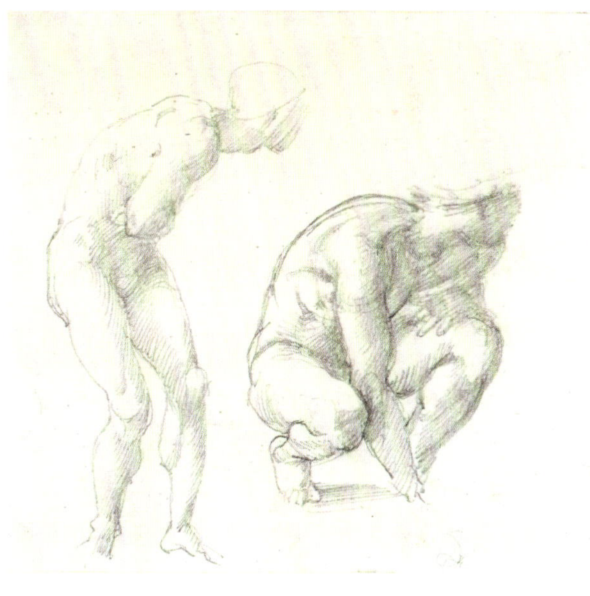

46
Study of a nude male crouching figure and a standing female nude with her arms tightly crossed, studies for *Souls on the Banks of the River Styx* c.1873
Graphite on paper, 14 × 13
Private collection courtesy of Peter Nahum. Renate Nahum. Agency

47
Study for The Masque of Cupid 1872
Graphite and charcoal on paper, 65 × 83.3
Amgueddfa Cymru – National Museum Wales

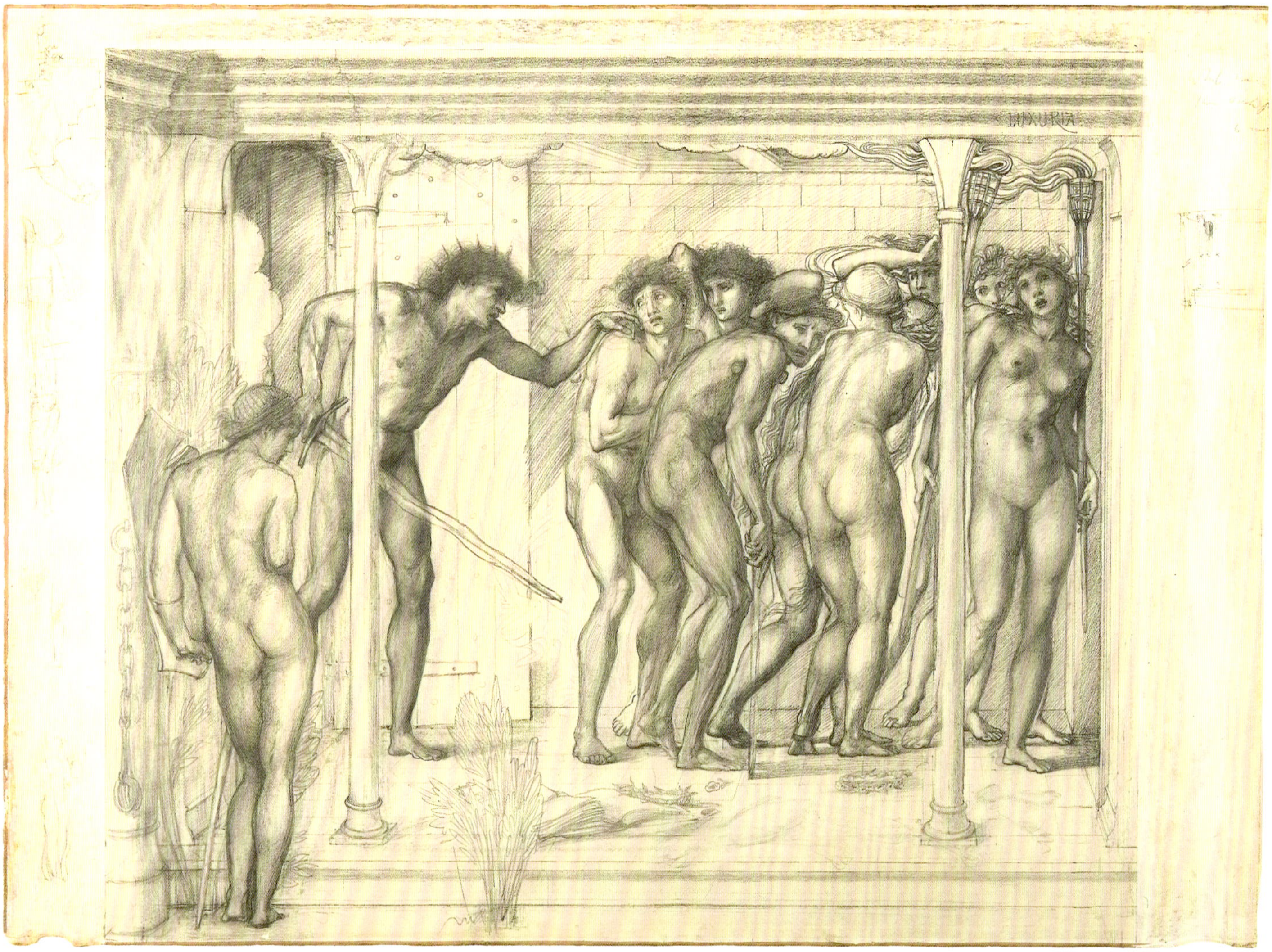

48
Souls on the Banks of the River Styx c.1873
Oil paint on canvas, 89 × 71
Private collection courtesy of Peter Nahum.
Renate Nahum. Agency

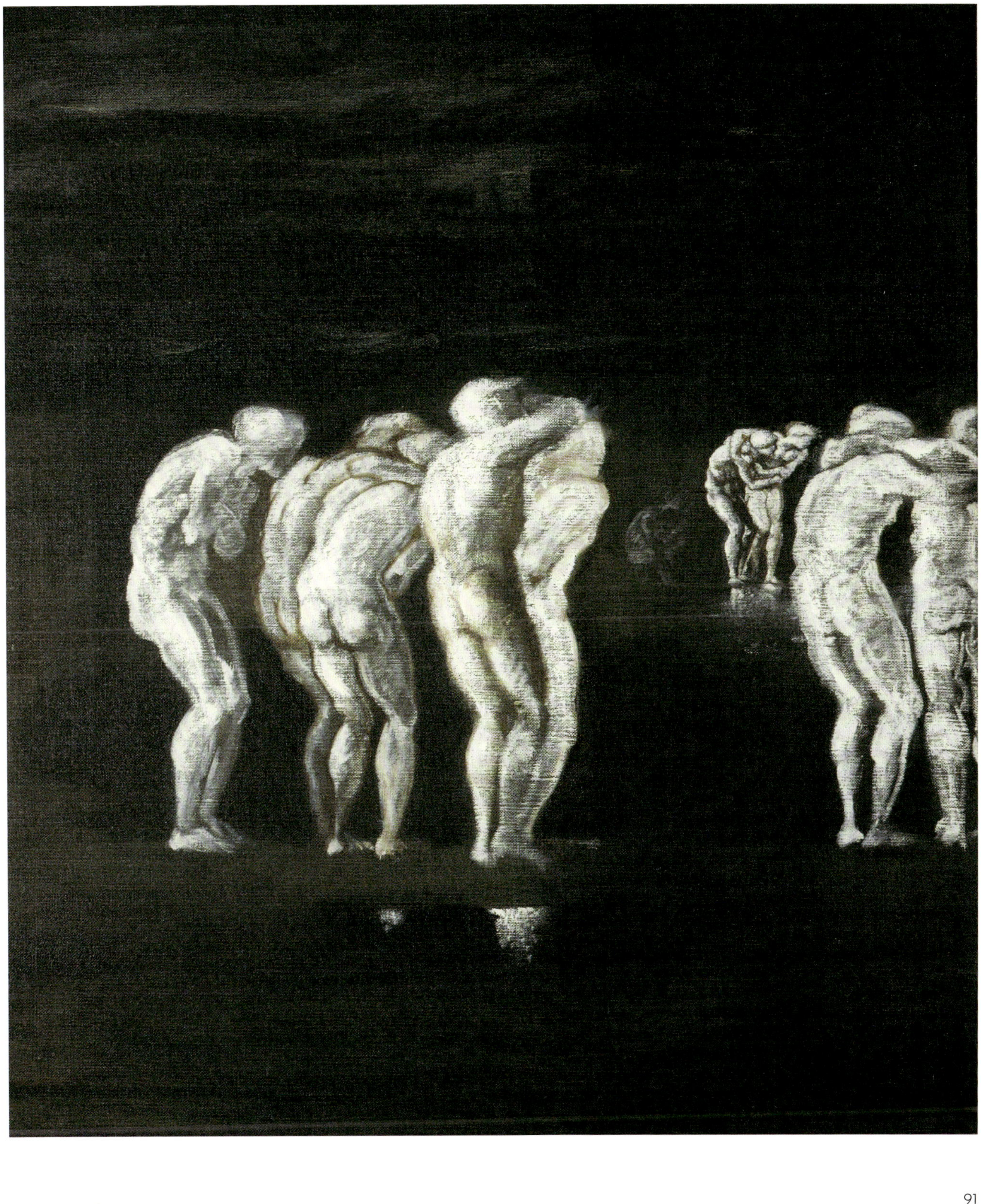

49
Venus Discordia c.1872–3
Oil paint on canvas, 128.2 × 209.8
Amgueddfa Cymru – National Museum Wales

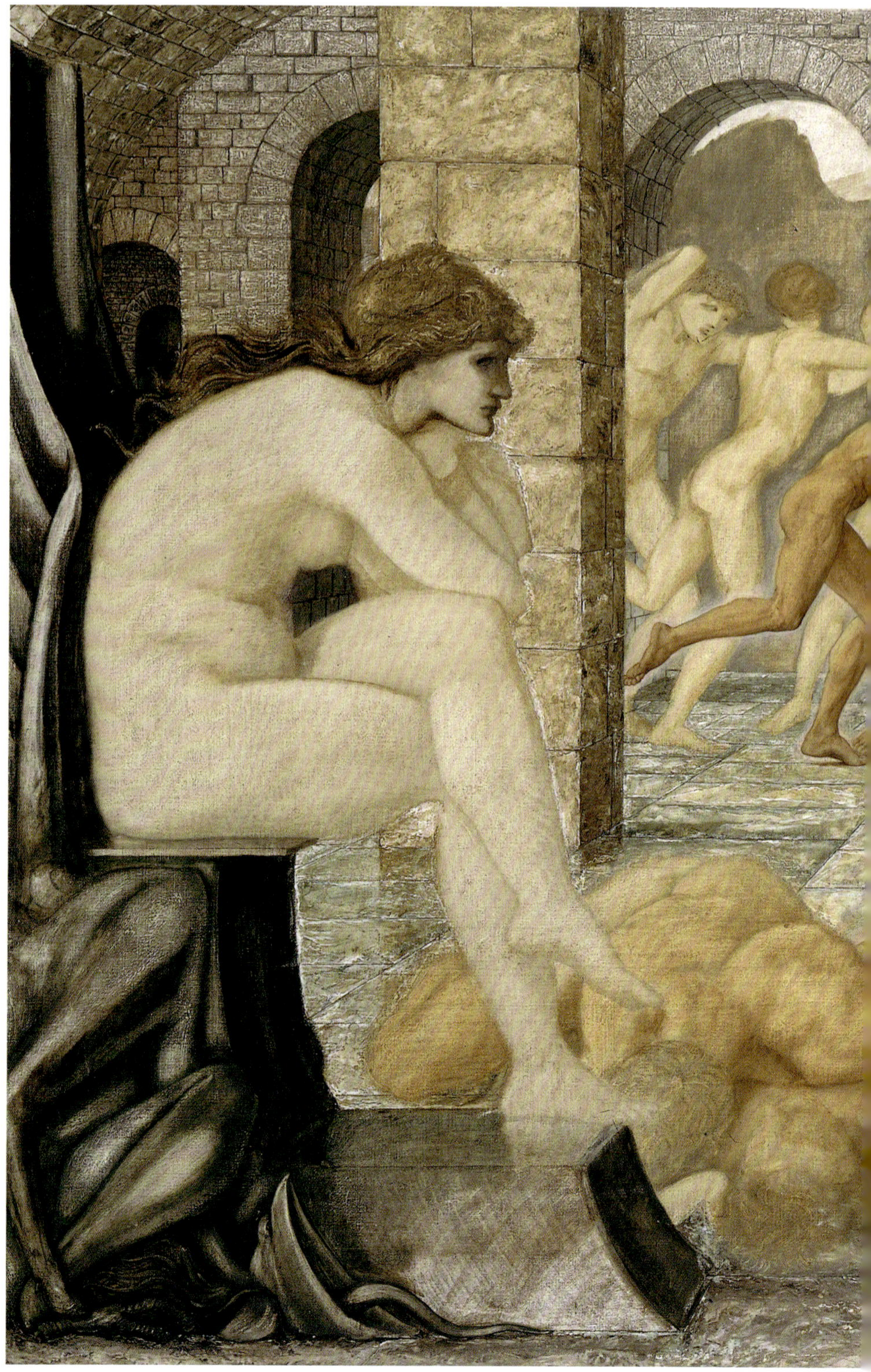

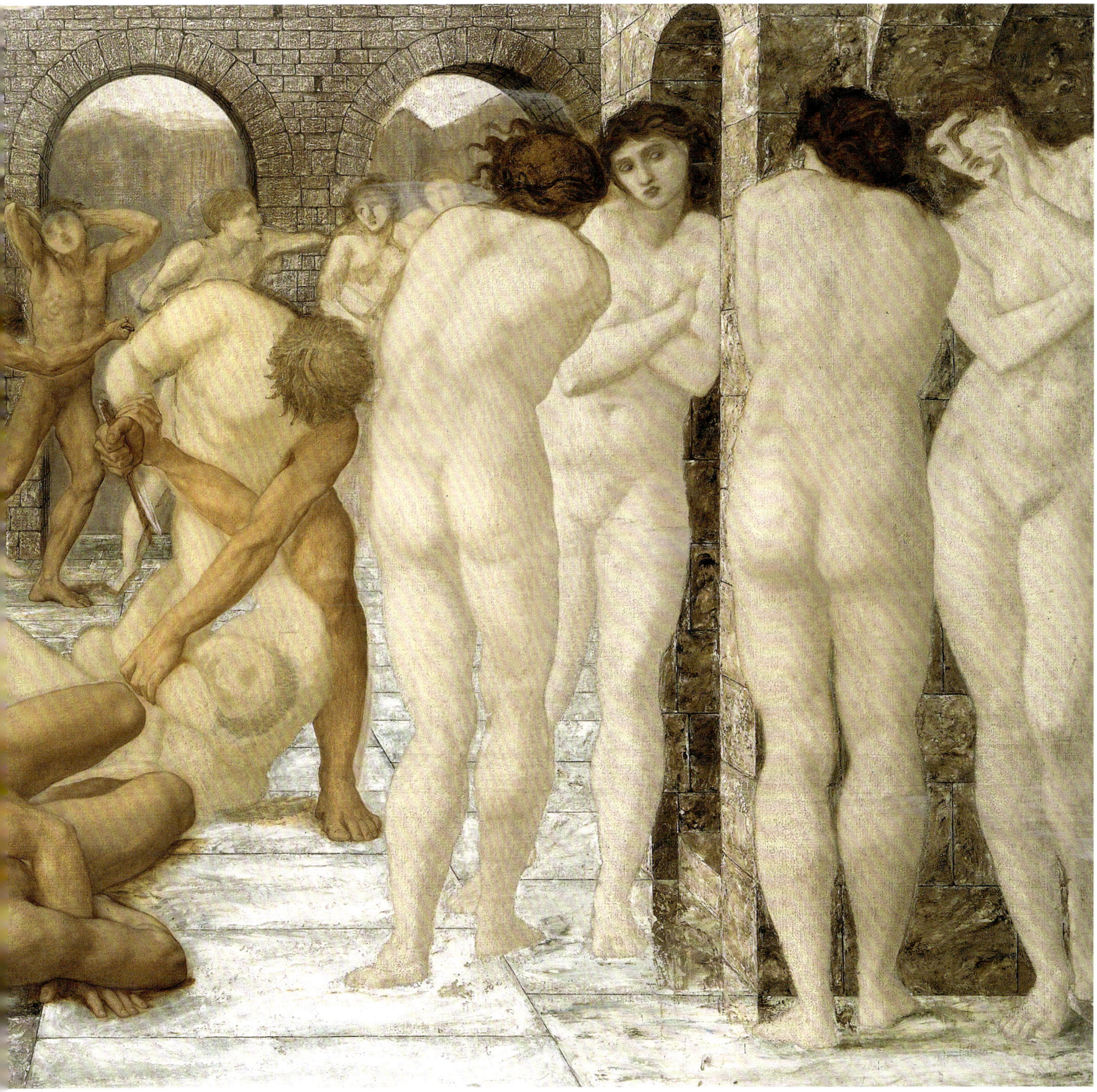

50
Stella Vespertina (The Evening Star) c.1880
Oil paint on canvas, 49 × 39
William Morris Gallery,
London Borough of Waltham Forest

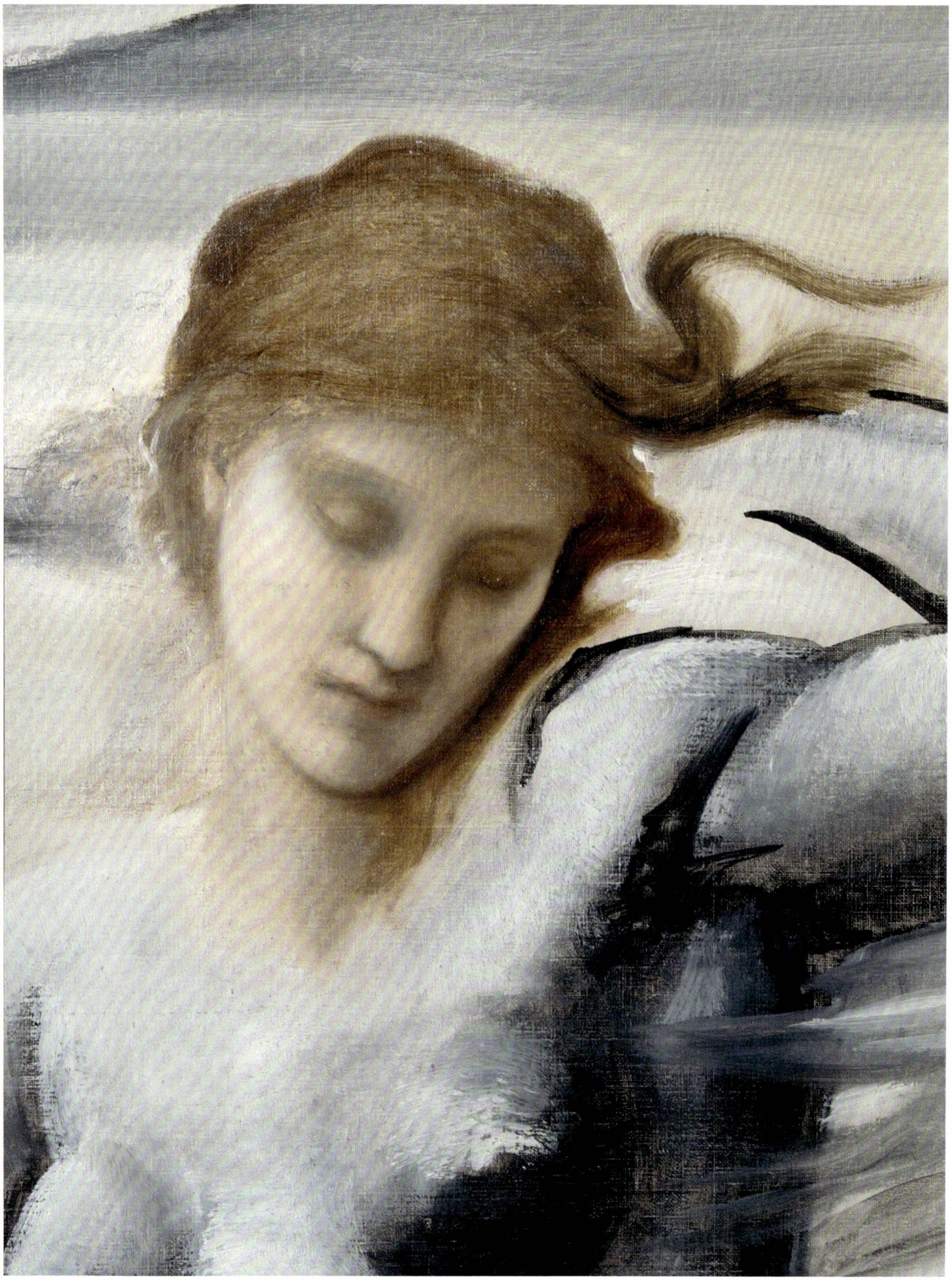

51
A Woman Playing a Cithara 1896
Tempera, gold paint and watercolour on paper, 35.3 × 21.3
Tate

52
Design for Embroidery 1890s
Watercolour on linen, 69 × 69 × 7
Private collection

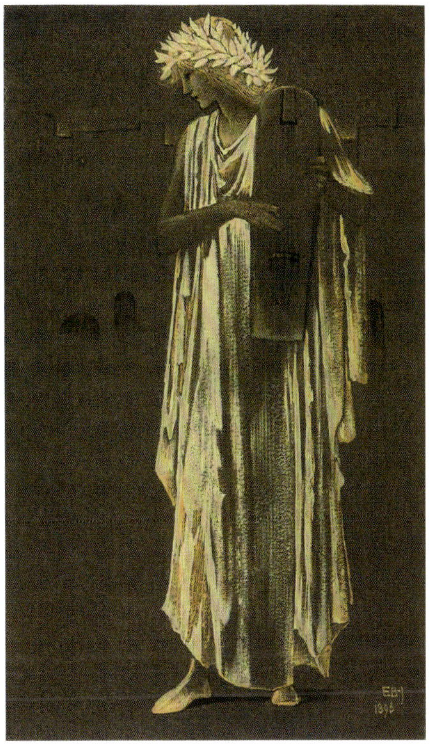

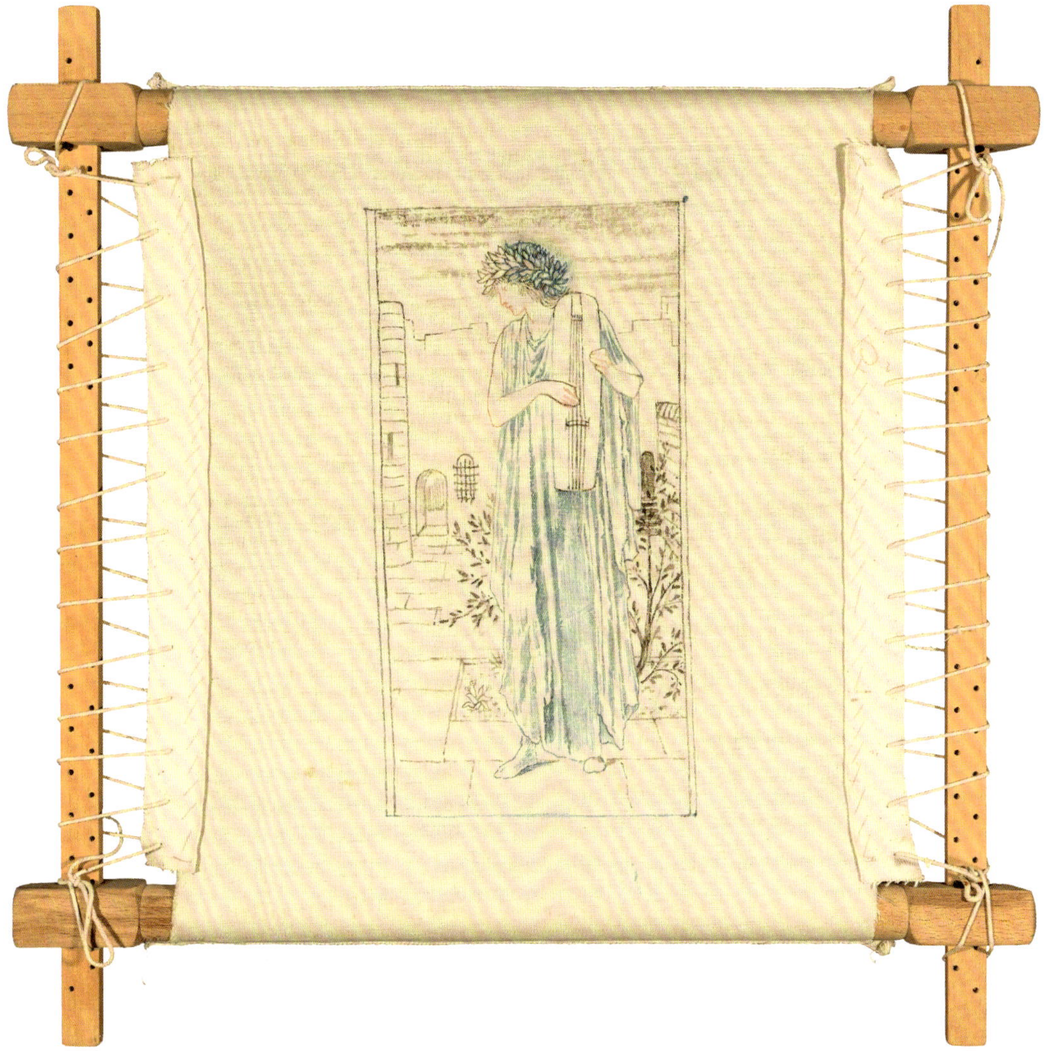

In one other key way Burne-Jones moved away from his earlier practices of making independent subject drawings. In undertaking designs for applied arts projects, notably stained glass, the artist developed a highly stylised linear description of figures with compacted compositions, their elements spread over the flattened picture plane. Although he began by emulating medieval stained glass – such as in *The Good Shepherd* (no.11) – by the time he designed windows depicting the Evangelists his compositions show a highly synthesised approach to designing for the medium. Some of the monumentality that he found in Michelangelo's frescos is visible in the cartoon for the *St Luke* window (no.54), one of his most frequently employed later designs.

53
Lot and his Daughters c.1874
Watercolour, bodycolour and coloured chalks on paper, 76.2 × 59.4
The Trustees of the Cecil Higgins Art Gallery (The Higgins Bedford)

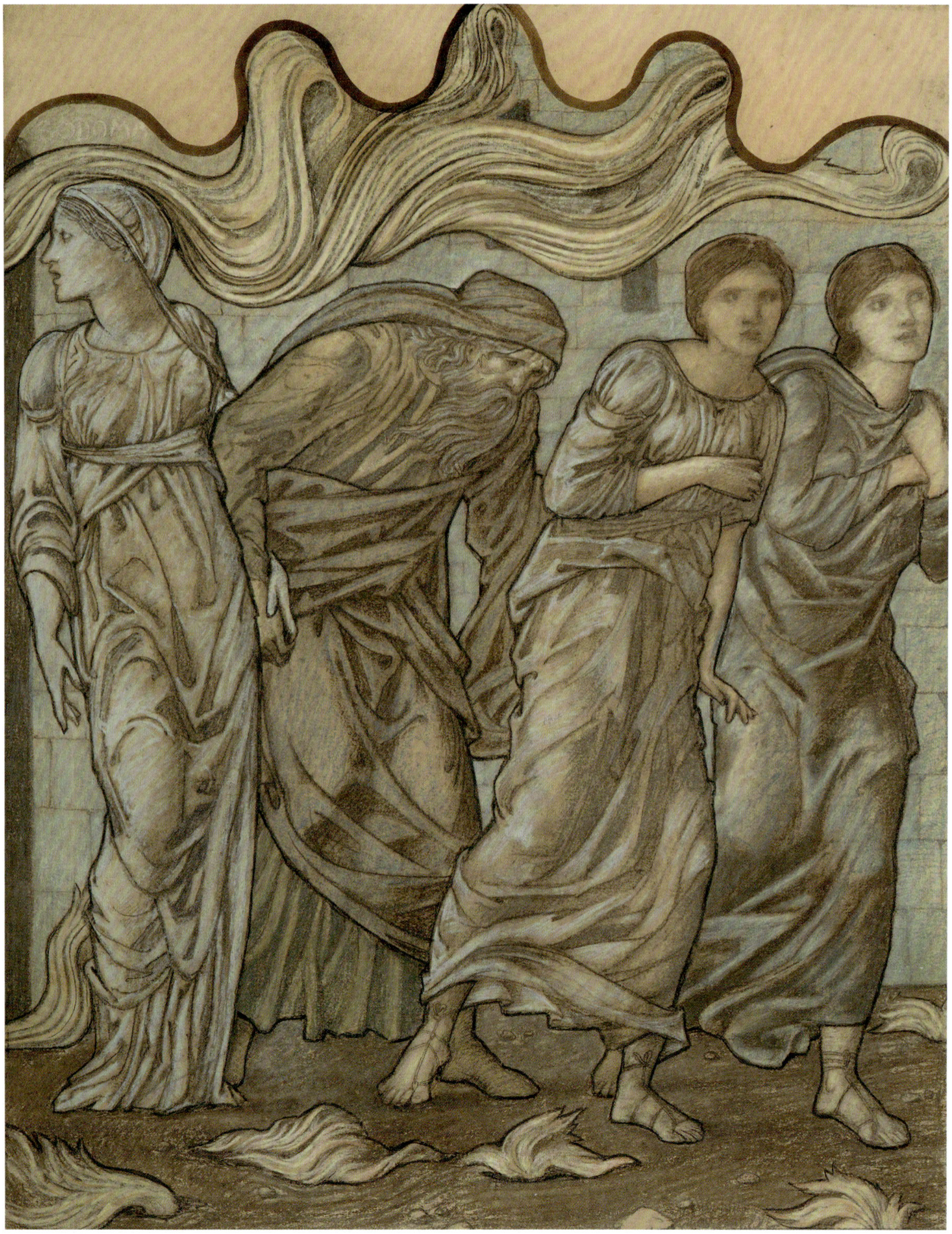

54
St Luke 1872
Graphite, pastel and gouache on paper, 122.4 × 51.6
Tate

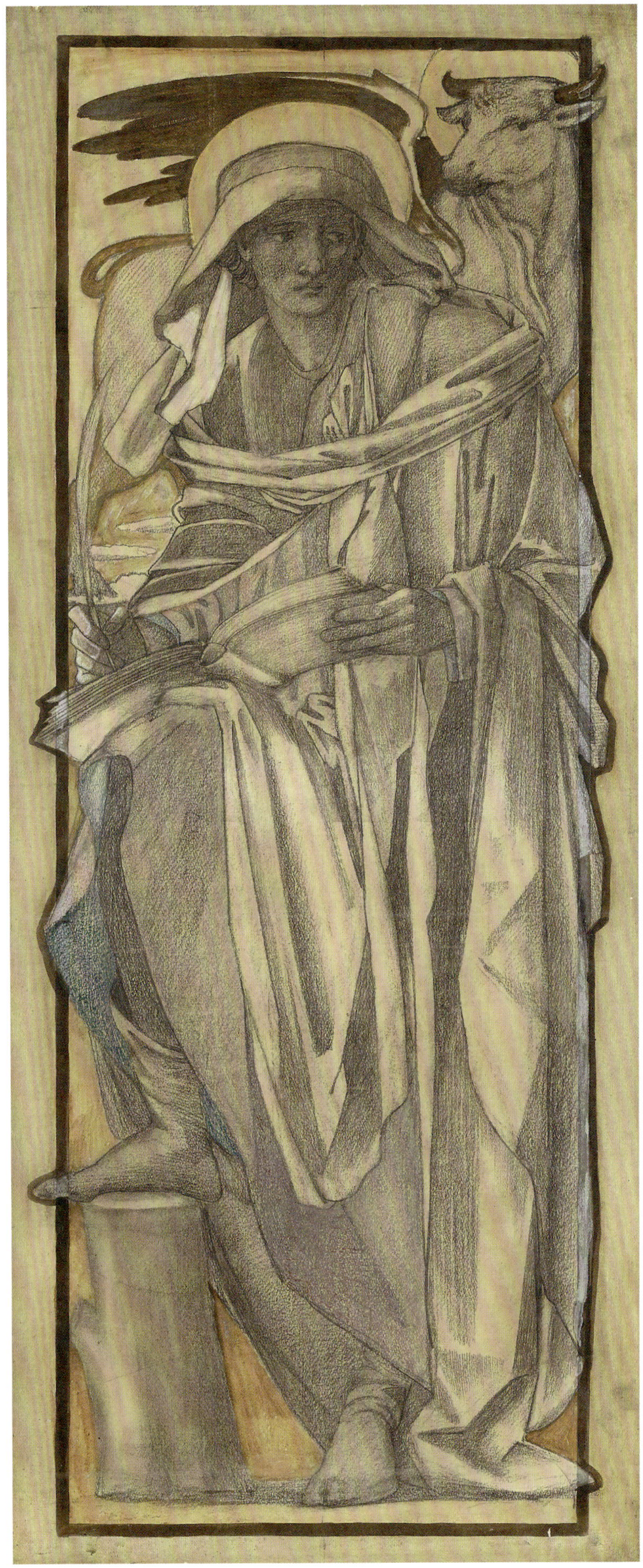

55
Studies of Drapery and the Figure of the Virgin for the *Annunciation* in the Church of St Martin's-on-the-Hill, Scarborough, Yorkshire c.1862
Graphite on paper, 34 × 36.2
Tate

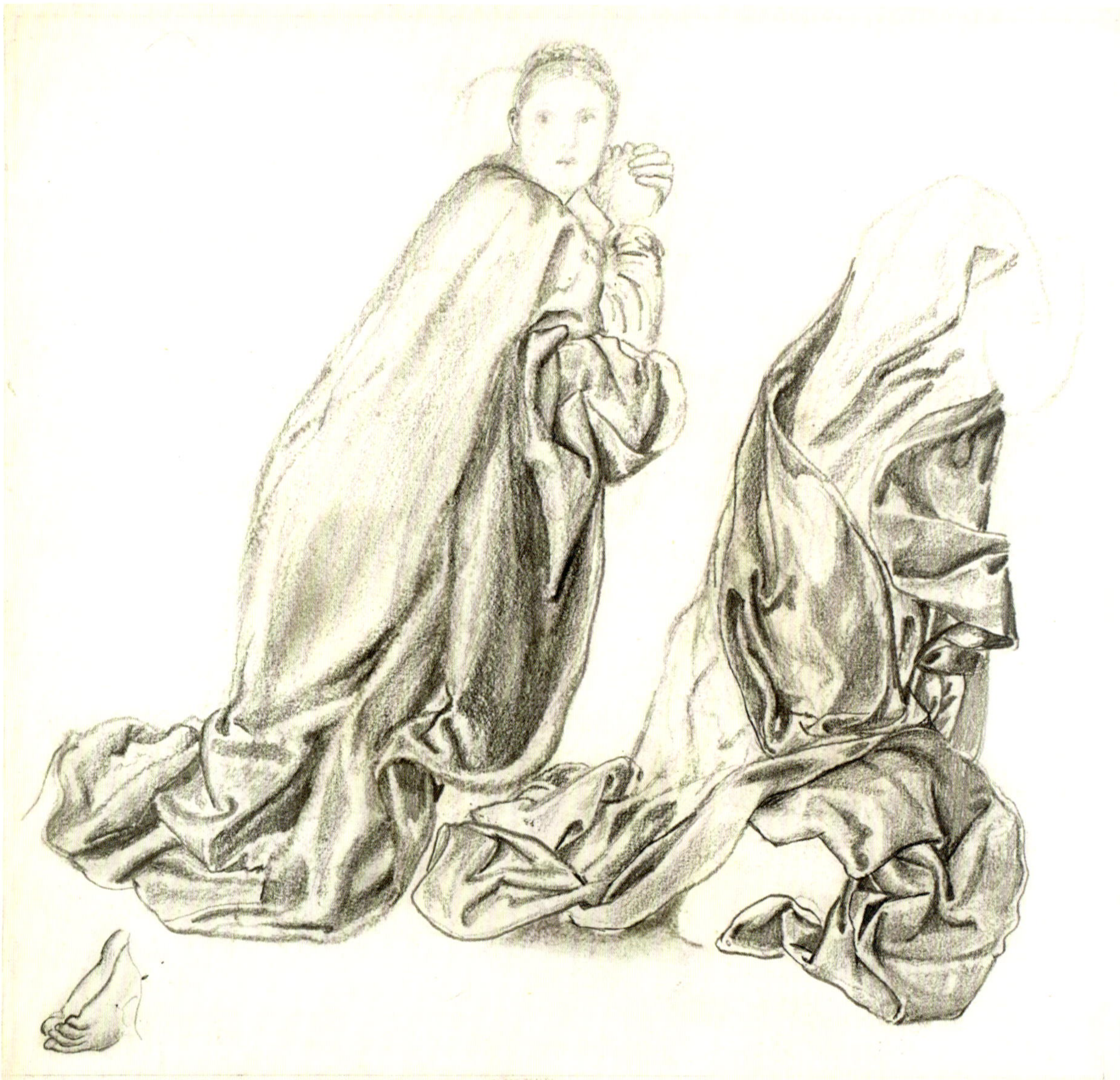

56
The Miracle of the Newborn Child, after Titian 1862
Watercolour and chalk on paper, 33 × 42
Private collection

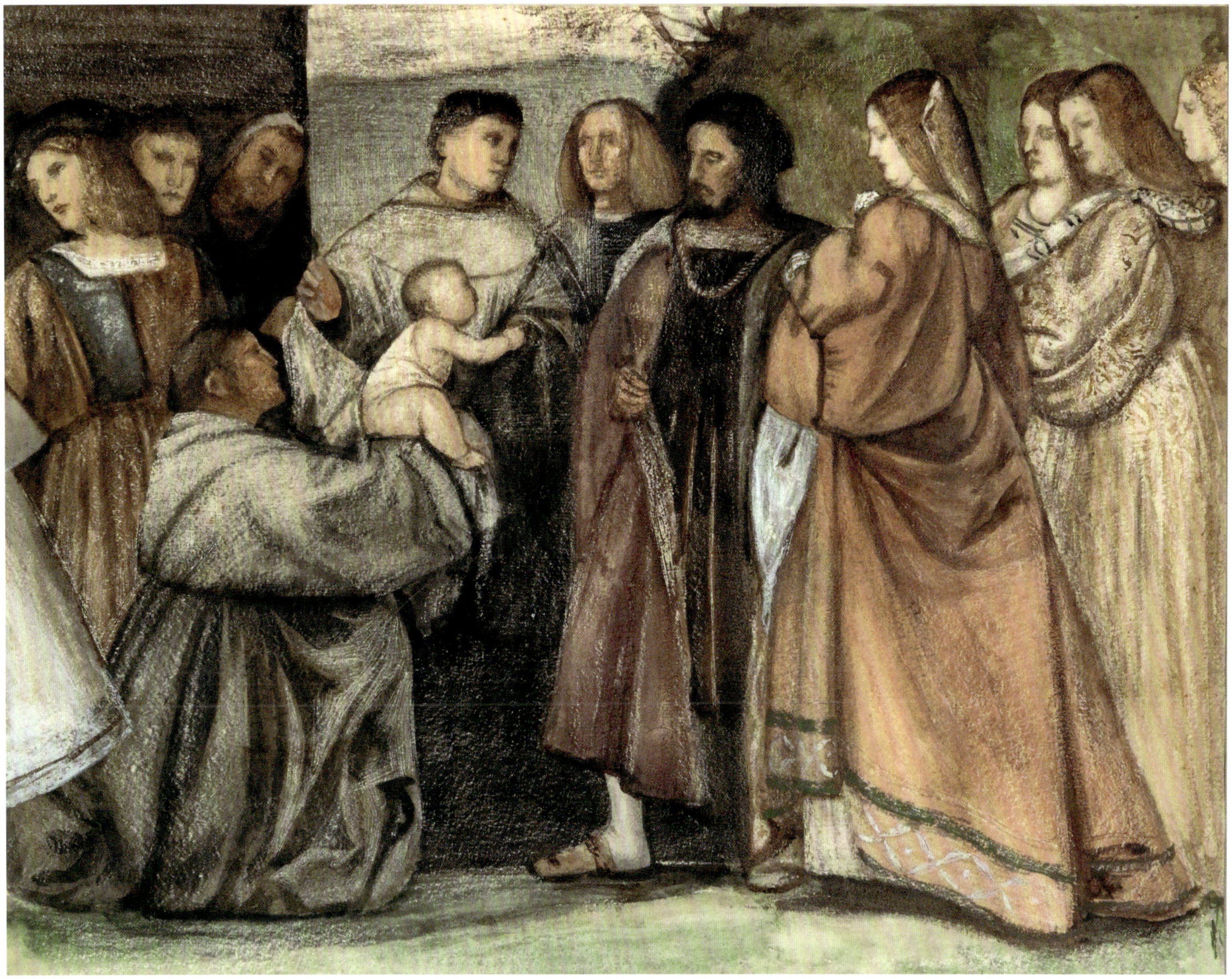

57
Study of the Head of Bacchus in Tintoretto's *The Marriage of Bacchus and Ariadne in the Presence of Venus*, before the picture was restored 1862
Graphite and chalk on paper, 27.1 × 41.5
The Ashmolean Museum, University of Oxford

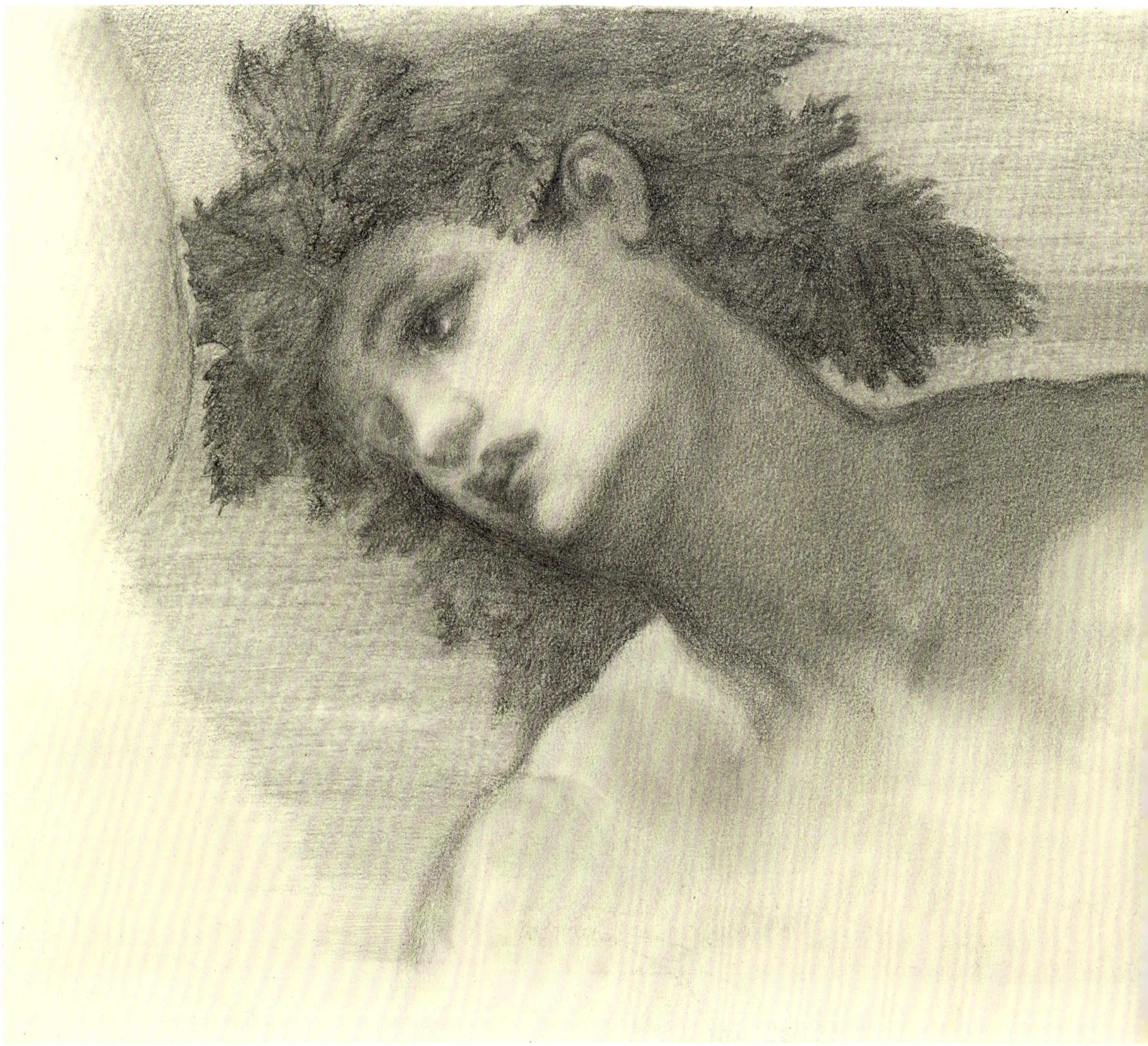

58
Study of a Man's Head 1866
Graphite on paper, 22.2 × 17.1
Tate

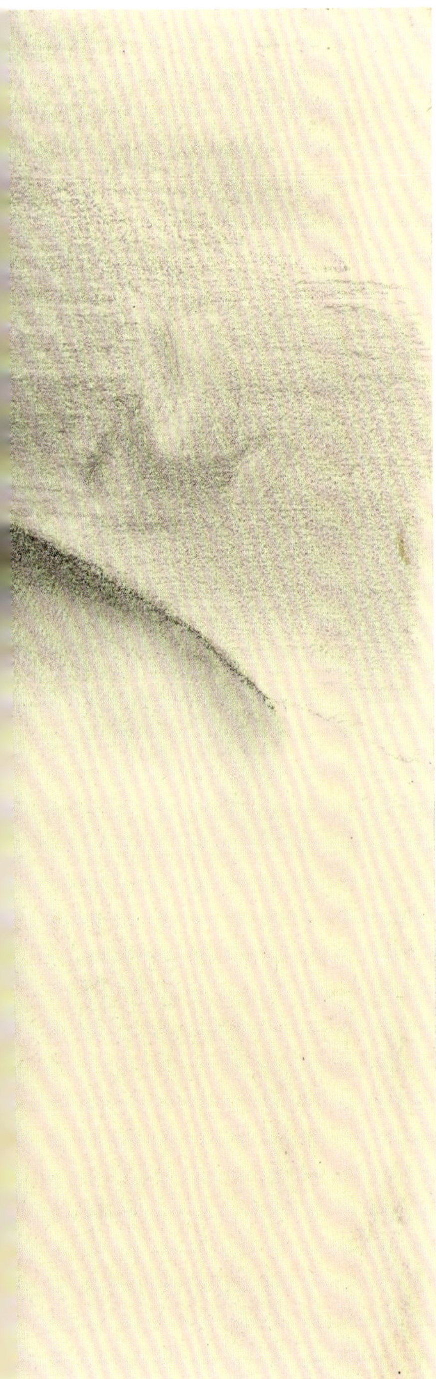

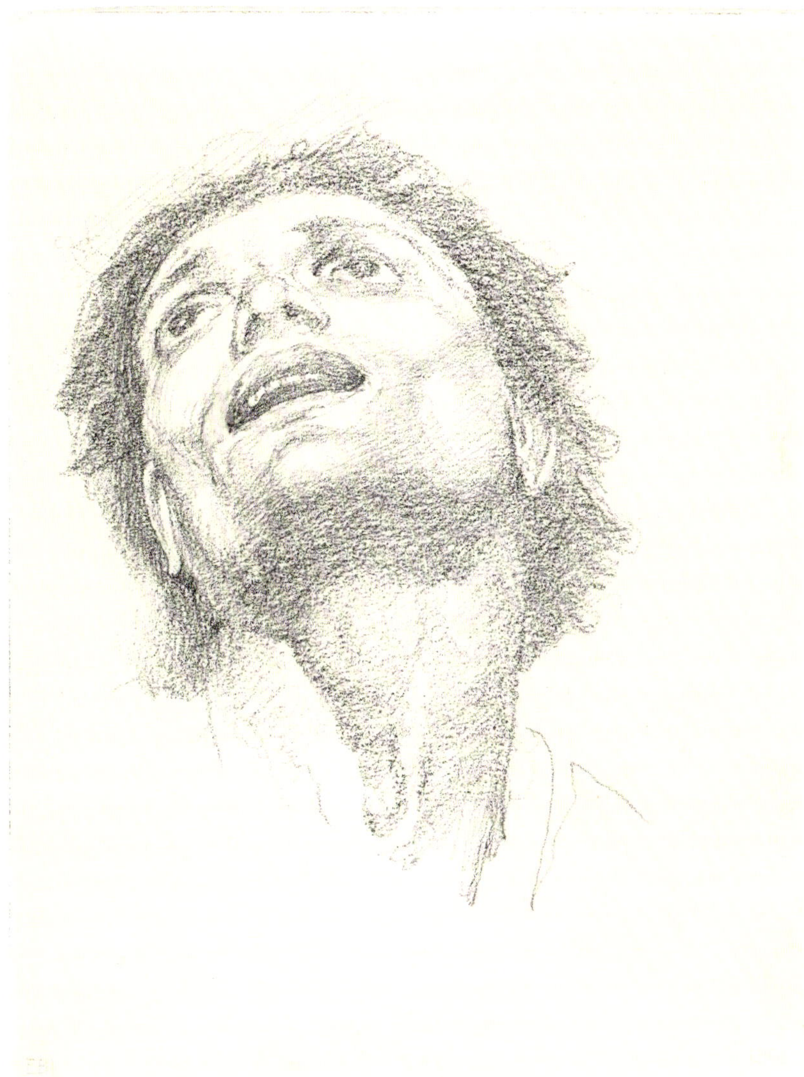

59
Study of the Pilgrim for *The Pilgrim outside the Garden of Idleness'* c.1872–7
Chalk and graphite on paper, 36.5 × 22.5
Tate

60
Studies of birds for *Love Leading the Pilgrim* c.1877–97
Chalk on paper, 30.4 × 20.2
Amgueddfa Cymru – National Museum Wales

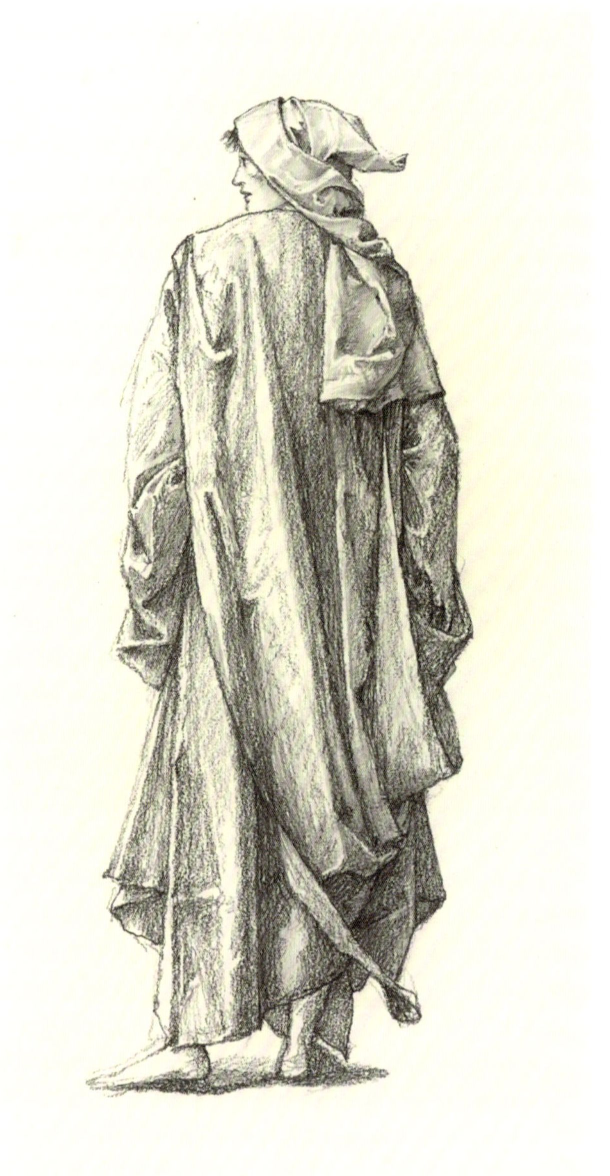

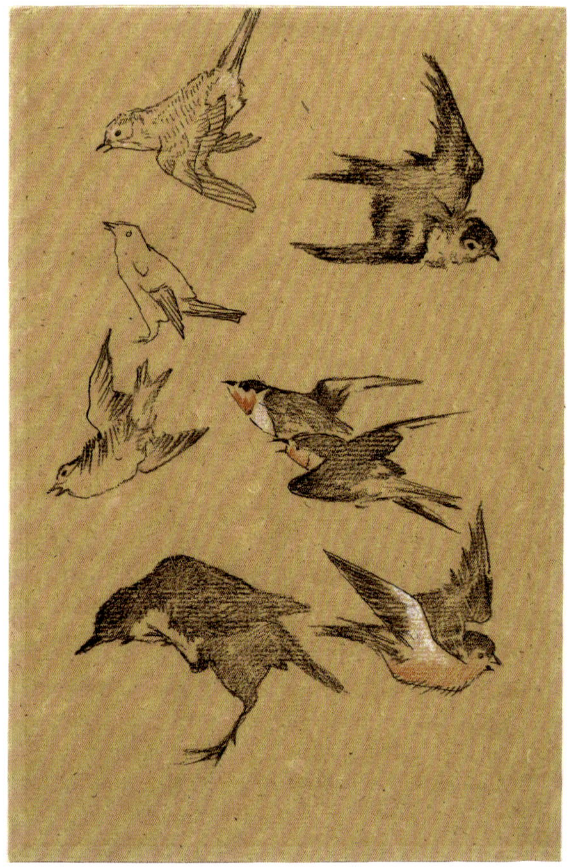

61
Studies for *Love Leading the Pilgrim*
Graphite on paper, 22.9 × 32.4
Tate

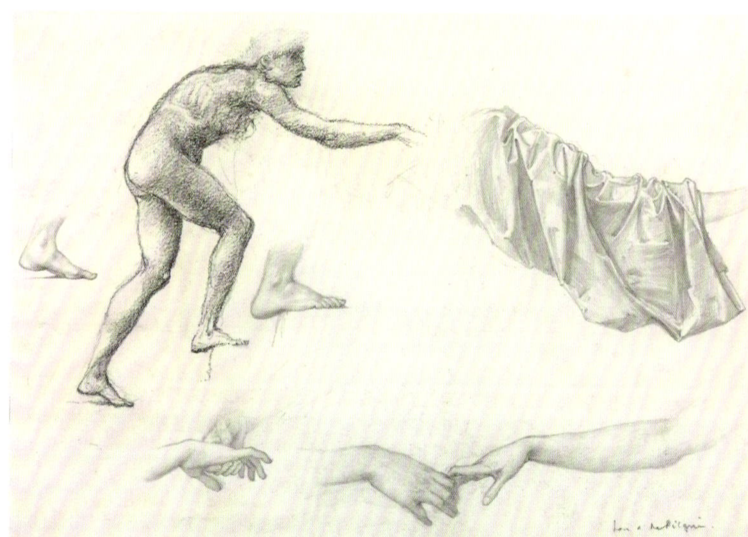

62
Study for the figure of Merlin in *Merlin and Nimue* 1861
Graphite and chalk on paper, 32.5 × 14.9
Victoria and Albert Museum

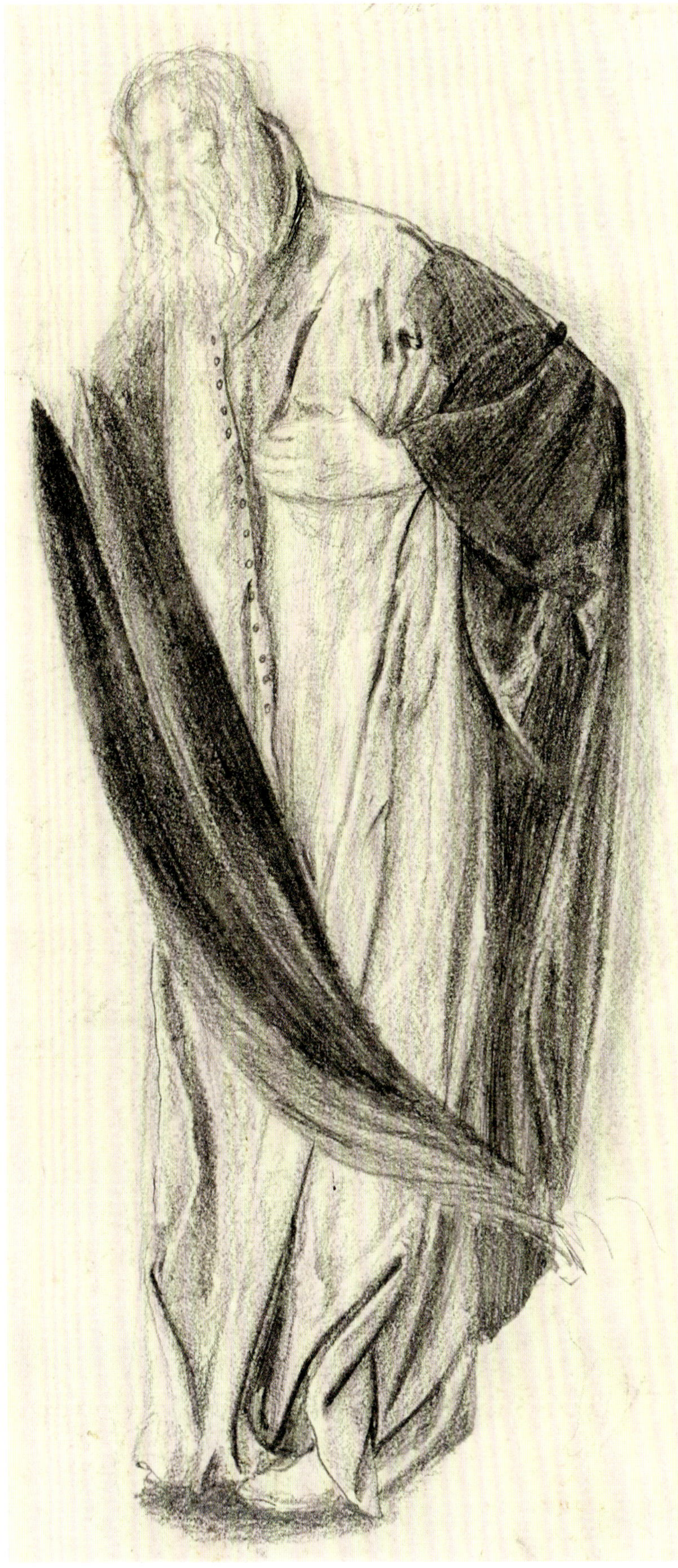

63
The Pilgrim Outside the Garden of Idleness
*(*Scene from *Roman de la Rose)* c.1893–8
Oil on canvas, 155.9 × 306.7
Victoria and Albert Museum

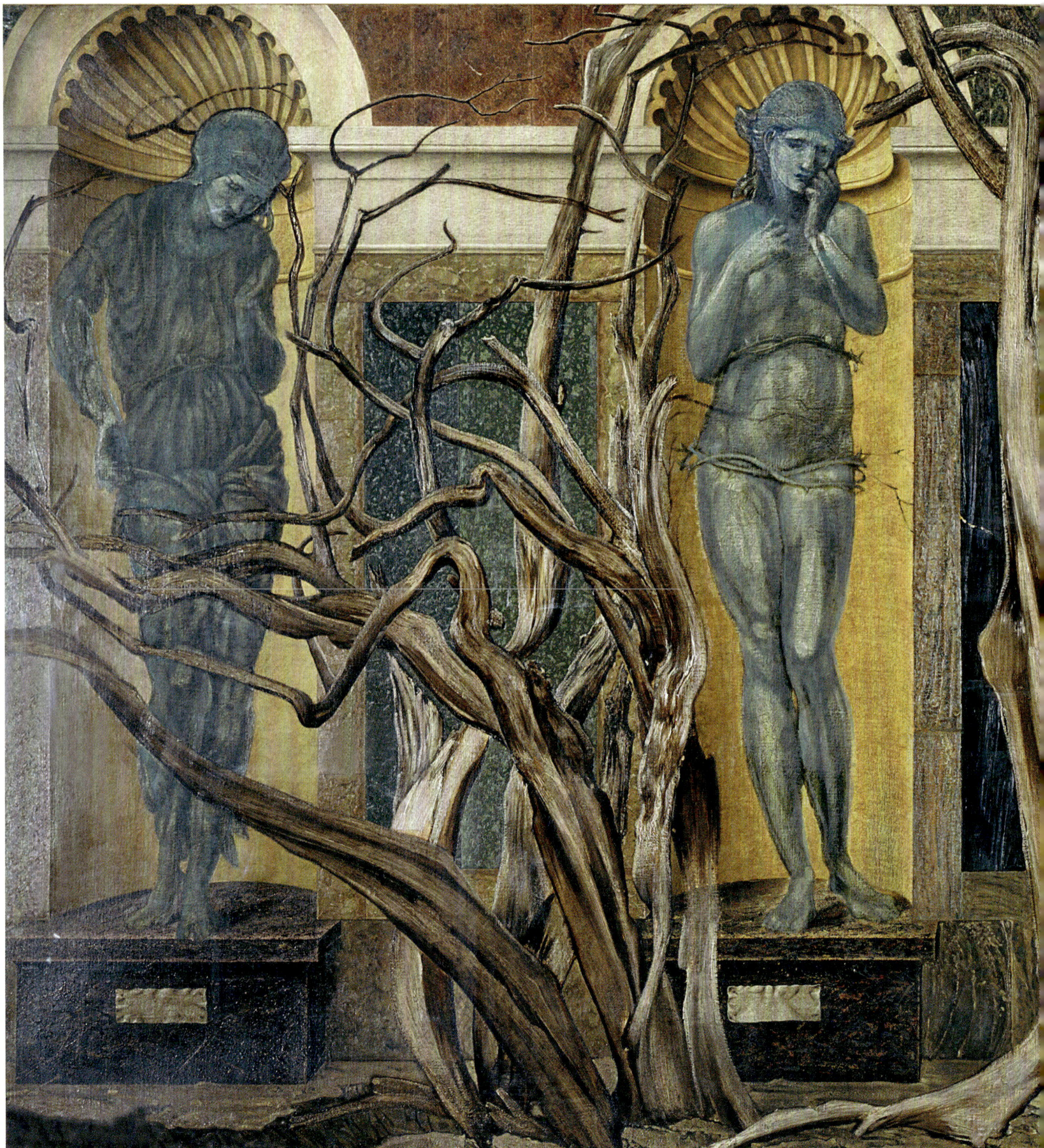

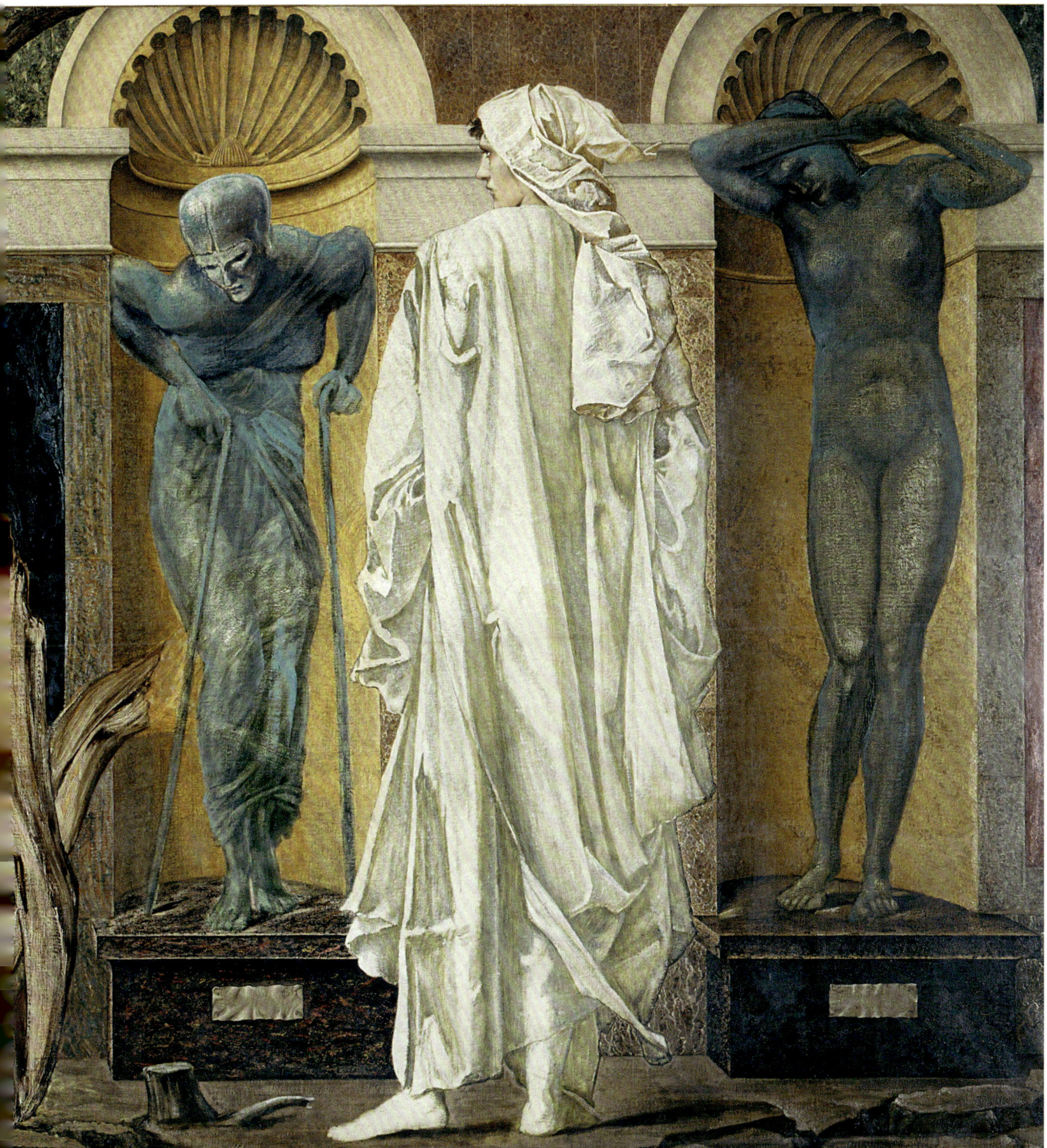

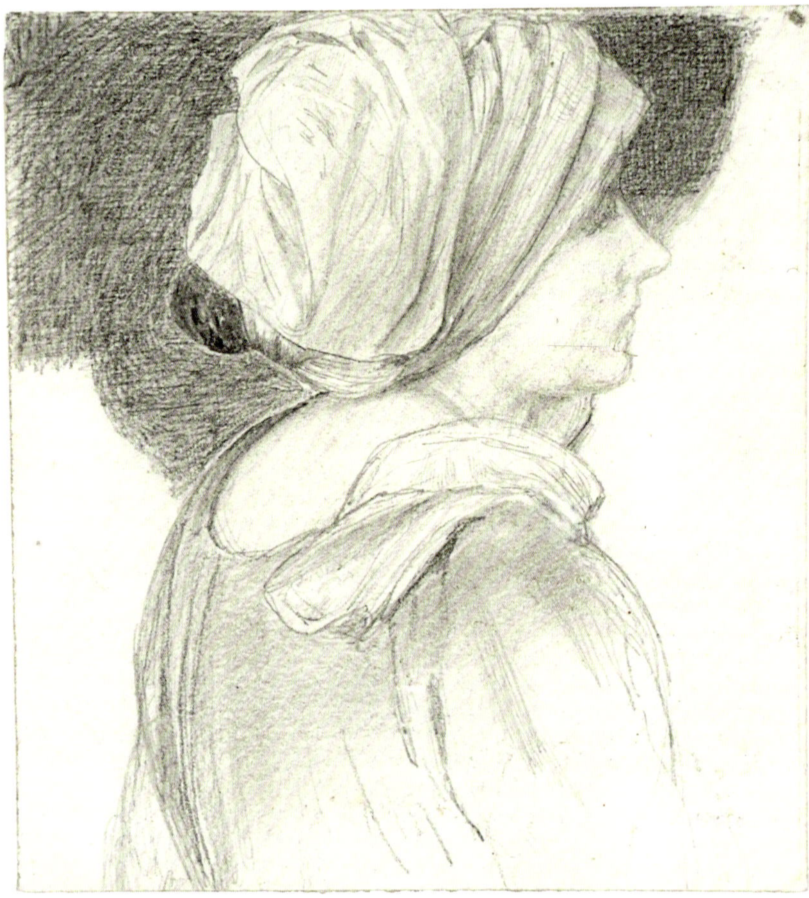

64
Study of the Head of a Female Attendant for *The Adoration of the Kings* c.1861
Graphite on paper, 15.4 × 14.2
Tate

65
Head of a Woman: possibly Georgiana Burne-Jones c.1861
Graphite on paper, 14 × 16.6
Tate

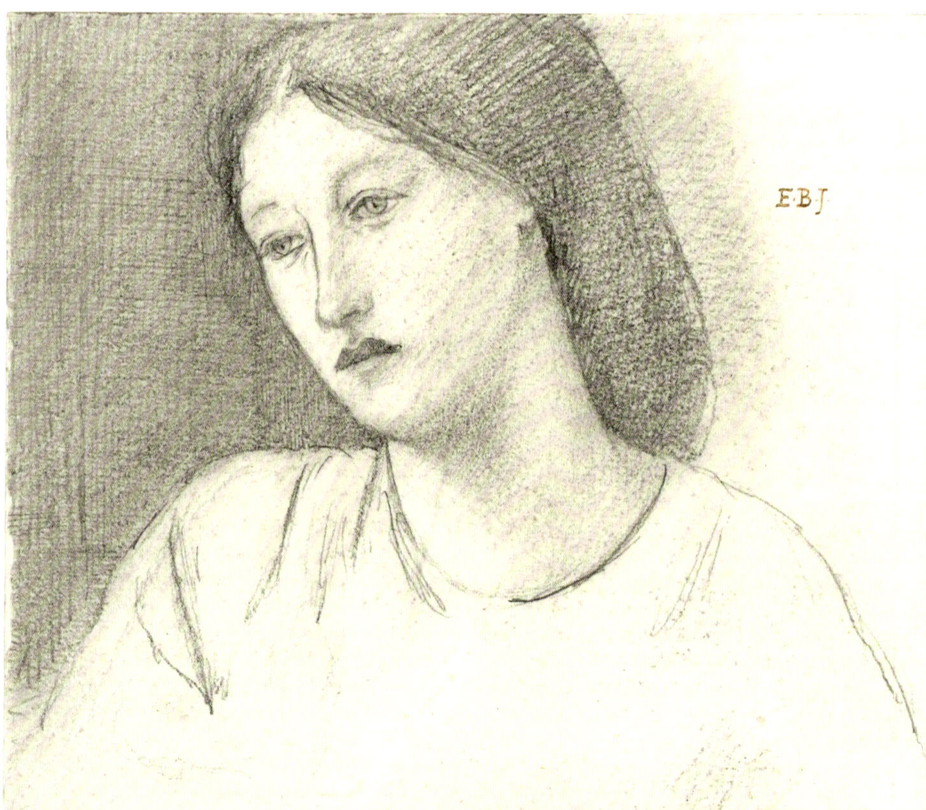

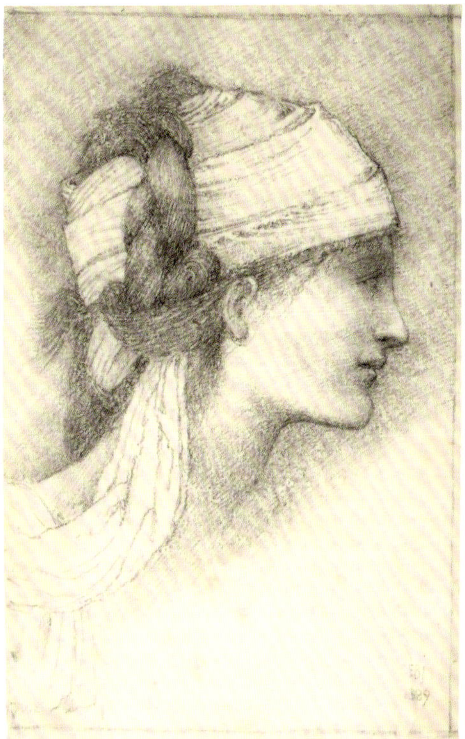

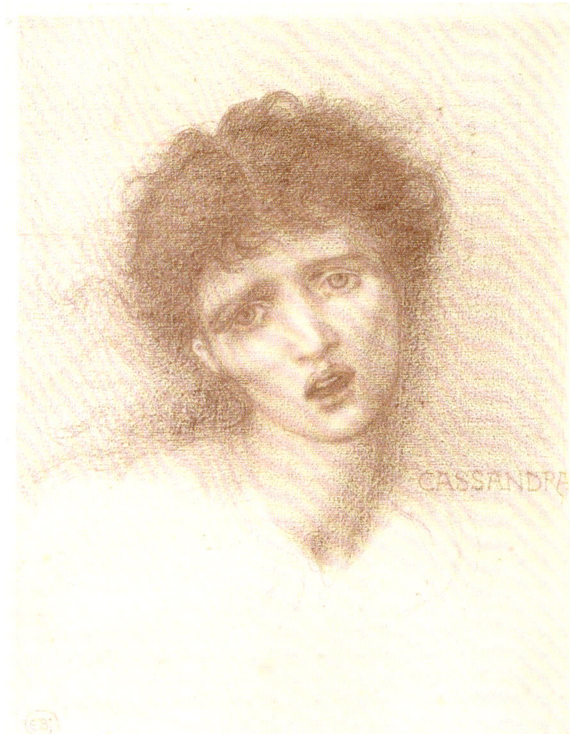

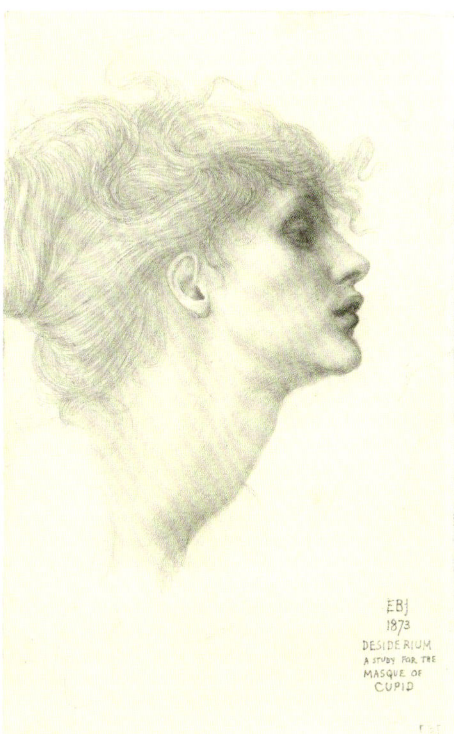

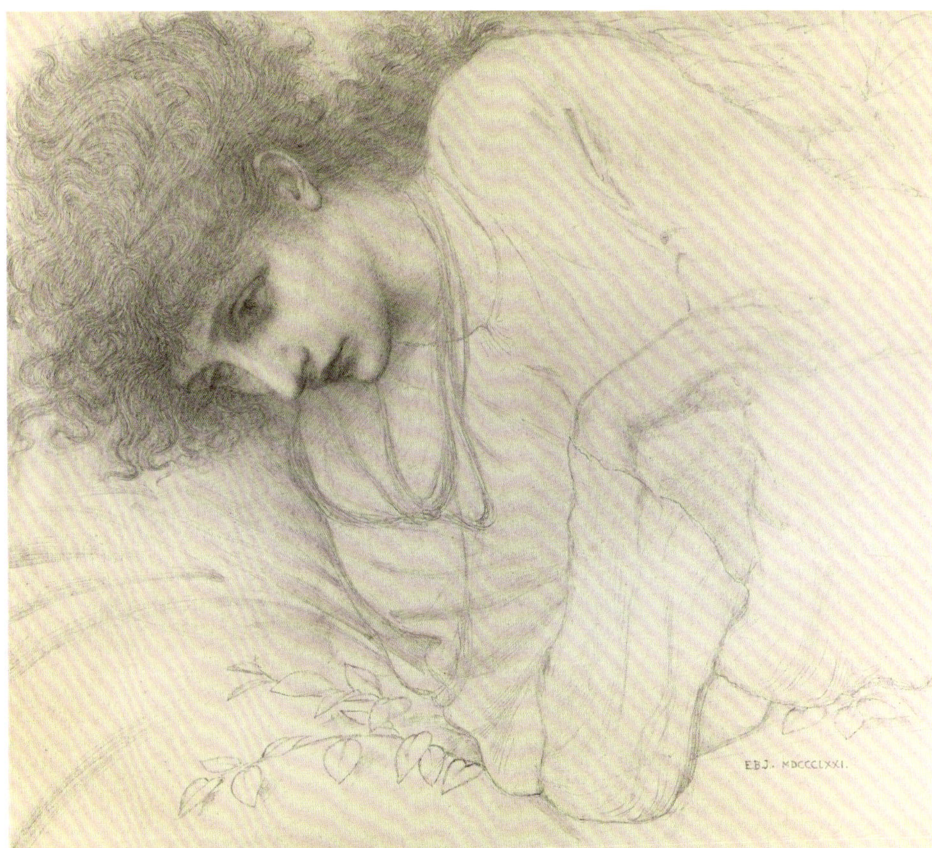

66 (top left)
Study of female head to right 1889
Charcoal on paper, 35.2 × 22.4
National Museums Liverpool, Lady Lever Art Gallery

67 (top right)
The Head of Cassandra 1866–70
Chalk on paper, 35.6 × 28
Victoria and Albert Museum

68 (below left)
Desiderium 1873
Graphite on paper, 21 × 13.3
Tate

69 (below)
Maria Zambaco 1871
Graphite on paper, 32 × 36.8
Private collection, Maas Gallery

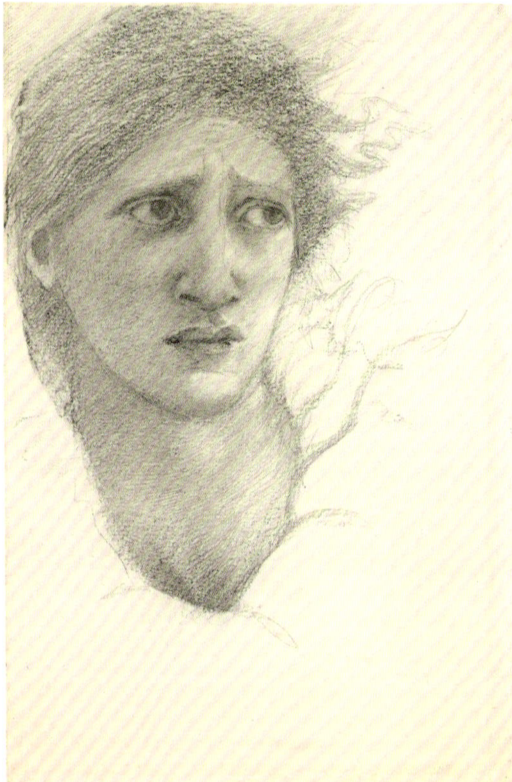

70
Head of a woman with furrowed brow, possibly a study for *Medusa* in *The Finding of Medusa* c.1875–7
Graphite on paper, 25.4 × 16.6
National Museums Liverpool, Lady Lever Art Gallery

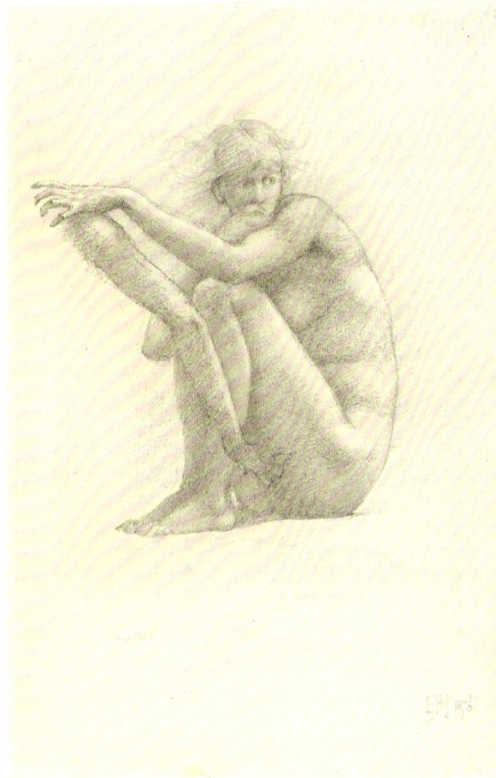

71
Study of a Gorgon in *The Finding of Medusa* 1876
Graphite on paper, 27.1 × 17.8
The Syndics of the Fitzwilliam Museum, University of Cambridge

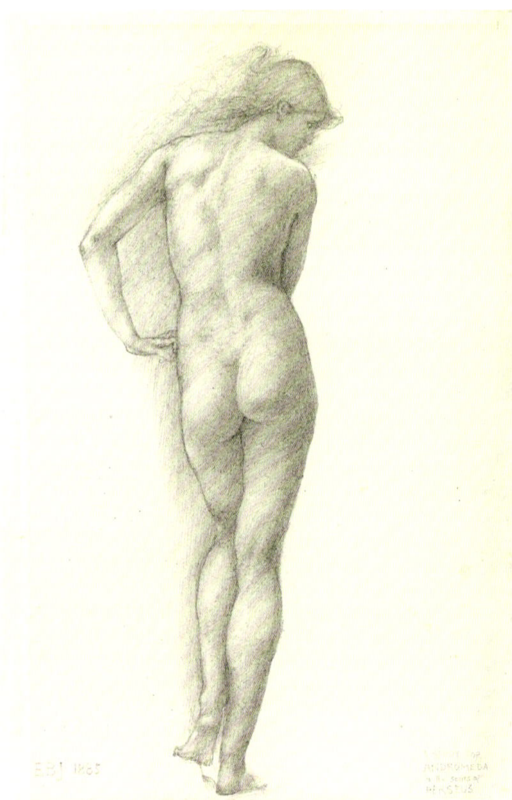

72
A Study for *Andromeda* for *The Doom Fulfilled* in the *Perseus* Series 1885
Graphite on paper, 27.3 × 18.2
The British Museum, London

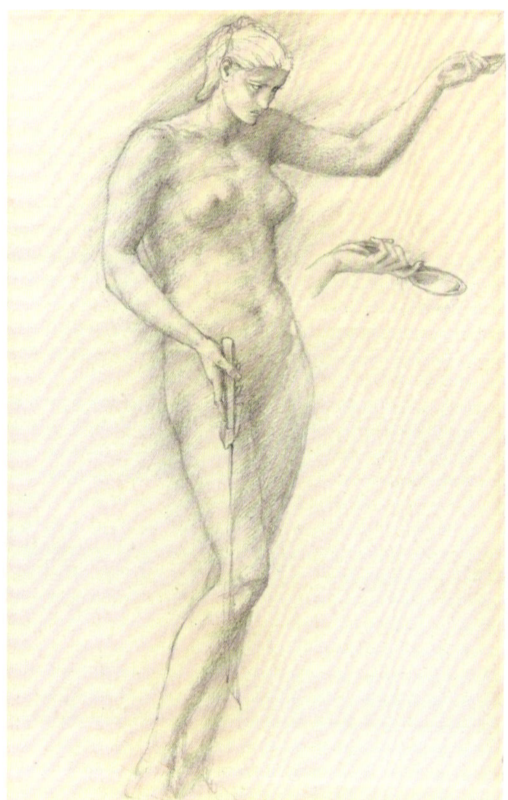

73
Study of *Athena* in *The Call of Perseus* 1876–7
Graphite on paper, 26.7 × 17.6
The Syndics of the Fitzwilliam Museum, University of Cambridge

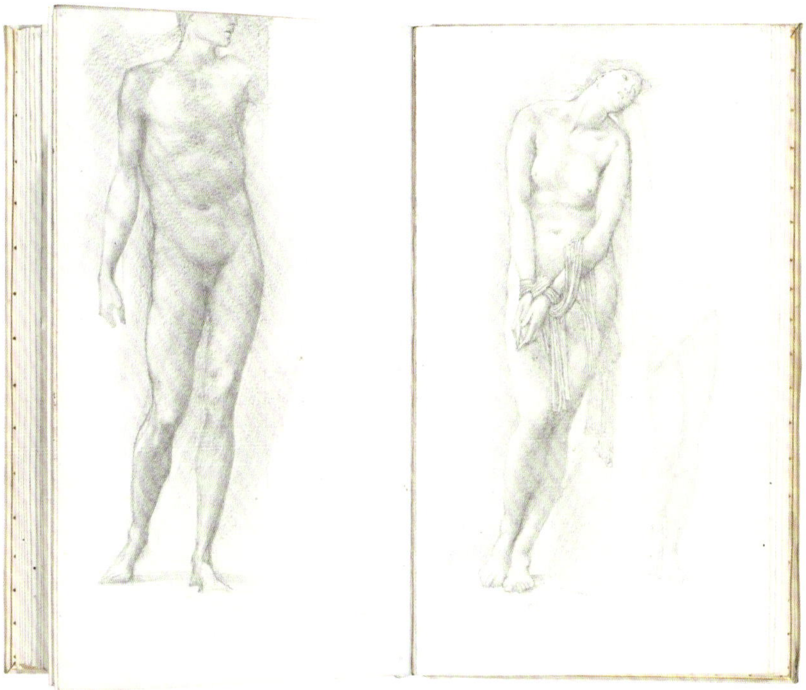

74
Sketchbook with studies of *Perseus* and *Andromeda* after 1875
Graphite on paper
Victoria and Albert Museum

75
Study for *Andromeda* c.1885
Chalk on paper, 38.1 × 27.9
Tate

76
Study for the head of *Medusa* in *The Baleful Head* 1876–7
Graphite on paper, 22.7 × 12.6
The Syndics of the Fitzwilliam Museum, University of Cambridge

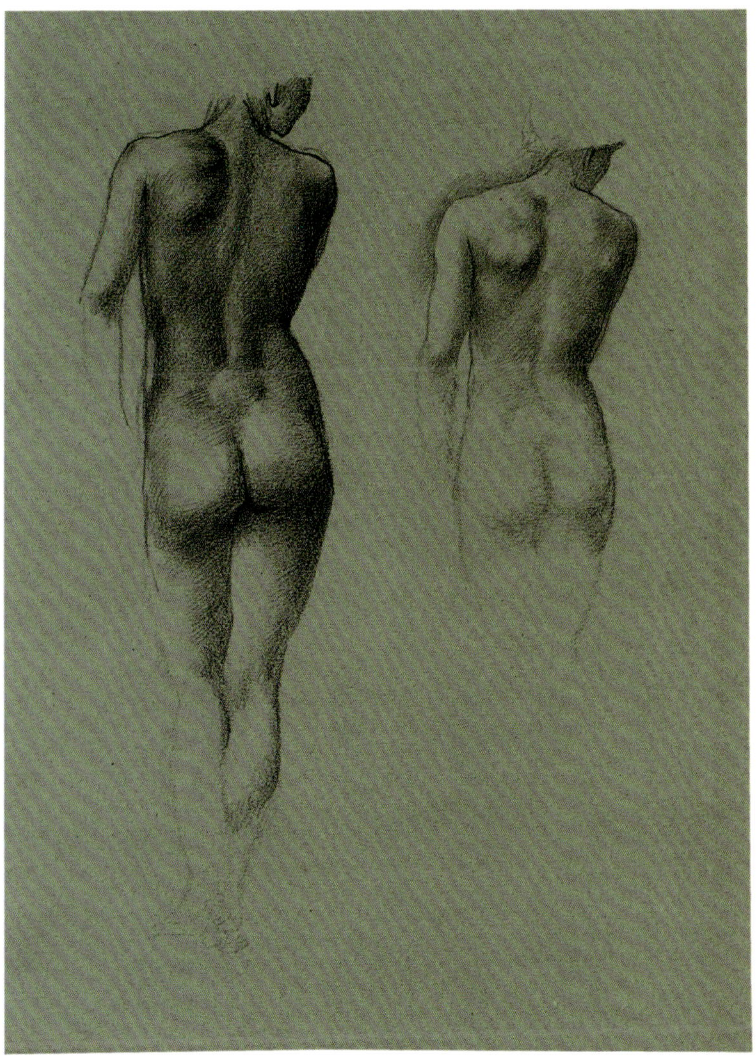

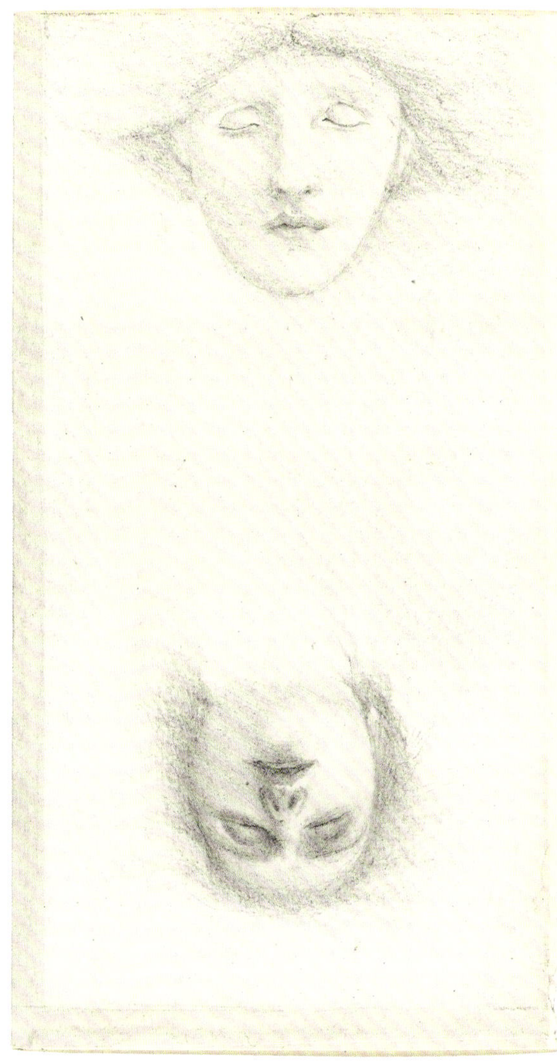

77
Study of Armour: Perseus in the *Finding of Medusa*
before 1880
Bodycolour on paper, 54 × 38.2
The Syndics of the Fitzwilliam Museum,
University of Cambridge

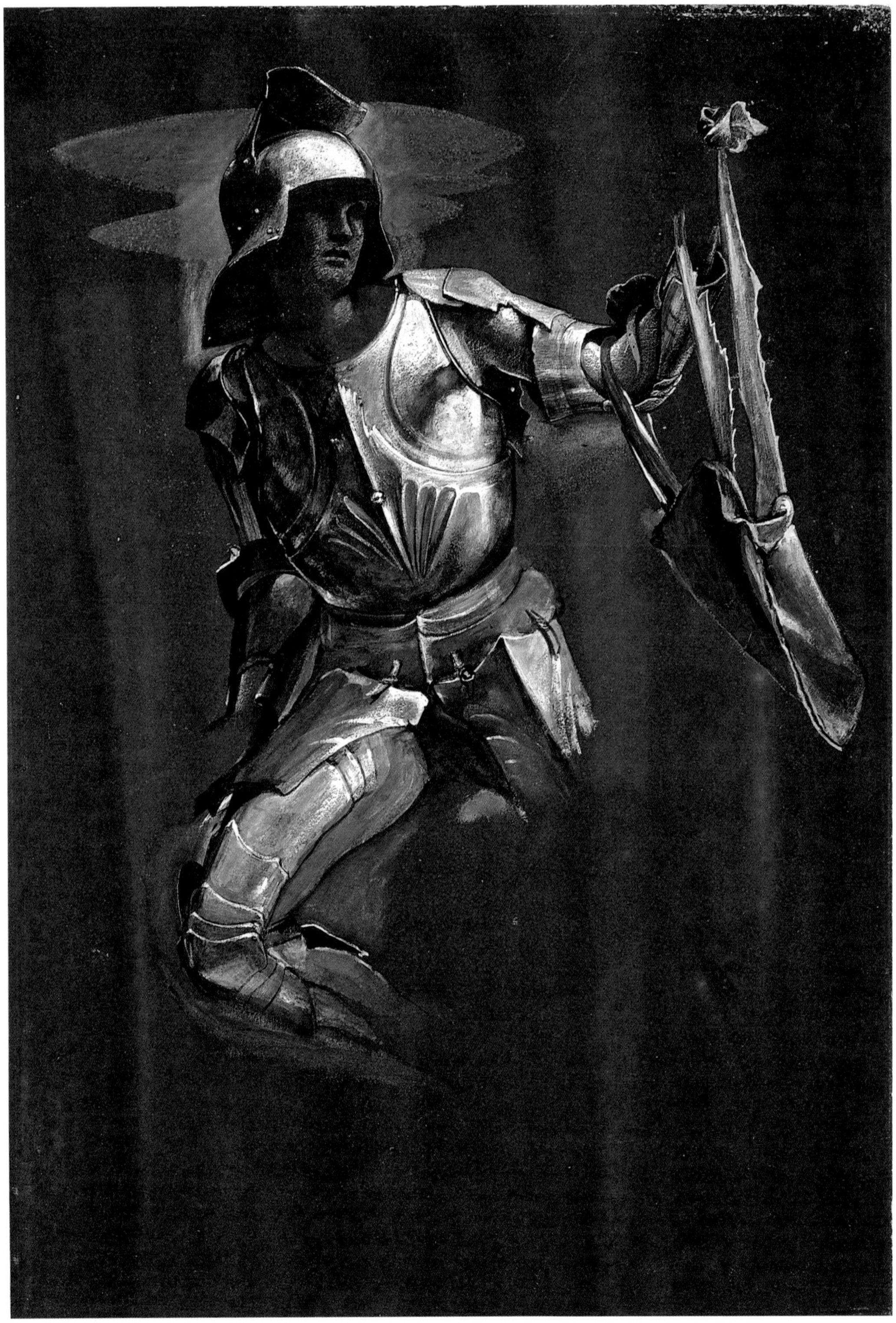

78
Nymphs of the Stars 1896
Bodycolour, gold pigment and pastel on paper, 35.5 × 24.8
Amgueddfa Cymru – National Museum Wales

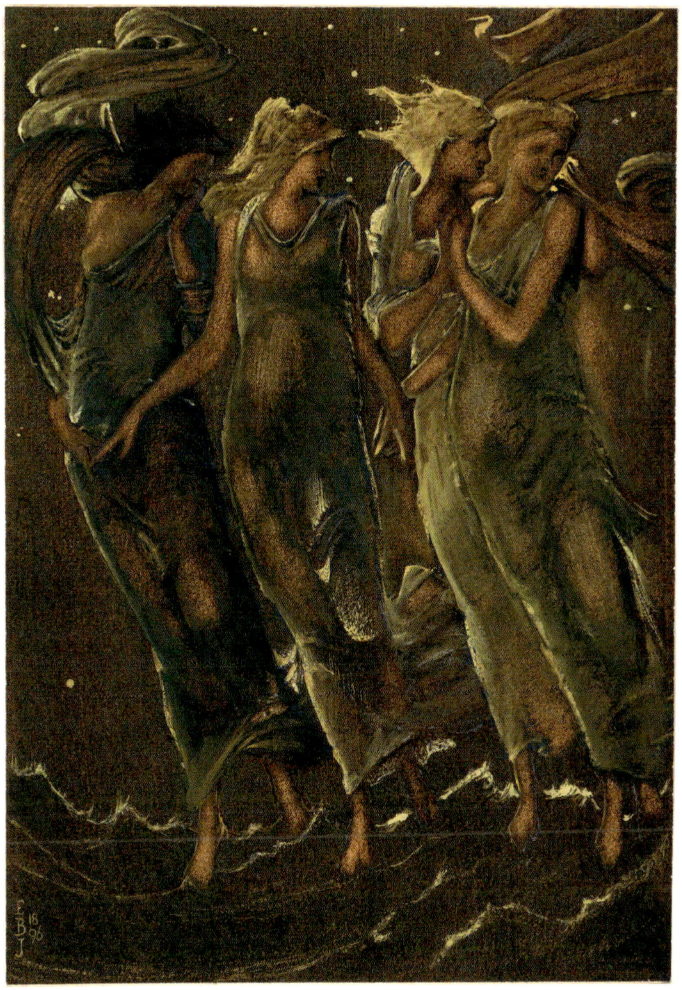

79
Nymphs of the Moon c.1896
Bodycolour and metallic pigments on prepared paper, 32.9 × 24.8
Amgueddfa Cymru – National Museum Wales

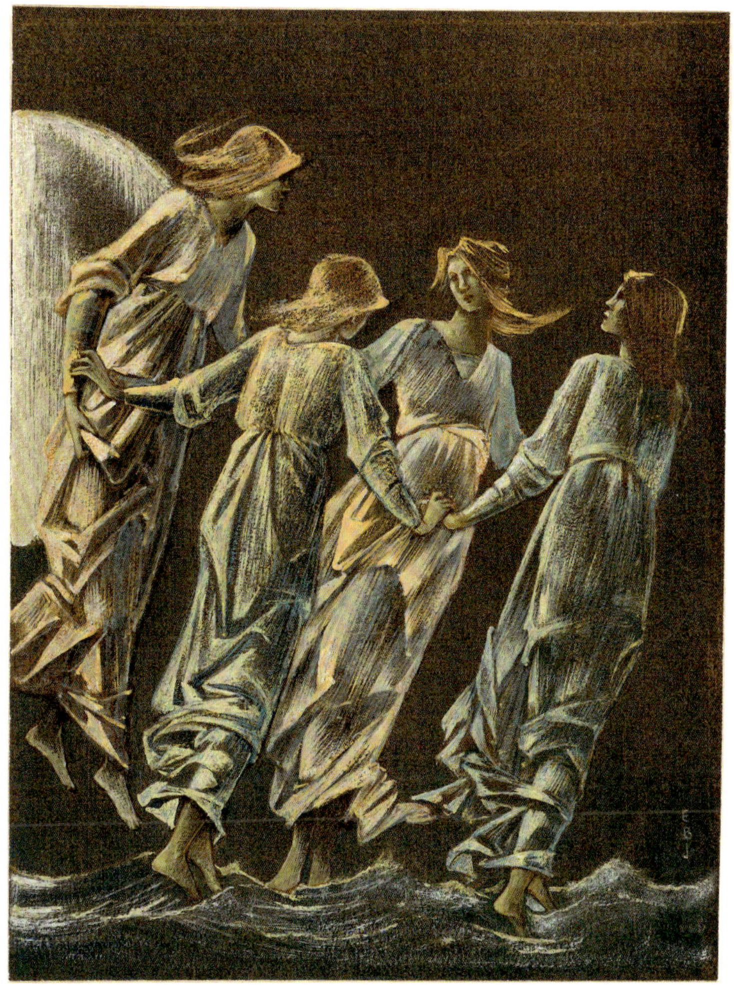

'Grotesque vigour'

The exceptions to this evolved refinement in Burne-Jones's work are the informal comic drawings, spontaneous in expression, both unguarded and inventive, a continuation of his adolescent practice of illustrating letters with amusing pictures. At the 1899 Burlington Fine Arts Club exhibition the most revelatory section was that devoted to humorous drawing. The works shown still belonged in the private collections of family members and close friends. In them we are presented with a striking contrast between the beautiful faces and graceful bodies depicted in exhibited works and the comic figures in caricatures. Old master examples are overturned or deliberately mocked. The Annunciation – one of the most highly aestheticised of the artist's religious themes – is made ludicrous by the excesses of his least favourite artist, Rubens, who peoples it with corpulent models (no.81).[16] In these, and in many other humorous drawings, the artist's etiolated figures are fattened up for comic effect. Burne-Jones's comically overweight characters owe a debt to the political satires of an earlier, less polite culture. The cruel depictions of Emma Hamilton in her plumper manifestation, published by James Gillray in the first decades of the century, spring to mind as prototypes of Burne-Jones's iconography of the 'fat lady' (no.89).

Yet we might detect a stronger link with the rediscovery of old master drawings by Burne-Jones and his circle, particularly in an acknowledgement of Leonardo's grotesques. Burne-Jones could have seen a key example at Christ Church Old Library, Oxford, while he was an undergraduate, well before his regular visits to the British Museum or his travels in Italy (fig.26). The relation of Burne-Jones's caricatures to Leonardo is further complicated by looking at *A Bathing Beauty* (no.80), which depicts Emma de Burgh, the famous American tattooed lady, with his *Last Supper* inked across her back. In such works 'low' culture threatens to suffocate the 'high' culture so carefully cultivated by Burne-Jones in his exhibited work.

In spirit the humorous drawings go back to his pre-Oxford days, to his childhood and early teens. One of the earliest influences on Burne-Jones's drawing style was the illustrator George Cruikshank. Writing about an example of the young artist's work decorating a letter from 1850, Georgiana Burne-Jones reveals in the *Memorials* that at this stage 'he had as yet seen no beautiful drawing, and though the grotesque vigour of Cruikshank had evidently affected him, that was not the language for which he was seeking.'[17] The mention of the beautiful is striking here: Burne-Jones might be said to start drawing with a vigorous and unschooled approach but, as he educated himself through looking and copying, he was led to an emulation of old master techniques and imagery and to ideals of physical beauty.

Cruikshank's tendency to depict skinny figures – as in his famous illustrations for Dickens – often contrasted for comic effect with plump ones, might have had a long-term effect on Burne-Jones's tastes. In his self-caricatures Burne-Jones depicted himself as both distrait and emaciated whereas Morris (as 'Topsy') is the opposite, rotund and irascible, his trousers bursting in rage or excess (nos.83, 85). In another of these drawings the distinction between the artist and another figure is even more telling. In a caricature (no.82) he sits, seemingly stunned, in wonder at the perfect face and figure of Maria Zambaco, recognisable from the many portrait drawings of her, such as no.69. The image is reminiscent of Rossetti's self-caricatures and his humorous drawings involving Jane Morris, in which her husband and the

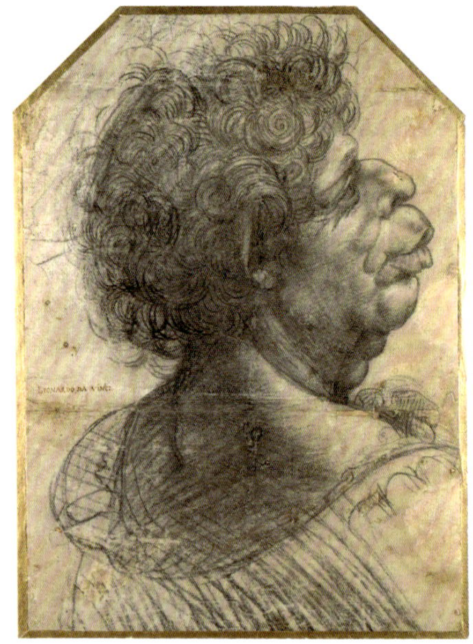

Fig.26
LEONARDO DA VINCI
Grotesque bust of a man in profile to right
c.1503–5
Chalk on paper, 38.2 × 27.5
Christ Church, Oxford

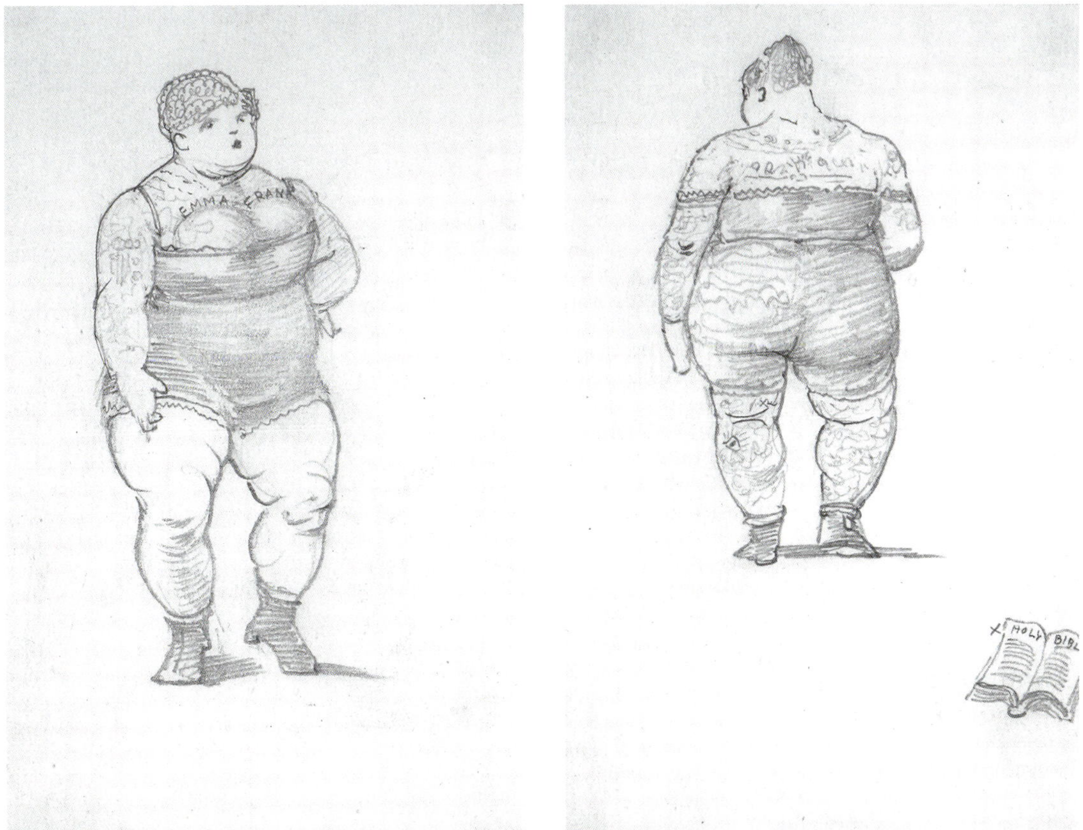

80
A Bathing Beauty: Two views, front and back, of Emma De Burgh, with Leonardo's 'Last Supper' tattooed on her back, whom the artist had seen that afternoon at the London Aquarium c.1893–5
Graphite on paper, 17.5 × 11.5 each
Peter and Renate Nahum

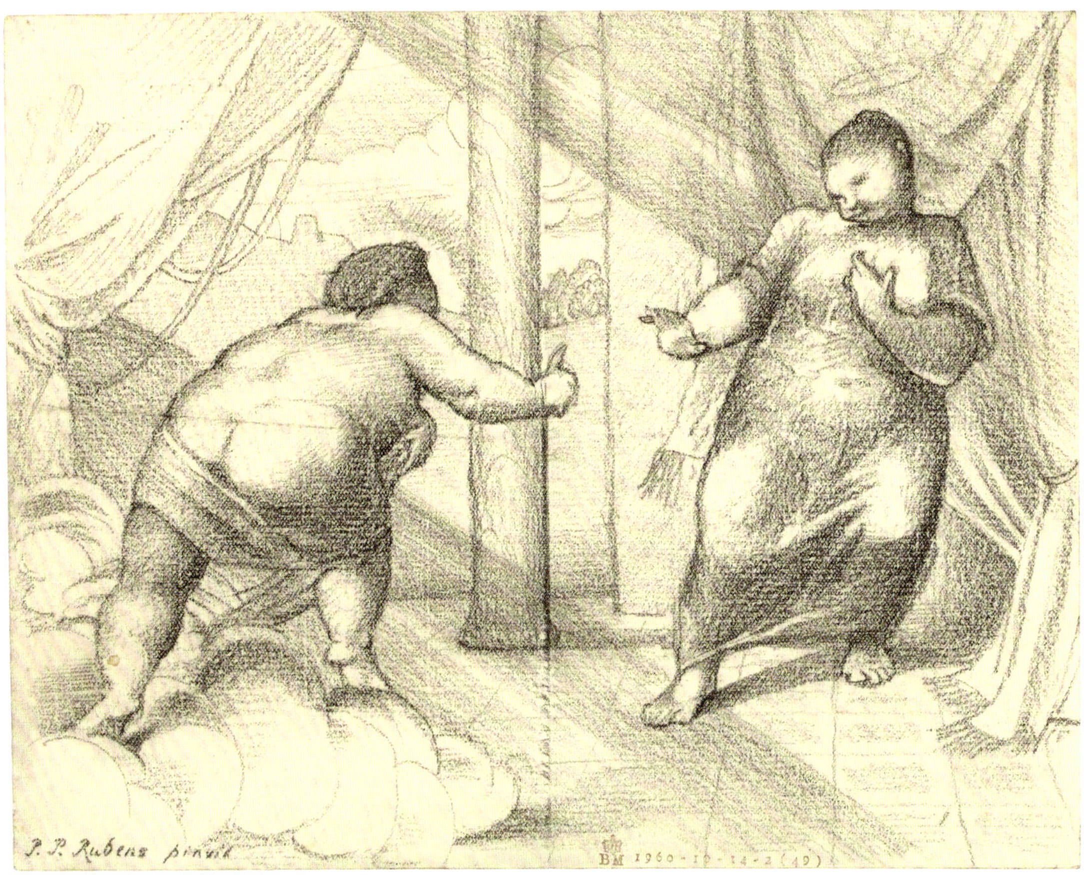

81
Caricature of an *Annunciation* by Rubens from the Album *Letters to Katie* 1883–9
Graphite on paper, 17.5 × 22.5
The British Museum, London

82
The Artist and Maria Zambaco
1866–72
Graphite on paper, 12 × 15
Private collection courtesy of Peter Nahum. Renate Nahum. Agency

83
William Morris Reading Poetry to Edward Burne-Jones 1861
Pen and ink on paper, 18 × 11.5
Victoria and Albert Museum

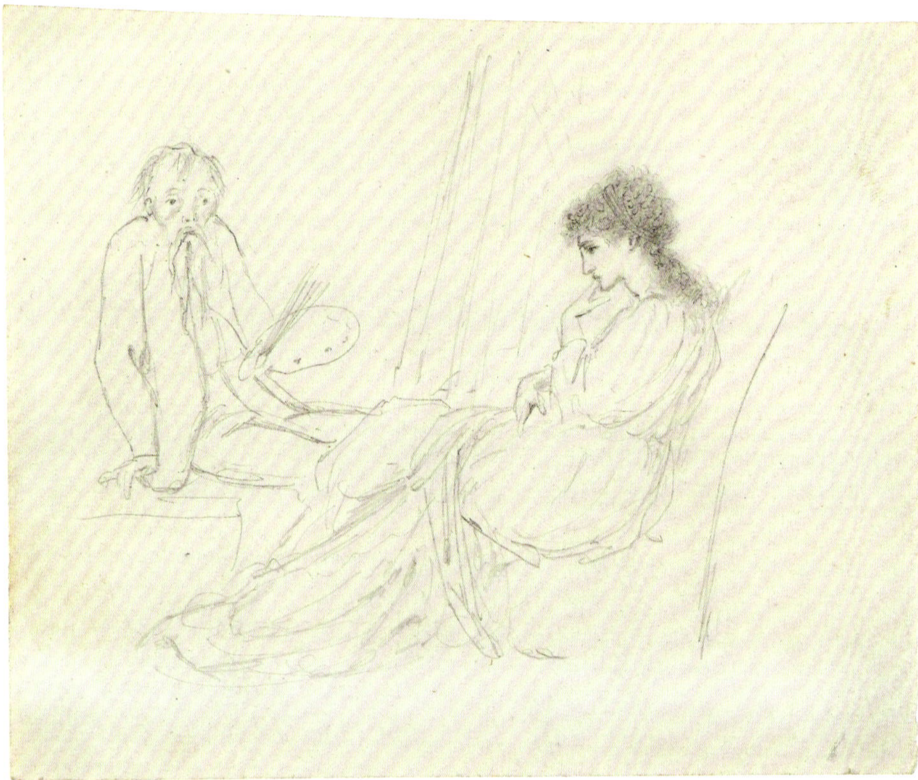

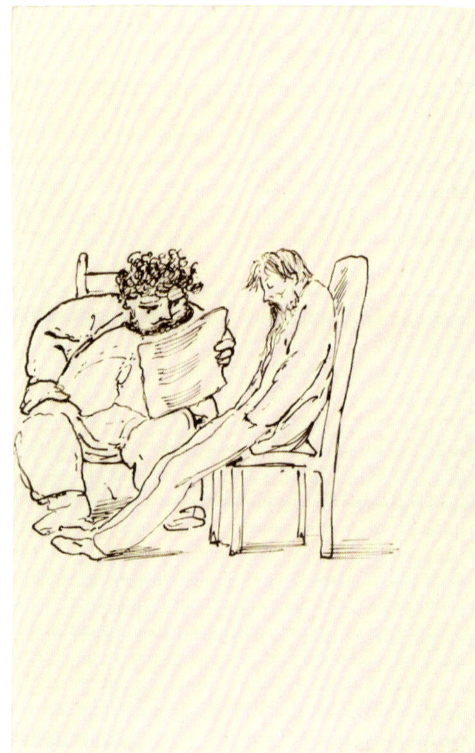

artist himself are represented comically while she retains her forbidding beauty. Both men dealt with their feelings about their own adulterous relationships not only in serious subject paintings but also, revealingly, in private caricatural drawings. We should note here that a group of pornographic sketches, based on bizarre sexual scenarios related by Swinburne and shared with the painter Simeon Solomon, is known to have existed but now appears to be lost.[18] Its very existence seems to offer a critical commentary on the 'ideal' works, by presenting the shadowed side of the artist's imagination.

* * *

T. Martin Wood, writing in the first book devoted solely to the study of Burne-Jones's drawings, cast doubt on the place his paintings would occupy in the future, 'judged merely from the standpoint of paint considered for its own sake'.[19] He thought that greater value would be put in his pencil studies. Certainly, in the last decades of his life Burne-Jones's studies became appreciated for their technical proficiency. Alfred Lys Baldry, reviewing an exhibition of the artist's drawings in 1895, noted that 'it would be difficult to find a better type of artistic endeavour to study ... These drawings show well with what power of design and with what sensitiveness of hand he puts down his conceptions.'[20] Such approval overturned the opinions expressed in the reception of his earlier works – in all media – which had been

84
Comic Drawing of four figures in long robes 1880s
Graphite on writing paper, 22.5 × 17.8
The British Museum, London

85
Account Book with Morris & Co with caricature frontispiece of the artist and William Morris 1883
Pen and ink on paper, 15.9 × 10.8 (each page)
The Syndics of the Fitzwilliam Museum, University of Cambridge

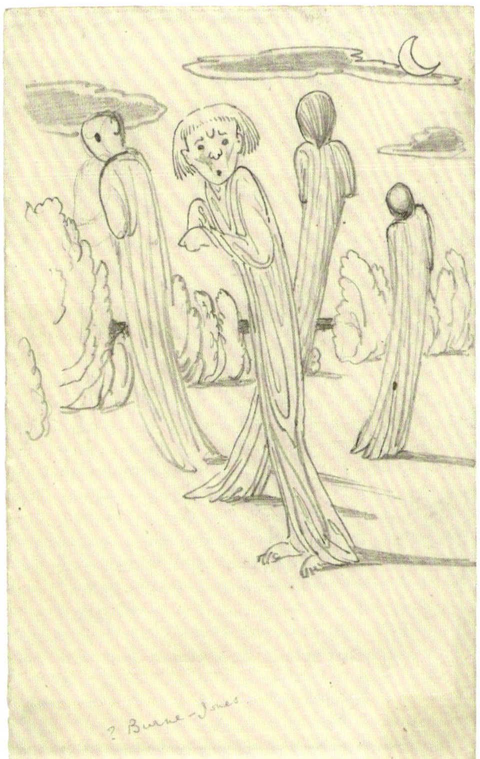

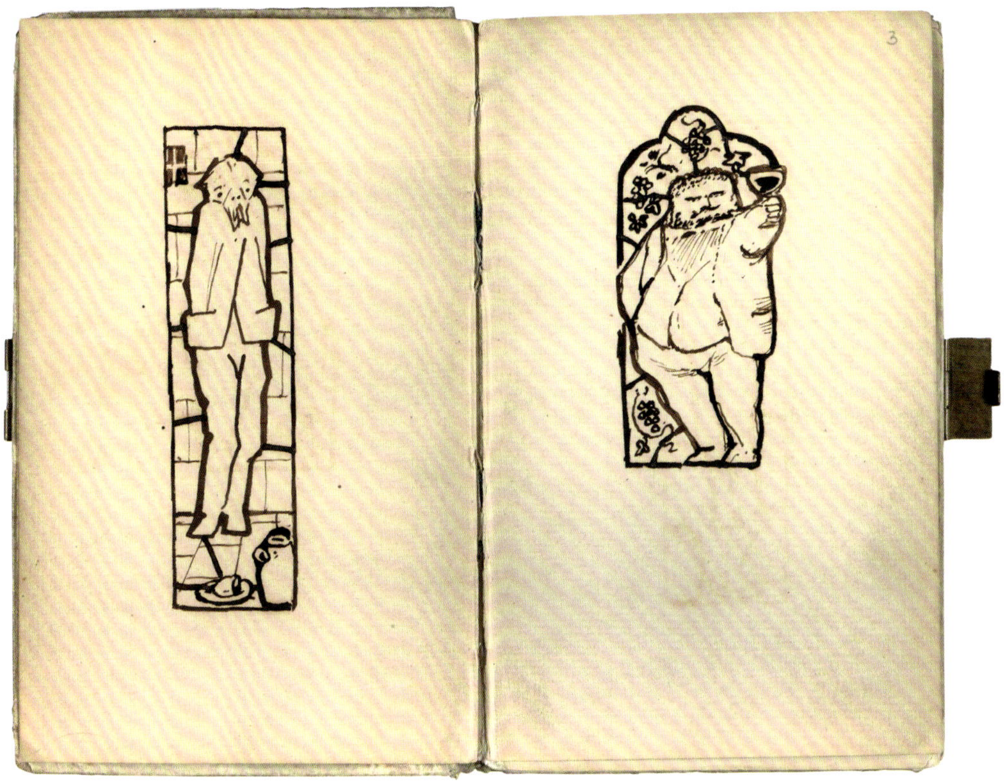

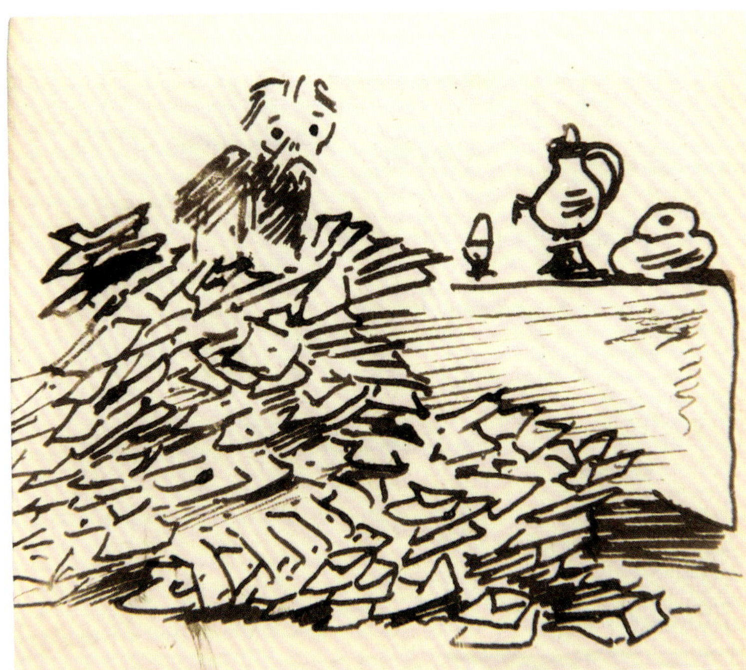

86
Self-portrait caricature in a letter to Cosmo Monkhouse 1894
Pen and ink on paper, 17.7 × 11.3
Collection of Stephen Calloway

87
Manuscript volume of illustrated letters and humorous drawings sent to Helen Mary Gaskell, 1897–8
18 × 12.5 (book closed)
Private collection

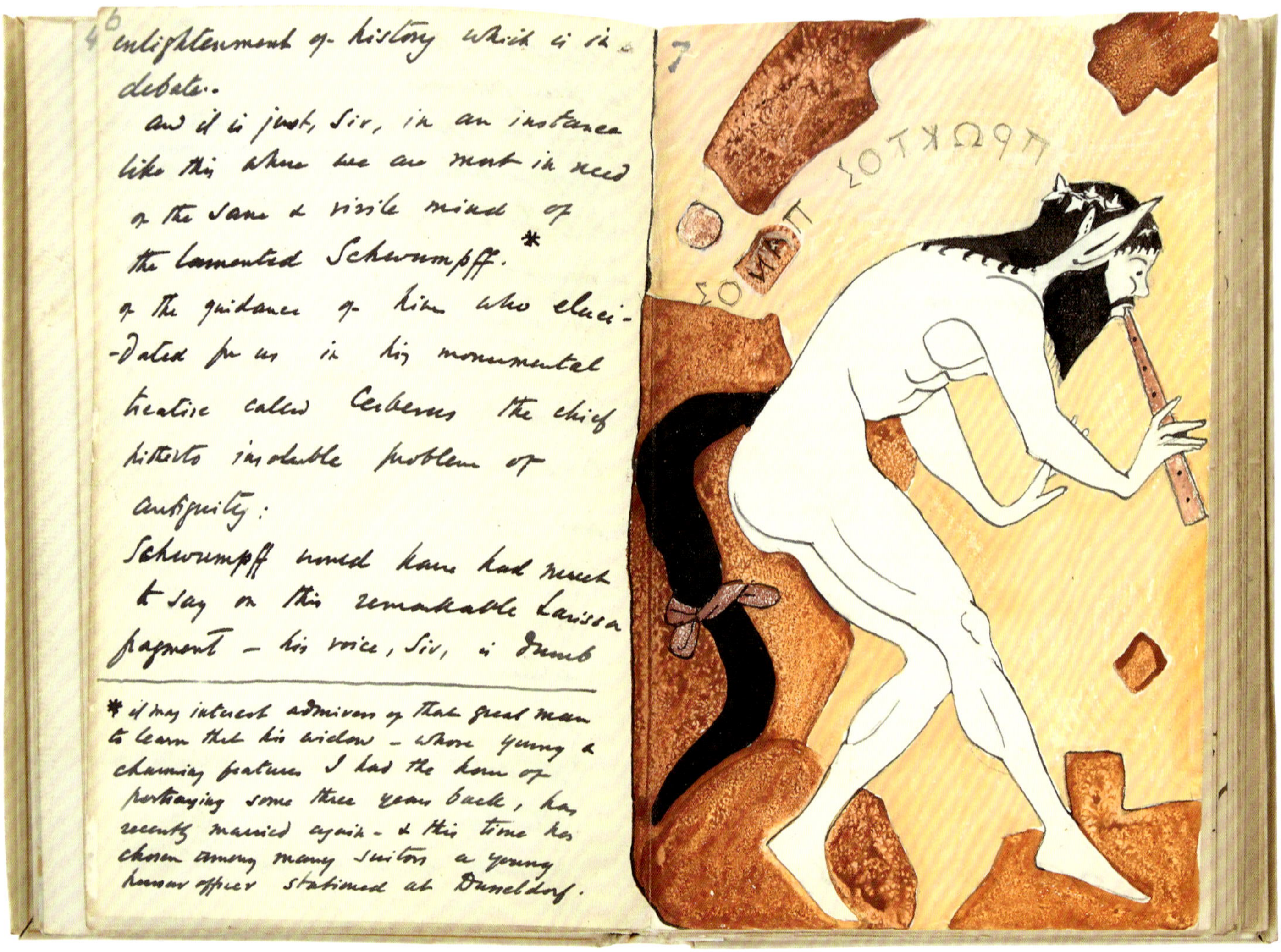
6 enlightenment of history which is in debate.
And it is just, Sir, in an instance like this where we are most in need of the sane & virile mind of the lamented Schwumpff.*
of the guidance of him who elucidated for us in his monumental treatise called Cerberus the chief hitherto insoluble problem of antiquity:
Schwumpff would have had much to say on this remarkable Larissa fragment – his voice, Sir, is dumb

* it may interest admirers of that great man to learn that his widow – whose young & charming features I had the honour of portraying some three years back, has recently married again – & this time has chosen among many suitors a young hussar officer stationed at Dusseldorf.

7

88
Illustrated Letter to Angela c.1896
Coloured pencil on paper, 18 × 12
Private collection

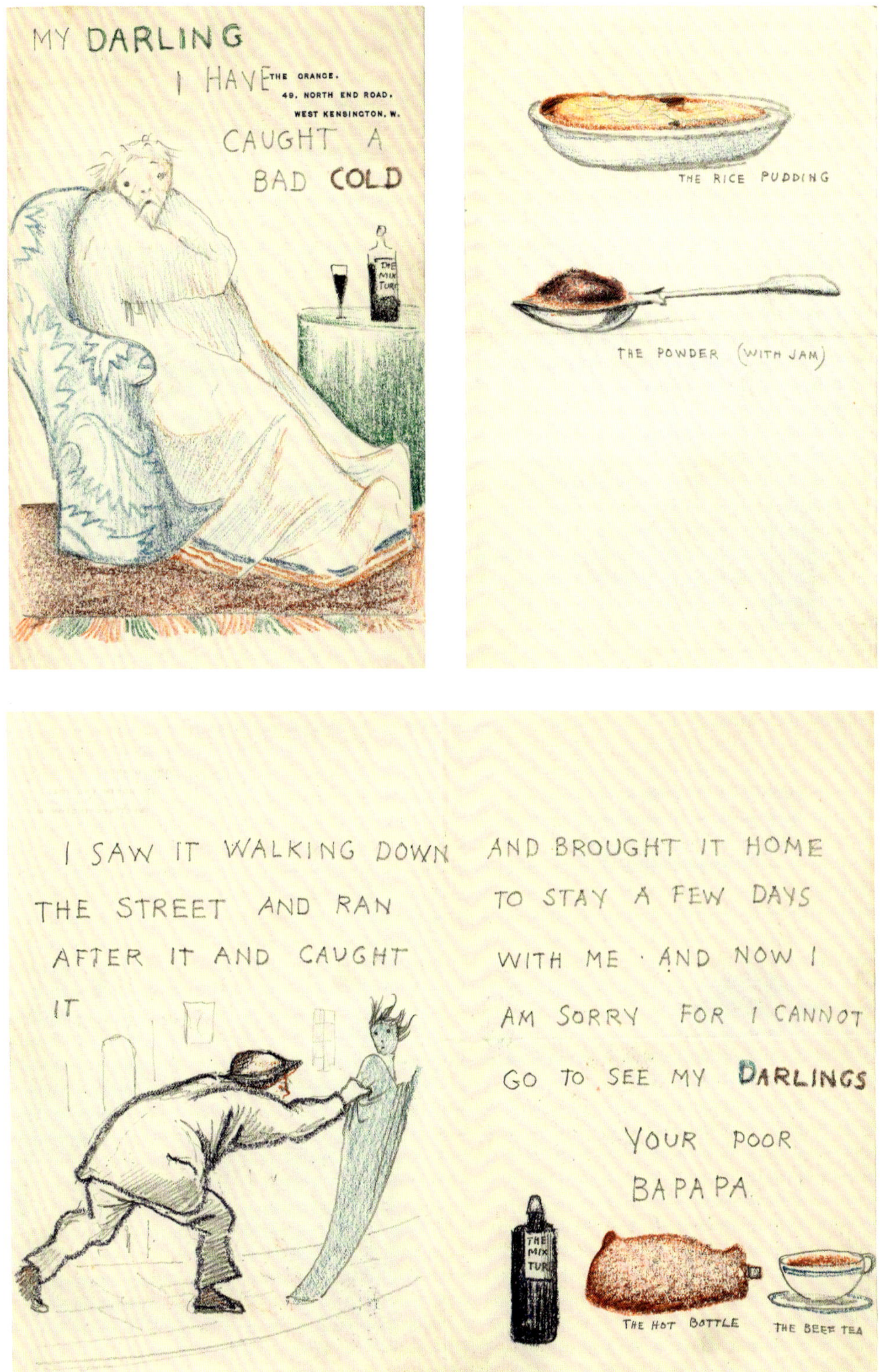

89
Album of illustrated letters to Mrs Gaskell 1893–8
Pen and ink and graphite on writing paper,
41.5 × 31 (album closed)
The Ashmolean Museum, University of Oxford

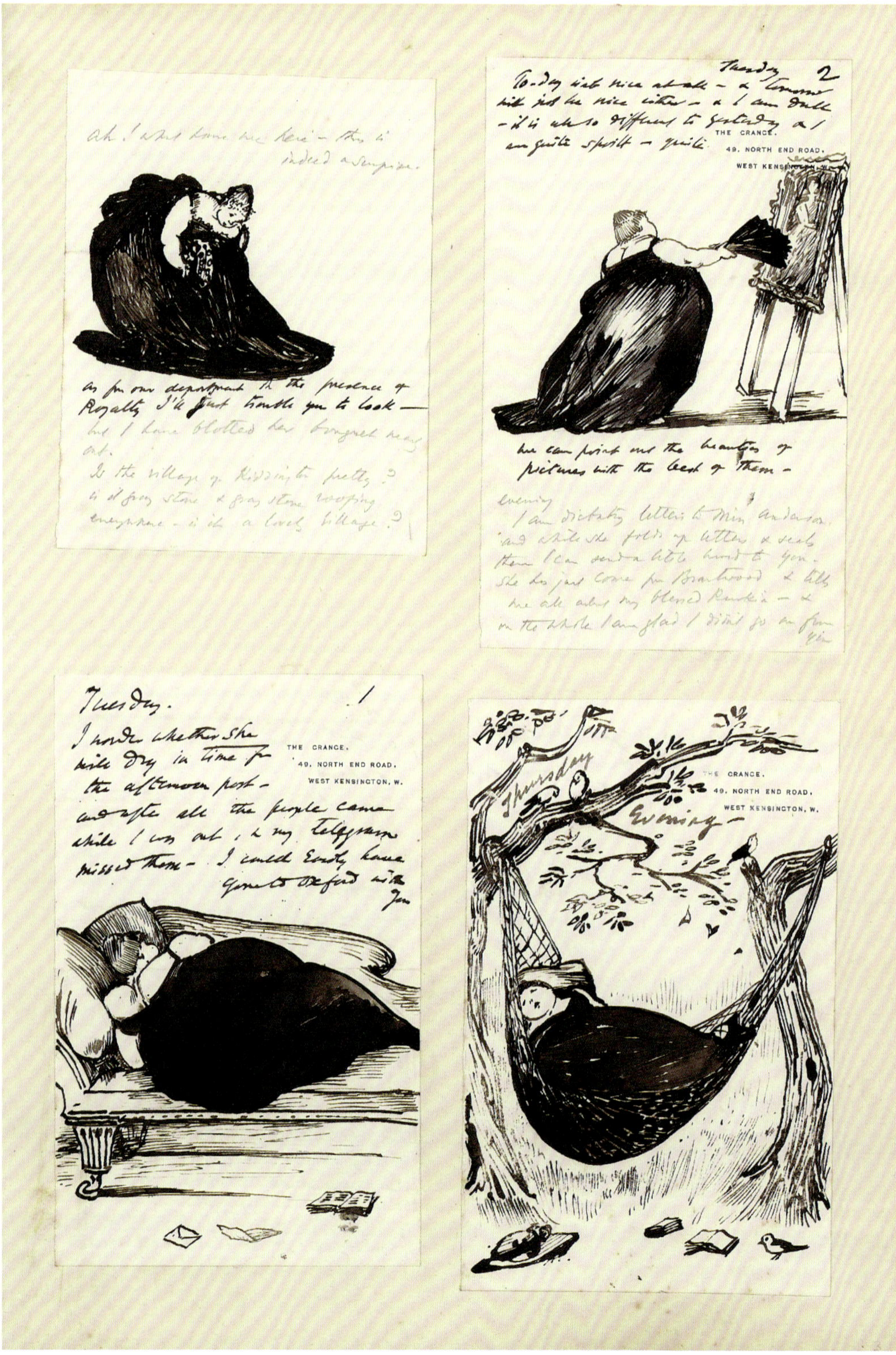

90
Head study for mermaid in
The Depths of the Sea 1886
Graphite on paper, 31.7 × 22.1
National Museums Liverpool,
Lady Lever Art Gallery

mocked or patronised. However, the trajectory of his career – from the awkward to the graceful – is the reverse of that undergone by most famous artists working at the end of the century; it is certainly in opposition to the tendencies of most pre- or early modernist art to reject finished, academic drawing practices and embrace the childlike and untutored. Yet Burne-Jones's 'impassioned imagination' was energetic and experimental in its own way throughout his life. His designs and studies are not merely imitative of old master draughtsmanship but inventive and personal, even troubling. Their surface beauty is a disguise that should alert us to look again, perhaps to discern what Swinburne found in Leonardo – mystery as well as grace.

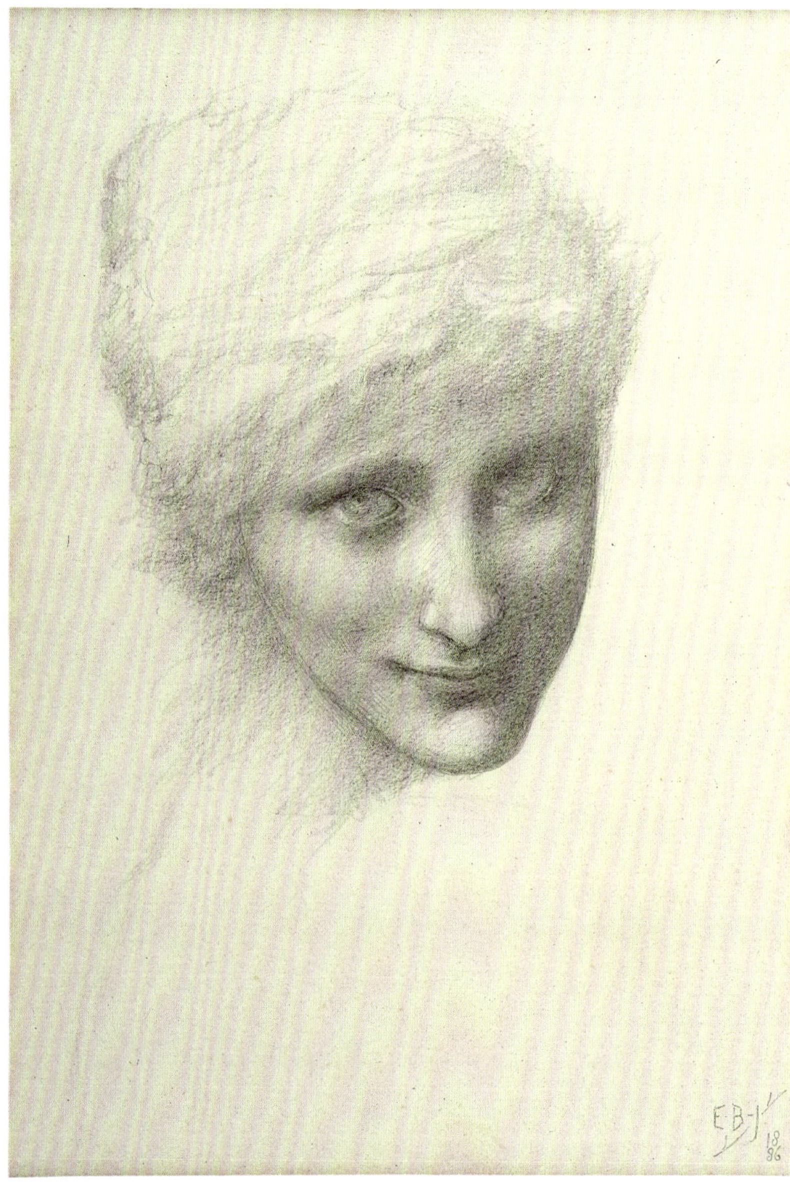

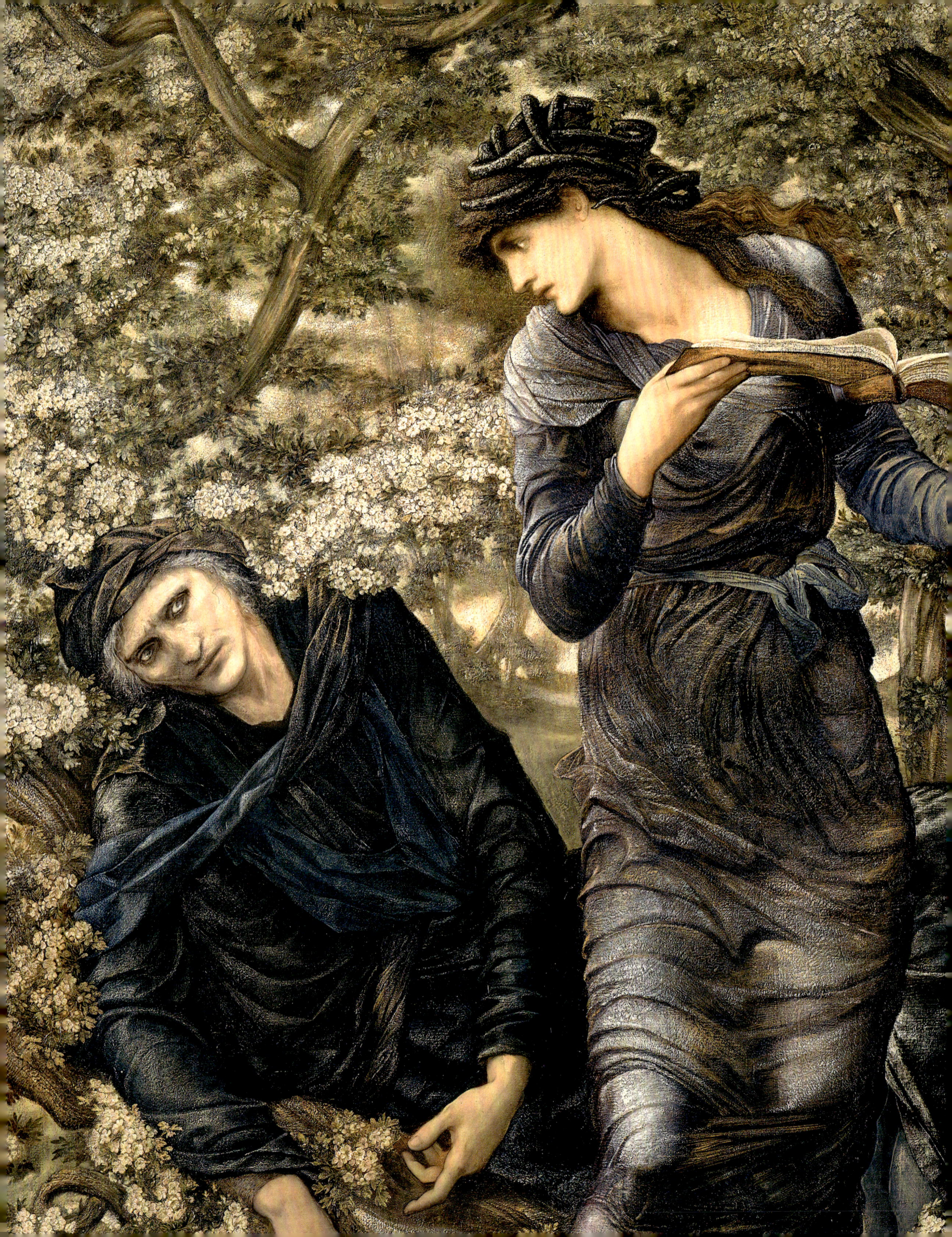

Burne-Jones on Show: Exhibition Pictures, 1877–98

ALISON SMITH

In an age when we expect exhibitions to be carefully selected and curated, the idea of the large-scale group exhibition does not perhaps have the same status or influence it did in the past. During the nineteenth century it was the hub around which so many reputations revolved and was crucial in establishing Burne-Jones's fame despite his contempt for the British exhibition scene as epitomised by the Royal Academy. He may have associated this institution with the mercantile bourgeois culture of his upbringing and, given his own connections, saw no need to cultivate the network of patronage the Academy was in theory supposed to open up to the aspiring artist. Like Rossetti, Burne-Jones possessed both the self-confidence, or recklessness, needed to go it alone. Indeed, apart from a couple of paintings – *Love among the Ruins* (no.91), shown at the Dudley Gallery in 1873, being the main exception – he exhibited no works in public between his controversial resignation from the Old Water Colour Society in 1870 and his dramatic reappearance at the new Grosvenor Gallery in 1877. This period has been seen as a time of liberation and enormous productivity, during which he worked on a multiplicity of projects without having to worry about deadlines, publicity or audience expectation. Two further visits to Italy in 1871 and 1873 allowed him to consolidate the example of the Renaissance masters who would inspire him for the rest of his life: Botticelli, Mantegna, Signorelli and Michelangelo.

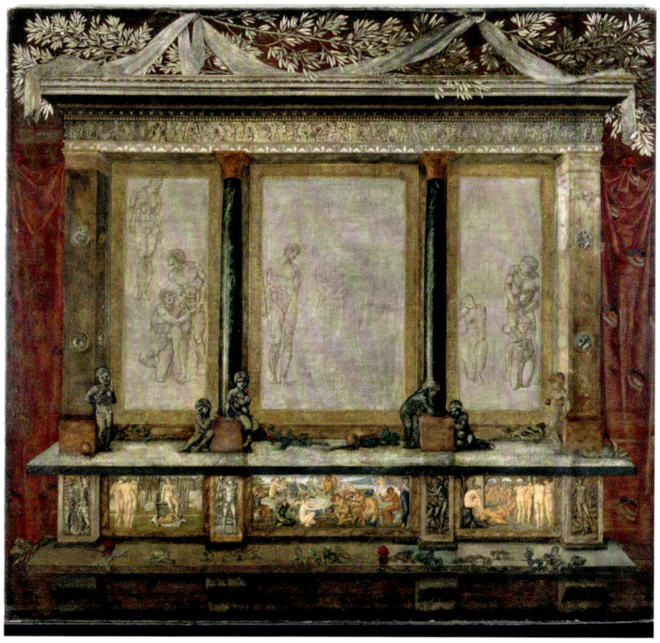

Fig.27 (right)
The Story of Troy 1872–98
Oil on canvas (unfinished)
273 × 294.6
Birmingham Museums and Art Gallery

The Beguiling of Merlin 1872–7 (detail, no.93)

91
Love among the Ruins 1870–3
Watercolour, bodycolour and gum arabic on paper, 96.5 × 152.4
Private collection

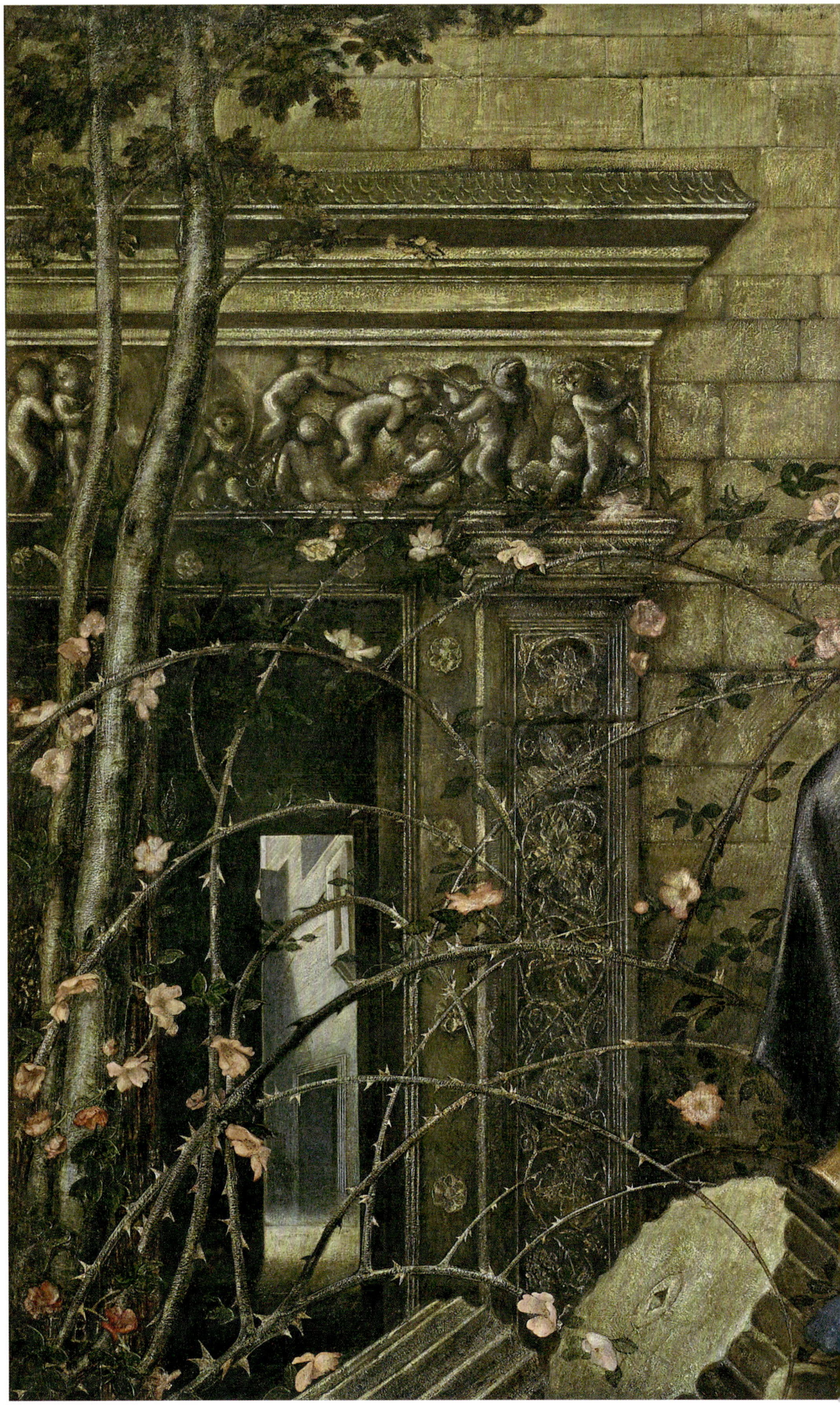

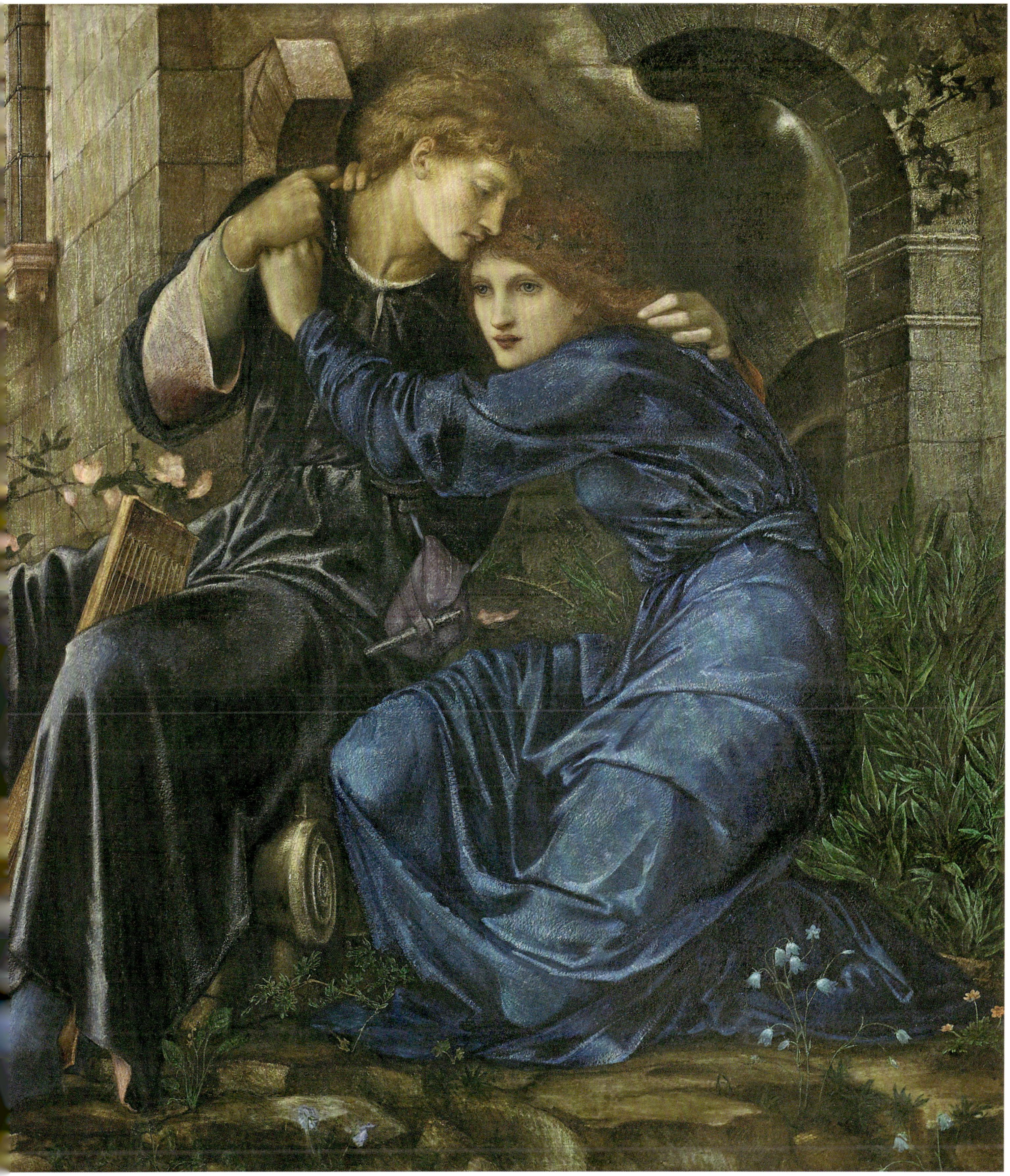

92
The Mill 1870–82
Oil paint on canvas, 90.8 × 197.5
Victoria and Albert Museum

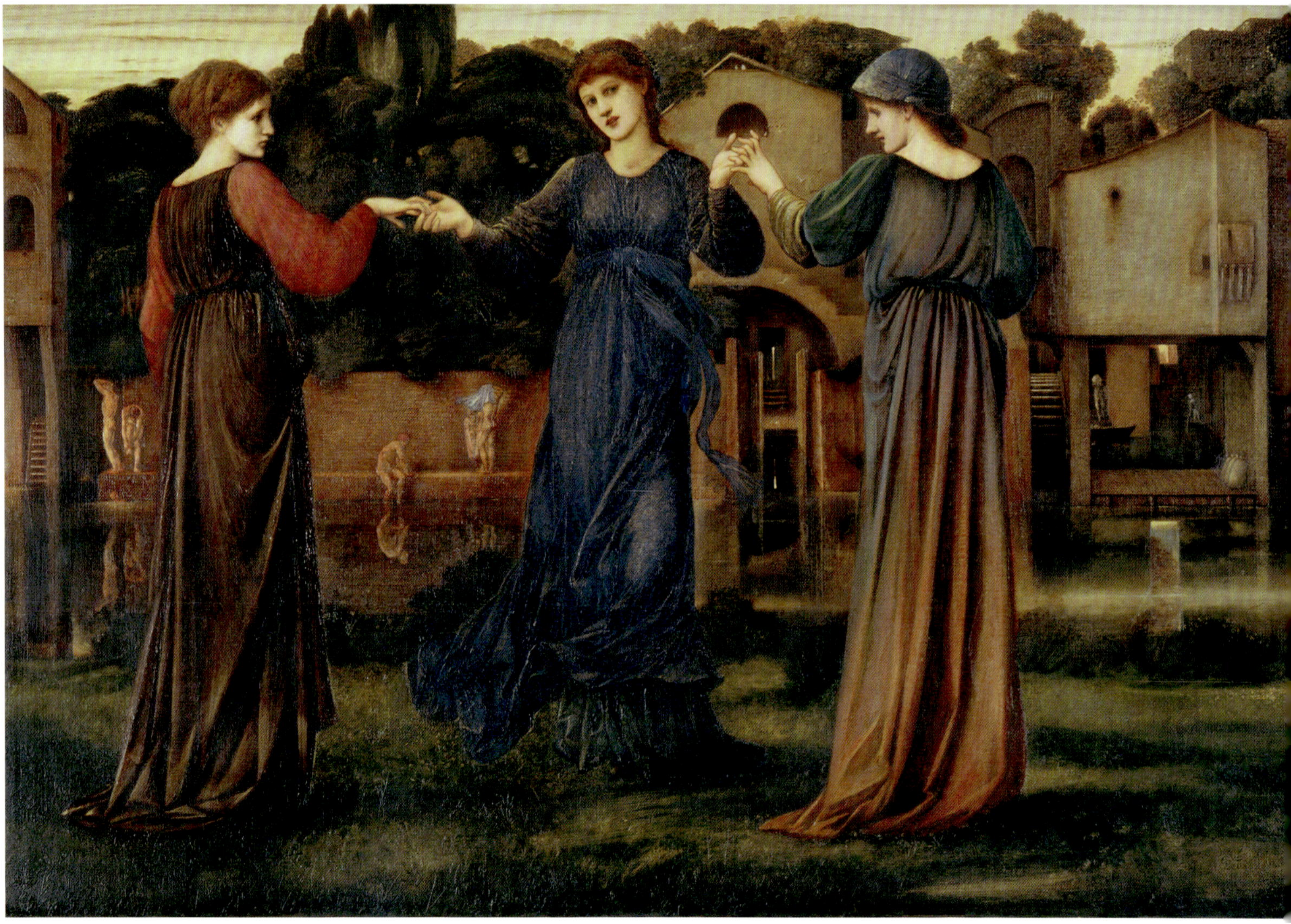

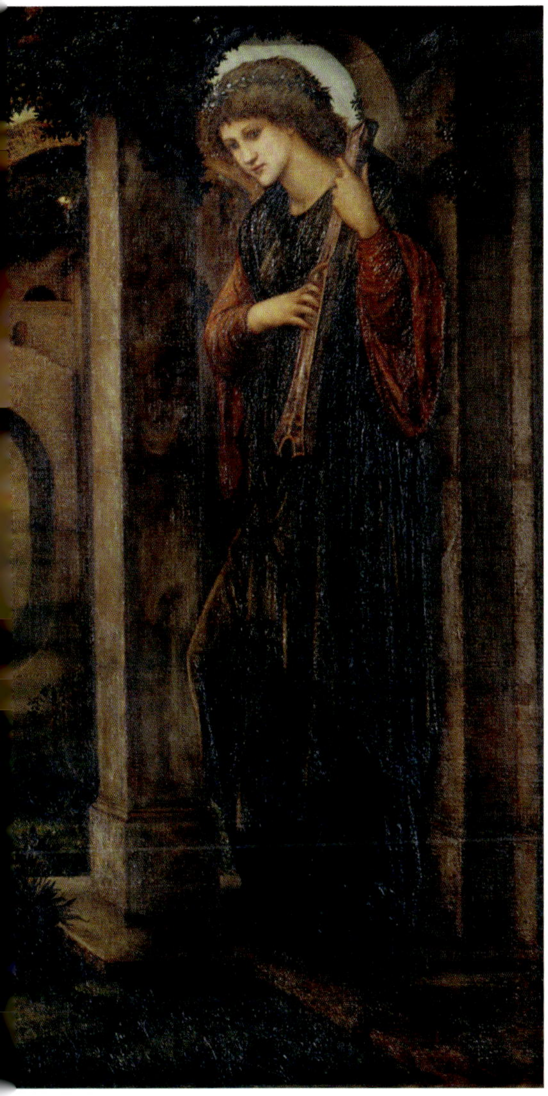

The influence of these artists runs through many of the works presented in this section, informing the nervy and attenuated body types and strong linear rhythms of the designs, as well as Burne-Jones's desire to paint on a large scale and in oil, a shift in emphasis facilitated by the large studio space available to him at the Grange, then isolated on the outskirts of London in Fulham.

During these years he saw less of Ruskin and Rossetti, falling out with the former in 1871 regarding differences of opinion over Michelangelo, and he was to see little of Rossetti following the latter's illness of 1872. Instead he became close to George Frederic Watts, another cultish outsider, similarly absorbed in his own projects regardless of public interest. Trusting in his own vision, Burne-Jones embarked on a number of ambitious unfinished schemes, including the *Troy Triptych* (fig.27), a vast and complex amalgamation of myth and allegorical narrative. Many of his greatest paintings were started at this time, including *The Mill* (begun in 1870), *The Beguiling of Merlin* (begun 1873–4), *Laus Veneris* (begun 1873–5), *The Golden Stairs* (designed 1872, painted 1876–80) and *The Wheel of Fortune*, initially conceived as one of four predella scenes in the *Troy Triptych* and worked on between 1875 and 1883.

In living what Henry James called 'a complete studio existence with doors and windows closed to the outside world', Burne-Jones was dependent for his livelihood on the income he earned through Morris & Co. and from devoted patrons such as William Graham, who, all too aware of 'the unmercenary spirit' with which his friend worked, was willing to spend a thousand pounds or more on a picture and to wait patiently until it was delivered.[1] Having sustained the artist during his self-imposed exile, his small circle of supporters were also partly responsible for his return to the exhibition stage. This happened in 1877 when Burne-Jones was invited to show eight pictures at the Grosvenor Gallery in New Bond Street, established that year as an alternative to the Royal Academy by the aristocratic connoisseur Sir Coutts Lindsay, with his wife Lady Blanche (a Rothschild) providing the essential backing. Setting itself apart from the mainstream exhibiting societies, the Grosvenor was a more private organisation that defined itself in terms of distinction. In contrast to the Academy, where pictures were jammed together in tiers, the Grosvenor aimed at a more aesthetic hang, isolating works in order to foreground the ideal of 'art for art's sake', upheld by the progressive artists whose work was selected for display by Lindsay's deputies, Sir Charles Hallé and the writer and critic Joseph Comyns Carr. Like Burne-Jones, most of these artists were inspired by Italian Renaissance culture to fashion an ideal that emphasised sensory experience and poetic feeling above prosaic naturalism and narrative. The Grosvenor promoted this exclusive group to market its own rarefied identity. Each painter's works were hung together with plenty of space around them on a rich damask background. Burne-Jones's were displayed on scarlet (rather to his consternation) in the west gallery, the main room on the first floor. With their unusual elongated horizontal and vertical formats, cold matt surfaces, sinuous rhythms and strange poetic subjects, these shone out among the other exhibits, projecting him into the limelight as the leader of a new aesthetic sensibility in British art. 'Mr. Burne-Jones stands forward both as a great inventive genius and as one of the most complete masters, not, in all instances, of the grammatical, but of the expressive, the designing, the combining, the characterising part of draughtsmanship', pronounced the critic Sidney Colvin, Burne-Jones's main champion at the time, acknowledging the fruits gained from the artist's years in hibernation.[2] From this point on the Grosvenor became key to Burne-Jones's success: the annual exhibitions forced him to bring his ideas to completion, and once installed on the gallery walls, his paintings demanded attention, as the German critic Richard Muther recalled: 'There was a cult of Burne-Jones at the Grosvenor Gallery, as there is a cult of Wagner at Bayreuth. One had to work one's way gradually through the crowd to see his pictures, which always occupied the place of honour in the principal room of the gallery.'[3]

Key among the pictures shown at the first Grosvenor exhibition was *The Beguiling of Merlin*, painted for Frederick Leyland, and a reprise of the earlier *Merlin and Nimue* (no.20), with the snake-crowned Nimue shown enchanting Merlin with his own sorcery by binding him into a hawthorn tree in the forest of Brocéliande in Brittany. Here the theme of Merlin's helplessness and entrapment is conveyed by the serpentine rhythms of the drapery and tree branches that literally and metaphorically imprison the wizard and deprive him of his power; his drooping hands and glassy-eyed demeanour reinforce the sense of paralysis and drug-induced stupor. Like so many of Burne-Jones's works to date, this is a painting about power relations in which a male protagonist falls victim to a hidden threatening female power, but here the drama is relayed through more abstract means with the faces and hands standing out against the flatness of the bodies and extreme linearity of the design, like panes in a stained-glass window. By finding a striking visual language to capture the ebb and flow of magic, the picture caught the imagination and was praised both for its bold design and subtle poetic conception.

The Beguiling of Merlin was the first of the artist's works to be shown on the Continent, initially in the form of Adolfe Lalauze's engraving that accompanied Comyns Carr's article in *L'Art* extolling Burne-Jones as a painter of great intensity and imagination, with the original painting appearing alongside *Love among the Ruins* at the Exposition Universelle of 1878.[4] This was just the start of what was to be a stellar rise to fame. In 1878 Burne-Jones was represented by eleven works at the Grosvenor, this time hung on the artist's preferred colour, a dull green, such was his sway over the institution. One of the highlights was *Laus Veneris* (no.94), painted for William Graham as a larger version of an earlier watercolour on the same theme.The oil is a densely wrought visualisation of the eponymous poem by Swinburne, whose controversial 1866 *Poems and Ballads*, in which it first appears, had been dedicated to Burne-Jones. A group of musicians prepare to entertain Venus as she languidly awaits the knight Tannhäuser.[5] As an elaborate synthesis of the decorative and fine arts, music and poetry, the picture overwhelms the eye with its rich saturated colour, indented surface texture and near-literal rendition of objects, from the busy Venus-themed tapestries on the wall to the convoluted forms of the metalwork music-stand with chimes in the foreground. The compression of forms into parallel horizontal bands is alleviated by the mere suggestion of perspective in the window frame and the objects scattered across the floor, creating a lavish claustrophobic effect that echoes the steamy hothouse atmosphere conjured by Swinburne in his verse. And like the latter, it was too much for conventional taste. The critic Frederick Wedmore thought the figure of Venus was unwholesome in the extreme, noting with disapproval: 'It is a soul that has known strange tortures: a body that has writhed with every impulse of sickness instead of health.'[6]

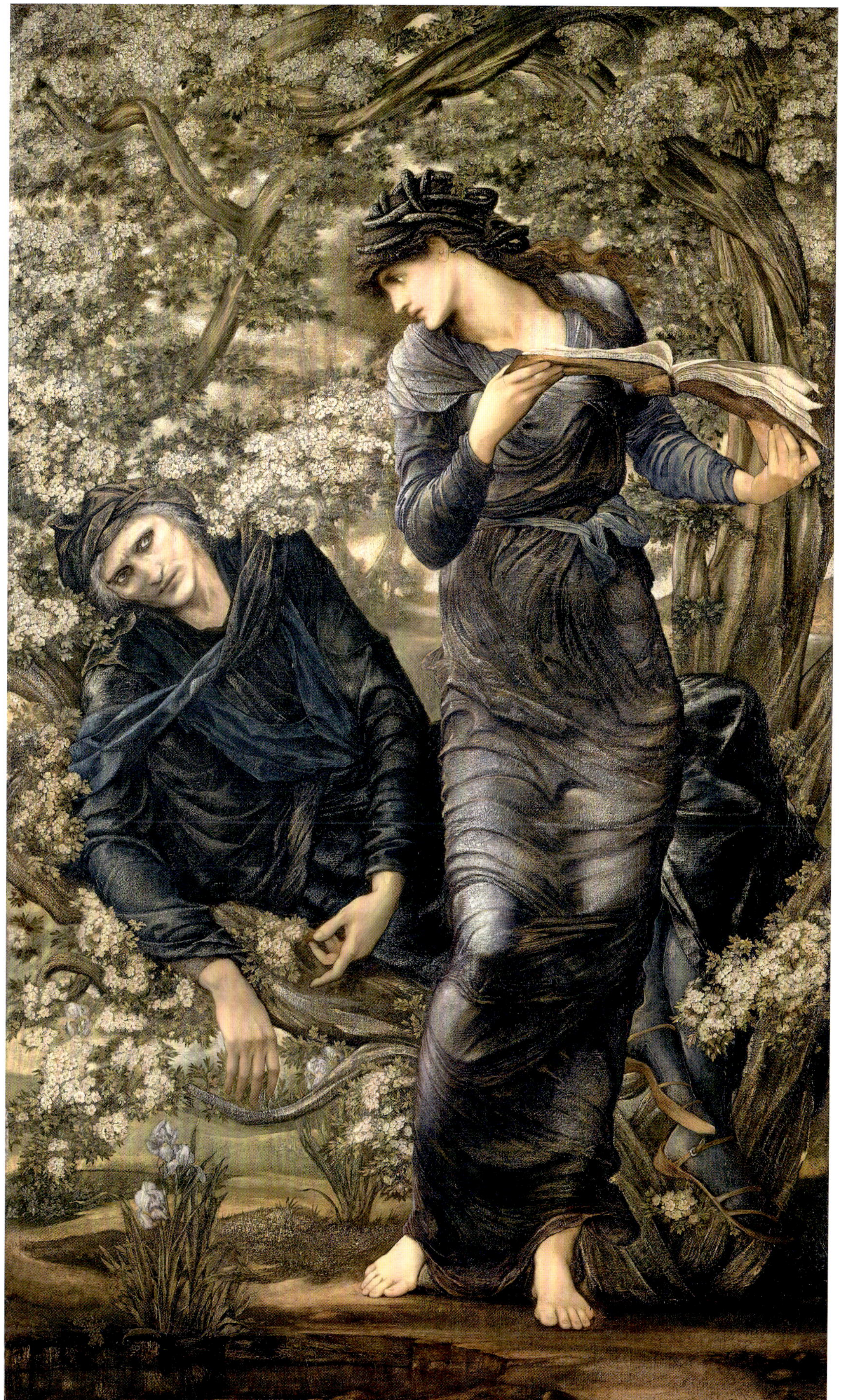

93
The Beguiling of Merlin 1872–7
Oil paint on canvas, 186 × 111
National Museums Liverpool,
Lady Lever Art Gallery

94
Laus Veneris 1873–8
Oil paint on canvas, 119.4 × 180.3
Laing Art Gallery (Tyne & Wear
Archives & Museums)

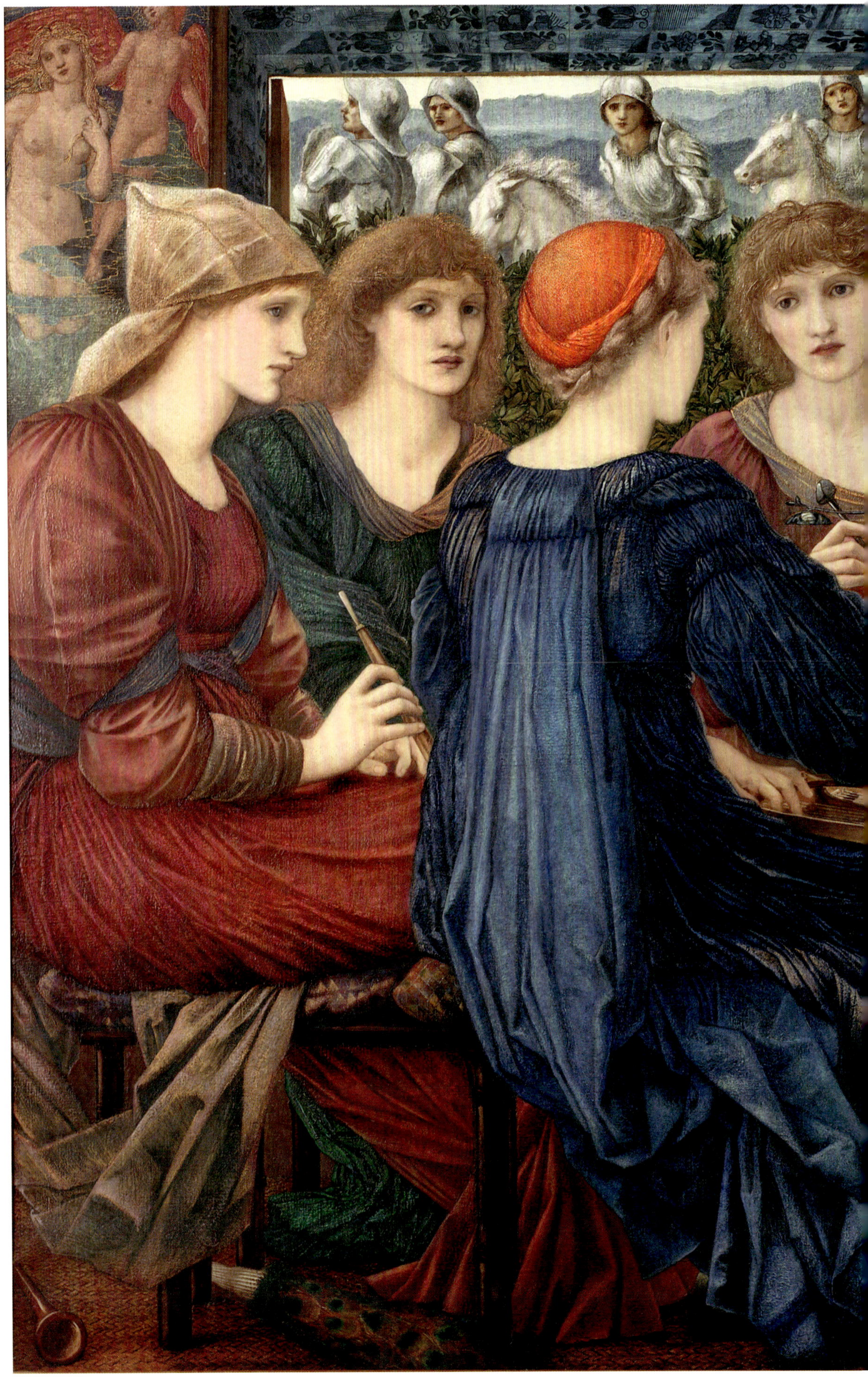

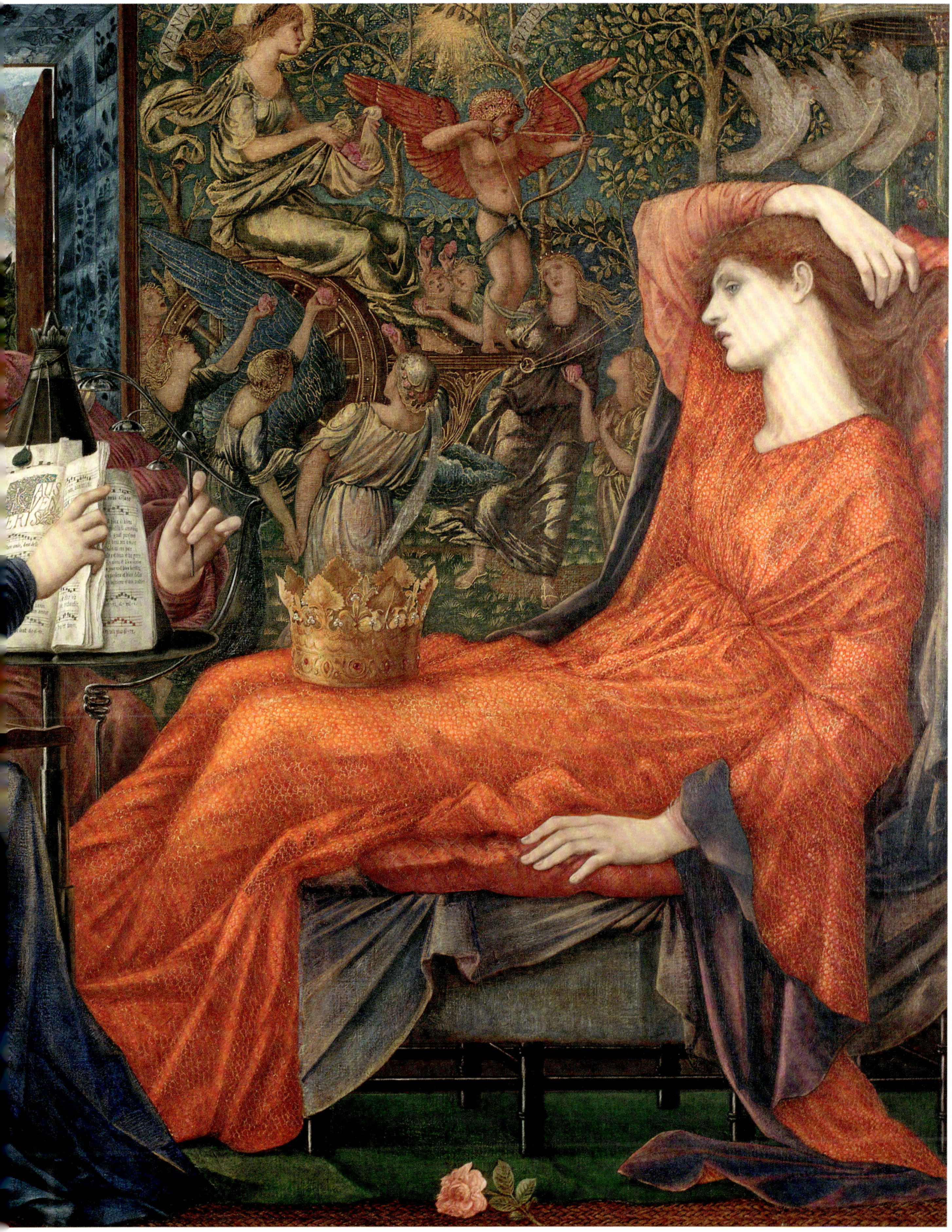

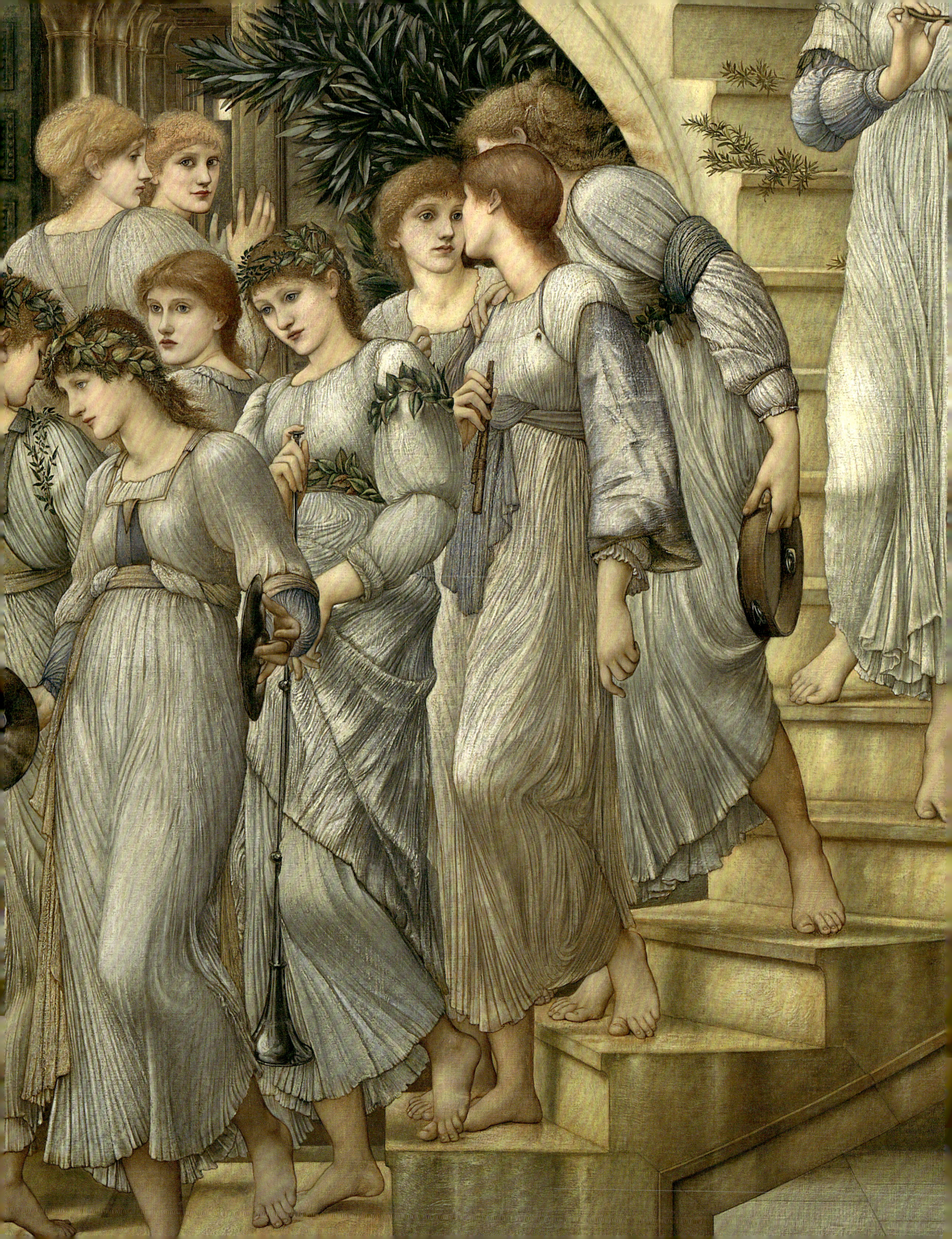

95
The Golden Stairs 1880
Oil paint on canvas, 269.2 × 116.8
Tate

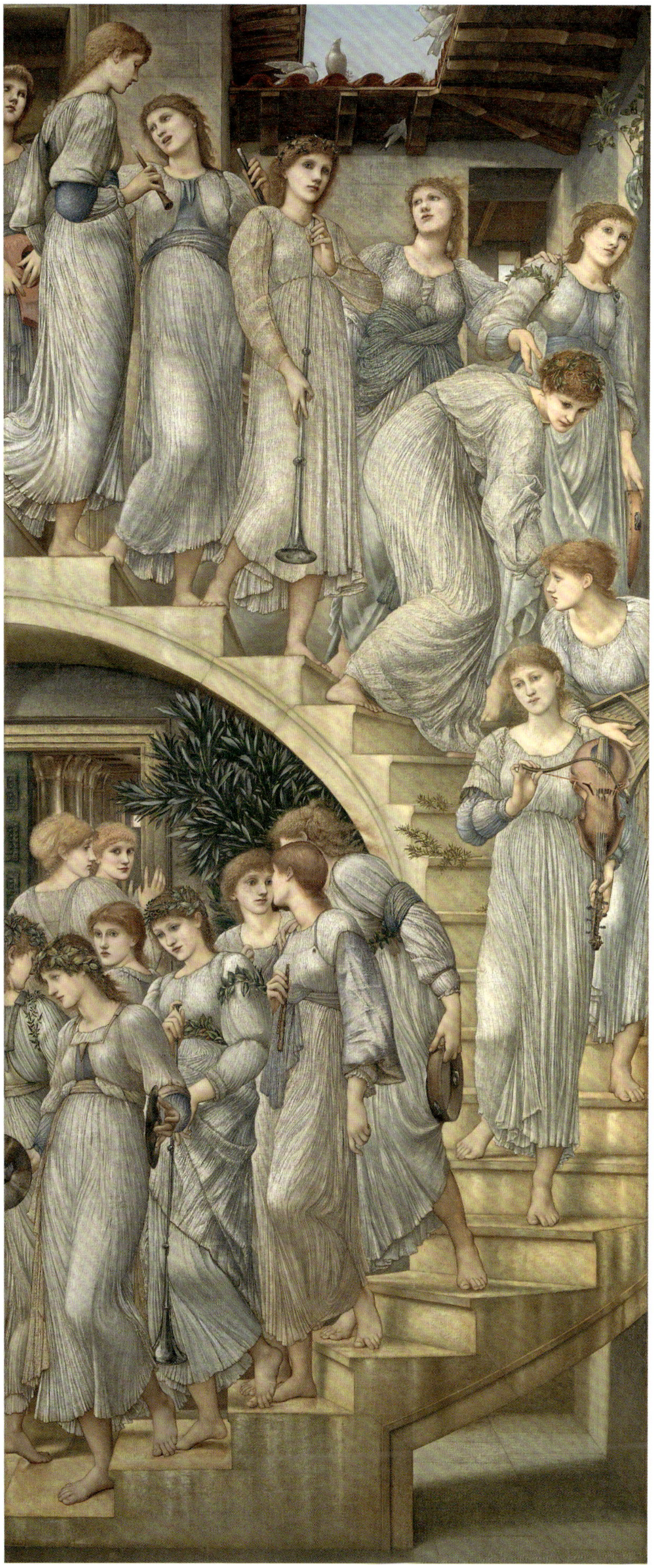

Burne-Jones struck a somewhat cerebral note at the Grosvenor in 1880 with *The Golden Stairs* – a refined Botticelli-inspired composition in a cool-silver colour key, in which the descending movement of music-playing maidens conveys a dream-like feeling of harmony and repose. The sheer subtlety and ambition of the design, not to mention the appearance of many artistic and well-connected women in it, gave it the cachet of being the image par excellence that encapsulated the spiritualised beauty of the aesthetic movement and the 'liberal dreaminess' upheld by the artist's main patrons and supporters, the 'Souls'.[7] It was parodied (most famously in Gilbert and Sullivan's 1881 comic opera *Patience* as well as in *Punch*) and adapted by artists across the world, from Bombay to Krakow.[8] Such was Burne-Jones's reputation by this time that he could afford not to exhibit in 1881, leading Henry James to comment 'a Grosvenor without Mr Burne-Jones is a *Hamlet* with Hamlet left out'.[9] He returned the following year with nine pictures including *The Tree of Forgiveness* (no.96) and *The Mill* (no.92). The former is a muscular Michelangelesque reworking of *Phyllis and Demophoön* (no.25), in which the convoluted 'art nouveau' rhythms of drapery and hair intensify Phyllis's passionate embrace as she bursts out of the tree to grasp the startled Demophoön, while the latter is a mood picture that evokes a wistful feeling for a lost past with its mysterious labyrinthine architecture, autumnal palette and limpid reflections, features that anticipate the inward-looking art of the European symbolists, notably Fernand Khnopff, the artist's main champion on the Continent.

The Wheel of Fortune (no.97) appeared at the Grosvenor in 1883. This is a tensely compartmentalised design with a vertiginous passage of perspective in which the colossal figure of Fortune, clad in tortuous metallic Mantegna-like drapes, is shown slowly turning a wheel on which the straining Michelangelesque bodies of a slave, king and poet lie suspended. In reworking a medieval *vanitas* emblem, the picture strikes a sombre, even political note, with the foot of the slave pressing down on the head of the king, paving the way for the painting that came to exemplify the artist's belief in the redemptive power of art, *King Cophetua and the Beggar Maid* (no.98). Inspired by an Elizabethan ballad as reinterpreted by Tennyson, this enormous, elaborately staged composition was shown to great acclaim at the Grosvenor in 1884, and went on to cause a sensation when exhibited at the 1889 Exposition Universelle in Paris, sealing Burne-Jones's reputation on the Continent as the greatest English painter of his time and a republican at heart with its message of love and beauty transcending all material power and wealth. For the critic Maurice Hamel it was a 'mysterious fantasy' that appealed to a sensitive elite, whereas for Robert de la Sizeranne, writing soon after the artist's death, Burne-Jones's dream vision of a social hierarchy in reverse presented a moral, even political corrective to all the worldly goods on display: it was 'the symbolic expression of the Scorn of Wealth', 'the Apotheosis of Poverty', expressing through its worship of beauty the radical idea of 'the revenge of art on life'.[10] The success of *King Cophetua* in Paris won Burne-Jones the respect of French symbolists including Gustave Moreau and Pierre Puvis de Chavannes and led to him being embraced by more liberal exhibiting societies such as the Salon of the Société Nationale des Beaux-Arts on the Champ de Mars. It was through this painting and its dissemination in print form that his work spread out from France and became known all over Europe.[11]

King Cophetua also marked a watershed in Burne-Jones's relationship with the Grosvenor. As Lindsay had become increasingly dependent on commercial

96
The Tree of Forgiveness 1881–2
Oil paint and chalk on canvas, 186 × 111
National Museums Liverpool, Lady Lever Art Gallery

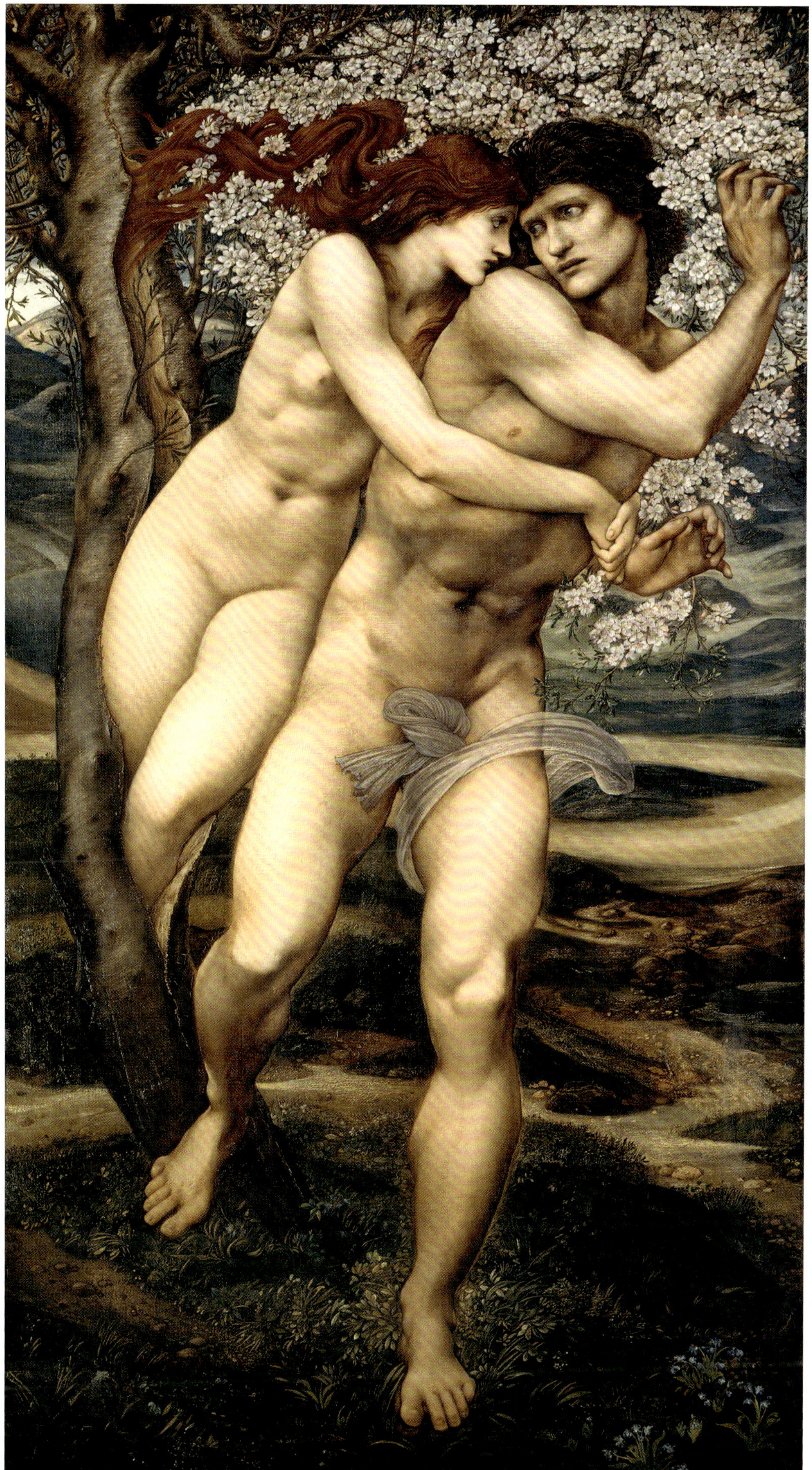

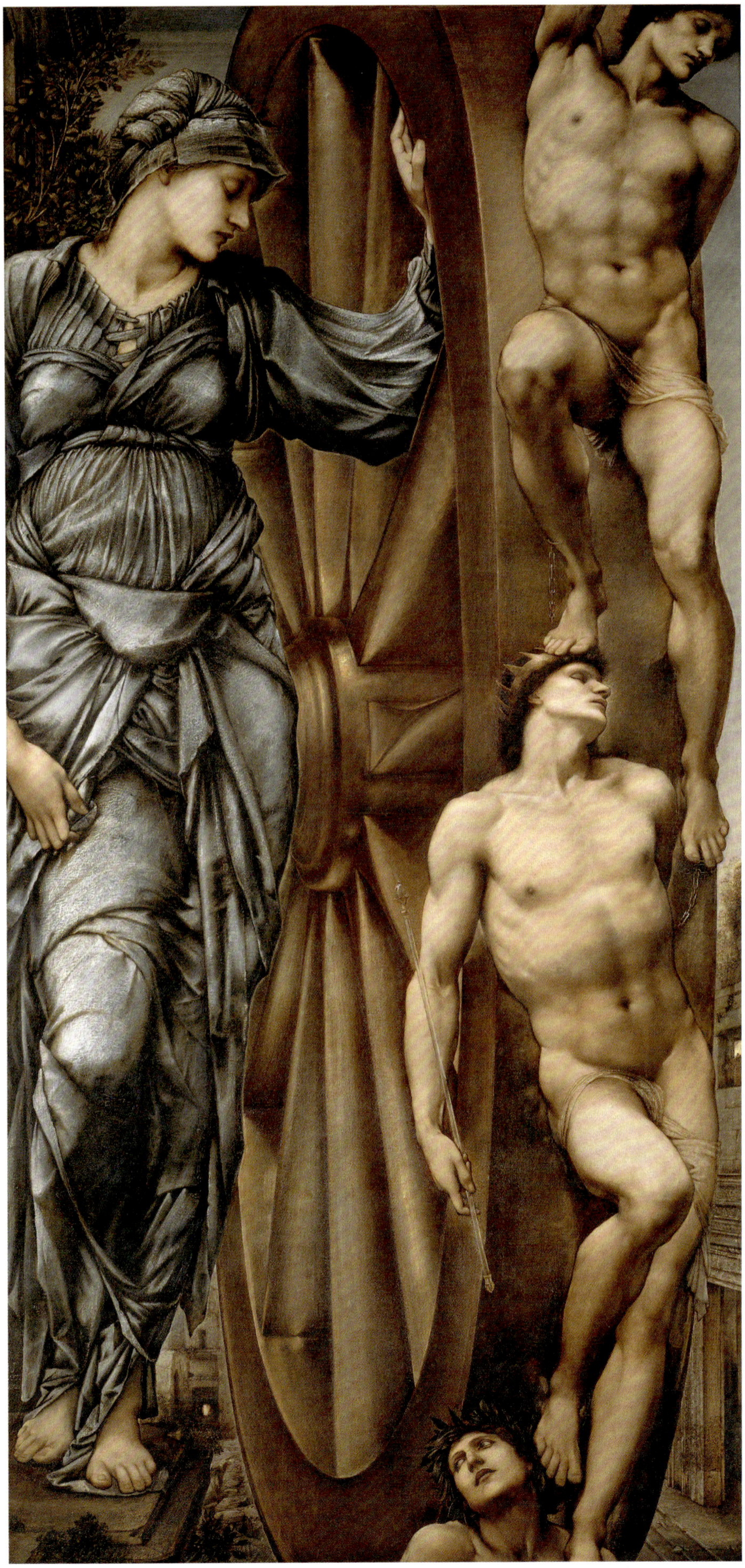

97
The Wheel of Fortune 1883
Oil paint on canvas, 259 × 151.5
Musée d'Orsay, Paris

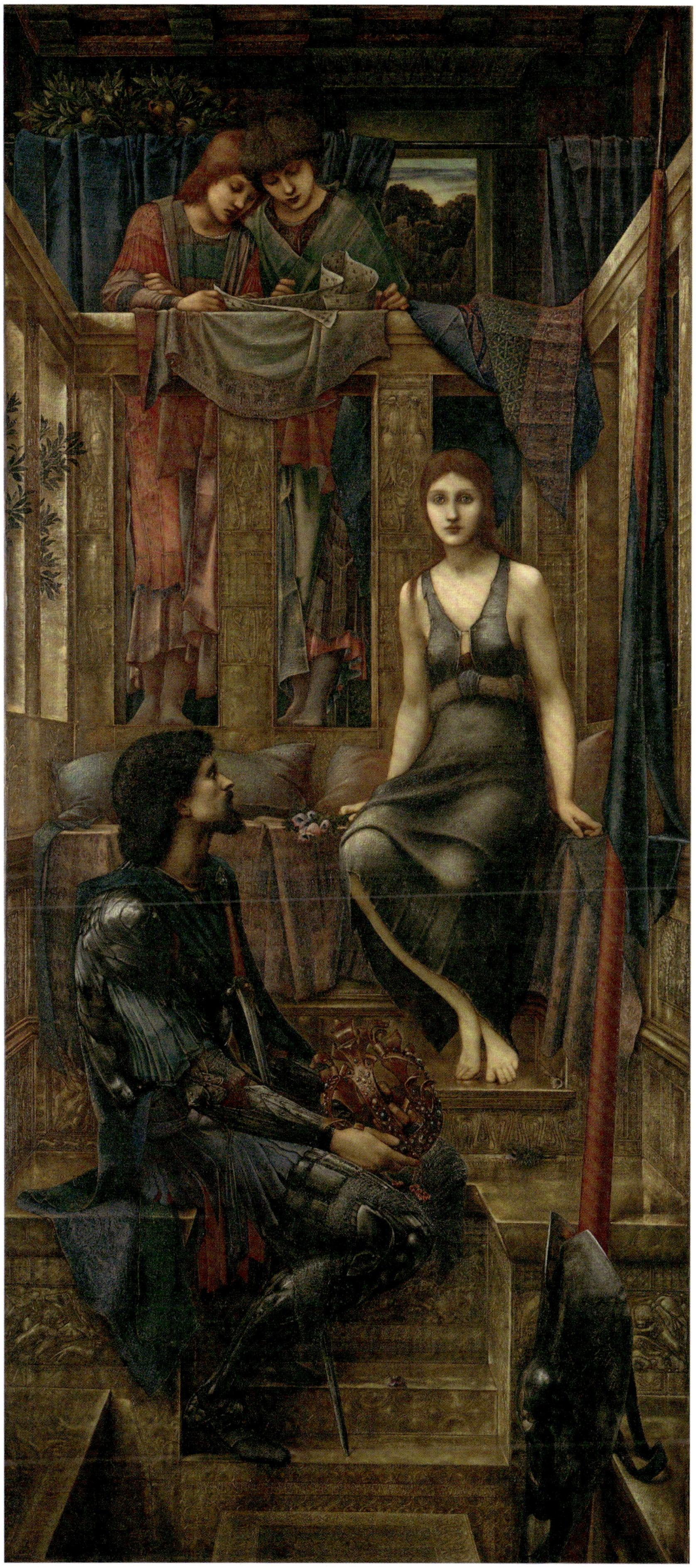

98
King Cophetua and the Beggar Maid 1884
Oil paint on canvas, 293.4 × 135.9
Tate

99
The Morning of the Resurrection 1886
Oil paint on wood, 84.5 × 151.1
Tate

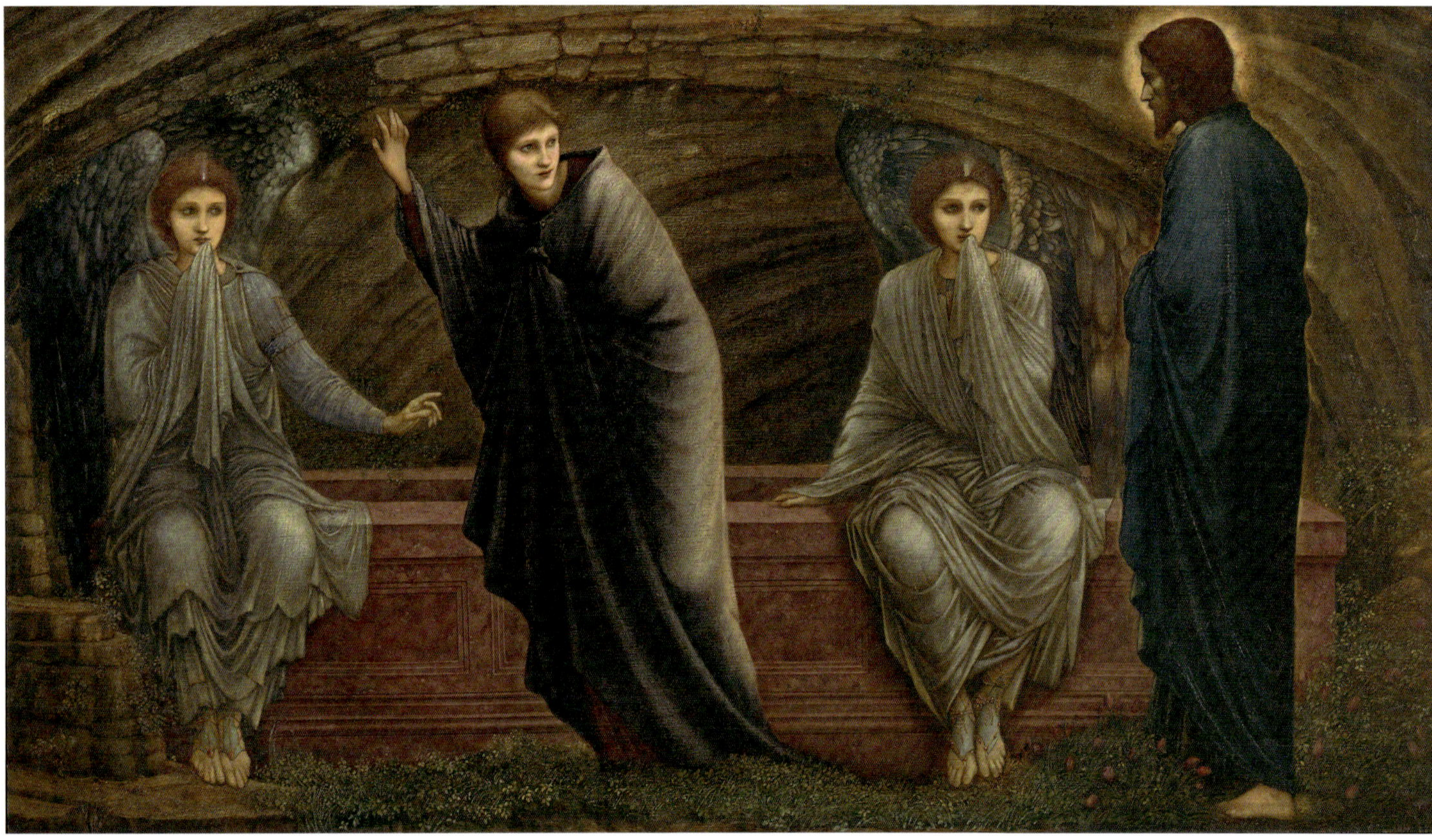

initiatives to keep the gallery afloat following his wife's separation from him in 1882, Burne-Jones's commitment waned. He showed nothing in 1885, asserting his independence the following year by moving away from the lushness of his earlier creations with the muted and spare *Morning of the Resurrection* (no.99), which depicts the penitent Magdalene at the tomb of Christ barely comprehending his resurrection. This was adapted from the panel installed in St Peter's Church, Vere Street, London, in memory of the Christian Socialist, F.D. Maurice, and the only non-Anglo-Catholic church for which Burne-Jones designed an altarpiece (the original is now in a private collection). In 1888 he decided to throw in his lot with Hallé and Comyns Carr when they resigned to form the New Gallery in nearby Regent Street, encouraging other artists to follow and thereby forcing the Grosvenor to close in 1890. The works Burne-Jones exhibited at the New Gallery were to become even more ascetic, signalling a drift towards what has been termed a 'self-absorbed abstraction', with elongated, spiritualised figures draped in heavy Gothic folds in barren settings.[12] Generally shadowy and monochromatic, these sober late works show just how little prepared Burne-Jones was to compromise his vision for critical praise and material gain. *The Dream of Launcelot at the Chapel of the San Graal* (exhibited New Gallery, 1896; no.100) is a dark, mystical picture against which the illuminated bodies of the knight and angel are shrouded in angular, leaden folds

100
The Dream of Launcelot at the Chapel of the San Graal 1895–6
Oil paint on canvas, 138.5 × 169.8
Southampton City Art Gallery

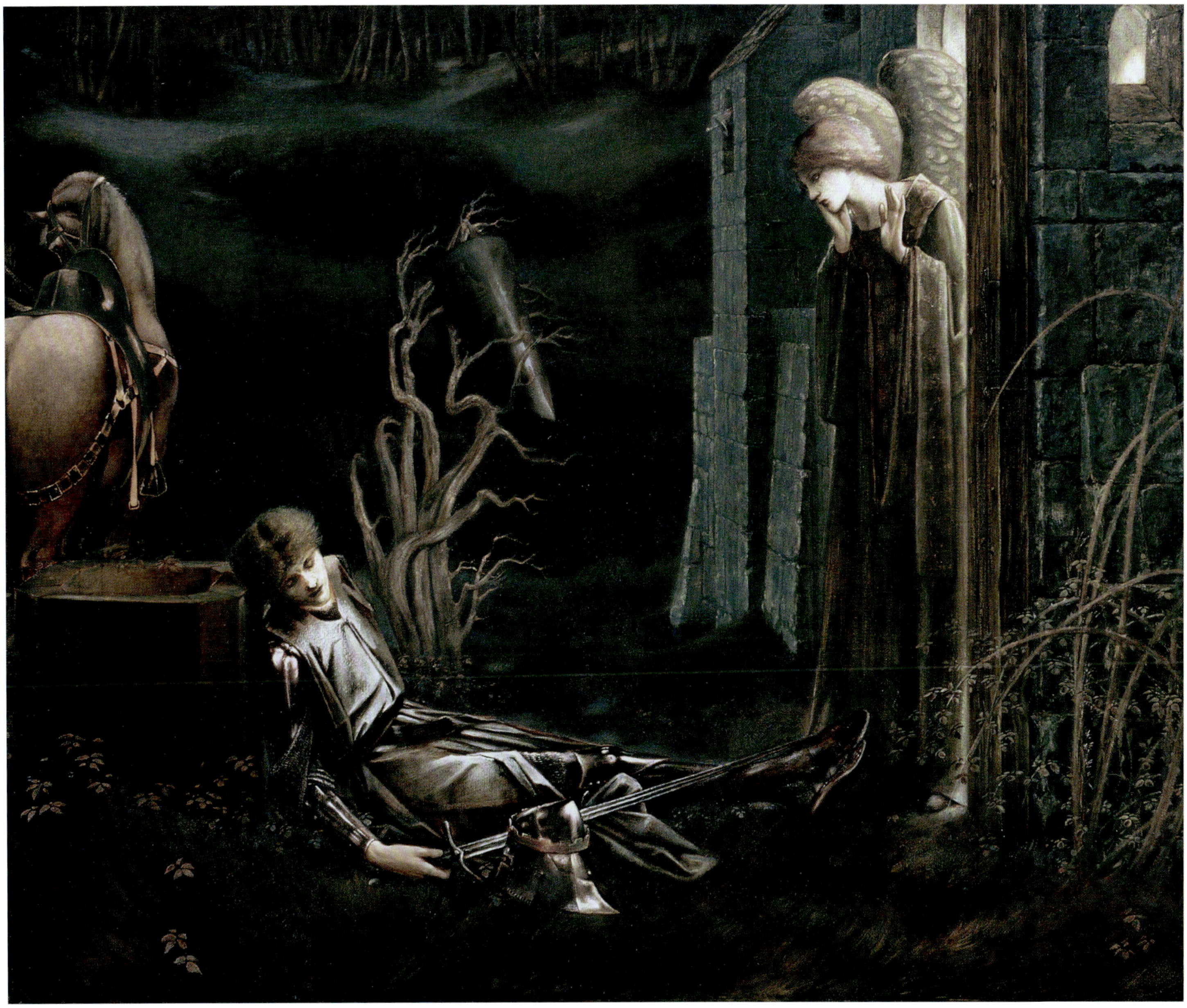

101
Love and the Pilgrim 1877–97
Oil paint on canvas, 157.5 × 304.8
Tate

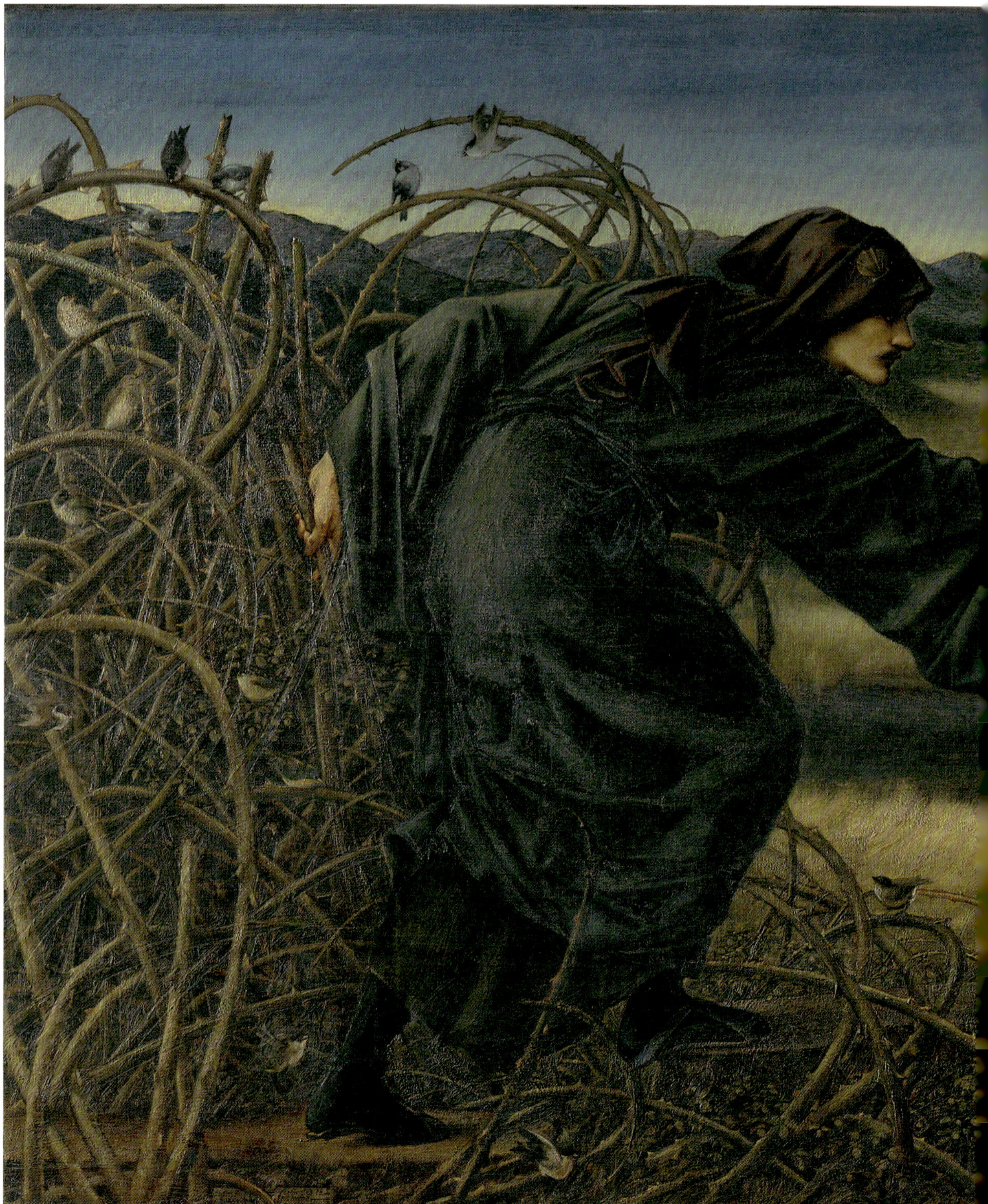

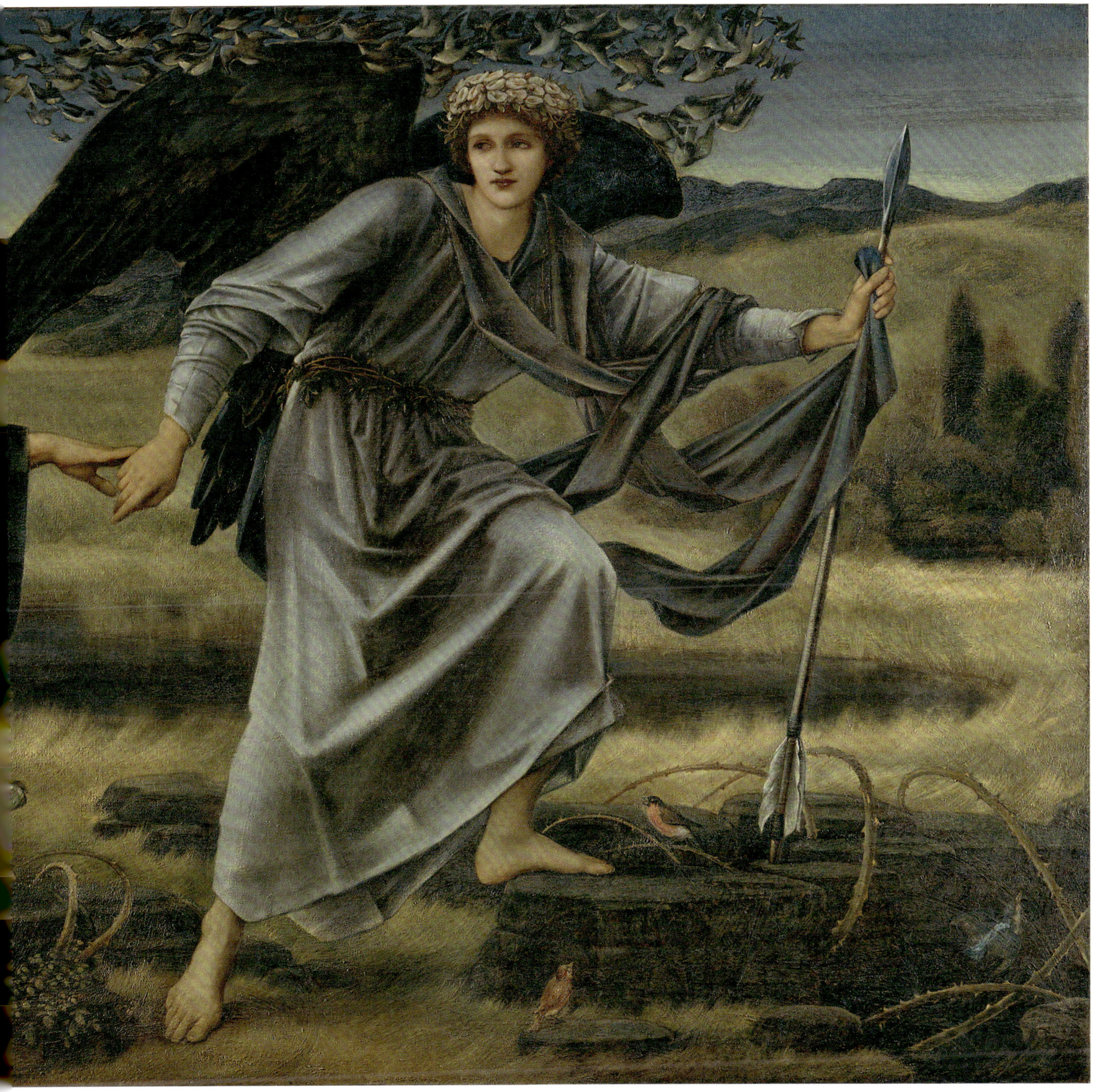

of drapery. The same is true of *Love and the Pilgrim* (no.101), derived from Chaucer's *Romaunt of the Rose* and the artist's last major finished oil, which he exhibited at the New Gallery in 1897. Like the *Dream of Launcelot*, it is stark and austere, the sense of desolation enhanced by the empty pool and barren mountains in the distance. Apart from the birds and hands touching in the centre of the composition, there are few tender elements to relieve the eye from the overarching theme of endurance. Despite hours spent perfecting the details and tonal effects, it did not sell, leading Burne-Jones to reflect in private that his works were now out of sympathy with the new vogue for impressionist art taking hold among collectors.[13]

Such fears have to be set against the high esteem with which he was held both in Britain and abroad at this time. Indeed, as Burne-Jones reached the peak of his fame around 1890, so he had become co-opted into the art establishment, something he found hard to resist even though it departed from the idea he had cultivated from his early years as a *pictor ignotus* working apart from the mainstream. In 1885 he was elected an Associate of the Royal Academy, also accepting in the same year the title of Honorary President of the Royal Birmingham Society of Artists in his home town, and in 1886 he was re-elected to the Old Water Colour Society. In 1892 the New Gallery hosted a retrospective exhibition of his work followed by another just after his death in 1898. In 1886, aged fifty-three, he made what must be one of the most delayed debuts at the Academy with *The Depths of the Sea* (no.102). Here the bodies of two interlocking nude figures plunge to the seabed, their descending movement echoed by the unusual vertical format of the composition. One is alive, smiling at the spectator in a mysterious Leonardo-like manner; the other appears dead, his musculature as taut as the surrounding rocks and his genitalia artificially obscured by the mermaid's arm. It was certainly an outlier amid the medley of other styles displayed on the Academy walls and was to be his only exhibit there: he resigned in 1893 having never been upgraded from associate status. Meanwhile the works Burne-Jones exhibited on the Continent were accompanied by honours: in 1889 he was awarded a first-class medal for *King Cophetua* and also received the Cross of the Légion d'honneur; three years later he was elected a corresponding member of the Académie des Beaux-Arts in Paris. The ultimate accolade came in 1894 when he accepted the offer of a baronetcy from the Queen, becoming Sir Edward Coley Burne-Jones, Bart. By this time William Graham had played a vital intermediary role in maximising the price requested for his major pictures, even intervening to negotiate a higher sum with the Earl of Wharncliffe for *King Cophetua* (to include copyright) and acting as an intermediary with Agnew's over the sale of the *Briar Rose* (nos.123–6).[14] In the final years of Burne-Jones's life, his son Philip became proactive in promoting his father's work, negotiating, for example, an exhibition of Burne-Jones's works at the Georges Petit Gallery in Paris.[15]

Another way in which Burne-Jones's pictures touched a broad audience was through reproductive photographs and prints. Frederick Hollyer's platinotypes and the photogravure reproductions issued by Colnaghi and Agnew's after *King Cophetua* and the *Briar Rose* only increased his reputation abroad stimulating a transnational symbolist aesthetic that radiated out from Britain and France to eastern Europe and beyond.[16] Burne-Jones himself abjured the commercial practice of reproducing works through the methodical means of steel engraving that had fuelled the reputation (and fortunes) of artists such as Millais, Holman Hunt and W.P. Frith, preferring

102
The Depths of the Sea 1886
Oil paint on canvas, 197 × 75
Private collection

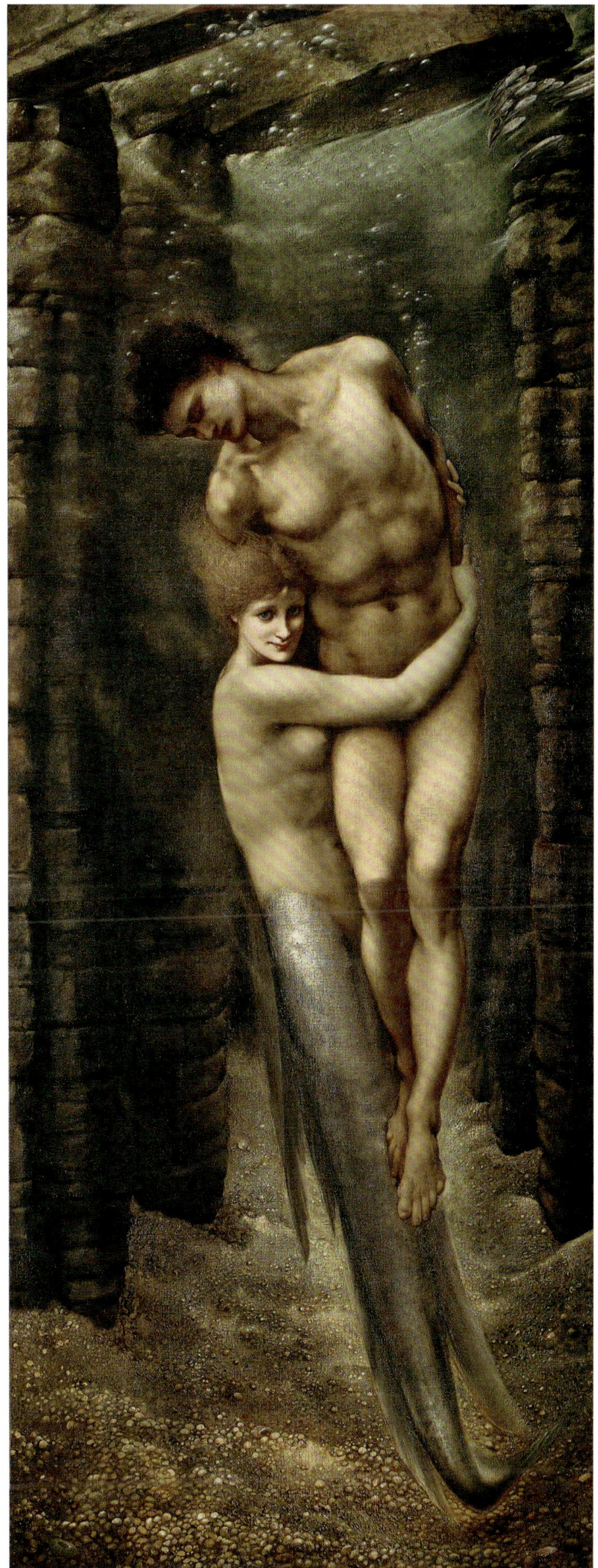

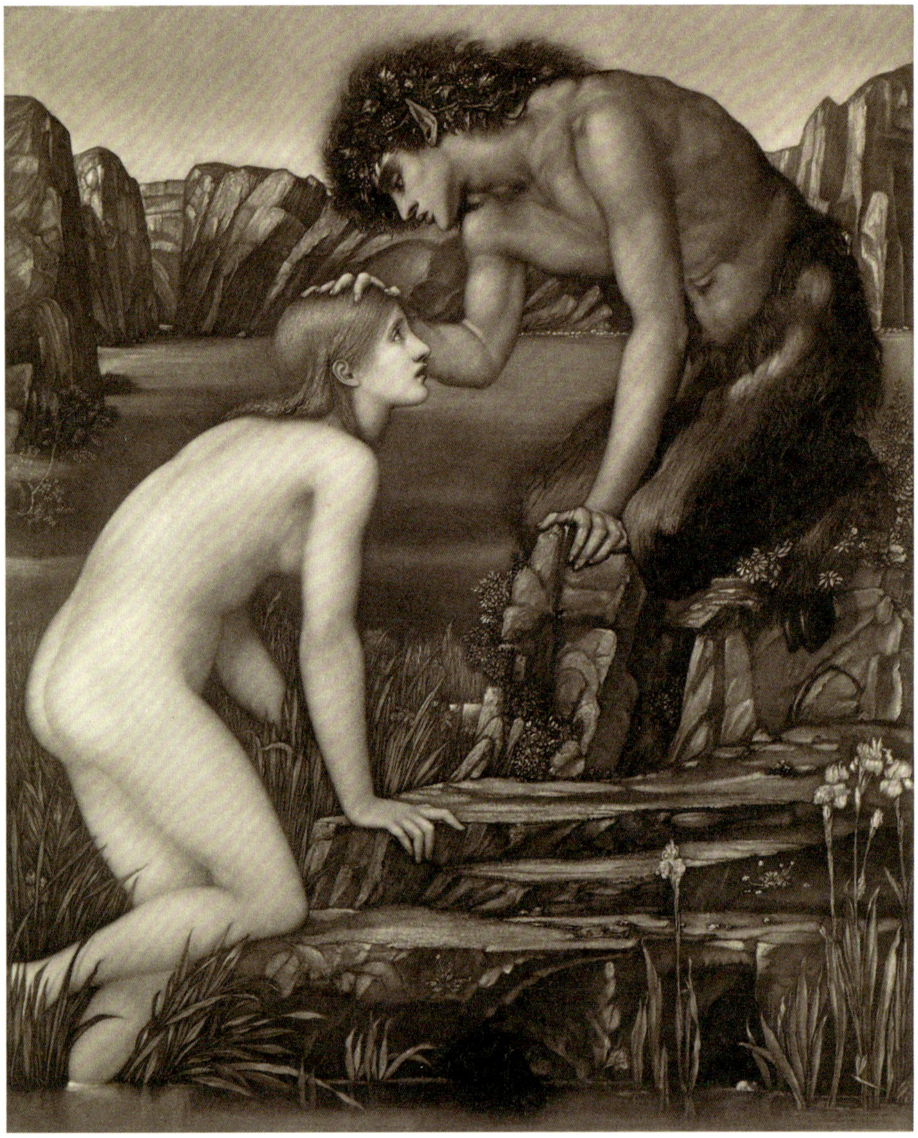

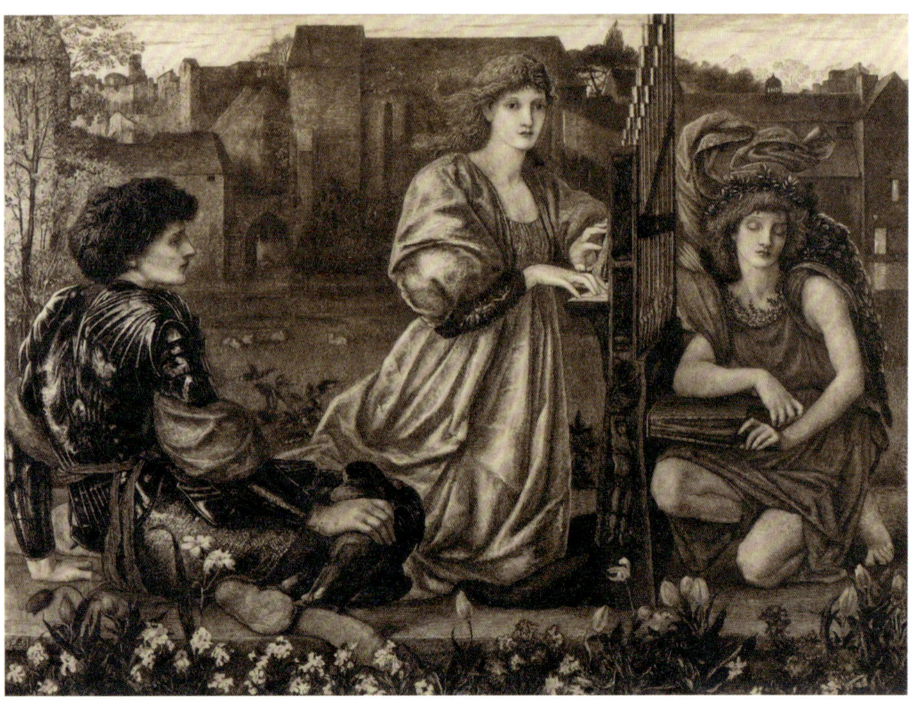

103
CHARLES WILLIAM CAMPBELL
after EDWARD BURNE-JONES
Pan and Psyche 1887
Mezzotint on paper, 35.6 × 29.9
The Maas Gallery

104
ROBERT WALKER MACBETH
after EDWARD BURNE-JONES
Le Chant d'Amour 1896
Etching on vellum, 38.4 × 53
The Maas Gallery

to work with printmakers who could reproduce the spirit of his paintings using the more 'artistic' processes of etching, dry point and mezzotint on copper plates, necessitating a limited print run. He was thrilled with the mezzotint after *Pan and Psyche* (no.103) by Charles William Campbell, published by Dunthorne in the year of the printmaker's untimely death in 1887. By contrast, there was disappointment with Robert Macbeth's etching after *Le Chant d'Amour* (no.104): Burne-Jones described it as 'clumsy' and 'brutal' – 'he can do ploughboys but knights & ladies & gods are far from him'.[17] On the whole he preferred Continental engravers to British ones and found the perfect translator in the Polish printmaker Feliks Stanisław Jasiński, whose six highly refined engravings on vellum, produced between 1894 and 1900 and published by Arthur Tooth & Sons, are reminiscent of Burne-Jones's early meticulously rendered drawings on vellum. Indeed, so entranced was he with Jasiński's fine quality of line and tone that he stipulated an exception be made to the rule of destroying a plate after an edition had been made in the case of Jasiński's copper plate after his *Annunciation* (no.105), which Burne-Jones gave to the V&A as a work of art in its own right. Jasiński's prints did much to establish Burne-Jones's reputation outside Britain as the greatest Pre-Raphaelite and as an essentially black-and-white artist, the absence of colour in the engravings reinforcing the remoteness and perfection of his vision.

In the midst of this adulation, Burne-Jones steered a fine line between passive acquiescence and an equally passive resistance, accepting his due but protesting in private against the 'pompous' and 'pedantic' culture of academies, the 'slave market' mentality of the sale room and shying away from attending exhibitions of his works due to ill health.[18] It may be that he found it difficult to navigate a moral path through the public arena now that the exhibition scene had become so complex, with competing organisational bodies and opportunities overseas, or that he believed his pictures were too personal for public exposure. Viewed as a group, the exhibition paintings do represent something of a paradox in that, although their size invites a public setting, they are essentially hermetic, their meaning not obvious to the viewer. Certainly in a culture where audiences expected pictures to be explained to them, critics found Burne-Jones's works impossible to comprehend, the *Art Journal* describing *The Mill* as 'difficult to understand if, indeed, he means it to be understood', and *The Morning of the Resurrection* to be as much a colour harmony as an illustration of a religious subject.[19] Burne-Jones's preference for having his pictures glazed, which gave them, he maintained, 'a kind of aetherial varnish', added to the overall sense of mystery and distance from the 'people' represented.[20] The same would apply to his habit of communicating *sub rosa* by embedding personal dedications into the fabric of a work, as with the tiny oblation to the 'Soul' member Laura Lyttelon, who died in childbirth, inscribed discreetly at the bottom left-hand corner of *The Morning of the Resurrection*, and the dedication to Swinburne along the lower edge of *Love and the Pilgrim*.[21]

In a sense the pictures were designed to elude interpretation, distilled as they were from disparate literary and visual sources. Figures are invariably represented disengaged from the thrust of narrative action, so the viewer is not encouraged to empathise with them as characters in a particular situation. Rather they appear endlessly static, imprisoned within the parameters of a composition as if victims of the artwork itself. By virtue of an overriding mood of ennui, Burne-Jones's works

105
FELIKS JASIŃSKI
after EDWARD BURNE-JONES
Copper plate for *The Annunciation* 1897
59.8 × 28.5
Victoria and Albert Museum

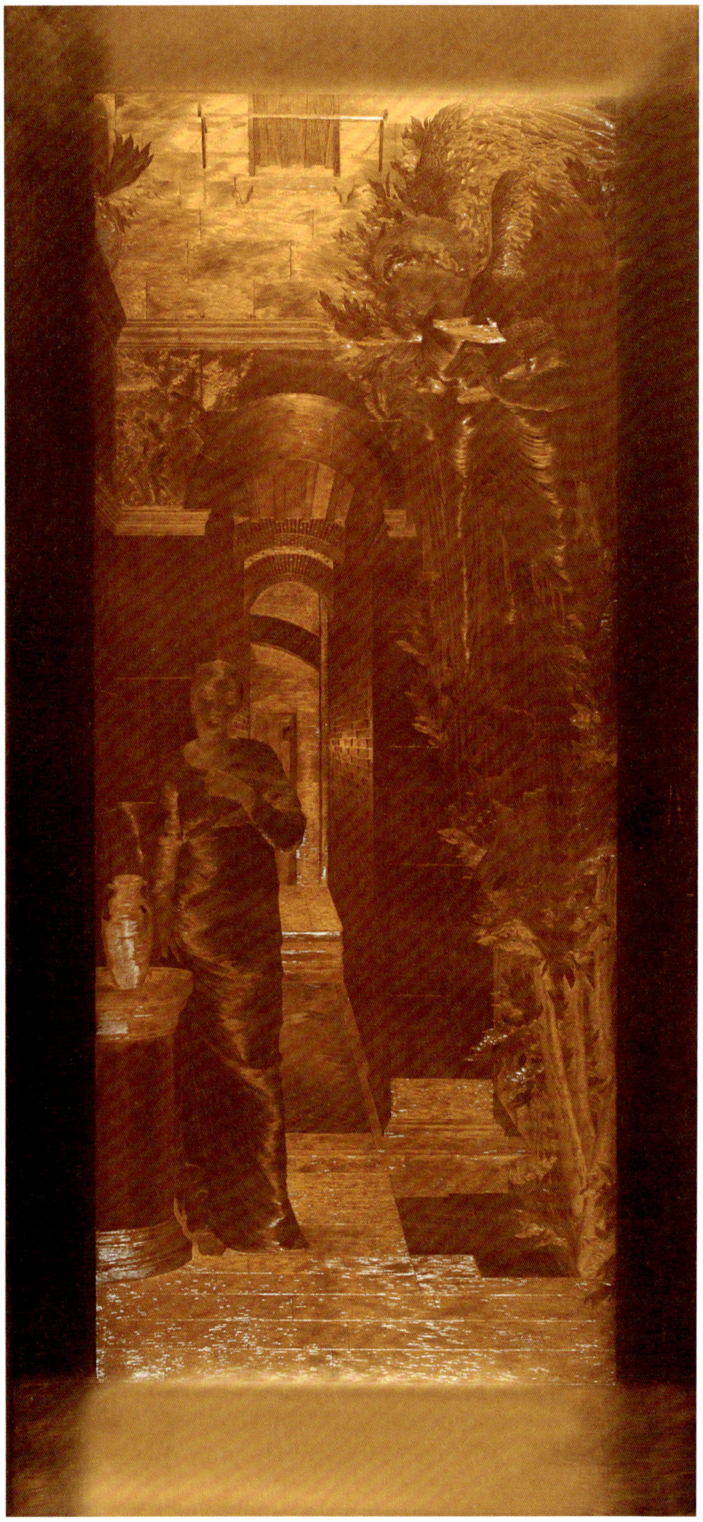

106
FELIKS JASIŃSKI
after EDWARD BURNE-JONES
Proof print for *The Annunciation* 1897
Etching on vellum, 47 × 20
Victoria and Albert Museum

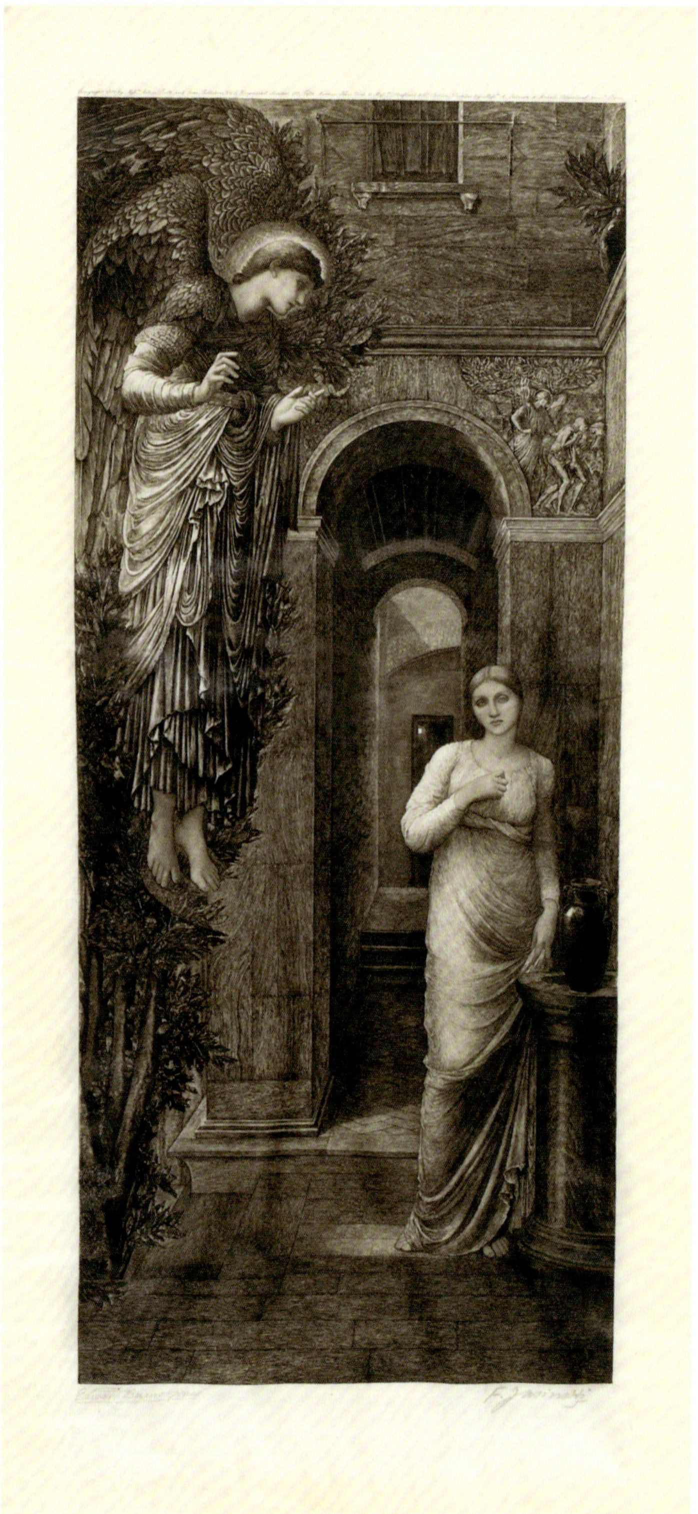

were often seen to encapsulate the doubtful religious mindset of the era, which would explain why he was regarded as a profoundly spiritual artist, one whose work was not so much conceived as an alternative to conventional religion and morality, but as a means of expressing a world-weariness and the kind of numinous experience lost to the world through science and materialism. The great early-twentieth-century writer G.K. Chesterton summed it up when he wrote of the pictures: 'They represent that sad satisfaction, that quietude, hopeless and yet not unhappy, which has been a dominant note in the intellectual class in our time.'[22]

Such pessimism does not of course suit the idea of public art and its communal appeal. This might explain why, by the time of his death, not one of Burne-Jones's paintings had been acquired for the new public galleries that were springing up all over Britain (the exception being the large watercolour *The Star of Bethlehem* commissioned in 1887 by the Corporation of Birmingham for the new municipal Museum and Art Gallery), in contrast to the ubiquity of his stained-glass windows that adorned churches of all denominations. Unlike his contemporaries – Millais, Leighton and Watts – Burne-Jones's work did not feature in the new National Gallery of British Art that opened on Millbank in 1897, prompting the artist to tell his studio assistant Thomas Rooke that Tate 'hates me and won't have anything of mine in his gallery'.[23] It was not until the next century that his paintings were acquired for public museums, *King Cophetua* leading the way when it was presented to the nation in 1900 via public subscription. The gift and bequest of works that followed had the effect of transforming the walls of our museums through their scale and mysterious beauty, establishing Burne-Jones as a public artist, something he had shied away from during his lifetime.

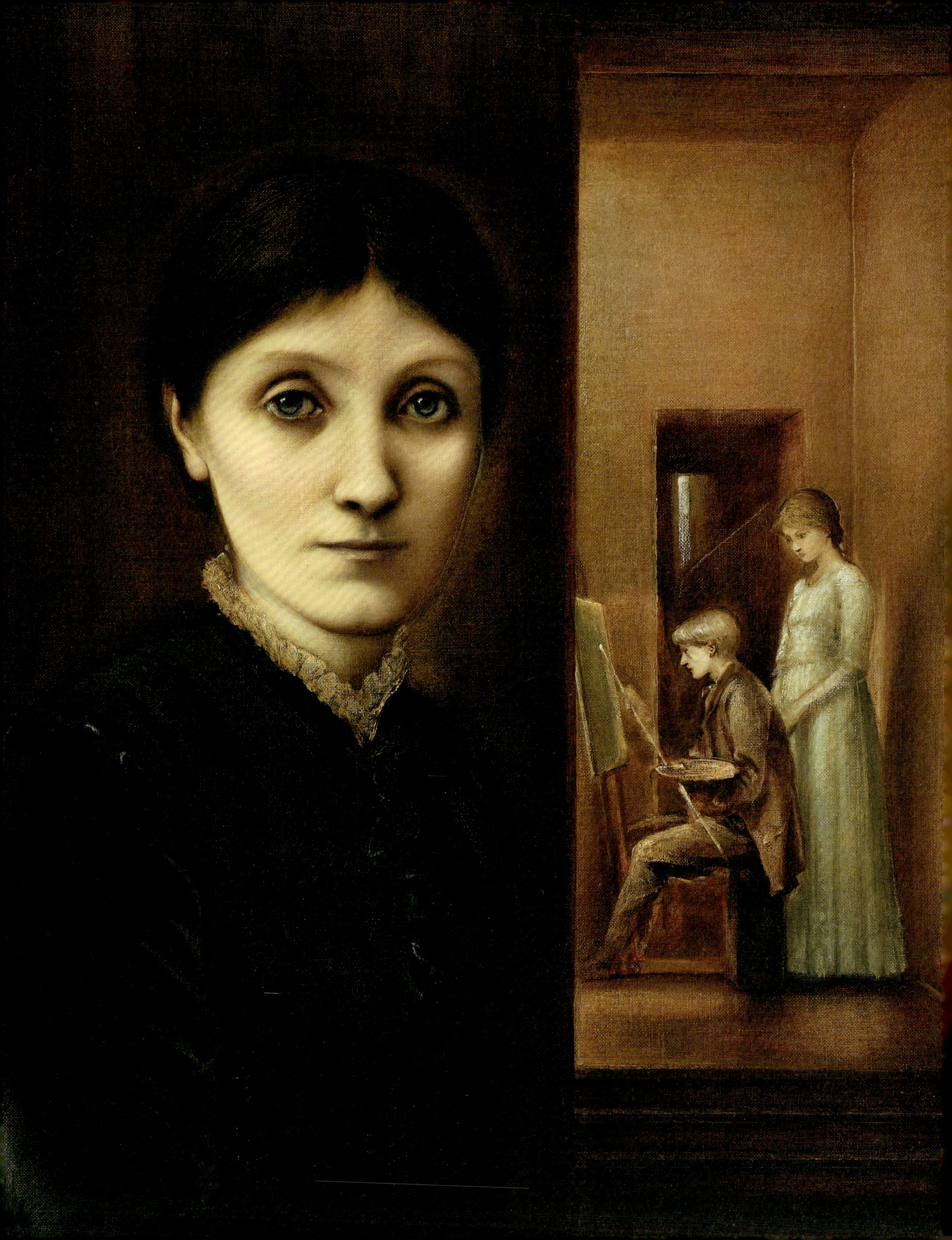

Portraits

CHARLOTTE GERE

The private and personal defined Pre-Raphaelite portraiture, with sitters drawn mainly from an intimate circle of family and friends. Burne-Jones succeeded in evading all but the most pressing commissions for formal portraits, and these he imbued with his special qualities of insight and empathy – even spirituality – rather than the indicators of social standing and worldly success required by a fashionable portrait practice. In 1895, in a much quoted letter, he wrote ruefully to Frances Horner of his shortcomings in capturing a likeness, but he does himself an injustice.[1] His best, it was generally agreed, were unselfconscious pencil portraits, made throughout his career in preparation for his imaginative works, or simply of a face that pleased him. The generally favourable notice in *The Times* of his portraits in the 1899 memorial exhibition, came with the usual caveat that they were 'delicate and beautiful things, but very often too full of the painter's own personality to be truly portraits. A few are really like their subjects, but all have a suggestion of that peculiar type of beauty which haunted Burne-Jones from the beginning to the end.'[2] After his death his wife Georgiana wrote in her *Memorials* of her husband: 'Truth to tell, portrait-painting was distasteful to Edward, who always said so on occasion, but special reasons over-came the feeling from time to time. He once wrote: "I do not easily get portraiture, and the perpetual hunt to find in a face what I like, and leave out what mislikes me, is a bad school for it."'[3]

He was striving for something beyond mere resemblance: 'The art of portraiture he considered very seriously from the point of what "expression" was allowable – a question he had settled with regard to his imaginative pictures at an early date.' He believed: 'The only expression allowable in great portraiture is the expression of character and moral quality, not of anything temporary, fleeting, accidental.'[4] This complex process of achieving heightened expression of personality is evident in comparing preparatory drawing and finished portrait. In the drawings and especially in photographs (often cruel reminders of his idealisation), the sitter's costume, ruched, ruffled and lace-trimmed, loosely corresponds to the fashions of the day.

For Burne-Jones portraiture had a drawback. The sitter expected to receive a completed work before too long, and his notorious hatred of letting go meant that some portraits remained unfinished – particularly of those closest to him, among them William Graham (no.107),[5] his most important early patron, and Georgiana with their children Philip and Margaret at the piano.[6] An abandoned portrait of John Ruskin provoked his wife's comments about his dislike of portraiture, quoted above. Notwithstanding his protestations, the results were among his most original and timeless works.

As with all his work, he half-jokingly exaggerated his difficulties with portraiture, but in the case of the commissions his agonies may be justified. In a letter to his young friend Katie Lewis he expressed his hatred of 'copying things', liking only

Portrait of Georgiana Burne-Jones 1883 (detail, no.112)

107
Portrait of William Graham c.1880
Oil paint on canvas, 59 × 43
Private collection

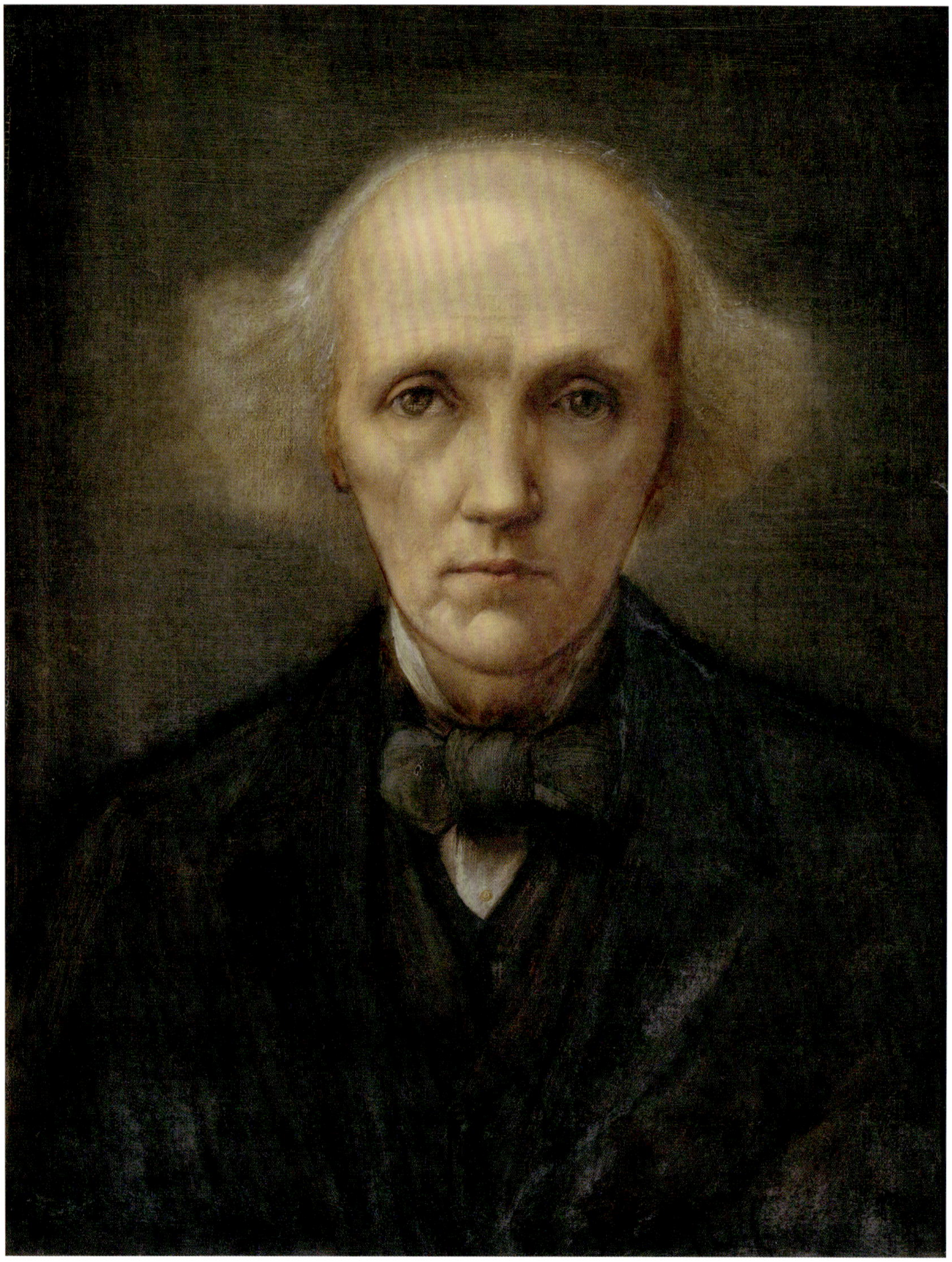

108
Portrait of Frances Graham 1879
Oil paint on canvas, 59.7 × 44.5
Private collection

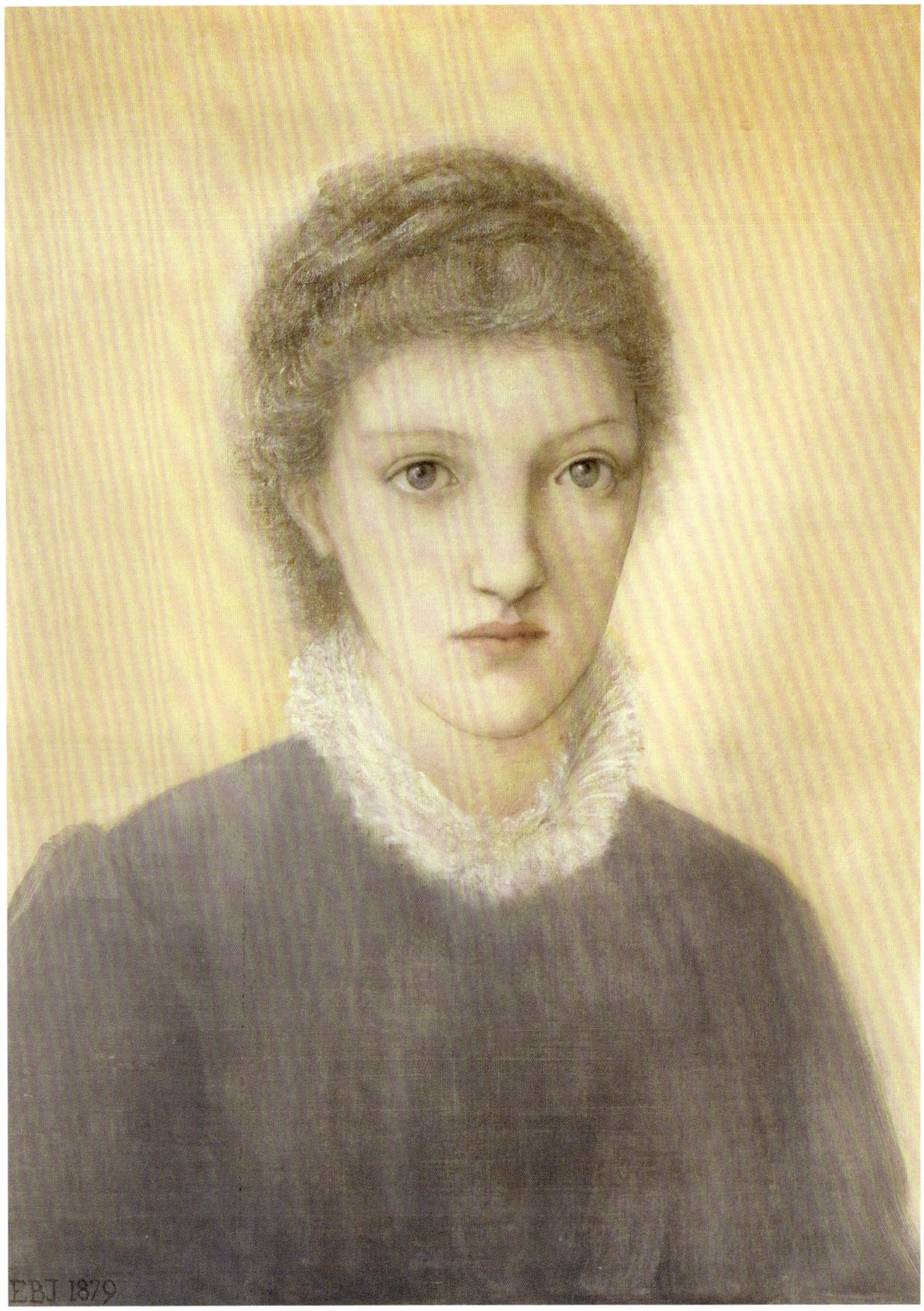

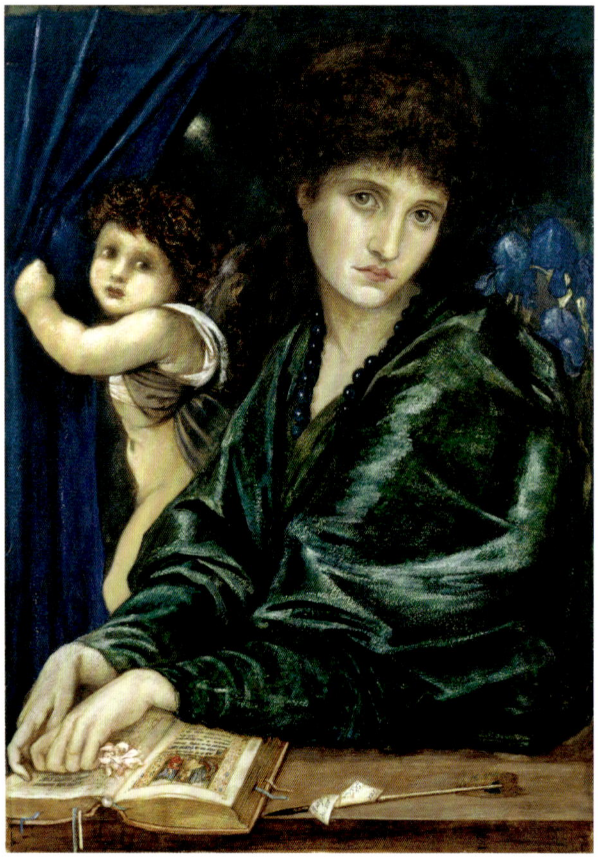

Fig.28
Maria Zambaco 1870
Bodycolour on paper
76.3 × 55
Clemens-Sels-Museum, Neuss, Germany

to draw 'out of my head'.[7] The portraits, entailing ugly (in his view) modern dress and requiring painfully sought likeness, nonetheless follow closely the successive phases of his career, from Rossettian late Pre-Raphaelitism (an endless succession of likenesses of Maria Zambaco, whose features haunted his work for years; fig.28, no.69), through aestheticism, to symbolism. Burne-Jones loved women so long as they were not fat or fashionable, but melancholy, pale faces afflict his portraiture. 'His portraits do not show his sitters as the world sees them, but as he sees, and to find portraiture in them one has to see as much as possible with his eyes – the eyes of an artist of the Renaissance, deepened and saddened by the accumulated experience of the modern world.'[8] It is hard to reconcile this pen-portrait with the merry author of comic illustrated letters and caricatures, displaying unexpectedly barbed humour towards his most treasured friends and obsessively concerned with the dreaded fat ladies (no.89).

Familiar faces people his imagined world; Georgiana is a constant presence in his early works, more carefree than in later portraits. She is the subject of her husband's one early attempt at formal portraiture, an unsuccessful, sad-featured essay in the 'Holbeinesque' dated 1863.[9] A poignant contrast with the youthful kneeling figure in the right-hand panel of *The Annunciation and the Adoration of the Magi* (no.12), the portrait was never finished or shown in public and the experiment was not repeated. In photographs, Georgiana looks solemn but not tragic (see fig.33); the portraits – possibly unconsciously – expose deeply buried emotions (see no.112). Alphonse Legros and G.F. Watts both painted Burne-Jones's portrait in old masterly guise (1868–70),[10] but he was not tempted back into portraiture on his own account until a serenely domestic family group, begun in 1879.

William Graham, and his sixth child and fourth daughter, Frances (no.108), are among the earliest formal portraits. William Graham, India merchant and Liberal

109
A Painted Casket Decorated with Angels 1877
Oil paint and gold on panel, 20.3 × 33.6 × 19
Private collection

MP for Glasgow, was Burne-Jones's most loyal and generous supporter through the years when he did not exhibit in public, and owner of his finest 'Venetian' works and the early *Briar Rose* panels. William Graham loaned him early Italian works from his collection for inspiration.[11] Georgiana remarked that 'his face was like that of a saint and at times like one transfigured'.[12] He had endured the deaths of two of his sons and was soon to be mortally ill. Provisionally dated c.1880, his portrait was probably worked on along with that of Frances. Throughout his illness he continued to oversee Burne-Jones's financial affairs and the sale of his pictures, matters to which the artist himself displayed a determined incompetence.

The most long-lasting and intense of the *amitiés amoureuses* pursued throughout his life inspired the ethereal and spiritual portrait of Frances Graham (later Lady Horner).[13] She is wearing an unstructured 'artistic' gown finished with a 'soft chemisette, frilled around the throat', as described by Mrs Haweis in *The Art of Dress*, the *vade mecum* of the artistic dresser published in 1879.[14] Frances had made studio visits to Burne-Jones with her father as a child, but dated their true friendship to when she was seventeen or eighteen. 'We went about with Burne-Jones everywhere. Aggie [Agnes, her younger sister] and I, and my father; to picture galleries, to circuses, to plays.'[15] The change was marked in 1875 by a valentine, about which Mary Gladstone reported: 'F[rances] has got such a beauty from Mr Burne-Jones – a big picture of Cupid dragging a maiden through all meshes and mazes of love.'[16]

In spite of her initial disappointment at visiting the Grange rather than Rossetti's romantic household in Chelsea, she loved Burne-Jones deeply and he made endless tokens of his feelings – little short of passion – for her, as he ruefully remarked to Ruskin: 'Many a patient design went to adorning Frances' ways. Sirens for her girdle, Heavens and Paradises for her prayer books, Virtues and Vices for her necklace boxes – ah! The folly of me from the beginning.'[17] The casket – perhaps intended for a 'necklace box' – decorated with Virtues and Hope with angels (no.109), was made for her birthday on 28 March 1877.[18]

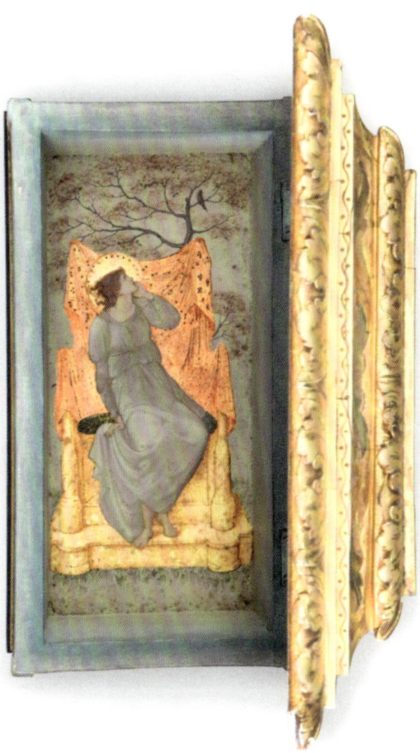

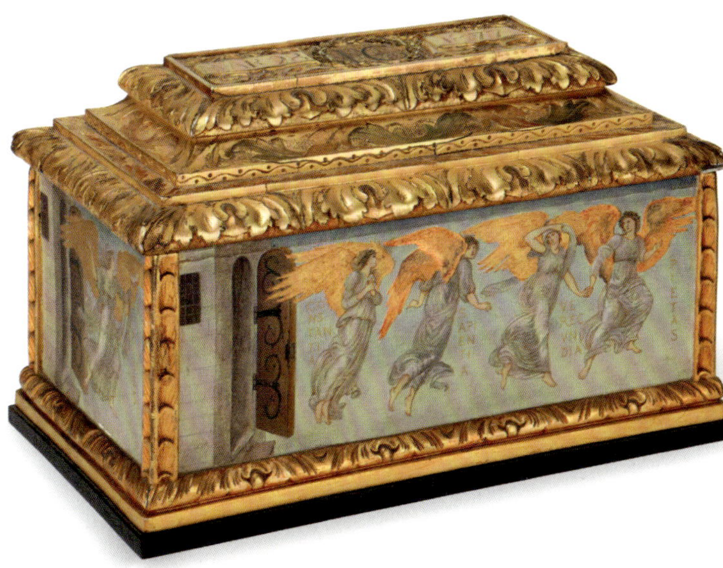

110
FRANCES HORNER (NÉE GRAHAM)
after a design by EDWARD BURNE-JONES
Embroidered Purse with the zodiac sign of Aries, mid 1870s
24 × 27.5 × 2
Private collection

111
WILLIAM MORRIS and
EDWARD BURNE-JONES
The Rubáiyát of Omar Khayyám 1872
Illuminated manuscript, 28.5 × 44 (open)
Private collection

Two modest examples stand for the embroidery designs that he lavished on her, a purse and a watercolour scheme for an embroidery of a woman playing a cithara (no.52). The motif of the silk purse (no.110) is Aries (21 March–19 April), the zodiac sign for her birthday. Frances, a skilled needlewoman, had mastered the innovative techniques required for the Morris/Burne-Jones style of embroidery, an important aspect of Burne-Jones's decorative practice. Burne-Jones does not mention among his offerings the Graham Piano (no.150), made by Broadwood and decorated by him with references to their relationship, and a self-portrait, probably because it was a commission from her father.

A substantial gift came in the form of an illuminated manuscript, Fitzgerald's 'Rubáiyát of Omar Khayyám' (no.111), lettered and ornamented by William Morris and with six large miniatures bordered with gold by Burne-Jones. The latter are composed of couples sitting or crouching, and three in moonlight, who are overshadowed by an air of sadness, loss, transience and the pains of love. Variously dated to 1871 or 1872, the images follow soon after the dramatic crisis in his affair with Maria. Although it was not conceived with her in mind, they foretell his frustrated and long-lasting relationship with Frances.[19]

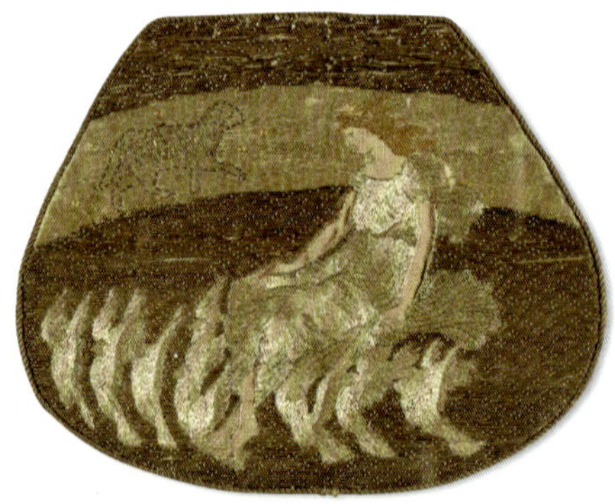

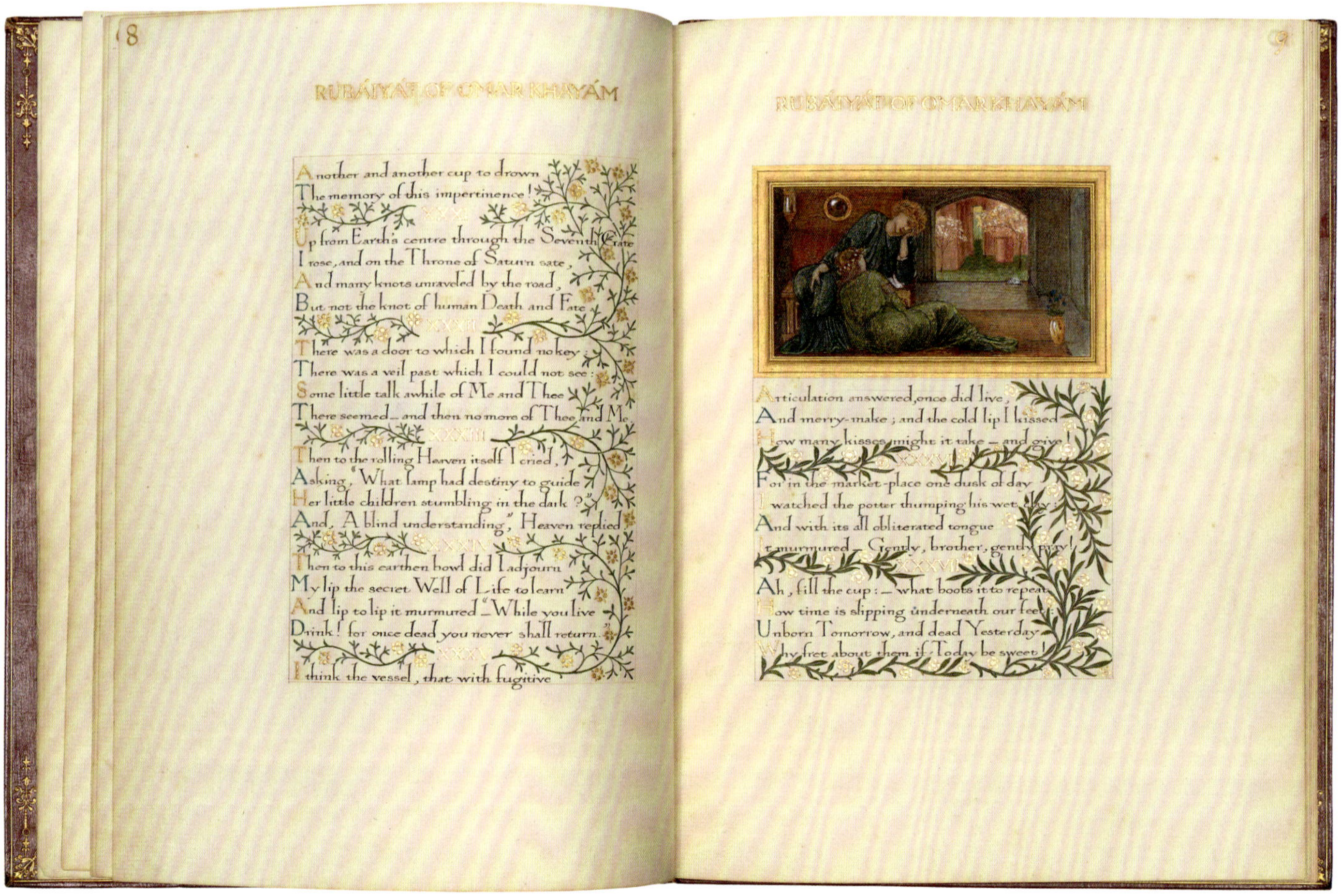

112
Portrait of Georgiana Burne-Jones, begun 1883
Oil paint on canvas, 76 × 53
Private collection

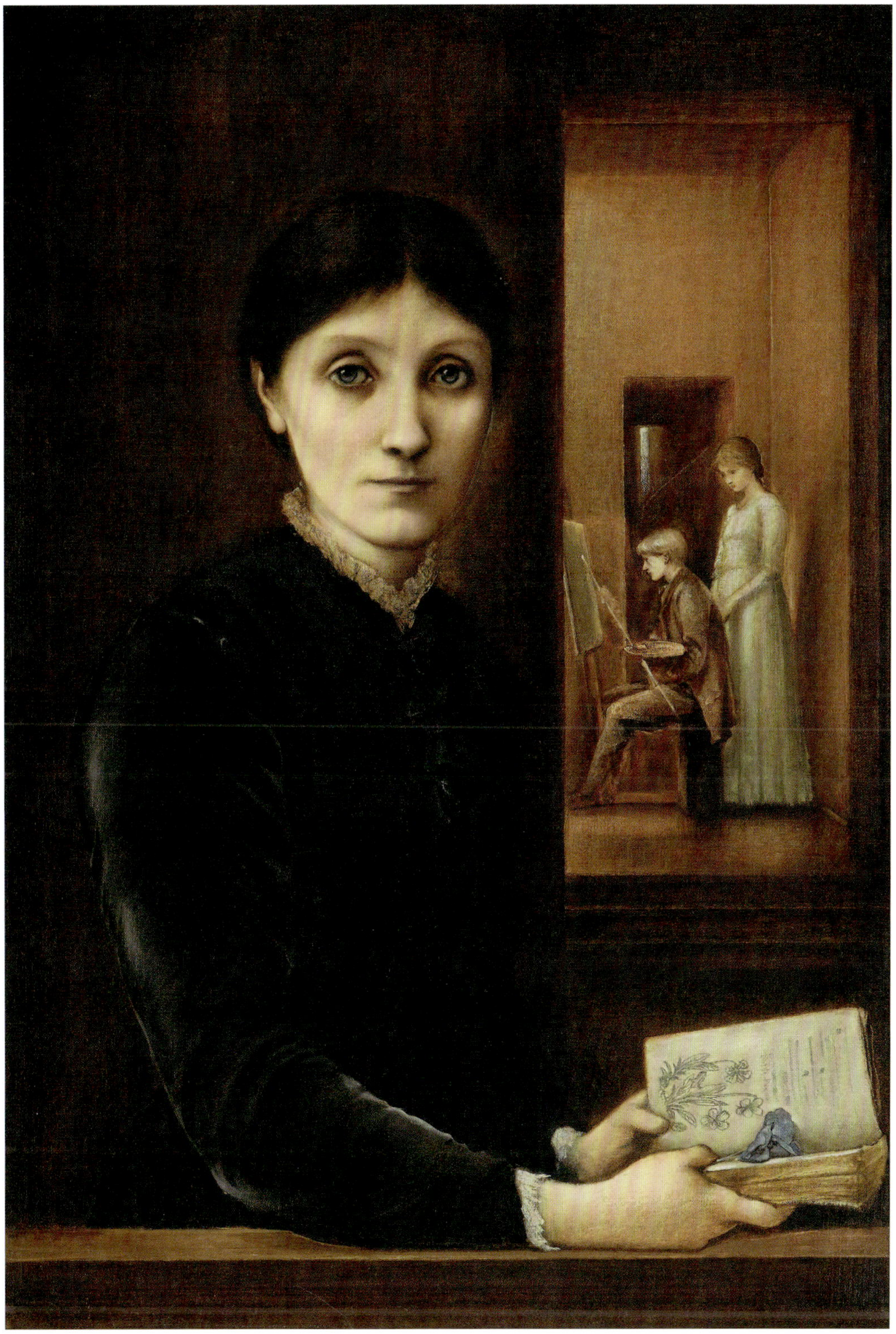

Frances keenly regretted her parents' disapproval of people 'in society', but membership of the intellectual and artistic coterie of the 'Souls' launched her into the milieu that would eventually produce her husband. Burne-Jones was devastated when she married a barrister, John Horner, of Mells in Wiltshire in 1883. Julia Cartwright saw one of his pencil profiles of Frances at Mells in 1894, describing it as 'a beautiful drawing of Mrs Horner herself, a profile done in 1879 which is one of the best heads of her I know. It is the face which has so entirely taken possession of his mind.'[20] The Hollyer plantinotype of the drawing was sent to friends, a common practice among owners of the drawings.[21]

In 1883 Burne-Jones embarked on another portrait of Georgiana with their two children (no.112). Georgiana dominates the foreground and Philip and Margaret are seen through an opening on the right; the setting recalls a painting of Isabella d'Este attributed to Giulio Romano, which he had admired on visits to Hampton Court (and was the source for the dress worn by Sidonia von Bork, no.18). Queen Victoria had allowed the neglected royal treasures at Hampton Court to be restored and put on show in 1843 (Windsor followed in 1845). Rossetti took Burne-Jones there; the Renaissance works in particular inspired their 'Venetian' figure subjects.

He has caught Georgiana's disquietingly penetrating gaze. Her eyes were a distinguishing feature, described by Graham Robertson as 'those wonderful eyes of clearest grey ... Their direct gaze would always cause me little sub-conscious heart-searchings, not from fear of criticism or censure, but lest those eyes in their grave wisdom, their crystal purity, should rest upon anything unworthy.'[22] A pansy, for 'thoughts' (*pensées* in French) and enduring love, lies on a copy of Gerard's *Herbal*. Gerard's definition of the 'paunsie' is strictly medical, including its efficacy in curing the 'French disease' (syphilis). Morris owned a copy and the bold woodcut illustrations inspired his pattern designing; perhaps it was borrowed from him and is tacit acknowledgment of his close friendship with Georgiana. She laid a posy of heartsease (a wild pansy) on the casket containing her husband's ashes when it was interred at Rottingdean in 1898.[23] The book is a reminder of hours spent in the studio reading aloud to her husband while he worked, a task shared by the children as soon as they were old enough.

Lengthy preparations for Burne-Jones's monumental *King Cophetua and the Beggar Maid* (no.98) included a highly finished study of the king, a portrait in its own right (no.113). The model was William Arthur Smith Benson, handsome member of a family renowned for their looks; other members also modelled for Burne-Jones. Benson, a metalworker, made the armour and crown for the painting from Burne-Jones's designs. An architect by training, he also supervised alterations to Burne-Jones's seaside home at Rottingdean.

The 'aesthetic' portraits are sparing of attributes and accessories: Margaret (no.114), Amy Gaskell (no.121) and Baronne Deslandes (no.123) swerve the conventions of Victorian storytelling that employed setting, clothes and jewels. The subliminal messages are subtle – a flower, a crystal ball – and are rarely mentioned in press coverage obsessed with the sitters' resemblance to his imaginary incarnations. Henry James criticised 'this languishing type ... which savours of monotony'.[24] Seemingly simple in plain colours (two are predominantly blue), unstructured and unadorned, the sitters cite the new style of dressing being adopted in circles to which they belonged. Habitué of Little Holland House and friend of the Prinseps,

113
Portrait Head of King Cophetua c.1883–4
Oil paint on canvas, 56 × 42
Private collection courtesy of Peter Nahum.
Renate Nahum. Agency

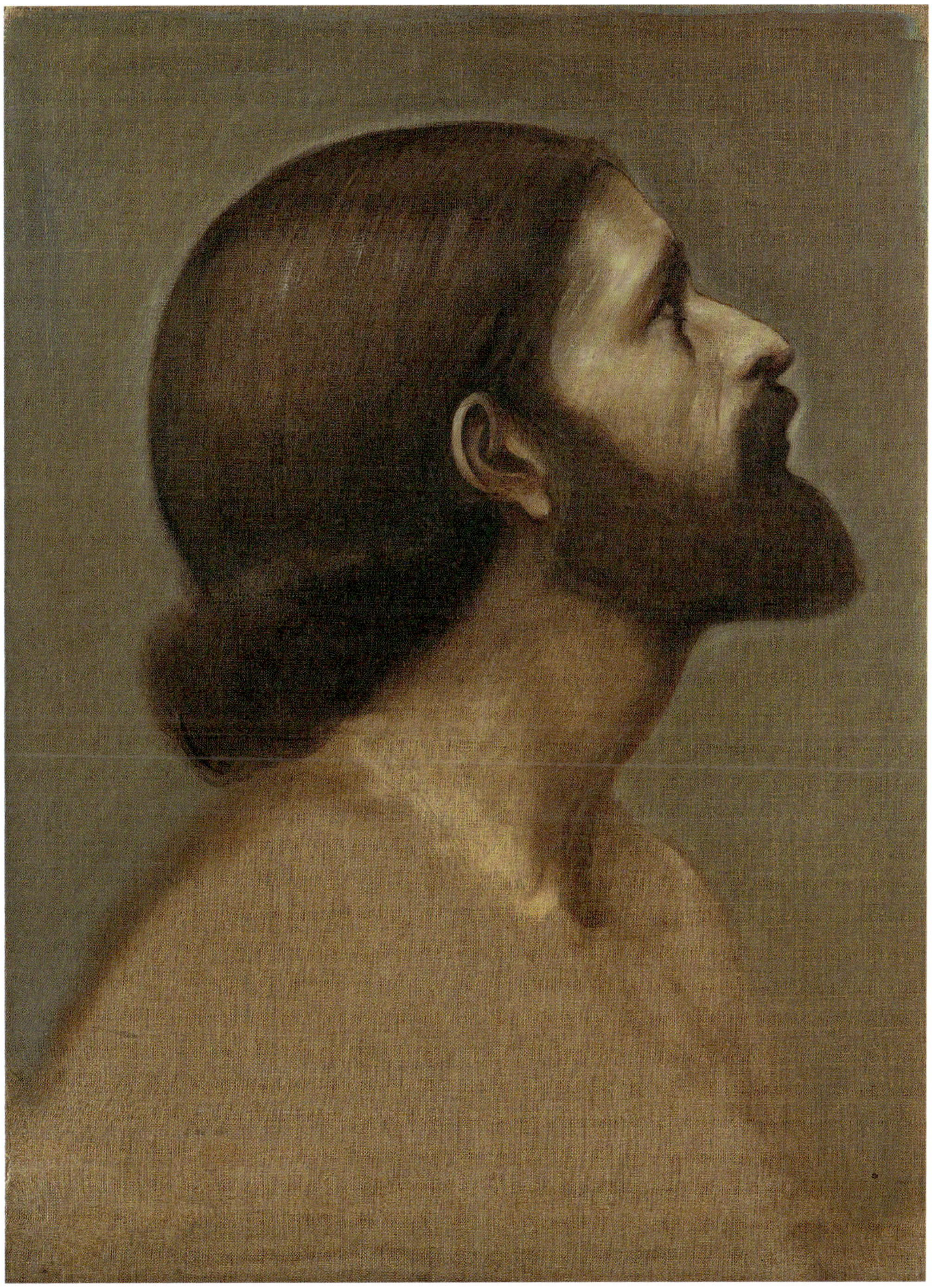

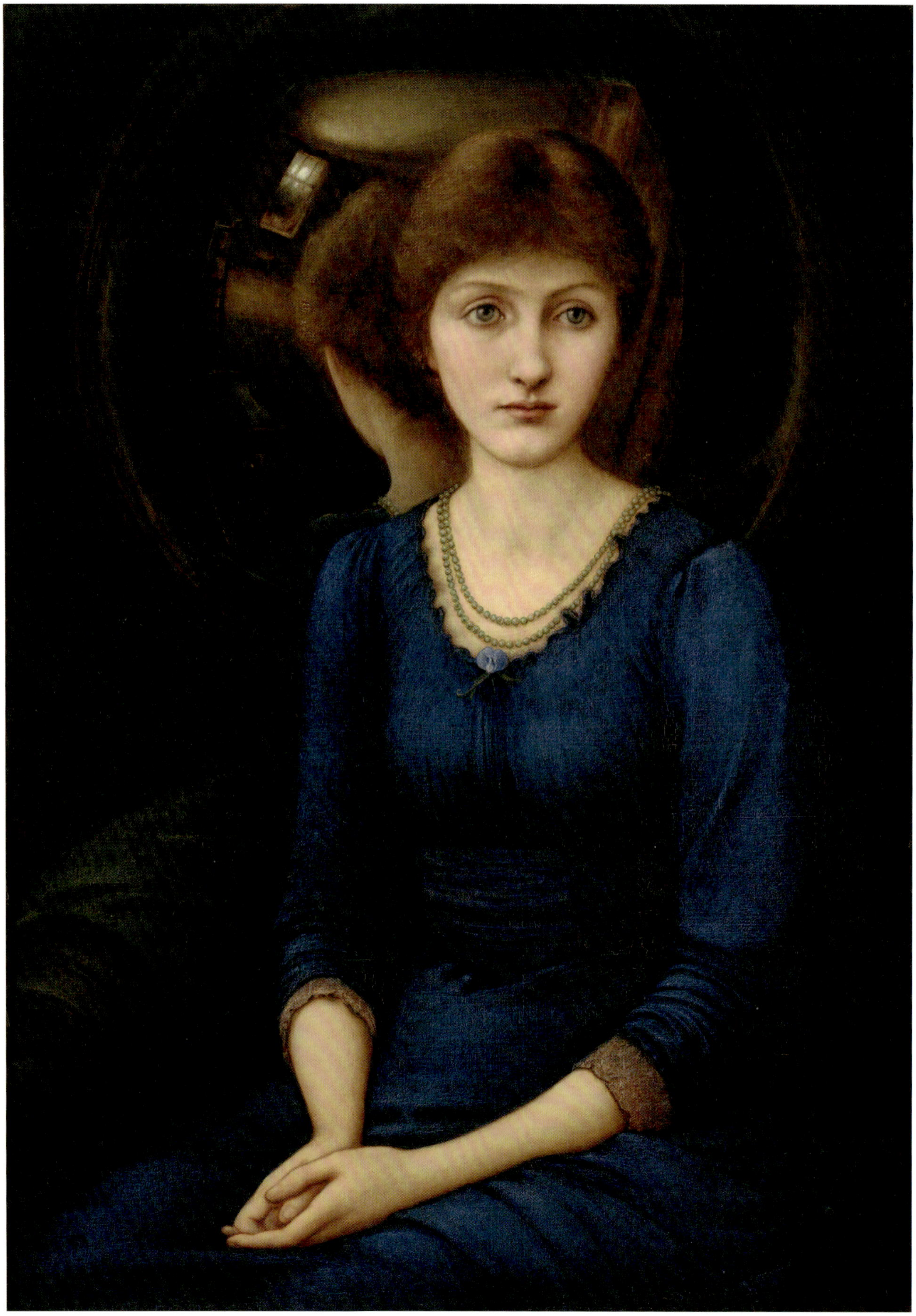

114
Margaret Burne-Jones 1885–6
Oil paint on canvas, 92 × 66
Private collection

115
CARLO GIULIANO after a design by EDWARD BURNE-JONES
Brooch pendant in the form of a singing bird 1885–95
Enamelled gold set with turquoise, coral, pearls and a ruby, 4.2 × 4.3 × 14
Victoria and Albert Museum

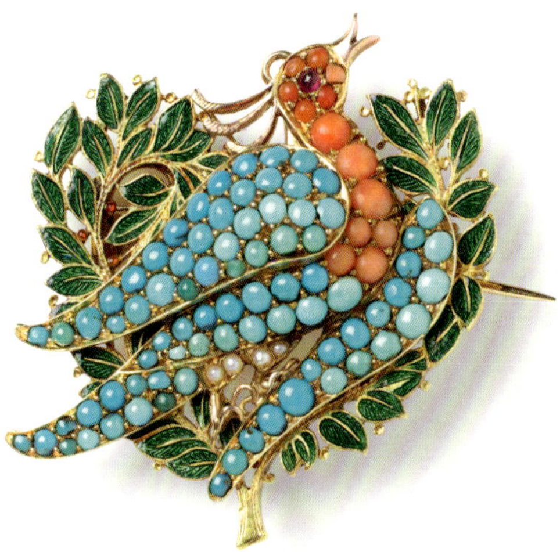

Burne-Jones must have known the photographs by Mrs Cameron, Sara Prinsep's sister. Maria Zambaco's cousin, Marie Spartali, sat for both painter and photographer, suggesting a shared aesthetic. Burne-Jones studied historic costume and illuminated manuscripts for his literary subjects, but the portraits most often refer to old masters, then freely accessible in the National Gallery and Hampton Court. These quotations were recognisable to an increasingly well-informed public.

Blue was Margaret's favourite colour; it matched her eyes, like the sweet-pea flower pinned to her neckline. A convex mirror, reflecting her room at the Grange, frames her head like a halo, or more probably is a reference to Van Eyck's *Arnolfini Portrait*, acquired in a blaze of publicity by the National Gallery in 1842.

He gave Margaret jewels and associated the magical attributes of gemstones with his love for her and his desire to keep her always with him. He reputedly designed a number of them, but Georgiana wrote: 'I only remember one thing which he carefully and completely designed and saw executed, a brooch representing a dove, made of pink coral and turquoise, surrounded by olive branches of green enamel' (no.115).[25] Three of these, of around 1884, were possibly bridesmaids' brooches; one made after 1895 was owned by the critic Harry Quilter.[26] Margaret's was handed on to her daughter Clare Mackail. Laura Lyttelton (née Tennant; see no.90) bequeathed hers to Frances Horner's daughter Cicely in 1885.[27] Jewels, real and imagined, such a feature in Victorian art, are deployed only rarely by Burne-Jones.

Exhibited simply as 'A Portrait', Margaret needed no identification, her face already familiar from her father's paintings.[28] As a sleeping princess with attendants, she pervades the later *Briar Rose* series (see nos.123–6). The fairy tale Sleeping Beauty had preoccupied him since the 1860s, but now it prompted thoughts of Margaret's impending marriage, the tangled thorny branches failing to ensure the princess remained untouched for ever. Bowing to the inevitable, he gave her a study of herself in the series for a wedding present.

Least complex emotionally, Burne-Jones's child portraits were less of a trial to him and usually well received. He liked children and got on well with them, particularly the irrepressible and strong-willed Katie Lewis. Hearing that her behaviour had improved, he wrote: 'If she does I shall no longer adore her: her

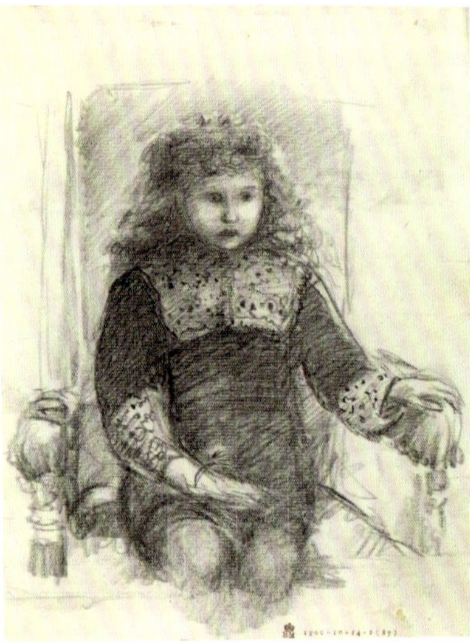

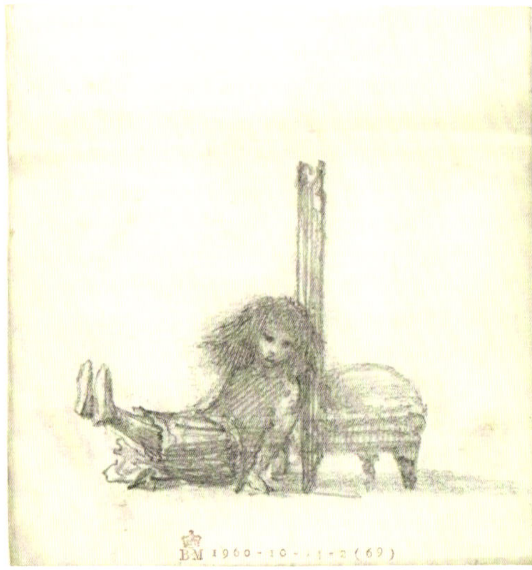

Fig.29a
Drawing or study from letter to Katie Lewis from the Album *Letters to Katie* 1883–9
Graphite
26.2 × 20
The British Museum, London

Fig.29b
Drawing from letter to Katie Lewis from the Album *Letters to Katie* 1883–9
Graphite
11.8 × 11.3
The British Museum, London

fascinating villainy touched my artistic soul.'[29] Katie's portrait (no.116) is the most original; apparently caught unawares, absorbed in the tale of St George and the Dragon, she ignores both artist and public gaze. With the dark dress against vibrant gold cushions and drapery, he was striving for the depth of colour and tone in the *Arnolfini Portrait* that he despaired of emulating; there are clues in motifs from it, such as the little dog and the orange.[30] Begun when Katie was four years old, it was completed when she was eight; drawings show her in rebellious, rumpled disarray, with wild hair (figs.29a & b).[31] Burne-Jones kept the portrait for ten more years, when he finally handed it over Sir George Lewis, who, at a loss as to how to thank him, thrust a box of cigars into his hand.[32]

In 1892 Malcolm Bell remarked: 'The truth of this needs no insisting on; and we find even in his portraits, such as that of Miss Norton, and the pencil drawing of the famous pianist Paderewski, a marked stamp of the painter's personality upon an unmistakable likeness.'[33] There are differing accounts of Burne-Jones's meeting with Paderewski. Whatever the circumstances, the delicacy of the Paderewski drawing had great appeal (fig.30); it was one of the most popular of Hollyer's platinotypes, which Paderewski sent to admirers, suitably dedicated and signed. Burne-Jones's dear friend Lawrence Alma-Tadema, then painting a very different portrait of Paderewski (1891), owned a copy. In his oil portrait (no.117) Burne-Jones translated his instinctive reaction to Paderewski's otherworldly beauty – likening him to the young Algernon Swinburne – into an expression of concentrated power. The daughter of the singer George Henschel saw in the Paderewski portrait a 'compelling atmosphere of inward dignity and nobility'.[34]

His most challenging portrait, of Lady Windsor ('Gay' Alberta Victoria Sarah Caroline, née Paget, no.118), and only full-length in the 'ancestral' manner, was commissioned by her husband (14th Baron Windsor). Even if the choice of artist was his, Gay's formidable mother, Walburga, Lady Paget, an ardent admirer of Burne-Jones's 'Venetian' subjects, must have endorsed it. She accompanied her

116
Portrait of Katie Lewis 1886
Oil paint on canvas, 61 × 127
Private collection

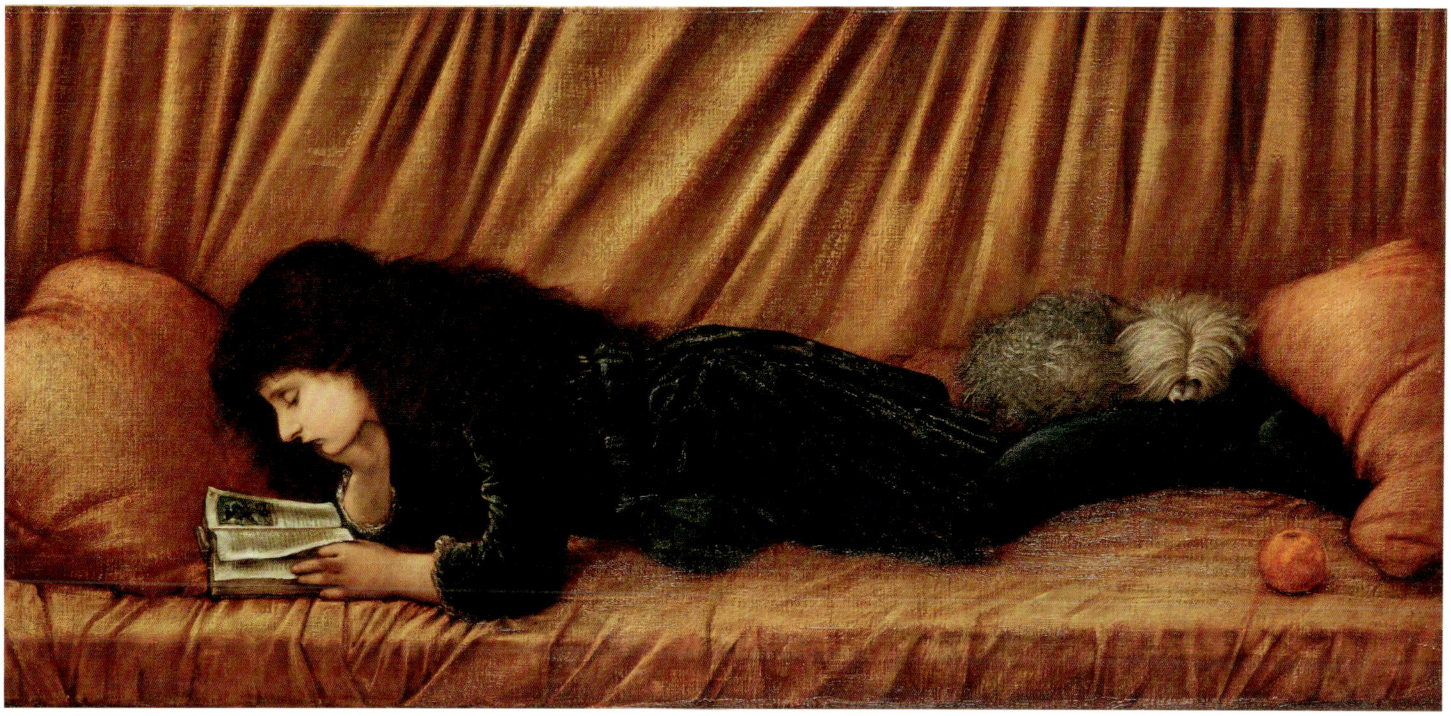

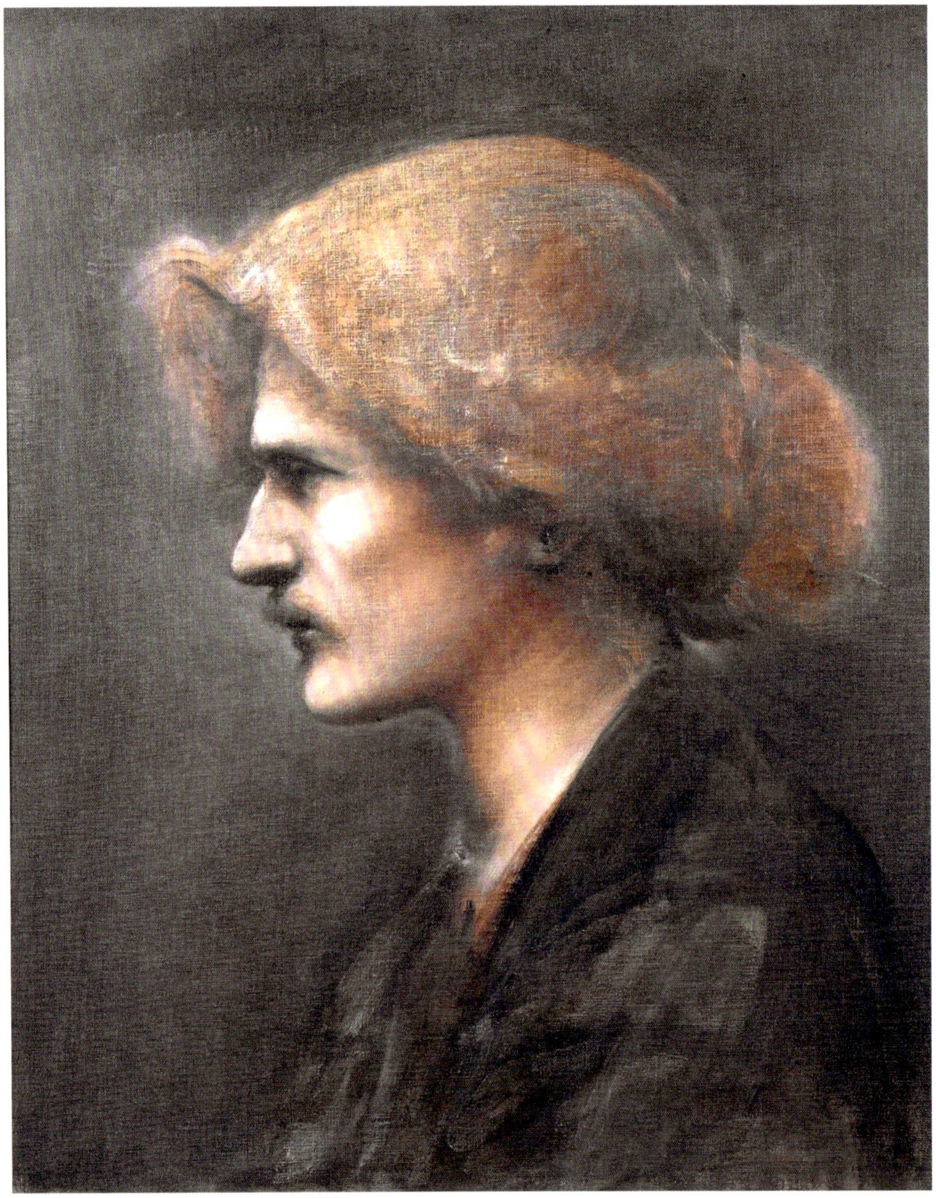

117
Ignacy Jan Paderewski 1890
Oil paint on canvas, 61 × 51
RCM Museum, Royal College of Music, London

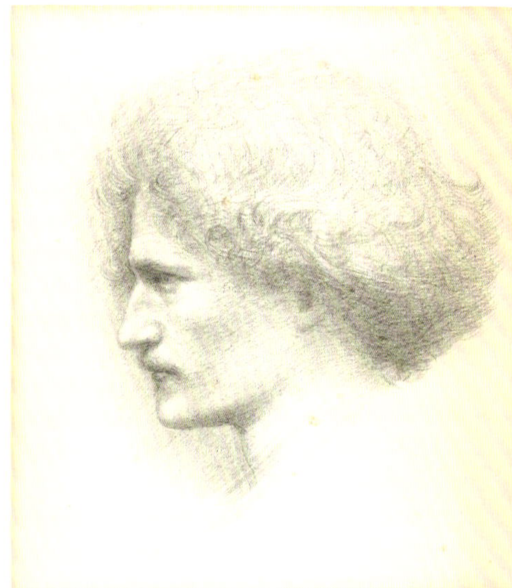

Fig.30
Portrait of Ignacy Jan Paderewski 1892
Graphite on paper, 34.7 × 31
National Museum, Warsaw

daughter to the sittings, chattering away to him as artist to artist. With her habitual downward gaze, Gay stands in a softly draped, blue-green dress, more to Burne-Jones's taste than Lady Paget's; her beautiful daughter needed the fashionable leg-of-mutton sleeves that 'give breadth and dignity to the figure, as in the old Venetian portraits, and make even a large head look small'.[35] Critics detected a striking and not altogether helpful resemblance to another exhibit at the New Gallery in 1895, the parade of grey-clad figures in *The Wedding of Psyche*. Lady Paget regretted the portrait had 'been much abused by the critics', probably referring to *The Times*: 'Spirituality in a portrait is an admirable thing, especially these days when it is rare; but why pervade a portrait, like that of Lady Windsor, with a world-weariness which would seem to imply that there was no joy left to be drawn either from the things of the senses or the things of the soul.'[36] In 1899 Lord Windsor acquired Burne-Jones's equally ethereal painting, then titled *The Uninterpreted Dream* (no.153), maybe to complement the portrait of his wife.[37]

Burne-Jones's homage to the Mona Lisa, *Vespertina Quies* (no.119), was exhibited at the New Gallery with Lady Windsor's portrait, ironically exemplifying exactly

118
Lady Windsor 1893–5
Oil paint on canvas, 199.5 × 95.5
Private collection, on loan to Birmingham Museums Trust on behalf of a Private Lender

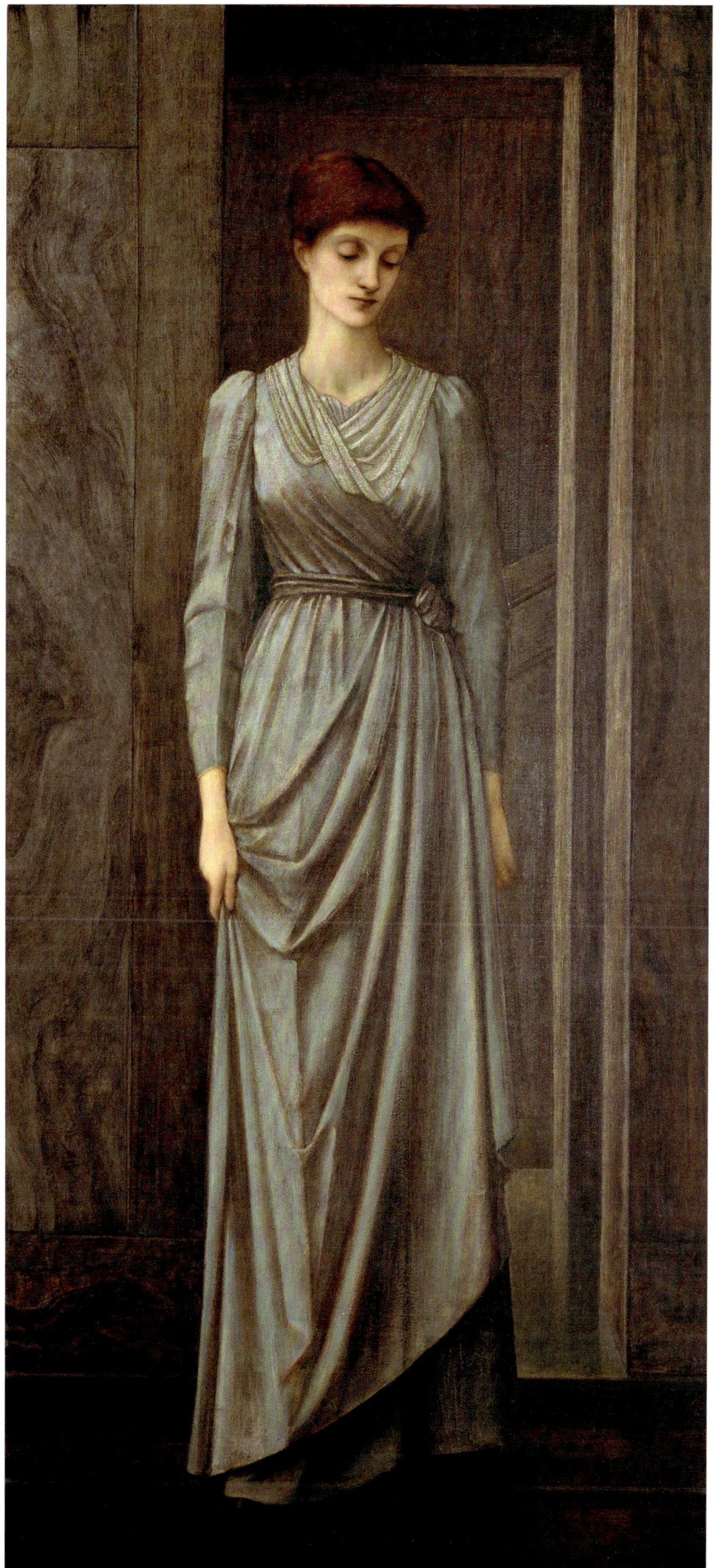

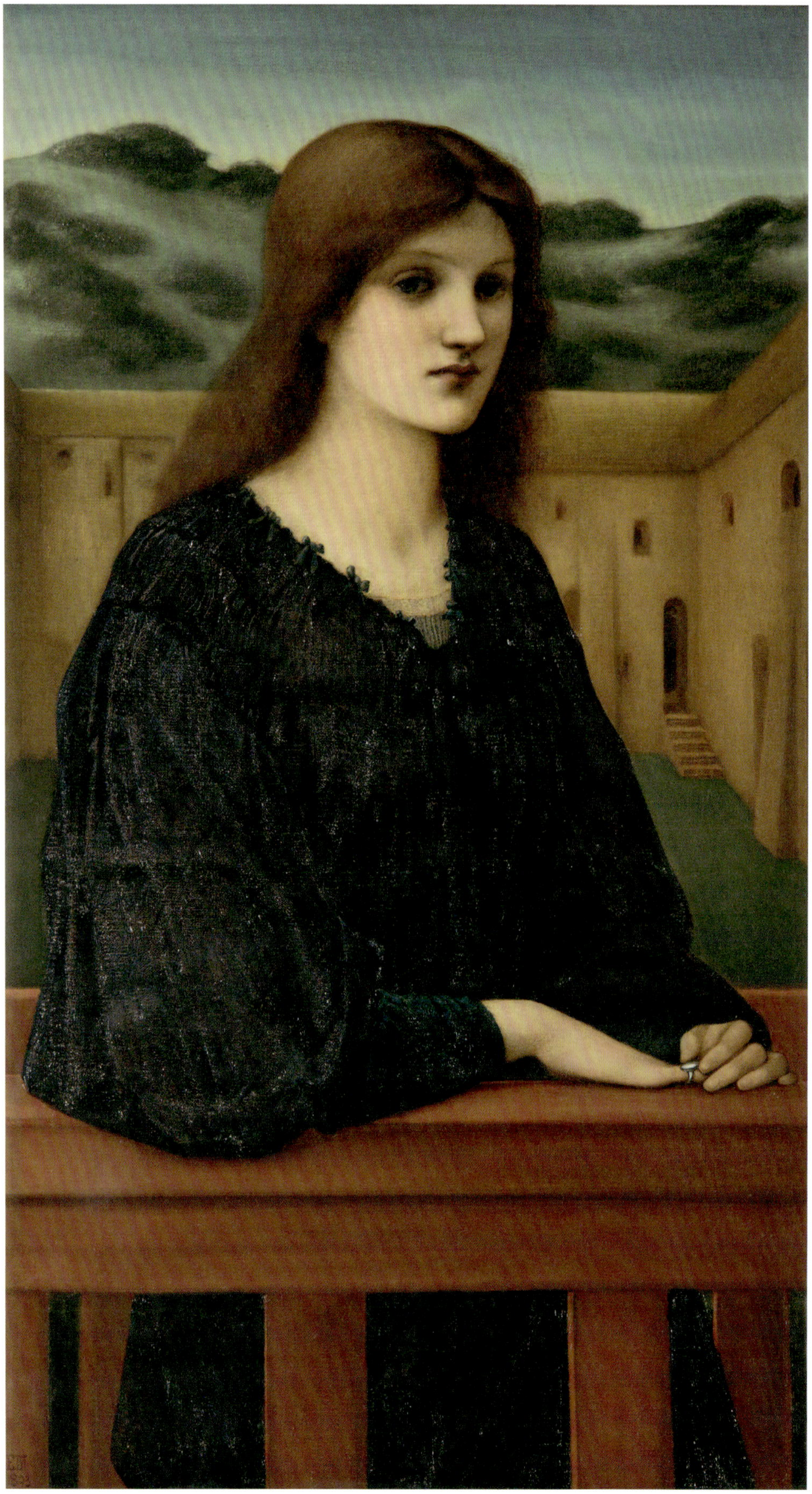

119
Vespertina Quies 1893
Oil paint on canvas, 107.9 × 62.2
Tate

120
Flamma Vestalis 1896
Oil paint on canvas, 107.9 × 37.4
Private collection

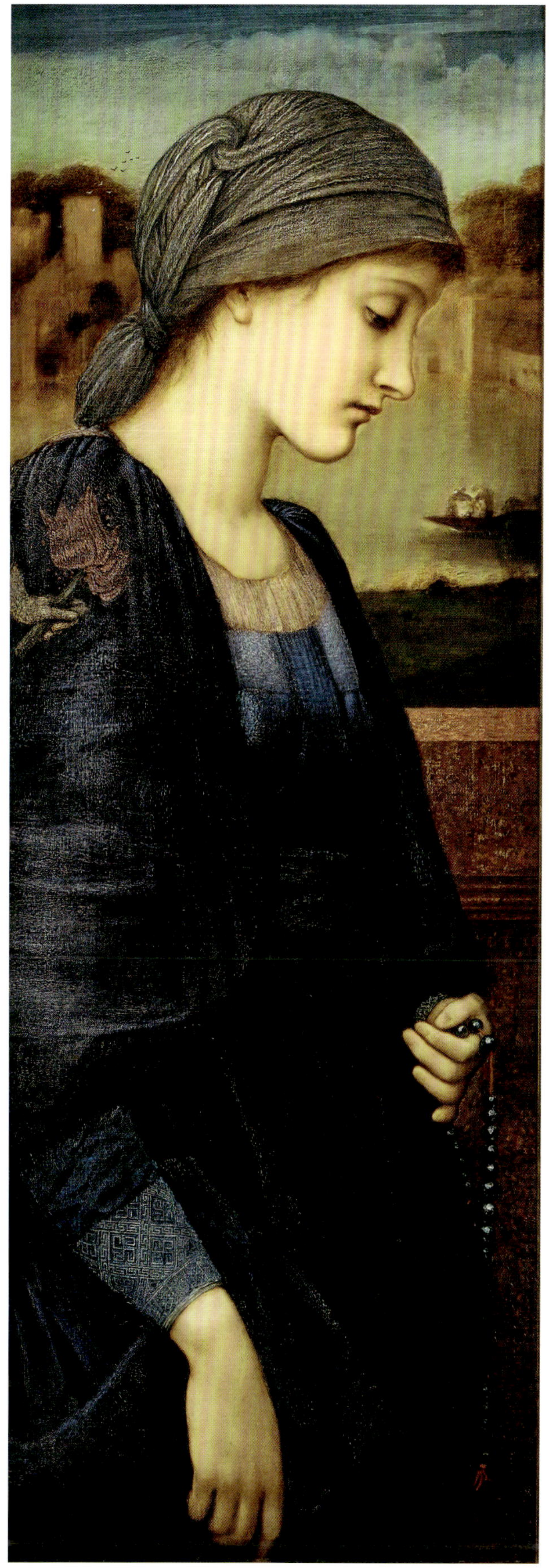

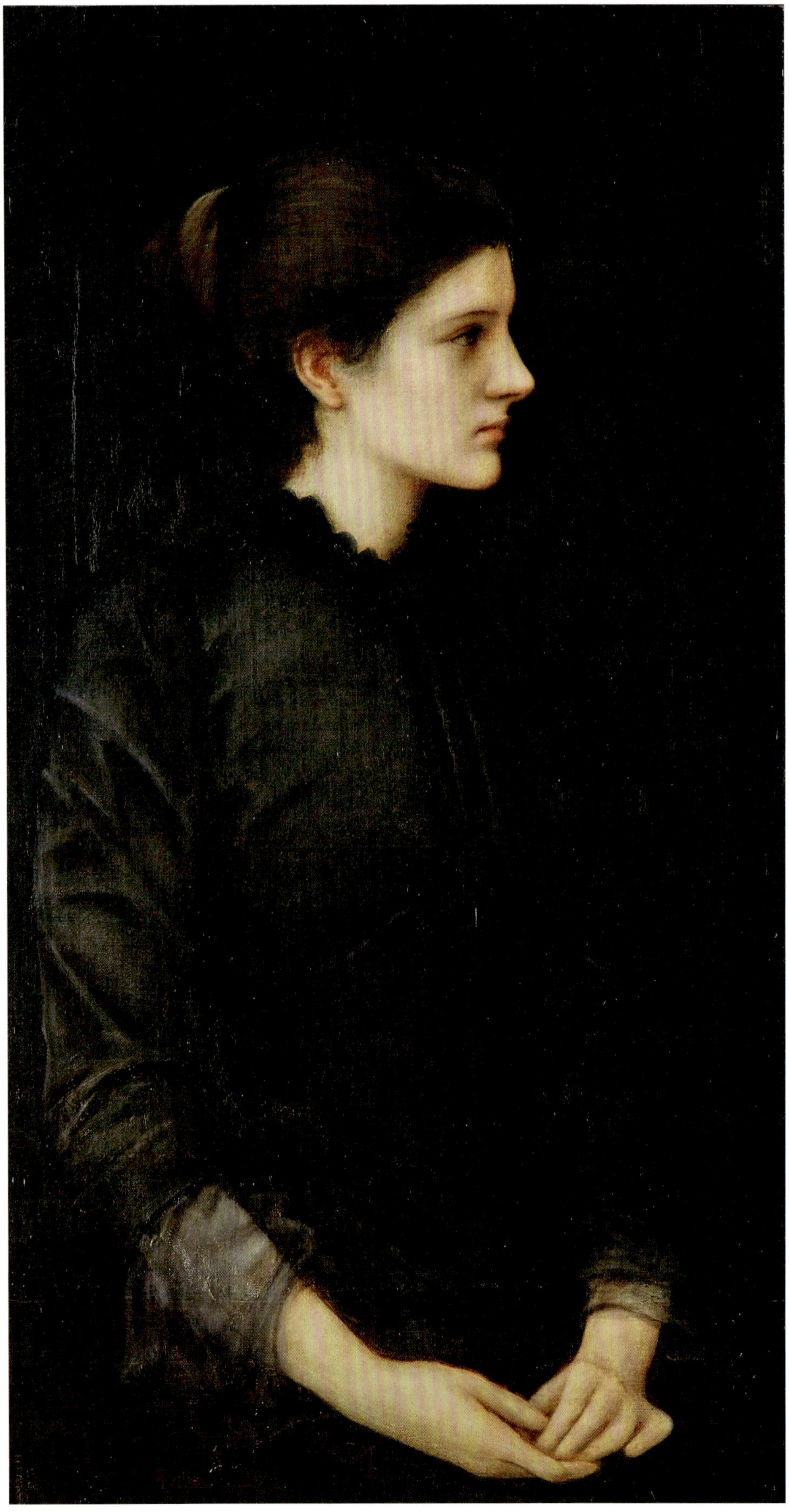

121
Portrait of Amy Gaskell 1893
Oil paint on canvas, 96.5 × 52
Private collection

122
Baronne Madeleine Deslandes 1895–6
Oil paint on canvas, 115.5 × 58.2 mm
National Gallery of Victoria, Melbourne

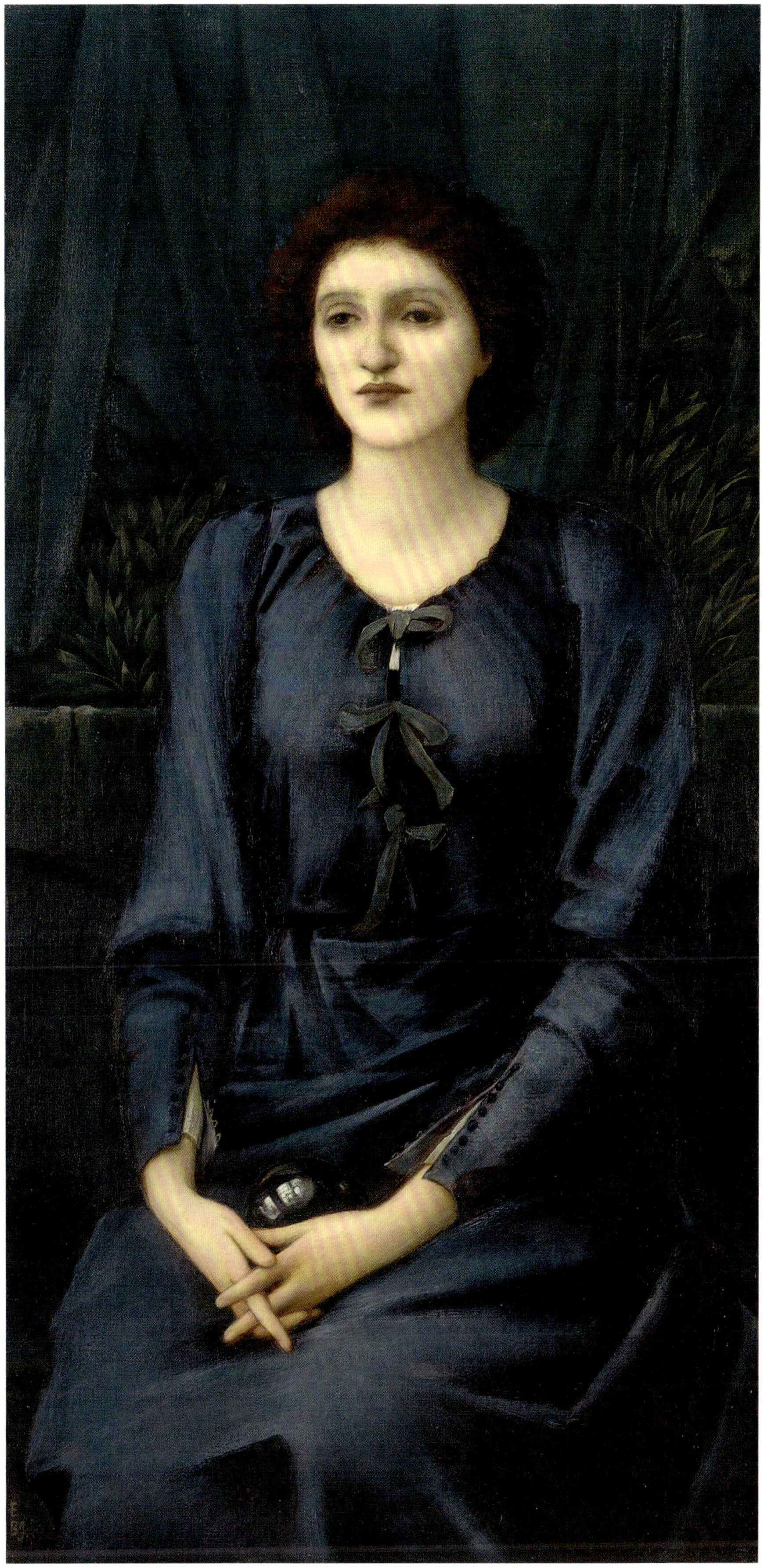

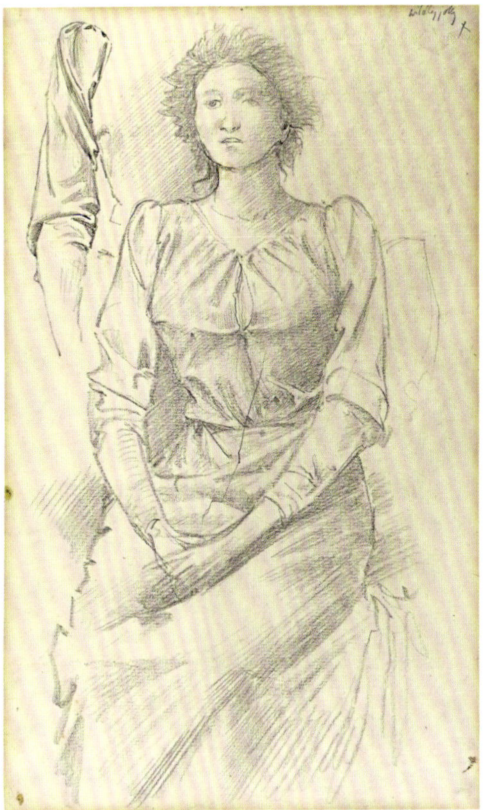

Fig.31
Study for Portrait of Baronne Madeleine Deslandes 1895
Graphite on paper
31.8 × 19
National Gallery of Victoria, Melbourne

the 'Venetian' character – even to the voluminous sleeves – regretted by Lady Paget in the muted tones of her daughter's dress. Of this portrait of Bessie Keene, one of Burne-Jones's favourite models, Graham Robertson wrote: 'She [Bessie] succeeded her mother as chief "angel and nymph" – and he produced one beautiful portrait of her; actually a portrait though he called the picture "Vespertina Quies." It showed her in a gown of deep blue against a background of grey walls under a quiet evening sky.'[38]

Baronne Madeleine Deslandes (*salonière* and symbolist writer under the pseudonym Ossit, no.122) bridges a shift from aestheticism to symbolism already hinted at in Lady Windsor's portrait and was well received in Paris. A much-used motif of laurel branches in the background emphasises its 'Renaissance' character: the crystal ball in her lap focuses light, like the convex mirror it resembles. A feature of Burne-Jones's *Days of Creation* series, this same motif, in his personification of 'art' for William Burges's Great Bookcase (shown at the International Exhibition in London in 1862), suggests yet another interpretation.[39]

> *It is perfectly true that [Burne-Jones] does not paint dress from Worth, or furniture from the stores. He should be congratulated thereon. But it is an immense error, made by realists in search of modern superficiality, to think that his works suggest fewer contemporary pictures, fewer existing interests, because they are further apart from our daily life than the illustrations in the* Graphic *and the* Illustrated London News.[40]

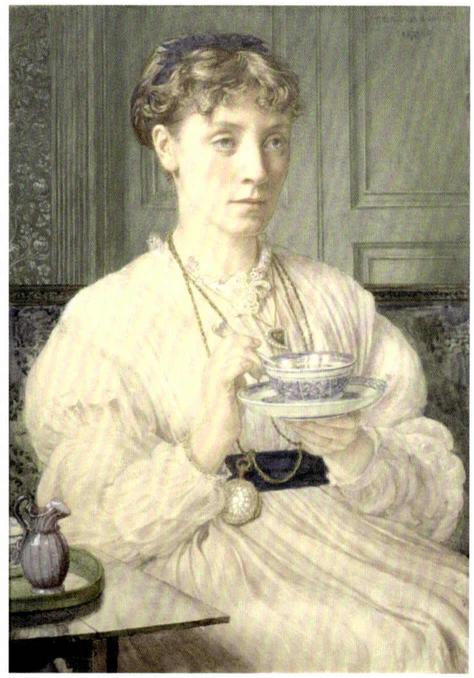

Fig.32
EDWARD POYNTER
Georgiana Burne-Jones 1870
Watercolour
35.5 × 25.4
Private collection

Baronne Deslandes's buttons and bows are carefully delineated, but there is little suggestion of the flamboyant, fashionable *belle époque* figure well known in France.[41] The Burne-Jones portrait reflects a wish, perhaps, to get away from those conventions. A preparatory drawing, with a study of a ruched sleeve and a deep neckline frill, reveals the many altered details (fig.31). Her choice of Burne-Jones probably followed on from her experience of seeing the exhibition of his works at the New Gallery in 1892, which she writes about in her article on Burne-Jones in *Le Figaro*, 7 May 1893 (front page). Here she describes the allegorical globes in *The Days of Creation* in symbolist terms as 'symbols of the immeasurable distress of creation'. Julia Cartwright saw the work in progress: 'He took us upstairs and showed us a charming portrait of a French lady with a Jewish look "From the Valley of Lebanon".'[42]

Amy, beautiful and troubled daughter of Burne-Jones's last passionate attachment, to Helen Mary Gaskell ('May', introduced to him by Frances Horner), is aged nineteen in her portrait and soon to be married (no.123). 'Very beautiful, too, is "The Portrait of Miss Amy Gaskell" (155), a profile of a girl in a dark dress painted against a dark background, against which the pale face and hands stand out with singular effectiveness and value,' according to *The Times*.[43] All extraneous details have been excised from the black dress requested by Burne-Jones, except for one fashionable detail, the corset-like waist; it looks forward to portraiture styles that would develop in the twentieth century. *The Times* critic compared it with *Flamma Vestalis* (the early three-quarter-length version of 1886 of which no.120 is a near replica, waist length, dating from 1896), a Renaissance-influenced portrait in all but name, with colouring that Burne-Jones had all but abandoned. Of the first 1886 version, he remarked that it was 'very like Margaret'.

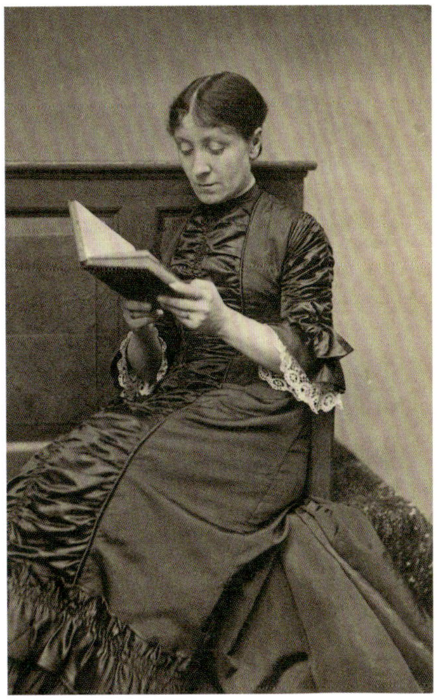

Fig.33
FREDERICK HOLLYER
Georgiana (née Macdonald), Lady Burne-Jones
c.1882
Platinotype cabinet card
National Portrait Gallery, London

With hindsight, Amy's exquisite portrait is only superficially comparable to *Flamma Vestalis*: it marks a maturity and the culmination of Burne-Jones's struggles with deeper expression in portraiture that he did not live to exploit. Mainly he painted women, of whom Henry James said: 'They live in a different world from ours – a fortunate world, in which young ladies may be slim, pale and "seedy" without discredit and (I trust) without discomfort. It is not a question of sickness and health; it is a question of grace, delicacy, tenderness, of the chord of association and memory.'[44] James's admiration for Burne-Jones was tempered by a certain sense of the absurd in his work.

Although he did not adopt the fashionable studio practice of annual 'Show Sundays' and 'days' when visitors were received in the afternoon or evening every week (known in French as '*jours*') – only a modified form of Sunday 'open house' was kept at the Grange – meetings took place there that might not have occurred in conventional high society circles. Through his friendship with William Graham and Frances Horner, Burne-Jones had infiltrated the Souls' circle to the extent that his children spoke their secret language. Many were frequent visitors; his work appealed to this set as it suggested culture and aesthetic refinement. Frances was known among her Souls friends as the 'Botticelli'. It was his recognised look: 'From Botticelli he took his type of female beauty.'[45] His daughter Margaret, Frances, Mary Gladstone and Laura Lyttelton are among the maidens descending *The Golden Stairs*, love letter to a veritable parade of aesthetes and Souls; it was gratifying to be recognised, a mark of their familiarity with artistic inner circles.[46] However, when it came to formal portraits, the choice of artist frequently fell to Watts, Millais, Poynter and J.S. Sargent; Rosalind Howard (wife of Burne-Jones's patron, Lord Carlisle) commissioned Poynter's portrait of Georgiana (fig.32). William Blake Richmond painted Margaret's most conventional likeness, in a white dress. It hung over the sitting-room fireplace at the Grange.[47]

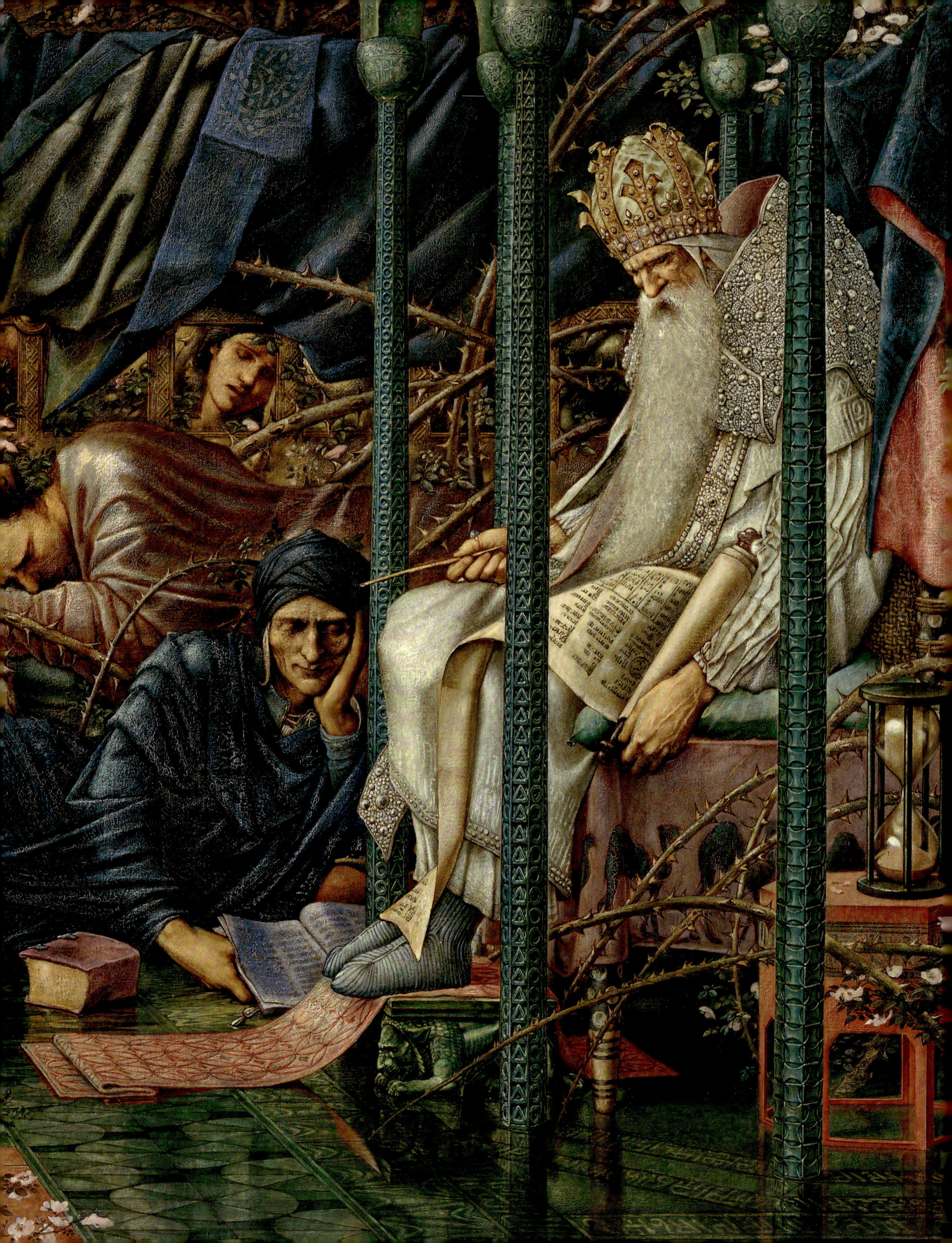

The Series Paintings

ELIZABETH PRETTEJOHN

Throughout the years of his successes at the Grosvenor and New Galleries, Burne-Jones returned, at intervals, to work on two great series of paintings. Like the pairs of stories in William Morris's verse epic of 1868–70, *The Earthly Paradise*, the two series address in turn classical mythology and northern legend: Perseus, who slew Medusa and rescued Andromeda from the sea-monster, and the princess who slept for a hundred years, surrounded by a hedge of thorns, until the arrival of her prince. One is a story of masculine endeavour, dramatised in ten scenes that emphasise verticals of movement and action, the other a tale of enchanted stillness, unfolding through four extended horizontal canvases that lead to a beautiful female figure. Perseus's world of rock, metal, sea and mist is dominated by blue, grey and tawny hues, whereas the princess inhabits the colour world of a medieval manuscript or stained-glass window. Everything in these immense sequences seems designed to contrast – classical and northern, masculine and feminine, vertical and horizontal, grey-blue and multi-coloured. Yet they share not only the grandeur of their scale and ambition, but also – and perhaps paradoxically – an immediacy of address. They retell stories that everyone knows: the Sleeping Beauty, most familiar of fairy tales from Charles Perrault in 1697 to Walt Disney in 1959, and the ancient myth of Perseus familiar in visual representations from Greek vase painting to Benvenuto Cellini and Titian. Victorian viewers would also have known Tennyson's Sleeping Beauty poem, 'The Day Dream' of 1842, and Charles Kingsley's version of the Perseus story in his best-selling collection for children, *The Heroes* of 1856. Then or now, the viewer's experience of Burne-Jones's series combines a recognition of something deeply familiar with the shock of its new realisation, one that is startlingly modern in significant respects.

Another similarity between the two series is the complexity with which they developed over the course of the artist's career. This may seem a merely prosaic point, not to mention a practical obstacle to clear exposition in an exhibition display or catalogue text. There is no full set of Perseus pictures that includes all of the proposed subjects in completed form, and the current exhibition accordingly juxtaposes four compositions from the final group of oil paintings (now in the Staatsgalerie, Stuttgart) with full-scale cartoons representing other subjects in the series (from the set of ten now in Southampton City Art Gallery), as well as a mixed-media version of one subject, *Perseus and the Graiae* (Amgueddfa Cymru – National Museum Wales, Cardiff). The *Briar Rose* series seems at first thought more straightforward: the four canvases seen in the exhibition constitute the full set completed by Burne-Jones and exhibited in 1890 at Agnew's, the London art-dealers, to an acclaim that marked the culmination of the artist's career. They are, moreover, supplemented by the ten additional canvases (no.127) that Burne-Jones subsequently made to adapt the sequence to the saloon at Buscot Park, where their purchaser,

The Council Chamber 1885–90 (detail, no.124)

123
The Briar Wood 1874–84
Oil paint on canvas, 125 × 231
The Faringdon Collection Trust

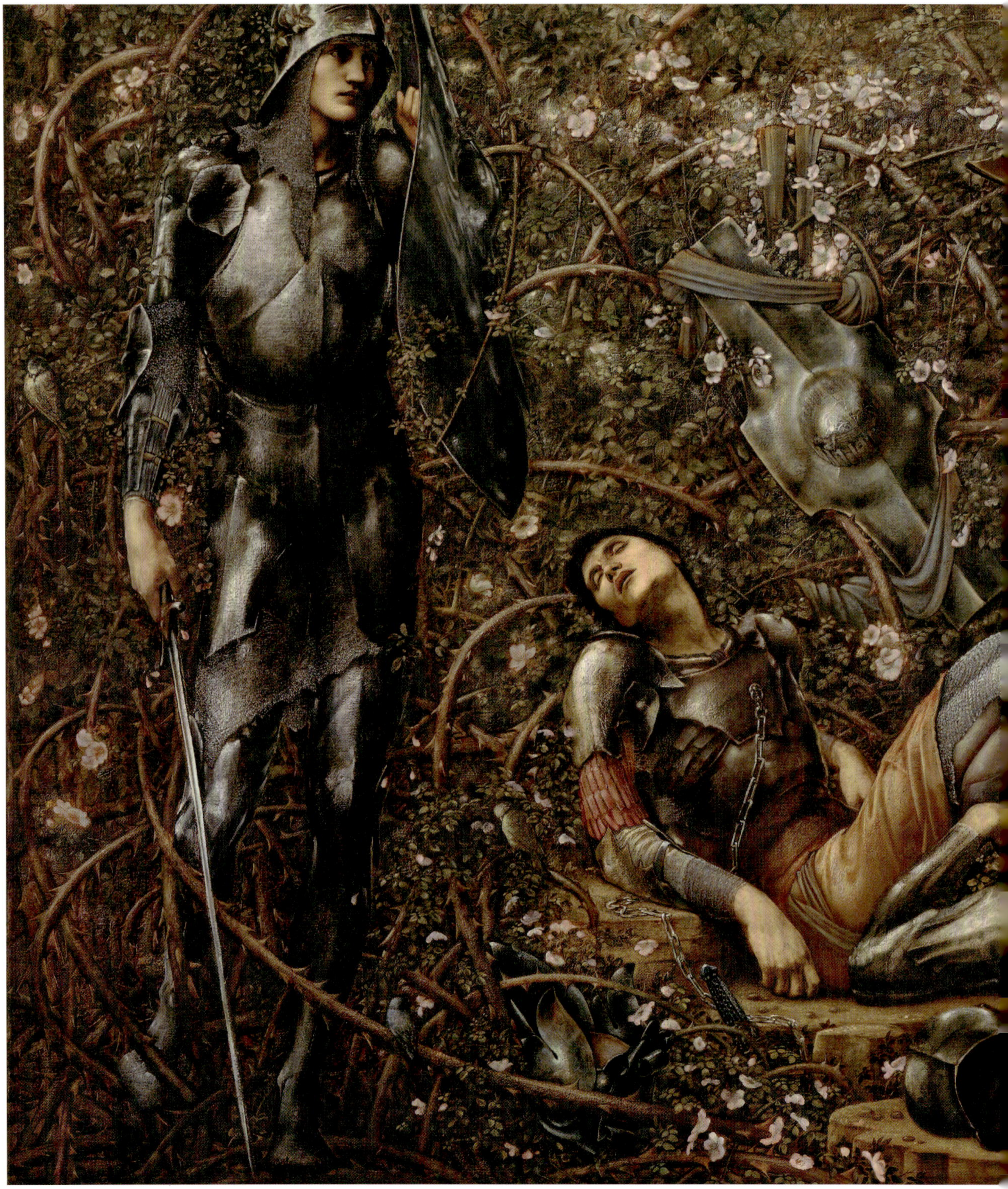

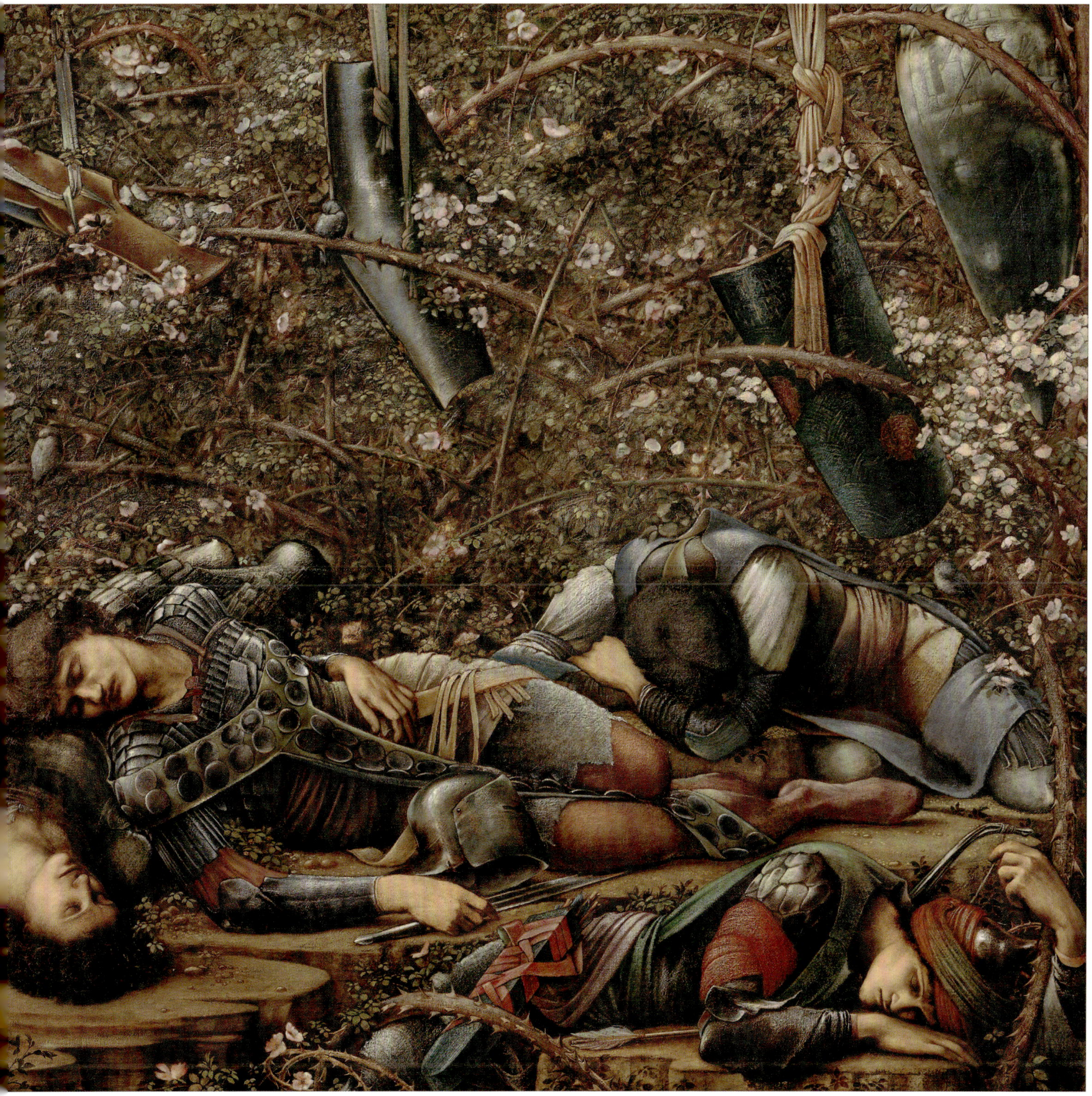

124
The Council Chamber 1885–90
Oil paint on canvas, 125 × 231
The Faringdon Collection Trust

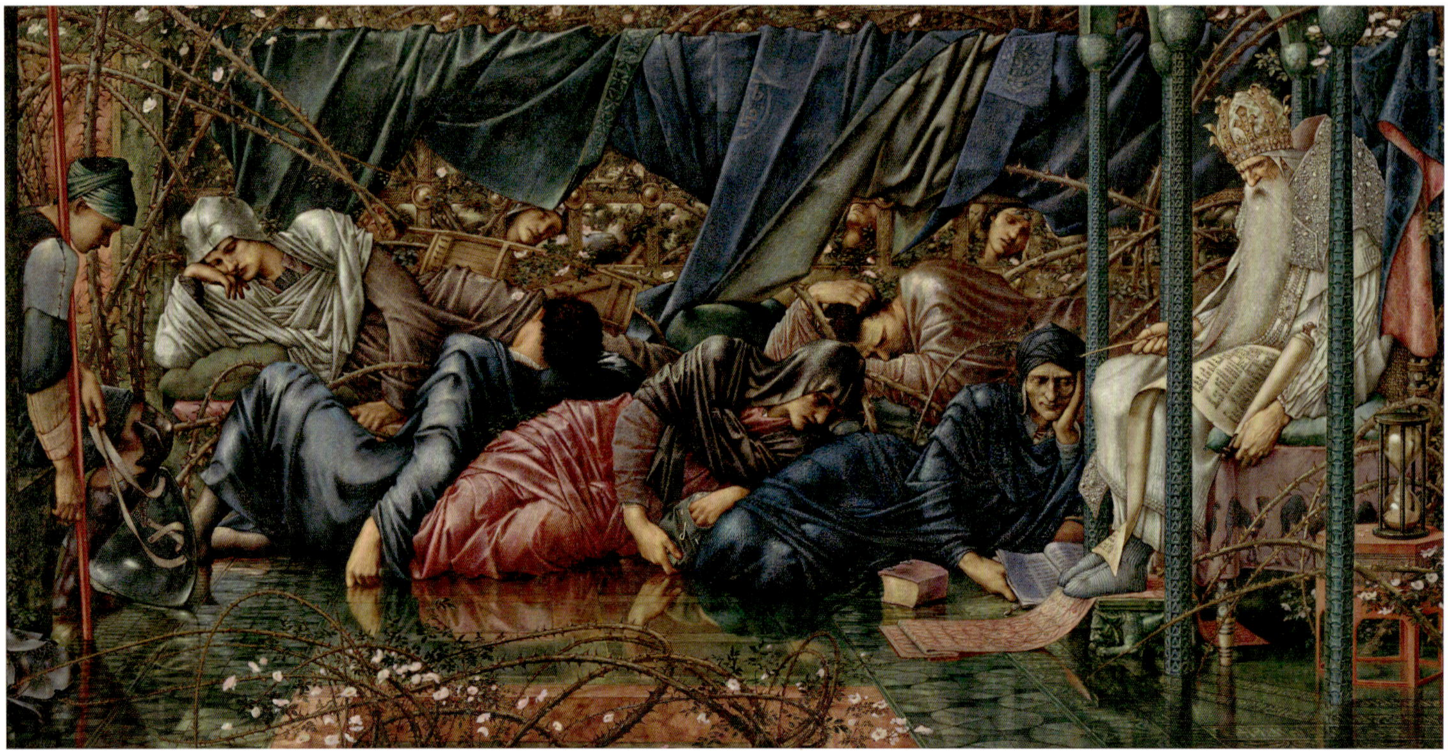

125
The Garden Court 1885–90
Oil paint on canvas, 125 × 231
The Faringdon Collection Trust

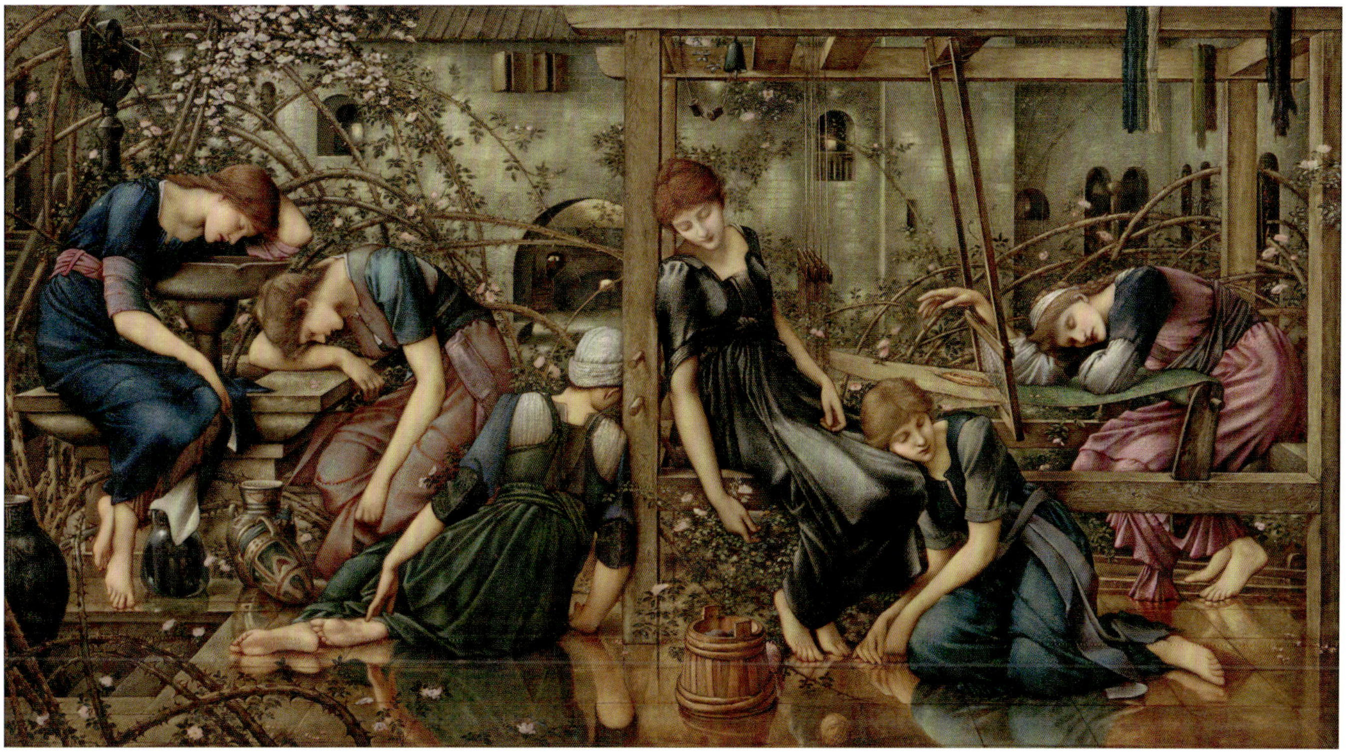

126
The Rose Bower 1886–90
Oil paint on canvas, 125 × 231
The Faringdon Collection Trust

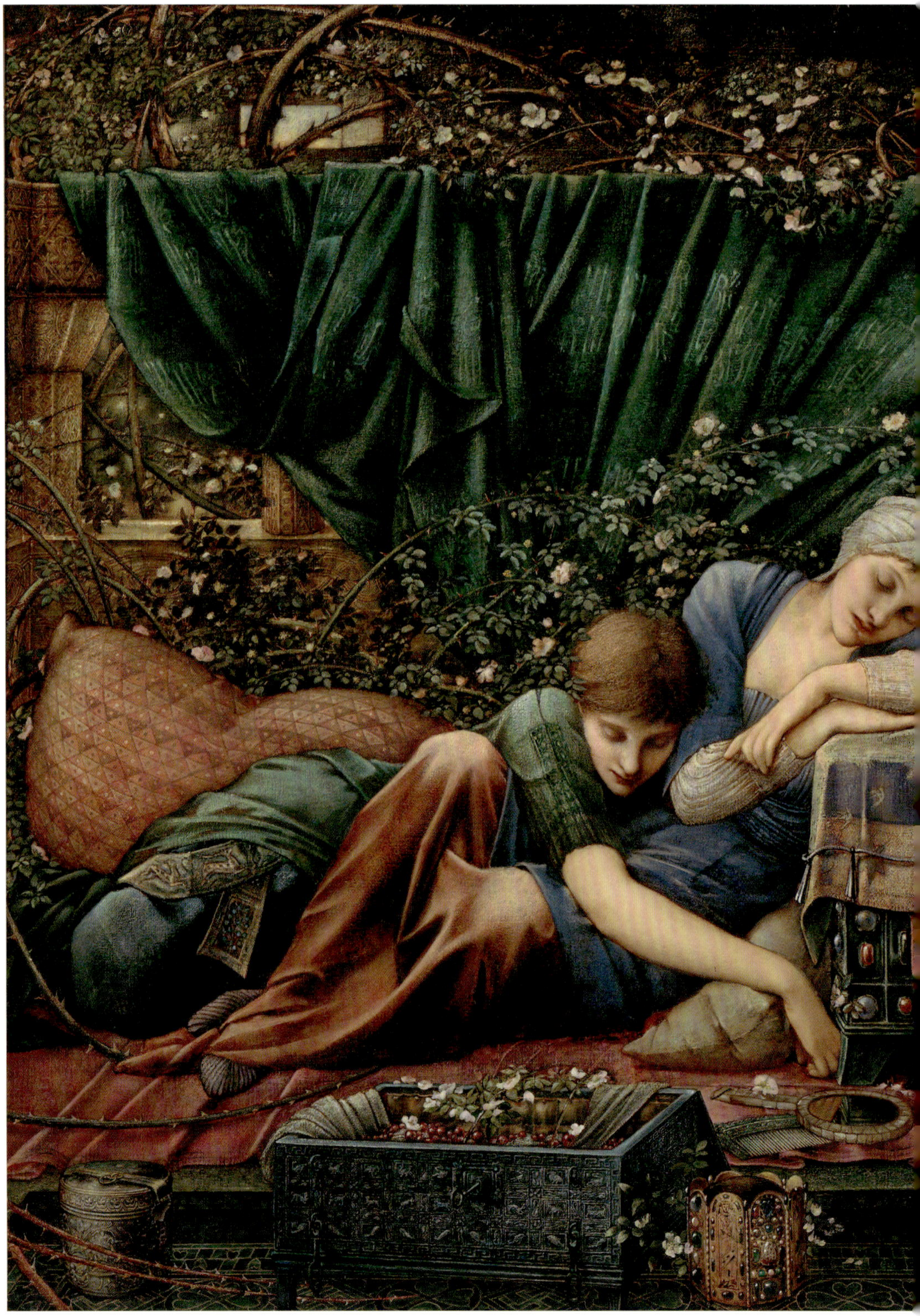

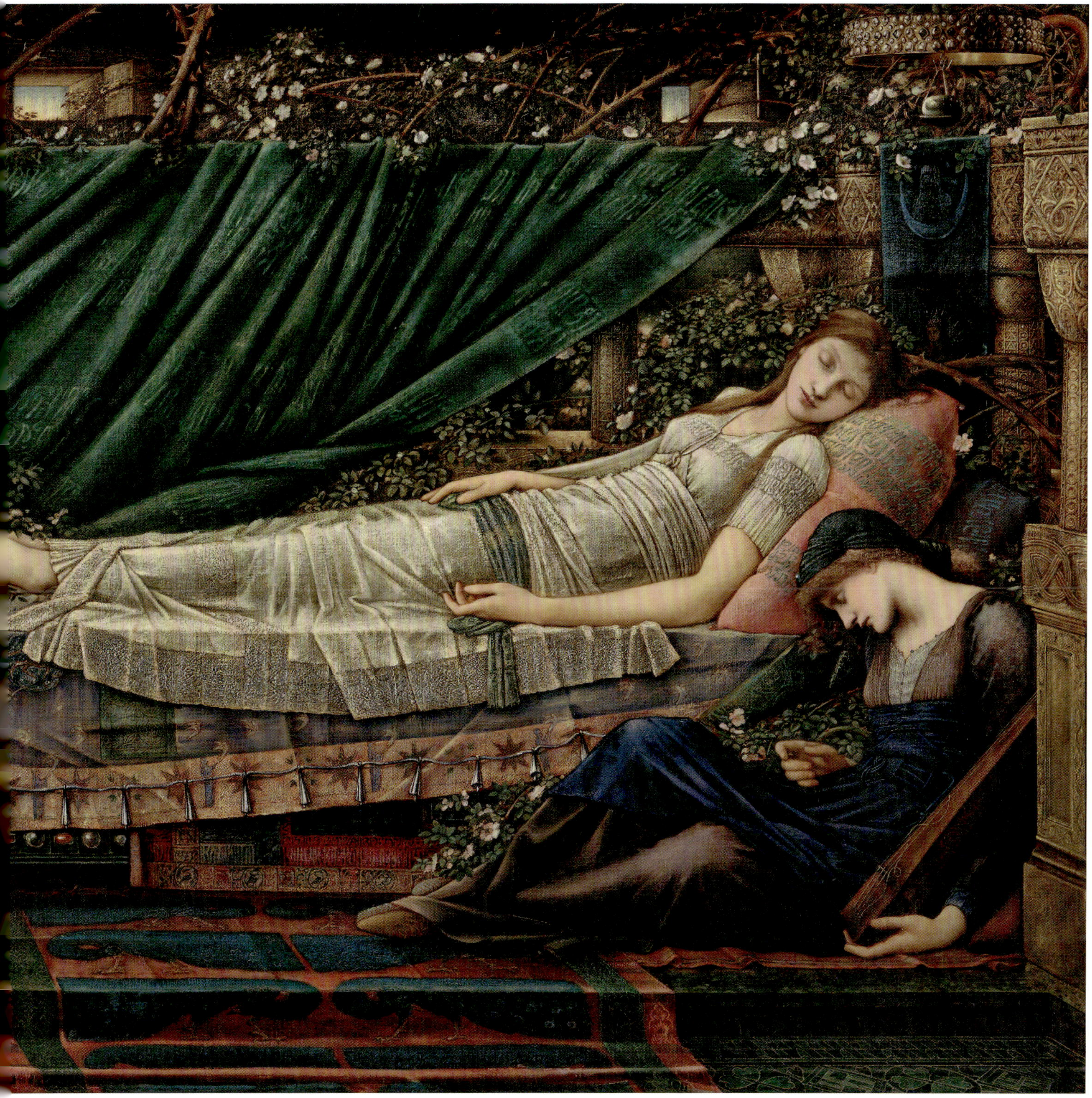

the financier and Liberal Unionist Member of Parliament Alexander Henderson, installed them (figs.34, 35); beneath the frames, verses newly composed by William Morris were added to elucidate the story. The exhibition therefore includes the full set of paintings, plus more. Yet these are neither the first nor the last of Burne-Jones's thoughts on the Sleeping Beauty legend. In the 1890s he took up three canvases, previously discarded from the set now at Buscot Park, and worked them up as independent works, now dispersed far and wide to collections in Delaware, Ireland and Bristol (UK).

The proliferation of versions cannot be dismissed as mere commercial expedients – or mere headaches for the exhibition curator and designer. The continuous process of multiplication and variation is integral to the history of the series paintings, which change and develop over the time span of Burne-Jones's career just as the myths and legends themselves evolve over the longer time frames of their life in the popular imagination. Perhaps, indeed, Burne-Jones's paintings – finished or unfinished – should be seen as episodes within the longer history of the myths.

Both series can be traced back, in Burne-Jones's oeuvre, to the early days of his collaboration with Morris and Rossetti in the 1860s, although their psychic roots no doubt reach further still, back to tales read or heard in the artist's childhood. The story of the Sleeping Beauty was the first to achieve material form, as a set of tiles made in 1864 for the house of Myles Birket Foster, himself an artist and an early patron of Morris, Marshall, Faulkner & Co.; the tiles are thought to have been painted (to Burne-Jones's design) by Lucy Faulkner, sister of one of the firm's partners (fig.37). Thus the telling of this story was a collaboration from the start. At this stage there were nine scenes – a comprehensive but also rambling and informal telling of the tale. Only the scene placed in the exact centre of the three-by-three

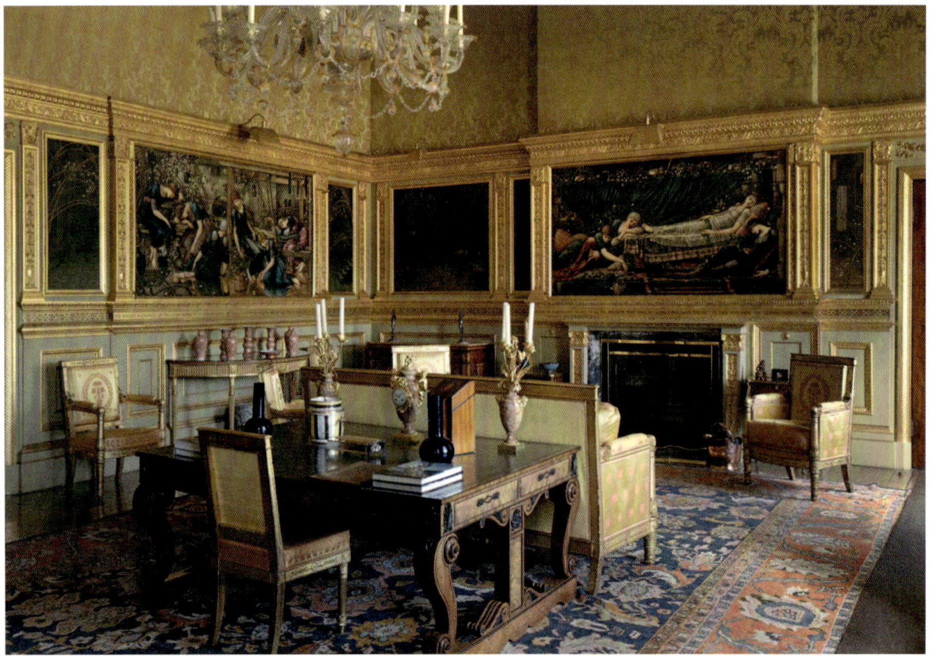

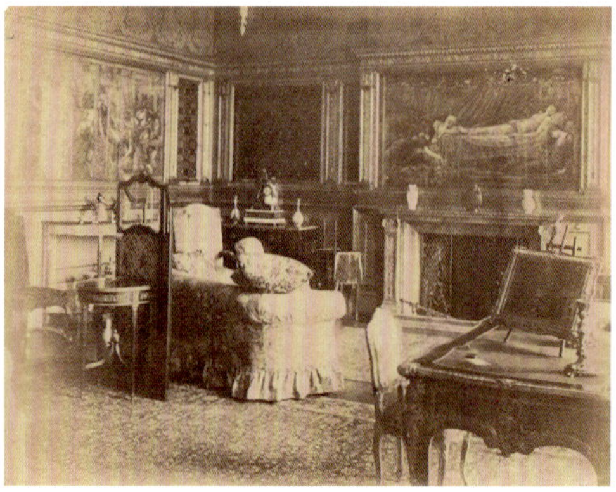

Fig.34
The saloon at Buscot Park before the side panels were painted and installed, 1891
The Faringdon Collection Trust

Fig.35
The Legend of the Briar Rose installed in the saloon at Buscot Park, 2018

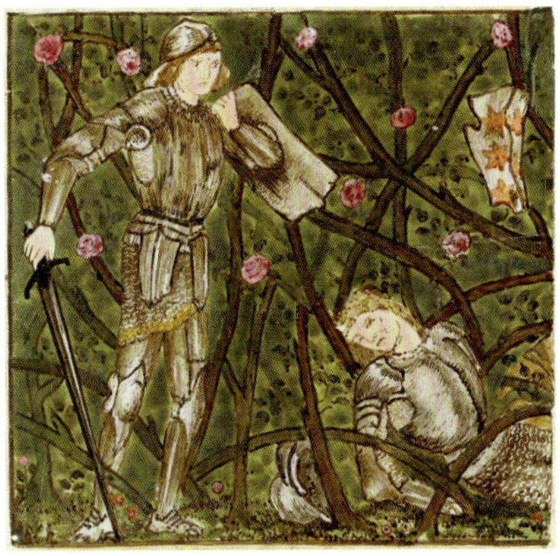

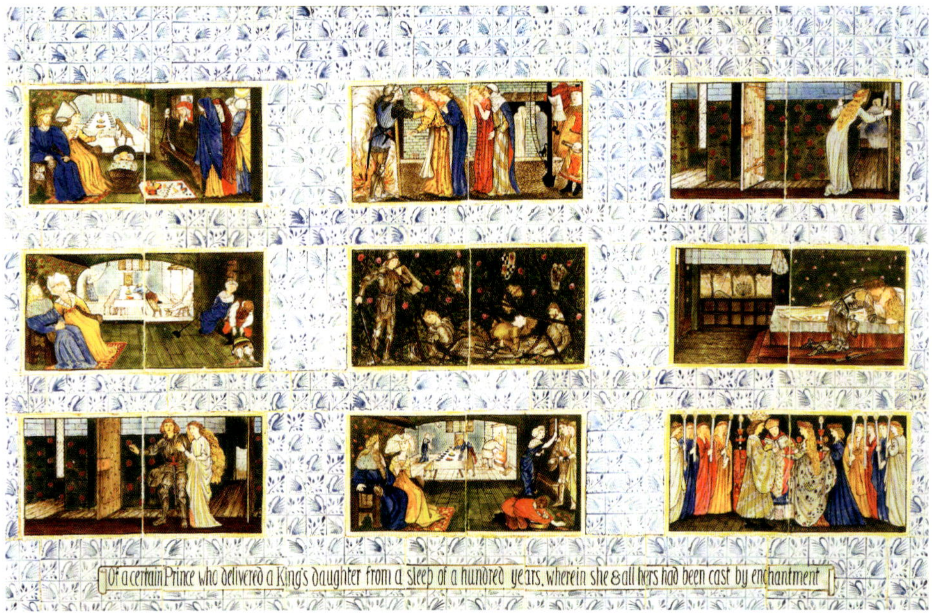

Fig.36
Detail of fig.37

Fig.37
Designed by Edward Burne-Jones, probably painted by Lucy Faulkner, and made by William Morris & Co.
Sleeping Beauty 1864
Ceramic tile panel
76.2 × 120.6
Victoria and Albert Museum

ensemble survived as the kernel from which the later versions grew: the scene of the prince entering the Briar Wood (fig.36), strewn with the armoured bodies of previous venturers, long since fallen asleep under the spell of the place. A piquant detail – the shields suspended in the tangle of briars while their owners slump beneath them – perhaps reads as humorous in the tile series. The shields reappear in all subsequent versions of this composition, but their heraldic devices become muted and their burnished metallic hues increasingly harmonise with the blue-greens of the foliage. The idea persists but its resonances change: the glinting shields, half-hidden in the tangle of briars, seem to be reclaimed by the natural world.

This scene, midway through the narrative in the tile series, becomes the first of the more concentrated final sequence of four compositions, and this reorientation, again, alters the import of the narrative as a whole: in subsequent versions the busy activity of the court, both before and after the hundred-years' sleep, is eliminated to dwell on the suspension of time and human volition in the moment before the spell is broken – the moment when the prince appears, but before his advent causes any other change. Burne-Jones first experimented with an independent oil painting of the scene, begun at large scale in 1869 and never finished (now at Houghton Hall). This led to the series of four, initiated in 1871 in medium-scale versions of about 60 cm high (now in the Museo de Arte de Ponce, Puerto Rico), and almost at once begun again on canvases at double that height – the set in the present exhibition.[1] In the independent scene and the first series, the prince's stance resembles that of the drawing of 1861, *Childe Roland* (no.6), striding forward with sword at the ready. In the final version he stands still with sword straight, better realising the revised conception of the story in which he is the sole waking figure and the only one to stand upright. He is like the time signature or clef at the beginning of a piece of music, or the initial letter of a manuscript: at extreme left, his role is to begin the

127
The Briar Rose side panels 1891
Oil paint on canvas, dimensions variable
The Faringdon Collection Trust

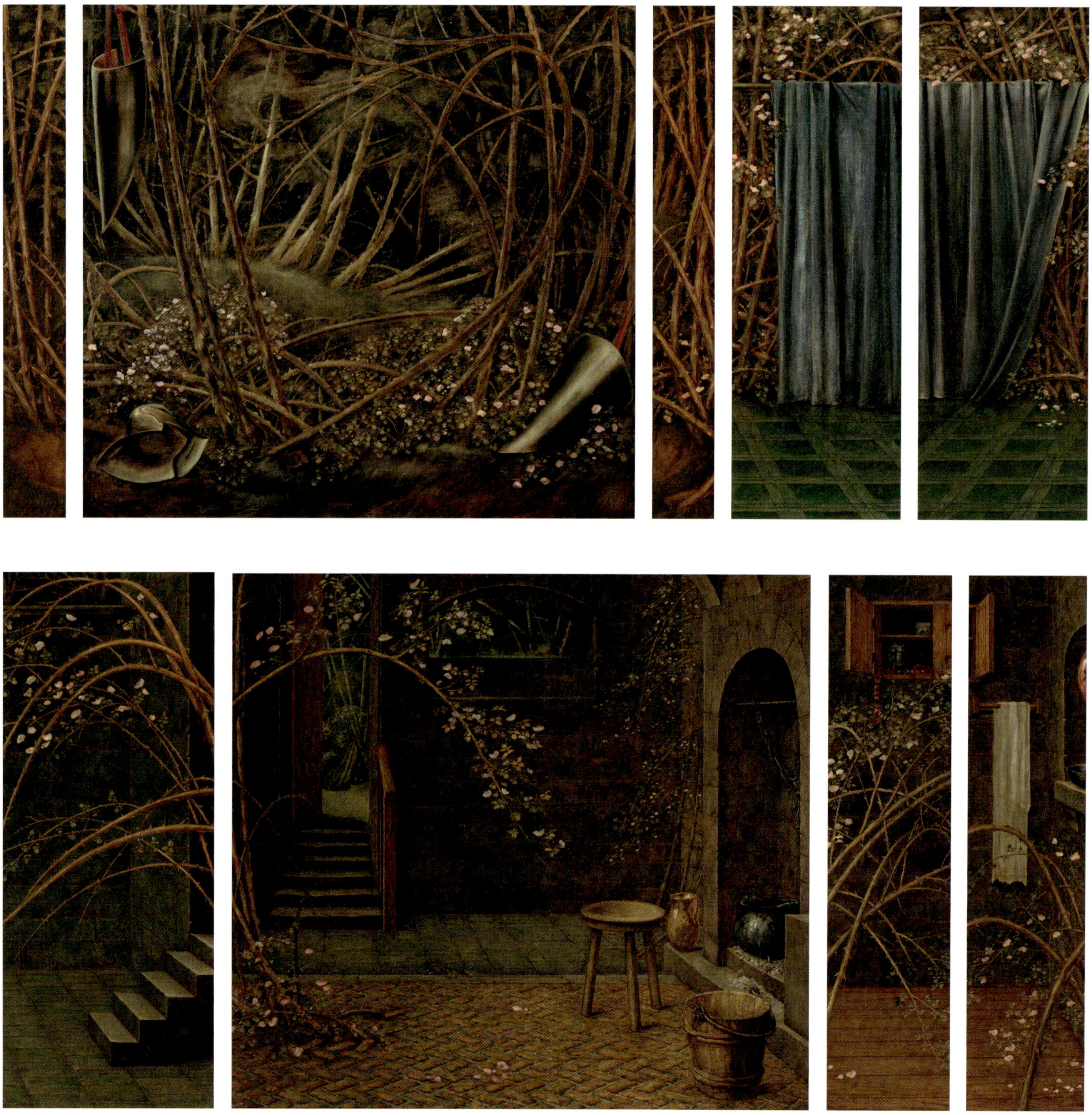

story, which unfolds from left to right in the manner of a child's storybook or comic strip, finally to reach the answering figure of the princess at the very end. In formal terms this is a complete narrative, from prince to princess, facing one another across the rhythmic array of approximately two dozen subsidiary figures. But it is a narrative in which nothing happens. Even the sand in the hourglass, beside the slumbering king in the second scene, is arrested halfway.

Writers on Burne-Jones have often interpreted this lack of action moralistically, as though it betrayed a reluctance on the artist's part to engage with the real world and its politics, or a refusal to acknowledge the awakening sexuality of the young princess, sometimes equated with Burne-Jones's daughter, Margaret (whose marriage in 1888 coincided with the final stages of work on the large series).[2] The French critic Robert de la Sizeranne discovered a moral in the failure of the previous knights to penetrate the briar before the hundred years have run their course: 'That the most righteous cause, the truest ideas, the most necessary reforms, cannot rise triumphant, however bravely we may fight for them, before the time fixed by the mysterious decree of the Higher Powers.'[3] That might seem to confirm the sense that the series somehow condones an escape from political or social reality. And yet the literal implication of the scene must be that – at last – the moment for decisive change has come, with the prince's arrival.

If that is so, it is not part of Burne-Jones's project to predict what that change might involve. In his own words, as reported by his wife Georgiana, 'I want it to stop with the Princess asleep and to tell no more, to leave all the afterwards to the invention and imagination of people, and tell them no more'.[4] This suggests a strong refusal to indulge art's potential to serve as propaganda. We viewers are presented with a whole world, complete in itself, but we are left free to imagine its destiny.

Tennyson's poem 'The Day-Dream' memorably figures the world awaking on the prince's arrival:

A touch, a kiss! the charm was snapt,
There rose a noise of striking clocks,
And feet that ran, and doors that clapt,
And barking dogs, and crowing cocks

If Burne-Jones declines to depict this moment, that may reflect the different exigencies of decorative painting, as opposed to the narrative movement of poetry: so abrupt a change in gear might destroy the visual coherence of the series. However, Burne-Jones may also be reflecting on Tennyson's own comments in the penultimate section of his poem, entitled 'Moral':

So, Lady Flora, take my lay,
And if you find no moral there,
Go, look in any glass and say,
What moral is in being fair.
Oh, to what uses shall we put
The wildweed-flower that simply blows?
And is there any moral shut
Within the bosom of the rose?

These lines adumbrate the ideas that would become associated with the slogan 'art for art's sake' by the time Burne-Jones painted his series.

The prince's arrival, then, opens the potential for change. In its refusal to specify that change – or to rule anything out – Burne-Jones's pictorial sequence permits the potential to be limitless, an idea more radical than any more narrowly political art. Yet there is no doubting the fact that Burne-Jones delights in painting the sleeping world with all its old-fashioned accoutrements, something about which he is characteristically self-conscious. In 1885, hard at work on the setting, he wrote to a landowning friend, Lady Leighton:

> *I wonder if in your land there grow stems of wild-rose such as I have to paint ... and if deep in some tangle there is a hoary, aged monarch of the tangle, thick as a wrist and with long, horrible spikes on it – and if three or four feet of such an one might be carved out for me by a 'feller' and sent to me.*[5]

This is a characteristic example of Burne-Jones's wit, with its touch of self-protective irony. It involves a highly ingenious – and hilarious – parody of first-generation Pre-Raphaelitism and the naive literalism of its 'truth-to-nature' project. The paintings of the *Briar Rose* series cannot be mistaken for early Pre-Raphaelite painting. Nonetheless, their spikes and tangles are quintessentially spiky and tangly; they are persuasively, or even obsessively, so. In some sense, the briars become the point of the story. When Burne-Jones came to execute the additional panels, to fit the series into Alexander Henderson's saloon, he filled them with briars (no.127).

The briar rose is Burne-Jones's distinctive annotation to the fairy tale, combining as it does the menace of the thorns with the beauty of the rose, symbol of the Virgin Mary and the goal of another of the artist's favourite quest narratives, the *Roman de la Rose*.[6] These natural objects leave behind early Pre-Raphaelite realism to enter a world of comparative mythology; one thinks of Wagner's Brünnhilde, put to sleep on a mountain top encircled by fire. Burne-Jones's Sleeping Beauty may have similarly far-reaching intellectual resonances, expressed in pictorial form: the briars and roses weave through all four horizontal canvases, and eventually through the supplementary canvases as well, in a world dense with circumstantial detail. Pre-Raphaelite realism does not vanish, but is transfigured.

The settings of the Perseus series, by contrast, are bare and barren, yet this effect was as hard won as all the circumstantial detail of the Sleeping Palace. In a letter of September 1876 Burne-Jones describes his work on the composition that represents Andromeda chained to a rock:

> *[A]ll the sick weeks I worked at it when I ought to have done nothing nearly ruined it. You see I began to play with it and filled it with little houses and fields and roads, and walled gardens and mills, and bushes and winding shores and islands, and one day the veil was lifted and I saw how every pretty incident helped to ruin the thing, and I had three days of havoc at it and took them all out; and now in their place is a grey, doleful rock, but for the first time there is hope in the picture.*[7]

The letter gives a vivid sense of the wrench required for Burne-Jones, so much at home in the fairy-tale environment of the Sleeping Beauty, to turn his imagination

128
The Call of Perseus; Perseus and the Graiae; Perseus and the Nereids 1875–6
Gouache, gold paint and ink on paper, 36.7 × 102.7
Tate

129
The Finding of Medusa; The Death of Medusa (The Birth of Pegasus and Chrysaor); Perseus Pursued by the Gorgons 1875–6
Gouache, gold paint and ink on paper, 36.8 × 128.4
Tate

130
Atlas Turned to Stone; The Rock of Doom and the Doom Fulfilled; The Court of Phineas; The Baleful Head 1875–6
Gouache, gold paint, graphite and chalk on paper, 36.7 × 148.7
Tate

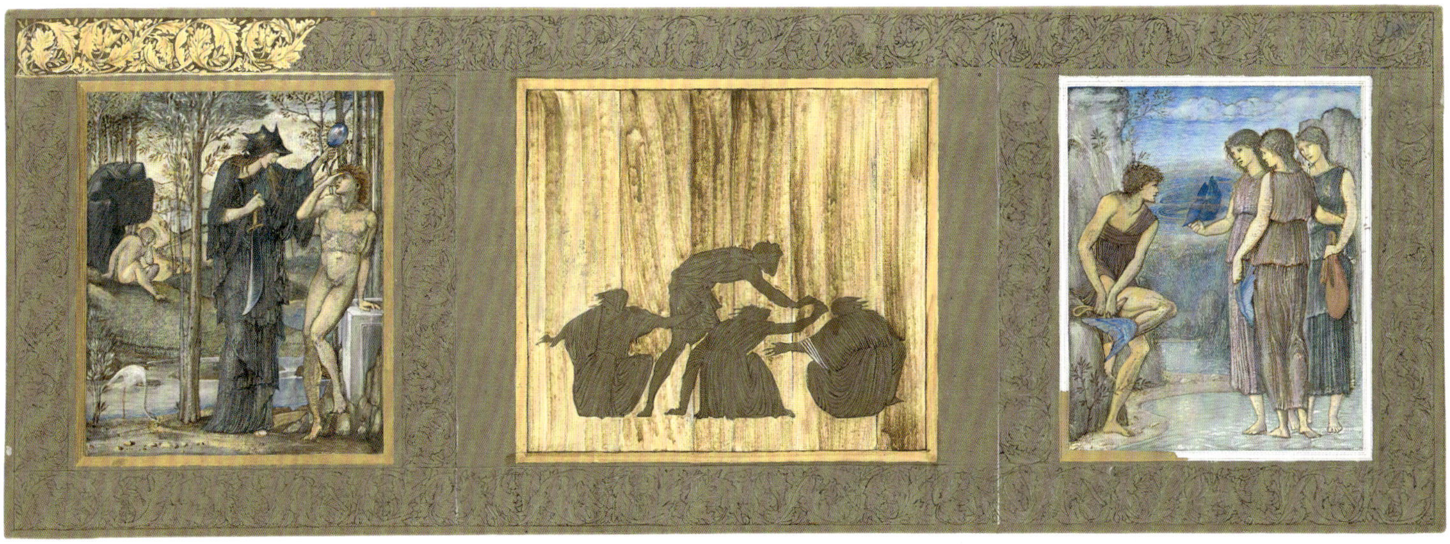

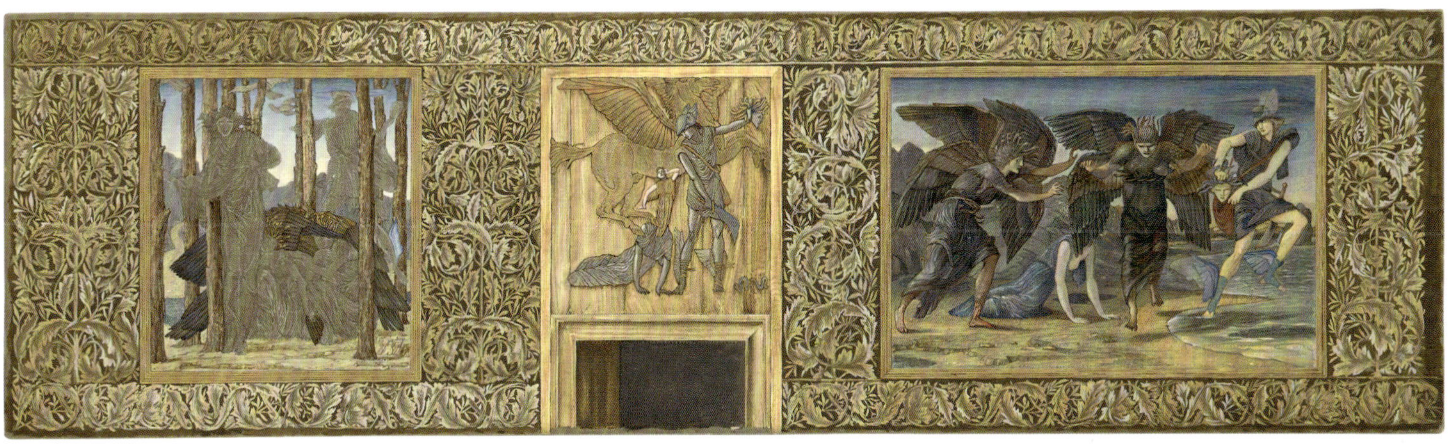

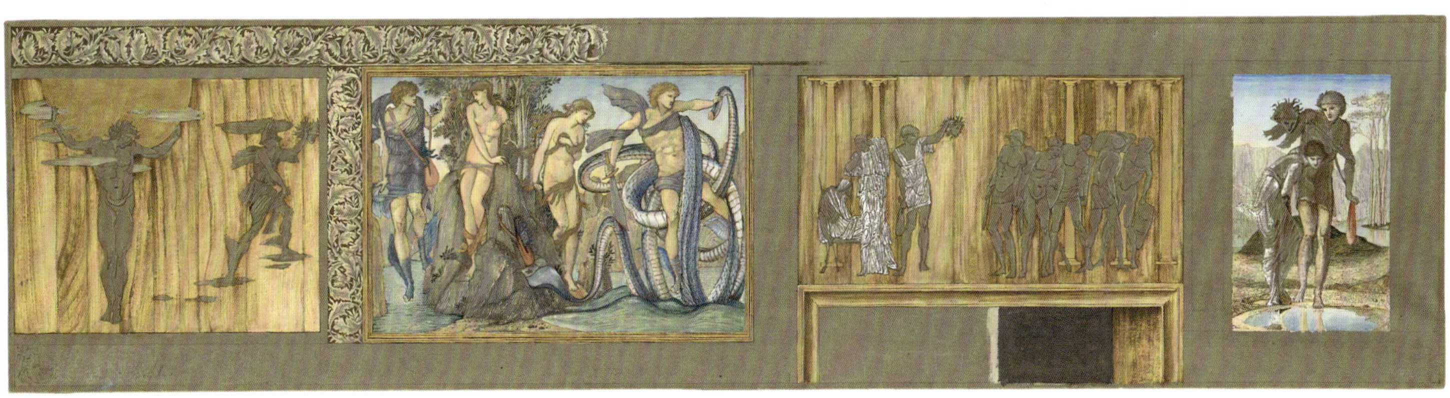

131
Perseus and the Graiae 1877–88
Silver and gold leaf, gesso, and oil paint on oak, 170.2 × 153.2
Amgueddfa Cymru-National Museum Wales

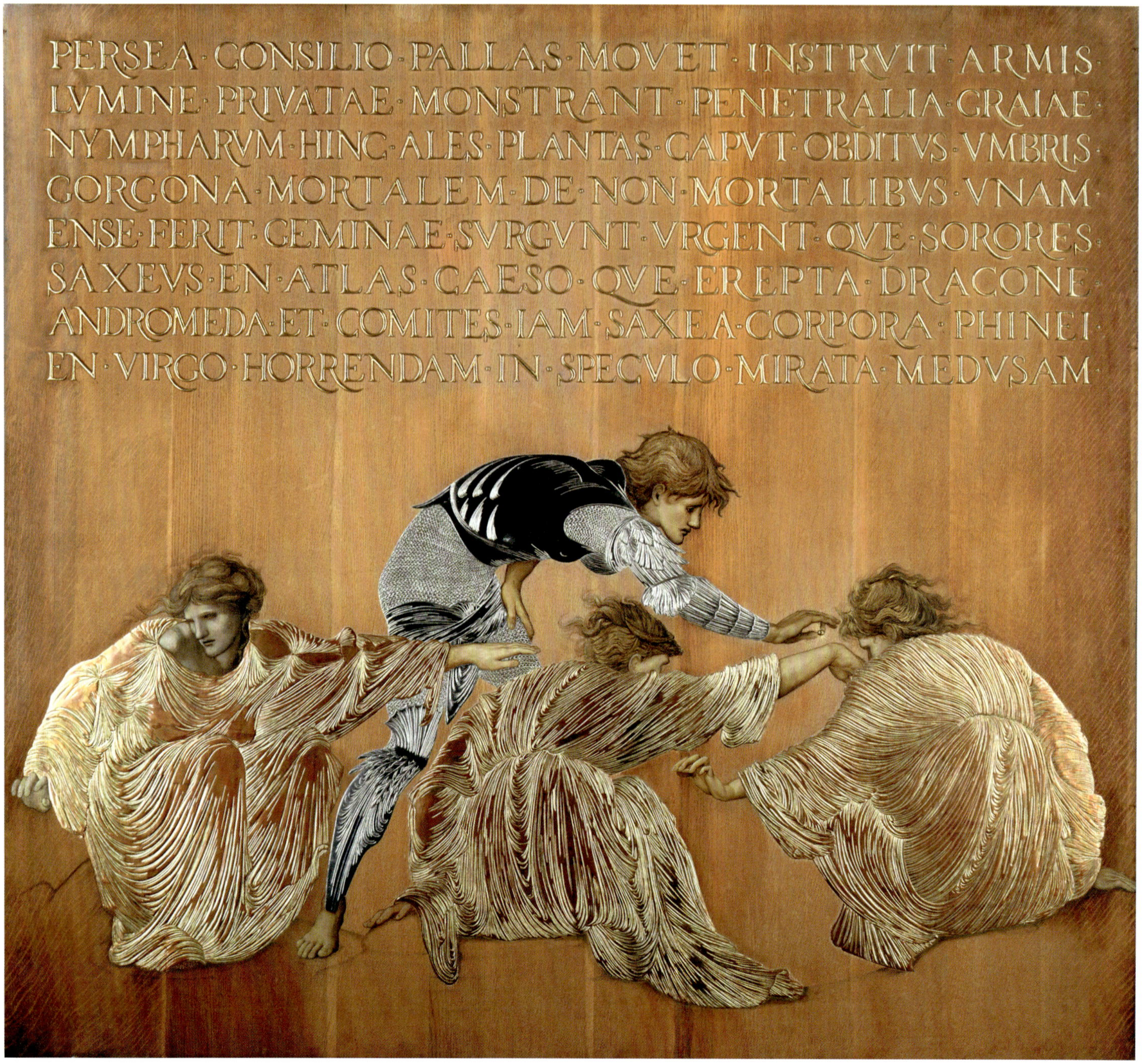

to creating a classical world sufficiently primeval for the adventures of Perseus. Yet this series also has its origins in the 1860s and in a collaboration with Morris: it derives from 'The Doom of King Acrisius', one of the Greek myths recounted in the first instalment of Morris's *Earthly Paradise*. Although the original plans for a publication lavishly illustrated by Burne-Jones ran into insoluble technical problems, the tales of *The Earthly Paradise* were premised from the outset on a union of word and image. In 1875, then, when Burne-Jones suggested to an enthusiastic new patron a series of paintings on the Perseus legend, he was resuming a collaborative project that had, in a sense, merely been interrupted for a decade.[8]

The patron was the twenty-six-year-old Arthur Balfour, later Prime Minister but at the time of the commission a brilliant young member of the artistic and hedonistic social group known as the 'Souls', and he was prepared to give the artist free rein.[9] Burne-Jones quickly worked out a design for the entire series in watercolour (nos.128, 129, 130). The design follows the complicated story of Morris's poem, omitting the framing narrative about King Acrisius (the grandfather whom Perseus unwittingly kills) and adjusting the order of the episodes into ten scenes organised on three long horizontal strips of paper, each of which concentrates on a phase of the story: the preparations for Perseus's quest, his slaying of the Gorgon Medusa, and his rescue of and marriage to Andromeda. Interspersed with fully coloured pictures are designs for four panels to be executed in relief, and the whole series is surrounded by an acanthus-leaf pattern in the style of Morris. Despite its origin in a narrative poem, the revised sequence perhaps makes sense only in the three-dimensional space of the interior for which it was designed, the drawing room of Balfour's London house, 4 Carlton Gardens. This was a very grand house indeed, in a cul-de-sac at the west end of Carlton House Terrace in the heart of Westminster and on land that had been part of the gardens of St James's Palace. Since the house was replaced by a new building in the 1930s, the original interior has been lost, and in any case only four of the paintings in the sequence were completed. The design, however, gives some sense of the sumptuousness of Burne-Jones's original idea for the series.

The relief panels formed a particularly innovative part of the design not only in their mixed media, but also in the stylisation of their figures, silhouetted in the shallowest of relief against a wood-grain pattern that makes no attempt to represent a natural setting. Burne-Jones tried out the idea for the first of the panels, representing Perseus's encounter with the Graiae (sisters of the Gorgons), in a work exhibited at the Grosvenor Gallery in 1878 (no.131), where he further complicated the mixture of representation and abstraction by adding a text that occupies nearly the entire top half of the composition. The text is of some importance, for it shows how Burne-Jones's treatment of the legend was beginning to develop beyond its initial conception. Rather than quoting lines from Morris's blank-verse poem in Chaucerian English, with its fast-moving narrative verve, Burne-Jones uses a new text composed in Latin for the occasion by the eminent classical scholar Richard Jebb, in stately dactylic hexameters, the metre of ancient epic poetry.[10] The eight lines summarise the entire story, transforming it from a narrative into something like a monument, and they are given the visual form of an ancient inscription, in Roman majuscule lettering with dots to separate the words. In literal translation the lines read:

Pallas urges on Perseus by her advice. She equips him with arms.
The Graiae, deprived of eyesight, show him the secret dwelling
Of the Nymphs. From here, his feet winged, his head hidden in shadow,
The Gorgon, alone mortal out of these non-mortals,
He strikes with his blade. The twin sisters rise, and press on him.
Behold Atlas stony, and, snatched from the slain dragon,
Andromeda, and the comrades of Phineus now stony bodies.
Behold the maiden wondering in a mirror at terrible Medusa.[11]

Despite the beauty of this experimental panel, with text and figures shimmering gold and silver on the oak grain, it was not favourably received at the Grosvenor, and Burne-Jones eventually reconceived the scene as an oil painting in which the text is replaced by a mountainous landscape swirling with mist (no.133). Arguably, though, the laconic formality of the Latin inscription, as well as the rhythmic lines of the relief, have left their traces on this scene. The darkened world, in which the Graiae reach for the single eye that Perseus has stolen (Jebb's Latin word *lumen* can mean 'light' as well as 'eye'), is both beautiful and terrible, and they must trade their wisdom to regain their vision.

Between the relief panel and the final version, Burne-Jones made yet another version of *Perseus and the Graiae* (Southampton City Art Gallery): a watercolour cartoon (in which the Latin text was retained) that represented the subject among the complete set of full-scale cartoons that formed a crucial part of Burne-Jones's complex working process for realising the series. The scene of the Graiae is the only one to have been refined through four successive versions – from the original design to the experimental relief panel shown at the Grosvenor, then the full-scale cartoon and finally the completed oil painting. That confirms its summative character, and the scene makes reference to many of the ideas that circulate, in mythic fashion, through the series as a whole. Despite the episodic character of the narrative, the series is held together by these recurring ideas. One is the wisdom of women, who instruct Perseus at every stage: Pallas Athene gives Perseus the first clues to start his quest (no.132) and tells him how to reach the Graiae, who, in their turn, lead him to the sea nymphs who reveal, at last, where the Gorgons reside (no.134). There are, then, three groups of three female figures, like the three Fates and three Graces of classical mythology or Wagner's Rhinemaidens and Norns; each of them has some form of knowledge or power that Perseus needs to draw upon. Another recurring idea revolves around the power of sight or vision: the Graiae with their single eye, the Medusa's head that turns to stone anyone who beholds it, the mirror that Perseus uses to look at Medusa unharmed. Finally, and most hauntingly, there is the mirroring surface of the well in the final scene, in which Perseus can finally show Andromeda the head of Medusa, making yet another group of three faces, seen twice (no.141). Burne-Jones's fascination with reflections – also evident in the polished reflective surfaces of the *Briar Rose* series – is echoed in the sheen of Perseus's armour and the pools of water that appear at intervals. These are only a few of the recurring ideas that thread through the series: the viewer may discover and follow many more.

The complexity with which ideas and visible forms weave through the individual works of the series perhaps suggests why it was so difficult to bring to conclusion. Any fresh start, moreover, brought with it a new set of ramifications. The set of ten

132
The Call of Perseus 1877–98
Oil paint and chalk on canvas, 152.5 × 127
Staatsgalerie Stuttgart

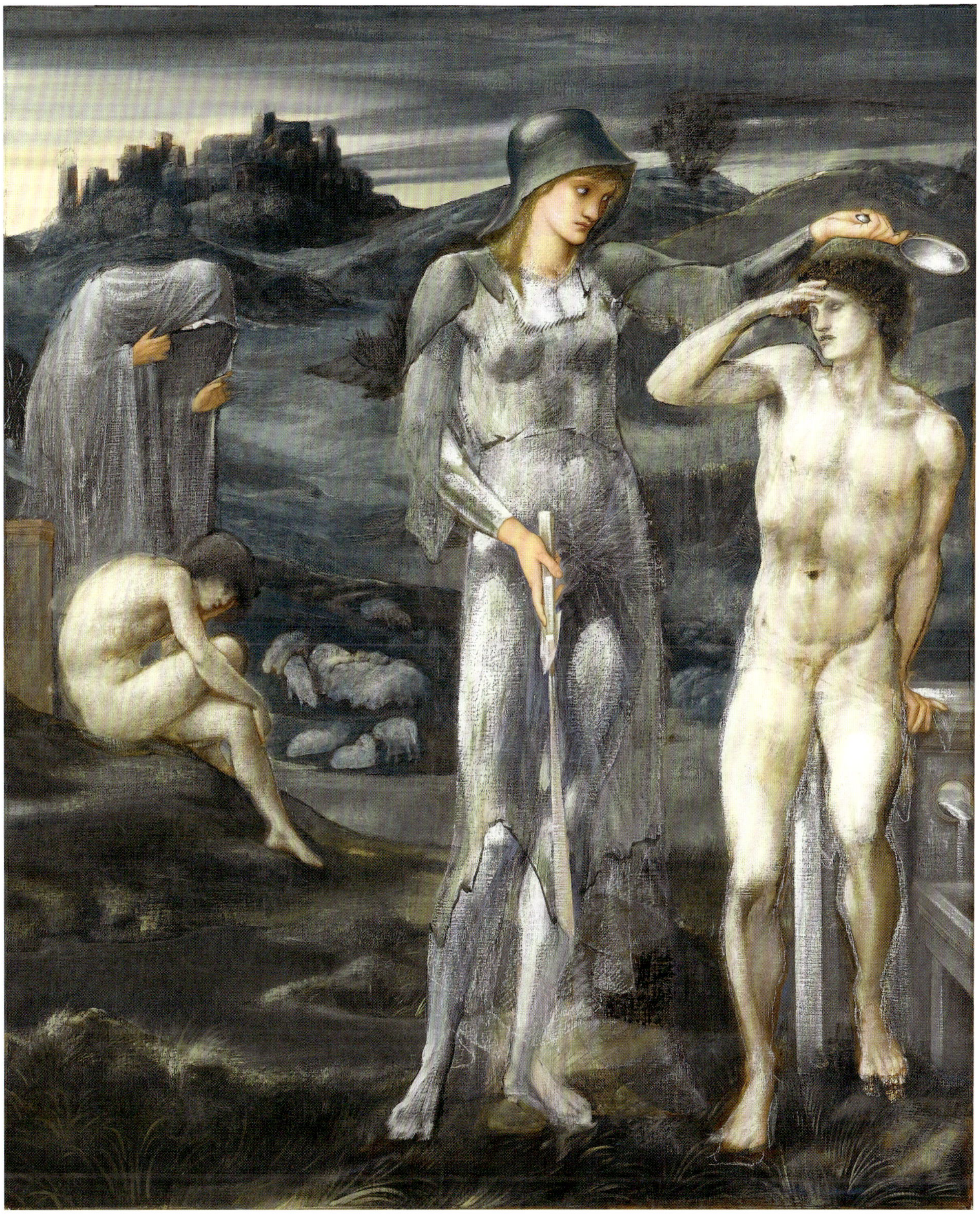

133
Perseus and the Graiae 1892
Oil paint on canvas, 153.5 × 170
Staatsgalerie Stuttgart

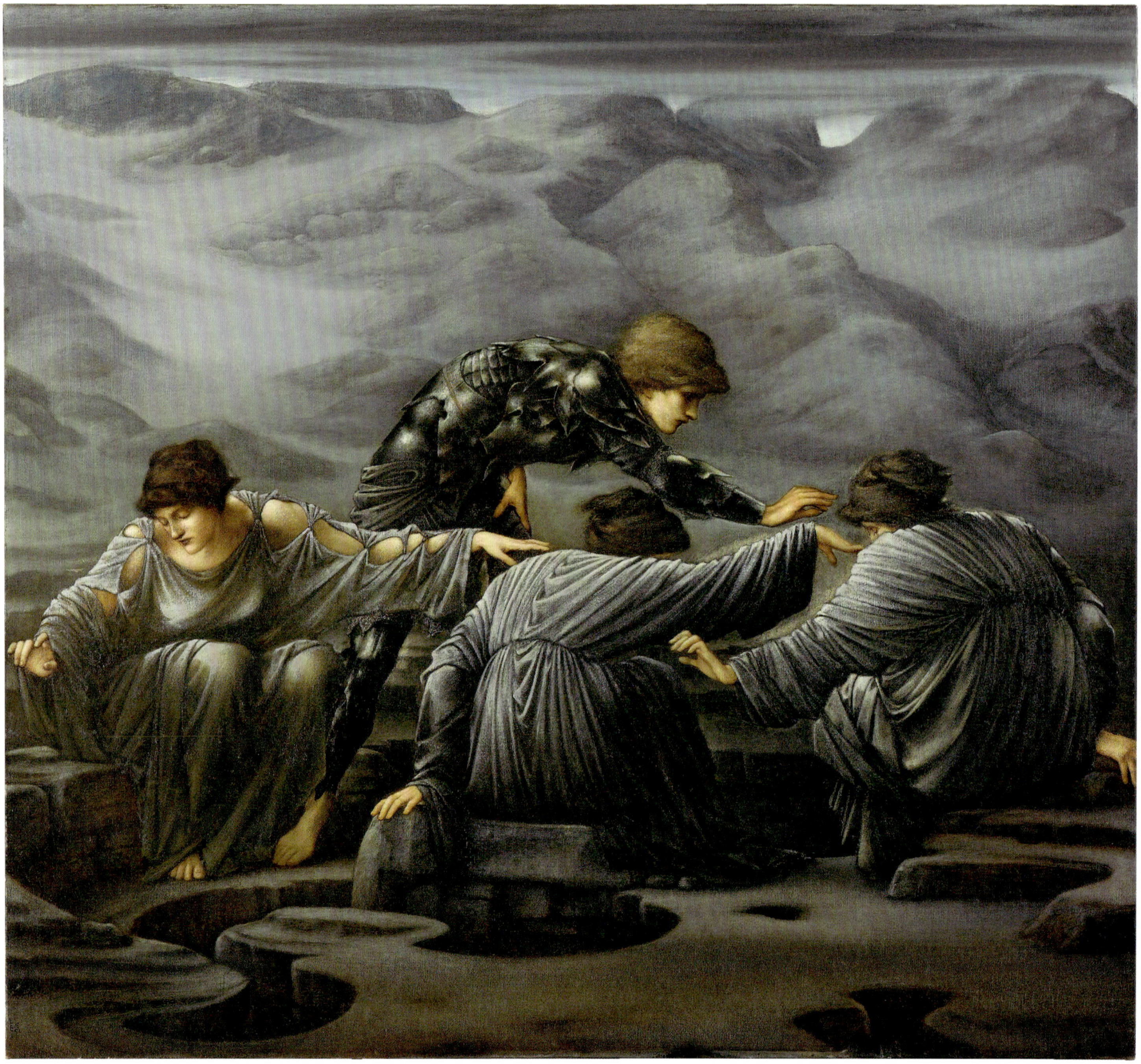

134
Perseus and the Sea Nymphs
(The Arming of Perseus) 1877
Bodycolour on paper, 152.8 × 126.4
Southampton City Art Gallery

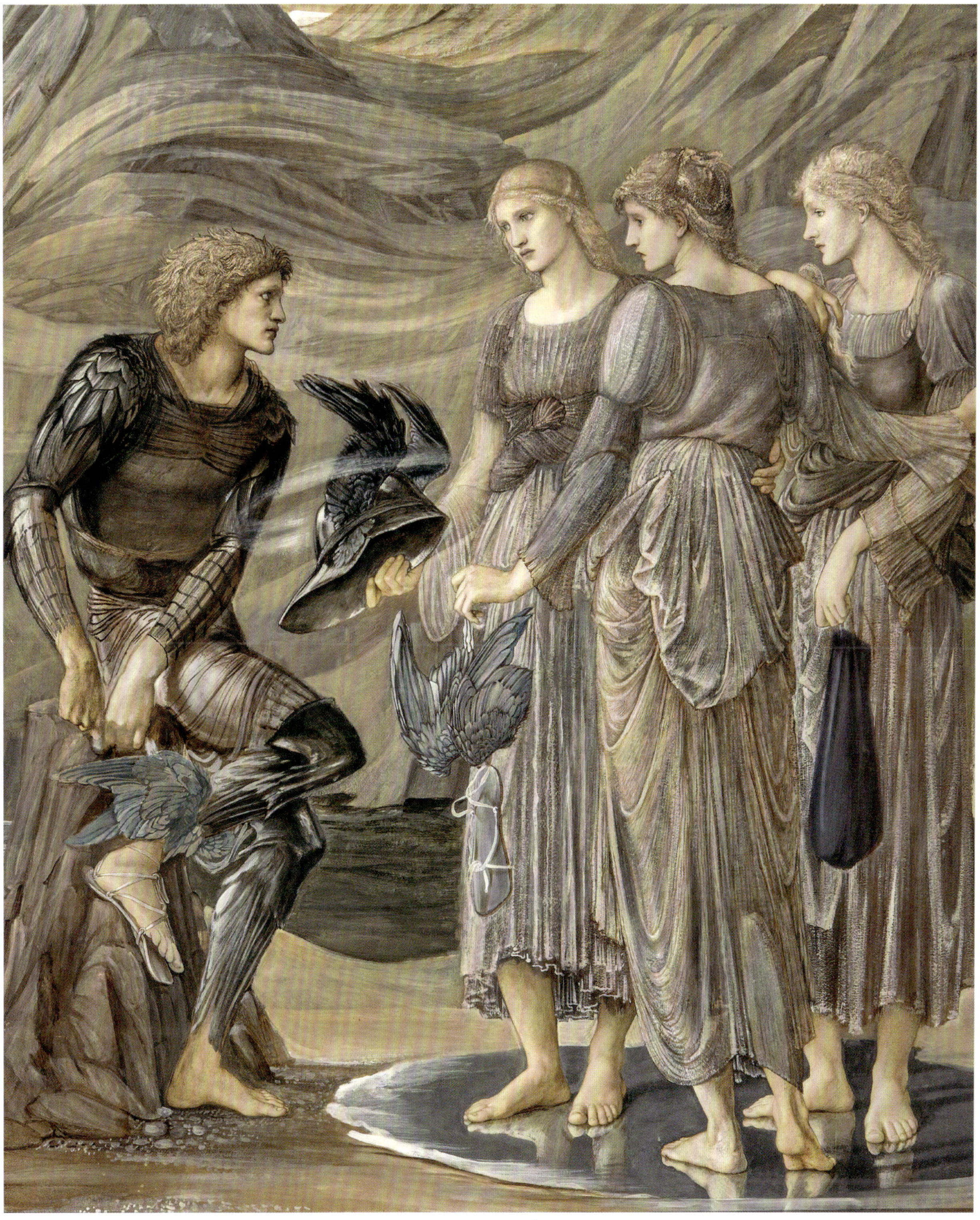

135
The Finding of Medusa c.1882
Bodycolour on paper, 152.5 × 137.7
Southampton City Art Gallery

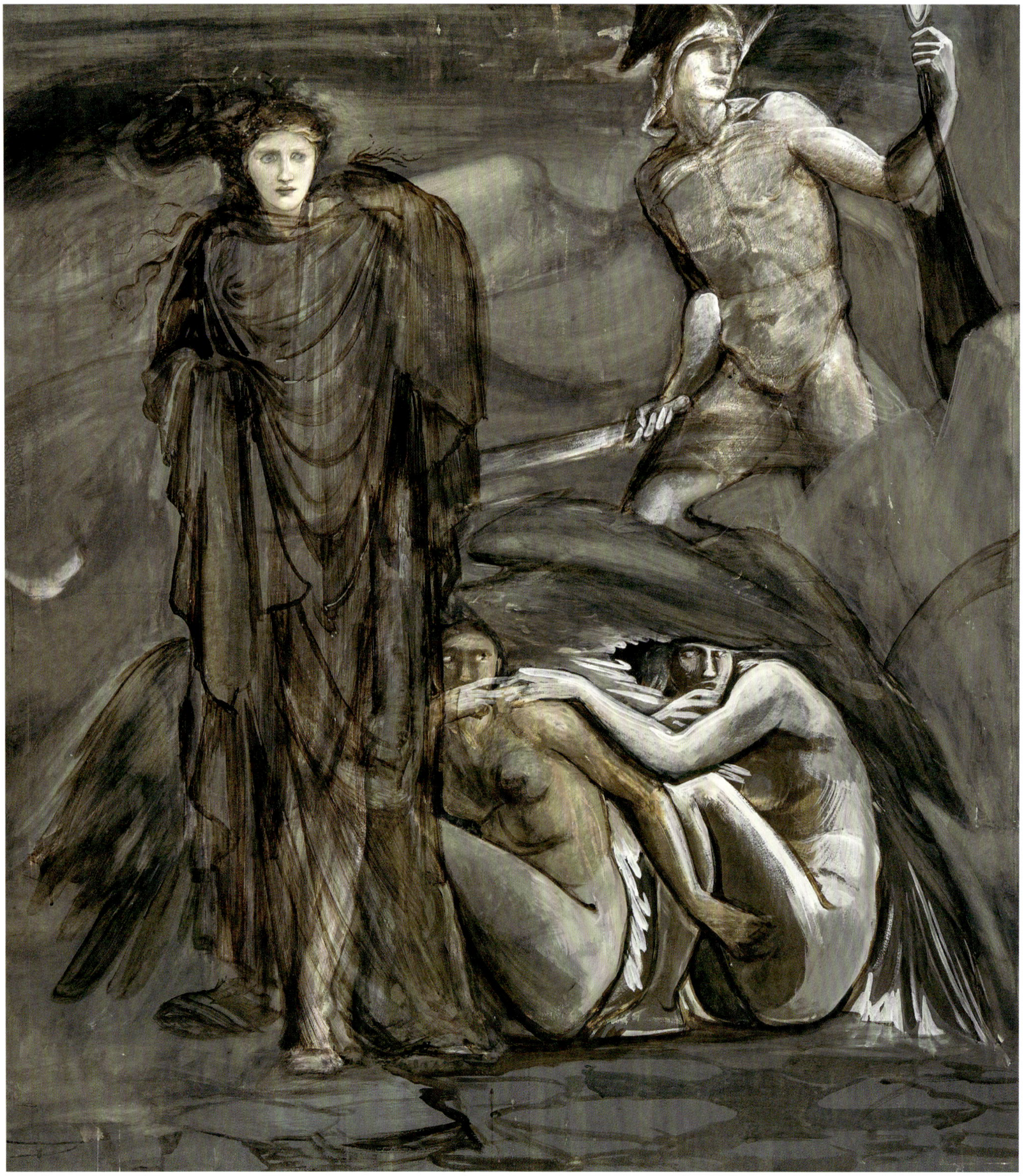

136
The Death of Medusa (I) c.1882
Bodycolour on paper, 124.5 × 116.9
Southampton City Art Gallery

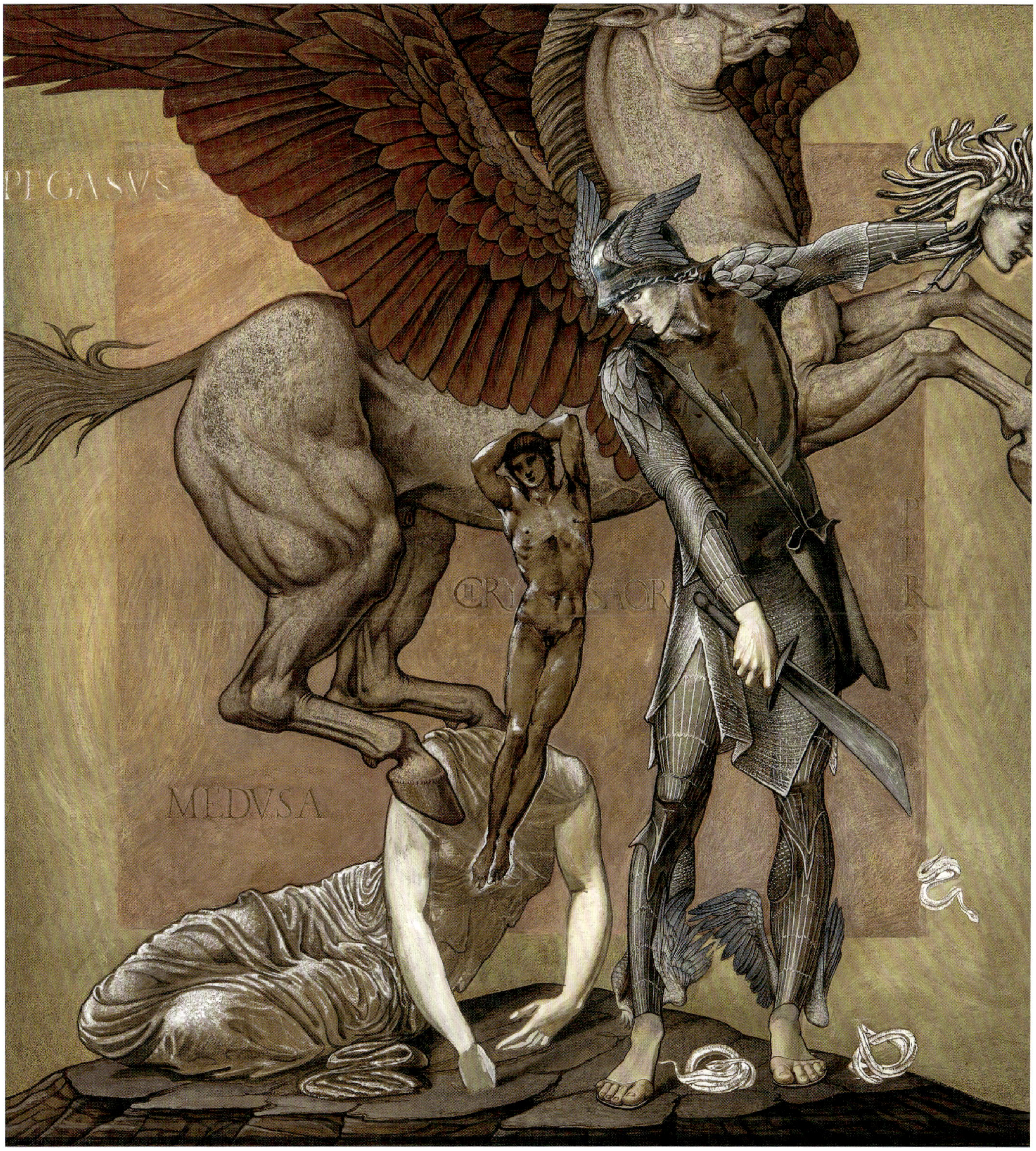

137
The Death of Medusa (II) c.1881–2
Bodycolour on paper, 152.5 × 136.5
Southampton City Art Gallery

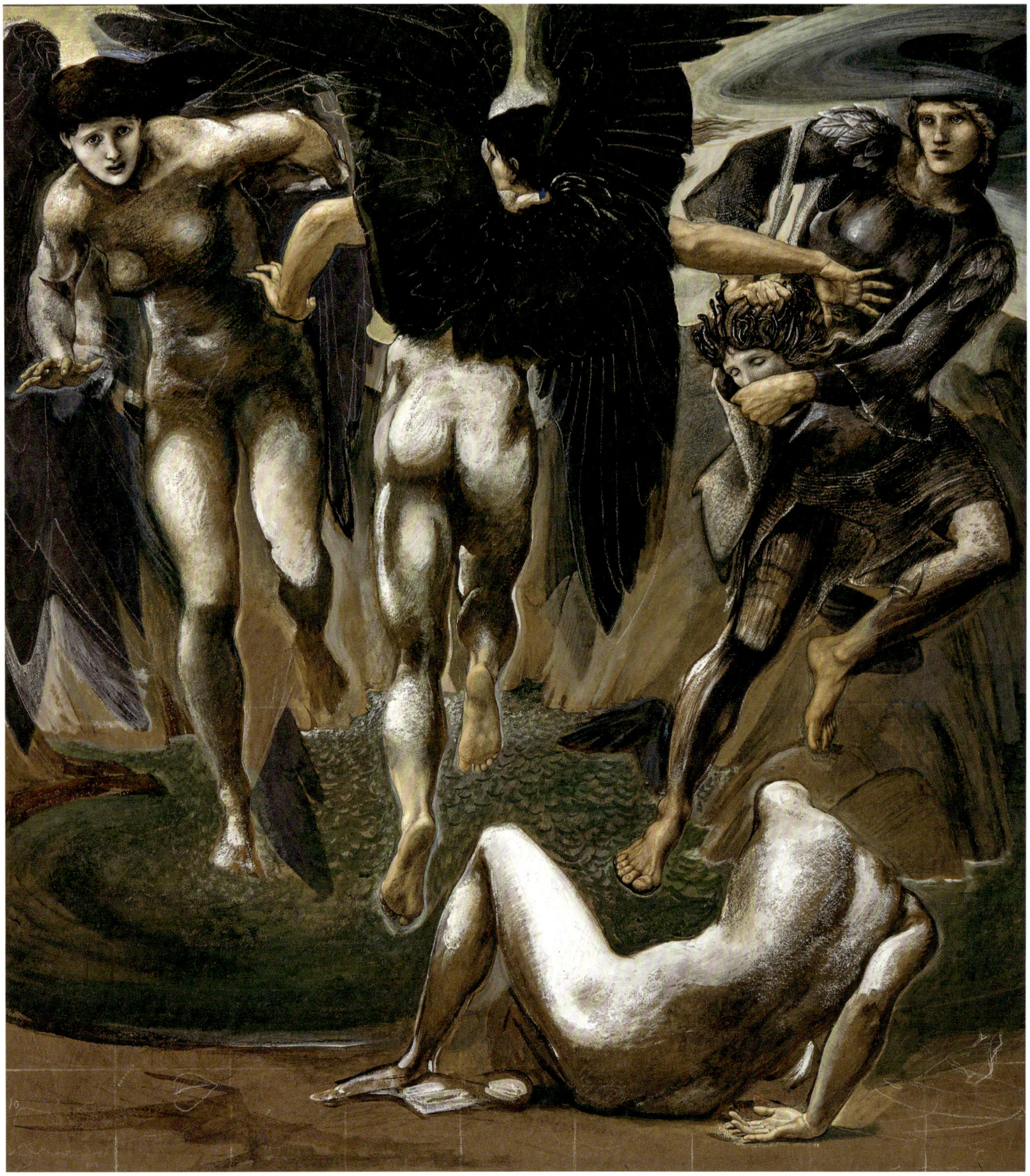

138
Atlas Turned to Stone c.1878
Bodycolour on paper, 150.2 × 190.2
Southampton City Art Gallery

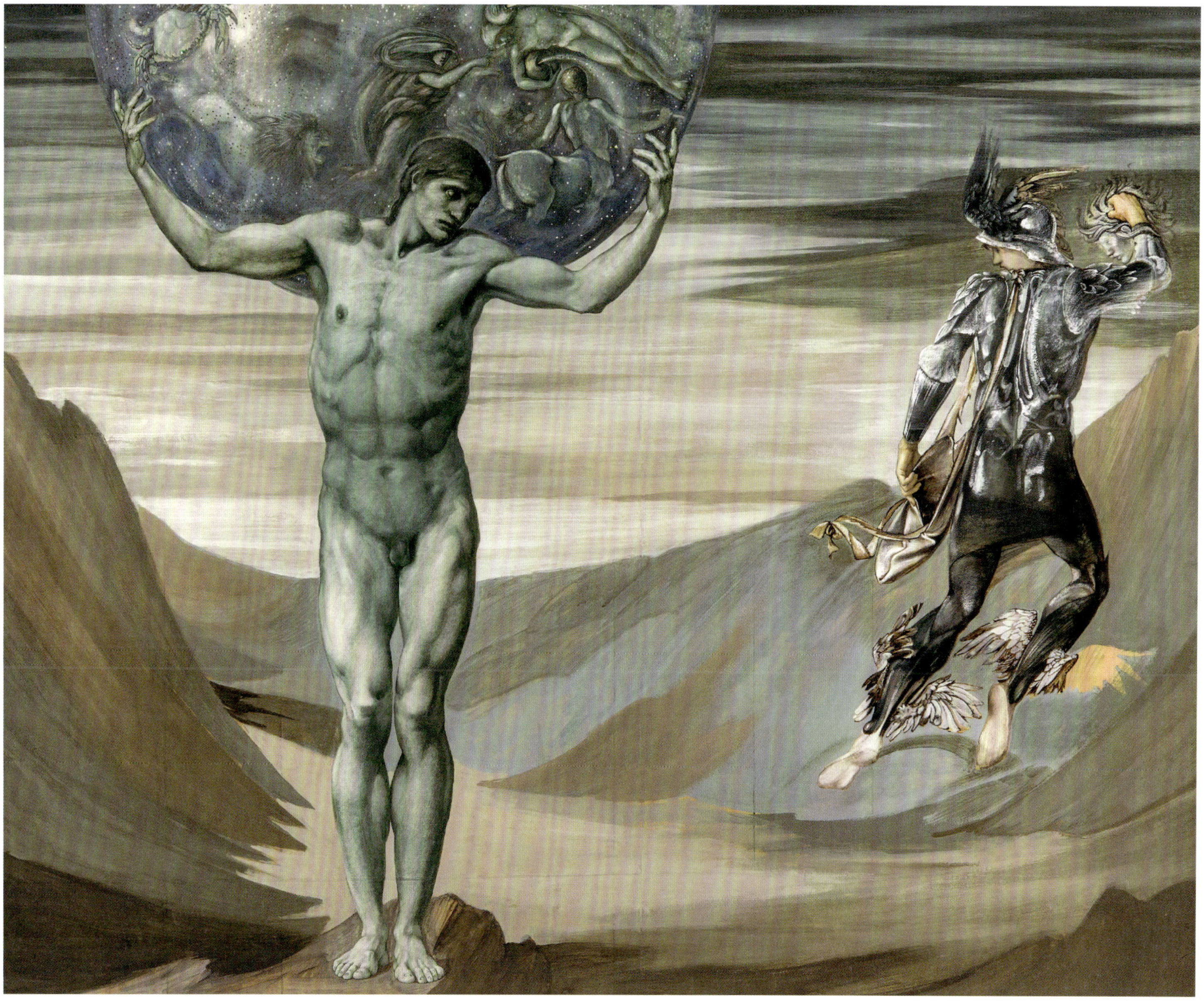

139
The Rock of Doom 1885–8
Oil paint on canvas, 155 × 130
Staatsgalerie Stuttgart

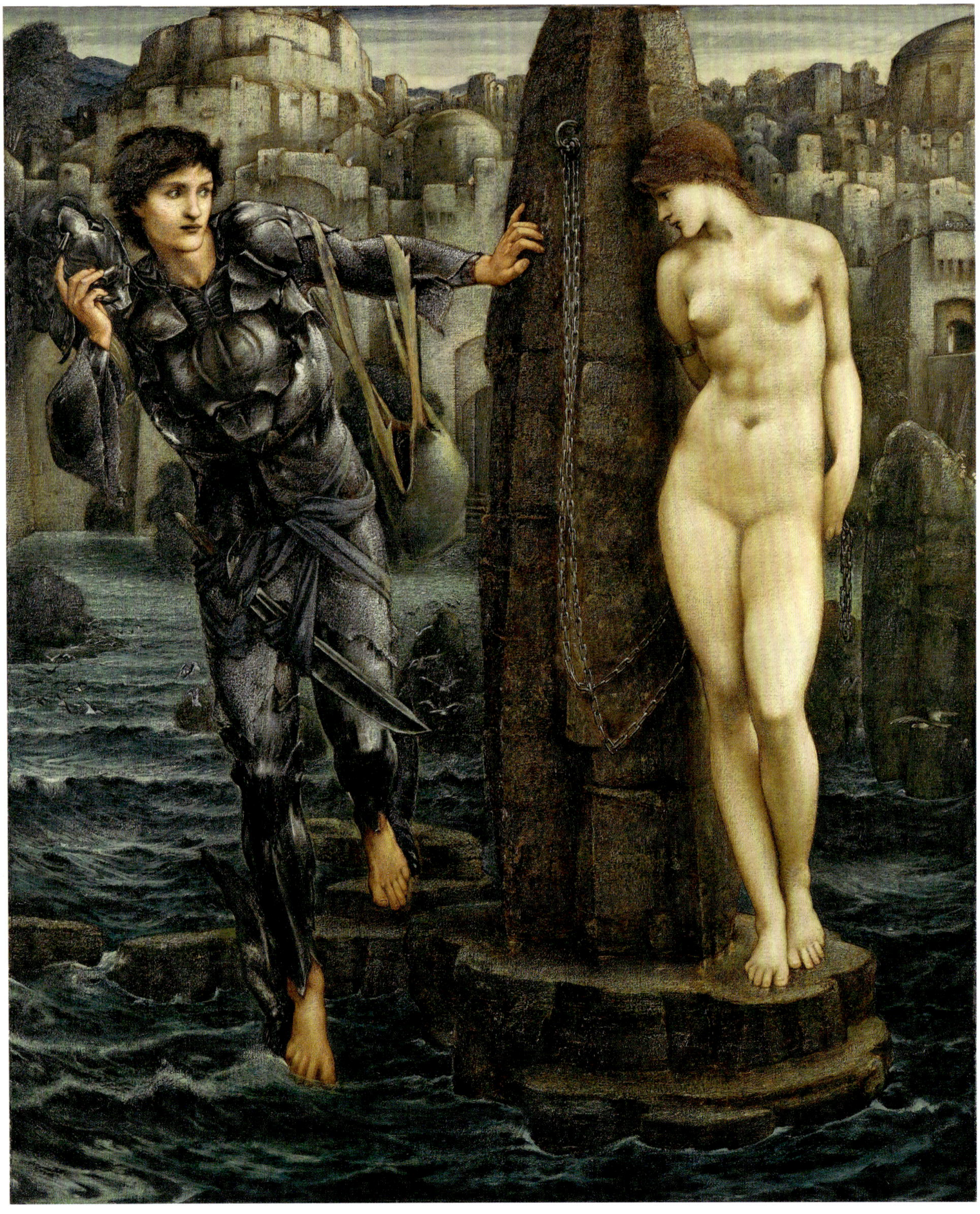

140
The Doom Fulfilled 1888
Oil paint on canvas, 155 × 140.5
Staatsgalerie Stuttgart

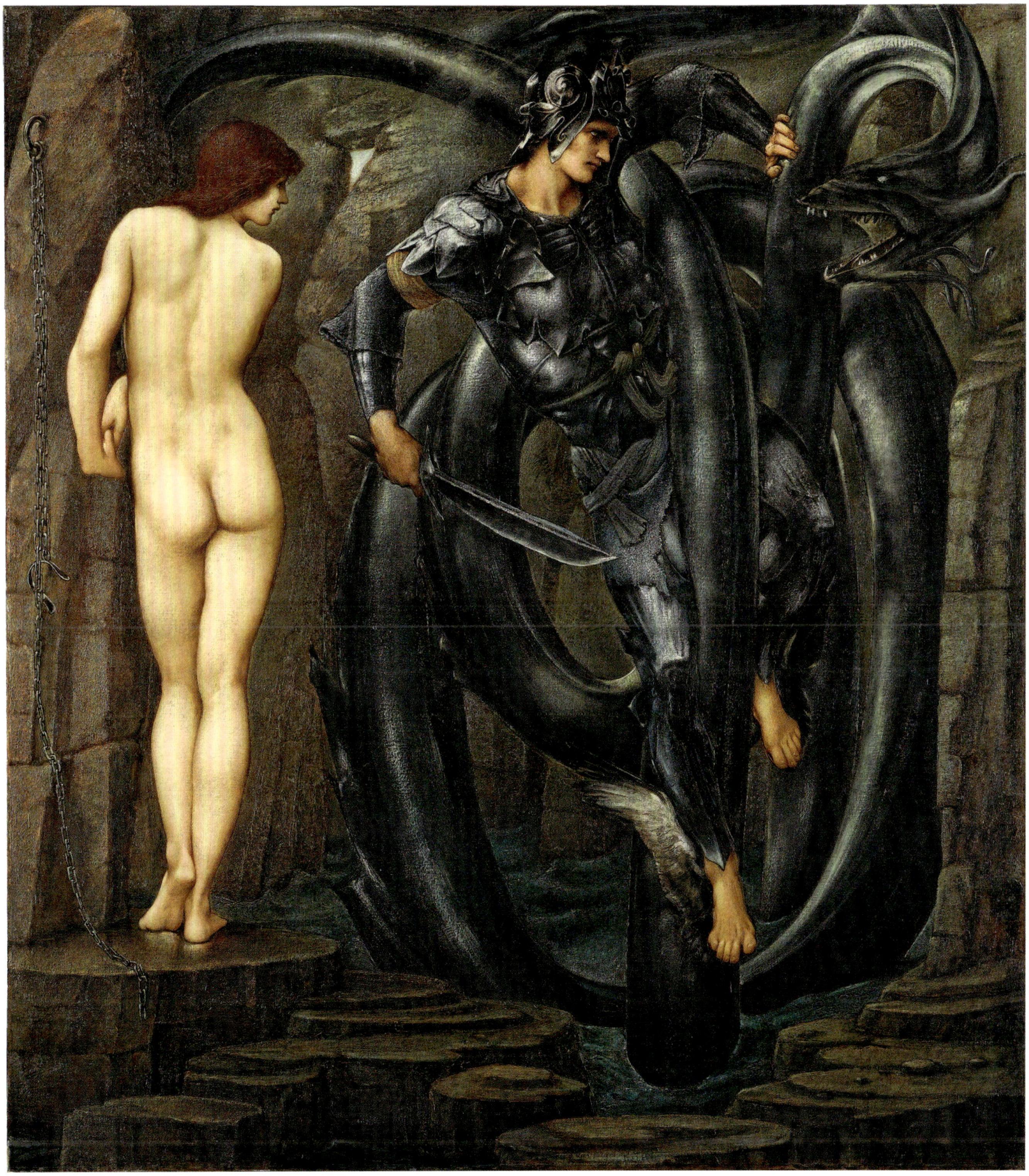

cartoons, now at Southampton, makes the most complete record of the series as a whole. Burne-Jones's practice seems to have been to make a new cartoon when his ideas changed; thus the scene of Perseus rescuing Andromeda, originally a long horizontal composition representing two stages in the struggle, was divided in two, for which both cartoons and final works survive: *The Rock of Doom* (Perseus's first encounter with Andromeda, no.139) and *The Doom Fulfilled* (his slaying of the sea monster, no.140). The cartoons are at the full scale intended for the final series – each scene, that is, 1.5 metres high.[12] Simultaneously, Burne-Jones made countless drawings and studies for the figures, settings, and accessories: this is the most extensively researched and carefully studied campaign of preparatory work ever carried out by the artist (see for example nos.70–76). The ten cartoons were installed in the garden studio of Burne-Jones's London house, the Grange, where they made a vivid impression on visitors, and with good reason (see fig.5). When the series was exhibited at the Whitechapel Art Gallery, in an exhibition of 1948 to mark the centenary of the Pre-Raphaelite Brotherhood, it caught the attention of Wyndham Lewis, then art critic for the *Listener*. Interestingly, the vorticist and strident modernist found Burne-Jones's work a revelation: 'I would far rather possess one of his Perseus series than a Botticelli. That series – or rather the full-size studies – is alone worth visiting Whitechapel to see.'[13]

It is only through this full set that we can grasp the scale and impact intended for the series – a true *Gesamtkunstwerk*, or total work of art. The Wagnerian term is not inappropriate to the mythic dimension of Burne-Jones's series paintings; Ruskin, too, chose the word 'mythic' to characterise Burne-Jones's art in his Oxford lecture series of 1883.[14] One might wish that Balfour had been a less sympathetic patron, and had demanded completion of the works he had commissioned. Certainly that would have provided the world with more masterworks by Burne-Jones. But it would not have brought closure to the myth. As in the case of the *Legend of the Briar Rose*, the completion of a series was only provisional; had Burne-Jones lived, he might have begun another set of canvases. Moreover, the myth lives on in the minds of its viewers, if we take seriously Burne-Jones's stated wish 'to leave all the afterwards to the invention and imagination of people'. The point is embedded in the project for *The Earthly Paradise*: for Morris and Burne-Jones, myth as the expression of the people should not be a thing of the past, but something that continues to unfold even in our sophisticated, scientific modern times. To the end of his life, Burne-Jones was still making work to encourage myth to thrive amongst the people.

141
The Baleful Head 1885
Bodycolour on paper, 153.7 × 129
Southampton City Art Gallery

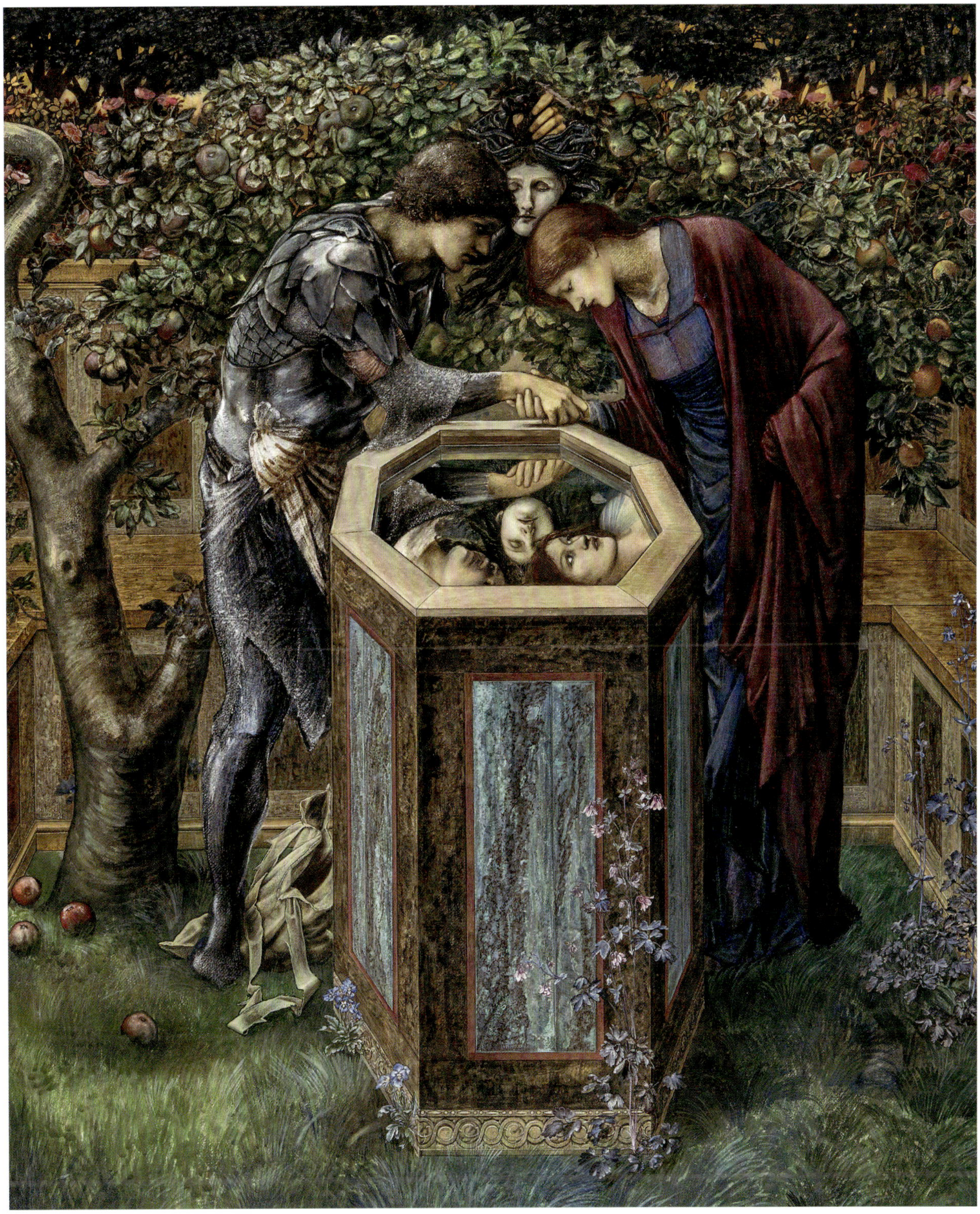

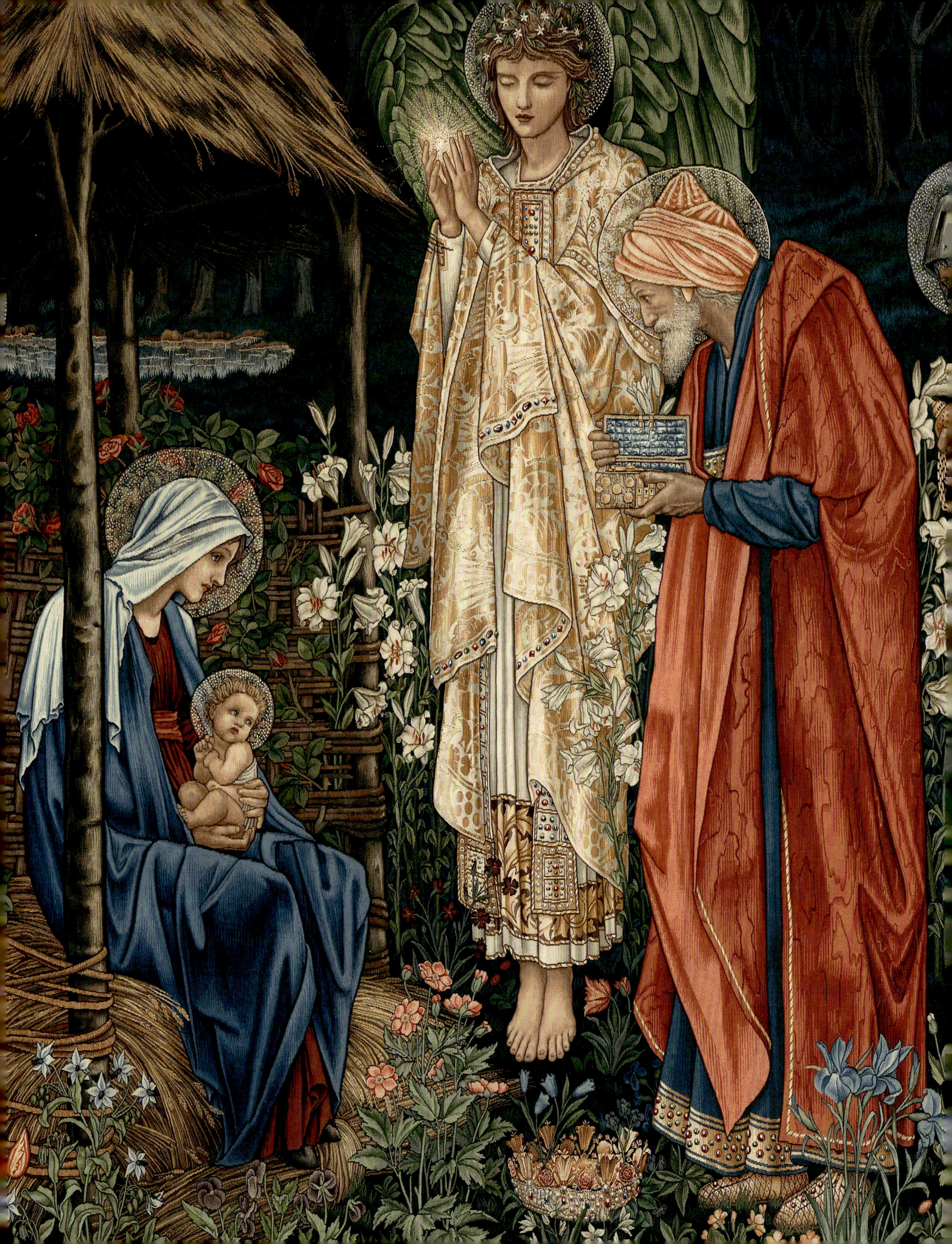

Burne-Jones as Designer

SUZANNE FAGENCE COOPER

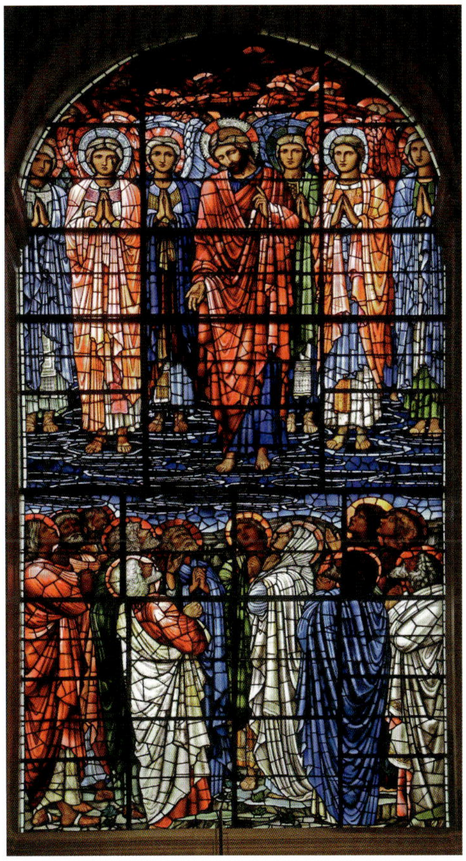

Fig.38
The Ascension 1885–97
Stained-glass window
St. Philip's Cathedral, Birmingham

In early 1897 Burne-Jones told his assistant it was 'a pity I was not born in the Middle Ages ... people then would have known how to use me'. He was mourning the loss of Morris and what he called 'the halving of my life'. They had shared a love of tapestries and manuscripts, 'two arts which others don't care for', as well as stained glass, beautiful printed books and embroideries.[1] Designs commissioned by Morris & Co. were his most regular source of income, reaching a far wider audience than his oil paintings: Burne-Jones enriched churches from Aberdeen to Cape Town, with his vision of 'heaven beginning six inches over the tops of our heads, as it really does'.[2]

To focus on the decorative arts in Burne-Jones's career raises a number of intriguing questions, about themes that resonate across multiple projects, and about collaboration and the boundaries of his art. Unlike his paintings for the Grosvenor or New Galleries, these works were meant to be touched, worn or woven into the liturgy of worship.

The majority of Burne-Jones's designs were church stained-glass commissions – 'as I live! another Nativity' – his figures squeezed between stone traceries (Christ's arms in many of Burne-Jones's *Crucifixions* are held up, painfully, almost above his head, to fit an elongated lancet window).[3] This was his bread-and-butter work. He drew the outlines in the evenings, as Georgiana remembered, when 'he made the designs without hesitation ... these large free drawings, which came out upon the paper so quickly that it seemed as if they must have already been there, and his hand were only removing a veil ... He always stood at this work.'[4] John Ruskin also insisted on the ease of Burne-Jones's mark-making: he told students it was 'only by trying to copy these ... outlines that you will fully feel the grandeur of action in the moving hand, tranquil and swift as a hawk's flight.'[5] However, the artist himself tells a different story. In an account book he described his work 'for St Philip's Church, Birmingham (my native town)' as 'a colossal design of the Ascension; perhaps my fiftieth treatment of the subject – involving much physical fatigue in addition to mental weariness', for which he was paid the 'flagrantly inadequate' sum of £200 in February 1884 (fig.38).[6]

The Firm had come to rely on him as the sole supplier of new designs for stained glass, and it was a complex business. There was regular consultation with Philip Webb, who choreographed the individual lights within the architectural setting. An assistant copied Burne-Jones's drawing, strengthening the outlines. Burne-Jones noted in an account book on 1 January 1866 that 'touching up' one of his cartoons 'cannot be paid for: it aged me – it blighted me'.[7] From 1874 the firm began to use photography, creating an enlarged image to be overpainted with watercolour and annotations. Then the lead lines were added. Burne-Jones explained that 'the leads are part of the beauty of the work ... the more of them, the deeper the colour'.[8] Finally the pot metal glass was selected, the faces were added in enamel by the firm's team of painters, and the whole soldered together.[9]

The Adoration of the Magi 1894 (detail, no.148)

142
Angeli Ministrantes 1878
Crayon and chalk on paper on canvas, 212.3 × 150.5
The Syndics of the Fitzwilliam Museum, University of Cambridge

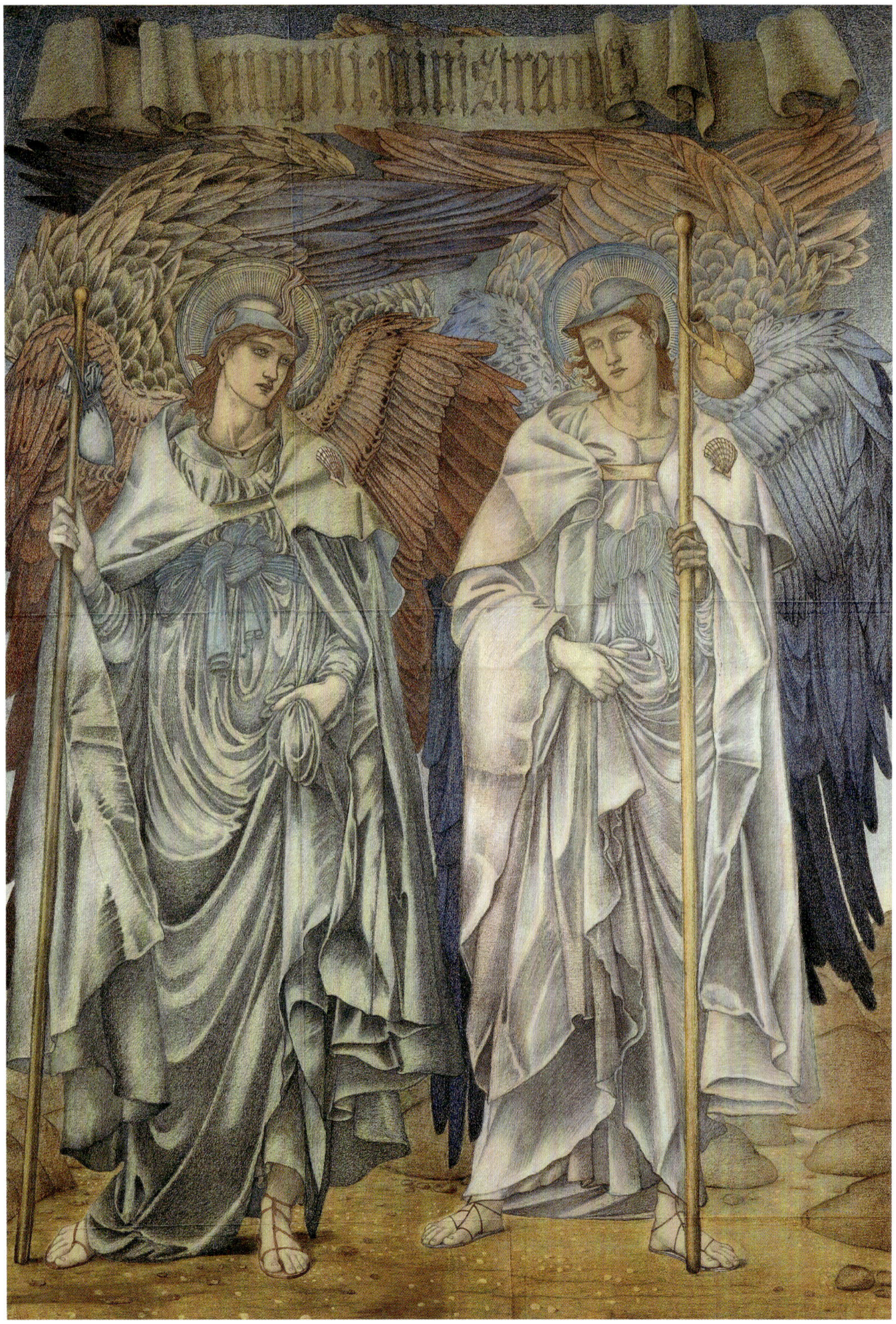

143
Angeli Laudantes 1878
Chalk on paper on canvas, 212.8 × 154.3
The Syndics of the Fitzwilliam Museum, University of Cambridge

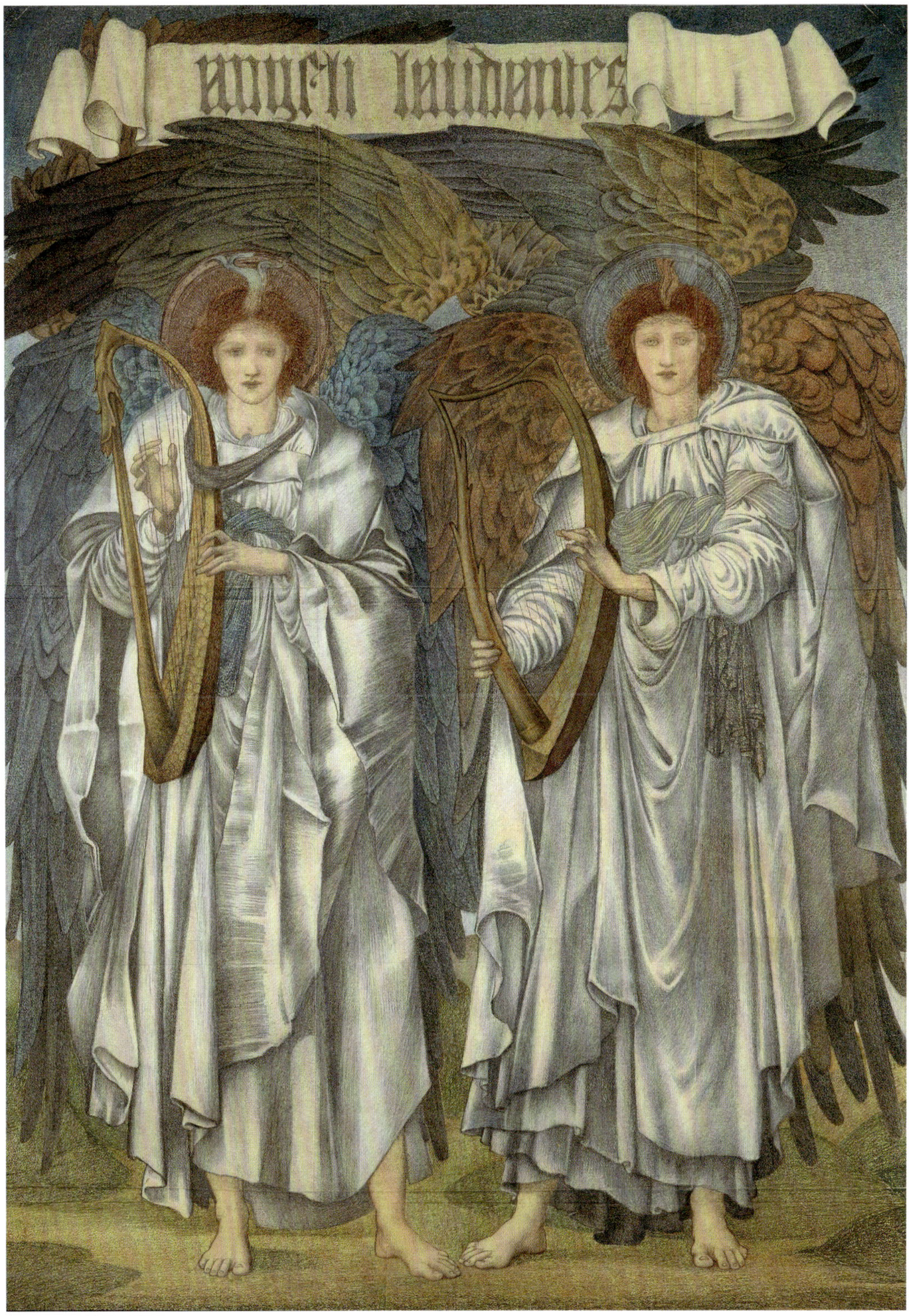

Burne-Jones's original drawings were often reused for other projects or reimagined as works of art in their own right. The fate of *Elijah in the Wilderness*, for instance, demonstrates how one idea was recycled over several decades. First created as a light in the west window of Calcutta Cathedral in 1874, *Elijah* was remade at least seventeen times during Burne-Jones's lifetime.[10] The taut Michelangelesque figure with his pair of ravens reappeared in Blackburn, Cromer and Chelsea, and a white robed *Elijah* was sent in 1883 to represent Morris & Co. at the Foreign Fair in Boston, Massachusetts. In 1897 *Elijah* became Prophecy standing beside Faith (a repurposed figure of Enoch) in Manchester College Chapel, Oxford. Meanwhile, the cartoon was returned to Burne-Jones's studio, where the artist, or one of his assistants, began to transform it into a stand-alone picture, with the addition of watercolour. It was left unfinished at his death.[11]

Other designs, like the *Angeli Laudantes* (no.143) and *Angeli Ministrantes* (no.142), crossed the boundaries between several media – from glass to independent large-scale drawings to tapestry. They were conceived in 1878 as lancet windows for Salisbury Cathedral.[12] As they were translated into new materials, the colour palettes shifted, from the saturated reds and peacock blues of stained glass to restrained silvery tones in the massive chalk drawings. Finally, there are the indigo-dyed wools, with shot-silk drapery linings, in the later woven tapestry version.[13] The backgrounds also changed in each reworking. The stained-glass angels appear before a pale network of scrolling vines. They tread lightly on fine blue waves, marking the borders of heaven. In the coloured exhibition drawing – what the artist called 'a travelling picture' – he brings the angels down to earth.[14] They now stand in a stony desert, a 'no man's land' that thirsts for the quickening touch of the divine. For the later tapestry version the space behind the angels was filled with woven millefleurs. John Henry Dearle, Morris & Co.'s studio manager, also simplified the wings, reducing the feathery layers that originally suggested a host of angels bursting the confines of the architectural framework. In the tapestry the outline of each angel is neatly defined. They are single and grounded. In each iteration the angels have become more tactile, less remote.

The impact of some stained-glass designs reached far beyond the congregations that saw them on a Sunday. *The Pelican in her Piety* (no.144), Burne-Jones's design for St Martin's, Brampton, Cumbria (1880), was never recreated for other projects.[15] However, it had a significant afterlife. *The Pelican* was a medieval symbol of Christ's sacrifice, resurrected by Morris and Burne-Jones from the illuminated bestiaries they loved: Burne-Jones remembered one book that had 'a pea-green donkey in it, quite big, standing all by itself'.[16] Like a medieval manuscript painting, *The Pelican* design reduced the natural world to its essentials. But for Nikolaus Pevsner, in his 1936 essays *Pioneers of Modern Design*, Burne-Jones's treatment of the twisting tree trunk also foreshadowed the fin de siècle.[17] The tension is seen more clearly in the drawing than in the finished glass, where the eye is dazzled by a rich background filled with bluebells, nightshade and tulips. However, Pevsner's focus on whiplash curves distracts from the origins of this cartoon. The condensed forms suited the glass and leading of the window. Only later did Burne-Jones smarten up his drawing with coloured chalks and gold leaf, when he knew it would not be needed in the workshop again.

Not all Burne-Jones's church commissions came through Morris & Co. His priestly training and his sympathy for ancient buildings brought him to the

144
The Pelican in her Piety 1880
Crayon, pastel and chalk on paper,
172.7 × 57.2
William Morris Gallery,
London Borough of Waltham Forest

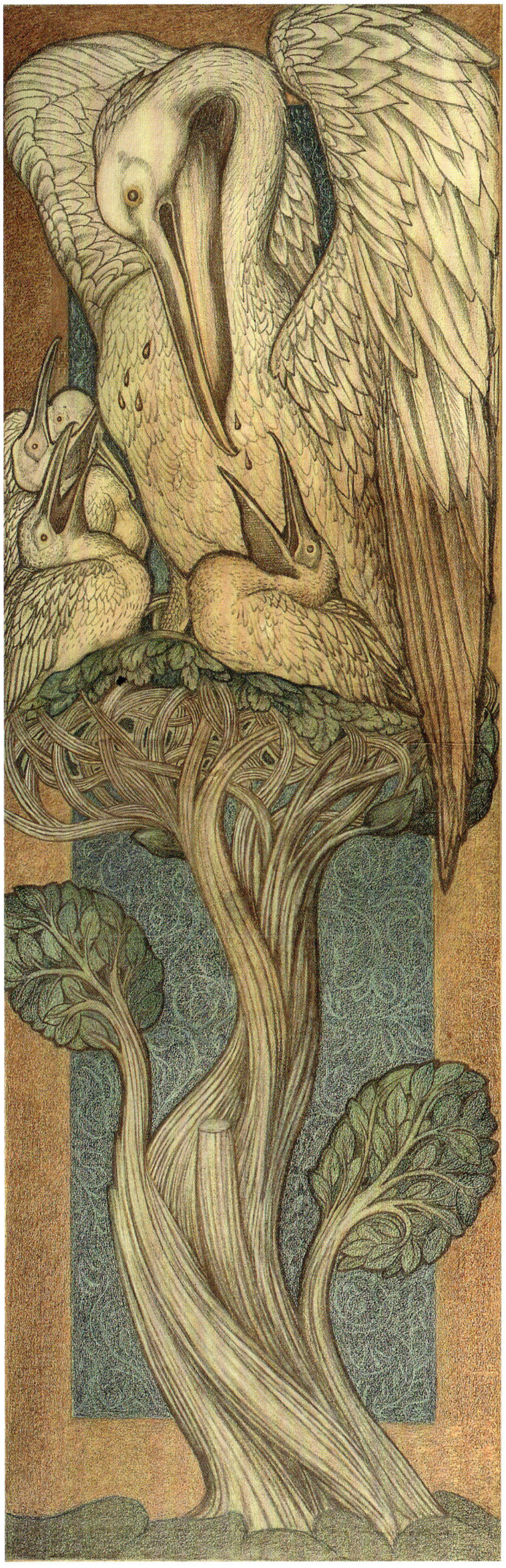

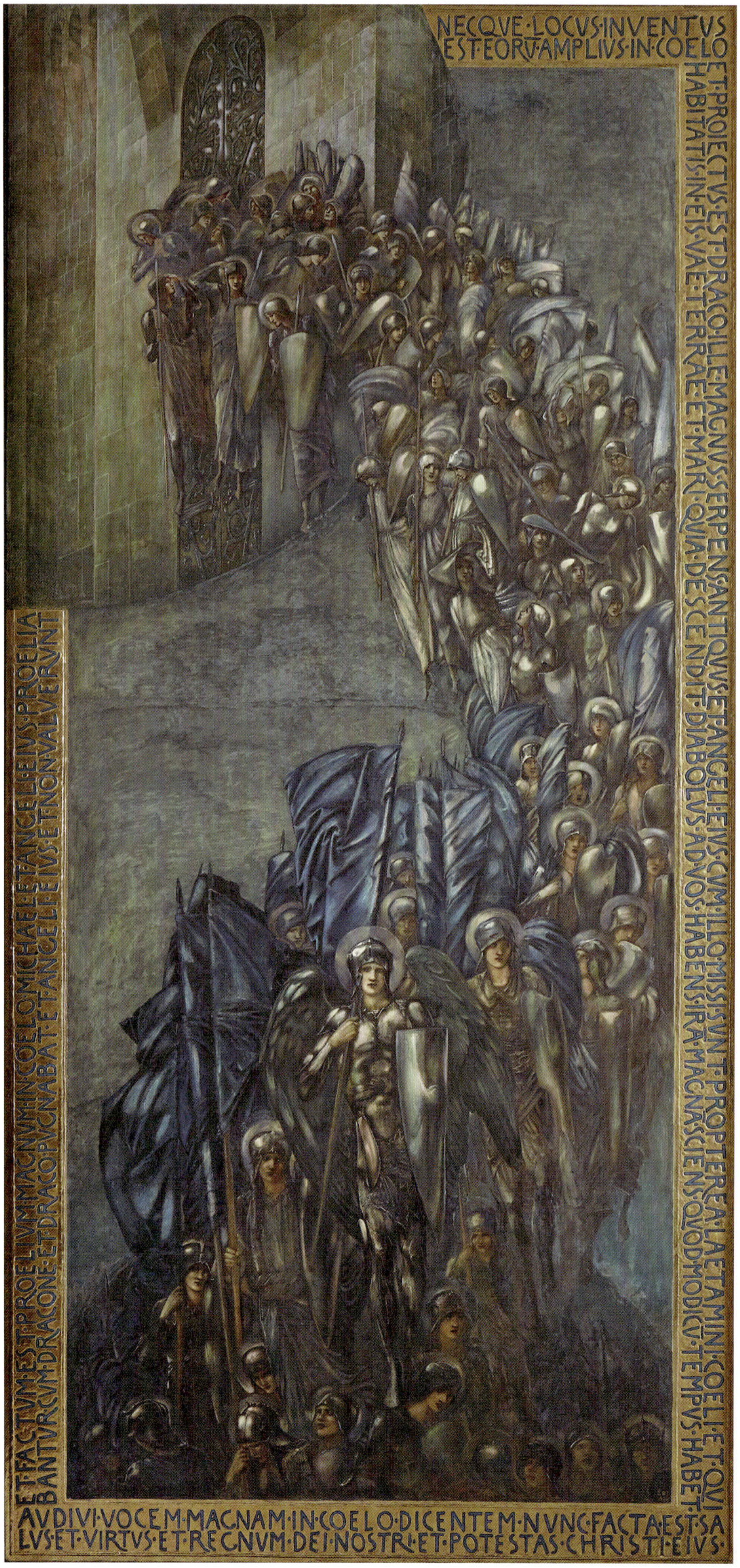

145
The Fall of Lucifer 1894
Bodycolour and paint on paper, 245 × 118
Private collection

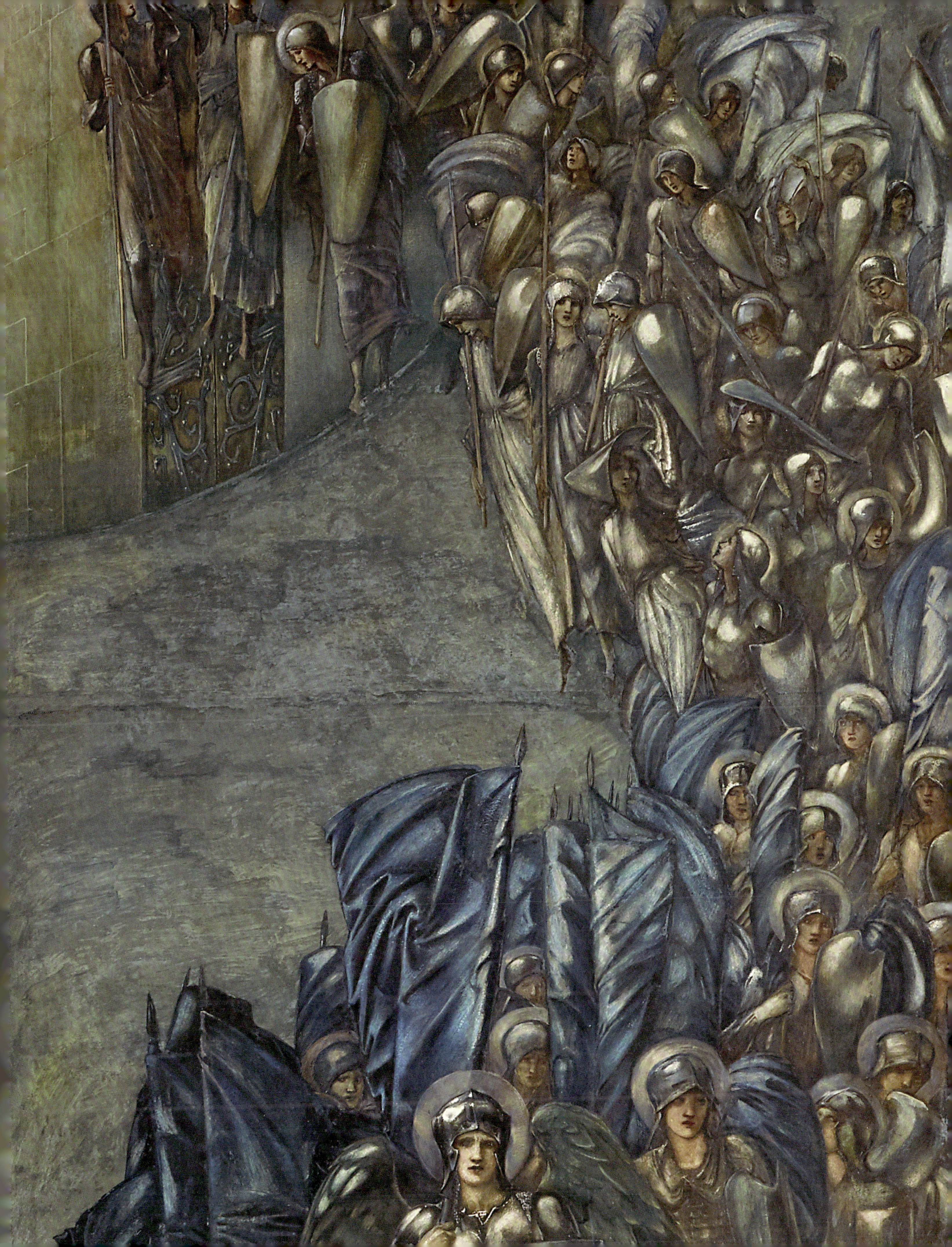

attention of other patrons like the rector of St Paul's Within-the-Walls, the new American Church in Rome, who invited him to decorate the apse and arches with mosaics (see fig.7).[18] Burne-Jones had written to Ruskin twenty years earlier of an ideal church with 'a barrel roof that should hold our hierarchies and symbols and gods'.[19] Burne-Jones remembered seeing the mosaics in San Vitale in Ravenna in 1873, discovering 'with wonder and delight the jewel-like brilliancy' of shimmering gold and blue angels that matched his imagination.[20] This was his ideal project.

Burne-Jones wanted his own designs to be 'VISIBLE, INTELLIGIBLE, at a distance, at a good height'. But his mosaics were made in Italy by the Venezia-Murano company, and the first attempt was dreadful. Burne-Jones told his assistant Thomas Rooke, who was visiting Venice, to 'scold them' until they could make 'the faces sweetly pale – the eyebrows straight, the darkness under them steady'.[21] He hoped that 'the great spaces of sky or water or golden wall' would look 'rich and cared for'. He created precise colour notes, numbering the 'little packets of tesserae' that he had been sent as samples: 'The wings will be of gold colour deeping [sic] towards the centre at the top and heightened with silver [,] outermost line brown.'[22]

Unexpected motifs surfaced from earlier works. The Pelican became a witness to the Annunciation, while the sinuous tree on which she sat sprouted to become a radical Tree of Life. In Burne-Jones's words, 'it's a mystical thing – Christ hanging with outspread arms but not crucified; the cross is turned into a big tree all over leaves, and the stems of the tree are gold'.[23]

In a letter to Frances Horner, Burne-Jones wrote: 'On one wall, there is a space of forty feet sheer down, where I mean to shoot Lucifer and his knights out of a glittering Heaven.' Although this mosaic panel was never completed, it was designed as a foil to the *Christ in Majesty* flanked by archangels above the altar. Burne-Jones left a rectangular void where Lucifer had been, before his rebellion. *The Fall of Lucifer* (no.145) took on a new life as an independent picture – a massive gouache with a gilded inscription. The buttresses of the New Jerusalem mark the beginning and end of the text.[24] Initially Burne-Jones envisioned a battle between the archangels Michael and Lucifer, but gradually his treatment became less black and white. The final version is carried out in many shades of grey and silver, with Lucifer as a knight, still haloed and wonderfully winged, carrying his banner undaunted. Perhaps this is why the design was never finally commissioned: it was too ambiguous. At first sight it is even unclear whether the central figure is Michael or his adversary. And the opening of Hell is not fiery red but dark and packed with angels, their puzzled faces turned upwards. Burne-Jones complained: 'Never was such an unruly crowd, but they are tamed at last and the doors shut tight and fast behind them.'[25] When the gouache was shown in the New Gallery in 1894, the shining bodies of the fallen angels seemed a disconcerting counterpoint to Burne-Jones's beautiful girls on *The Golden Stairs*.

Certain stories, from the Book of Revelation, Chaucer and Malory to Morris's *Earthly Paradise* poems, provided Burne-Jones with ideas that grew from household objects, stitched on linen or glazed on earthenware, to emerge as oil paintings years later. His treatment of Arthurian subjects follows this pattern. In the first months of his marriage, Burne-Jones designed four large figures – *Arthur*, *Merlin*, *Morgan le Fay* and *Lancelot* – for Georgiana to embroider in wools and gold thread 'to decorate a room of our own'.[26] This project was never completed, but he returned to Malory's tales in the 1880s with four stained-glass windows for his home at Rottingdean (fig.39).[27] Burne-Jones emphasised the elemental eruption of men into the sacred space of the San Graal chapel. Waves crash from one window to the next, and the bare earth lifts beneath Galahad's feet. 'How that San Graal story is ever in my mind and thoughts continually', he wrote towards the end of his life. 'Was ever anything in the world as beautiful as that is beautiful?'[28]

This intense imaginative engagement culminated in his designs for five large Arthurian tapestries. Morris and Burne-Jones were invited to decorate Stanmore Hall, 'a new-fangled place' in Middlesex (*The Arming and Departure of the Knights* and *The Attainment*, nos.146, 147).[29] Morris had experimented with tapestry weaving since 1879, setting up his own loom in Kelmscott House.[30] But this was the firm's first large narrative series of tapestries made on the high loom in the medieval manner. Burne-Jones was delighted: he thought tapestry was 'beautifully half way between painting and ornament – I know nothing that's so deliciously half way.'[31] It was a medium particularly suited to Malory's vivid, dreamlike writing.

From *The Summons* to *The Attainment*, Burne-Jones was able to clothe and arm the worthy knights, design Arthur's feast hall and an ancient chapel. He and Morris discussed how to work in wool and silk to create 'the sheen of metal' or the effect of damask in Guenevere's gown.[32] The compositions relied on the rhythmic interplay of colours: rosy pinks and golds for women and angels, silver and blood red for men. The robust energy of the Rottingdean windows was now restrained, the waters tamed, the mood prayerful.

To work on this scale needed time and materials. All three looms at Merton Abbey were employed from 1891 to 1895 on the first set.[33] The tapestries hung around the dining room at Stanmore Hall, with verdure panels placed beneath the main narrative, and *The Attainment* tapestry was specially shaped to fit over an awkwardly

Fig.39
The Quest for the Sanc Grael 1880–90
Four stained-glass panels designed by Edward Burne-Jones and made by William Morris & Co.
Victoria and Albert Museum

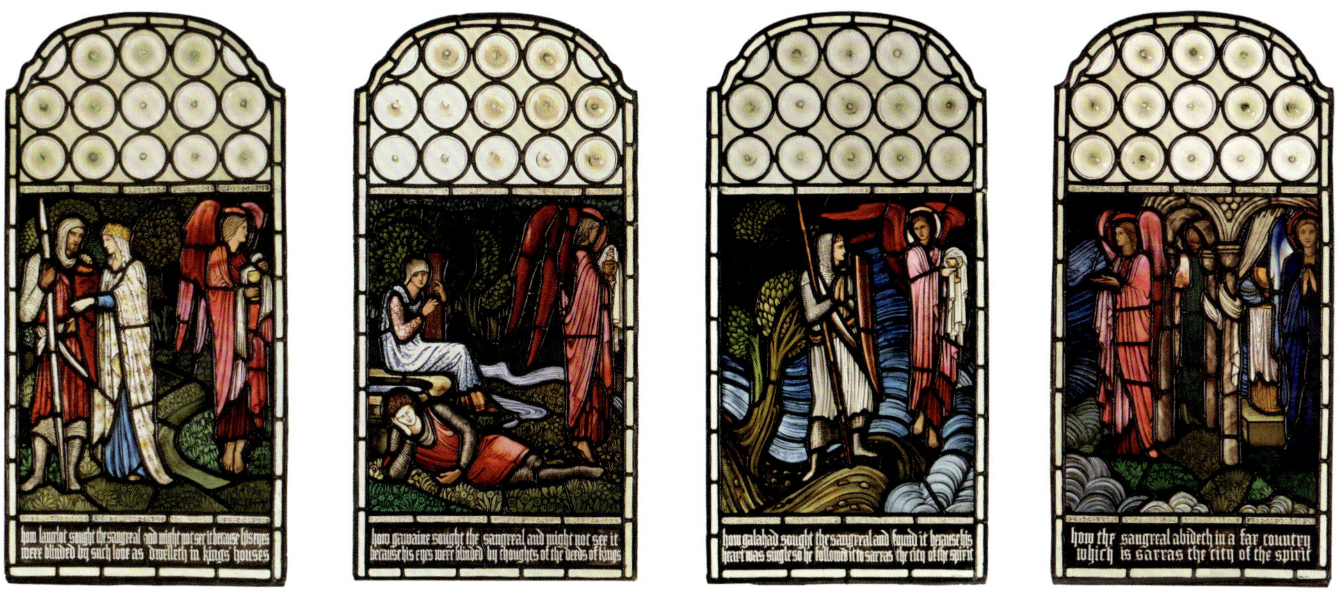

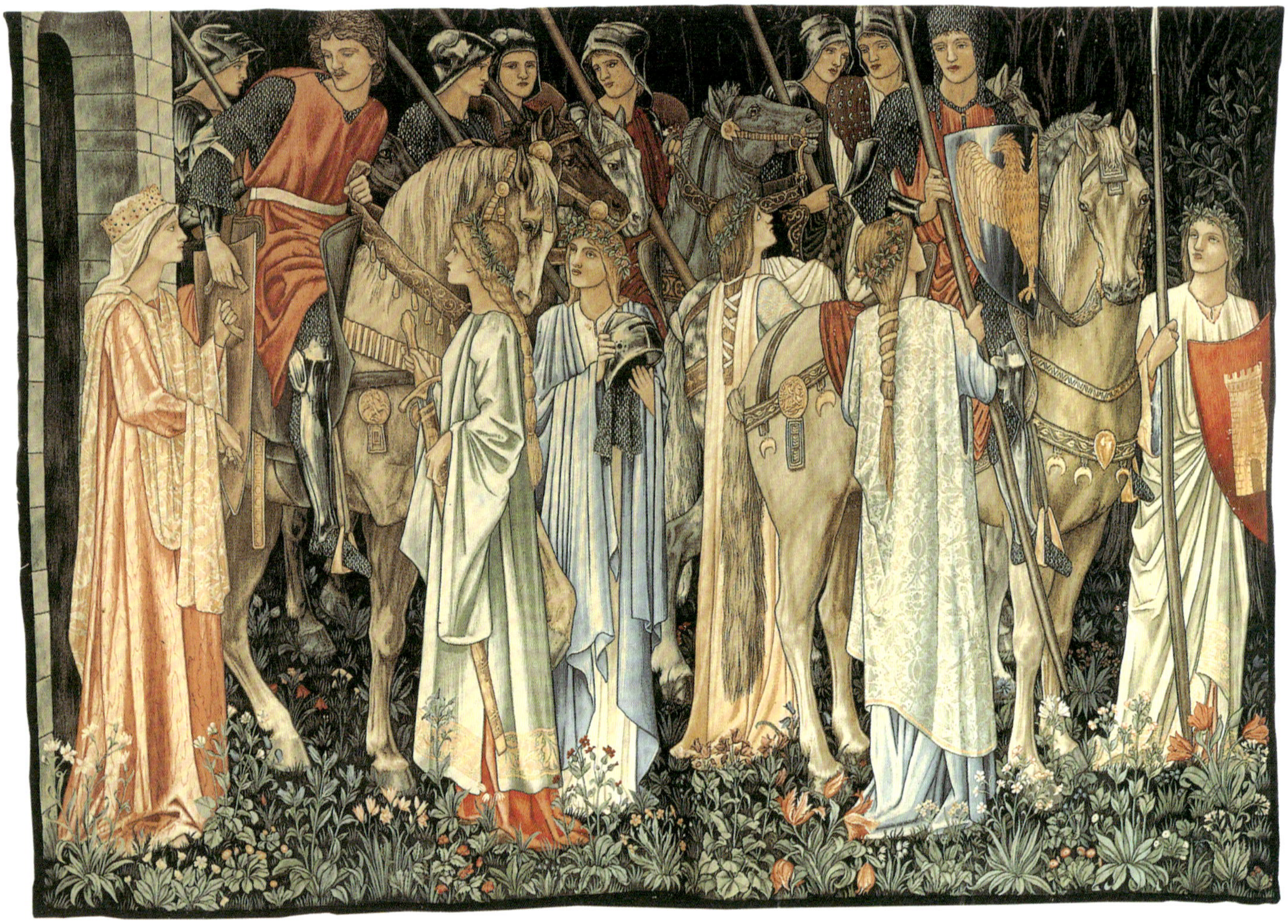

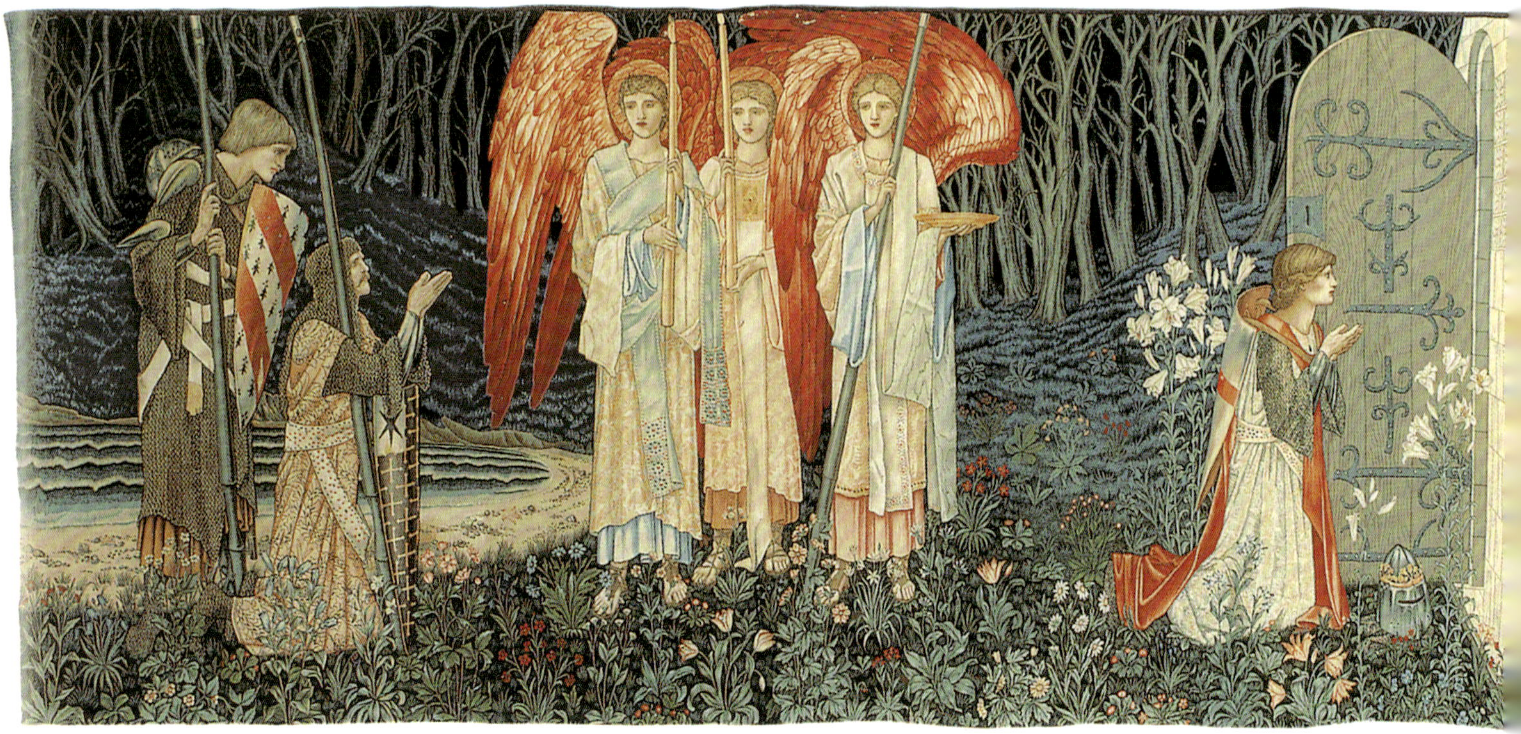

146
The Arming and Departure of the Knights of the Round Table on the Quest for the Holy Grail 1890–4
Cotton, wool and silk, 240 × 347
Collection Jimmy Page courtesy Paul Reeves London

147
The Attainment: The Vision of the Holy Grail to Sir Galahad, Sir Bors and Sir Perceval 1890–4
Cotton, wool and silk, 239 × 749
Collection Jimmy Page courtesy Paul Reeves London

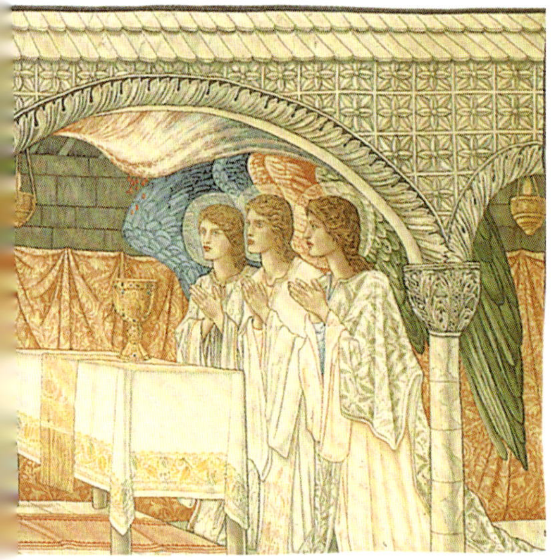

placed door. Morris charged £3,500 for the tapestries, and Burne-Jones was paid £1,000 as the principal designer. His drawings were photographed and enlarged 'to the full size, mounted on stretchers', and Dearle put in the flowers and accessories, before a final tracing was passed to the weavers.[34]

The firm had perfected the system of overlapping Burne-Jones's figures and Dearle's floral details in the late 1880s, when Morris agreed to make a tapestry for Exeter College, Oxford. The full-size composite photographic cartoon for *The Star of Bethlehem*, with watercolour additions by Burne-Jones, is preserved in the V&A. It shows the essential symbolic objects, the briar rose and the floral crown at the Virgin's feet, that later became lost among Dearle's millefleurs.[35] In early sketches the kings laid their gifts before the Virgin and Child, but still wore their crowns. Burne-Jones changed this detail and moved the angel bearing the star to hover in the centre, bringing heaven down to within touching distance of earth. The *Art Journal* suggested that the angel was a 'strange, radiant figure, resembling a statue from Chartres or Rheims'.[36] This reverential otherworldly design proved the most popular of his tapestries. The weavers made nine further copies, from the 1880s to 1906, including the third example created at Merton for the calico manufacturer, William Simpson in 1894, which he then presented to the City of Manchester.

The size and complexity of *The Star of Bethlehem* and *Morte d'Arthur* tapestries made them unaffordable for many potential clients. But Burne-Jones's single-figure designs like Flora and Pomona were also offered as half-size versions. They were his earliest attempts at working in tapestry: Botticellian girls, with the minimum of movement or expression.[37] *Pomona* (no.149) was recreated as a large embroidered hanging by the Royal School of Needlework soon after its first weaving. The school was set up in 1872 to revive 'a beautiful and practically lost art', by training 'reduced or distressed Gentlewomen', but the standard of work produced in the first years was 'an incongruous motley of indigested decorative ideas'.[38] Sympathetic designers like Burne-Jones and Walter Crane were recruited to improve standards, and *Pomona* was chosen as a suitable subject. Burne-Jones painted the faces and hands directly onto the linen support, with the needlewomen stitching around his brushwork. Morris added verses emphasising her mystical character as 'the ancient Apple-Queen', and vast, swirling acanthus leaves for the background. These scrolls were criticised as 'too large in relation to the figure', but Morris was sufficiently pleased with the results to send this work to the Chicago International Exhibition in 1893.[39]

Embroidery kits for cushions and ready-made church decorations created by May Morris and her team became a mainstay of the firm. But Burne-Jones also made bespoke designs for friends like Frances Horner (née Graham). Many were small, personal projects, like the embroidery design of a woman playing a cithara (no.52). As Burne-Jones explained sadly to Ruskin, he was constantly designing new delights for Frances (see p.151), and when Burne-Jones died, Herbert Asquith wrote to console her: 'He gave you always of his best, and it must be some solace to you to remember that up to the end you above all others lightened and enriched his difficult life.'[40] His most magnificent tribute was a decorated piano,[41] for which his pictures provided half the pleasure; she supplied the other half when she lifted the lid and touched the keys.

The *Graham Piano* (no.150) was part of Burne-Jones's plan to work with Broadwood to produce instruments for the 'House Beautiful'.[42] It was commissioned by Frances's father, William Graham, in 1879, probably as a gift for her birthday.

148
The Adoration of the Magi 1894
Tapestry, 258 × 384
Manchester Metropolitan University Special Collections

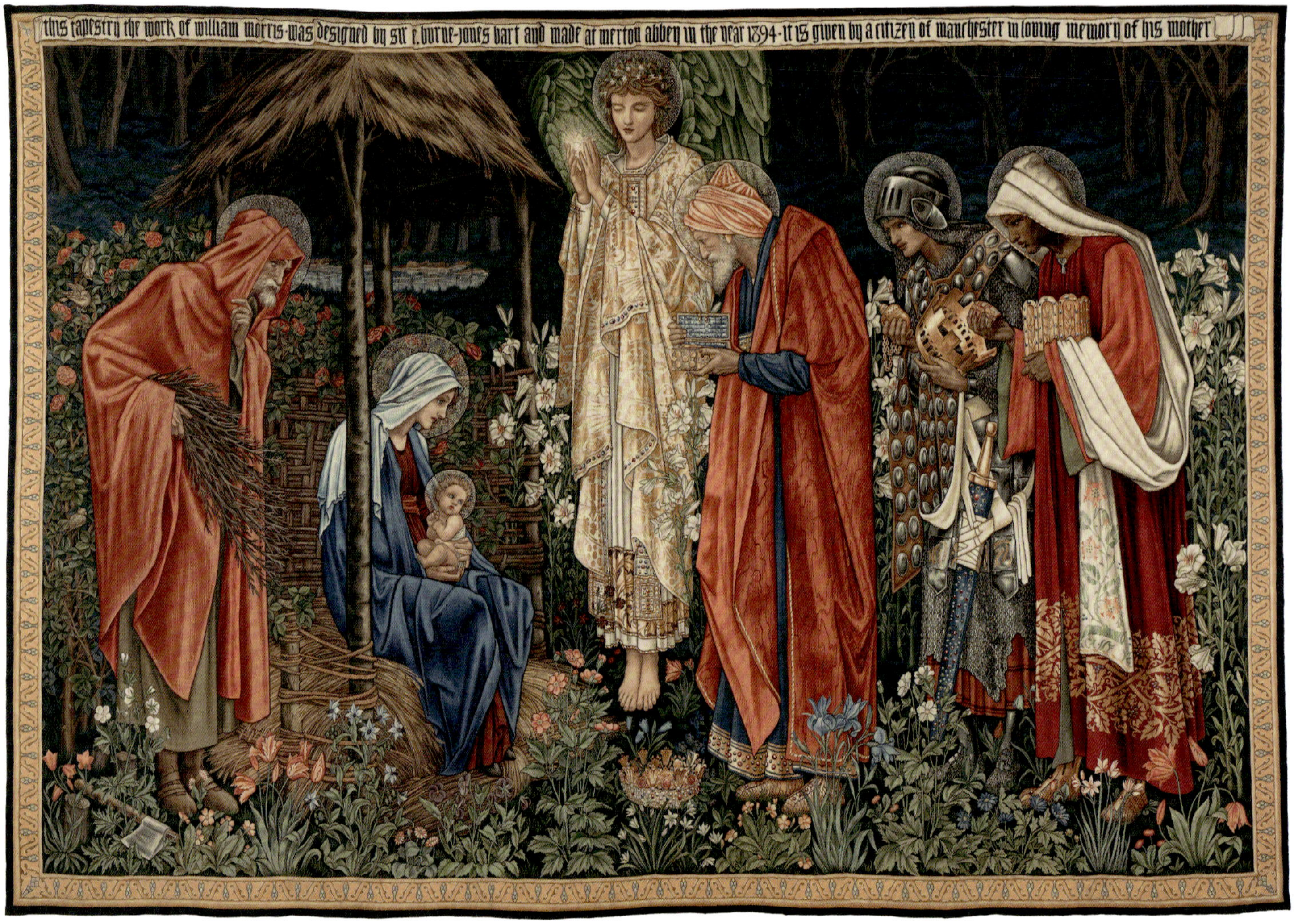

Burne-Jones had been working on the narrative roundels of Orpheus and Eurydice since 1872, as illustrations for a poem by Morris.[43] Now the musical legend could be wrapped around the body of the piano. Burne-Jones painted the figures in muted ivories and greys. He created movement and tension through the swirling, pleated robes, and by allowing his figures ever so slightly to break their bounds, with a toe or lock of hair overlapping the roundel edge.

The conflict between confinement and release, at the heart of the story, was emphasised by the tightly bound draperies. They were also a nod towards a shared passion for Mantegna's pictures: 'If ever they would look at me as I have looked at Mantegna', he wrote to Frances, 'what a well-rewarded ghost mine would be.'[44] William Graham encouraged Burne-Jones's enthusiasm by lending him works by Mantegna and Carpaccio from his own collection. The relationship can be felt, for

149
Pomona c.1885
Embroidered wall hanging;
linen embroidered with floss silks
Central panel 321 × 281.5 × 4
Side panels 271 × 28 × 2.5 each
Private collection

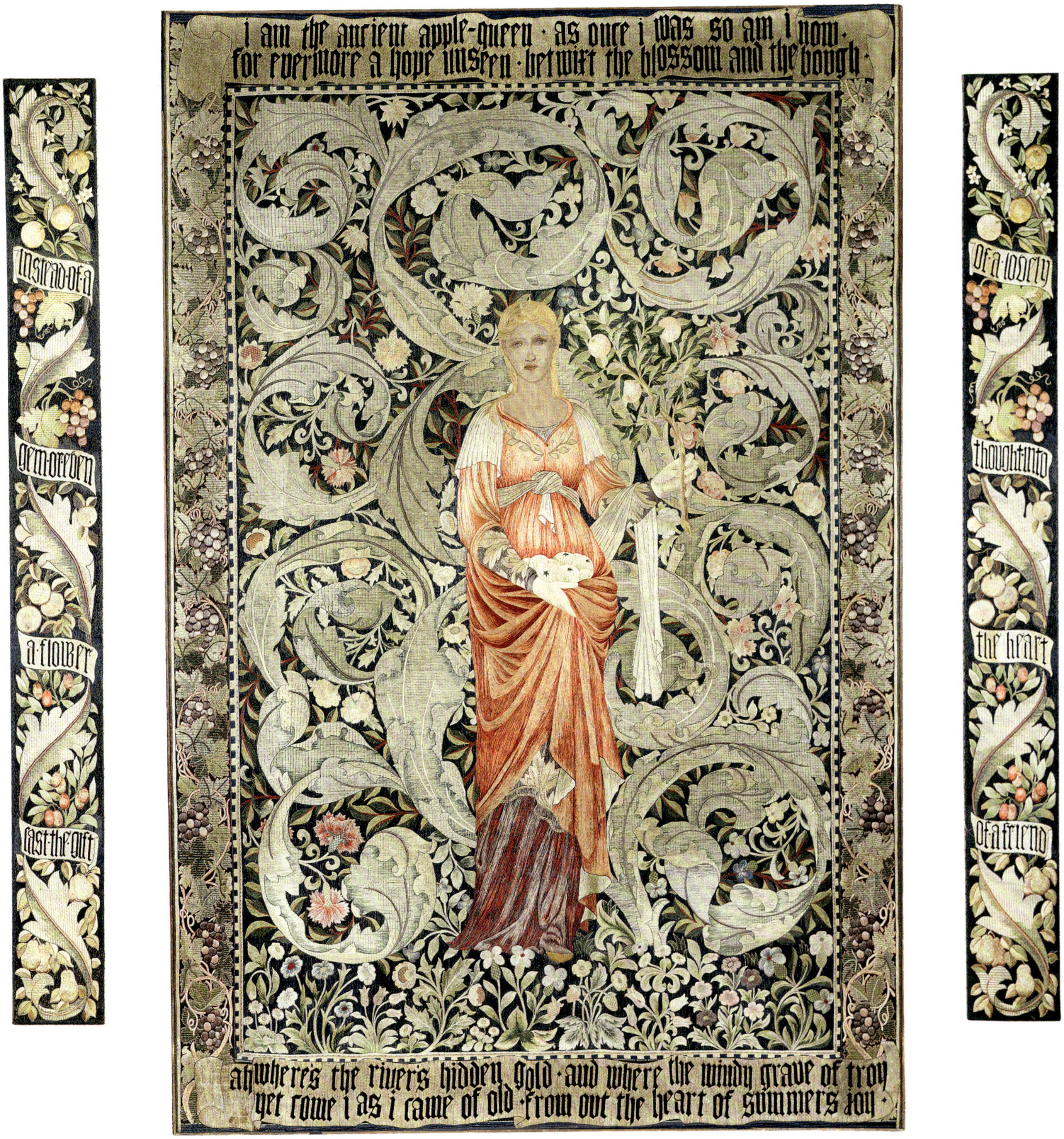

example, in Burne-Jones's design for *Orpheus at the Gates of the Underworld*, where the hunched figure echoes Mantegna's *Christ's Descent into Limbo* (engraving, c.1475–80).

The decoration of the piano divides into three distinct sections: the grey-toned Underworld on the main body; Mother Earth under the lid, with her dimpled disorder of putti, some peaceful, some destructive; and a celestial muse on top of the lid. The nude figure of Earth nurturing her children could only have been seen when Frances was performing, creating an unexpected disjunction between the painted female body and the young woman seated at the keyboard. Burne-Jones's pleasure in a visual joke among friends extended to scattering painted petals beneath the strings of the keyboard, as if they had blown in from a neighbouring picture of the *Briar Rose*.[45]

With the lid closed, the focus moves to the chivalric world of Guido Cavalcanti, (d.1300). His verses, beginning 'Fresca rosa novella ...', appear on a scroll next to the reclining figure of the poet himself.[46] An idealised portrait of Frances appears as a disembodied, semi-divine woman, in striking contrast to the fecund figure of Mother Earth below. The image of the poet/lover resonated with Frances. Burne-Jones drew the same hooded figure, as Chaucer's *Pilgrim* searching for the 'Heart of the Rose', in a large valentine's picture he sent her in 1877 (fig.40). This composition evolved into the major oil painting of *Love and the Pilgrim* (no.101), which he dedicated to another poet, Swinburne. Chaucer, like Cavalcanti, reinterpreted earlier courtly love texts for audiences of his own day. Burne-Jones was following closely in their traditions, imagining himself as the melancholy lover, reframing stories for new generations.

The interweaving of words and images was fundamental to Burne-Jones's friendships. This was especially true with Morris: from 1866 they spent their Sunday mornings planning illustrations for *The Earthly Paradise*, Morris's series of poems from classical and Norse traditions. Morris envisaged printing the work himself, with over 500 woodcuts designed by Burne-Jones. (Morris's retellings of 'Pygmalion' and 'The Hill of Venus' reappeared in Burne-Jones's art to the end of their lives.) 'Cupid and Psyche', the poem for the month of May, particularly appealed to Burne-Jones, with the winged figure of Cupid as a sensual counterpart to the angels of his stained-glass designs. And *The Wedding of Pysche*, filled with music in a minor key, suggested

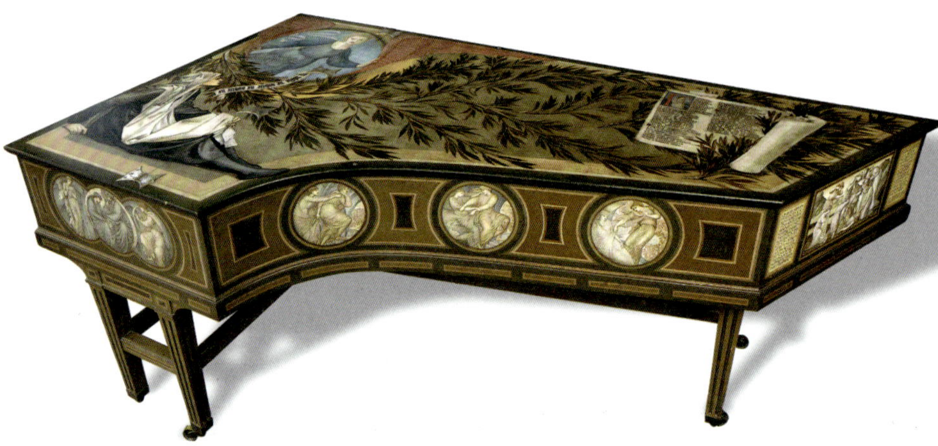

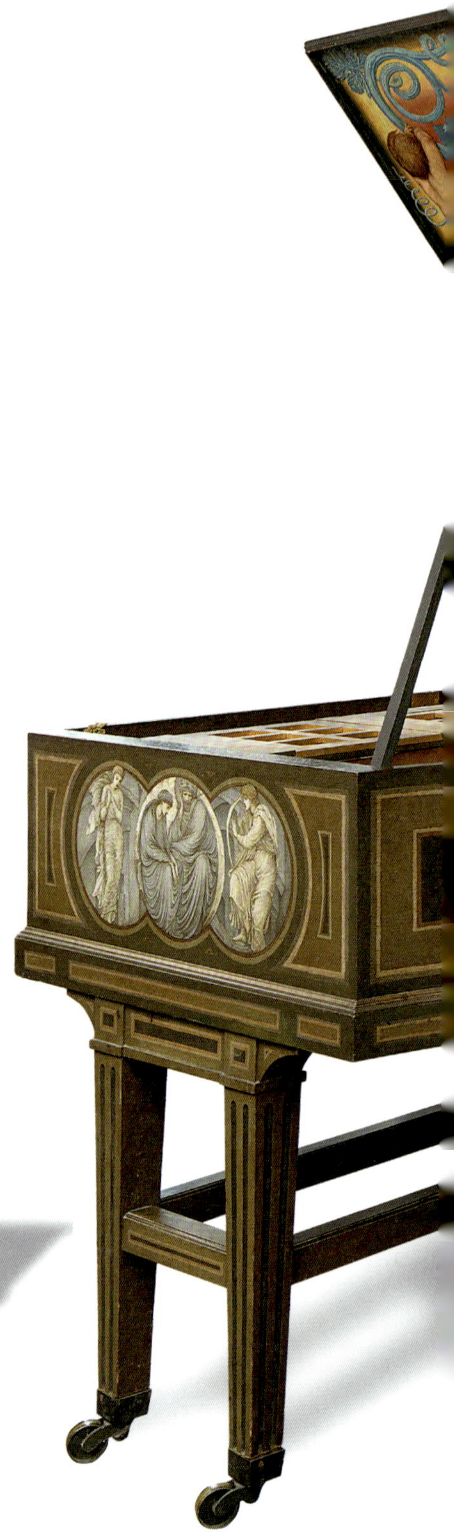

150
The Graham Piano 1879–80
Painted wood, 98 × 142 × 260
Private collection

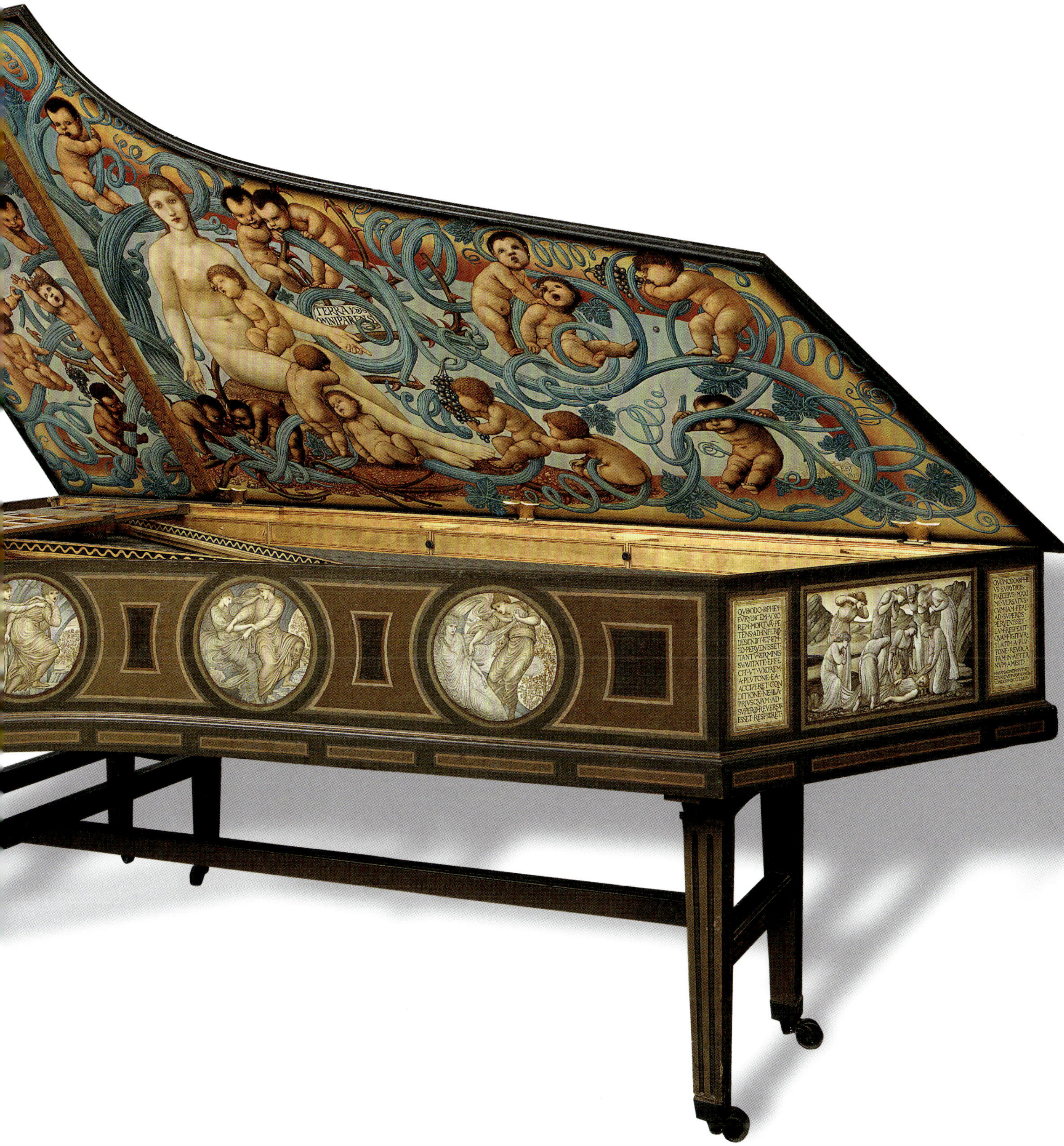

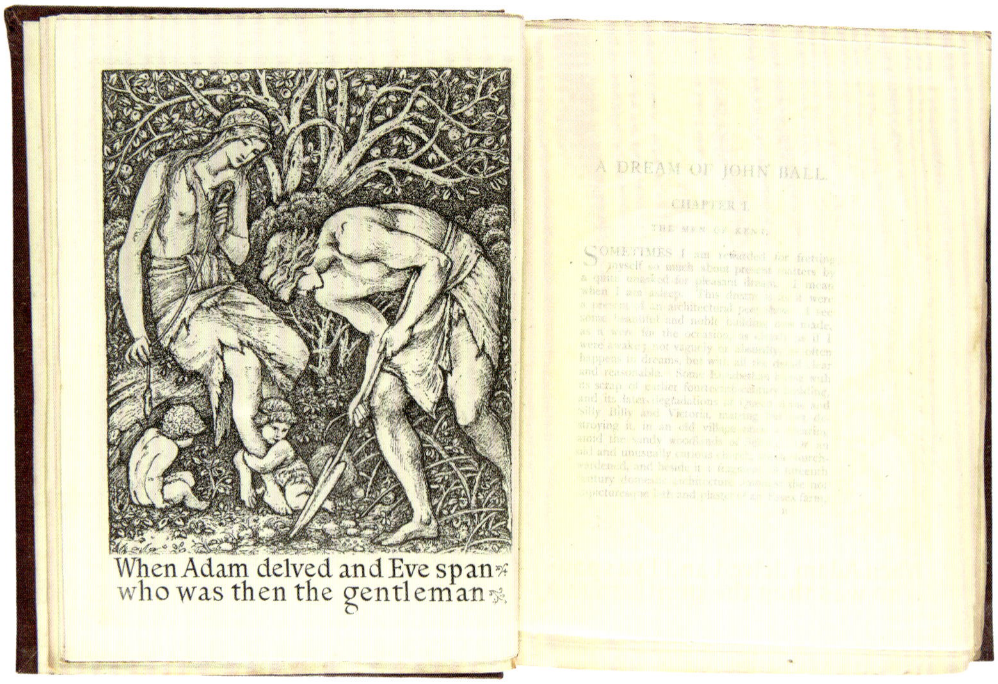

151
WILLIAM MORRIS
The Dream of John Ball 1888
Frontispiece by Edward Burne-Jones
Book, 17 × 13.5 × 1.6 (book closed)
Collection of Stephen Calloway

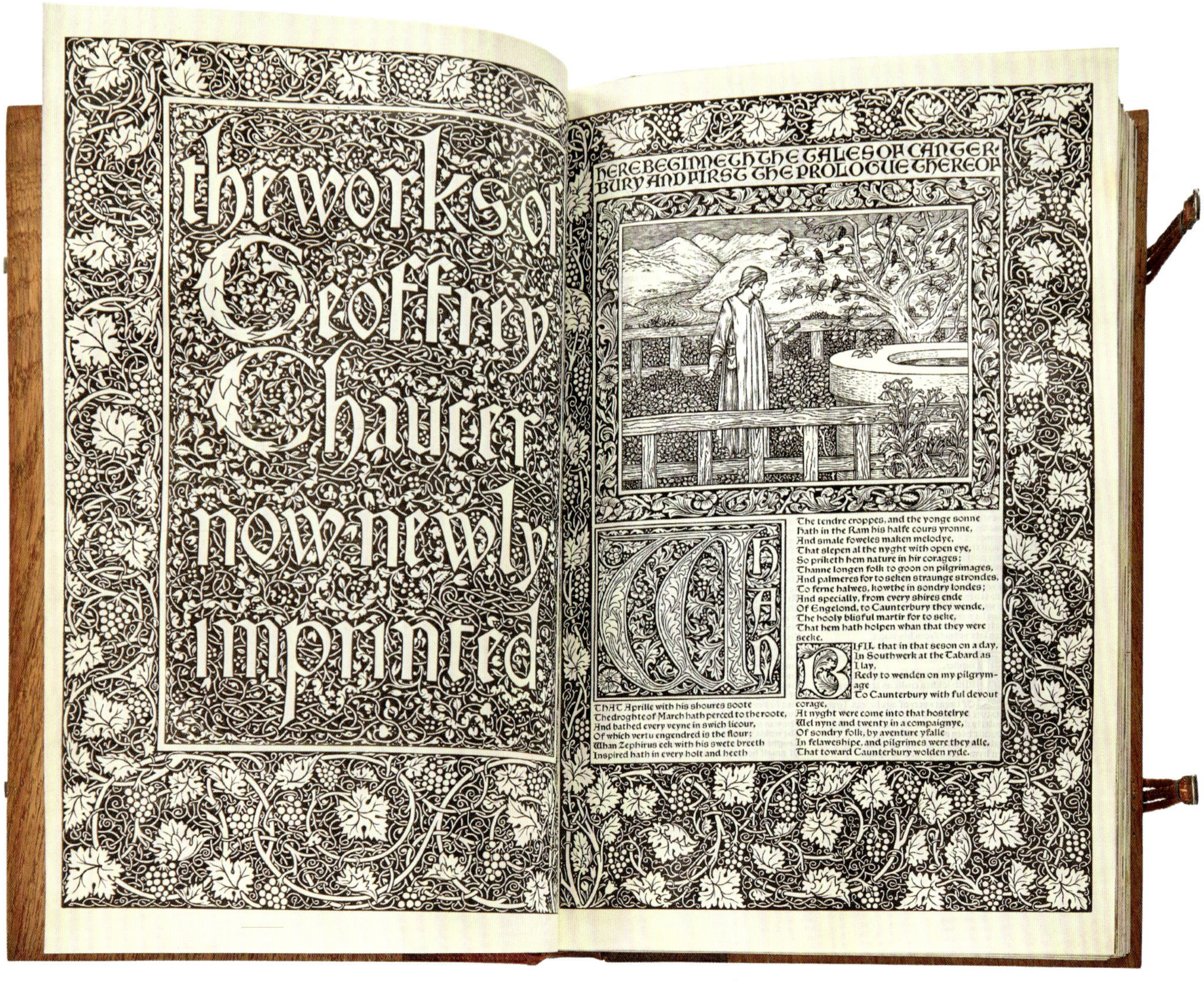

152
WILLIAM MORRIS and
EDWARD BURNE-JONES
The Works of Geoffrey Chaucer 1896
Printed book, 44 × 32
Private collection

Fig.40
Love and the Pilgrim 1874–5
Drawing for Frances Graham,
91.2 × 180.5
Private collection

Fig.41
Trial proof sheet of *The Golden Legend* 1892
Illustration by William Morris and
Edward Burne-Jones.
Wood engraving in ink on paper
Victoria and Albert Museum

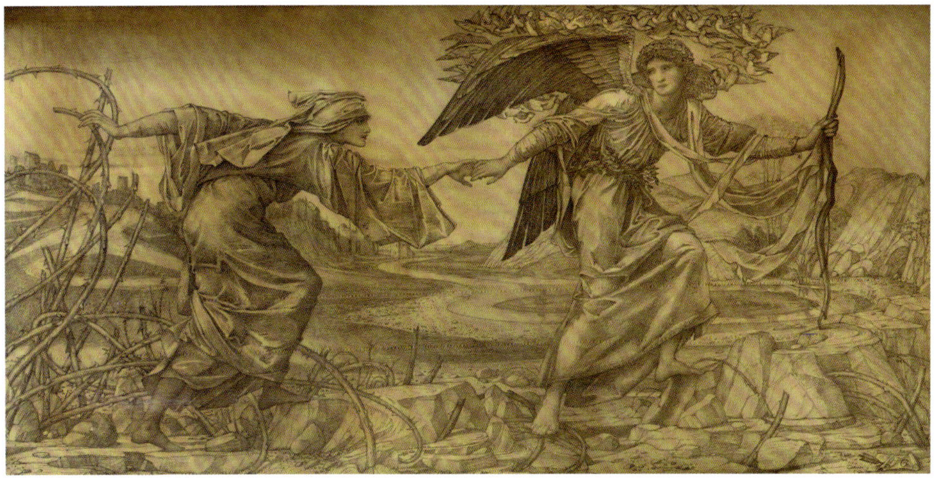

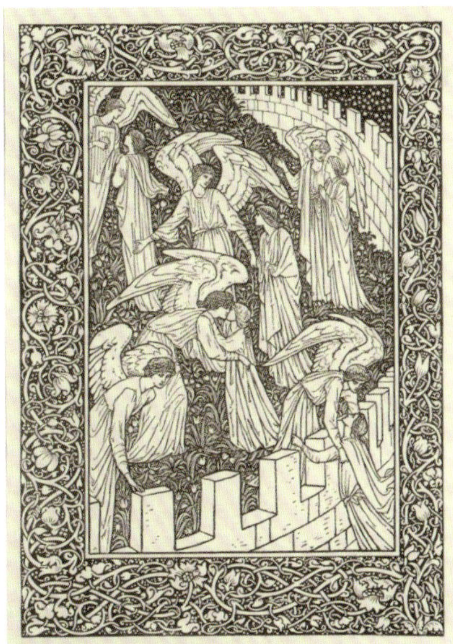

a processional structure – like a theme and variations – that remained a favourite compositional device.

Morris cut fifty woodblocks for Burne-Jones's illustrations for *The Earthly Paradise* (no.1), but the scale of the project was overwhelming and left unfinished. The dream of printing stayed with Morris, and colleagues like Emery Walker helped him perfect layouts and fonts, the balance of text and illustration, papers, inks and bindings. Finally in May 1891 Morris began printing his own books at the Kelmscott Press in Hammersmith. He designed the borders – 'they were *stroked* into place, as it were, with a sensation like that of smoothing a cat'[47] – and made 'Blooming-letters'.[48] Morris intended to publish his own work, including the abandoned *Earthly Paradise* (1896–7) and his tale of the Peasants' Revolt, *The Dream of John Ball* (1892; no.151), alongside texts that had shaped his life's work like *The Nature of Gothic* (1892), a chapter from Ruskin's *Stones of Venice*.

From the outset Morris hoped to publish Chaucer, but the *Kelmscott Complete Works* (no.152) was not finished until June 1896, shortly before his death. It was embellished with eighty-seven illustrations by Burne-Jones.[49] Now Burne-Jones felt at home, his pictures 'snugly cased in borders and buttressed up by the vast initials'.[50] Elongated figures, draped, winged and crowned, dance across the pages with slow rhythmical steps. Burne-Jones pauses at moments of greeting and parting, watching and wondering. With the *Pilgrim*, we contemplate entering the Garden of Idleness. We study the stars or stand alongside the Knights, yearning for Emelye. It was a vast undertaking – what Burne-Jones called 'a pocket cathedral' – yet these are intimate pictures, to be held in the hand, traced with a finger, animated by the enfolding texts.

If Chaucer was the last Kelmscott project that Morris and Burne-Jones completed together, *The Golden Legend* (1892; fig.41) was the first. This compendium of saints' lives offered glimpses of the medieval landscape of the imagination, and Burne-Jones's full-page illustration reveals with great clarity the elements that mattered most to him.[51] An angel leans over the edge of heaven to lift a young soul into the walled garden. This is his vision of Paradise, where mortals and angels embrace and walk side by side.

In one of his earliest writings Morris described seeing 'even very far off things clearer than we see real material things on earth'.[52] These 'far-off things' were Burne-Jones's favourite subjects, seen clearly and truthfully, and made in collaboration with old friends who understood his experimental visual vocabulary.

153
Spirits, or *The Uninterpreted Dream* 1890s
Oil paint on canvas, 127 × 85
Etienne Bréton, Saint-Honoré Art Consulting, Paris

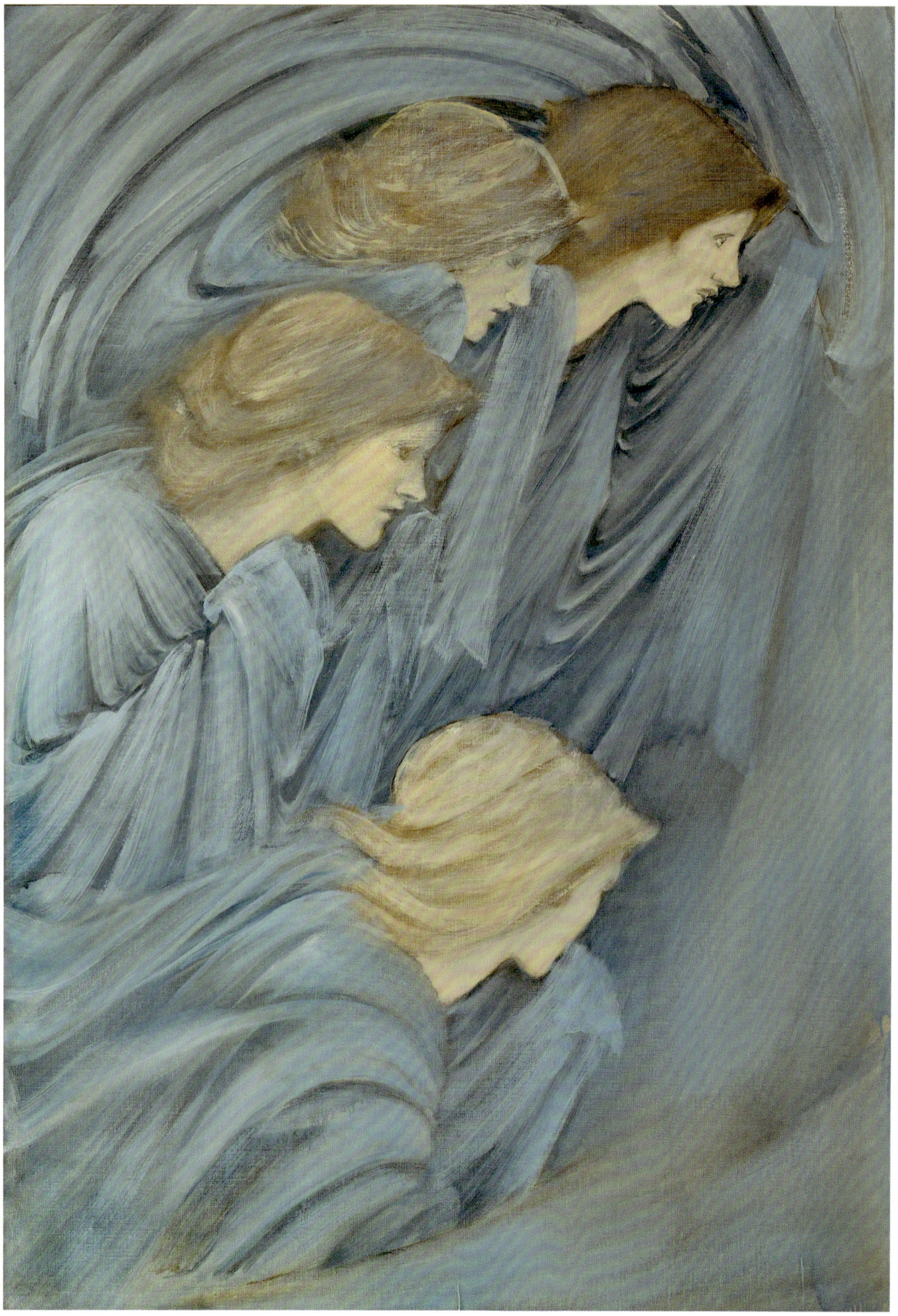

Chronology

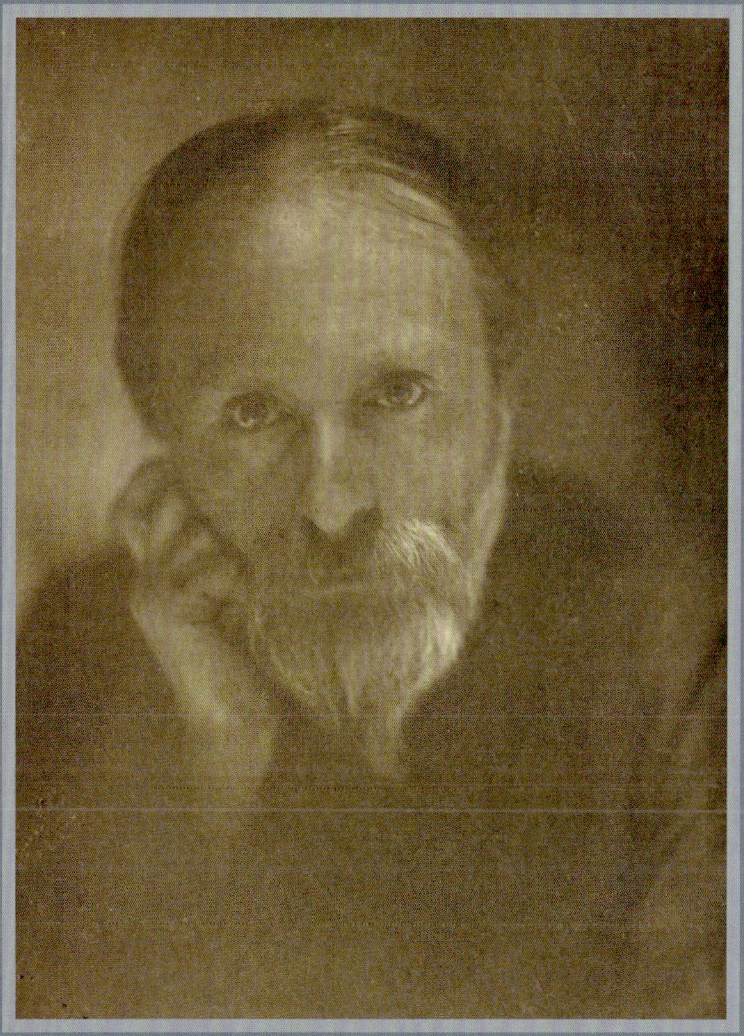

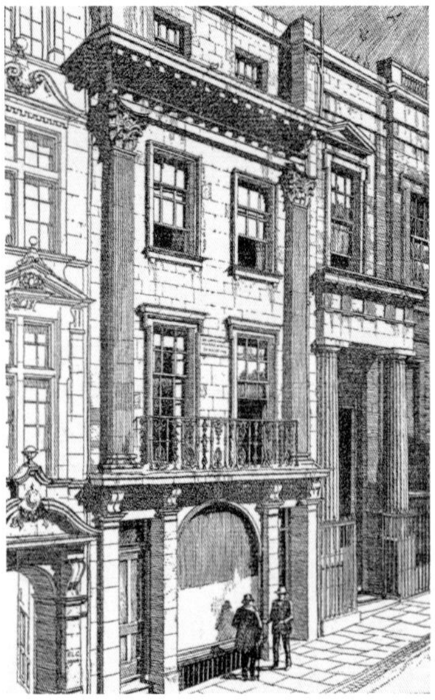

Bennett's Hill, Birmingham, birthplace of Edward Burne-Jones

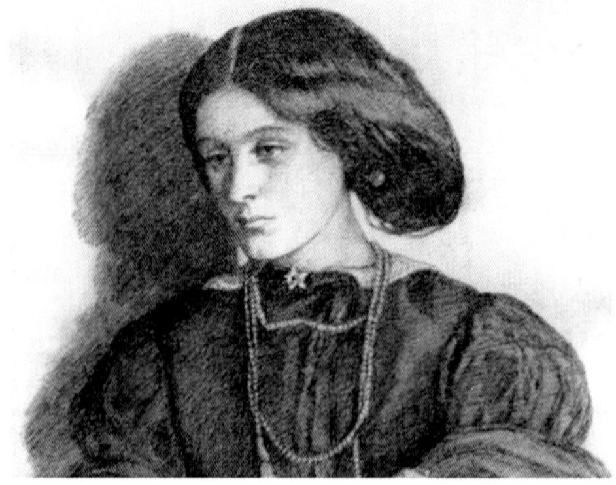

Dante Gabriel Rossetti
Georgiana Burne-Jones 1860

1833
Born 28 August at 11 Bennett's Hill, Birmingham, the son of Edward Richard Jones, framer and gilder. His mother Elizabeth (née Coley) dies within a week of his birth, and he is brought up by his father's housekeeper, Ann Sampson. Baptised Edward Coley Burne Jones (the 'Burne' after his aunt), and known mostly as Edward Jones.

1844–52
Educated at King Edward's School, New Street, Birmingham, and from 1848 attends drawing classes at Birmingham Government School of Design three evenings a week.

Introduced to the ideas of Tractarianism and the writings of John Henry Newman. Under these influences decides to read theology at Exeter College, University of Oxford.

1851
Meets Georgiana Macdonald for the first time, the daughter of a Methodist minister and the sister of school friend Henry ('Harry') Macdonald.

1853
Goes up to Exeter College, Oxford, where he meets William Morris, also studying there and destined for the Church. A close friendship develops based on a shared interest of literature and poetry. With friends from Birmingham studying at Pembroke College, they form a 'Brotherhood', later referred to as the 'Birmingham Set'. Starts to read the writings of John Ruskin, including *The Stones of Venice* and early volumes of *Modern Painters*.

Engrossed in religion, Burne-Jones and Morris plan to establish a religious order.

1854
Sees his first Pre-Raphaelite paintings in the collection of Thomas Combe in Oxford. Dante Gabriel Rossetti's watercolour *Dante Drawing an Angel on the Anniversary of Beatrice's Death* makes the deepest impression (fig.23).

Visits the Royal Academy and sees William Holman Hunt's *The Light of the World* and *The Awakening Conscience*.

Commissioned to produce illustrations for *The Fairy Family* for Archibald Maclaren (published 1857).

Comes up with the nickname of 'Topsy' for William Morris, who in turn calls Burne-Jones 'Ned'.

1855
Discovers in a Birmingham bookshop Robert Southey's 1817 edition of Thomas Malory's *Le Morte d'Arthur*, the 15th-century retelling of the legend of King Arthur, which would have a profound influence on him.

Travels to northern France with William Morris and William Fulford to study Gothic cathedrals. In Paris is overwhelmed by Fra Angelico's *Coronation of the Virgin* at the Louvre. On the journey home, at the quay of Le Havre, Morris and Burne-Jones resolve to devote their lives to art – Morris as an architect, Burne-Jones as a painter. He would later describe that moment as the 'most memorable night of my life'.

1856
Visits Rossetti in his studio at Chatham Place, Blackfriars. Subsequently abandons his degree studies in Oxford and moves to London to study with Rossetti. Attends Leigh's art school in Bloomsbury, though later writes he learned nothing there.

Takes lodgings with William Morris at 17 Red Lion Square. Morris designs heavy oak furniture, which is decorated by Burne-Jones and Rossetti with designs from Arthurian legend.

Becomes integrated into the wider Pre-Raphaelite circle, meeting Millais, Holman Hunt and Madox Brown. Introduced to the Prinsep family at Little Holland House and G.F. Watts, who has a studio there.

Corresponds with John Ruskin, finally meeting him later in the year – the beginning of a life-long friendship.

Becomes engaged to Georgiana Macdonald.

1857
Receives his first commission as a professional artist, painting *The Blessed Damozel* in oil for Thomas Plint of Leeds, though it remains unfinished.

At the suggestion of Rossetti, makes his first design for stained glass, *The Good Shepherd*, for James Powell and Sons (executed in 1861).

Together with Rossetti, Morris and others, decorates the debating chamber of the new Oxford Union building (now the Union Library). Paints scenes from Malory's *Le Morte d'Arthur* in fresco from the late summer into early 1858. Meets Algernon Charles Swinburne, then an undergraduate at Balliol.

Grows a beard, which he would keep for the rest of his life.

1858
Produces designs for the large *St Frideswide* stained-glass windows at Christ Church Cathedral, Oxford, working under contract to James Powell and Sons.

Suffers his first serious illness and recuperates over the summer at Little Holland House, where he is looked after by Mrs Prinsep and her family. Meets important literary figures, including Alfred Tennyson, and gains further insight into painting from G.F. Watts.

Attends the Hogarth Club (1858–61), where he exhibits stained-glass designs.

Produces his first important pen-and-ink drawings, including *Going to the Battle*.

1859
Teaches drawing at the Working Men's College (until 1861), first as assistant to Ford Madox Brown, later with his own classes.

Attends the wedding of Morris and Jane Burden in Oxford, with Georgiana and her sisters.

Produces *The Tree of Jesse* and *Christ in Majesty* designs for the east window of Waltham Abbey, Essex, commissioned by architect William Burges, who was appointed to restore the great medieval church.

Makes his first trip to Italy, travelling with Charles Faulkner and Val Prinsep via Paris to Genoa, Pisa, Florence and Venice, where he makes studies of the works of Botticelli, Ghirlandaio, Mantegna and Gozzoli. Returns via Milan after four weeks.

1860
Produces his first serious works in watercolour, *Sidonia von Bork* and *Clara von Bork*, the figure of Clara modelled on Georgiana.

Marries Georgiana on 9 June in Manchester. The honeymoon to Paris is abandoned due to Burne-Jones's ill health.

The couple move to Burne-Jones's rooms at 24 Russell Place, Fitzroy Square, where he had lived since 1858. They are regular visitors to the Morris residence, Red House, near Bexleyheath.

Starts to paint a triptych altarpiece for St Paul's Church, Brighton: *The Adoration of the Magi* (centre) and *The Annunciation* (wings). On completion and installation the following year, he decides it requires revision and paints a second version for the church.

1861
The Burne-Joneses move to 62 Great Russell Street, opposite the British Museum; their son Philip is born on 21 October.

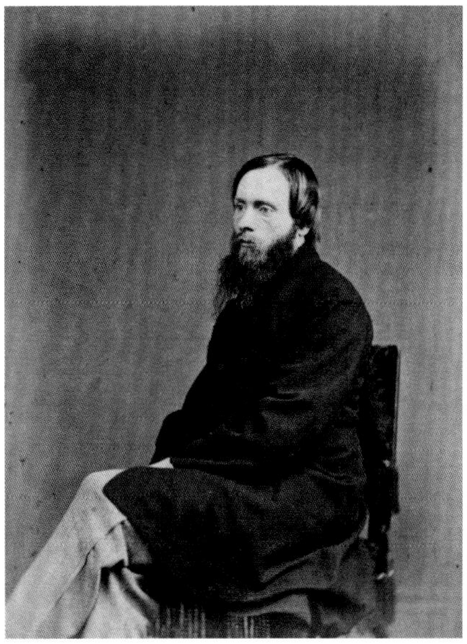

Edward Burne-Jones, 1864

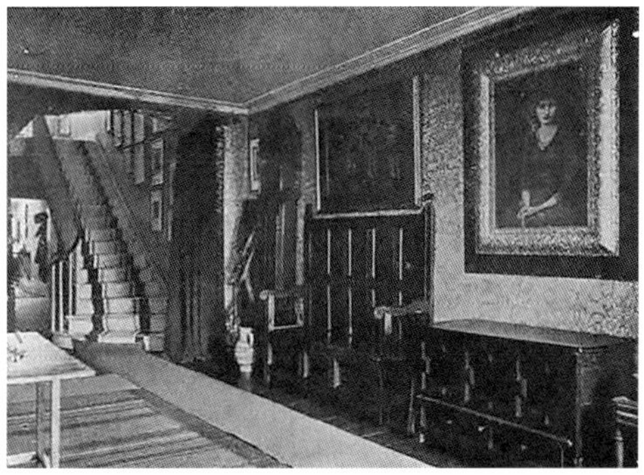

The Grange, entrance hall c.1887

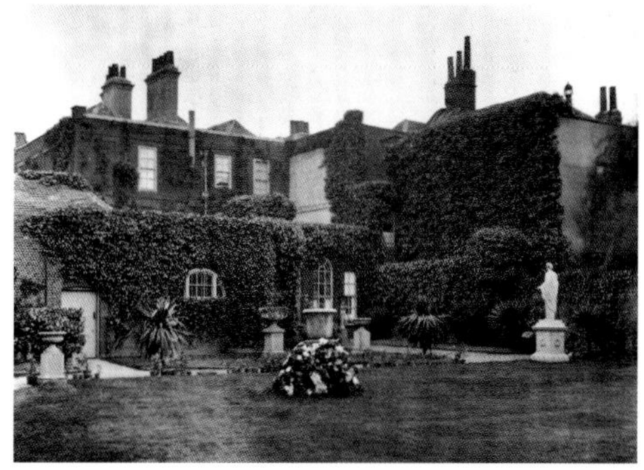

The Grange, c.1900

Produces *Childe Roland* for Ruskin, the last in a sequence of elaborate pen-and-ink drawings.

Becomes founding partner of Morris, Marshall, Faulkner & Co. (aka 'the Firm'), together with Rossetti, Philip Webb, Madox Brown and others. Produces stained-glass designs for the Firm from now on.

1862
Travels to Italy with Georgiana and Ruskin, via Paris and Basel. Leaving Ruskin in Milan, the couple journey via Verona and Padua to Venice where they stay for three weeks, returning to Milan before heading back to London. Burne-Jones studies the Venetian old masters, Titian, Tintoretto and Veronese, making copies for Ruskin.

Painted furniture by the Firm is displayed in the Medieval Court at the International Exhibition held in South Kensington.

Between 1862 and 1865 produces designs for three large earthenware tile panels, *Sleeping Beauty*, *Cinderella* and *Beauty and the Beast*. The painting of the tiles is largely carried out by Kate and Lucy Faulkner (sisters of Charles Faulkner) following Burne-Jones's designs.

Burne-Jones's early patron Thomas Plint dies unexpectedly. The executors of his estate accept the first version of *The Adoration of the Magi* and *The Annunciation* (1860–1) in lieu of money advanced.

1863
Paints the large watercolours *The Merciful Knight* and *The Annunciation (The Flower of God)*, two of the four works he exhibits the following year at the Old Water Colour Society.

Visits Winnington Hall, Northwich, Cheshire, a finishing school for girls supported by Ruskin. Designs cartoons for needlework based on Chaucer's poem *The Legend of Good Women*, to be embroidered by the girls. This turns out to be too ambitious and is abandoned.

Begins the watercolour *The Wine of Circe* for Ruskin.

1864
Elected Associate of the Society of Painters in Water-Colours (Old Water Colour Society) and exhibits four works.

Revises designs for *The Legend of Good Women* for production as a set of seven stained-glass panels for Myles Birkett Foster's house The Hill in Witley, Surrey. Duplicates are made for inclusion in the Exhibition of Stained Glass, Mosaics, etc. held at the South Kensington Museum, where they are bought by the museum.

Plans are made to extend Red House and for the Burne-Jones family to move there with the Morrises. These are abandoned after Georgiana gives birth to their second child, Christopher, who dies tragically three weeks later.

1865
The Burne-Joneses move to 41 Kensington Square.

The watercolourist Myles Birkett Foster commissions a set of seven canvases to hang in the dining room of his house in Surrey, illustrating the legend of St George and the Dragon. In 1897 they are exhibited in Munich, winning a gold medal.

Begins illustrations for William Morris's cycle of narrative poems *The Earthly Paradise*.

At Little Holland House meets George Howard (later 9th Earl of Carlisle), who becomes a good friend and patron. Establishes a friendship with Alphonse Legros, recently arrived from Paris and teaching at the South Kensington School of Art. Meets James Abbot McNeil Whistler.

The Morrises moves to Queen Square, Bloomsbury.

1866
Completes *The Lament*, started the previous year.

His daughter Margaret is born at Kensington Square in June.

Invited by the poet William Allingham to Lymington in Hampshire and takes a trip over to the Isle of Wight to visit Tennyson.

Misses the joint wedding of Georgiana's sisters in Wolverhampton. Agnes (Aggie) Macdonald marries the artist Edward Poynter (later President of the Royal Academy) and Louisa (Louie) Macdonald marries Alfred Baldwin, businessman and later Conservative MP, the couple's son Stanley Baldwin later becoming Prime Minister.

Poems and Ballads by Algernon Charles Swinburne is published, dedicated to Burne-Jones. The collection includes the poem 'Laus Veneris', begun four years earlier.

Works with Morris and Webb on designs to decorate the Green Dining Room at the South Kensington Museum (now 'The Morris Room' at the V&A).

Takes on his first studio assistant, Charles Fairfax Murray.

Meets Maria Zambaco (née Cassavetti), the model and aspiring artist from a wealthy Greek family living in London, and is immediately struck by her beauty.

Meets Frederick Leyland and William Graham via the Old Water Colour Society, both of whom become two of his most important patrons and supporters.

1867
Begins an affair with Maria Zambaco; the intense emotional experience brings on a bout of depression that leaves him unable to work, even for the Firm.

Moves to the Grange, North End Lane, Fulham, then a long cab-ride from the city and virtually in the countryside. Burne-Jones later adds a large studio at the end of the garden. The Grange remains their family home for the next thirty years.

Opens his first bank account at Praeds & Co. in Fleet Street, but struggles to manage his finances and is helped by Frederick Leyland, and later by William Graham.

1868
The illness brought on by his relationship with Maria Zambaco impedes his ability to work.

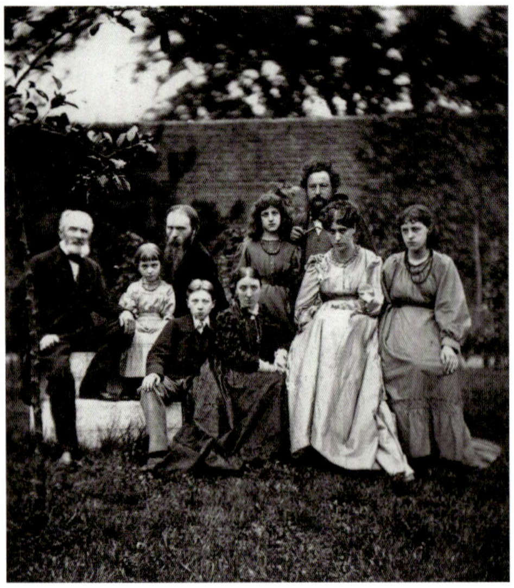

The Burne-Jones and Morris families, 1874

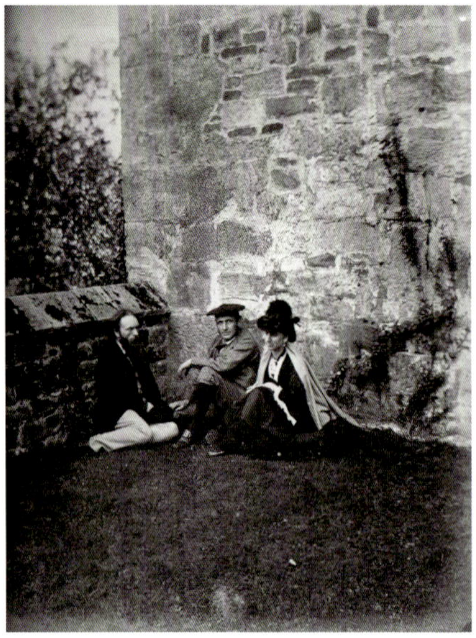

Edward Burne-Jones with George and Rosalind Howard, Naworth Castle, c.1874

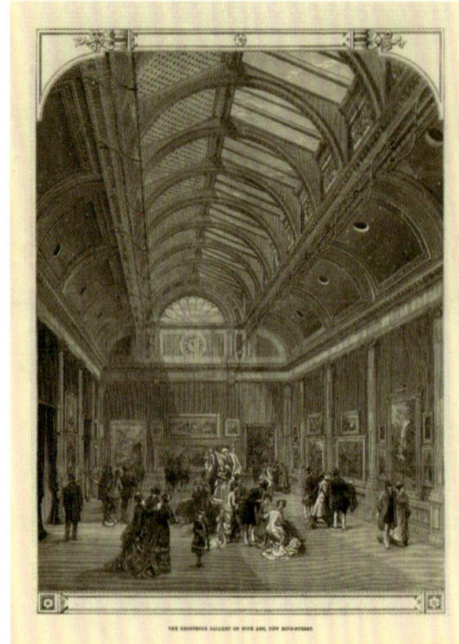

Interior of Grosvenor Gallery, 1877

1869
Attempts to end his relationship with Maria but her attempted suicide becomes a public scandal. Georgiana leaves London for Oxford with the children.

Thomas Matthews Rooke succeeds Charles Fairfax Murray as Burne-Jones's new studio assistant, remaining with him for the rest of his life.

1870
Phyllis and Demophoön is badly reviewed at the Old Water Colour Society, leading Burne-Jones to resign his membership of the society. He withdraws from public exhibition, later describing this new freedom as the 'seven blissfullest years of work that I ever had; no fuss, no publicity, no teasing about exhibiting, no getting pictures done against time'.

Reconciled with Georgiana, and begins painting *Love among the Ruins* and *The Mill.*

1871
Falls out with Ruskin over the latter's lecture disparaging Michelangelo, which Burne-Jones interprets as a criticism of his own work.

Makes his third trip to Italy, visiting, among other places, Florence, Pisa, Siena and Rome. Sketches works of the early Renaissance masters, including Giotto, Uccello and Piero della Francesca, and studies Michelangelo's frescos in the Sistine Chapel.

1872
Embarks on many pictures, including scenes for the *Briar Rose* series, *The Golden Stairs*, and *Venus Discordia.*

George Howard commissions the *Cupid and Psyche* frieze for the dining room of his new house, 1 Palace Green, Kensington, designed by Philip Webb. Burne-Jones has completed little of the work by 1876, so Walter Crane is brought in to finish the canvas panels, with Burne-Jones making final alterations in 1881.

Completes illustrations for *The Rubáiyát of Omar Khayyám*, which he gifts to Frances Graham. Morris presents another version to Georgiana.

Starts cartoons for stained glass for Christ Church Cathedral, Oxford, and Jesus College Chapel, Cambridge.

The Morrises move out of 26 Queen Square to Horrington House, Turnham Green, Chiswick, only a half-hour walk from the Grange. Morris visits Burne-Jones regularly on Sundays for breakfast and to work on current projects.

1873
Burne-Jones is one of the few friends of Simeon Solomon who speak out in support of him following his arrest and charge of indecent behaviour in a public lavatory.

Frances Graham visits the Grange with her father, William Graham, meeting Burne-Jones for the first time.

Exhibits two watercolours, *Love among the Ruins* and the *Hesperides*, at the Dudley Gallery.

Makes his final visit to Italy, with William Morris. They travel via Paris, visiting Maria Zambaco, who had moved there to work as a sculptor and medallist. In Florence they visit Spencer Stanhope, and in Siena call on Fairfax Murray. Morris returns to England, but Burne-Jones stays on a few weeks and develops a fever. It takes him months to recover once he returns to London.

1874
Starts corresponding with Frances Graham, illustrating his letters to her.

Produces designs for a long embroidered frieze, based on Chaucer's *Romaunt of the Rose*, to decorate the dining room of Rounton Grange, another house designed by Philip Webb, this time for the northern industrialist Lowthian Bell.

Visits Naworth Castle, Cumberland, the home of George and Rosalind Howard.

1875
Through Frances Graham meets Mary Gladstone (daughter of the former Prime Minister, William Ewart Gladstone), who becomes a lifelong friend.

Receives a commission from the young Conservative MP and future Prime Minister, Arthur Balfour, to paint the Perseus series.

The Firm is reconstituted under Morris's ownership and Burne-Jones takes on more figurative and stained-glass work as a result. He falls out with Madox Brown in the process of reorganisation, who never speaks to him again.

1876
Following the massacre of Christians in the Balkans, is drawn into the 'Eastern Question Affair', a cause championed by Gladstone. Though relatively brief, this is the most politically active part of his life; he joins the massed crowds in protest along with Georgiana and William Morris. He later becomes disillusioned after Gladstone changes his position and regrets the time spent away from painting.

1877
Exhibits eight pictures at the newly opened Grosvenor Gallery, including *The Beguiling of Merlin*. His work is praised by critics, including Ruskin in *Fors Clavigera*, the same article in which he attacks the work of Whistler, leading the artist to sue for libel.

Attends rehearsals for the Wagner concerts at the Royal Albert Hall, where he contrives to meet Margaret Benson (later Mrs Drummond), who poses for the head of Medusa in the Perseus series, among other works. Her brother, the metalworker W.A.S. Benson, was also to model for Burne-Jones.

Deepens his friendship with the writer George Eliot (Mary Anne Evans), initially Georgiana's friend.

Employs Matthew Webb as junior studio assistant.

1878
Exhibits eleven pictures at the Grosvenor Gallery, including *Laus Veneris* and the oil version of *Le Chant d'Amour.*

Visits Paris with Morris, where *The Beguiling of Merlin* is exhibited at the Exposition Universelle. It is praised by critics but not awarded a prize.

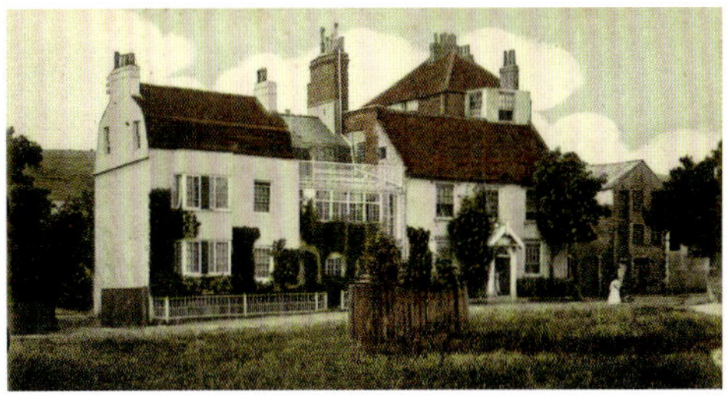

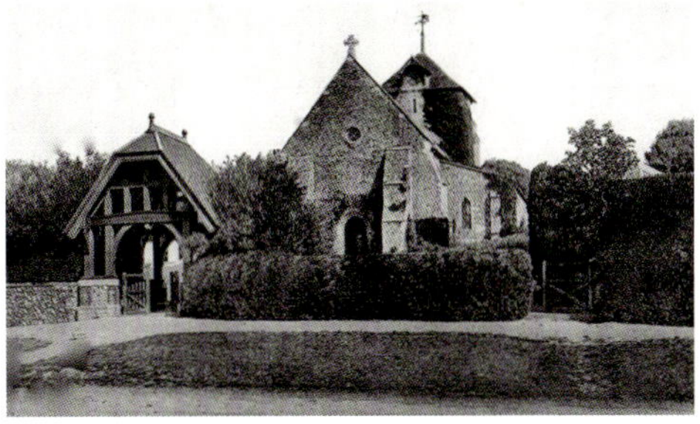

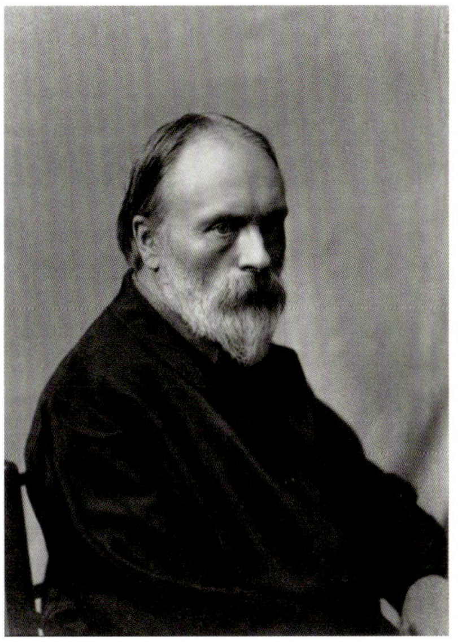

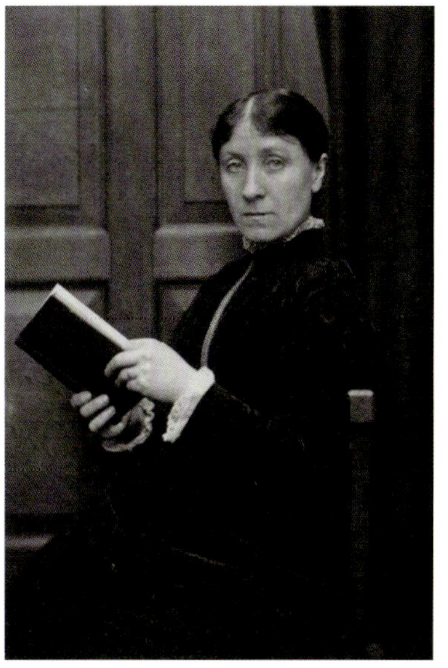

North End House, Rottingdean

Edward Burne-Jones, c.1885

Georgiana Burne-Jones, c.1890

St Margaret's Church, Rottingdean

Brief holiday at Bonneville and Annecy.

Around this time meets George Lewis, a famous solicitor, and his second wife Elizabeth. The Burne-Joneses are regular visitors to the Lewises' house in Portland Place and Ashley Cottage, their country house at Walton-on-Thames.

Called as a witness at the Ruskin trial, where he reluctantly takes the stand in defence of Ruskin against Whistler. Whistler never speaks to Burne-Jones again.

Produces stained-glass designs *Angeli Ministrantes* and *Angeli Laudantes* for Salisbury Cathedral, as well as five cartoons for the windows of St Martin's, Brampton, and three of St Catherine for Christ Church Cathedral, Oxford.

1879

Pygmalion and the Image is exhibited at the Grosvenor Gallery, along with *The Annunciation*.

Travels to Hawarden Castle, Flintshire, Wales, the home of Mary Gladstone, where he develops a friendship with her father, William Ewart Gladstone, the Liberal MP and Prime Minster.

Joins the campaign, led by Ruskin and Morris, to prevent the so-called 'restoration' of the facade of St Mark's Cathedral, Venice. Morris asks him to speak on the subject at a meeting in the Sheldonian Theatre, Oxford, his one and only formal public speech.

William Graham commissions scenes from the Orpheus legend to decorate a grand piano for his daughter Frances. He also commissions a portrait of her, possibly to mark Frances's twenty-first birthday.

1880

Completes *The Golden Stairs* for exhibition at the Grosvenor Gallery, where it causes a sensation.

Last meeting with George Eliot before her death later that year.

Through George and Elizabeth Lewis, meets and befriends Oscar Wilde.

After a 'fiasco of a holiday' in the summer travelling around Wiltshire, Devon and Somerset, the Burne-Joneses buy North End House in the small village of Rottingdean, just outside Brighton, as a summer retreat.

1881

Commissioned by G.E. Street to produce designs for mosaics for the apse and choir of the American Episcopal Church in Rome, St Paul's Within-the-Walls. The designs are finished three years later, but parts of the scheme are not completed until after the artist's death.

Begins work on his magnum opus, *The Sleep of King Arthur in Avalon*, as a commission from George Howard.

Awarded an Honorary Doctorate degree from the University of Oxford.

1882

After not exhibiting any works the previous year, he returns to the Grosvenor Gallery exhibiting nine works including *The Mill* and *The Tree of Forgiveness*.

Dante Gabriel Rossetti dies having suffered a mild stroke, aged only fifty-three, at the house of an old friend in Birchington-on-Sea in Kent.

Commissioned by his friend, the physician Dr Charles Bland Radcliffe, to paint an altarpiece at St Peter's, Vere Street, London, in memory of the Christian Socialist, F.D. Maurice. The subject is *Mary Magdalene at the Sepulchre* (installed early 1883).

Moves his aged father to London, who unexpectedly marries a young servant maid. The couple leave London for Birmingham.

Builds the garden studio at the Grange.

Produces his first design for tapestry, *Pomona*, which is woven at the Morris & Co. tapestry works, recently moved to Merton Abbey.

1883

Burne-Jones and Morris are made Honorary Fellows of Exeter College, University of Oxford, their old college.

Exhibits *The Wheel of Fortune* and *The Hours* at the Grosvenor Gallery.

In the second of his *Art of England* lectures, Ruskin celebrates Burne-Jones as a painter of mythology.

Writes a series of illustrated letters to Katie Lewis, the five-year-old daughter of George Lewis, later published as *Letters to Katie*.

Grows slightly estranged from Morris, on account of his political activism and involvement with the Democratic Federation.

Stained-glass designs by Burne-Jones exhibited on the Morris & Co. stand at the Foreign Fair, Boston, USA.

1884

King Cophetua and the Beggar Maid is exhibited at the Grosvenor Gallery.

Produces the first of four major designs for the stained-glass windows at St Philip's Cathedral, Birmingham, as well as *The Quest for the Sanc Grael* for his house at Rottingdean.

1885

Decides to hyphenate his surname, much to the scorn of his friends, including Morris.

Elected Associate of the Royal Academy of Arts.

Long-standing patron and friend, William Graham dies. Burne-Jones sends some small pictures to Glasgow to be buried with him in his coffin.

Paints portrait of his daughter Margaret Burne-Jones.

Accepts the honorary title of President of the Royal Birmingham Society of Artists, and visits Birmingham in October.

First mosaic unveiled at the American Episcopal church of St Paul's Within-the-Walls, Rome.

1886

Reluctantly accepts re-election to the Old Water Colour Society.

The Depths of the Sea is exhibited at the Royal Academy summer exhibition at Burlington House, the only time he showed a picture there.

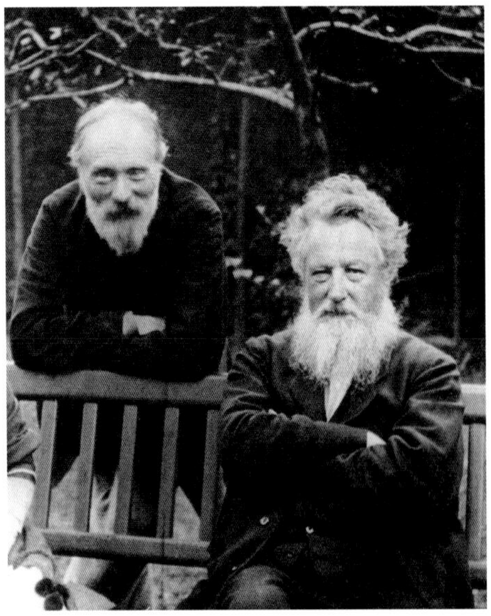

Edward Burne-Jones and William Morris, 1890

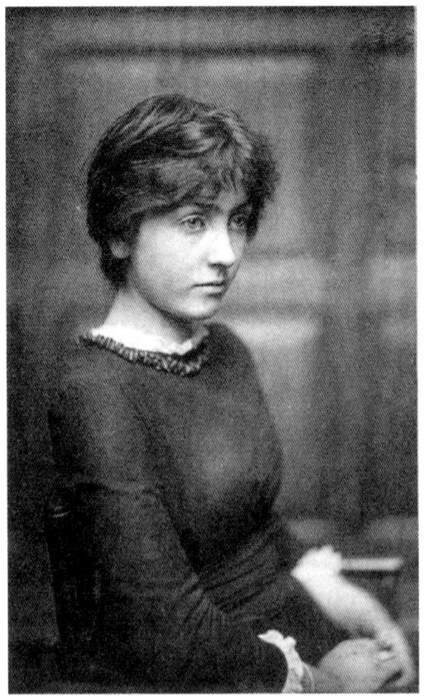

Margaret Burne-Jones, c.1885, taken before her marriage to J.W. Mackail

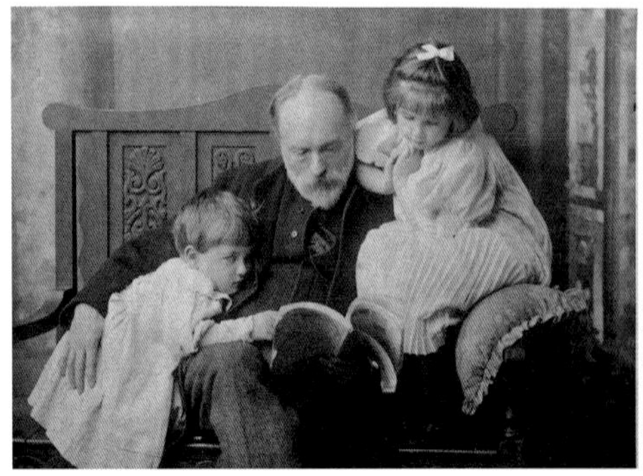

Edward Burne-Jones with Denis and Angela Mackail, 1895

His version of the Vere Street St Peter's altarpiece exhibited at the Grosvenor Gallery as *The Morning of the Resurrection.*

Laura Lyttelton (née Tennant), friend of Frances Graham and one of the best loved of the Souls, dies after giving birth, much to Burne-Jones's distress.

William Graham's pictures are sold at auction; those by Burne-Jones command high prices.

1887
Final exhibition at the Grosvenor Gallery before its closure includes his memorial tablet to Laura Lyttelton and *The Garden of Pan.*

Begins painting *The Star of Bethlehem*, a large-scale watercolour commissioned by the Corporation of Birmingham for the new municipal Museum and Art Gallery. He would use the same composition as a design for the *Adoration of the Magi*, a tapestry commissioned for the chapel of Exeter College, Oxford.

1888
The New Gallery, Regent Street, is opened by J. Comyns Carr and Charles Hallé (former Directors at the Grosvenor Gallery), with works by Burne-Jones including two paintings from the Perseus series: *The Rock of Doom* and *The Doom Fulfilled.* The New Gallery becomes his main exhibiting gallery for the rest of his career.

Margaret marries the academic, poet and historian John William (Jack) Mackail at the church of St Margaret of Antioch, Rottingdean. He would later produce a biography of William Morris.

Continues work on the *Briar Rose* series.

First exhibition of the Arts & Crafts Exhibition Society at the New Gallery, including decorative work from Morris & Co.

1889
His father dies and is buried in Brompton Cemetery, alongside his aunt Keturah Catherwood and little Christopher.

Absorbed by the *Briar Rose* series, he does not exhibit at the second exhibition at the New Gallery. Morris steps back slightly from his political activities and their friendship is renewed.

Frederic Leighton persuades Burne-Jones to lend *King Cophetua and the Beggar Maid* and *The Depths of the Sea* to the British Section of the Exposition Universelle in Paris. *King Cophetua* is received with great acclaim and he is later awarded the Cross of the Légion d'honneur.

Buys the adjoining house in Rottingdean. This provides a studio and snug smoking-room he calls the Merry Mermaid.

1890
The *Briar Rose* series is exhibited at Agnew's, Bond Street, to great acclaim, and subsequently (with free admission) at Toynbee Hall, Whitechapel, East London. The paintings are bought by Alexander Henderson (later Lord Faringdon) and installed in the saloon of his new house, Buscot Park, west Oxfordshire. Burne-Jones supervises the hanging of the pictures and offers to paint connecting link panels to complete the room.

Paints the portrait of the Polish musician, composer, politician and campaigner for independence, *Ignacy Jan Paderewski.*

Granddaughter Angela Mackail (later Thirkell) born.

Begins designs for the *Holy Grail* series of tapestries, commissioned for the dining room of Stanmore Hall, the home of the wealthy financier and colonial mining speculator William Knox D'Arcy.

1891
The Star of Bethlehem is included in the Pre-Raphaelite exhibition at Birmingham Museum and Art Gallery, and at the New Gallery, London.

Begins producing illustrations for the Kelmscott Press.

Aubrey Beardsley visits his studio with his sister, to show Burne-Jones his portfolio. Oscar and Constance Wilde are there the same afternoon.

Declines a commission to decorate the dome of St Paul's Cathedral with mosaics.

1892
Grandson Denis Mackail is born.

Death of his long-standing patron Frederick Leyland. Burne-Jones designs his tomb for Brompton Cemetery in the form of a Byzantine sarcophagus.

Develops an obsessive friendship with Helen Mary (May) Gaskell, having been introduced to her at the Grange by Frances Horner (née Graham).

Elected a corresponding member of the Académie des Beaux-Arts, Paris. Declines invitation to exhibit at the Salon de la Rose + Croix, which he describes as 'silly'.

Retrospective exhibition of his work is held at the New Gallery.

1893
Resigns as Associate of the Royal Academy.

Forms close friendship with two young sisters, Violet and Olive Maxse, whom he teaches to draw.

Love among the Ruins is damaged in France. Decides to paint a replacement in oils.

Completes *Vespertina Quies.*

Three stained-glass windows designed by Burne-Jones depicting the three archangels Gabriel, Michael and Raphael are installed in St Margaret's, Rottingdean, as a gift to mark the wedding of his daughter Margaret there.

Sees Emma de Burgh, otherwise known as the American Tattooed Lady, at the Royal Aquarium with Leonardo's *Last Supper* tattooed on her back and the American Eagle and Union Jack on each kneecap.

Presents three drawings to the Musée du Luxembourg, Paris.

1894
Gladstone offers him a baronetcy 'in recognition of the high position which you have obtained by

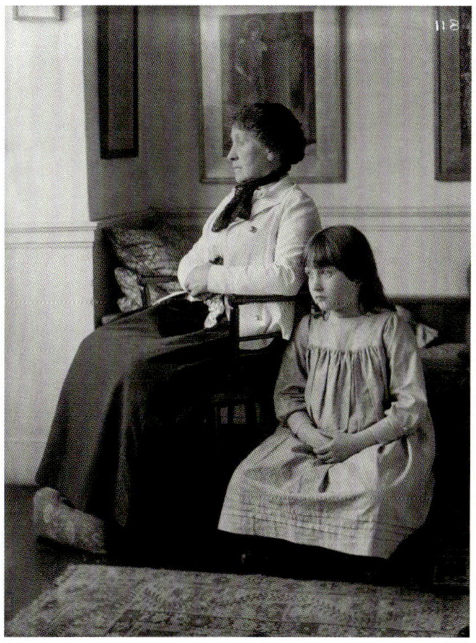

Georgiana Burne-Jones and Angela Mackail, c.1900

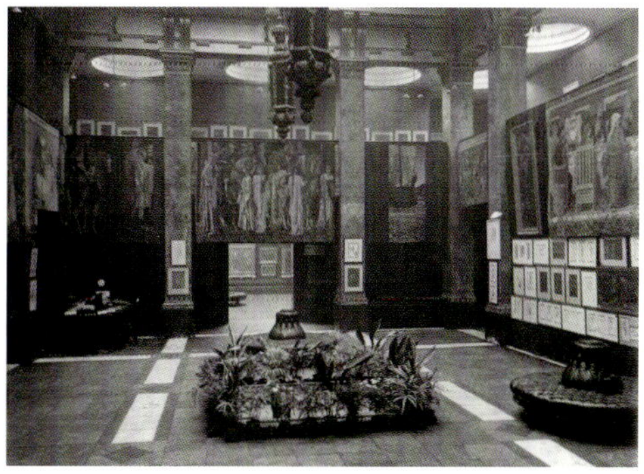

Burne-Jones Memorial Exhibition at New Gallery 1898–9

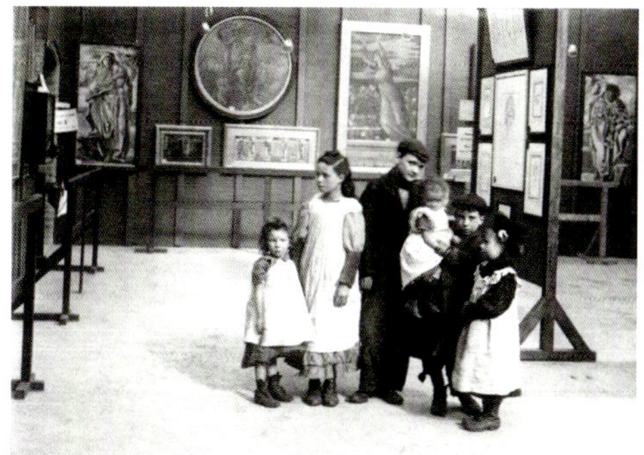

'Spitalfields Nippers' visiting *Modern Pictures by Living Artists...* at the Whitechapel Gallery, 1901

your achievement in your noble art'. He accepts and legalises the name of Burne-Jones.

Finishes his replacement version of *Love among the Ruins.*

Completion of the *Holy Grail* and the *Adoration of the Magi* tapestries, as well as the large painting in gouache of *The Fall of Lucifer.*

Visits W.E. Gladstone at Hawarden.

Early indications of heart trouble.

1895

Portrait of *Lady Windsor* exhibited at the New Gallery.

Designs scenery and costumes for J. Comyns Carr's production of *King Arthur* at the Lyceum Theatre, with his friend Ellen Terry as Guinevere.

Lends Constance Wilde money to tide her over following the trial of Oscar Wilde.

1896

Exhibition of drawings at the Fine Art Society.

Publication of the Kelmscott *Chaucer.*

Visits the Society of Antiquaries to view manuscripts with Morris.

Paints *Flamma Vestalis* and *The Dream of Launcelot at the Chapel of the San Graal.*

Third grandchild, Clare Mackail born.

William Morris dies on 3 October at Kelmscott House, Hammersmith. The funeral is held at St George's Church, Kelmscott, Oxfordshire.

1897

Finishes *Love and the Pilgrim,* which is shown at the New Gallery in the spring.

Taken by Georgiana to Malvern Spa to recuperate from influenza.

Georgiana visits the cathedrals of northern France with the Mackails. Burne-Jones remains at Rottingdean, where his nephew Rudyard Kipling is staying.

Two lancet windows designed by Burne-Jones, *Jacob's Dream* and *The Tree of Jesse*, are installed in St Margaret's, Rottingdean.

Makes last designs for the Kelmscott Press. Continues work on *The Sleep of King Arthur in Avalon*, now at St Paul's Studios, close to the Grange.

Declines an invitation to Queen Victoria's Diamond Jubilee celebration dinner.

The *Last Judgement* window is installed in St Philip's Church, Birmingham (later Birmingham Cathedral).

1898

Helps to organise the Rossetti retrospective at the New Gallery.

Begins his last major design for the *Passing of Venus* tapestry.

W.E. Gladstone dies. Attends his state funeral at Westminster Abbey. His stained-glass memorial to Gladstone is installed in St Deiniol's Church, Hawarden.

Burne-Jones dies of angina during the night of 16–17 June at the Grange. His ashes are buried in Rottingdean churchyard, and a memorial plaque is placed on the outside wall of the church. A memorial service is held at Westminster Abbey, the first ever held there in honour of a painter, as a result of a signed petition sponsored by the Prince of Wales.

A retrospective exhibition of his work is held at the New Gallery.

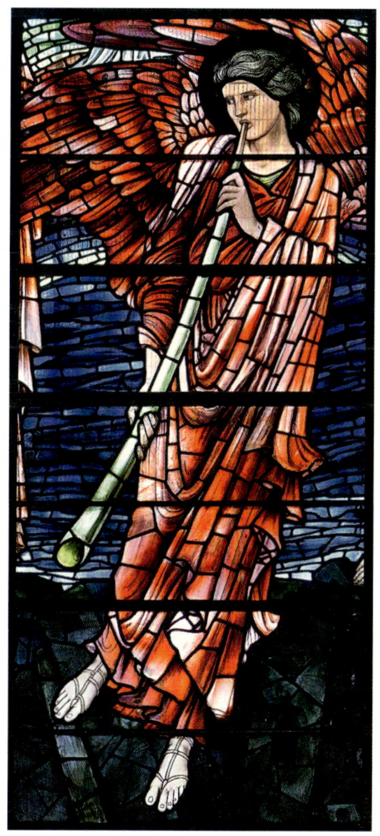

Last Judgement 1897 (detail)

Notes

Burne-Jones: Intellectual, Designer, People's Man

I am grateful to Charles Martindale, Charlotte Gere and Katherine Hinzman for insights, comments and research that have informed my thinking for this essay.

1 Lago 1982, p.147.
2 John Christian, 'A Critical Somersault', in Wildman and Christian 1998, pp.3–4.
3 Sewter 1974–5, vol.1, p.46. See also Alan Crawford, 'Burne-Jones as a Decorative Artist', in Wildman and Christian 1998, pp.5–23.
4 William Morris, 'The Lesser Arts' (1877), in *Hopes and Fears for Art* (1882), repr. in Morris 1914, pp.3–27.
5 Exceptions might be Paul Gauguin and Vincent Van Gogh, who had little formal art training, but they were not university educated.
6 See Kris and Kurz 1979, pp.26–38 (on 'the discovery of talent'). A story about Burne-Jones, in which a family friend, Mr Caswell, praises his childhood drawings, draws on this archetypal myth, but the episode fails to lead directly to an artistic career (G. Burne-Jones 1904, vol.1, p.6).
7 Immanuel Kant, *The Critique of Judgement* (1790). On the importance of this key text in British art, see Prettejohn 2007, pp.17–19 and passim.
8 He was christened 'Edward Coley Burne Jones' ('Burne' was the name of an aunt) and did not adopt the hyphenated form until late in his career; see G. Burne-Jones 1904, vol.1, p.4, vol.2, pp.241–2.
9 Ruskin 1883, p.297.
10 Lago 1982, p.27.
11 G. Burne-Jones 1904, vol.1, pp.22–6.
12 Barthes 1977, p.146.
13 See for example John Christian, 'The Compulsive Draughtsman', in Birmingham Museums and Art Gallery 2007, p.7.
14 George Du Maurier, in a letter to Burne-Jones dated 9 February 1893 (Fitzwilliam Museum, Cambridge), quoted in MacCarthy 2011, p.536.
15 Robertson 1931, p.84.
16 Lago 1982, p.138. I am grateful to Alison Smith for alerting me to Burne-Jones's interesting comment on the relationship between design and colour in his work (Lago 1982, p.51).
17 Lago 1982, p.147.
18 Robertson 1931, p.83.
19 G. Burne-Jones 1904, vol.2, p.26.
20 'Art made by the people and for the people as a joy to the maker and the user': William Morris, 'The Beauty of Life' (1880), in Morris 1914, p.73.
21 Lago 1982, p.29.
22 Allingham 1908, p.139.
23 G. Burne-Jones 1904, vol.2, p.13.
24 G. Burne-Jones 1904, vol.2, p.13; the wording echoes the directions in *The Book of Common Prayer* (1662): 'In Quires and Places where they sing, there followeth the Anthem' (after the collects, in both Morning and Evening Prayer); see Cummings 2011, pp.248, 256.
25 G. Burne-Jones 1904, vol.1, p.130.
26 Quoted, for example, by Laurence Binyon in his entry on Burne-Jones for *Encyclopaedia Britannica*, 1911, vol.4, p.850. The first published appearance of the quotation seems to be in Burlington Fine Arts Club 1899, p.vii; see Wildman and Christian 1998, p.320.
27 See Weliver 2017, pp.55–63.
28 Lewis 1948, p.672.
29 Wood 1907, pp.10–11.
30 Letter to *The Times*, 13 May 1851, repr. in Ruskin 1903–12, vol.12, p.322.
31 G. Burne-Jones 1904, vol.2, p.209.

At Work: Burne-Jones's Studio, Materials and Techniques

1 G. Burne-Jones 1904, vol.2, p.187; Lago 1982, pp.122–4; 182.
2 Burne-Jones to Mary Elcho, c.1888–98, cited in Dakers 1988, p.499.
3 G. Burne-Jones 1904, vol.2, p.159.
4 Wilson 1934, p.89.
5 Ruskin to G.F. Watts, 13 February 1873, Bodleian Library Collection, Mss eng.lett.c50.
6 https://www.spectator.co.uk/2017/07/the-victorian-artist-who-was-more-jackson-pollock-than-pre-raphaelite.
7 Letter dated 13 May 1893, British Library, Add MS 54217, ff.71–4.
8 M. Bell 1909, p.62.
9 Letter to Helen Mary Gaskell, 20 September 1894, British Library, Add MS 54217, ff.282–7; P. Burne-Jones 1900, p.161.
10 Robertson 1931, p.76.
11 Benson was also responsible for adding a studio to the family property, North End House, in Rottingdean: MacCarthy 2011, p.200.
12 Others included Henry Ellis Wooldridge, Matthew Webb, Garstin Harvey Osmond Weeks, the American Francis Lathrop and James Melhuish Strudwick.
13 The full reference is in the typescript copy of Rooke's diary in the National Art Library, V&A (4 volumes).
14 Lago 1982, p.22; Comyns Carr 1914, p.81.
15 Lago 1982, p.20; pp.197–98 n.2; G. Burne-Jones 1904, vol.2, p.61.
16 As described in Charles Fairfax Murray, 'Notes on Techniques', unpublished manuscript, Birmingham Museum and Art Gallery, inv.no.2006.1330.
17 Tate Gallery conservation report N04390 by Sheila Fairbrass, 31 March 1978.
18 Lago 1982, pp.46–7.
19 Mann 2014, p.658.
20 Mann 2014, p.660.
21 Murray op. cit.; for zinc white see Townsend 2004, p.46.
22 Robertson 1931, p.83.
23 G. Burne-Jones 1904, vol.2, pp.61–2.
24 *Love among the Ruins*, Christie's sale catalogue, Thursday 11 July 2013, p.23.
25 *Art Journal*, 1873, p.87.
26 Rothenstein 1935, p.114; see also Binyon 1946, p.163.
27 Roberson ledgers, Hamilton Kerr Institute, Cambridge, 18 November 1891 (MS 250-1993), p.281. I am grateful to Fiona Mann for this reference.
28 G. Burne-Jones 1904, vol.2, pp.38–9.
29 Correspondence with author, 30 January 2018.
30 Murray op. cit. See also M. Bell 1901, p.56.
31 Burne-Jones to Harry Quilter, n.d. 1891, Huntington Library HM 32301, cited in Munro 1992, p.95.
32 Tate Gallery conservation record for *King Cophetua and the Beggar Maid* (Joyce Townsend), January 2017; P. Burne-Jones 1900, p.160. Burne-Jones made his first order of turpentine from Roberson's in 1888 and then regular orders from 1893 to 1898 (Fiona Mann to author 30 January 2018).
33 P. Burne-Jones 1900, p.160. See also G. Burne-Jones 1904, vol.2, pp.321–22.
34 P. Burne-Jones 1900, p.160.
35 G. Burne-Jones 1904, vol.2, p.323.
36 A label on the reverse of *The Garden Court* from the *Briar Rose* series (version in Bristol Museum and Art Gallery) reads: 'if it is thought desirable to varnish it, please let five or six years go by – and then let only mastic varnish be used' (I am grateful to Jenny Gaschke for this reference).
37 P. Burne-Jones 1900, p.160.
38 Tate Gallery conservation record for *King Cophetua*.
39 Benson's objects are Illustrated in Vallance 1900, pp.28–30 and Philip Burne-Jones's 'Notes on some unfinished works of Sir Edward Burne-Jones, Bt.,' *Magazine of Art*, 1900, pp.161–2; Burne-Jones to George Howard, n.d. (Howard correspondence, Castle Howard, Yorkshire).
40 G. Burne-Jones 1904, vol.2, p.261.
41 Burne-Jones to May Gaskell, 1 August 1893, British Library, Add MS 54217, ff.93–4.

'Girlish Dreams': Burne-Jones in the Twentieth Century

1 MacCarthy 2011, p.511.
2 Smith 1996, p.180; and see Alison Smith's essay in this book, p.23. For analysis of Burne-Jones's androgynous bodies, see Bullen 1998, ch.4, and Andres 2005, ch.5.
3 New Gallery 1898, pp.27–8.
4 Kipling 2004, p.342 (23 June 1898).
5 Mahood 2009, p.80; Proust 1955, p.645.
6 See Bénédite 1998; Des Cars 1998.
7 Bénédite 1998, pp.40–6, 56.
8 Busine 1992; Khnopff 1898, p.526.
9 Penrose 1981, p.56.
10 Fitzgerald 1975, pp.258, 279.
11 For a survey of this strand in British art, see Christian 1989.
12 See Crossman 2015.
13 See his letters to *The Times*, 17 November 1910, p.4, and 24 January 1913, p.10. In 1912 Philip was invited to speak in New York on 'degeneracy in art' and duly condemned what he saw as 'scribbles of the nursery, enlivened by the delirium of the madhouse' produced by 'the hysteric and epileptic schools' (*New York Times*, 20 February 1912, p.3). The excesses of his rhetoric were criticised in Macfall 1912.
14 'The Great Illusion', *Manchester Guardian*, 2 October 1920, p.7.
15 Robertson 1931, pp.73–85; Burne-Jones 1925.
16 Thirkell 2012, p.58.
17 Carpenter 1977, p.177. As it happens, Tolkien and Burne-Jones attended the same school in Birmingham and the same Oxford college.
18 Sheridan 1921, p.13 (many thanks to Jonathan Black for this reference); Askari 2014, p.63 (*The Beggar Maid*, dir. Herbert Blaché, USA 1921). Fifty years later *King Cophetua* appeared in *Rendez-vous à Bray* by the Belgian director André Delvaux (Colvile 2006, p.127). As early as 1910, one of the very first vampire films (*The Vampire*, Selig Polyscope Co., USA) was advertised as being based on a famous painting by Edward Burne-Jones: but the source was in fact the most original work of his son Philip, showing a female vampire in action and now recognised as a key ingredient in the invention of the 'vamp' of the twenties.
19 There was a brief exhibition at Fulham Library in 1928 of material lent from the Grange, and another there in 1967. Hopes to preserve the Grange as some kind of memorial to the painter ended with its demolition in the fifties. On the planning of the 1933 exhibition, see Lago 1975.
20 *The Times*, 16 June 1933, p.15.
21 *The Times*, 17 June 1933, p.10.
22 *Daily Mail*, 28 August 1933, p.8.
23 R. Bell 1933, p.620; Fincham 1933.
24 Wilenski 1933, pp.224–5; *Apollo* review of 1933 Tate exhibition quoted by John Christian in Wildman and Christian 1998, p.1, where Christian also refers to the books by Wilenski and Collins Baker.
25 Collins Baker 1933, p.206.
26 See Hilliard 1982.
27 In fact the gist of Lewis's suggestion had already been taken up in 1932 by Charles de Noailles, the distinguished French collector of surrealism, who in that year acquired Burne-Jones's *Wheel of Fortune* now in the Musée d'Orsay (as noted by Elizabeth Prettejohn in a lecture given at the British Academy, 6 March 2018).
28 *Observer*, 7 December 1969, p.40.
29 Hilton 1970, p.190.
30 Harrison and Waters 1989, p.xiv.
31 Lee 2013, p.214.
32 Fitzgerald 1977, p.57.
33 Lohf 1972; Hartnoll 1972.
34 Royal Academy 2003, no.30 (acquired 1972).
35 John Christian in Wildman and Christian 1998, pp.3–4.
36 Jones 2017, p.83. For a recent study of the significance of Bowie's projection of shifting gender, see Bradley and Page 2017. Gill Perry (2016) has compared news photographs of the spontaneous gatherings at makeshift shrines, following the death of Bowie in January 2016, to Burne-Jones's *Last Sleep of Arthur in Avalon*.
37 MacInnes 1976; he died a few days after the publication of this article.
38 Baldwin 1935, pp.178–9.

Apprentice to Master: 1856–70

1 Cited in G. Burne-Jones 1904, vol.1, p.36.
2 Cited in Horner 1933, p.120.
3 The later drawings for this book were made around the time Burne-Jones first met Rossetti and reflect more of his influence. The drawings are reproduced in Maclaren 1985.
4 Cited in G. Burne-Jones 1904, vol.1, p.149.
5 The drawing was previously identified as an Arthurian incident, possibly the Lady of Shalott; see Harrison and Waters 1989, p.23.
6 Rossetti 2002–9, vol.2, p.171; G. Burne-Jones 1904, vol.1, p.225.
7 Burne-Jones, unpublished 'List of Designs', Fitzwilliam Museum, Cambridge.
8 See Harrison and Waters 1989, p.28; Vallance 1900, p.2.
9 *The Good Shepherd* became one of Powell's standard designs. The version shown here was commissioned by H.H. Dobney, editor of the *Christian Spectator* and an artist, and installed as the centre light of the east window of the King Street Congregational Church in Maidstone, Kent (Christian 1968, pp.30–46). In the 1970s the church

was demolished to make way for the Stoneborough Shopping Centre. *The Calling of St Peter* was made for the top of a lancet in an as yet unidentified church.

10 Possible sources include Simone Martini's *Annunciation*, Uffizi, Florence; the *Annunciation* by Giotto, Arena Chapel, Padua; Carpaccio's *St George* in the Scuola di San Giorgio degli Schiavoni, Venice. The central panel may also have been prompted by Hugo van der Goes's *Portinari Altarpiece*, which Burne-Jones would have seen in Florence. See Parkinson 1975; Staley 2011, p.349.

11 For a more detailed consideration of the iconography in relation to the liturgical programme of the church, see Crossman 2007, pp.169–72. For the second version (now in a private collection), see the entry by Christopher Newall in the Sotheby's sale catalogue, 3 November 1993 (192). Rachel Scott's technical analysis of the first version will be the focus of a forthcoming Tate paper.

12 Burne-Jones Account Books with Morris & Co., Fitzwilliam Museum, Cambridge. See also Schoenherr 2011, p.116.

13 Burne-Jones to Ford Madox Brown, December 1859, cited in Munro 1992, p.85.

14 'The Society of Painters in Watercolour', *Art Journal*, 1865, pp.173–4.

15 Ruskin 1903–12, vol.36, p.468. For an in-depth analysis of Ruskin's programme for Burne-Jones, see John Christian's essay, '"A Serious Talk": Ruskin's Place in Burne-Jones's Artistic Development', in Parris 1984a, pp.184–205.

16 Studies for the former exist in a sketchbook in the V&A; see Parris 1984b, p.304, for details.

17 *The Times*, 27 April 1870, p.4; *Illustrated London News*, 30 April 1870, p.459.

'An impassioned imagination': Burne-Jones as a Draughtsman

1 Monkhouse 1899, p.xvii. A friend of Burne-Jones, Monkhouse had previously written an essay on the artist published in *Scribner's Magazine*, vol.XV, no.2, 2 February 1894, pp.135–54. X64770 is an illustrated letter from Burne-Jones to Monkhouse from 1894.

2 In Monkhouse 1899 (p.6, where it is listed as item 15) the work is entitled 'Going to the Battle', as inscribed on the 'oaken mount', and the date is given as 1859, although in later publications it is amended to 1858.

3 Monkhouse 1899, p.43.

4 Swinburne 1875, p.316. Pater's essays were collected in his most famous book, *Studies in the History of the Renaissance* (1873), a key work of aesthetic movement art criticism.

5 Symonds 1901, pp.284–5.

6 *Athenaeum*, 16 November 1889, p.680.

7 For an overview of the artist's approaches to drawing, see John Christian, 'The Compulsive Draughtsman', in Birmingham Museums and Art Gallery 2007, pp.7–27.

8 This version, now in the Tate, was exhibited as 'The Parable of the Boiling Pot' at the Burlington Fine Arts Club in 1899. It was then still in the possession of Georgiana Burne-Jones. The 'oaken mount' was inscribed with verses from Ezekiel 16: 49 and 14: 10–12. The studies, showing Ezekiel crouching rather than standing upright, were incorporated into the design commissioned by the Dalziel Brothers in 1859 for their *Bible Gallery*, published in 1881.

9 Harrison 2010, p.16.

10 For the story of the encounter see G. Burne-Jones 1904, vol.1, p.129. For the Rossetti watercolour see Surtees 1971, vol.1, pp.41–2.

11 Quoted in G. Burne-Jones 1904, vol.1, p.195.

12 For Ruskin's gift see G. Burne-Jones 1904, vol.1, p.287.

13 In the autumn of 1874, writing to his son Philip at boarding school, the artist reflected on the Dürer print – given to him in 1865 by Ruskin – and the use made of it by F. de la Motte Fouqué in his novel *Sintram and his Companions* (1814): '[Of Fouqué's stories] I believe Undine is the best, but I used to like Sintram most – it is a story made out of the engraving I have by Albert Dürer, of the Knight riding by a rock and horribles all about him. And it shews what a treasure such a design is in the world that it can suggest such beauty to another man' (G. Burne-Jones 1904, vol.2, p.49). A reduced copy of the engraving was reproduced as the frontispiece of several English translations published in the mid-nineteenth century. Burne-Jones listed the book as one of the favourites of his undergraduate years (G. Burne-Jones 1904, vol.1, p.142). The Dürer print is also referenced in Burne-Jones's drawing *Sir Galahad* (1858, Fogg Gallery, Cambridge, Mass.).

14 For an account of this moment in Burne-Jones's friendship with Ruskin, see John Christian, '"A Serious Talk": Ruskin's Place in Burne-Jones's Artistic Development', in Parris 1984a, p.198.

15 The photographic reproductions survive and are now housed in the University College London Library, Special Collections.

16 The drawing is bound into a volume of illustrated letters sent by the artist to Katherine (Katie) Lewis. The volume also contains a pastiche version of Burne-Jones's major painting of his later career *King Cophetua and the Beggar Maid* 1884 (no.98). It is also imagined as if redone by Rubens in a drawing of c.1885, reproduced in Harrison and Waters 1973, p.139.

17 G. Burne-Jones 1904, vol.1, p.44.

18 See MacCarthy 2011, p.196, where there is a quote from a long letter to 'My dear but Infamous Pote', which discusses Burne-Jones illustrating Swinburne's erotic fantasies.

19 Wood 1907, p.3.

20 *Magazine of Art*, January 1896, pp.43–4.

Burne-Jones on show: Exhibition Pictures, 1877–98

1 Lubbock 1920, vol.1, p.126; letter from William Graham to Edward Burne-Jones, 9 January 1871 (private collection).

2 Colvin 1877, p.828.

3 Muther 1907, Vol.3, p.177.

4 Comyns Carr 1877, pp.78–9.

5 The painting also derives from the German legend of Tannhäuser and William Morris's poem 'The Hill of Venus' in *The Earthly Paradise* (1868–70).

6 'Some Tendencies in Recent Painting', *Temple Bar*, July 1878, p.339.

7 As discussed in Weliver 2017.

8 The international reach of its influence can be seen in works as varied as Stanisław Wyspiański's *Apollo* window at the Medical Society, Kraków, 1904; Shapoor Bhedwar's pictorialist photograph, *On the Temple Step* 1890s (Alkazi Foundation); and Marcel Duchamp's Cubist *Nude Descending a Staircase* 1912 (Philadelphia Museum of Art).

9 James 1956, p.205.

10 Hamel 1889, p.230; La Sizeranne 1898b, p.515. The painting's glorification of the Ethiopian king would have made a dramatic contrast with the 'human zoo' exhibits on display in the 'Negro Village' at the Exposition, although this was not commented on at the time.

11 It should be mentioned that the more outlandish exhibiting societies were too much for Burne-Jones, which would explain why he declined an invitation to exhibit at Joséphin (Sâr) Péladan's 'Salon de la Rose + Croix' in 1892, being suspicious of its aims (letter to G.F. Watts, n.d., microfiche Tate Gallery Archive).

12 Wildman and Christian 1998, p.315.

13 See his conversations recorded by Rooke in Lago 1982, pp.102, 122–4, 179, 182.

14 See Garnett 1999/2000, pp.169–71.

15 The exhibition never materialised. Philip Burne-Jones to Georges Petit, 4 March 1897, Fondation Custodia, Paris (I am grateful to Mariela Saldias for this reference).

16 See, for example, Tobin 2006, Szczerski 2015 and Smith 2009.

17 Burne-Jones to May Gaskell cited in Christopher Newall, 'Burne-Jones and his Printmakers', in Hartnoll 1988 p.11.

18 Letters from Burne-Jones to May Gaskell, 15 February 1893, and Frances Horner, June 1897 (private collection). According to Madeleine Deslandes (*Le Figaro*, 7 May 1897), Burne-Jones had not once visited the large retrospective exhibition of his work at the New Gallery.

19 'The Grosvenor Gallery', *Art Journal*, 1882, p.189, and 1886, p.188.

20 Lago 1982, p.138.

21 Burne-Jones to Frances Horner, June 1886 (private collection).

22 Chesterton 2008, p.49.

23 Cited in Christian 1975, p.29.

Portraits

1 Horner 1933, p.132. Frances lent her letters from Burne-Jones to his widow for her biography (see note 3) and in 1915 circulated a selection in typescript among her friends, under the title 'A Book of Beauty', before they were published in her memoir, *Time Remembered*, in 1933.

2 *The Times*, 9 January 1899, p.8.

3 G. Burne-Jones 1906, vol.1, p.299.

4 G. Burne-Jones 1906, vol.2, pp.140–1, referring to the commissioned portrait of Caroline Fitzgerald, 1884, oil on canvas, University of Toronto Collection, Toronto.

5 'From an unfinished drawing by Sir Edward Burne-Jones' (Horner 1933, pl. facing p.6, which is in fact an oil painting).

6 G. Burne-Jones 1906, vol.2, pl. facing p.106, 'Family Group': 'From an unfinished oil painting by Edward-Burne-Jones, begun October, 1879, in the possession of Lady Burne-Jones'.

7 Christian 1988, p.33.

8 *The Times*, 28 April 1894, p.10.

9 Elisa Korb, 'Models, Muses and Burne-Jones's Continuous Quest for the Ideal Female Face', in Birmingham Museums and Art Gallery 2007, p.41 (illus.), cat. no.20 (presented by Colin MacInnes, Burne-Jones's great-grandson, in 1956).

10 Alphonse Legros, *Portrait of Edward Burne-Jones* 1868–9, oil on panel, Aberdeen Art Gallery; George Frederic Watts, *Portrait of Edward Burne-Jones* 1870, oil on canvas, Birmingham Museums and Art Gallery.

11 On their Italian travels, Ruskin had obliged a bored and resentful Burne-Jones to copy old master paintings; see Burne-Jones 1906, vol.1, ch.XIII, pp.241ff.

12 Burne-Jones 1906, vol.1, p.296, where Georgiana also said: 'He had an inborn perception about painting and an instinct for old pictures that was marvellous.' See Garnett 1999/2000.

13 Reynolds 2004. The portrait was shown at the New Gallery, 1898–9, described as a 'sketch'.

14 Haweis 1879, pp.102–3.

15 Horner 1933, pp.105–6. The chronology is hard to establish because Frances gives her age as if she was born in 1858 rather than 1854/5 (established in the ODNB entry, see note 13).

16 Masterman 1930, entry dated Sunday, 4 February 1875, p.94. 'Loved by Burne-Jones, Mary Gladstone was the daughter of the Prime Minister, William Gladstone and an "occasional Soul"'.

17 Burne-Jones 1906, vol.2, pp.130–1; the original letter is dated 1883, the year of Frances's marriage to John Horner.

18 Christie's, King Street, London, 13 July 2016, lot 117, described as a gift for her nineteenth birthday. She was born in 1854/5 (established in the ODNB entry, Reynolds 2004), so she was really at least twenty-two.

19 One of four illuminated versions of the poem by Morris and Burne-Jones, it has no title page. The first was given to Georgiana in 1872, but the exact date when this version was given to Frances seems not to be recorded. J.W. Mackail (1890, vol.1, p.279) described the watercolours as 'six extraordinarily beautiful pictures' ('Love Among the Ruins', p.5, is a version of his 1870 watercolour of that title): Wildman and Christian 1998, cat. no.59, pp.162–4.

20 Emanuel 1989, p.189. Burne-Jones features frequently in these diaries, as Julia Cartwright was writing an account of his work, completed in 1894.

21 See Abdy and Gere 1984, pl. opp. p.131.

22 Robertson 1931, p.75. Her photograph, by Frederick Hollyer, was taken just a year before the commencement of the portrait.

23 *The Times*, 22 June 1898.

24 Henry James, 'The picture season in London, 1877', in Sweeney 1956, p.146.

25 Burne-Jones 1906, vol.2, p.132. A brooch-pendant, featuring a dove on a heart-shaped olive branch in enamelled gold, set with turquoise, coral, pearls and ruby, marked by Carlo Giuliano, about 1884: Margaret's brooch was shown at the exhibition of her father's work at the New Gallery in 1892.

26 Gere and Munn, pp.137–8. Both the British Museum and the Victoria and Albert Museum sketchbooks have designs in pencil for heart and bird jewels (BM, Secret Book of Designs, P&D, 1899,0713.322–544; V&A, Sketchbook, E.8-1955). The dove on an olive branch bears conventional messages of love in use in 'bird' message jewels throughout the Victorian period.

27 Cicely's younger sister, Katherine Asquith (née Horner), wears the brooch in a portrait photograph (National Portrait Gallery, NPG G3CR68).

28 It was shown at the Grosvenor Gallery in 1887 as 'A Portrait', and everyone in their circle must have

recognised her; see John Christian in Wildman and Christian 1998, cat. no.117, p.260.
29 Christian 1988, p.21.
30 Lago 1982, pp.132, 136.
31 British Museum, with the Album of MS Letters to Katie, P&D 1960,1014.2.69, 1960,1014.2.87.
32 Lago 1982, p.164.
33 M. Bell 1892, p.96.
34 Henschel 1944, p.87; she said her father introduced Paderewski to Burne-Jones.
35 Paget 1924, vol.1, p.161. Not everyone shared her view of the dress, which was imitated by artistic dressers.
36 *The Times*, 27 April 1895, p.12.
37 See *Illustrated catalogue of the highly important collection of master works*, Chickering Hall, New York, 1899, lot 119.
38 Robertson 1931, p.282; he notes that Mrs Keene sat for *The Days of Creation* and *Vivien and Merlin.*
39 Ashmolean Museum, University of Oxford, William Burges (1827–1881), Great Bookcase, oak, carved, painted and gilt, 1856–62.
40 La Sizeranne 1898a, pp.239–40.
41 Wubben 2015.
42 Quoted in Emanuel 1989, p.200, diary entry for Sunday, 16 February 1896.
43 *The Times*, 28 April 1894, p.10 (exhibited at the New Gallery, 1894).
44 Henry James on the Grosvenor Gallery, 'London Pictures, 1882', in Sweeney 1956, p.204.
45 La Sizeranne 1898a, p.222.
46 The rediscovery in 2016 of a group of studies for the painting originally owned by Sir George and Lady Lewis established further identities; see Christie's, King Street, London, 14 December 2016, lots 15–24.
47 Sitting room at the Grange, photographed by Frederick Hollyer, National Monuments Record. The portrait is one of three painted by Richmond.

The Series Paintings

1 For a full history see John Christian, 'The Briar Rose Series', in Conrad and Zettel 2009, pp.137–55.
2 See for example Lutchmansingh 1989. For revisionist views see Pascu-Tulbure 2012 and Rager 2009.
3 La Sizeranne 1898b, p.516.
4 G. Burne-Jones 1904, vol.2, p.195.
5 G. Burne-Jones 1904, vol.2, p.145.
6 See further Arscott 2008, ch.5 (pp.105–25).
7 G. Burne-Jones 1904, vol.2, pp.68–9.
8 For fuller histories see Fabian Frölich, 'The Perseus Series', in Conrad and Zettel 2009, pp.103–35; and Löcher 1973.
9 See Abdy and Gere 1984, pp.30–45 (ch.2, on Arthur Balfour).
10 Jebb's papers in the Wren Library at Trinity College, Cambridge, include the Latin text; he may have been introduced to Burne-Jones by Balfour (also a Trinity College graduate) or by Sidney Colvin, Slade Professor at Cambridge (1873–85) and a friend of Burne-Jones. I am grateful to Chistopher Stray for information about Jebb.
11 Translation by Charles Martindale.
12 Except for the two panels designed to surmount doors, and therefore slightly shorter.
13 Lewis 1948, p.672. The series of ten cartoons was purchased by Alexander Henderson, the owner of the Briar Rose series, before being sold by his heirs to Southampton City Art Gallery. For details see Anne Anderson and others, *The Perseus Series: Sir Edward Coley Burne-Jones*, exh. cat, Southampton City Art Gallery 1998, p. 49.
14 Ruskin 1883.

Burne-Jones as Designer

1 Burne-Jones, conversations with his studio assistant Thomas Rooke, typescript in the National Art Library, V&A, pp.398, 144 & 396 (29 May 1897, 5 Feb 1896 & 26 May 1897).
2 Burne-Jones, quoted in Burne-Jones 1904, vol.2, p.65.
3 Burne-Jones, notes in his Account Books in the Fitzwilliam Museum, Cambridge, quoted in Schoenherr 2011, p.139 (June 1872, commission for Castle Howard). Sewter (1974–5, vol.1, passim) recorded more than 660 of his individual compositions made by Morris & Co., as well as a handful produced in the early days for other manufacturers.
4 G. Burne-Jones 1904, vol.2, p.6.
5 John Ruskin, 'The Mythic School: The Art of England', in Ruskin 1903–12, vol.33, p.301.
6 Schoenherr 2011, p.166.
7. Schoenherr 2011, p.131 (1 January 1866).
8 Edward Burne-Jones, quoted by Peter Cormack, *MORRIS & COMPANY'S STAINED GLASS for THE CHAPEL OF CHEADLE ROYAL HOSPITAL: An Illustrated Catalogue*, London 2008, p.3.
9 Sewter (1974–5, vol.1, p.49) identifies a number of glass painters from the Account Books, including Pozzi, Campfield and Bowman.
10 The popularity of this image was in part due to the contemporary enthusiasm for Mendelssohn's oratorio, *Elijah*, premiered in Birmingham in 1846 and performed for Queen Victoria in London in April 1847.
11 The design for *Elijah in the Wilderness*, watercolour and bodycolour, 1874–98, was presented to Birmingham Museum and Art Gallery, 1898P18.
12 Schoenherr 2011, p.154 (between March and August 1878).
13 Both panels were rewoven in 1905 for Eton College Chapel as memorials of the Boer War: Parry 1996, p.290.
14 Burne-Jones explained to his studio assistant: 'I never could understand but a picture painted in the place it's intended to fill – never cared for a travelling picture, though mine are all that' (conversations with Thomas Rooke, National Art Library, V&A, p.412, 12 June 1897).
15 A different design for this subject, also by Burne-Jones, is noted by Sewter (1974–5, vol.2, p.99) in St Mary's, Ingestre. Burne-Jones was paid £80 for 'Pelican & 2 Angels' in October 1889.
16 Burne-Jones, conversations with Thomas Rooke, National Art Library, V&A, p.203 (11 May 1896).
17 Nikolaus Pevsner, *Pioneers of Modern Design* (1936), London 1991, p.21 (illus.). Burne-Jones explored similar forms in his depiction of the hawthorn tree in *The Beguiling of Merlin* (no.93).
18 For a full account of the project, see Dorment 1976 and 1978.
19 Burne-Jones to John Ruskin, May/June 1862, quoted in Dorment 1976, p.100.
20 M. Bell 1901, p.83.
21 Burne-Jones quoted in MacCarthy 2011, p.xxxvi and p.xxxv.
22 Dorment 1976, p.275 and p.263 (letters from Burne-Jones to Castellani, 1890 and 1884).
23 Dorment 1976, p.81.
24 Letter to Frances Horner, June 1887. The final text is taken from *Revelation* 12: 7–10. Dorment 1976, pp.42–44.
25 *Magazine of Art*, 1894, pp.257–8.
26 Parry 1996, p.238, cat. no.M.11.
27 Burne-Jones, *The Quest for the Sanc Grael*, four panels, stained glass, 1880–90, V&A, C.623, 624, 625 & 626-1920.
28 Burne-Jones claimed, when he heard Wagner's *Parsifal* performed in London in 1884, that the composer had recreated 'the very sounds that were to be heard in the Sangraal Chapel', adding 'and I ought to know' (G. Burne-Jones 1904, vol.2, p.333 and p.43).
29 Burne-Jones to Lady Leighton, 23 Dec 1890, quoted in Parry 1996, p.294.
30 Morris's first attempt at tapestry weaving, *Acanthus and Vine* (Society of Antiquaries/ Kelmscott Manor), took him 516½ hours, between May and September 1879 (Parry 1996, p.286.)
31 Burne-Jones, conversations with Thomas Rooke, National Art Library, V&A, 11 June 1896, p.231.
32 Burne-Jones quoted by A.B. Bence-Jones, 'The Holy Grail Tapestries', 1895, manuscript, National Art Library, V&A, in Wildman and Christian 1998, p.302.
33 Once the Stanmore Hall set was complete, Morris & Co. produced several other weavings of these designs, including a partial set of three panels in 1895–6 for Compton Hall, Wolverhampton, and all five narrative panels for George McCulloch of Queen's Gate, London. This group was shown in Edwin Lutyens's pavilion at the 1900 Paris Exposition. The last weaving was made in 1932.
34 A.B Bence-Jones, quoted in Wildman and Christian 1998, p.298.
35 The crown was copied from Van Eyck's Ghent altarpiece of 1432.
36 *Art Journal*, June 1891, p.185, quoted in Wildman and Christian 1998, p.295.
37 Burne-Jones was paid £25 for the *Pomona* design in December 1882. Morris told his daughters that 'Uncle Ned has done me two lovely figures for tapestry, but I have got to design a background for them. I shall probably bring them down [to Kelmscott Manor] next time I come for my holiday task' (Parry 1996, p.291).
38 *The Queen*, 25 April 1874, quoted by Lynn Hulse, 'Elizabeth Burden and the Royal School of Needlework', *Journal of the William Morris Society*, Winter 2014, p.27. Both Elizabeth Burden (Morris's sister-in-law, who taught at the RSN intermittently between 1873 and 1877) and Madeline Wyndham were critical of the quality of the work.
39 W.G. Paulson Townsend (Design Master of the RSN), *Embroidery or the Craft of the Needle*, London 1899, p.173.
40 Quoted in Christie's sale catalogue, *Victorian, Pre-Raphaelite and Impressionist Art Sale*, 13 July 2016.
41 Burne-Jones to Frances Horner, 13 Sept. 1892 and 6 Nov. 1892, quoted in Dakers 2001, pp.16, 20.
42 Burne-Jones to Kate Faulkner, quoted in Wildman and Christian 1998, p.276. He worked with Broadwood in 1878 to design a piano for Georgie and Margaret following the lighter form of the harpsichord. Examples of this reformed design were commissioned by friends and patrons, including A.C. Ionides for his home at 1 Holland Park. His piano, decorated by Kate Faulkner in 1883, is now in the V&A.
43 The finished pencil drawings, dated 1875, are in the Ashmolean Museum, Oxford. The legend originally came from Ovid's *Metamorphoses*, which also inspired Burne-Jones's *Pygmalion* series and *The Tree of Forgiveness*. Morris's narrative poem was published posthumously in 1915 in his *Collected Works*, vol.24.
44 MacCarthy 2011, p.234, and Burne-Jones to Frances Horner, quoted in Robinson 1982, p.27. Burne-Jones had long admired Mantegna's *Triumphs of Caesar* (1484–92) at Hampton Court, and in 1871 he had surreptitiously copied his *Allegories* in the Louvre.
45 Burne-Jones had completed a small series of Sleeping Beauty paintings (now in the Museo de Arte de Ponce, Puerto Rico) for William Graham in 1875.
46 Cavalcanti's verse was not included in Dante Gabriel Rossetti's *Early Italian Poets* (1861). However it was a reworking of an earlier dialogue between a lover and a lady by Ciullo D'Alcamo, 'Rosa fresca aulentissima', which was the opening poem in Rossetti's translations, 'Part One: poets chiefly before Dante'.
47 W.R. Lethaby, quoted in Parry 1996, p.332.
48 Note by William Morris, quoted in Parry 1996, p.319.
49 Morris set trial passages from 'The Franklin's Tale' in his 'Troy' type in the first year of production. Most of Burne-Jones's drawings for the illustrations are now in the Fitzwilliam Museum, Cambridge. For decades they had reimagined these tales and poems, from the *Prioress's Tale* wardrobe Burne-Jones decorated in 1859, to the massive *The Romaunt of the Rose* embroideries, stitched by the women of Rounton Grange (1874–82).
50 Burne-Jones, quoted in Parry 1996, p.331. For more details of the production methods see Robert Catterson-Smith's account, quoted in Parry 1996,, p.334, and Suzanne Fagence Cooper, *Pre-Raphaelite Art in the V&A Museum*, London 2003, p.92.
51 Burne-Jones, proof page for *The Golden Legend*, 1892, V&A, 1784-1920. Morris had intended *The Golden Legend* to be the first publication from his press, but it took longer than anticipated and was not released until November 1892.
52 William Morris, 'The Story of an Unknown Church', *The Oxford and Cambridge Magazine*, 1856, quoted by Jerome McGann, '"A Thing to Mind": The Materialist Aesthetic of William Morris', *Huntington Library Quarterly*, vol.55, no.1, Winter 1992, p.59.

Bibliography

Abdy and Gere 1984
Jane Abdy and Charlotte Gere, *The Souls*, London 1984

Allingham 1908
William Allingham, *A Diary*, ed. H. Allingham and D. Radford, London 1908

Andres 2005
Sophia Andres, *The Pre-Raphaelite Art of the Victorian Novel*, Columbus, OH 2005

Arscott 2008
Caroline Arscott, *William Morris and Edward Burne-Jones: Interlacings*, New Haven and London 2008

Askari 2014
Kaveh Askari, *Making Movies into Art: Picture Craft from the Magic Lantern to Early Hollywood*, London 2014

Baldwin 1935
Stanley Baldwin, 'Burne-Jones' (1933), in *This Torch of Freedom: Speeches and Addresses*, London 1935, pp.173–9

Barthes 1977
Roland Barthes, 'The Death of the Author' (1968), in *Image Music Text*, trans. Stephen Heath, London 1977

M. Bell 1892
Malcolm Bell, *Sir Edward Burne-Jones: A Record and Review*, London 1892

M. Bell 1901
Malcolm Bell, *Sir Edward Burne-Jones*, London 1901

M. Bell 1909
Malcolm Bell, 'A Biographical Study', in *Sir Edward Burne-Jones*, London 1909

R. Bell 1933
Robert Anning Bell, 'Burne-Jones', *Saturday Review*, 24 June 1933, pp.620–1

Bénédite 1998
Léonce Bénédite, *L'Idéalisme en France et en Angleterre. Gustave Moreau & E. Burne-Jones*, La Rochelle 1998 (originally published as: 'Deux idéalistes: Gustave Moreau et E. Burne-Jones', in *Revue de l'art ancien et moderne*, 5, 1899, pp.265–90, 357–78; 6, 1899, pp.57–70)

Binyon 1946
Laurence Binyon, *English Water-Colours*, London 1946

Birmingham Museums and Art Gallery 2007
Hidden Burne-Jones: Works on Paper by Edward Burne-Jones from Birmingham Museums and Art Gallery, exh. cat., Birmingham Museums and Art Gallery, 2007

Bradley and Page 2017
Peri Bradley and James Page, 'David Bowie – the trans who fell to earth: cultural regulation, Bowie and gender fluidity', *Continuum*, vol.31, no.4 (2017), pp.583–95

Bullen 1998
J. B. Bullen, *The Pre-Raphaelite Body: Fear and Desire in Painting, Poetry and Criticism*, Oxford 1998

Burlington Fine Arts Club 1899
Exhibition of Drawings and Studies by Sir Edward Burne-Jones, Bart, intro. Cosmo Monkhouse, exh. cat., Burlington Fine Arts Club, London, 1899

E. Burne-Jones 1925
Edward Burne-Jones, *Letters to Katie*, with an introductory note by W. Graham Robertson, London 1925

G. Burne-Jones 1904
Georgiana Burne-Jones, *Memorials of Edward Burne-Jones*, 2 vols., London 1904

G. Burne-Jones 1906
Georgiana Burne-Jones, *Memorials of Edward Burne-Jones*, 2 vols., London 1906

P. Burne-Jones 1900
Philip Burne-Jones, 'Notes on some unfinished works of Sir Edward Burne-Jones, Bt. By His Son', *Magazine of Art*, 1900

Busine 1992
Laurent Busine, 'From Edward Burne-Jones to Fernand Khnopff', in *Burne-Jones (1833–1898). Dessins du Fitzwilliam Museum de Cambridge*, exh. cat., Musée des Beaux-Arts, Nantes 1992, pp.59–68

Carpenter 1977
Humphrey Carpenter, *J.R.R. Tolkien: A Biography*, London 1977

Chesterton 2008
G.K. Chesterton, 'Five Painters and a Critic', *The Bookman*, April 1902, reprinted in *G.K. Chesterton on Watts*, Watts Gallery, Compton 2008, pp.49–50

Christian 1968
John Christian, 'The Archives of the Whitefriars Studios, London', *Artifex Journal of the Crafts* I, 1968, pp.30–46

Christian 1975
John Christian, *Burne-Jones: The Paintings, Graphic and Decorative Work of Sir Edward Burne-Jones 1833–98*, exh. cat., Hayward Gallery, London 1975

Christian 1988
John Christian (ed.), *Letters to Katie from Edward Burne-Jones*, London 1988

Christian 1989
John Christian (ed.), *The Last Romantics: The Romantic Tradition in British Art, Burne-Jones to Stanley Spencer*, exh. cat., Barbican Art Gallery, London 1989

Collins Baker 1933
C. H. Collins Baker, *British Painting*, London 1933

Colvile 2006
Georgiana M.M. Colvile, 'Between Surrealism and Magic Realism: The Early Feature Films of André Delvaux', *Yale French Studies*, no.109 (2006), pp.115–28

Colvin 1877
Sidney Colvin, 'The Grosvenor Gallery', *Fortnightly Review*, 1877

Comyns Carr 1877
Joseph Comyns Carr, 'La Saison d'Art à Londres: La Grosvenor Gallery', *L'Art*, 1877

Comyns Carr 1914
Joseph Comyns Carr, *Coasting Bohemia*, London 1914

Crossman 2007
Colette Crossman, 'Art as Lived Religion: Edward Burne-Jones as Painter, Priest, Pilgrim and Monk', PhD thesis, University of Maryland, 2007

Crossman 2015
Colette Crossman, 'Seeing the Sacred: Burne-Jones's Reception as a "Great Religious Painter"', *Nineteenth-Century Art Worldwide*, vol.14, no.2, Summer 2015 (www.19thc-artworldwide.org/summer15/crossman-on-burne-jones-s-reception-as-a-great-religious-painter – accessed 26 February 2018)

Cummings 2011
Brian Cummings (ed.), *The Book of Common Prayer: The Texts of 1549, 1559, and 1662*, Oxford 2011

Dakers 1988
Caroline Dakers, 'Culture and the Country House 1880–1940', MA thesis, Royal College of Art, 1988

Dakers 2001
Caroline Dakers, 'Yours affectionately, Angelo: The letters of Edward Burne-Jones (1833–98) & Frances Horner (1858–1940)', *British Art Journal*, vol.2, no.3, 2001

Des Cars 1998
Laurence Des Cars, 'Edward Burne-Jones and France', in Wildman and Christian 1998, pp.25–39

Dimbleby 2004
Josceline Dimbleby, *A Profound Secret: May Gaskell, her Daughter Amy, and Edward Burne-Jones*, London 2004

Dorment 1976
Richard Dorment, 'Burne-Jones and the Decoration of St. Paul's American Church, Rome', PhD thesis, Columbia University, 1976

Dorment 1978
Richard Dorment, 'Burne-Jones's Roman Mosaics', *Burlington Magazine*, vol.120, no.899, Feb. 1978, pp.72–82

Dorment 2003
Richard Dorment, 'Realists and Romantics, Storytellers and Symbolists: Changing Attitudes towards Victorian Art', in *Pre-Raphaelite and other Masters: The Andrew Lloyd Webber Collection*, exh. cat., Royal Academy, London, 2003, pp.11–25

Emanuel 1989
Angela Emanuel (ed.), *Bright Remembrance: The Diaries of Julia Cartwright*, London 1989

Fincham 1933
David Fincham, 'The Painter of Dreams', *Observer*, 27 August 1933, p.13

Fitzgerald 1975
Penelope Fitzgerald, *Edward Burne-Jones: A Biography*, London 1975

Fitzgerald 1977
Penelope Fitzgerald, *The Knox Brothers*, London 1977

Garnett 1999/2000
Oliver Garnett, 'The letters and collection of William Graham – Pre-Raphaelite patron and Pre-Raphaelite collector', *The Walpole Society* 1999/2000, pp.145–343

Gere and Munn 1989
Charlotte Gere and Geoffrey C. Munn, *Artists' Jewellery, Pre-Raphaelite to Arts and Crafts*, Woodbridge 1989

Hamel 1889
Maurice Hamel, 'Exposition Universelle de 1889: Grande-Bretagne', *Gazette des Beaux-Arts*, July–December 1889, p.230

Harrison 2010
Colin Harrison, 'The Pre-Raphaelites and Italian Art before and after Raphael', in Colin Harrison and Christopher Newall, *The Pre-Raphaelites and Italy*, Oxford 2010

Harrison and Waters 1973
Martin Harrison and Bill Waters, *Burne-Jones*, London 1973

Harrison and Waters 1989
Martin Harrison and Bill Waters, *Burne-Jones*, 2nd edn, London 1989

Hartnoll 1972
Julian Hartnoll, *Burne-Jones et l'influence des préraphaélites*, exh. cat., Galerie du Luxembourg, Paris 1972

Hartnoll 1988
Julian Hartnoll, *The Reproductive Engravings after Sir Edward Coley Burne-Jones*, London 1988

Haweis 1879
Mary Eliza Haweis, 'Pre-Raphaelitism', in *The Art of Dress*, London 1879

Henschel 1944
Helen Henschel, *When Soft Voices Die*, London 1944

Hilliard 1982
David Hilliard, 'Unenglish and Unmanly: Anglo-Catholicism and Homosexuality', *Victorian Studies*, vol.25, no.2 (1982), pp.181–210

Hilton 1970
Timothy Hilton, *The Pre-Raphaelites*, London 1970

Hoffmann 1972
Edith Hoffmann, 'Burne-Jones and the Pre-Raphaelite Influence, in Paris', *Burlington Magazine*, May 1972, pp.354–7

Horner 1933
Frances Horner, *Time Remembered*, London 1933

Ironside 1940
Robin Ironside, 'Burne-Jones and Gustave Moreau', *Horizon*, June 1940, pp.406–24

James 1956
Henry James, *The Painter's Eye: Notes and Essays on the Pictorial Arts*, ed. John L. Sweeney, London 1956

Jones 2017
Dylan Jones, *David Bowie: A Life*, London 2017

Khnopff 1898
Fernand Khnopff, 'A Tribute from Belgium', *Magazine of Art*, vol.22 (1898), pp.520–6

Kipling 2004
The Letters of Rudyard Kipling, 2: 1890–99, ed. Thomas Pinney (1990), Basingstoke 2004

Kris and Kurz 1979
Ernst Kris and Otto Kurz, *Legend, Myth, and Magic in the Image of the Artist: A Historical Experiment*, New Haven and London 1979

La Sizeranne 1898a
Robert de La Sizeranne, *English Contemporary Art*, London 1898

La Sizeranne 1898b
Robert de La Sizeranne, 'In Memoriam: Sir Edward Burne-Jones, Bart.: A Tribute from France', *Magazine of Art* 22 (1898)

Lago 1975
Mary M. Lago, 'A Golden Age Revisited: Ernest S. Thomas and the Burne-Jones Centenary', *Apollo*, November 1975, pp.358–61

Lago 1982
Mary Lago (ed.), *Burne-Jones Talking: His Conversations 1895–1898 Preserved by his Studio Assistant Thomas Rooke*, London 1982

Laver 1933
James Laver, 'The World of Burne-Jones', *Listener*, 23 August 1933, pp.261–3, 287

Lee 2013
Hermione Lee, *Penelope Fitzgerald: A Life*, London 2013

Lewis 1948
Wyndham Lewis, 'The Brotherhood', *Listener*, 22 April 1948, p.672

Löcher 1973
Kurt Löcher, *Der Perseus-Zyklus von Edward Burne-Jones*, Stuttgart 1973

Lohf 1972
Kenneth A. Lohf, 'The Burne-Jonesiness of Burne-Jones. A Collector's Discovery of an Artist's Life and Works', *Gazette of the Grolier Club*, no.17 (1972), pp.43–52

Lubbock 1920
Percy Lubbock (ed.), *The Letters of Henry James*, London 1920, vol.1

Lucie-Smith 1975
Edward Lucie-Smith, 'The Burne-Jones Revival', *Illustrated London News*, vol.263, October 1975, pp.90–4

Lutchmansingh 1989
Larry D. Lutchmansingh, 'Fantasy and arrested desire in Edward Burne-Jones's Briar-Rose series', in Marcia Pointon (ed.), *Pre-Raphaelites Re-Viewed*, Manchester 1989, pp.123–39

MacCarthy 2011
MacCarthy, Fiona, *The Last Pre-Raphaelite: Edward Burne-Jones and the Victorian Imagination*, London 2011

Macfall 1912
Haldane Macfall, 'Of Decadence in Art', *Academy and Literature*, 6 April 1912, pp.430–2

MacInnes 1976
Colin MacInnes, 'A Tardy Revival', *Spectator*, 17 April 1976, p.26

Mackail 1890
J.W. Mackail, *Life of William Morris*, 2 vols., London 1890

Maclaren 1985
Archibald Maclaren, *The Fairy Family*, illustrated by Edward Burne-Jones, with an introduction by John Christian, London 1985

Mahood 2009
Linda Mahood, *Feminism and Voluntary Action: Eglantyne Jebb and Save the Children, 1876–1928*, London 2009

Mann 2014
Fiona Mann, 'A "born rebel": Edward Burne-Jones and watercolour painting 1857–80', *Burlington Magazine*, October 2014, pp.657–64.

Marsh 1985
Jan Marsh, *Pre-Raphaelite Sisterhood*, London 1985

Masterman 1930
Lucy Masterman (ed.), *Mary Gladstone: Diaries and Letters*, London 1930

Morris 1914
May Morris (ed.), *The Collected Works of William Morris*, vol.22, London 1914

Munro 1992
Jane A. Munro, '"This hateful letter-writing": Selected Correspondence of Sir Edward Burne-Jones in the Huntington Library', in Malcolm Warner, *Pre-Raphaelites in Context*, San Marino, CA 1992

Muther 1907
Richard Muther, *The History of Modern Painting*, 4 vols., London 1907

New Gallery 1898
Exhibition of the Works of Sir Edward Burne-Jones 1898–1899 (with an essay by Joseph Comyns Carr), exh. cat., New Gallery, London 1898

Paget 1924
Lady Walburga Paget, *In My Tower*, 2 vols., London 1924

Parkinson 1975
Ronald Parkinson, 'Two early Altar-Pieces by Burne-Jones', *Apollo*, November 1975, pp.320–23

Parris 1984a
Leslie Parris (ed.), *Pre-Raphaelite Papers*, London 1984

Parris 1984b
Leslie Parris (ed.), *The Pre-Raphaelites*, exh. cat., Tate Gallery, London 1984

Parry 1996
Linda Parry (ed.), *William Morris*, exh. cat., Victoria and Albert Museum, London 1996

Pascu-Tulbure 2012
Cristina Pascu-Tulbure, 'Burne-Jones's *Briar Rose*: New Contexts', *English* 61, no. 233 (2012), pp.151–75

Penrose 1981
Roland Penrose, *Picasso: His Life and Work* (1958), 3rd edn, Berkeley and Los Angeles, CA 1981

Perry 2016
Gill Perry, 'What Connects David Bowie with King Arthur?', 2016 (www.bbc.com/culture/story/20160115-what-connects-david-bowie-with-king-arthur – accessed 1 March 2018)

Prettejohn 2007
Elizabeth Prettejohn, *Art for Art's Sake: Aestheticism in Victorian Painting*, New Haven and London 2007

Proust 1955
Marcel Proust, *Jean Santeuil*, trans. Gerard Hopkins, London 1955

Rager 2009
Andrea Wolk Rager, '"Smite this Sleeping World Awake": Edward Burne-Jones and *The Legend of the Briar Rose*', *Victorian Studies* 51, no. 3 (Spring 2009), pp.438–50

Reynolds 2004
K.D. Reynolds, 'Horner, Frances Jane, Lady Horner (née Graham)', *Oxford Dictionary of National Biography*, Oxford 2004: http://www.oxforddnb.com/view/10.1093/ref:odnb/9780198614128.001.0001/odnb-9780198614128-e-49524

Robertson 1931
W. Graham Robertson, *Time Was: The Reminiscences of W. Graham Robertson*, London 1931

Robinson 1982
Duncan Robinson, *William Morris, Edward Burne-Jones and the Kelmscott Chaucer*, London 1982

Rossetti 2002–9
Dante Gabriel Rossetti, *The Correspondence of Dante Gabriel Rossetti*, ed. William E. Fredeman, vols. I–VIII, London 2002–9

Rothenstein 1935
William Rothenstein, *Men and Memories*, vol.1, London 1935

Royal Academy 2003
Pre-Raphaelite and Other Masters from the Andrew Lloyd Webber Collection, exh. cat., Royal Academy, London 2003

Ruskin 1883
John Ruskin, 'Lecture II: Mythic Schools of Painting: E. Burne-Jones and G.F. Watts', *The Art of England* (1883), repr. in Ruskin 1903–12, vol.33, pp.287–305

Ruskin 1903–12
Ruskin, John, *Library Edition of the Collected Works of John Ruskin*, ed. E.T. Cook and A. Wedderburn, 39 vols, 1903–12

Schoenherr 2011
Douglas E. Schoenherr, 'Edward Burne-Jones's Account Books with Morris & Company (1861–1900): an annotated edition', *Journal of Stained Glass*, vol.35, 2011, pp.78–241.

Sewter 1974–5
A. Charles Sewter, *The Stained Glass of William Morris and his Circle*, 2 vols., New Haven, CT 1974–5

Sheridan 1921
Clare Sheridan, *Russian Portraits*, London 1921

Smith 1996
Alison Smith, *The Victorian Nude: Sexuality, Morality and Art*, Manchester 1996

Smith 2009
Alison Smith (ed.), *Symbolist Art in Poland*, exh. cat., Tate Britain, 2009

Staley 2011
Allen Staley, *The New Painting of the 1860s: Between the Pre-Raphaelites and the Aesthetic Movement*, New Haven and London, 2011

Surtees 1971
Virginia Surtees, *The Paintings and Drawings of Dante Gabriel Rossetti (1828–1882)*: A Catalogue Raisonné, 2 vols., London 1971

Sweeney 1956
John L. Sweeney (ed.), *The Painter's Eye: Notes and Essays on the Pictorial Arts by Henry James*, London 1956

Swinburne 1875
A.C. Swinburne, 'Notes on Designs of the Old Masters at Florence', in *Essays and Studies*, London 1875

Szczerski 2015
Andrzej Szczerski, *Views of Albion: The Reception of British Art and Design in Central Europe, 1890–1918*, Oxford 2015

Symonds 1901
J.A. Symonds, *The Life of Michelangelo Buonarotti* (1893), New York 1901

Thirkell 2012
Angela Thirkell, *Three Houses* (1931), London 2012

Tobin 2006
Thomas J. Tobin (ed.), *Worldwide Pre-Raphaelitism*, New York 2006

Townsend 2004
Joyce H. Townsend, Jacqueline Ridge and Stephen Hackney, *Pre-Raphaelite Painting Techniques*, London 2004

Vallance 1900
Aymer Vallance, 'The Decorative Art of Sir Edward Burne-Jones, Baronet', *Easter Art Annual*, London 1900, pp.28–30

Weliver 2017
Phyllis Weliver, 'Liberal Dreaminess and *The Golden Stairs* of Edward Burne-Jones (1833–1898)', *British Art Journal*, vol.XVII, no.3, Spring 2017, pp.55–63

Wildman and Christian 1998
Stephen Wildman and John Christian, *Edward Burne-Jones: Victorian Artist-Dreamer*, exh. cat., Metropolitan Museum of Art, New York 1998

Wilenski 1933
R. H. Wilenski, *English Painting*, London 1933

Wilson 1934
R.N.D. Wilson, *The National and Tate Galleries*, London 1934

Wilton and Upstone 1997
Andrew Wilton and Robert Upstone (eds.), *The Age of Rossetti, Burne-Jones & Watts: Symbolism in Britain 1860–1910*, exh. cat., Tate Gallery, London 1997

Wood 1907
T. Martin Wood, *The Drawings of Sir E. Burne-Jones*, London and New York n.d. [1907]

Wubben 2015
Emily Wubben, 'Artistic souls: Edward Burne-Jones and his portrait of Baronne Deslandes', *Art Journal of the National Gallery of Victoria*, no.54, 2015

List of Exhibited Works

All works are by Edward Burne-Jones (1833–1898) unless otherwise stated. Information is correct at time of printing but is subject to change.

01
Archibald Maclaren 1819–1884
The Fairy Family: A Series of Ballads and Metrical Tales Illustrating the Fairy Mythology of Europe
1857
Book
19.9 × 14 × 3 (book closed)
Collection of Stephen Calloway
(no.4, p.48)

Cupid's Daughter by his Forge
c.1857
Graphite, pen and ink on paper
13.8 × 12.1
William Morris Gallery, London Borough of Waltham Forest
(no.2, p.46)

The Calling of St Peter
c.1857
Stained and painted glass
107.2 × 35.6
Victoria and Albert Museum
(no.10, p.54)

The Good Shepherd
1857–1861
Stained-glass panel
132 × 50.8
Birmingham Museums Trust on behalf of Birmingham City Council
(no.11, p.54)

Going to the Battle
1858
Pen and ink with grey wash on vellum
22.3 × 19.5
The Syndics of the Fitzwilliam Museum, University of Cambridge
(no.5, p.48)

The Wise and Foolish Virgins
c.1859
Pen and ink and grey wash
45.5 × 60.5
Private collection
(no.8, p.52)

Buondelmonte's Wedding
1859
Pen and ink with some grey wash on vellum
25.5 × 77
The Syndics of the Fitzwilliam Museum, University of Cambridge
(no.7, p.50)

Ladies and Death
1860
Painted wooden panel on an upright piano made by Frederick Priestley, painted gilt and gesso on wood, with a layer of shellac over gilded areas
33 × 125.7
Victoria and Albert Museum. Given by Mrs J.W. Mackail, daughter of the artist
(no.16, p.62)

Sidonia von Bork 1560
1860
Watercolour and gouache on paper
33.3 × 17.1
Tate. Bequeathed by W. Graham Robertson 1948
(no.18, p.63)

Clara von Bork 1560
1860
Watercolour and gouache on paper
34.2 × 17.9
Tate. Bequeathed by W. Graham Robertson 1948
(no.17, p.63)

Childe Roland
1861
Pen and ink and wash on paper
43 × 24
The Trustees of the Cecil Higgins Art Gallery (The Higgins Bedford)
(no.6, p.49)

The Annunciation and the Adoration of the Magi
1861
Oil paint on three canvases
108.6 × 73.7, 108.6 × 156.2, 108.6 × 73.7
Tate. Presented by G.H. Bodley in memory of George Frederick Bodley 1934
(no.12, p.56)

Clerk Saunders
1861
Watercolour on paper
69.9 × 41.8
Tate. Presented by Mrs Wilfred Hadley through the Art Fund 1927
(no.19, p.64)

Merlin and Nimue
1861
Watercolour and bodycolour on paper
64.2 × 52.1
Victoria and Albert Museum
(no.20, p.65)

Cupid's Forge
1861
Watercolour, bodycolour and gum arabic laid down on linen
32.5 × 50
Private collection courtesy of Peter Nahum. Renate Nahum. Agency
(no.3, p.46)

The God of Love and Alceste from Chaucer's *Legend of Good Women*
1861–64
Stained and painted glass
46.8 × 50.7 × 3.2
Victoria and Albert Museum
(no.13, p.59)

Dido and Cleopatra from Chaucer's *Legend of Good Women*
1861–64
Stained-glass panel
47 × 43.2
Victoria and Albert Museum
(no.14, p.60)

The Annunciation (The Flower of God)
1862
Gouache on paper
61 × 53.3
Private collection
(no.21, p.68)

Edward Burne-Jones (1833–1898) and William Morris (1834–1896)
Geoffrey Chaucer
1863
Ceramic tile
15.3 × 15.3
Victoria and Albert Museum
(no.15, p.61)

The Return of the Dove to the Ark
1863
Pen and ink on paper
10.2 × 8.9
Victoria and Albert Museum. Given by Sir Philip Burne-Jones, Bart., on behalf of the executors of the late Sir Edward Burne-Jones
(no.9, p.53)

The Wine of Circe
1863–9
Watercolour and bodycolour on paper
71.1 × 101.6
Private collection
(no.23, p.70)

Le Chant d'Amour (The Love Song)
1865
Transparent and opaque watercolour on paper
54.9 × 77.7
Museum of Fine Arts, Boston. Bequest of Martin Brimmer
(no.22, p.69)

The Lament
1865–6
Watercolour and bodycolour on paper mounted on canvas
47.5 × 79.5
William Morris Gallery, London Borough of Waltham Forest. Brangwyn gift, 1941
(no.24, p.72)

Phyllis and Demophoön
1870
Gouache and watercolour on paper
91.5 × 45.8
Birmingham Museums Trust on behalf of Birmingham City Council
(no.25, p.73)

02
Gualdrada Donati Presenting Her Daughter to Buondelmonte
c.1860
Pen and ink with graphite on paper
23.3 × 39.3
The Ashmolean Museum, University of Oxford. Purchased 1951
(no.40, p.84–5)

Composition Study for *Ezekiel and the Boiling Pot*
c.1860
Graphite on paper
17.8 × 13.3
Tate. Bequeathed by J.R. Holliday 1927
(no.37, p.82)

Composition Study for *Ezekiel and the Boiling Pot*
c.1860
Graphite on paper
18.1 × 13.3
Tate. Bequeathed by J.R. Holliday 1927
(no.38, p.82)

Study of Ezekiel's Hand for *Ezekiel and the Boiling Pot*
c.1860
Graphite on paper
4.4 × 11.7
Tate. Bequeathed by J.R. Holliday 1927
(no.35, p.82)

Study of Ezekiel's Arm and Hand for *Ezekiel and the Boiling Pot*
c.1860
Graphite on paper
3.5 × 5.7
Tate. Bequeathed by J.R. Holliday 1927
(no.36, p.82)

Ezekiel and the Boiling Pot
1861
Ink and watercolour on vellum mounted on canvas
26 × 15.2
Tate. Purchased 1923
(no.39, p.83)

Composition Study for *Clerk Saunders*
c.1861
Graphite on paper
40.3 × 18.5
Tate. Bequeathed by J.R. Holliday 1927
(no.41, p.86)

Head of a Woman: possibly Georgiana Burne-Jones
c.1861
Graphite on paper
14 × 16.6
Tate. Bequeathed by J.R. Holliday 1927
(no.65, p.106)

Sketch of Two Seated Figures for possibly *The Backgammon Players*
c.1861
Graphite on paper
21 × 22.5
Tate. Bequeathed by J.R. Holliday 1927
(no.42, p.87)

Study for the Figure of Merlin in *Merlin and Nimue*
1861
Graphite and chalk on paper
32.5 × 14.9
Victoria and Albert Museum.
Bequeathed by J.R. Holliday
(no.62, p.103)

Study of the Head of a Female Attendant for *The Adoration of the Kings*
c.1861
Graphite on paper
15.4 × 14.2
Tate. Bequeathed by J.R. Holliday 1927
(no.64, p.106)

William Morris Reading Poetry to Edward Burne-Jones
1861
Pen and ink on paper
18 × 11.5
Victoria and Albert Museum
(no.83, p.114)

Studies of Drapery and the Figure of the Virgin for the *Annunciation* in the Church of St Martin's-on-the-Hill, Scarborough, Yorkshire
c.1862
Graphite on paper
34 × 36.2
Tate. Bequeathed by J.R. Holliday 1927
(no.55, p.98)

Study of the Head of *Bacchus* in Tintoretto's *The Marriage of Bacchus and Ariadne in the Presence of Venus,* before the picture was restored
1862
Graphite and chalk on paper
27.1 × 41.5
The Ashmolean Museum, University of Oxford.
Presented by John Ruskin to the Ruskin Drawing School (University of Oxford), 1875
(no.57, p.100–1)

The Miracle of the Newborn Child, after Titian
1862
Watercolour and chalk on paper
33 × 42
Private collection
(no.56, p.99)

Sketch of Two Seated Figures for *Chant d'Amour*
c.1862–5
Graphite on paper
19 × 30
Tate. Bequeathed by J.R. Holliday 1927
(no.43, p.87)

Study of a Man's Head
1866
Graphite on paper
22.2 × 17.1
Tate. Bequeathed by A.N. MacNicholl 1916
(no.58, p.101)

The Head of Cassandra
1866–70
Chalk on paper
35.6 × 28
Victoria and Albert Museum.
Bequeathed by Constantine Alexander Ionides
(no.67, p.107)

The Artist and Maria Zambaco
1866–72
Graphite on paper
12 × 15
Private collection courtesy of Peter Nahum.
Renate Nahum. Agency
(no.87, p.114)

Maria Zambaco
1871
Graphite on paper
32 × 36.8
Private collection, Maas Gallery
(no.69, p.150)

Study for *The Masque of Cupid*
1872
Graphite and charcoal on paper
65 × 83.3
Amgueddfa Cymru – National Museum Wales
(no.47, p.90)

St Luke
1872
Graphite, pastel and gouache on paper
122.4 × 51.6
Tate. Purchased 1919
(no.54, p.97)

Venus Discordia
c.1872–3
Oil paint on canvas
128.2 × 209.8
Amgueddfa Cymru – National Museum Wales
(no.49, p.92–3)

Study of the Pilgrim for *The Pilgrim Outside the Garden of Idleness*
c.1872–7
Chalk and graphite on paper
36.5 × 22.5
Tate. Presented by Lord Duveen 1924
(no.59, p.102)

Desiderium
1873
Graphite on paper
21 × 13.3
Tate. Presented by Sir Philip Burne-Jones Bt 1910
(no.68, p.107)

Two Studies on One Sheet for the Left-hand Figure and Central Crouching Figure in *Souls on the Banks of the River Styx*
c.1873
Graphite on paper
24.1 × 16.5
Private collection courtesy of Peter Nahum.
Renate Nahum. Agency
(no.45, p.89)

Study of a Nude Male Crouching Figure and a Standing Female Nude with her Arms Tightly Crossed, for *Souls on the Banks of the River Styx*
c.1873
Graphite on paper
14 × 13
Private collection courtesy of Peter Nahum.
Renate Nahum. Agency
(no.46, p.89)

Souls on the Banks of the River Styx
c.1873
Oil paint on canvas
89 × 71
Private collection courtesy of Peter Nahum.
Renate Nahum. Agency
(no.48, p.91)

Study of Seated Figure for *The Garden Court* in the *Briar Rose* Series
c.1873
Graphite on paper
12.6 × 17.9
Tate. Bequeathed by A.N. MacNicholl 1916
(no.33, p.81)

Lot and his Daughters
c.1874
Watercolour, bodycolour and coloured chalks on paper
76.2 × 59.4
The Trustees of the Cecil Higgins Art Gallery (The Higgins Bedford)
(no.53, p.96)

Sketchbook
1875
Graphite on paper
Victoria and Albert Museum. Given in accordance with the wishes of the late Lady Horner by her daughters Mrs Raymond Asquith and the Hon Mrs Cecily Lambton
(no.74, p.109)

Possibly a study for Medusa in *The Finding of Medusa*
c.1875–7
Graphite on paper
25.4 × 16.6
National Museums Liverpool, Lady Lever Art Gallery
(no.70, p.108)

Study of a Gorgon in *The Finding of Medusa*
1876
Graphite on paper
27.1 × 27.8
The Syndics of the Fitzwilliam Museum, University of Cambridge
(no.71, p.108)

Study for the head of *Medusa* in *The Baleful Head*
1876–7
Graphite on paper
22.7 × 12.6
The Syndics of the Fitzwilliam Museum, University of Cambridge
(no.76, p.109)

Study of *Athena* in *The Call of Perseus*
1876–7
Graphite on paper
26.7 × 17.6
The Syndics of the Fitzwilliam Museum, University of Cambridge
(no.73, p.108)

Study for *The Golden Stairs: Frances Graham at the Foot of the Stairs*
c.1876–80
Graphite on paper
25.4 × 14
Courtesy of Mrs Dianne Roberts
(no.26, p.76)

Study for *The Golden Stairs*
c.1876–80
Graphite on paper
25.2 × 13.8
Courtesy of Mrs Dianne Roberts
(no.27, p.76)

Study for *The Golden Stairs*
c.1876–80
Graphite on paper
25.2 × 13.8
Courtesy of Mrs Dianne Roberts
(no.28, p.77)

Study for *The Golden Stairs*
c.1876–80
Graphite on paper
25.2 × 13.8
Courtesy of Mrs Dianne Roberts
(no.29, p.77)

Studies of Birds for *Love Leading the Pilgrim*
c.1877–97
Chalk on paper
30.4 × 20.2
Amgueddfa Cymru – National Museum Wales
(no.60, p.102)

Studies for *Love Leading the Pilgrim*
Graphite on paper
22.9 × 32.4
Tate. Presented by Lord Duveen 1924
(no.61, p.102)

Study of Hands with Cymbals and Holding a Violin for *The Golden Stairs*
c.1878
Graphite on paper
26.3 × 17.5
The Syndics of the Fitzwilliam Museum, University of Cambridge
(no.31, p.79)

Study of Feet for *The Golden Stairs*
c.1878
Graphite on paper
26.4 × 17.5
The Syndics of the Fitzwilliam Museum, University of Cambridge
(no.30, p.79)

Plant Study for *Love and the Pilgrim*
1877–97
Graphite on paper
31.2 × 21.6
The Syndics of the Fitzwilliam Museum, University of Cambridge
(no.32, p.79)

Study of the King in *The Wheel of Fortune*
1879
Graphite on paper
27.2 × 18
The British Museum, London.
Bequeathed by Eric George Millar 1967
(no.44, p.89)

Comic Drawing of Four Figures in Long Robes
1880s
Graphite on writing paper
22.5 × 17.8
The British Museum, London.
Donated by Robert Steele 1941
(no.84, p.115)

Stella Vespertina (The Evening Star)
c.1880
Oil paint on canvas
49 × 39
William Morris Gallery,
London Borough of Waltham Forest
(no.50, p.94)

Study of Armour: Perseus in the *Finding of Medusa*
Before 1880
Bodycolour on paper
54 × 38.2
The Syndics of the Fitzwilliam Museum, University of Cambridge
(no.77, p.110)

Account Book with Morris & Co with caricature frontispiece of the artist and William Morris
1883
Pen and ink on paper
15.9 × 10.8 (each image)
The Syndics of the Fitzwilliam Museum, University of Cambridge
(no.85, p.115)

Caricature of an *Annunciation* by Rubens from the Album *Letters to Katie*
1883–9
Graphite on paper
17.5 × 22.5
The British Museum, London.
Bequeathed by Katherine Lewis 1960
(no.81, p.113)

Study of the Maid for *King Cophetua and the Beggar Maid*
1883
Graphite on paper
30.2 × 19.1
Tate. Purchased 1963
(no.34, p.81)

Study for *Andromeda*
c.1885
Chalk on paper
38.1 × 27.9
Tate. Presented by Lord Duveen 1924
(no.75, p.109)

A Study for *Andromeda* for *The Doom Fulfilled* in the *Perseus* series
1885
Graphite on paper
27.3 × 18.2
The British Museum, London.
Bequeathed by Eric George Millar 1967
(no.72, p.108)

Head Study for Mermaid in *The Depths of the Sea*
1886
Graphite on paper
31.7 × 22.1
National Museums Liverpool, Lady Lever Art Gallery
(no.90, p.119)

A Bathing Beauty: Two views, Front and Back, of Emma De Burgh, with Leonardo's 'Last Supper' Tattooed on her Back, whom the Artist had Seen that Afternoon at the London Aquarium
c.1893–5
Graphite on paper
17.5 × 11.5 each
Peter and Renate Nahum
(no.80, p.113)

The Pilgrim Outside the Garden of Idleness (Scene from *Roman de la Rose)*
c.1893–8
Oil on canvas
155.9 × 306.7
Victoria and Albert Museum. Given by Sir Philip Burne-Jones and Mrs J.W. Mackail, children of the artist
(no.63, p.104)

Study of Female Head to Right
1889
Charcoal on paper
35.2 × 22.4
National Museums Liverpool, Lady Lever Art Gallery
(no.66, p.107)

Album of Illustrated Letters to Mrs Gaskell
1893–8
Pen and ink and graphite on writing paper
41.5 × 31 (album closed)
The Ashmolean Museum, University of Oxford. Purchased 2015
(no.89, p.118)

Self-Portrait Caricature in a Letter to Cosmo Monkhouse
1894
Pen and ink on paper
17.7 × 11.3
Collection of Stephen Calloway
(no.86, p.115)

Illustrated Letter to Angela
c.1896
Coloured pencil on paper
18 × 12
Private collection
(no.88, p.117)

A Woman Playing a Cithara
1896
Tempera, gold paint and watercolour on paper
35.3 × 21.3
Tate. Bequeathed by Miss Maud Beddington 1940
(no.51, p.95)

Design for Embroidery
1890s
Watercolour on linen
69 × 69 × 7
Private collection
(no.52, p.95)

Nymphs of the Moon
c.1896
Bodycolour and metallic pigments on prepared paper
32.9 × 24.8
Amgueddfa Cymru – National Museum Wales
(no.79, p.111)

Nymphs of the Stars
1896
Bodycolour, gold pigment and pastel paper
35.5 × 24.8
Amgueddfa Cymru – National Museum Wales
(no.78, p.111)

Manuscript Volume of Illustrated Letters and Humorous Drawings sent to Helen Mary Gaskell
1897–8
Bound volume of illustrated letters
18 × 12.5 (book closed)
Private collection
(no.87, p.116)

03

Love among the Ruins
1870–3
Watercolour, bodycolour and gum arabic on paper
96.5 × 152.4
Private collection
(no.91, p.112–3)

The Mill
1870–82
Oil paint on canvas
90.8 × 197.5
Victoria and Albert Museum. Bequeathed by Constantine Alexander Ionides
(no.92, p.124–5)

The Beguiling of Merlin
1872–77
Oil paint on canvas
186 × 111
National Museums Liverpool, Lady Lever Art Gallery
(no.93, p.127)

Laus Veneris
1873–78
Oil paint on canvas
119.4 × 180.3
Laing Art Gallery (Tyne & Wear Archives & Museums)
(no.94, p.128)

The Golden Stairs
1880
Oil paint on canvas
269.2 × 116.8
Tate. Bequeathed by Lord Battersea 1924
(no.95, p.131)

The Tree of Forgiveness
1881–82
Oil paint and chalk on canvas
186 × 111
National Museums Liverpool, Lady Lever Art Gallery
(no.96, p.133)

The Wheel of Fortune
1883
Oil paint on canvas
259 × 151.5
Musée d'Orsay, Paris
(no.97, p.134)

King Cophetua and the Beggar Maid
1884
Oil paint on canvas
293.4 × 135.9
Tate. Presented by subscribers 1900
(no.98, p.135)

The Morning of the Resurrection
1886
Oil paint on wood
84.5 × 151.1
Tate. Bequeathed by Mrs S.G. Potter 1937
(no.99, p.136)

The Depths of the Sea
1886
Oil paint on canvas
197 × 75
Private collection
(no.102, p.141)

The Dream of Launcelot at the Chapel of the San Graal
1895–6
Oil paint on canvas
138.5 × 169.8
Southampton City Art Gallery
(no.100, p.137)

Love and the Pilgrim
1896–7
Oil paint on canvas
157.5 × 304.8
Tate. Presented by the Art Fund 1942
(no.100, p.138–9)

Charles William Campbell 1855–1887
after Edward Burne-Jones
Pan and Psyche
1887
Mezzotint on paper
35.6 × 29.9
The Maas Gallery
(no.103, p.142)

Feliks Jasiński 1862–1901
after Edward Burne-Jones
Copper plate for *Annunciation*
1897
59.8 × 28.5
Victoria and Albert Museum
(no.105, p.144)

Robert Walker Macbeth 1848–1910
after Edward Burne-Jones
Le Chant d'Amour
1896
Etching on vellum
38.4 × 53
The Maas Gallery
(no.104, p.144)

Feliks Jasiński
after Edward Burne-Jones
Proof print for *Annunciation*
1897
Etching on vellum
47 × 20
Victoria and Albert Museum
(no.106, p.144)

04

Portrait of Frances Graham
1879
Oil paint on canvas
59.7 × 44.5
Private collection
(no.108, p.149)

Portrait of William Graham
c.1880
Oil paint on canvas
59 × 43
Private collection
(no.10, p.148)

Portrait Head of King Cophetua
c.1883–4
Oil paint on canvas
56 × 42
Private collection courtesy of Peter Nahum. Renate Nahum. Agency
(no.113, p.155)

Portrait of Georgiana Burne-Jones
1883
Oil paint on canvas
76 × 53
Private collection
(no.112, p.153)

Margaret Burne-Jones
1885–6
Oil paint on canvas
92 × 66
Private collection
(no.114, p.156)

Portrait of Katie Lewis
1886
Oil paint on canvas
61 × 127
Private collection
(no.116, p.159)

Ignacy Jan Paderewski
1890
Oil paint on canvas
61 × 51
RCM Museum, Royal College of Music, London
(no.117, p.160)

Vespertina Quies
1893
Oil paint on canvas
107.9 × 62.2
Tate. Bequeathed by Miss Maud Beddington 1940
(no.119, p.162)

Portrait of Amy Gaskell
1893
Oil paint on canvas
96.5 × 52
Private collection
(no.121, p.164)

Lady Windsor
1893–5
Oil paint on canvas
199.5 × 95.5
Birmingham Museums Trust on behalf
of a Private Lenderl
(no.118, p.161)

Baronne Madeleine Deslandes
1895–6
Oil paint on canvas
115.5 × 58.2 mm
National Gallery of Victoria, Melbourne, Australia.
Purchased with funds donated by Andrew Sisson,
2005
(no.122, p.165)

Flamma Vestalis
1896
Oil paint on canvas
107.9 × 37.4
Private collection
(no.120, p.163)

Morris, William 1834–1896
The Rubáiyát of Omar Khayyám
1872
Illuminated manuscript
28.5 × 44 (open)
Private collection
(no.111, p.152)

Horner, Frances (née Graham) 1855–1940
after a design by Edward Burne-Jones
Embroidered Purse with the zodiac sign of Aries
mid-1870s
24 × 27.5 × 2
Private collection
(no.110, p.152)

A Painted Casket Decorated With Angels
1877
Oil paint and gold on panel
20.3 × 33.6 × 19
Private collection
(no.109, p.151)

Carlo Giuliano 1826–1895
Brooch pendant in the Form of a Singing Bird
1885–95
Enamelled gold set with turquoise, coral,
pearls and a ruby
4.2 × 4.3 × 14
Victoria and Albert Museum. Given by Geoffrey
and Caroline Munn through the Art Fund
(no.115, p.157)

05
The Call of Perseus; Perseus and the Graiae;
Perseus and the Nereids
1875–6
Gouache, gold paint and ink on paper
36.7 × 102.7
Tate. Presented by the Trustees of the Chantrey
Bequest 1919
(no.128, p.181)

The Finding of Medusa; The Death of Medusa
(The Birth of Pegasus and Chrysaor); Perseus
Pursued by the Gorgons
1875–6
Gouache, gold paint and ink on paper
36.8 × 128.4
Tate. Presented by the Trustees of the Chantrey
Bequest 1919
(no.129, p.181)

Atlas Turned to Stone; The Rock of Doom
and the Doom Fulfilled; The Court of Phineas;
The Baleful Head
1875–6
Gouache, gold paint, graphite and chalk on paper
36.7 × 148.7
Tate. Presented by the Trustees of the Chantrey
Bequest 1919
(no.130, p.181)

The Call of Perseus
1877–98
Oil paint and chalk on canvas
152.5 × 127
Staatsgalerie Stuttgart
(no.132, p.185)

Perseus and the Graiae
1877–88
Silver and gold leaf, gesso, and oil paint on oak
170.2 × 153.2
Accepted by HM Government in Lieu of Inheritance
Tax and allocated to Amgueddfa Cymru-National
Museum Wales with additional contributions from
The Art Fund
(no.131, p.182)

Perseus and the Graiae
1892
Oil paint on canvas
153.5 × 170
Staatsgalerie Stuttgart
(no.133, p.186)

Perseus and the Sea Nymphs
(The Arming of Perseus)
1877
Bodycolour on paper
152.8 × 126.4
Southampton City Art Gallery
(no.134, p.187)

The Finding of Medusa
c.1882
Bodycolour on paper
152.5 × 137.7
Southampton City Art Gallery
(no.135, p.188)

The Death of Medusa (I)
c.1882
Bodycolour on paper
124.5 × 116.9
Southampton City Art Gallery
(no.136, p.189)

The Death of Medusa (II)
c.1881–2
Bodycolour on paper
152.5 × 136.5
Southampton City Art Gallery
(no.137, p.190)

Atlas Turned to Stone
c.1878
Bodycolour on paper
150.2 × 190.2
Southampton City Art Gallery
(no.138, p.191)

The Baleful Head
1885
Bodycolour on paper
153.7 × 129
Southampton City Art Gallery
(no.141, p.195)

The Rock of Doom
1885–8
Oil paint on canvas
155 × 130
Staatsgalerie Stuttgart
(no.139, p.192)

The Doom Fulfilled
1888
Oil paint on canvas
155 × 140.5
Staatsgalerie Stuttgart
(no.140, p.193)

06
The Briar Wood
1874–84
Oil paint on canvas
125 × 231
The Faringdon Collection Trust
(no.123, p.170–1)

The Council Chamber
1885–90
Oil paint on canvas
125 × 231
The Faringdon Collection Trust
(no.124, p.172)

The Garden Court
1885–90
Oil paint on canvas
125 × 231
The Faringdon Collection Trust
(no.125, p.173)

The Rose Bower
1886–90
Oil paint on canvas
125 × 231
The Faringdon Collection Trust
(no.126, p.174)

Briar Rose Infill Panel – Left of 'The Briar Wood'
1891
Oil paint on canvas
114.9 × 14.6
The Faringdon Collection Trust
(no.127, p.178)

Briar Rose Infill Panel – Right of 'The Briar Wood'
1891
Oil paint on canvas
115.6 × 14.6
The Faringdon Collection Trust
(no.127, p.178)

Briars with Helmet and Greave – Infill Panel
1891
Oil paint on canvas
114.9 × 127.6 mm
The Faringdon Collection Trust
(no.127, p.178)

Briar Rose Infill Panel – Left of 'The Council Chamber'
1891
Oil paint on canvas
114.9 × 39.4
The Faringdon Collection Trust
(no.127, p.179)

Briar Rose Infill Panel – Right of 'The Council Chamber'
1891
Oil paint on canvas
114.9 × 39.4
The Faringdon Collection Trust
(no.127, p.178)

Briar Rose Infill Panel – Left of 'The Garden Court'
1891
Oil paint on canvas
114.9 × 47.6
The Faringdon Collection Trust
(no.127, p.178)

Briar Rose Infill Panel – Right of 'The Garden Court'
1891
Oil paint on canvas
114.9 × 47.6
The Faringdon Collection Trust
(no.127, p.178)

A Stone Kitchen Overgrown with Briars – Infill Panel
1891
Oil paint on canvas
114.9 × 127.6
The Faringdon Collection Trust
(no.127, p.178)

Briar Rose Infill Panel – Left of 'The Rose Bower'
1891
Oil paint on canvas
114.9 × 27.3
The Faringdon Collection Trust
(no.127, p.178)

Briar Rose Infill Panel – Right of 'The Rose Bower'
1891
Oil paint on canvas
115.6 × 27.3
The Faringdon Collection Trust
(no.127, p.178)

07
Angeli Ministrantes (Salisbury Cathedral)
1878
Crayon and chalk on paper on canvas
212.3 × 150.5
The Syndics of the Fitzwilliam Museum, University of Cambridge
(no.142, p.198)

Angeli Laudantes (Salisbury Cathedral)
1878
Crayon and chalk on paper on canvas
212.8 × 154.3
The Syndics of the Fitzwilliam Museum, University of Cambridge
(no.143, p.199)

The Graham Piano
1879–80
Painted wood
98 × 142 × 260
Private collection
(no.150, p.211)

The Pelican in her Piety
1880
Crayon, pastel and chalk on paper
172.7 × 57.2
William Morris Gallery,
London Borough of Waltham Forest
(no.144, p.201)

Elijah in the Wilderness
1883
Stained, painted and leaded glass
164.5 × 64.5
Birmingham Museums Trust on behalf of Birmingham City Council
Presented by Mrs J.H. Francis, 1920
(not illustrated)

Pomona
c.1885
Embroidered wall hanging; linen embroidered with floss silks
Central panel 321 × 281.5 × 4
Side panels 271 × 28 × 2.5 each
Private collection
(no.149, p.209)

The Fall of Lucifer
1894
Bodycolour and paint on paper
245 × 118
Private collection
(no.145, p.202)

The Adoration of the Magi
1894
Tapestry
258 × 384
Manchester Metropolitan University Special Collections
(no.148, p.208)

The Attainment: The Vision of the Holy Grail to Sir Galahad, Sir Bors and Sir Perceval
1890–94
Cotton, wool and silk
239 × 749
Collection Jimmy Page courtesy Paul Reeves London
(no.147, p.206)

The Arming and Departure of the Knights of the Round Table on the Quest for the Holy Grail
1890–94
Cotton, wool and silk
240 × 347
Collection Jimmy Page courtesy Paul Reeves London
(no.146, p.206)

William Morris 1834–1896
The Earthly Paradise
1868
Book
18.8 × 13.5 × 4 (book closed)
Collection of Stephen Calloway
(no.1, p.16)

William Morris 1834–1896
The Dream of John Ball
1888
Book
17 × 13.5 × 1.6 (book closed)
Collection of Stephen Calloway
(no.151, p.212)

The Works of Geoffrey Chaucer
1896
Printed book
44 × 32
Private collection
(no.152, p.212)

Frederick Hollyer 1838–1933
Album of 21 Photographs Recording the Burne-Jones Memorial Exhibition at the New Gallery in 1898–9
Album of photographs laid down on card
33.5 × 52 × 2.5 (book closed)
Peter and Renate Nahum
(p.221, centre)

08
Spirits, or *The Uninterpreted Dream*
1890s
Oil paint on canvas
127 × 85
Etienne Bréton, Saint-Honoré Art Consulting, Paris
(no.153, p.214)

Index

Photo Credits

Art Collection 2/ Alamy Stock Photo p.216 (right)

© Ashmolean Museum, University of Oxford fig.23; nos. 40, 57, 89

bpk/ Staatsgalerie Stuttgart nos. 132, 133, 139, 140

© Bednorz Images/ Bridgeman Images p.221 (far right, bottom)

Mario Bettella fig.9; nos. 103, 104

© Birmingham Museums Trust fig.27; pp.10–11 (detail); nos. 11, 25, 118

© 2018 Museum of Fine Arts, Boston no.22

Bridgeman Images figs.28, 38; p.9 (detail); no.149

© The Trustees of the British Museum figs.29a, 29b; nos. 44, 72, 81, 84

By permission of the Governing Body of Christ Church, Oxford fig.26

© Christie's Images Ltd. 2018 nos. 26, 27, 28, 29, 88, 109

© Christie›s Images Ltd./ Bridgeman Images no.108

© The Faringdon Collection, Buscot Park fig.34

© The Faringdon Collection, Buscot Park. Photo: Tate Photography/ Marcus Leith fig.35; pp.2–3, 168 (detail); nos. 123, 124, 125, 126, 127

© The Fitzwilliam Museum, Cambridge figs.2 (detail), 25; nos. 5, 7, 30, 31, 32, 71, 73, 76, 77, 85, 142, 143

Courtesy George Eastman Museum fig.18

Rex Harris fig.7

Historic England Archive fig.10

The History Collection/ Alamy Stock Photo p.220 (centre)

Hulton Archive/ Getty Images p.217 (far right)

Alex Jamison pp.42–3 (detail); no.8

Iain Lewis nos. 52, 110

© Look and Learn/ Bridgeman Images p.219 (far left, top)

© Look and Learn/ Peter Jackson Collection/ Bridgeman Images p.218 (far right)

Courtesy the Maas Gallery no.69

© Manchester Metropolitan University Special Collections. Photo: Tony Richards p.196 (detail); no.148

Christian Markel/ National Gallery of Victoria, Melbourne no.122

Courtesy Peter & Renate Nahum pp.218 (centre), 221 (centre); nos. 3, 45, 46, 48, 80, 82

© National Museum Wales nos. 47, 49, 60, 78, 79, 131

Courtesy National Museum, Warsaw fig.30

© National Museums Liverpool pp.4, 120 (detail); nos. 66, 70, 90, 93, 96

© National Portrait Gallery, London figs.1, 8, 11, 33

© National Portrait Gallery, London. Photo: Frederick Hollyer p.218 (far left)

© National Portrait Gallery, London. Photo: Alfred James Philpott (Phillpot) (suggested) p.219 (centre)

© National Portrait Gallery, London. Photo: Henry and Richard Stiles p.220 (far right)

© National Portrait Gallery, London. Photo: Sir Emery Walker pp.220 (far left, after Frederick Hollyer), 221 (far left)

© National Portrait Gallery, London. Photo: John Watkins p.217 (far left)

Selina Ou/ National Gallery of Victoria, Melbourne fig.31

David Parmiter Photography cover (hardback); fig.15 (detail); p.203 (detail); nos. 21, 87, 91, 102, 116, 120, 121, 145, 152

Private collection/ Bridgeman Images fig.32

Prudence Cuming Associates fig.16 (detail); no.113

© RMN-Grand Palais (musée d'Orsay)/ Gérard Blot p.12 (detail); no.97

Gerhard Richter Archive fig.21

© Royal College of Music/ ArenaPAL no.117

Courtesy Sotheby's, London fig.12; p.146 (detail); no.112

Southampton City Art Gallery/ Bridgeman Images nos. 100, 134, 135, 136, 137, 138, 141

Courtesy Spitalfields Life Books p.221 (far right, top)

David Stubbs nos. 6, 53

© Tate, 2018 fig.13 (detail); pp.34 (detail), 74 (detail), 130 (detail); nos. 12, 17, 18, 19, 33, 34, 35, 36, 37, 38, 39, 41, 42, 43, 51, 54, 55, 58, 59, 61, 64, 65, 68, 75, 95, 98, 99, 101, 119, 128, 129, 130

© Tate, 2018. Photo: David Lambert & Rod Tidnam no.56

© Tate, 2018. Photo: Marcus Leith fig.40; nos. 107, 111, 114, 150

© Tyne & Wear Archives & Museums/ Bridgeman Images cover (paperback); no.94

© Victoria and Albert Museum, London figs.3 (detail), 19, 36, 37, 39, 41; pp.44 (detail), 215; nos. 9, 10, 13, 14, 15, 16, 20, 62, 63, 67, 74, 83, 92, 105, 106, 115

© Victoria and Albert Museum, London. Photo: Frederick Hollyer p.219 (far right)

Scott Wicking fig.14 (detail); no.23

Copyright Credits

© 1979 National Film Trustee Company Ltd. Courtesy Python (Monty) Pictures Ltd. fig.22

© Estate of Roger Perry fig.19

© Gerhard Richter 2018 fig.21

© Mick Rock 1975, 2018 fig.20

Supporting Tate

Tate relies on a large number of supporters – individuals, foundations, companies and public sector sources – to enable it to deliver its programme of activities, both on and off its gallery sites. This support is essential in order for Tate to acquire works of art for the Collection, run education, outreach and exhibition programmes, care for the Collection in storage and enable art to be displayed, both digitally and physically, inside and outside Tate. Please contact us at:

Development Office
Tate
Millbank
London SW1P 4RG

Tel: +44 (0)20 7887 4900
Fax: +44 (0)20 7887 8098

Tate Americas Foundation
520 West 27 Street Unit 404
New York, NY 10001
USA

Tel: 001 212 643 2818
Fax: 001 212 643 1001

Donations, no matter the size, are gratefully received, either to support particular areas of interest, or to contribute to general activity costs.

Legacies
A legacy to Tate may take the form of a residual share of an estate, a specific cash sum or item of property such as a work of art. Legacies to Tate are free of inheritance tax, and help to secure a strong future for the Collection and galleries. For further information please contact the Development Office.

Offers in lieu of tax
Inheritance Tax can be satisfied by transferring to the Government a work of art of outstanding importance. In this case the amount of tax is reduced, and it can be made a condition of the offer that the work of art is allocated to Tate. Please contact us for details.

Tate Members
Tate Members enjoy unlimited free admission throughout the year to all exhibitions at Tate, as well as a number of other benefits such as exclusive use of our Members' Rooms and a free annual subscription to *Tate Etc.* Whilst enjoying the exclusive privileges of membership, members also help secure Tate's position at the very heart of British and modern art. Members support actively contributes to new purchases of important art, ensuring that Tate's collection continues to be relevant and comprehensive, as well as funding projects in London, Liverpool and St Ives that increase access and understanding for everyone.

Tate Patrons
Tate Patrons share a passion for art and are committed to supporting Tate on an annual basis. The Patrons help enable the acquisition of works across Tate's broad collecting remit, support the staging of major exhibitions in the galleries, and also give their support to vital conservation, learning and research projects. The scheme provides a forum for Patrons to share their interest in art and meet curators, artists and one another in an enjoyable environment through a regular programme of events. These events take place both at Tate and beyond and encompass curator-led exhibition tours, visits to artists' studios and private collections, art trips both in the UK and abroad, and access to art fairs. The scheme welcomes supporters from outside the UK, giving the programme a truly international scope. For more information, please contact the Patrons Office on +44(0)20 7887 8740 or at patrons.office@tate.org.uk.

Corporate Membership
Corporate Membership at Tate offers companies opportunities for corporate entertaining and the chance for a wide variety of employee benefits. These include special private views, special access to paying exhibitions, out-of-hours visits and tours, invitations to VIP events and talks at members' offices.

Corporate Investment
Tate has developed a range of imaginative partnerships with the corporate sector, ranging from international interpretation and exhibition programmes to local outreach and staff development programmes. We are particularly known for high-profile business to business marketing initiatives and employee benefit packages. Please contact the Corporate Partnerships team for further details.

Charity Details
The Tate Gallery is an exempt charity; the Museums & Galleries Act 1992 added the Tate Gallery to the list of exempt charities defined in the 1960 Charities Act. Tate Foundation is a registered charity (number 1085314).

Tate Americas Foundation
Tate Americas Foundation is an independent charity based in New York that supports the work of Tate in the United Kingdom. It receives full tax exempt status from the IRS under section 501(c)(3) allowing United States taxpayers to receive tax deductions on gifts towards annual membership programmes, exhibitions, scholarship and capital projects. For more information please contact the Tate Americas Foundation office.

Tate Britain Donors to the Centenary Development Campaign
The Annenberg Foundation
The Asprey Family Charitable Foundation
Ron Beller and Jennifer Moses
Alex and Angela Bernstein
The Charlotte Bonham-Carter Charitable Trust
Lauren and Mark Booth
Ivor Braka
The CHK Charitable Trust
The Clore Duffield Foundation
Sadie Coles
Giles and Sonia Coode-Adams
Alan Cristea
Thomas Dane
The D'Oyly Carte Charitable Trust
Sir Harry and Lady Djanogly
The Dulverton Trust
Maurice and Janet Dwek
Friends of the Tate Gallery
Bob and Kate Gavron
Sir Paul Getty, KBE
Alan Gibbs
Mr and Mrs Edward Gilhuly
Helyn and Ralph Goldenberg
Nicholas and Judith Goodison
Richard and Odile Grogan
Pehr and Christina Gyllenhammar
Heritage Lottery Fund
Jay Jopling
Mr and Mrs Karpidas
Howard and Lynda Karshan
Peter and Maria Kellner
Madeleine Kleinwort
Brian and Lesley Knox
The Kresge Foundation
Catherine and Pierre Lagrange
Mr and Mrs Ulf G Linden
Ruth and Stuart Lipton
Anders and Ulla Ljungh
Lloyds TSB Foundation for England and Wales
David and Pauline Mann-Vogelpoel
Sir Edwin and Lady Manton
Nick and Annette Mason
Viviane and James Mayor
Anthony and Deirdre Montagu
Sir Peter and Lady Osborne
Maureen Paley
William A Palmer
Mr Frederik Paulsen
The Pet Shop Boys
The P F Charitable Trust
The Polizzi Charitable Trust
John and Jill Ritblat
Barrie and Emmanuel Roman
Lord and Lady Sainsbury of Preston Candover
Mrs Coral Samuel, CBE
David and Sophie Shalit
Mr and Mrs Sven Skarendahl
Pauline Denyer-Smith and Paul Smith
Mr and Mrs Nicholas Stanley
The Jack Steinberg Foundation
Charlotte Stevenson
Tate Gallery Centenary Gala
Carter and Mary Thacher
Mr and Mrs John L Thornton
The Trusthouse Charitable Foundation
David and Emma Verey
Dinah Verey
Clodagh and Leslie Waddington
Gordon D Watson
Mr and Mrs Anthony Weldon
The Duke of Westminster, OBE TD DL
Sam Whitbread
Mr and Mrs Stephen Wilberding
Michael S Wilson
The Wolfson Foundation

and those who wish to remain anonymous

Donors to The Tate Britain Millbank Project
Alan Cristea Gallery
The Deborah Loeb Brice Foundation
Clore Duffield Foundation
Sir Harry and Lady Djanogly
The Gatsby Charitable Foundation
J Paul Getty Jr Charitable Trust
Heritage Lottery Fund
The Hiscox Foundation
James and Clare Kirkman
The Linbury Trust and The Monument Trust
The Manton Foundation
The Mayor Gallery
Ronald and Rita McAulay
Midge and Simon Palley
PF Charitable Trust
The Porter Foundation
The Dr Mortimer and Theresa Sackler Foundation
Mrs Coral Samuel, CBE
Jake and Hélène Marie Shafran
Tate Members
The Taylor Family Foundation
Sir David and Lady Verey
Sir Siegmund Warburg's Voluntary Settlement
Garfield Weston Foundation
The Wolfson Foundation

and those who wish to remain anonymous

Tate Britain Benefactors and Major Donors
We would like to acknowledge and thank the following benefactors who have supported Tate Britain prior to June 2018.

Alireza Abrishamchi
Abrishamchi Family Collection
Raad Zeid Al-Hussein
Dilyaya Allakhverdova
Princess Alia Al-Senussi
Olga de Amaral
The Ampersand Foundation
The Fagus Anstruther Memorial Trust in memory of the late Hartley Ramsden and Margot Eates
Miss Mary Louise Archibald
Art Fund
Arts Council England
Arts & Humanities Research Council
ArtSocial Foundation
Charles Asprey
Celia Atkin
Axel Vervoordt Gallery
Miroslaw Balka, in honour of Sir Nicholas Serota
Roger Ballen
Lionel Barber
The Estate of Peter and Caroline Barker-Mill
Wilhelmina Barns-Graham Trust through the Art Fund
Hannah Barry
Big Lottery Fund
Blavatnik Family Foundation
Bloomberg Philanthropies
Harry and Fabiana Bond
The Charlotte Bonham-Carter Charitable Trust
Pontus Bonnier
John Botts, CBE
Estate of Louise Bourgeois
Elena Bowes
Barbara Hepworth Estate
Dr Luther Brady
The Deborah Loeb Brice Foundation
Laurel and Paul Britton
Rory and Elizabeth Brooks Foundation
Beatrice Bulgari | In Between Art Film
Byucksan Foundation
Calouste Gulbenkian Foundation

Trustees of the Chantrey Bequest
David and Rose Cholmondeley
The Estate of Mrs Anne Christopherson
The Clore Duffield Foundation
Sadie Coles
Carla Emil and Richard Silverstein
Connolly
Contemporary Art Society
The Ernest Cook Trust
Corinne Bellow Charity
Douglas S Cramer
Alan Cristea
Harry G David
Tacita Dean
Jeremy Deller, in honour of Sir Nicholas Serota
Tiqui Atencio Demirdjian and Ago Demirdjian
Department for Business, Innovation and Skills
James E Diner
Anthony and Anne d'Offay
Peter Doig, in honour of Sir Nicholas Serota
Joe and Marie Donnelly
Robert Drake
Lonti Ebers
Maryam and Edward Eisler
John Ellerman Foundation
European Collection Circle
European Union
Monir Shahroudy Farmanfarmaian
The Estate of Maurice Farquharson
Estate of Paul Feiler
Wendy Fisher
Eric and Louise Franck
Dorothy Free
The Estate of Lucian Freud
Amanda and Glenn Fuhrman and The FLAG Art Foundation
Gagosian
Frank Gallipoli
The Garcia Family Foundation
Candida and Zak Gertler
Georg Geyer
Adrian Ghenie
Glenstone Foundation
Milly and Arne Glimcher
Anna and Ralph Goldenberg
Nan Goldin, in honour of Sir Nicholas Serota
Antony Gormley
Lydia and Manfred Gorvy
Noam Gottesman
The Granville-Grossman Bequest
Mr Andre Guilherme Brandão
Tae Won Hahn
The Hakuta Family
Alexandra and Guy Halamish
Maggi Hambling, in honour of Maria Balshaw
Paul Hamlyn Foundation
Susan Hayden
Hazlitt Holland-Hibbert
The Estate of Barbara Hepworth
Heritage Lottery Fund
The Hintze Family Charitable Foundation
Damien Hirst
David Hockney
The Estate of Howard Hodgkin
Rebecca Horn
Tierney Horne
Michael and Ali Hue-Williams
The Estate of Malcolm Hughes
Mr Kyung-soo Huh
Huo Family Foundation (UK) Limited
The Estate of Bert and Beatrice Irvin
The J Isaacs Charitable Trust
Tim Jefferies, in honour of Sir Nicholas Serota
Georg Geyer
Pamela Joyner and Alfred J Giuffrida
Rasha Said Khawaja
Sung Moon Kwon
Catherine Lagrange
The Estate of Fay Elspeth Langford
David and Amanda Leathers
Fondation Walter & Nicole LeBlanc
Agnès and Edward Lee
Legacy Trust UK
The Leverhulme Trust
James Lindon
Galleria Lorcan O'Neill
Andrew Lugg
Roland Augustine and Lawrence Luhring
LUMA Foundation
Caro MacDonald
The Estate of Sir Edwin Manton
The Manton Foundation
Danica and Eduard Maták
Lord McAlpine of West Green
Mark McCain
The Estate of Kenneth McGowan
Steve McQueen
The Andrew W. Mellon Foundation
The Paul Mellon Centre for Studies in British Art
Gustav Metzger
Boris and Vita Mikhailov
Naomi Milgrom Foundation
Sir Geoffroy Millais
Victoria Miro
Henry Moore Foundation
The Estate of Jenifer Ann Murray
Fayeeza Naqvi
National Heritage Memorial Fund
The National Trust
New Carlsberg Foundation
Catherine Opie
Simon and Midge Palley
The Pasmore Estate
Patio Bullrich
Catherine Petitgas
Stanley Picker Trust
The Pictet Group
The Pivovarov Family
Courtney Plummer
David W. Posnett, OBE
Gilberto Pozzi
Emilio Prini
Carla Rapoport
The Robert Rauschenberg Foundation
Rennie Foundation
Andrea Rosen
The Estate of Eugene and Penelope Rosenberg
Edward Ruscha
Sean Ryerson
Keith and Katherine Sachs
The Estate of Simon Sainsbury
Per Sandven
The Estate of Khadija Saye
Carolin Scharpff-Striebich
Gregor Schneider
The Finnis Scott Foundation
Jake and Hélène Marie Shafran
Komal Shah
Jack Shear
Dasha Shenkman
Taryn Simon
Andy Simpkin
The Estate of Sylvia Sleigh
Matthew Slotover and Emily King
Stephen Friedman Gallery
The Estate of Michael Stoddart
Surgo Donor Advised Fund
Tamares Real Estate Holdings Inc. in collaboration with the Zabludowicz Collection
Tate 1897 Circle
Tate Africa Acquisitions Committee
Tate Americas Foundation
Tate Asia-Pacific Acquisitions Committee
Tate International Council
Tate Latin American Acquisitions Committee
Tate Members
Tate Middle East and North Africa Acquisitions Committee
Tate North American Acquisitions Committee
Tate Patrons
Tate Photography Acquisitions Committee
Tate Russia and Eastern Europe Acquisitions Committee
Tate South Asia Acquisitions Committee
Terra Foundation for American Art
The Estate of Mr Nicholas Themans
Thomas Dane Gallery
Wolfgang Tillmans, in honour of Sir Nicholas Serota
Russell Tovey
Robert and Matthew Travers, PIANO NOBILE (Works of Art) Limited
Tuplin Fine Art Ltd
Luc Tuymans
Francis Upritchard
V-A-C Foundation
The Estate of Mollie Winifred Vickers
Mercedes Vilardell
Marie-Louise von Motesiczky Charitable Trust
Mark Wallinger
David and Maria Wilkinson
Jane and Michael Wilson
The Lord Leonard and Lady Estelle Wolfson Foundation
Erwin Wurm
The Estate of Mr Anthony Zambra

and those who wish to remain anonymous

Platinum Patrons
Eric Abraham
Ghazwa Mayassi Abu-Suud
Maria Adonyeva
Mr Shane Akeroyd
Basil Alkazzi
Bobby Arora
Celia and Edward Atkin, CBE
Alex Beard
Beecroft Charitable Trust
Jacques Boissonnas
Natalia Bondarenko
John Booth
Rory and Elizabeth Brooks
The Lord Browne of Madingley, FRS, FREng
Karen Cawthorn Argenio
Mr Stephane Custot
Pascale Decaux
Sophie Diedrichs-Cox
Valentina Drouin
Ashiya Dudhia
Mr David Fitzsimons
Edwin Fox Foundation
Stephen Friedman
Mrs Lisa Garrison
Hugh Gibson
Mr Florian Gutzwiller
Alexis and Anne-Marie Habib
David Herro
Misha and Theresa Horne
Mr and Mrs Yan Huo
Mr Phillip Hylander
Ms Natascha Jakobs
Mrs Gabrielle Jungels-Winkler
Maria and Peter Kellner
Anna Korshun
Lali Marganiya
Mira Dimitrova and Luigi Mazzoleni
Scott and Suling Mead
Mr Donald Moore
Mary Moore
Afsaneh Moshiri
Anthony and Jacqueline Orsatelli
Hussam Otaibi
Simon and Midge Palley (Chair)
Jan-Christoph Peters
Mr and Mrs Paul Phillips
Mr Gilberto and Mrs Daniela Pozzi
Frances Reynolds
Jake and Hélène Marie Shafran
Andrée Shore
Maria and Malek Sukkar
Pierre Tollis and Alexandra Mollof
Annie Vartivarian
Miss Cheyenne Westphal
Michael and Jane Wilson
Lady Wolfson of Marylebone
Brian T K Yim
Poju Zabludowicz and Anita Zabludowicz, OBE
Meng Zhou

and those who wish to remain anonymous

Gold Patrons
Ms Mila Askarova
Lars Bane
Francesca Bellini Joseph
Shoshana Bloch
Elena Bowes
Louise and Charlie Bracken
Angela Choon
Beth and Michele Colocci
Harry G David
Ms Miel de Botton
Mr Frank Destribats
Mrs Maryam Eisler
Michael Herzog
Fiona Mactaggart
Alison Myners
Mr Francis Outred
Mariela Pissioti
Richard Portes CBE FBA
Mathew Prichard
Garance Primat
Valerie Rademacher
Jordana Reuben
Almine Ruiz-Picasso
Ralph Segreti
Carol Sellars
Mr and Mrs Stanley S Tollman
Manuela and Iwan Wirth
Chizuko Yoshida

and those who wish to remain anonymous

Silver Patrons
Sharis Alexandrian
Ryan Allen and Caleb Kramer
Gregor Alpers
Mrs Malgosia Alterman
Dina Amin
The Anson Charitable Trust
Toby and Kate Anstruther
Mr and Mrs Zeev Aram
Hannah Armstrong
Shalni Arora
Mrs Charlotte Artus
Aspect Charitable Trust
Tracy Barakat
Peter Barham
Mrs Jane Barker
Oliver Barker
Mr Edward Barlow
Victoria Barnsley, OBE
Hazel Barratt
Jim Bartos
Dr Amelie Beier
Ms Anne Berthoud
Madeleine Bessborough
Janice Blackburn
David Blood and Beth Bisso
Bruno Boesch
Harry and Fabiana Bond
Mr Brian Boylan
Viscountess Bridgeman
Mr Dan Brooke
Ben and Louisa Brown
Beverley Buckingham
Michael Burrell
Mrs Marlene Burston
Piers Butler
Mrs Aisha Cahn
Sarah Caplin
Timothy and Elizabeth Capon
Mr Francis Carnwath and Ms Caroline Wiseman
Countess Castle Stewart
Roger Cazalet
Lord and Lady Charles Cecil
Dr Peter Chocian
Cynthia Clarry
Frank Cohen
Mrs Jane Collins
Dr Judith Collins
Terrence Collis
Mr and Mrs Oliver Colman
Mayte Comin
Carole and Neville Conrad
Giles and Sonia Coode-Adams
Cynthia Corbett
Mark and Cathy Corbett
Pilar Corrias
Tommaso Corvi-Mora
Mr and Mrs Bertrand Coste
Kathleen Crook and James Penturn
James Curtis
Richard Cyzer
Daniella Luxembourg Art
Fiona Davies
Sir Howard Davies
Sir Roger and Lady De Haan
Elisabeth De Kergorlay
Giles de la Mare
Mr Damon and The Hon Mrs de Laszlo
Alexander de Mont
Anne Chantal Defay Sheridan
Jackie Donnelly Russell
Joan Edlis
Lord and Lady Egremont
Margaret Erbe
John Erle-Drax
Dr Nigel Evans
Stuart and Margaret Evans
Eykyn Maclean LLC
Leonie Fallstrom
Mrs Heather Farrar
David Fawkes
Mrs Margy Fenwick
Laurie Fitch
The Sylvie Fleming Collection
Lt Commander Paul Fletcher
Katherine Francey Stables
Mr and Mrs Laurent Ganem
Mala Gaonkar
Geoffrey and Julian Charitable Trust
Elena Geuna
Mr Mark Glatman
Ms Emily Goldner and Mr Michael Humphries
Emma Goltz
Aphrodite Gonou
Kate Gordon
Dimitri Goulandris
Penelope Govett
Svitlana Granovska
Jennifer Greenberg
Judith and Richard Greer
Martyn Gregory
Richard and Odile Grogan
Carol Grose
John Howard Gruzelier
Mrs Helene Guerin-Llamas
Jill Hackel Zarzycki
Louise Hallett
Arthur Hanna
Mark Harris
Michael and Morven Heller
Christian Hernandez and Michelle Crowe Hernandez
Paul Higgins
Muriel Hoffner
James Holland-Hibbert
Lady Hollick, OBE
Holtermann Fine Art
Jeff Horne
John Huntingford
Helen Janecek
Sarah Jennings
Mr Haydn John
Mr Michael Johnson
Mike Jones
Jay Jopling
Mrs Brenda Josephs
Tracey Josephs
Mr Joseph Kaempfer
Andrew Kalman
Ghislaine Kane

Dr Martin Kenig
Mr David Ker
Mr and Mrs Simon Keswick
Mrs Mae Khouri
David Killick
Mr and Mrs James Kirkman
Brian and Lesley Knox
David P Korn
Kowitz Trust
Mr and Mrs Herbert Kretzmer
Linda Lakhdhir
Simon Lee
Tiina Lee
Leonard Lewis
Sophia and Mark Lewisohn
Yuandao Liu
Mr Gilbert Lloyd
Mrs Elizabeth Louis
Mark and Liza Loveday
Jeff Lowe
Alison Loyd
Mrs Ailsa Macalister
Mr William MacDougall
Kate MacGarry
Sir John Mactaggart
Audrey Mandela
Marsh Christian Trust
Stephen and Sharon Mather
Daniele Mattogno
Ms Fiona Mellish
Mrs R W P Mellish
Professor Rob Melville
Dr Helen Metcalf
Dr Basil Ross Middleton
Victoria Miro
Jan Mol
Mrs Bona Montagu
Mrs William Morrison
Louise Nathanson
Ms Deborah Norton
Julian Opie
Pilar Ordovás
Sayumi Otake
Desmond Page
Maureen Paley
Michael Palin
Mrs Kathrine Palmer
Mathieu Paris
Mrs Véronique Parke
Olga Pavlova
Frans Pettinga
Trevor Pickett
Frederique Pierre-Pierre
John Pluthero
Graham Powell
Susan Prevezer, QC
Mr and Mrs Ryan Prince
Ivetta Rabinovich
Patricia Ranken
Mrs Phyllis Rapp
Lady Ritblat
David Rocklin
Frankie Rossi
Mr David V Rouch
Mr James Roundell
Mr Charles Roxburgh
Hakon Runer and
Ulrike Schwarz-Runer
Mr Alex Sainsbury and
Ms Elinor Jansz
Mr Richard Christo Salmon
Mr Richard Saltoun
Cherrill and Ian Scheer
Sylvia Scheuer
Mrs Cara Schulze
Melissa Sesana
Ellen Shapiro
The Hon Richard Sharp
Neville Shulman, CBE
Ms Julia Simmonds
Simon C Dickinson Ltd
David Solo
Louise Spence
Mr Nicos Steratzias
Marie-Claude Stobart
Mrs Patricia Swannell
Mr James Swartz
The Lady Juliet Tadgell
Tot Taylor
Isadora Tharin
Elaine Thomas
Anthony Thornton
Marita Thurnauer
Ian Tollett
Victoria Tollman O'Hana
Karen Townshend
Andrew Tseng
Melissa Ulfane
Mrs Jolana Vainio and
Dr Petri Vainio
Celine Valligny
Mrs Cecilia Versteegh
Gisela von Sanden
Andreas Vourecas-Petalas
Audrey Wallrock
Offer Waterman
Mrs Sian West
Professor Sarah Whatmore
Victoria Wilks
Mr David Wood
Mr Douglas Woolf
Sharon Zhu

and those who wish to remain anonymous

Young Patrons
10 Hanover
Yasmine Abou Adal
Nadine Adams
Letizia Afentakis Cramer
Maria Lorena Aisaguer
Miss Noor Al-Rahim
HRH Princess Alia Al-Senussi
Miss Sharifa Alsudairi
Lucy Attwood
Miss Olivia Aubry
Flavie Audi
Charles and Tetyana Banner
Mr Richard Bazzaz
Katrina Beechey
Sophie Beeftink
Penny Johanna Beer
Dr Maya Beyhan
Roberto Boghossian
Georgina Borthwick
Chantal Bradford
Kit Brennan
Kate Bryan
Verena Butt d'Espous
Alexandre Carel
David Carpenter
Lauren Carpenter
Sean Carpenter
Federico Martin Castro Debernardi
Marie-Louise Chaldecott
Alexandra and Kabir Chhatwani
Yoojin Choi
Aidan Christofferson
Bianca Chu
Harriet Clapham
Julia Clemente
Thamara Corm
Tara Wilson Craig
Sophie Da Gama Campos
Henry Danowski
Grantland D'Avino
Mr Joshua Davis
Countess Charlotte de la
Rochefoucauld
Giacomo De Notariis
Agnes de Royere
Raphaele Deghaye
Indira Dyussebayeva
Alexandra Economou
Eleanor A Edelman
Mr Will Elliott
Olivia Farry
Danae Filioti
Dr L Foley
Jane and Richard Found
Sylvain Fresia
Laurie Frey
Brian Fu
Magdalena Gabriel
Mr Andreas Gegner
Elissa Goldstone
Molly Grad
Mr Taymour Grahne
Beth Greenacre
Alex Haidas
Sara Harrison
Alexis Hervieu-Causse
Simona Houldsworth
Stephen Howe
Kyu Hwang
Kamel Jaber
Karim Jalbout
Aled Jones
Miss Meruyert Kaliyeva
Mrs Vasilisa Kameneva
Miss Tamila Kerimova
Imogen Kerr
Zena Aliya Khan
Marika Kielland
Ms Chloe Kinsman
Maria Korolevskaya
Daria Kravchenko
Zoe Kuipers
Nicholas M Lamotte
Ms Aliki-Marcadia Lampropoulos
Patricia Lara
Nadja Laub
Madame Henriette Poppy Lefort
John Lellouche
Alexander Lewis
Claire Livingstone
Lucy Loveday
Mr J Lueddeckens
Thomas Luypaert
Yusuf Macun
Stephanie Magistretti
Frederic Maillard
Ms Sonia Mak
Dr Christina Makris
Mr Jean-David Malat
Kamiar Maleki
Daria Manganelli
Ignacio Marinho
Zain Masud
Magnus Mathisen
Charles-Henri McDermott
Fiona McGovern
Mary McNicholas
Chelsea Menzies
Miss Nina Moaddel
Mr Fernando Moncho Lobo
John-Christian Moquette
Jacopo Moretti
Vanita Nathwani
Ikenna Obiekwe
Aurore Ogden (Co-Chair, Young
Patrons Ambassador Group)
Reine and Boris Okuliar
Berkay Oncel
Chloe O'Sullivan
Periklis Panagopoulos
Christine Chungwon Park
Alexander V Petalas (Co-Chair,
Young Patrons Ambassador
Group)
Victor Petitgas
Robert Phillips
Mr Mark Piolet
Sébastien Plantin
Christopher Pullen
Chelsea Purvis
Ms Catherine Quin
Georgina Rees
Mr Eugenio Re Rebaudengo
Sydney Rogers
Ms Nadja Romain
Nour Saleh
Sophie Samuelson
Paola Saracino Fendi
Franz Schwarz
Count Indoo Sella Di Monteluce
Nasiha Shaikh
Robert Sheffield
Henrietta Shields
Ms Marie-Anya Shriro
Amar Singh
Evgenia Slyusarenko
Zoe Karafylakis Sperling
Dominic Stolerman
Daniel Story
Melisa Tapan
Nayrouz Tatanaki
Vassan Thavaraja
Mr Leo Thetiot
Soren S K Tholstrup
Ross Thomas
Omer Tiroche
Simon Tovey
Mr M Travers
Mr Giancarlo Trinca
Mr Philippos Tsangrides
Ms Navann Ty
Mr Lawrence Van Hagen
Steffan Vaughan Griffiths
Damian Vesey
Alina Voronova
Luning Wang
Alexandra Werner
Ewa Wilczynski
Anna Wilkie
Elizabeth Wilks
Kim Williams
Alexandra Wood
Edward Woodcock
Tyler Woolcott
Vanessa Wurm
Ms Eirian Yem
HRH Princess Eugenie of York
Nadia Zayan
Evgeny Zborovsky
Marcelo Osvaldo Zimmler

and those who wish to remain anonymous

International Council Members
Mr Segun Agbaje
Staffan Ahrenberg,
Editions Cahiers d'Art
Mr Geoff Ainsworth, AM
Ricard Akagawa and
Frances Reynolds
Mrs Maria Baibakova and
Mr Adrien Faure
Anne H Bass
Nicolas Berggruen
Pontus Bonnier
Paloma Botín O'Shea
Frances Bowes
Ivor Braka
The Deborah Loeb Brice Foundation
The Broad Art Foundation
Andrew Cameron, AM
Nicolas and Celia Cattelain
Mrs Christina Chandris
Richard Chang (Vice Chair)
Pierre Chen, Yageo Foundation,
Taiwan
Mr Attilio Codognato
Sir Ronald Cohen and Lady Cohen
Mr Dimitris Daskalopoulos
Mr and Mrs Michel David-Weill
Ms Miel de Botton
Tiqui Atencio Demirdjian and
Ago Demirdjian
Joseph and Marie Donnelly
Mrs Olga Dreesmann
Barney A Ebsworth and
Rebecca L Ebsworth
Füsun and Faruk Eczacibasi
Stefan Edlis and Gael Neeson
Mr and Mrs Edward Eisler
Fares and Tania Fares
Mrs Doris Fisher
Mrs Wendy Fisher
Dr Kira Flanzraich
Amanda and Glenn Fuhrman
The Gaudio Family Foundation (UK)
Limited
Candida and Zak Gertler
Mrs Yassmin Ghandehari
Alan Gibbs
Lydia and Manfred Gorvy
Mr Laurence Graff
Konstantin Grigorishin
Mr Xavier Guerrand-Hermès
Mimi and Peter Haas Fund
Margrit and Paul Hahnloser
Andy and Christine Hall
Mrs Susan Hayden
Ms Ydessa Hendeles
Marlene Hess and James D. Zirin
André and Rosalie Hoffmann
Ms Maja Hoffmann
Vicky Hughes
Ishikawa Foundation
Dakis and Lietta Joannou
Sir Elton John and Mr David Furnish
Pamela J Joyner
Monica Kalpakian
Mr Chang-Il Kim
Jack Kirkland
C Richard and Pamela Kramlich
Mrs Grażyna Kulczyk
Andreas and Ulrike Kurtz
Catherine Lagrange
Mr Pierre Lagrange
The Lauder Foundation -
Leonard and Judy Lauder Fund
Agnès and Edward Lee
Jacqueline and Marc Leland
Ms Joyce Liu
Panos and Sandra Marinopoulos
Mr and Mrs Donald B Marron
Mr Ronald and The Hon
Mrs McAulay
Mark McCain and Caro MacDonald
Mr Leonid Mikhelson
Naomi Milgrom, AO
Mr Donald Moore
Simon and Catriona Mordant
Mrs Yoshiko Mori
Mr Guy and The Hon Mrs Naggar
Fayeeza Naqvi
Mrs Judith Neilson, AM
Dr Mark Nelson
Mr and Mrs Takeo Obayashi
HRH Princess Firyal of Jordan
Mr and Mrs Eyal Ofer
Andrea and José Olympio Pereira
Hideyuki Osawa
Irene Panagopoulos
Young-Ju Park
Yana and Stephen Peel
Daniel and Elizabeth Peltz
Catherine Petitgas (Chair)
Sydney Picasso
Jean Pigozzi
Lekha Poddar
Miss Dee Poon
Ms Miuccia Prada and Mr Patrizio
Bertelli
Laura Rapp and Jay Smith
Maya and Ramzy Rasamny
Rennie Foundation
Patrizia Sandretto Re Rebaudengo
and Agostino Re Rebaudengo
Sir John Richardson, KBE
Michael Ringier
Lady Ritblat
Ms Hanneli M Rupert
Ms Güler Sabanci
Dame Theresa Sackler, DBE
Mrs Lily Safra
Muriel and Freddy Salem
Rajeeb and Nadia Samdani
Alejandro Santo Domingo
Dasha Shenkman, OBE
Dr Gene Sherman, AM
Jon and Kimberly Shirley
Uli and Rita Sigg
Norah and Norman Stone
Julia Stoschek
John J Studzinski, CBE
Maria and Malek Sukkar
Mr Christen Sveaas
Lorraine Tarabay
Mr Robert Tomei
The Hon Robert H Tuttle and
Mrs Maria Hummer-Tuttle
Mrs Ninetta Vafeia
Paulo A W Vieira
Mercedes Vilardell
Robert and Felicity Waley-Cohen
The Hon Hilary M Weston
Angela Westwater and David Meitus
Diana Widmaier Picasso
Christen and Derek Wilson
Mrs Sylvie Winckler

The Hon Dame Janet Wolfson de Botton, DBE
Poju Zabludowicz and Anita Zabludowicz, OBE
Michael Zilkha

and those who wish to remain anonymous

Africa Acquisitions Committee
Kathy Ackerman Robins
The African Arts Trust
Anshu Bahanda
Adnan Bashir
Priti Chandaria Shah
Mrs Kavita Chellaram
Harry G David
Mr and Mrs Michel David-Weill
Robert and Renee Drake
Mrs Wendy Fisher
Diane B. Frankel
Andrea Kerzner
Samallie Kiyingi
Alexander Klimt
Othman Lazraq
Matthias and Gervanne Leridon
Caro Macdonald
Dale Mathias
Professor Oba Nsugbe, QC
Ms Ndidi Okpaluba
Mr Hussam Otaibi
Pascale Revert Wheeler
Emile Stipp
Pulane Tshabalala Kingston
Liese Van Der Watt and Stephan Pretorius
Mr Varnavas A Varnava
Josef Vascovitz and Lisa Goodman
Mercedes Vilardell (Chair)
Alexa Waley-Cohen
Peter Warwick
Ms Isabel Wilcox
Marwan G Zakhem

and those who wish to remain anonymous

Asia-Pacific Acquisitions Committee
Sara A Alireza
Matthias Arndt
Bonnie and R Derek Bandeen
Mrs Bambi Blumberg
Mr and Mrs John Carrafiell
Jasmine Chen
Adrian Cheng
Jonathan Cheung
Lawrence Chu
Marcel Crespo
Mr Yan d'Auriol
Dani Duclos
Mrs Yassmin Ghandehari
Philippa Hornby
Mr Yongsoo Huh
Shareen Khattar Harrison
Mr Chang-Il Kim
Mr Jung Wan Kim
Ms Yung Hee Kim
Ms Ellie Lai
Alan Lau (Co-Chair)
Woong-Yeul Lee
Jasmine Li
Mr William Lim
Lin Qi
Ms Dina Liu
Alan and Yenn Lo
Ms Kai-Yin Lo
Anne Louis-Dreyfus
Lu Xun
Elaine Forsgate Marden
Marleen Molenaar
Mr John Porter
The Red Mansion Foundation
Mr Reade and Mrs Elizabeth Griffith
Dr Gene Sherman, AM (Co-Chair)
Leo Shih
Arif Suherman
Ed Tang
Chikako Tatsuuma
Dr Andreas Teoh
Rudy Tseng
Yang Bin
Jenny Yeh
Fernando Zobel de Ayala

and those who wish to remain anonymous

Latin American Acquisitions Committee
Monica and Robert Aguirre
José Antonio Alcantara
Celia Birbragher
Estrellita and Daniel Brodsky
Simone Coscarelle Parma
HSH the Prince Pierre d'Arenberg
Tiqui Atencio Demirdjian (Co-Chair)
Renata Dias de Moraes
Marta Regina Fernandez Holman
Katherine Francey
Barbara Hemmerle Gollust
Julian Iragorri
Countess Nicole Junkermann Brachetti Peretti
Aimee Labarrere de Servitje
José Luis Lorenzo
Felipe and Denise Nahas Mattar
Susan McDonald
Gabriela Mendoza
Veronica Nutting
Victoria and Isaac Oberfeld
Silvia Paz-Illobre
Catherine Petitgas
Claudio Federico Porcel
Mr Thibault Poutrel
Frances Reynolds
Erica Roberts (Co-Chair)
Alin Ryan Lobo
Catalina Saieh Guzman
Teresa Sapey
Lilly Scarpetta
Camila Sol de Pool
Teresita Soriano Zucker
Juan Carlos Verme

and those who wish to remain anonymous

Middle East and North Africa Acquisitions Committee
Ahmad and Sirine Abu Ghazaleh
HRH Princess Alia Al-Senussi
Abdelmonem Bin Eisa Alserkal
Mehves Ariburnu
Marwan T Assaf
Niloufar Bakhtiar Bakhtiari
Perihan Bassatne
Family Boghossian
Banu Çarmikli
Ms Isabelle de la Bruyère
Füsun Eczacibasi
Shirley Elghanian
Delfina Entrecanales, CBE
Noor Fares
Hossein and Dalia Fateh
Negin Fattahi-Dasmal
Raghida Ghandour Al Rahim
Mareva Grabowski
Maryam Eisler (Co-Chair)
Aysegül Karadeniz
Mr Elie Khouri
Maha and Kasim Kutay
David Maupin
Tansa Mermerci Eksioglu
Basma Haout Monla
Falak Naqvi
Dina Nasser-Khadivi
Shulamit Nazarian
Mr Moshe Peterburg
Ramzy and Maya Rasamny (Co-Chair)
Thomas Rom
Mrs Madhu Ruia
Mrs Karen Ruimy
Shihab Shobokshi
Maria and Malek Sukkar
Faisal Tamer
Berna Tuglular
Ayse Umur
Sebnem Unlu
Mahdi Yahya
Mr Zahid and Ms Binladin
Roxane Zand

and those who wish to remain anonymous

North American Acquisitions Committee
Alizera Abrishamchi
Jacqueline Appel and Alexander Malmaeus
Abigail Baratta
Dorothy Berwin
Dillon Cohen
Michael Corman and Kevin Fink
Theo Danjuma
James E Diner
Mala Gaonkar
Jill Garcia
Victoria Gelfand-Magalhaes
Shari Glazer
Amy Gold
Nina and Dan Gross
Pamela J Joyner
Monica Kalpakian
Elisabeth and Panos Karpidas
Christian Keesee
Naznin and Mahmood Khimji
Miyoung Lee
Marjorie and Michael Levine
James Lindon
Sheryl and Eric Maas
Kathleen Madden and Paul Frantz
Rebecca Marks
Nancy McCain
Jeff Menashe
Stavros Merjos
Gregory R Miller (Co-Chair)
Rachelli Mishori and Leon Koffler
Sami Mnaymneh
Shabin and Nadir Mohamed
Jenny Mullen
Amy and John Phelan
Laura Rapp and Jay Smith
Carolin Scharpff-Striebich
Komal Shah
Francis and Eleanor Shen
Dasha Shenkman, OBE
Kimberly Richter Shirley and Jon Shirley
Beth Swofford
Juan Carlos Verme
Christen Wilson (Co-Chair)
Derek Wilson

and those who wish to remain anonymous

Photography Acquisitions Committee
Ryan Allen
Artworkers Retirement Society
Nicholas Barker
Cynthia Lewis Beck
Carolin Becker
Pierre Brahm
Mrs William Shaw Broeksmit
Elizabeth (Co-Chair) and Rory Brooks
Nicolas (Co-Chair) and Celia Cattelain
Beth and Michele Colocci
Mr and Mrs Michel David-Weill
Anthony Diamandakis
Mr Hyung-Teh Do
Nikki Fennell
David Fitzsimons
Lisa Garrison
Ms Emily Goldner and Mr Michael Humphries
Ann Hekmat
Alexandra Hess
Bernard Huppert
Jack Kirkland
David Knaus
Mr Scott Mead
Sebastien Montabonel
Mr Donald Moore
Kristin Rey
David Solo
Saadi Soudavar
Nicholas Stanley
Maria and Malek Sukkar
Francois Trausch, in memory of Caroline Trausch
Annie Vartivarian
Michael and Jane Wilson

and those who wish to remain anonymous

Russia and Eastern Europe Acquisitions Committee
Dmitry Aksenov
Dilyara Allakhverdova (Co-Chair)
David Birnbaum
Maria Rus Bojan
Maria Bukhtoyarova
Francise Hsin-Wen Chang
Lyuba Galkina
Konstantin Grigorishin
Cees Hendrikse
Mr Vilius Kavaliauskas and Rita Navalinskaite
Carl Kostyál
Mrs Grazyna Kulczyk
Peter Kulloi (Co-Chair)
Eniko Leányvári and Gábor Illés
Eduard Maták
Luba Michailova
Maarja Oviir-Neivelt
Florin Pogonaru
Petr Pudil
Neil K Rector
Valeria Rodnyansky
Robert Runták
Ovidiu Sandor
Zsolt Somlói
Elena Sudakova
The Tretyakov Family Collection
Miroslav Trnka
Jo Vickery
Veronika Zonabend
Mr Janis Zuzans

and those who wish to remain anonymous

South Asia Acquisitions Committee
Shohidul Ahad-Choudhury
Mrs Sheetal Ansal
Maya Barolo-Rizvi
Krishna Bhupal
Dr Arani and Mrs Shumita Bose
Akshay Chudasama
Jai Danani
Shalini Amerasinghe Ganendra
Zahida Habib
Shalini Hinduja
Deepanjana Klein
Simran Kotak and Vir Kotak
Ms Aarti Lohia
Yamini Mehta
Mr Yogesh Mehta
Mohammad N. Miraly
Mr Rahul Munjal and Mrs Pooja Munjal
Mrs Chandrika Pathak
Puja and Uday Patnaik
Lekha Poddar (Co-Chair)
Sameer Sain
Nadia Samdani
Rajeeb Samdani (Co-Chair)
Mrs Tarana Sawhney
Osman Khalid Waheed
Manuela and Iwan Wirth

and those who wish to remain anonymous

The 1897 Circle
Marilyn Bild
David and Deborah Botten
Geoff Bradbury
Charles Brett
Sylvia Carter
Eloise and Francis Charlton
Mr and Mrs Cronk
Alex Davids
Jonathan Davis
Professor Martyn Davis
Sean Dissington
Ronnie Duncan
Joan Edlis
V Fabian
Lt Cdr Paul Fletcher
Mr and Mrs R.N. and M.C. Fry
Tom Glynn
Richard S. Hamilton
L.A. Hynes
John Janssen
Dr Martin Kenig
Isa Levy
Theo Matoff
Jean Medlycott
Miss Sue Novell and Mr Graham Smith
Martin Owen
Simon Reynolds
Dr Claudia Rosanowski
Ann M Smith
Deborah Stern
Jennifer Toynbee-Holmes
Estate of Paule Vézelay
D. Von Bethmann Hollweg
Audrey Wallrock
Prof. Brian Whitton
Kay and Dyson Wilkes
Simon Casimir Wilson
Andrew Woodd
Mr Zilberberg

and those who wish to remain anonymous

European Collection Circle
Jacques Boissonnas
Karen Cawthorn Argenio
Lonti Ebers
Trustees of the Gaudio Family Foundation (UK) Limited
Agnès and Edward Lee (Chair)

and those who wish to remain anonymous

Tate Britain Corporate Supporters
BNP Paribas
Bloomberg LP
Christie's
Deutsche Bank AG
EY
Laurent Perrier
Loewe
Qantas
RSM
Sotheby's

and those who wish to remain anonymous

Tate Britain Corporate Members
Bank of America Merrill Lynch
BCS Consulting
Clifford Chance LLP
Deutsche Bank AG
Ernst & Young
Finsbury
Holdingham Group
HSBC
Hyundai Card
Imperial College Healthcare Charity
JATO Dynamics
Linklaters
Morgan Stanley
Oliver Wyman
Siegel + Gale

and those who wish to remain anonymous